THE ONE YEAR BOOK OF
Family Devotions

VOLUME 3

THE
ONE
YEAR
BOOK OF
Family Devotions

VOLUME
3

Tyndale House Publishers, Inc.

Stories written by Katherine Ruth Adams, Jean Burns, Brenda
Decker, Harriet A. Durrell, Jan Hansen, Ruth Jay, Gail L. Jenner,
Nance E. Keyes, Phyllis Klomparens, Sherry Kuyt, Dolores A.
Lemieux, Agnes Livezey, Dawn E. Maloney, Deborah Marett, Hazel
Marett, Lorna B. Marlowe, Ruth McQuilkin, Sara Nelson, Matilda
Nordtvedt, Ellen Orr, Raelene Phillips, Victoria Reinhardt, Phyllis
Robinson, Deana Rogers, Catherine Runyon, Marilyn Sentefitt,
Lois A. Teufel, Charlie VanderMeer, Geri Walcott, Linda Weddle,
Barbara Westberg, and Carolyn Yost. Authors' initials appear at the
end of each story. All stories are taken from issues of *Keys for Kids,*
published bimonthly by the Children's Bible Hour, Box 1, Grand
Rapids, Michigan 49501.

Library of Congress Catalog Card Number 88-71950
ISBN 0-8423-2617-0

Printed in the United States of America

00 99 98 97
14 13 12 11 10 9 8 7

CONTENTS

YOU HAVE in your hands a year's worth of delightful stories, all taken from *Keys for Kids,* a devotional magazine published by the Children's Bible Hour. For years the Children's Bible Hour has made *Keys* available free of charge to any family requesting a copy. Their fine ministry to families has been much appreciated over the years, and Tyndale House was proud to present *The One Year Book of Family Devotions* and *The One Year Book of Family Devotions, Volume 2.* So well received were those books that Tyndale now presents this third volume of stories from *Keys for Kids.*

Each day's story provides a contemporary illustration of the day's Scripture reading. Following each story is a "How About You?" section that asks children to apply the story to themselves. Following this is a memory verse, usually taken from the Scripture reading. Each devotion ends with a "key," a 2–5 word summary of the day's lesson.

The stories here are geared toward families with children ages 8 to 14. Children can enjoy reading these stories by themselves, but we hope that you will use them in a daily devotional time for the whole family. Like the many stories in the Bible that teach valuable lessons about life, the stories here will speak not only to children but to adults. They are simple, direct, and concrete, and, like Jesus' parables, they speak to all of us in terms we can understand. Like all good stories, they are made for sharing, so look at them as the basis for family sharing and growth.

This book includes a Scripture index and a topical index. The Scripture index is helpful if you want to locate a story related to a passage that you want to draw your family's attention to. The topical index is here because certain concerns arise spontaneously and unexpectedly in any family—illness, moving, a new baby, for example. We hope you will use the book faithfully every day, but the indexes are here so that you will not just be locked into the daily reading format. Feel free to use any story at any time it relates to a special situation in your family.

CHRIS WAS FRIGHTENED. It was his very first day at Jefferson School, and he didn't know anyone! As he walked down the unfamiliar hallway to his class, he prayed, "Lord, help me make a friend!"

Some of the boys and girls in Chris' class smiled at him, but hardly anyone said anything. By lunch time, he was very discouraged. The teacher showed him where to pay for his lunch and pointed out the section of tables reserved for the fifth graders. Chris sat down and looked around at the other boys and girls. They all seemed to know one another. Laughing and talking went on all around him.

Then Chris noticed something. One boy was praying! Right there in the cafeteria, he had bowed his head and closed his eyes and was praying. *He must be a Christian,* thought Chris. Getting up, he took his tray and went to sit next to the other boy. "Hi. I'm Chris," he said. "Were you praying just now?"

"Yes, I was," the boy answered. "I was thanking the Lord for my food. I'm a Christian."

"So am I!" exclaimed Chris. "We just moved to town, and I've been praying that the Lord would help me meet a new friend."

"Wow! That's great!" The boy grinned at Chris. "My name is Jason, and there are some other Christian kids around, too. You'll like it here."

Silently, Chris prayed, "Thank You, Lord—thank You for helping me meet Jason."

HOW ABOUT YOU? Are you sometimes ashamed to talk to the Lord in front of your friends? You don't need to feel that way. Talking to God is a very special privilege that a Christian has. Dare to pray in public, as Daniel did. It will be a testimony to those who are unsaved. It's also an encouragement to other Christians. □ L.W.

TO MEMORIZE: *Rejoicing in hope, patient in tribulation, continuing steadfastly in prayer.* Romans 12:12, NKJV

A New Friend

FROM THE BIBLE:
Daniel so distinguished himself . . . by his exceptional qualities that the king planned to set him over the whole kingdom. At this, the administrators and the satraps tried to find grounds for charges against Daniel. . . . So the administrators and the satraps went as a group to the king and said: "O King Darius, live forever! The royal administrators, prefects, satraps, advisers and governors have all agreed that the king should issue an edict and enforce the decree that anyone who prays to any god or man during the next thirty days, except to you, O king, shall be thrown into the lions' den. Now, O king, issue the decree and put it in writing. . . ." Now when Daniel learned that the decree had been published, he went home to his upstairs room where the windows opened toward Jerusalem. Three times a day he got down on his knees and prayed, giving thanks to his God, just as he had done before.
Daniel 6:3-10, NIV

Praying is a privilege

2

The Invitation

"Do not let your hearts be troubled. Trust in God; trust also in me. In my Father's house are many rooms; if it were not so, I would have told you. I am going there to prepare a place for you. And if I go and prepare a place for you, I will come back and take you to be with me that you also may be where I am. You know the way to the place where I am going." Thomas said to him, "Lord, we don't know where you are going, so how can we know the way?" Jesus answered, "I am the way and the truth and the life. No one comes to the Father except through me."
John 14:1-6, NIV

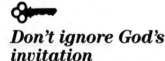

Don't ignore God's invitation

WHEN ELLEN RETURNED to school after Christmas vacation, it seemed so good to see all her friends again. As they chatted happily together, she noticed that several of them referred to Marilee's party.

Marilee's party? thought Ellen. *That was going to be after Christmas.* She vaguely remembered being handed an invitation, but since it wasn't happening right away and she was very busy, she hadn't paid much attention just then. What had she done with the invitation? She hurried to look in her desk. There it was—a small square envelope sticking out of her math book. She quickly pulled it out and read, "Please come to a party." The details were on the inside. She read only the first line. "We'll look for you on December 28, 7:00 . . . ." Oh no! December 28! The party *was* after Christmas, but it was last week! Just then two girls came over to her desk. "You really missed it!" exclaimed Sue. "Marilee's dad took us out to her grandparents' place in the country, and we had a real sleigh ride."

"And we pulled taffy afterward," added Brenda. As the two girls walked away singing "Jingle Bells," Ellen bit her lip to keep from crying. But when she told her parents about it that evening, she did shed a few tears. "It sounded like so much fun, and I could have gone," she sniffed. "I was invited, but I didn't read the invitation carefully. Now it's too late. I missed it."

"Oh, I'm sorry," sympathized Mother.

"Yes, it is too bad," agreed Dad. "This reminds me of another invitation that is carelessly ignored. God invites us all to spend eternity in heaven with Him, but many people pay no attention. The day will come when it will be too late to accept that invitation, too."

Ellen nodded. "I'm glad I won't miss that," she said. "It would be lots worse than missing Marilee's party."

HOW ABOUT YOU? Have you been careless with God's invitation to heaven? Have you been too busy to think about it? Do you intend to have a look at it later? Accept the invitation which God is patiently offering now. □ H.M.

TO MEMORIZE: *And the Lord said, "My Spirit shall not strive with man forever."* Genesis 6:3, NKJV

"IF I WATCH anything as violent as that, Daddy, you make me turn the TV off," observed Jill as her father was watching the evening news.

"You're right," he agreed, and he snapped off the set. "I do like to keep up on what's happening in the world, but frankly, I think it would be better if they wouldn't show some of those pictures. Maybe I should rely more heavily on my newspaper."

"Did I hear someone say they want a newspaper?" asked Andy as he came in the back door. "Well, now, I just happen to have one for you. Here you are, Sir." He handed his dad a paper. "I just finished my paper route," he said. "Seems like everybody I saw remarked about the number of articles on crime and war these days. I felt like the bearer of bad news!"

"Well, *I'm* the bearer of good news—dinner's ready!" announced Mother as she joined them. Laughing, they trooped to the table and together thanked God for the food they were about to eat. "Ummmm, this lasagne sure is good news," commented Andy as he took a large portion. "Too bad I can't tell my customers about this."

Dad looked at him thoughtfully. "There is some good news that all of us should be telling," he said. "Who knows what it is?"

Jill and Andy looked puzzled. "I'll give you a clue," said Dad. "It's found in the Bible."

"Oh, I know—it's the good news of Jesus!" exclaimed Jill. "We're supposed to tell everybody about Him."

"Right," agreed Dad. "We are to tell others the gospel message. 'Gospel' means 'good news.' Perhaps there's so much bad news in the world today because not enough people know the good news of the gospel. Let's all make an effort to tell it to at least one person tomorrow."

HOW ABOUT YOU? When was the last time you shared the good news of Jesus with someone? If you are a Christian, it's your responsibility to tell others that Jesus died on the cross for our sins, that He was buried, and that He rose again. Invite your friends to trust in Jesus. □ H.M.

TO MEMORIZE: *He said to them, "Go into all the world and preach the good news to all creation."* Mark 16:15, NIV

3

Good News!

FROM THE BIBLE:
He told his disciples, "I have been given all authority in heaven and earth. Therefore go and make disciples in all the nations, baptizing them into the name of the Father and of the Son and of the Holy Spirit, and then teach these new disciples to obey all the commands I have given you; and be sure of this—that I am with you always, even to the end of the world."
Matthew 28:18-20, TLB

Share the gospel

Good News!

(Continued from yesterday)

FROM THE BIBLE:
Now let me remind you,
brothers, of what the gospel
really is, for it has not
changed—it is the same Good
News I preached to you before.
You welcomed it then and still
do now, for your faith is squarely
built upon this wonderful
message; and it is this Good
News that saves you if you still
firmly believe it, unless of
course you never really believed
it in the first place. I passed on
to you right from the first what
had been told to me, that Christ
died for our sins just as the
Scriptures said he would, and
that he was buried, and that
three days afterwards he arose
from the grave just as the
prophets foretold.
1 Corinthians 15:1-4, TLB

Believe the gospel

AS ANDY DELIVERED his papers, he thought of what Dad had said about telling the good news of Jesus to someone. Andy really meant to do it. Just as he was placing a paper on Mr. Watkins' steps, the door opened, and there was Mr. Watkins himself.

"Saw you coming," he greeted Andy. "I suppose you're bringing me gloomy news again tonight." He accepted the paper from Andy's hand.

"Evening, Sir," said Andy, and he began to move away.

But Mr. Watkins was still talking. "Sure would be nice if you'd bring me some good news for a change."

Andy gulped. Here was his chance to tell the good news! If only Mr. Watkins would go in . . . but he seemed to be waiting for a reply. "Why, ah, actually, I do know some good news. . . ." Andy began fearfully.

"You do? What's that?" questioned Mr. Watkins.

Andy didn't know how to proceed. "Well, it's found in the Bible. Jesus died on the cross."

Mr. Watkins look surprised. "He did, eh? Well that doesn't sound like such good news to me— another death."

"Oh, but He died for you," explained Andy. "He paid the price for your sins. And . . . and he didn't stay dead. He rose again, and lots of people saw Him. If you'll believe in Him, you'll go to live with Him someday."

To Andy's surprise, Mr. Watkins was listening carefully. "Well, now, young fella, I suppose I've not always done the right thing, but I'm not so bad," he argued. "I don't think it was necessary for anybody to die for me."

"You have to believe the gospel if you want to go to heaven," Andy told him firmly.

Mr. Watkins smiled. "You're a very persuasive young man," he said. "I learned about Jesus when I was a boy, but I never did anything about it. I'm going to think about this a lot more. Thanks for reminding me." Andy hurried home with a smile on his face.

HOW ABOUT YOU? Perhaps you've heard the "good news" many times, but have you ever done anything about it? Have you accepted what Jesus did for you? If not, acknowledge your need today. □ H.M.

TO MEMORIZE: *The time is fulfilled, and the kingdom of God is at hand. Repent, and believe in the gospel.* Mark 1:15, NKJV

I SURE WISH Dad could come to my basketball game tonight," complained Bud to his older brother Troy. "He's had to work every Friday night. It's not fair!"

Troy tried to cheer him. "Mom and I have been there, Bud, and you've been doing great!"

"But it's not the same," Bud replied. Just then Mother called them to supper, and the discussion ended.

"Mmmmm, this roast beef is delicious!" exclaimed Troy. "Remember how often we wished for a roast when Dad was out of work?"

"I sure do," replied Mother, "and I'm glad you reminded me. I've been grumbling lately about Dad working the second shift, forgetting that no work means no gravy." She glanced at Bud, but he refused to smile. All evening he remained gloomy.

The next evening, the family lingered over supper, glad to have Dad with them. "Since I'm only here on Saturday and Sunday evenings," said Dad, "I really miss our family devotions. Troy, did you choose something for tonight?"

Troy grinned as he replied, "I've got it all planned, Dad, and I think we all need it." Troy took the Bible and read from Exodus and Numbers. Then he looked up and grinned. "Today is an anniversary," he announced. "Anybody know what for?"

"I do," responded Dad promptly. "It's just three months ago that I got called back to work."

"Oh, that's right!" said Mom. "I remember how thrilled we were." She paused, then exclaimed, "Oh, I see your point, Troy! We've been like the Israelites. At first they were thrilled with manna, just like we were with Dad's job. But then they began to loathe it. I'm afraid we did that, too, and I confess that I was probably the first to complain. I hope you'll all forgive me. May God forgive us, too! Thank you for teaching us a lesson, Troy."

HOW ABOUT YOU? Is there some blessing in your life that you've begun to despise? Perhaps you prayed for a brother or sister, but now that you have one you sometimes wish you didn't. Or maybe you prayed that your Sunday school class would grow, and now that it has, you don't like it because a new member does better than you. Be careful. Never despise God's blessings. □ R.P.

TO MEMORIZE: *We sinned when we spoke against the Lord.* Numbers 21:7, NIV

5

Dad's Job

FROM THE BIBLE:
When the dew was gone, thin flakes like frost on the ground appeared on the desert floor. When the Israelites saw it, they said to each other, "What is it?" For they did not know what it was. Moses said to them, "It is the bread the Lord has given you to eat. This is what the Lord has commanded: 'Each one is to gather as much as he needs. Take an omer for each person you have in your tent.' " The Israelites did as they were told; some gathered much, some little. And when they measured it by the omer, he who gathered much did not have too much, and he who gathered little did not have too little. Each one gathered as much as he needed. Exodus 16:14-18, NIV

They traveled from Mount Hor along the route to the Red Sea, to go around Edom. But the people grew impatient on the way; they spoke against God and against Moses, and said, "Why have you brought us up out of Egypt to die in the desert? There is no bread! There is no water! And we detest this miserable food!" Numbers 21:4-6, NIV

Appreciate God's blessings

6

Ah-choo

FROM THE BIBLE:

Surely the arm of the Lord is not too short to save, nor his ear too dull to hear. But your iniquities have separated you from your God; your sins have hidden his face from you, so that he will not hear. For your hands are stained with blood, your fingers with guilt. Your lips have spoken lies, and your tongue mutters wicked things. No one calls for justice; no one pleads his case with integrity. They rely on empty arguments and speak lies; they conceive trouble and give birth to evil.
Isaiah 59:1-4, NIV

Sin separates us from God

"AH-CHOO!" KAREN SNEEZED as she settled down in her seat. She felt lousy, but she hadn't wanted to stay home. She was too mad. Mom had caught her copying a book report that her brother had written last year, and she had put up a big fuss. She insisted that Karen read the book herself and do her own report. Besides that, she was grounded for a whole week. "Copying is cheating and stealing," Mom said. Karen knew she should be sorry, but she wasn't.

As the hours passed, Karen continued to sneeze and sniff. Her nose was so stuffy. As she sniffed, she noticed that several of her neighbors gave her scowling looks. Her throat was sore, too, and she coughed a lot. Finally recess came. "Let's go jump rope," she suggested to Suzie, but Suzie shook her head and hurried away.

"Karen," said Miss Wilson, "don't you think you ought to go home? Your cold sounds terrible!" Reluctantly Karen agreed, so Miss Wilson arranged for Mother to pick her up.

Later, when Karen was settled at home, she let out a long sigh. "It's sure good to be here," she said. "Everybody avoided me at school."

Mom smiled. "You can't blame them," she said. "Nobody wanted to catch your cold, so they stayed away. Your cold separated you from your friends. It reminds me of sin." Karen looked at her mother in surprise. "You see," Mom went on, "sin separates us from fellowship with God. He always loves us, but He cannot fellowship with us when we refuse to do anything about our sin."

Karen knew it was true. Ever since she had gotten mad at Mom, she had felt far away from God. No, it was before that. It was ever since she decided to copy that she felt guilty and alone. "I know what you mean," she told Mom. "I need to confess some things to God, and I'm sorry I got mad at you, too."

HOW ABOUT YOU? Is there a sin that is separating you from God? Those who never accept Jesus as Savior will be separated from God forever. But even if you are a Christian, you need to confess any sin in your life. □ H.M.

TO MEMORIZE: *Your iniquities have separated you from your God; your sins have hidden his face from you, so that he will not hear.* Isaiah 59:2, NIV

KAREN'S COLD WAS keeping her home a second day, but she was feeling better. Towards noon, the phone rang, and Mom answered it. "For you," she called to Karen.

"Hello," said Karen, wondering who would be calling her during school hours. There was a moment of silence and then, "Ah-choo!" she heard. She was puzzled until she heard Suzie's voice. "You too?" laughed Karen. "I'm sorry. I'm afraid you caught that cold from me. How are you feeling?"

"Not so great," answered Suzie, "but I'll live. I should be mad at you, though. This cold isn't all I caught from you!" Karen listened in surprise as Suzie explained that she, too, had tried Karen's idea of copying her older brother's book report. And she, too, had been caught at it and punished for her dishonesty. "Next time you have a dumb idea, keep it to yourself, please," she said.

"Oh, no!" groaned Karen. "I'm sorry I got you in trouble." She apologized to Suzie and shared what she had learned from her experience. "And now I've learned something else," she concluded. "Sin is like my cold in another way. It's contagious."

As Karen hung up the phone, her mother smiled at her. "I think you've learned a couple of valuable lessons," she said. "Every time you get a cold, let it remind you of the seriousness of sin."

HOW ABOUT YOU? Did you notice that even the sin of our first parents was something of a "copy cat" affair? First one sinned, and the other followed. Perhaps you think that your lying, cheating, disobedience, or pride affects only you. Never forget there are always others watching you. When you sin in any way, you influence them whether you mean to or not. □ H.M.

TO MEMORIZE: *None of us lives to himself, and no one dies to himself.* Romans 14:7, NKJV

Ah-choo

(Continued from yesterday)

FROM THE BIBLE:
Now the serpent was more crafty than any of the wild animals the Lord God had made. He said to the woman, "Did God really say, 'You must not eat from any tree in the garden'?" The woman said to the serpent, "We may eat fruit from the trees in the garden, but God did say, 'You must not eat fruit from the tree that is in the middle of the garden, and you must not touch it, or you will die.' " "You will not surely die," the serpent said to the woman. "For God knows that when you eat of it your eyes will be opened, and you will be like God, knowing good and evil." When the woman saw that the fruit of the tree was good for food and pleasing to the eye, and also desirable for gaining wisdom, she took some and ate it. She also gave some to her husband, who was with her, and he ate it.
Genesis 3:1-6, NIV

Sin is contagious

JANUARY

8

Disobedient Duke

FROM THE BIBLE:
The Lord your God commands you this day to follow these decrees and laws; carefully observe them with all your heart and with all your soul. You have declared this day that the Lord is your God and that you will walk in his ways, that you will keep his decrees, commands and laws, and that you will obey him. And the Lord has declared this day that you are his people, his treasured possession as he promised, and that you are to keep all his commands.
Deuteronomy 26:16-18, NIV

Obey God's commandments

DAWN WAS DELIGHTED when her parents gave her a puppy for her birthday. He wriggled in her arms as she hugged him tight. "I'll call him Duke!" she announced.

"Well, Duke has lots of things to learn," her father said. "You'll need to reward him when he's good and spank him when he does something bad, so he'll learn right away which things he's not supposed to do."

Dawn frowned. "He won't be bad, Daddy. I'll love him so much that he'll want to be really good. Duke's going to be the best dog in the world!"

But Duke was not a good dog. He dug up the flower bed and chewed on shoes. He ran away when he was called. Dawn scolded and spanked until she was tired of it, but it seemed to do no good. Duke went right on getting into places where he wasn't supposed to be.

One day Dawn came into the living room looking very sad. "Why is Duke so bad?" she burst out. "I scold him and scold him, and he acts like he's sorry. He licks my face and wags his tail, so I pet him and hug him. And then he turns right around and is bad all over again. I love him so much. Why does he keep on being bad?"

Dad put down his paper and pulled Dawn onto his lap. "Sometimes it takes a long time to train a puppy," he said. What you just told me reminds me an awful lot of what happens between us and God."

"What do you mean?" asked Dawn.

"Well, remember when you got Duke? You said you would love him so much that he'd want to be good to please you, but instead he's been a lot of trouble," replied Dad. "Very often we're the same way with God. He loves us so much that we should all want to be good to please Him, but instead we want to do things our own way." Dad shook his head. "You just told me about how bad it makes you feel when Duke insists on disobeying you," he added. "Think how bad it must make God feel when the people He cares about so much keep on ignoring His teaching."

HOW ABOUT YOU? Are you an obedient child of God? He loves you so much and wants only the very best for you. Stop hurting Him by disobeying. Listen to His Word and do what it says. God will be pleased, and you will be happy, too. □

TO MEMORIZE: *If you love me, you will obey what I command.* John 14:15, NIV

M OM," CALLED CATHY as she returned from school one day, "can we go get my birthday party invitations?"

Mother shook her head. "I'm sorry, Honey, but I promised Mrs. Kettering I'd drive her to the doctor's office this afternoon. Ever since she broke her leg last year, she's had a hard time getting around."

"Well," said Cathy, "we'd better get the invitations soon. It's only two weeks till my birthday."

Mother smiled. "Have you decided who you'll invite?" she asked. "Remember, five guests is the limit."

Cathy nodded. "I want to invite Susie, Lori, Lena, Emily and Joanne."

Mother looked surprised. "What about Pam from next door?" she asked. "I thought you two were best friends!"

"Oh, we are," Cathy said, "but I can see her any time. I want someone different for a change. I suppose Pam might be mad about it when she finds out, but she'll get over it."

Mother was quiet for a minute. "I'm thinking of Mrs. Kettering's broken leg," she said. "Even though the fracture did heal, her leg will never be quite the same. Sometimes it hurts, and she has to be careful not to put too much stress on it. She can't trust it fully. It's the same way with friendship."

"Friendship?" asked Cathy. "What do you mean?"

"If you hurt a friend out of selfishness or carelessness, she may be willing to forgive you. But she may never be able to fully trust you again, and your relationship will suffer." Mother sighed. "I learned that lesson the hard way—I once lost a good friend because of a cruel, thoughtless remark I made. Friends are a precious gift from God, Cathy—don't take them for granted."

Cathy looked thoughtful. "I think I'd better go over my guest list again," she decided. "Pam is too important to risk hurting her feelings."

HOW ABOUT YOU? Do you take your friends for granted? Do you assume that they'll always be willing to forgive you, no matter what? Even a strong friendship can be broken, and healing can be difficult. Treat your friends as you want them to treat you—with kindness and respect. □ S.K.

TO MEMORIZE: *Do not forsake your friend and the friend of your father.* Proverbs 27:10, NIV

Fractured Friendship

FROM THE BIBLE:
It was not an enemy who taunted me—then I could have borne it; I could have hidden and escaped. But it was you, a man like myself, my companion and my friend.
Psalm 55:12-13, TLB

Wounds from a friend can be trusted, but an enemy multiplies kisses. He who is full loathes honey, but to the hungry even what is bitter tastes sweet. Like a bird that strays from its nest is a man who strays from his home. Perfume and incense bring joy to the heart, and the pleasantness of one's friend springs from his earnest counsel. Do not forsake your friend and the friend of your father, and do not go to your brother's house when disaster strikes you—better a neighbor nearby than a brother far away.
Proverbs 27:6-10, NIV

Treat friends with care

10

God and Me

FROM THE BIBLE:

This is what God the Lord says—he who created the heavens and stretched them out, who spread out the earth and all that comes out of it, who gives breath to its people, and life to those who walk on it: "I, the Lord, have called you in righteousness; I will take hold of your hand. I will keep you and will make you to be a covenant for the people and a light for the Gentiles, to open eyes that are blind, to free captives from prison and to release from the dungeon those who sit in darkness. I am the Lord; that is my name! I will not give my glory to another or my praise to idols. See, the former things have taken place, and new things I declare; before they spring into being I announce them to you." Sing to the Lord a new song, his praise from the ends of the earth, you who go down to the sea, and all that is in it, you islands, and all who live in them. Let the desert and its towns raise their voices; . . . let them shout from the mountaintops. Let them give glory to the Lord and proclaim his praise in the islands.
Isaiah 42:5-12, NIV

*Glorify God,
not self*

WE'LL ALL BE late for church if Bette doesn't hurry up," complained Peter. "She takes forever to fix her hair!"

Finally they were on their way. "Dad!" cried Bette, "make Peter close his window. The wind makes my hair a mess."

Before going into the church service, Bette went to comb her hair again. Peter, Mother, and Dad sat down. Mother and Dad frowned as she tiptoed into the pew during the first hymn.

After church that night, Peter got out a magnifying glass. "It's fun to look at stuff under this," he said. "It really makes everything look big."

"Oh, let me see, too," said Bette, and he shared the magnifying glass with her.

Observing them, Dad wrote something on two small pieces of paper, which he placed on the table with some other things Peter had lined up to look at. He watched as Peter put the first paper under the magnifying glass. Peter looked at it and shrugged. Then Bette looked. "Why did you write *God* on the paper for us to see?" she asked her father.

"Because God should be magnified," explained Dad. "Whoa, there," he added as Peter picked up the second piece of paper. "Don't put that one under your glass, Son. It's not supposed to be magnified."

Peter read it and handed it to his sister. Written in small letters was the word *me*.

"You see," continued Dad, "sometimes we tend to magnify 'me' instead of God. If we do that, we might spend too much time on appearance."

"Yeah," broke in Peter with a grin, "we comb our hair all the time and make everybody late for church."

"On the other hand," said Dad, "when we magnify God instead of 'me' we try to please Him in our behavior and we don't point the finger at someone else."

HOW ABOUT YOU? Do you spend too much time in front of your mirror? God wants you to look neat, clean, and as attractive as possible, but remember that real beauty is seen in actions more than in appearance. □ H.A.D.

TO MEMORIZE: *Glorify the Lord with me; let us exalt his name together.* Psalm 34:3, NIV

JULIE FELT GROUCHY as she sat on the couch at the home of her Sunday school teacher, Mrs. Watson. She didn't really want to be on what she called "this stupid old Parents' Night planning committee." She had to miss her favorite TV program to attend this meeting. Marla and Danny, the other committee members, seemed to be enjoying it, however—or at least they *had* been. They had made several suggestions, but Julie just scowled about all of them. Now the others seemed to be losing a lot of their enthusiasm, too.

"Julie," said Mrs. Watson finally, "why don't you help me prepare the snacks? Marla and Danny, I like your ideas. Keep thinking."

Glumly, Julie followed Mrs. Watson into the kitchen and arranged cookies on a plate while Mrs. Watson prepared hot chocolate. "Maybe I'll add just a little lemon juice to this chocolate," Mrs. Watson said.

"Lemon juice?" Julie was surprised. "That'll make it sour!"

Mrs. Watson looked at the bottle of lemon juice she held in her hand. "You're right, of course," she agreed. "And you know, Julie, just like a little lemon juice can ruin this hot chocolate, so too a bad attitude from just one person can ruin the special night we're planning. We want this to be a good Parents' Night, especially since we know there will be unsaved dads and moms attending. Marla and Danny have come up with some good ideas, but you've 'soured' them all."

Julie bit her lip and stared at the floor. "I'm sorry," she said at last, and she really was. "I'll apologize to Marla and Danny. I really do like their ideas. Oh, and Mrs. Watson?" she added.

"Yes, Julie?"

Julie grinned. "Please put the lemon juice away."

HOW ABOUT YOU? Are you a complainer? Do you often "get into moods" if things don't go the way you want? You might be surprised how quickly your moods can spread. The Lord wants you to be joyful and get along with others. □ L.W.

TO MEMORIZE: *Do all things without murmuring and disputing.* Philippians 2:14, NKJV

FROM THE BIBLE:
Moses also said, "You will know that it was the Lord when he gives you meat to eat in the evening and all the bread you want in the morning, because he has heard your grumbling against him. Who are we? You are not grumbling against us, but against the Lord." Then Moses told Aaron, "Say to the entire Israelite community, 'Come before the Lord, for he has heard your grumbling.' " While Aaron was speaking to the whole Israelite community, they looked toward the desert, and there was the glory of the Lord appearing in the cloud. The Lord said to Moses, "I have heard the grumbling of the Israelites. Tell them, 'At twilight you will eat meat, and in the morning you will be filled with bread. Then you will know that I am the Lord your God.' "
Exodus 16:8-12, NIV

Don't be a complainer

JANUARY

12

A Witness

FROM THE BIBLE:

He told them, "This is what is written: The Christ will suffer and rise from the dead on the third day, and repentance and forgiveness of sins will be preached in his name to all nations, beginning at Jerusalem. You are witnesses of these things."
Luke 24:46-48, NIV

God helps you witness

CHRISTY HAD TO walk four blocks to get home from Bible club, but she didn't mind. It was such a beautiful day. As she walked, she thought about her good friend Maribeth who didn't go to Bible club or church. Christy knew she should witness to Maribeth about Jesus, but how could she do it? Maribeth might laugh!

As Christy waited at the intersection for the light to change, she saw an old man start across the street against the light. Suddenly a truck came through the intersection and hit him. Then everything happened quickly, and soon the injured man was on his way to the hospital.

A few nights later, Christy's dad read in the newspaper, "The police are looking for the little red-haired girl who witnessed an accident on the corner of Clay and Main at 2:50 P.M. on Tuesday." Dad looked at Christy. "It seems that they need you as a witness."

"But why do they want me?" asked Christy. "I didn't do anything wrong."

"Of course not," Dad assured her. "They're probably looking for someone to tell them exactly what happened. Someone must have seen you there."

"But I don't want to say anything," protested Christy.

"You know what happened, so you must tell about it," her father said. "But you needn't be afraid. I'll go with you. You won't be alone."

When Christy went to bed that night, the scene of the accident went through her mind. She remembered that she had been thinking about witnessing to Maribeth, but she had been scared. Now it seemed she was going to have to be a different kind of witness. She was scared about that, too, but Dad would be with her. Suddenly she realized that just as her earthly father would be with her when she witnessed at the police station, so her heavenly Father would be with her when she witnessed to Maribeth. If she could trust her earthly father, how much more she should trust her heavenly Father!

HOW ABOUT YOU? Are you afraid to witness, or tell others, about Jesus? You know what Jesus did for you and you should tell your friends. Remember, you're not alone. Jesus has told you to go and be His witness, and He has also promised to go with you. Trust him. □ J.H.

TO MEMORIZE: *I am with you always, even to the end of the age.* Matthew 28:20, NKJV

SOME TIME AFTER Christy went to the police station with her father, she had to appear in court and tell exactly what she had seen and heard. "The truck driver could be convicted—and sued—for hitting the man unless he has a witness to testify that he was driving in a proper manner," the police chief had explained. "Your job, Christy, is just to tell what happened."

Again Christy was nervous. She had never been inside a courtroom before. Then she remembered her father's advice: "Just tell the truth about what you saw."

Finally Christy gave her testimony. It wasn't hard. The words came quite easily, once she got started. After the case was presented, the truck driver was cleared of any wrongdoing. He came over to shake hands with Christy. "I'm really sorry that man got hurt," the driver said, "but I'm thankful that you stood up and told the truth, Christy. It takes away the guilt—and the punishment, too. I could have been sent to jail if I were convicted. Thanks, Christy. I'll always be grateful."

On the way home, Christy and her dad stopped for hot fudge sundaes. "You're quiet, Christy. What are you thinking about?"

"I was thinking about my friend Maribeth," Christy explained. "I've wanted to talk to her about Jesus, but I didn't know what to say. Now I do. When I gave my testimony about the accident, I just told what happened. And I'll just tell Maribeth what happened, too. I'll tell her what Jesus has done for me and how I've seen Him working in my life."

"Great!" said Dad as he gave her a big hug. "Remember how grateful the truck driver was for your testimony which helped save him from punishment? Perhaps some day Maribeth will be grateful for your testimony, too."

HOW ABOUT YOU? Do you want to witness, but you just don't know what to say? A witness simply gives his testimony. He tells the truth about what happened. You can do that. Remember, Jesus has saved you! Tell somebody. □ J.H.

TO MEMORIZE: *You will be his witness to all men of what you have seen and heard.* Acts 22:15, NIV

A Witness

(Continued from yesterday)

FROM THE BIBLE:
Christ was alive when the world began, yet I myself have seen him with my own eyes and listened to him speak. I have touched him with my own hands. He is God's message of life. This one who is life from God has been shown to us and we guarantee that we have seen him; I am speaking of Christ, who is eternal Life. He was with the Father and then was shown to us. Again I say, we are telling you about what we ourselves have actually seen and heard, so that you may share the fellowship and the joys we have with the Father and with Jesus Christ his son. And if you do as I say in this letter, then you, too, will be full of joy, and so will we. This is the message God has given us to pass on to you: that God is Light and in him is no darkness at all.
1 John 1:1-5, TLB

Give your testimony

14

A Witness

(Continued from yesterday)

FROM THE BIBLE:

Who is going to harm you if you are eager to do good? But even if you should suffer for what is right, you are blessed. "Do not fear what they fear; do not be frightened." But in your hearts set apart Christ as Lord. Always be prepared to give an answer to everyone who asks you to give the reason for the hope that you have. But do this with gentleness and respect, keeping a clear conscience, so that those who speak maliciously against your good behavior in Christ may be ashamed of their slander.

1 Peter 3:13-16, NIV

Witness by actions

AS CHRISTY BOWED her head in the school lunchroom and silently thanked God for the food, Jenny poked Ellen. "Look!" she said loudly. "Christy's falling asleep at the table." Ellen giggled, and Jenny continued to poke fun at Christy. Suddenly her elbow hit her plate. It slid off the table, spattering Christy's skirt with spaghetti sauce.

"Jenny, look what you did now!" the other girls exclaimed in horror.

Christy carefully wiped the spots on her skirt. "It's all right," she said. "The skirt will wash. I'm sorry you spilled your lunch. You may have some of mine."

Jenny tossed her head. "Miss Do-Gooder," she snorted. "I've had more than I can take!" With that she left the table and Ellen soon followed.

"Jenny burns me up," Maribeth said. "She's so mean! How can you be nice to her, Christy?"

Christy took a deep breath. Here was a chance to give her testimony. "I'd be mean, too, if I didn't have Jesus to help me," she said.

"What do you mean?" asked Maribeth.

"I used to do lots of bad things," Christy admitted, "before I accepted Jesus as my Savior. He gives me power to do the things that are right."

"What do you mean—accepted Jesus as your Savior?" Maribeth questioned.

"It's like ABC," Christy explained. "A, I admitted I was a sinner. B, I believed Jesus died on the cross to pay for my sins. C, I confessed my sins and asked Jesus to forgive me. You can ask Him to be your Savior, too."

Maribeth looked thoughtful as she pushed back her plate. "And that's why you don't lose your temper when Jenny's mean to you?" she asked. "There must really be something to it. You'll have to tell me more about that!"

HOW ABOUT YOU? Are you a good witness? A good witness must be reliable in word and character. Do your talk and your walk (or actions) produce enough evidence to show you are a Christian? Christ must be seen in your actions before others will be willing to listen and accept the testimony from your mouth. □ J.H.

TO MEMORIZE: *In your hearts set apart Christ as Lord. Always be prepared to give an answer to everyone who asks you to give the reason for the hope that you have.* 1 Peter 3:15, NIV

"DO YOU REALLY think this thing is ever going to turn into something beautiful, Grandma?" asked Nathan, bringing a jar to the sofa where his grandmother was resting. He had caught a caterpillar, and it had spun itself into a cocoon. Nathan liked to share things with Grandma. She was always interested even though she was sick.

Grandma smiled as she looked at the dried-up, greenish thing in the jar Nathan held. "Oh, yes. Just wait," she answered. "Sit down a minute, Nathan, and let's talk." She patted the seat beside her. "Nathan, someday soon I'm going to be like the pupa inside that cocoon," Grandma continued. "The doctor says I won't be here much longer—I will die soon." A big lump came into Nathan's throat, and tears sprang to his eyes. Grandma patted his hand. "I don't want you to feel too bad when that happens, Nathan, because I'll be going to heaven. My old body will be buried in the ground, but the real me will be with Jesus, because I have received Him as my Savior. And some day I'll get a wonderful new body that won't get sick anymore. You keep watching the cocoon, and when you see the beautiful creature that comes out of it, think about the beautiful new body your grandma is going to get."

One night while Nathan was asleep, Grandma died. When Nathan saw her lying so still in her casket, he knew it was only her body. Grandma was with Jesus. Thinking about that helped, but he still felt sad.

The morning after Grandma's funeral, Nathan noticed something that made him very excited. "Mom! Dad!" he called. "Look at my butterfly!" Sure enough, a beautiful butterfly had emerged from the cocoon.

As they admired the lovely creature together, Nathan decided to let it go free. "Just like Grandma," he said as he watched the butterfly stretch its wings and fly away. "Someday she'll have a new body, too."

HOW ABOUT YOU? Do you realize that you don't need to fear death when you have trusted Jesus to be your Savior? Just as the caterpillar turned into a beautiful butterfly, so you will receive a new body that will live forever. Thank God for this wonderful hope. □ M.N.

TO MEMORIZE: *In a flash, in the twinkling of an eye, at the last trumpet. For the trumpet will sound, the dead will be raised imperishable, and we will be changed.* 1 Corinthians 15:52, NIV

17

Grandma and the Butterfly

FROM THE BIBLE:

Listen, I tell you a mystery: We will not all sleep, but we will all be changed—in a flash, in the twinkling of an eye, at the last trumpet. For the trumpet will sound, the dead will be raised imperishable, and we will be changed. For the perishable must clothe itself with the imperishable, and the mortal with immortality. When the perishable has been clothed with the imperishable, and the mortal with immortality, then the saying that is written will come true: "Death has been swallowed up in victory." "Where, O death, is your victory? Where, O death, is your sting?" The sting of death is sin, and the power of sin is the law. But thanks be to God! He gives us the victory through our Lord Jesus Christ.

1 Corinthians 15:51-57, NIV

Christians live forever

18

Lava Lips

FROM THE BIBLE:

We put bits in horses' mouths that they may obey us, and we turn their whole body. Look also at ships: although they are so large and are driven by fierce winds, they are turned by a very small rudder wherever the pilot desires. Even so the tongue is a little member and boasts great things. See how great a forest a little fire kindles! And the tongue is a fire, a world of iniquity. The tongue is so set among our members that it defiles the whole body, and sets on fire the course of nature; and it is set on fire by hell. For every kind of beast and bird, of reptile and creature of the sea, is tamed and has been tamed by mankind. But no man can tame the tongue. It is an unruly evil, full of deadly poison. With it we bless our God and Father, and with it we curse men, who have been made in the similitude of God. Out of the same mouth proceed blessing and cursing. My brethren, these things ought not to be so.

James 3:3-10, NKJV

Control your mouth

HI, MOM," called Tracie as she opened the front door. "We had the best class today! We learned about volcanos."

"That sounds interesting," replied Mother. "Volcanos are a fascinating part of nature."

Tracie nodded. "My teacher, Mr. Hoover, had a small model of a volcano. He could even make it erupt. Do you know what erupts from a real volcano?"

"Lava, hot gasses, and rock fragments," answered Tracie's brother Jason, who had also come in from school.

Tracie frowned. "I asked Mom, not you," she growled. Then she went on telling about the volcano. "Pressure builds up and the red hot ash blasts through the surface. Do you know where it erupts from?" she asked, looking at her mother.

Jason answered again. "From the mouth. It's at the top of a cone-shaped mountain," he said.

"Wrong!" declared Tracie triumphantly. "That's what it looks like, but the actual opening is lower than the top, or mouth. It's called a vent." She made a face at her brother. "Shows how much you know, Dummy. Next time mind your own business and don't answer unless I ask you."

"Tracie," Mother scolded, "a volcano isn't the only thing with a mouth. We have mouths, too. Perhaps eruptions don't come from the mouth of the volcano, but our mouths can erupt with hot, vicious, unkind words that hurt other people. I'm afraid you've been allowing that to happen. We can't control volcanic eruptions, but we *can* learn to control our tongues and our mouths."

HOW ABOUT YOU? Do unkind words sometimes slip out of your mouth? Remember that God made your mouth to praise and glorify Him. Words that hurt others don't please God. Ask Him to help you control your tongue when you feel a hot, vicious eruption building up. □ N.E.K.

TO MEMORIZE: *Out of the same mouth proceed blessing and cursing. My brethren, these things ought not to be so.* James 3:10, NKJV

TOM SCOWLED as he furiously raked leaves. He had been grumpy all afternoon. "I was gonna collect aluminum cans today to make a little money for a new skateboard," he muttered to himself. "Instead, here I am, doing stupid yard work." It was their first Saturday at their new home, and Dad insisted that Tom help with the work.

On the far side of a big tree, Tom noticed a large hole in the base of the tree. "Look, Dad," he called as he knelt to peer inside. "This would be a good place to hide stuff."

Dad walked over to look. "Maybe there's a cache of jewels or a sack of stolen money inside," he whispered teasingly. He poked his rake into the hole, and they heard a scraping sound as the rake hit a metal object.

"Something *is* hidden in there!" cried Tom. Plunging his hand inside the cavity, he felt around and finally pulled out a small box. Eagerly, Tom opened the old box and looked inside. Then he let out a disappointed groan. The "treasure" turned out to be a handful of multicolored stones, a rusty pocket knife, and a soggy, mildewed book of children's poems.

"Somebody must have treasured these things but then forgot about them," said Dad. "I hope he stored some of his treasures in a better place."

Maybe he put things in a safe deposit box when he got older," suggested Tom.

"I was thinking of an even better place than that," said Dad. "As Christians we should 'lay up treasures' in heaven, where they'll never be ruined or stolen."

Tom thought about the skateboard he wanted so much. He'd teased and begged for it. He'd grumbled when his parents didn't buy it for him. As he looked at the rusty pocket knife, he realized that all material things were bound to wear out or break down. Somehow, a skateboard didn't seem quite so important anymore.

HOW ABOUT YOU? Is there something you want very much? Maybe it's a toy like some of your friends have or something you saw on television. Earthly treasures don't last. Serving Christ brings treasure you will never lose. It's more priceless than all the possessions in the world. □ E.D.

TO MEMORIZE: *Store up for yourselves treasures in heaven, where moth and rust do not destroy, and where thieves do not break in and steal. For where your treasure is, there your heart will be also.* Matthew 6:20-21, NIV

19

Priceless Treasure

FROM THE BIBLE:
Do not store up for yourselves treasures on earth, where moth and rust destroy, and where thieves break in and steal. But store up for yourselves treasures in heaven, where moth and rust do not destroy, and where thieves do not break in and steal. For where your treasure is, there your heart will be also. . . . No one can serve two masters. Either he will hate the one and love the other, or he will be devoted to the one and despise the other. You cannot serve both God and Money.
Matthew 6:19-21, 24, NIV

Heavenly treasure is priceless

JANUARY

20

In the Beehive

FROM THE BIBLE:

God has arranged the parts in the body, every one of them, just as he wanted them to be. If they were all one part, where would the body be? As it is, there are many parts, but one body. The eye cannot say to the hand, "I don't need you!" And the head cannot say to the feet, "I don't need you!" On the contrary, those parts of the body that seem to be weaker are indispensable, and the parts that we think are less honorable we treat with special honor. And the parts that are unpresentable are treated with special modesty, while our presentable parts need no special treatment. But God has combined the members of the body and has given greater honor to the parts that lacked it, so that there should be no division in the body, but that its parts should have equal concern for each other. If one part suffers, every part suffers with it; if one part is honored, every part rejoices with it. Now you are the body of Christ, and each one of you is a part of it.

1 Corinthians 12:18-27, NIV

You are needed

LISA SLAMMED the door behind her. "I was looking forward to having the lead part in our youth pageant, but instead I have to make stupid props," she complained to her father, who was putting on his bee-keeper's outfit. "Carrie got picked for the lead." Lisa jumped up. "I want to go with you to the beehives," she said. They exchanged smiles as Lisa, too, slipped into a "bee suit."

At the beehive, Lisa watched as Dad pulled out a honeycomb from one of the hives. "Oh! Good!" he said. "I'm relieved to see that there aren't just queen bees in this hive, aren't you?"

Lisa was puzzled. "There's never more than one queen in a hive, Dad. You know that." she said.

"Yes, well, I'm just glad they're not *all* queens," repeated Dad. "Then there wouldn't be any workers to make the honey, and I like honey!" He checked each of the remaining honeycombs. "The Bible says that every member of the body has a job to do. In the beehive, each one needs to do his own job so the whole thing works together efficiently. The bees can't all be drones. They can't all be worker bees. And they can't all be queens. Each kind of bee is needed. It's that way in life, too."

"Oh, I think I know what you're trying to say, Dad." Lisa's eyes sparkled. "You're trying to tell me that making props is just as important as Carrie's position. Without props you can't have a good play."

Dad hugged Lisa. "Exactly."

"Then I'll be a bu-z-z-zy bee making props," Lisa giggled as she slid her hand into Dad's.

HOW ABOUT YOU? Are you content with what God has given you to do? Or do you often wish for a greater, more important position? God says each one is needed. He doesn't list any position as greater than another. He just asks you to do your best in whatever job you are given. Do whatever you do "as unto the Lord." □ D.A.L.

TO MEMORIZE: *God has arranged the parts in the body, every one of them, just as he wanted them to be.* 1 Corinthians 12:18, NIV

WHEN JEFF'S PARENTS had announced that they were moving to Taiwan to help the missionaries, Jeff hadn't realized that everything would be so strange. He was glad he had at least one friend who spoke English. George was his age, and he attended English classes at the mission. He had even taken an American name.

"I show you town," the friendly black-haired boy said one day in his best English. The boys hopped on their bikes. Dodging people, other bikes, and trucks on the narrow streets, they pedaled around the small town. "Come," said George as he parked his bike in front of a large building.

When George pushed open the door, Jeff gasped at what he saw. "God factory," explained George waving his hand at the rows and rows of half-made idols stacked on the floor of the warehouse. "My father makes. He paints faces. Very nice. Many people buy."

Jeff got a sick feeling in his stomach. He could not believe that people would make their own gods. How could man-made gods help anybody, when they were only pieces of wood? "Your father makes gods?" asked George.

Jeff shook his head slowly. Trying to make George understand, he found himself talking just like him. "No, George," he said, "we not make gods. Our God make us!"

Jeff had always known that God had made him, but he had never thought that was anything so special before. Now he realized what a wonderful God he had! He was so glad he knew the true God. Silently he prayed, "Thank You, God, for making me. Help me tell George and other people about You so they won't have to worship a man-made god who can't even hear their prayers."

HOW ABOUT YOU? Aren't you glad you can know the living God? He's the creator of the whole universe. But there are still many people who don't know that. Will you share this knowledge with them? Begin in your own neighborhood. Maybe someday God will even allow you to carry His message to other lands. □ M.N.

TO MEMORIZE: *Declare his glory among the nations, his marvelous deeds among all peoples.* 1 Chronicles 16:24, NIV

Who Made Whom?

FROM THE BIBLE:
Sing to the Lord, all the earth; proclaim his salvation day after day. Declare his glory among the nations, his marvelous deeds among all peoples. For great is the Lord and most worthy of praise; he is to be feared above all gods. For all the gods of the nations are idols, but the Lord made the heavens. Splendor and majesty are before him; strength and joy in his dwelling place. Ascribe to the Lord, O families of nations, ascribe to the Lord glory and strength, ascribe to the Lord the glory due his name. Bring an offering and come before him; worship the Lord in the splendor of his holiness. Tremble before him, all the earth! The world is firmly established; it cannot be moved. Let the heavens rejoice, let the earth be glad; let them say among the nations, "The Lord reigns!"
1 Chronicles 16:23-31, NIV

Tell about the living God

22

Side Effects

FROM THE BIBLE:

Happy is the man who doesn't give in and do wrong when he is tempted, for afterwards he will get as his reward the crown of life that God has promised those who love him. And remember, when someone wants to do wrong it is never God who is tempting him, for God never wants to do wrong and never tempts anyone else to do it. Temptation is the pull of man's own evil thoughts and wishes. These evil thoughts lead to evil actions and afterwards to the death penalty from God.
James 1:12-15, TLB

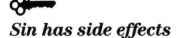

Sin has side effects

HI, SKIPPY." Jordan plopped his homework on the table as he greeted the bouncing puppy. Then he stared at his little sister. Her face and arms were covered with red splotches. "Boy, you look funny," he said.

"I don't feel funny," Melody snapped. "I itch all over."

Mother looked up from her needlework. "Melody had a reaction to the medicine she was taking. It's one of the side effects the doctor said could occur. 'Side effects' refers to problems caused by the medication," Mother explained.

Jordan had lost interest. "I'm going over to Butch's for a while," he said.

Mother shook her head. "Oh, no, you aren't. Your dad told you to clean the patio yesterday, and you didn't do it."

Jordan scowled. The look Mother gave him told Jordan not to say another word, and he stomped out to the patio, with Skippy eagerly running ahead. Angrily, Jordan picked up a horseshoe and threw it.

"Hoooowww!" Skippy howled as the horseshoe hit him.

Jordan ran to the whimpering puppy crumpled on the ground. "Oh, Skippy, I'm so sorry." Tears wet Jordan's cheeks as he yelled, "Mother! Mother! Skippy's hurt."

Much later, Jordan told his dad about it. "The vet said it was a miracle Skippy's back wasn't broken," he said.

"A temper out of control is a dangerous thing," said Dad.

Mother gently patted the puppy, who lay in Melody's red-splotched arms. "Medicine isn't the only thing that has side effects," said Mother. "Sin does, too." Jordan looked at his toes, as Mother continued, "Skippy is suffering the side effects of your sin, Jordan." She handed a bill to her husband and smiled. "And so is your dad. The vet's bill was fifty-two dollars."

Jordan brushed a tear from his eye as his father hugged him. "It's worth it, if you've learned your lesson, Son."

HOW ABOUT YOU? The next time you're tempted to do something wrong, ask yourself, What would be the side effects if I do this? It might save you and someone you love a lot of pain. □ B.W.

TO MEMORIZE: *The wages of sin is death, but the gift of God is eternal life in Christ Jesus our Lord.*
Romans 6:23, NKJV

SANDRA HEAVED a big sigh. "I sure wish we could go to Iowa for Grandma and Grandpa's twenty-fifth anniversary party," she said. "All my cousins will be there. Why does your boss have to be so mean and not let you off, Dad?"

"He's not being mean, Sandra," replied Dad. "It's just that too many other people requested that week off before I did."

"Why don't we pray about this?" suggested Mother cheerfully.

"Pray about it?" asked Sandra. "Do you think we ought to? My friend Clara says we shouldn't bother God with unimportant things, because He's busy running a whole universe. Does He want to be bothered with a family trip? I try not to bother Him with little things anymore."

Dad frowned. "Sandra, remember last December when I told you to make a list of what you'd like for Christmas?" he asked. Sandra nodded, and Dad continued, "You didn't say, 'Oh, I couldn't do that. You have your job to think about, and repairs to make on the house, and so many more important things.' "

"But you're my dad!" interrupted Sandra.

Dad nodded. "That's right," he said, "and I'd feel bad if you weren't comfortable giving me that list." He reached for his Bible and turned to Romans 8:14. He looked at Sandra. "God is your heavenly Father, Sandra, and He feels grieved when you don't confide in Him. Now, let's pray about that trip."

HOW ABOUT YOU? Did you know that God is interested in all your requests—even the "little" ones? It may be that you have a father who you feel really doesn't care about you. Well, you can be sure that your heavenly Father cares. He loves His children even more than an earthly father would. Even though His answer may be "no" or "wait a while," your requests are very important to Him. □ P.R.

TO MEMORIZE: *Be anxious for nothing, but in everything by prayer and supplication, with thanksgiving, let your requests be made known to God.* Philippians 4:6, NKJV

Trips and Small Things

FROM THE BIBLE:

And so it is with prayer—keep on asking and you will keep on getting; keep on looking and you will keep on finding; knock and the door will be opened. Everyone who asks, receives; all who seek, find; and the door is opened to everyone who knocks. You men who are fathers—if your boy asks for bread, do you give him a stone? If he asks for fish, do you give him a snake? If he asks for an egg, do you give him a scorpion? [Of course not!] And if even sinful persons like yourselves give children what they need, don't you realize that your heavenly Father will do at least as much, and give the Holy Spirit to those who ask for him?

Luke 11:9-13, TLB

Bring requests to God

24

The Whole Flower

FROM THE BIBLE:

Oh, the depth of the riches both of the wisdom and knowledge of God! How unsearchable are His judgments and His ways past finding out! "For who has known the mind of the Lord? Or who has become His counselor? Or who has first given to Him and it shall be repaid to him?" For of Him and through Him and to Him are all things, to whom be glory forever. Amen. . . . I beseech you therefore, brethren, by the mercies of God, that you present your bodies a living sacrifice, holy, acceptable to God, which is your reasonable service. And do not be conformed to this world, but be transformed by the renewing of your mind, that you may prove what is that good and acceptable and perfect will of God.

Romans 11:33-36; 12:1-2, NKJV

Give God your whole life

"MOTHER-R-R!" wailed Alyce. "Mrs. Purdy gave me a flower from her garden, and Kirk took it and wouldn't give it back. He tore it all up!"

"I gave it back," insisted Kirk.

"One petal at a time!" exclaimed Alyce.

"Kirk, you had no business taking your sister's flower," said Mother. "Since you did, you can stop at the florist's and use your own money to buy her another one when you go to get these things I need." She handed him a list.

After Kirk was gone, Mother mentioned that the youth pastor from church had called. "He'd like you to play the piano for youth meeting Sunday," she told Alyce.

Alyce shook her head. "I'm already working in the nursery on Sunday," she said. "That's enough."

That evening, Kirk asked Alyce if she planned to attend the special junior choir practice to prepare a number for the missionary meetings which were coming up soon. Alyce shook her head. "I have to work in the nursery at church on Sunday," she said. "I'm busy enough."

"Well, do you want to help me hunt for pop cans at the park to make some money for the special offering?" asked Kirk. "We usually do pretty well with that."

Alyce sighed. "I told you—I'm busy enough this week," she replied. "I shouldn't have to do everything!"

"One petal at a time," murmured Mother softly.

"What?" asked Alyce.

"You wanted a whole flower, not just one petal at a time," explained Mother. "God wants a whole life—a whole person. It seems to me that you want to give Him your baby-sitting services one week, your money another time, and maybe your voice the week after that—'one petal at a time.' Now it may be that that's all God will require in any given week, but He wants your whole life to be available to Him all the time."

Alyce was thoughtful as she glanced at the flower her brother had bought for her.

HOW ABOUT YOU? Is your whole life available for God's use every day of the week? Be ready to serve Him in as many ways as He may ask of you. Serve Him with your whole heart and life. □ H.M.

TO MEMORIZE: . . . *not lagging in diligence, fervent in spirit, serving the Lord.* Romans 12:11, NKJV

As CHAD HELPED his father dig up a small part of their grassy yard for a garden, they heard little Jenny coming across the lawn. "Me, too!" Jenny cried in her small voice. "I wanna help, Daddy! Me help."

"Jenny, you're too small for this job," said Dad. "Look! The shovel is bigger than you are."

Jenny stood watching for a moment, then ran off to her sand box. When she came back she had a little plastic shovel. She began poking it into the grass. "Oh, Dad, look!" said Chad. "Jenny thinks she can dig up the sod with that toy shovel."

Dad wiped perspiration from his forehead. "This is hard enough even with the right tools, Jenny," he said. "That shovel won't do the job."

After dinner that evening, Chad got his Bible and Sunday school book. "For Sunday school this week, I have to look up some verses on serving God," he said. "Can you help me, Dad?"

"Well, today you saw the importance of using the right tool for digging in the garden," said Dad, "and when you have to 'dig' in the Bible, it's a good idea to use the right tool, too. Look in the back of your Bible at the part called the 'concordance.' You'll find words listed there in alphabetical order, like in a dictionary." He helped Chad find the right section. "Here's the word *serve* and a list of references where the word is used," continued Dad. "You might see if those are what you need."

"Hey! All right!" exclaimed Chad. "It's neat to have them listed like that."

"There are several tools that make Bible study much easier and more enjoyable," said Dad. "A concordance, Bible dictionary, commentary, and maps are friends and helpers as we study God's Word."

HOW ABOUT YOU? Are there words in the Bible that you don't understand? Do you wonder where Bible people lived or what they ate and wore? Do you sometimes skip Bible reading because it seems strange? Using study tools can help you and your family enjoy God's Word. □ C.R.

TO MEMORIZE: *They received the word with all readiness, and searched the Scriptures daily to find out whether these things were so.* Acts 17:11, NKJV

Gardens and God's Word

FROM THE BIBLE:
Every young man who listens to me and obeys my instructions will be given wisdom and good sense. Yes, if you want better insight and discernment, and are searching for them as you would for lost money or hidden treasure, then wisdom will be given you, and knowledge of God himself; you will soon learn the importance of reverence for the Lord and of trusting him. Proverbs 2:1-5, TLB

Use Bible study tools

JANUARY

26

Dumb Excuses

FROM THE BIBLE:

*God loved the world so much
that he gave his only Son so that
anyone who believes in him
shall not perish but have eternal
life. God did not send his Son
into the world to condemn it,
but to save it. There is no
eternal doom awaiting those
who trust him to save them. But
those who don't trust him have
already been tried and condemned for not believing in the
only Son of God. Their sentence
is based on this fact: that the
Light from heaven came into the
world, but they loved the
darkness more than the Light,
for their deeds were evil. They
hated the heavenly Light because
they wanted to sin in the
darkness. They stayed away
from that Light for fear their
sins would be exposed and they
would be punished. But those
doing right come gladly to the
Light to let everyone see that
they are doing what God wants
them to.*

John 3:16-21, TLB

Go to God for help

BARBI STUBBORNLY shook her head. "My
dad and mom are going to the college playoffs on
the Saturday of the youth retreat," she said. "I
want to go with them."

"But that's just for one day," persisted Molly.
"The retreat is for the whole weekend. Why don't
you come?"

Barbi shrugged. "I don't have the right clothes
for it."

"Oh, honestly!" fumed Molly. "You make up the
dumbest excuses."

Barbi grinned. "Besides, it costs too much."

"Barbi Edwards!" exclaimed Molly. "You know
that's not true. A couple of families offered to
sponsor the group, so it doesn't cost a thing.
They've already paid for twenty kids to go, and so
far only fourteen are going."

But in spite of Molly's best efforts to persuade
Barbi to go to the retreat, she refused.

After Bible club one day, Barbi was quiet as she
and Molly walked home. "I don't get it," she said
suddenly. "Miss Ellis is always bugging us to 'be
saved.' I don't think I've done anything so bad."

Molly was thoughtful. "Well," she answered
slowly, "even though you think you're not so bad,
you're not good enough for heaven. No sin at all
can enter there, so even the 'little' bad things
you've done have to be forgiven."

"Maybe so," said Barbi with a shrug, "but Miss
Ellis said that Jesus paid the price for everyone
to go to heaven. If that's so, the price is paid for
my salvation, right? So I don't need to worry about
it."

Molly hesitated. "Remember the retreat?" she
asked.

"Retreat?" repeated Barbi. "I didn't go."

"No," said Molly, "but the price was paid for
you to go. You just made dumb excuses for not
accepting the offer. It's like that with salvation,
too. Jesus paid the price for you to go to heaven,
but unless you receive the gift God offers, you
won't go there. That makes sense, doesn't it?"

Barbi hesitated. "Yes, I guess it does," she
admitted. "I guess I need to accept the offer."

HOW ABOUT YOU? Have you accepted God's offer
of salvation? Or are you saying, "I'll think about
it," or "I want to do some fun things first?" Stop
making "dumb excuses." □ H.M.

TO MEMORIZE: *To all who receive him, to those who
believed in his name, he gave the right to become
children of God.* John 1:12, NIV

27

A Light Matter

"WHAT'S NEXT?" asked Christine as she walked into Aunt Rose's kitchen. Christine was helping her aunt do some fall housecleaning.

"This light fixture," said Aunt Rose as she climbed up a stepladder. "It hasn't been cleaned for a very long time." Christine watched her aunt loosen screws from the globe around the kitchen light. Aunt Rose removed the globe and looked inside it. "The dirt has certainly built up inside this fixture," she said. She handed the globe to Christine, who put it into some sudsy water.

"I'll give it a nice, hot, soapy bath," Christine said. "Then I bet it will give off twice as much light as before."

"I wouldn't be surprised," agreed Aunt Rose. "Light fixtures give off less light if they aren't cleaned regularly. And Christians are the same way."

"They are?" asked Christine. "Well, I should give off lots of light then. I shower every day."

Aunt Rose laughed. "I think you know that's not the kind of cleaning I'm talking about," she said, "nor the kind of light. Jesus is the Light of the world, and others should see Him in us. But if we don't wash often with the Word of God, it becomes hard for His love to shine through us. Our testimonies for Him generally become dimmer and dimmer." She dried the clean globe as she added, "We aren't effective lights for Jesus when the cares of the world build up inside us."

Aunt Rose replaced the globe and tightened the screws. Then Christine switched on the light, and it was easy to see that it was much brighter than before.

HOW ABOUT YOU? Have you been brightening up the world or casting shadows? Can others see the light of Jesus shining through you? Regular church attendance, private devotions, and time spent in prayer will help you to be a cheerful Christian who brightens the lives of others. □ D.E.M.

TO MEMORIZE: *Let your light shine before men, that they may see your good deeds and praise your Father in heaven.* Matthew 5:16, NIV

FROM THE BIBLE:
Before anything else existed, there was Christ, with God. He has always been alive and is himself God. He created everything there is—nothing exists that he didn't make. Eternal life is in him, and this life gives light to all mankind. His life is the light that shines through the darkness—and the darkness can never extinguish it. God sent John the Baptist as a witness to the fact that Jesus Christ is the true Light. John himself was not the Light; he was only a witness to identify it. Later on, the one who is the true Light arrived to shine on everyone coming into the world. John 1:1-9, TLB

Let Jesus shine through you

28

Deadly Flea Bite

FROM THE BIBLE:

Do not be yoked together with unbelievers. For what do righteousness and wickedness have in common? Or what fellowship can light have with darkness? What harmony is there between Christ and Belial? What does a believer have in common with an unbeliever? What agreement is there between the temple of God and idols? For we are the temple of the living God. As God has said: "I will live with them and walk among them, and I will be their God, and they will be my people." "Therefore come out from them and be separate, says the Lord. Touch no unclean thing, and I will receive you." "I will be a Father to you, and you will be my sons and daughters, says the Lord Almighty."

2 Corinthians 6:14-18, NIV

Watch the little things

A BLAST OF rock music hit Mother's ears as she entered the house. "Russell, turn that off!" she called. *Click.* "Blessed quietness," Mother sighed. "I wish you could understand the damage that kind of music is doing to you."

Russell's lip curled. "Awww, it's not hurting me, and I wish you'd quit bugging me about it. Can't Christians enjoy life?"

"You know they can," Mother replied, "but it worries me when you enjoy the wrong things."

Russell shook his head. "You'll never understand. You belong to a different generation."

The telephone interrupted him, and Mother went to answer it. "Hello. How are you, Mildred? Tom is in the hospital?" Russell followed his mother into the den and listened. "Bubonic plague? Are they sure? I though bubonic plague was wiped out years ago. Certainly we'll pray for him. As soon as Phillip gets home, we'll meet you at the hospital. Don't give up, Mildred. We serve a big God. Tell Tom we're praying for him, okay? Good-bye."

"What's bubonic plague?" Russell asked.

Mother collapsed into a chair. "It's a terrible disease. In the Middle Ages it was called the Black Plague, and it killed thousands. The doctor told Aunt Mildred about a few cases in the States the last few years."

"What causes it?" Russell asked.

"Fleas from infected rats are the carriers," Mother answered grimly.

"Fleas?" Russell was astounded. "Little bitty fleas?"

"Little things can be deadly," Mother told him. "We are much more afraid of a rattlesnake than a flea, yet a flea bite can be just as deadly. Little things can be just as dangerous as big things— sometimes more so because we tend to overlook them." She paused and looked directly at him. "Little sins can cause spiritual epidemics."

Russell took a deep breath. "Little things like rock music?" Mother nodded. "You might be right," Russell admitted.

HOW ABOUT YOU? Are little things creeping into your life which will weaken you spiritually? What about the music you listen to, the books you read, the words you say? Check your life now for little sins that you need to destroy. □ B.W.

TO MEMORIZE: *Let us purify ourselves from everything that contaminates body and spirit, perfecting holiness out of reverence for God.* 2 Corinthians 7:1, NIV

MIKE HARDLY RAISED his eyes when Dad called. "Come, Son. We have to clean the basement now." A moment later, Mike slowly put down the book he was reading and went to the basement. Dad handed him a broom, and Mike began dusting cobwebs out of corners, while Dad cleaned a shelf. "That must be a good book," Dad said.

"It sure is, Dad," agreed Mike as he reached into a musty corner with the broom. "It's about some enemy spies on a 'search and destroy' mission. They want to blow up a bridge, cutting the good guys off from escape. I just hope those spies can be kept from destroying the bridge." He stopped working while his mind went back to the story.

"Well, you'd better get on with your own 'search and destroy' mission," laughed Dad.

"You're right, Dad," said Mike, waving the broom. "Watch out, spiders! I'm coming after you!"

Dad dumped some trash in a container. "Every Christian has an enemy on a 'search and destroy' mission against him," he said. "Satan's goal is to steal, kill, and destroy. He tries to steal your love for God, kill your desire to serve Him, and destroy your witness for Him."

Mike was thoughtful. "Yeah," he said finally, "like the time I wanted to stay home and watch a TV program instead of going to Bible club. I guess he stole my love for God."

Dad said, "You know, there's only one way to fight Satan, and that's to stay close to Jesus. Then Satan can't harm you." Dad gave the basement an approving glance. "Thanks for helping. You've done a good job. Now you can go back to your book and see how it turns out," he added with a smile.

Mike grinned. "OK. But I'm going to do my Sunday school lesson first. I don't want to give Satan a chance to use that book to keep me from staying close to God!"

HOW ABOUT YOU? Are you aware of Satan's secret mission against you? He knows just how to turn you away from loving God fully. But you can fight him. When you want to disobey Mom, skip church, tell a lie, or do any wrong thing, it's Satan attacking you. Realize that, and ask Jesus to help you follow Him. □ C.Y.

TO MEMORIZE: *He who is in you is greater than he who is in the world.* 1 John 4:4, NKJV

Search and Destroy

FROM THE BIBLE:
If God is on our side, who can ever be against us? Since he did not spare even his own Son for us but gave him up for us all, won't he also surely give us everything else? Who dares accuse us whom God has chosen for his own? Will God? No! He is the one who has forgiven us and given us right standing with himself. Who then will condemn us? Will Christ? No! For he is the one who died for us and came back to life again for us and is sitting at the place of highest honor next to God, pleading for us there in heaven. Who then can ever keep Christ's love from us? When we have trouble or calamity, when we are hunted down or destroyed, is it because he doesn't love us anymore? . . . Nothing can ever separate us from his love. Death can't, and life can't. The angels won't, and all the powers of hell itself cannot keep God's love away. Our fears for today, our worries about tomorrow, or where we are—high above the sky, or in the deepest ocean— nothing will ever be able to separate us from the love of God. Romans 8:31-39, TLB

Fight Satan

JANUARY

30

Experienced Comforter

FROM THE BIBLE:

Blessed be the God and Father of our Lord Jesus Christ, the Father of mercies and God of all comfort, who comforts us in all our tribulation, that we may be able to comfort those who are in any trouble, with the comfort with which we ourselves are comforted by God. For as the sufferings of Christ abound in us, so our consolation also abounds through Christ. Now if we are afflicted, it is for your consolation and salvation, which is effective for enduring the same sufferings which we also suffer. Or if we are comforted, it is for your consolation and salvation. And our hope for you is steadfast, because we know that as you are partakers of the sufferings, so also you will partake of the consolation.
2 Corinthians 1:3-7, NKJV

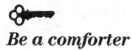

Be a comforter

"MAMA!" CALLED Janice loudly, "Kenny isn't helping me. Why should I have to pick up all the toys by myself?"

Mother found Kenny sitting on the floor, breathing hard. "Why, Janice—look at your brother! The dust must have triggered his asthma," Mother said with concern. "Go lie down, Ken, and I'll give you your medicine."

"Oh, Mom," complained Janice, "Kenny always gets out of everything just because he has asthma. It's not fair!"

Mother gave Janice a hug. "I know it seems that way at times," she said, "but it isn't his fault. I'm sure he would get rid of his asthma in a minute if he could."

"I'm not so sure," grumbled Janice.

A few days later, Janice developed a bad cough. Because she also had a high fever, Mother took her to the doctor. "It's bronchitis," he said. "I'll prescribe some medicine, and you'll need lots of rest for the next week or two, Janice."

Janice stayed inside for four days. She didn't like the medicine, and she missed playing with her friends. Worst of all, it was hard for her to breathe. She had to sleep propped up on pillows, the way Kenny slept sometimes. *Imagine feeling like this as often as he does*, Janice thought. Right then, she bowed her head and prayed—for herself, and especially for Kenny.

Finally Janice was able to go back to school. Right after school, she hurried home and entered the kitchen with a big smile. "It's so neat to be feeling good again," she told Mother.

"I imagine you're eager to go out and play with your friends, too," said Mother, grinning.

But Janice hung up her coat instead. "I think I'll go play a game with Kenny," she said. "I noticed that he acts tired lately, so I thought I'd try to cheer him up a while. I know now what it feels like to be sick."

HOW ABOUT YOU? Are you as sympathetic with others as you should be? Do you sincerely pray for them? Think of times you've been sick or have had problems. Try to remember little things people did for you which you liked. Give others the same kind of help you experienced. □ S.K.

TO MEMORIZE: . . . *who comforts us in all our tribulation, that we may be able to comfort those who are in any trouble, with the comfort with which we ourselves are comforted by God.* 2 Corinthians 1:4, NKJV

AFTER TRAVELING all day, Janet and her parents stopped at a motel. "Dear God," Janet prayed at bedtime, "please help my friends Donna, Jean, and Bill to accept You as their Savior."

"Have you ever told your friends about Jesus?" Dad asked as he tucked a blanket under Janet's chin.

"Well, no," Janet replied, "but I pray for them."

"Prayer is important," Mom said, "but we also need to share the gospel with others."

Before long the travelers were asleep. But suddenly, a loud, blaring noise burst into the night. Janet, Dad, and Mom jolted straight up in their beds. "The car horn must be stuck," Dad grumbled, half asleep. He grabbed his bathrobe and dashed to the door as the blaring sound continued. Dad ran out and yanked at the door of the car parked outside their room. "Get the keys," he yelled frantically. "I need to get in the car to unlock the hood."

Neither Mom nor Janet could hear him, so Dad raced back into the room. He dug into the pockets of the pants he had worn all day. Finally he zipped back outside and fumbled in the dark to get the key in the car door. By then, people in neighboring rooms were stirring.

"That isn't going to work." A man spoke loudly at Dad's shoulder. "You're trying to open *my* car." Dad was embarrassed. In the dark, the man's car looked just like his own, which was parked in the next space.

At bedtime the next day, Janet again prayed, "Please help my friends accept Jesus as Savior."

Mom looked at her thoughtfully. "Remember how all Dad's frantic efforts to turn off the horn last night were of no use at all?" she asked. "Just as Dad needed someone to point out his problem, your friends need you. Pray for them, and then witness to them."

HOW ABOUT YOU? Are you afraid to share the gospel at school because kids might laugh? Do you realize the importance of telling others about Jesus? Rather than sitting quietly while your friends run around seeking happiness in things that will not last, you need to pray and then obey God's command to tell others. □ N.E.K.

TO MEMORIZE: *Go therefore and make disciples of all the nations, baptizing them in the name of the Father and of the Son and of the Holy Spirit.* Matthew 28:19, NKJV

31

Go and Teach Them

FROM THE BIBLE:
In your hearts set apart Christ as Lord. Always be prepared to give an answer to everyone who asks you to give the reason for the hope that you have.
1 Peter 3:15, NIV

"The time has come," he said. "The kingdom of God is near. Repent and believe the good news!"
Mark 1:15, NIV

Tell others about Jesus

FEBRUARY

1

All God's Creatures

FROM THE BIBLE:

He waters the mountains from his upper chambers; the earth is satisfied by the fruit of his work. He makes grass grow for the cattle, and plants for man to cultivate—bringing forth food from the earth: wine that gladdens the heart of man, oil to make his face shine, and bread that sustains his heart. The trees of the Lord are well watered, the cedars of Lebanon that he planted. There the birds make their nests; the stork has its home in the pine trees. The high mountains belong to the wild goats; the crags are a refuge for the coneys. The moon marks off the seasons, and the sun knows when to go down. You bring darkness, it becomes night, and all the beasts of the forest prowl. The lions roar for their prey and seek their food from God. The sun rises, and they steal away; they return and lie down in their dens. Then man goes out to his work, to his labor until evening. How many are your works, O Lord! In wisdom you made them all; the earth is full of your creatures.
Psalm 104:13-24 NIV

Be kind to animals

THE DOG YELPED as Dale brought the stick down on its back. There was a rope around its neck, and the rope was attached to a wagon. "We'll get this dog trained," said Dale with a determined look on his face.

"Get going, dog!" shouted one of the boys. The poor dog struggled to get loose, but the rope tightened around its neck, and it made choking noises.

"What are you kids doing?" The boys stepped back when they saw Mr. Griffin coming across the street. Quickly he loosened the rope and set the dog free. Exhausted and frightened, it lay panting on the ground.

"We didn't mean to hurt him," stammered Dale. "We were just trying to train him to pull the wagon."

"Anyway, it's just a stray mutt," put in one of the others.

Mr. Griffin frowned. "Only a stray, you say. But it's still one of God's creatures. God cares about animals, and He doesn't want us to harm any of them."

"Animals are supposed to help people," said one of the boys, scuffing his shoe in the dirt.

"God gave us certain animals to help us in certain ways," replied Mr. Griffin. "He gave us big, strong ones to do heavy work, and he gave us little fellows like this dog to give us love and happiness. But all animals are part of God's creation, and God loves His creation. He wants us to be kind to all animals."

"I'm sorry I hurt the puppy," said Dale, and several other boys nodded.

"All right," said Mr. Griffin. "Now I'm going to take this little fellow home with me and see if I can find a good home for him."

HOW ABOUT YOU? Are you kind to animals? It's easy to be kind to your own pets, but what about stray animals or those that aren't very pretty or clean? God made them, too, and they have feelings and can be hurt just as much as a pampered pet. Don't cause pain or unhappiness to any creature. □ C.Y.

TO MEMORIZE: *How many are your works, O Lord! In wisdom you made them all; the earth is full of your creatures.* Psalm 104:24, NIV

A Look at the Heart

"WOW, MOM! I never knew all this stuff before." Keith was sitting on the floor, looking through an encyclopedia. "I'm doing a report on the heart for school. It's amazing how complicated God has made us!"

"Sounds interesting, Keith," responded Mother. "What did you learn?"

"Well, it says here that because of the heart, our blood circulates over a thousand times in just twenty-four hours, and it pumps over 5,000 quarts of blood in that time, too. And listen to this! If all our blood vessels were laid end to end, they would stretch almost 100,000 miles! And the most amazing thing is that the heart is only as big as our fist, yet it can do all that stuff." Keith paused as he wrote the facts on his paper.

"The Bible talks about the heart, too, Keith— but in the Bible the word *heart* represents our thoughts, attitudes, values, and emotions instead of the actual organ in our bodies. In Jeremiah we read that the heart is deceitful and wicked."

"That bad?" Keith asked, already knowing the answer.

"Right. We're all born with a sin nature," replied Mother. "God loved us so much, however, that He gave His Son to take the punishment for our sins. We couldn't do that ourselves. All we have to do is believe in Christ as Savior, and God will give us a new, clean heart."

Keith nodded. He had heard about the need for a new heart as long as he could remember, and a few years ago he had accepted Jesus as his Savior. "Mom, do you know what I'm going to do?" he said. "I'm going to write about the Bible in my report, too. Our teacher says we're supposed to put down everything we can find about our subject. What a great chance to tell him about the Lord!"

HOW ABOUT YOU? Do you have a new heart? In Jeremiah we read about the sinfulness of the heart. That sinfulness can only be taken care of by believing in Christ as our Savior. If you have never taken care of your sinful heart, why not do so today? □ L.W.

TO MEMORIZE: *Create in me a clean heart, O God, and renew a steadfast spirit within me.* Psalm 51:10, NKJV

FROM THE BIBLE:

This is what the Lord says: "Cursed is the one who trusts in man, who depends on flesh for his strength and whose heart turns away from the Lord. He will be like a bush in the wastelands; he will not see prosperity when it comes. He will dwell in the parched places of the desert, in a salt land where no one lives. But blessed is the man who trusts in the Lord, whose confidence is in him. He will be like a tree planted by the water that sends out its roots by the stream. It does not fear when heat comes; its leaves are always green. It has no worries in a year of drought and never fails to bear fruit. The heart is deceitful above all things and beyond cure. Who can understand it? "I the Lord search the heart and examine the mind, to reward a man according to his conduct, according to what his deeds deserve." Jeremiah 17:5-10, NIV

Ask Christ into your heart

3

A Memorial Rock

FROM THE BIBLE:

When the Philistines heard that Israel had assembled at Mizpah, the rulers of the Philistines came up to attack them. And when the Israelites heard of it . . . they said to Samuel, "Do not stop crying out to the Lord our God for us, that he may rescue us from the hand of the Philistines." Then Samuel took a suckling lamb and offered it up as a whole burnt offering to the Lord. He cried out to the Lord on Israel's behalf, and the Lord answered him. . . . The Philistines drew near to engage Israel in battle. But that day the Lord thundered with loud thunder against the Philistines and threw them into such a panic that they were routed before the Israelites. The men of Israel rushed out of Mizpah and pursued the Philistines, slaughtering them along the way to a point below Beth Car. Then Samuel took a stone and set it up between Mizpah and Shen. He named it Ebenezer, saying, "Thus far has the Lord helped us." 1 Samuel 7:7-12, NIV

Remember God's goodness

THE JOHNSON FAMILY stood looking at the big oak tree lying across their yard. During the night, a fierce storm had blown the tree down. Mark was the first to speak. "God sure did take good care of us, didn't He, Dad?"

"He surely did," Dad replied placing his hand on Mark's shoulder. "That really makes me stop and praise him."

Mark looked at their house standing just a short distance from the fallen tree, yet not harmed at all. "Yeah," he said in awe. "I hope I never forget all the things God has done for us. Whenever I'm scared of something, it helps to remember how God took care of me in the past."

"We had a story in Bible club about how Samuel once set up a stone as a memorial of how God had won a battle for Israel," commented Susan. "It had kind of a funny name, but it meant something like 'God has helped us.' "

"You're thinking of the name 'Ebenezer,' " said Mother. "Were you thinking of setting up a memorial rock of your own?"

Susan laughed. "Well, not exactly, but I thought maybe we could make a notebook of all the times God helps us. We could add to it whenever we get the chance."

"Hey, that's a good idea," agreed Mark. "Maybe we could put in a picture of all of us standing in front of this big tree. Whenever we see the picture we'll be reminded of God's help."

Mother and Dad both smiled approvingly. "We can call it our 'Ebenezer Book,' " suggested Dad. "What a good way to remember all that God has done for us."

HOW ABOUT YOU? Do you have a way of remembering the things the Lord has done for you? Have you received some special answers to prayer, or has God protected you in a dangerous situation? Maybe He's helped you through a hard class at school. Why don't you try to keep a record of what God has done for you? Don't do it to dwell on the past, but do it to be reminded of God's great help when you're faced with a difficult situation. □ D.R.

TO MEMORIZE: *I will sing of Your power; yes, I will sing aloud of Your mercy in the morning; for You have been my defense and refuge in the day of my trouble. Psalm 59:16, NKJV*

A Wonderful Meal

KAREN PICKED UP her Bible and carefully brushed off any dust that might have gathered since she used it last Sunday. This Bible had been a gift from the church for perfect attendance, and Karen wanted to keep it looking new as long as possible.

"But it won't do you much good if you don't read from it," her mother cautioned. Karen knew what her mother said was true. She had heard the same statement in church, but if she read from it, she might crease the page or bend the cover. And she didn't want that.

One day she picked up her mother's Bible and leafed through it with special care. "How come you let your Bible get so old-looking?" she asked seriously.

Mother smiled. "You don't mean an 'old-looking,' Bible," she corrected. "You mean 'used-looking,' don't you?"

Karen shrugged her shoulders. Suddenly she broke out in laughter. "Look what you wrote in it," she said, showing her mother the Bible. "It says 'Another wonderful meal.'"

"You'll find that all through the Bible," Mother replied without looking at the pages to which Karen pointed.

"Why would you put that in your Bible?" Karen asked, as she flipped through some other pages.

"God's Word is food for my spiritual life just like the meals I make are food for my physical needs," Mother explained. "The Bible gives strength, life, and maturity. It helps us to grow in love, and it keeps us from sin."

Karen thought about her mother's words. Her Sunday school teacher had said almost the same thing last week in class. Slowly Karen got up and went to her room. She picked up her beautiful Bible and opened it carefully. It was nice to keep it looking new, but it was more important to use it and benefit from God's teaching. She began to read and think about the words she was reading. Maybe someday she, too, would write in her Bible: "Another wonderful meal."

HOW ABOUT YOU? Are you keeping your Bible looking nice but unused? Is the Bible a part of your everyday life? Remember, it's your spiritual food. Don't neglect those meals. □ R.J.

TO MEMORIZE: *I meditate on your precepts and consider your ways.* Psalm 119:15, NIV

FROM THE BIBLE:
How can a young man keep his way pure? By living according to your word. I seek you with all my heart; do not let me stray from your commands. I have hidden your word in my heart that I might not sin against you. Praise be to you, O Lord; teach me your decrees. With my lips I recount all the laws that come from your mouth. I rejoice in following your statutes as one rejoices in great riches. I meditate on your precepts and consider your ways. I delight in your decrees; I will not neglect your word.
Psalm 119:9-16, NIV

Read the Bible

5

Better than a Phone

FROM THE BIBLE:

"He made the world and everything in it, and since he is Lord of heaven and earth, he doesn't live in man-made temples; . . . His purpose in all of this is that they should seek after God, and perhaps feel their way toward him and find him—though he is not far from any one of us. For in him we live and move and are! As one of your own poets says it, 'We are the sons of God.'"
Acts 17:24, 27-28, TLB

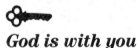

God is with you

ANN WAS A little nervous about baby-sitting way out in the country, but Mrs. King greeted her with a smile. She showed Ann a list of emergency numbers on a bulletin board near the phone. "As they say, help is as close as the telephone," she told Ann. Then with a wave and a smile, the Kings were gone.

Ann and the two children in her charge got along very well. Before sending them to bed, Ann fixed some toast and jelly as Mrs. King had instructed her to do. One slice burned, but she fixed a new one. She was buttering the last piece when they were all startled by the loud buzzing of the smoke alarm located in the hall. Ann gasped. *Lord, please show me what to do,* she prayed silently. Grasping each child by a hand, she hurried to the door and sent them to wait for her on the far side of the yard. As she watched them go, she picked up the phone and dialed the fire department. Then she hurried to join the children.

Soon the firemen came and hurried into the King's house. Before long, they came back out, grinning. "It's all right," they said. "We've checked everything. There's no fire, but smoke from a piece of bread caught in the toaster apparently tripped the smoke alarm." Ann was relieved, but she was also embarrassed because of having called the fire department over burned toast. "You did exactly the right thing," the firemen told Ann. "Never take a chance when there could be a fire."

"Know what?" Ann said later that night, after telling her mother about the excitement. "Mrs. King said help was as close as the phone, but it still took the firemen a little time to get here. I found out help was even closer than that. I asked the Lord to show me what to do, and He helped me right away."

HOW ABOUT YOU? Have you discovered that prayer is even better than a telephone? It takes time for people to come after you call them on the phone. God, on the other hand, is with you right now, and help is as near as He is. When you feel the need for help, call on Him. He wants you to do that. □ H.M.

TO MEMORIZE: *"I live in a high and holy place, but also with him who is contrite and lowly in spirit, to revive the spirit of the lowly and to revive the heart of the contrite."* Isaiah 57:15, NIV

As JANET WALKED into the nursing home with her mother, she wrinkled her nose. "What's that awful smell?" she asked. She had not really wanted to come here in the first place, and the smell of medication and illness didn't do anything to change her mind!

"These people are old and sick," Mother replied, "and a sickroom often has an unpleasant odor. But I think you'll be glad you came after you've visited Grandma Harper and some of the other people here. They're always such a blessing to me."

Janet could not imagine getting a blessing from being around these people. But she had promised to give a report next Sunday on her nursing home visit, so she just sighed and followed her mother down the hall.

They had hardly entered the room when Grandma Harper called out cheerily, "Oh, you brought your precious daughter!" Then she turned to Janet. "Honey, you'll have to forgive that outburst, but around here we seldom see such young and beautiful girls. Most of us have so many wrinkles we've forgotten what it was like to be young." She laughed pleasantly as she spoke, and Janet began to smile, too. Before long, she was telling the elderly woman about her school activities, her Sunday school class, and even about her birthday party. By this time there were several other people in the room, and at their urging, she sang a song for them. When they asked for another, Mother suggested that she sing an old, familiar one. Janet did, and soon several quavering, old voices joined the clear, young one in some well-loved hymns.

When they were ready to leave, Janet promised to bring other members of her class with her the next time. "You should hear them sing," she smiled.

Back in the car, Janet turned to her mother. "You were right, Mom," she said, "I'm the one who got the blessing."

HOW ABOUT YOU? Are there some elderly people in your hometown who would enjoy a visit from a group of young people? Many of the sick and elderly are not able to go to church. Will you visit them and share some of God's blessings with them? Remember, you, too, will be blessed. □ R.J.

TO MEMORIZE: *It is more blessed to give than to receive.* Acts 20:35, NKJV

Blessed and a Blessing

FROM THE BIBLE:
The righteous shall flourish like a palm tree, he shall grow like a cedar in Lebanon. Those who are planted in the house of the Lord shall flourish in the courts of our God. They shall still bear fruit in old age; they shall be fresh and flourishing, to declare that the Lord is upright; He is my rock, and there is no unrighteousness in Him.
Psalm 92:-12-15, NKJV

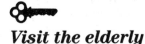

Visit the elderly

7

Guiding Stars

FROM THE BIBLE:

Do not enter the path of the wicked, and do not walk in the way of evil. Avoid it, do not travel on it; turn away from it and pass on. For they do not sleep unless they have done evil; and their sleep is taken away unless they make someone fall. For they eat the bread of wickedness, and drink the wine of violence. But the path of the just is like the shining sun, that shines ever brighter unto the perfect day. The way of the wicked is like darkness; they do not know what makes them stumble.

Proverbs 4:14-19 NKJV

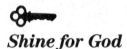

Shine for God

Don LOOKED AROUND at the darkening shadows. He was on a camp-out with some boys from church and their leader, Mr. Jordan. They had gone for a walk, and it had turned quite dark. The boys were starting to feel a little frightened. Don shivered and asked, "How are we going to find our camp, Mr. Jordan?"

An eerie sound made shivers run up and down their spines, and the boys stepped closer to their leader. "Now, boys, that was just an owl," said Mr. Jordan. "We'll be at camp in no time at all." He looked up and pointed. "Just what we need to guide us—the North Star!" He showed them how to find it and explained how it could help them find their way. Then they started off across a deserted field, keeping an eye on the bright star. Soon they were back at camp, sitting around a cozy campfire.

"Good thing we had that star to lead us," said Don.

"That's right," agreed Mr. Jordan. "Years ago, travelers and sailors used the stars to guide them." Then he added, "I'd like to see each of you boys shine for God like a guiding star, so you can lead others to know Him. Can you guess how you might do that?"

"Ah-h," began Don, thinking hard, "obey our parents?"

"Be nice to our brothers and sisters," one boy added.

"Play fair," said another boy.

"Obey the rules at school," offered still another.

"Those are great suggestions," Mr. Jordan agreed. "As you live in a way that pleases God, you have a good start in guiding others to him."

HOW ABOUT YOU? Are you willing to be a guiding light for God? When you do what God wants you to do, those who are watching will be pointed in the right direction. God will bless you for shining for Him. □ C.Y.

TO MEMORIZE: *The path of the just is like the shining sun, that shines ever brighter unto the perfect day.* Proverbs 4:18, NKJV

"Mommy!" SOBBED KELLI as she struggled through the doorway with her backpack, lunch pail, and doll.

Mother quickly dried her hands and hugged her little girl. "What's wrong, Honey?" she asked as she untied her daughter's hood and unzipped her coat.

"The big kids on the bus called me 'Four-eyes.' " Kelli sniffled as she took off her glasses to wipe away her tears. "I-I don't want to wear my glasses anymore." Mother sighed as she pulled Kelli's coat and boots off. "They said I was blind, too!" Kelli exclaimed. "I'm not blind, am I?"

"No, Honey," answered Mother. "You just need a little help so you can see clearly. Isn't it wonderful to be able to see better now? And you look very nice in your new glasses, too. The kids just like to tease—it doesn't mean anything. Ignore them, and they'll soon get tired of it."

Kelli looked at the glasses in her hand and then slipped them back on. "Being teased isn't as bad as not seeing," she decided.

Mother got up to answer the phone. When she returned a little later, she sat down with a sigh. "My friend Rachel reminds me of you," she said.

"Why, Mommy?" asked Kelli. "Does she get teased about wearing glasses?"

"No," Mother shook her head, "she sees well enough with her eyes. But I guess she has what the Bible calls 'blindness of heart.' She worries that she'll get teased about being a Christian. I'm so glad she has come to know the Lord, but when she's with her old friends, she often acts and talks just the way they do. She's afraid they'll tease her and laugh at her if she speaks up for the Lord. She's not as brave as you are, Kelli."

Kelli smiled. "I'll be braver tomorrow!" she declared.

HOW ABOUT YOU? Are you afraid of being teased and laughed at because you're a Christian? Are you afraid of being a little different from your friends? Don't be blind to what God wants you to do. The blessings He'll give as you live for Him are worth any teasing you may be asked to endure. □ V.R.

TO MEMORIZE: *You must no longer live as the Gentiles do, in the futility of their thinking.* Ephesians 4:17, NIV

FEBRUARY

8

Heart Blindness

FROM THE BIBLE:
So I tell you this, and insist on it in the Lord, that you must no longer live as the Gentiles do, in the futility of their thinking. They are darkened in their understanding and separated from the life of God because of the ignorance that is in them due to the hardening of their hearts. Having lost all sensitivity, they have given themselves over to sensuality so as to indulge in every kind of impurity, with a continual lust for more. You, however, did not come to know Christ that way. Surely you heard of him and were taught in him in accordance with the truth that is in Jesus. You were taught, with regard to your former way of life, to put off your old self, which is being corrupted by its deceitful desires; to be made new in the attitude of your minds; and to put on the new self, created to be like God in true righteousness and holiness. Ephesians 4:17-24, NIV

Don't be blind to God's ways

Hidden Treasure

FROM THE BIBLE:

"O you simple ones, understand prudence, and you fools, be of an understanding heart. Listen, for I will speak of excellent things, and from the opening of my lips will come right things; for my mouth will speak truth; wickedness is an abomination to my lips. All the words of my mouth are with righteousness; nothing crooked or perverse is in them. They are all plain to him who understands, and right to those who find knowledge. Receive my instruction, and not silver, and knowledge rather than choice gold; for wisdom is better than rubies, and all the things one may desire cannot be compared with her. I, wisdom, dwell with prudence, and find out knowledge and discretion. The fear of the Lord is to hate evil; pride and arrogance and the evil way and the perverse mouth I hate. Counsel is mine, and sound wisdom; I am understanding, I have strength."

Proverbs 8:5-14, NKJV

Wisdom is a treasure

PAUL LAID HIS report card on the table and picked up the newspaper. He raced upstairs, plopped down on his bed, and hurried through each page till he found what he was searching for. It was Part 3 of "Hidden Treasures"—a five-part article about the discovery of different treasures found in the seas. Paul eagerly read and then cut out the article. He often daydreamed about all the hidden treasures that hadn't been found yet—and what it would be like to find one and get rich!

After dinner, Paul's father picked up the paper. "What's been so interesting in the newspaper lately?" he asked. "I see that another article has been cut out."

Paul's eyes got big and dreamy as he told his dad all about the treasure articles and how he yearned to become a treasure hunter some day.

Dad smiled, but Mother raised her eyebrows and brought out Paul's report card. "It looks to me as if you've been concerned with the wrong kind of treasure lately," she observed. "Your school grades have gone down."

Paul sighed. "Oh, well, treasure hunters don't have to be so smart—just lucky!"

"The report card isn't all," said Mother. "Your Sunday school teacher says you've not done as well as usual there, either. You know, Proverbs says we must seek for wisdom with the same persistence that a treasure hunter searches for silver with. Wisdom is a treasure, Paul. The Bible describes it as being 'more precious than rubies.' "

"Your mother's right," agreed Dad. "The Bible also says that the 'fear of the Lord is the beginning of wisdom.' I think you need to get your treasure-hunting priorities in order, Son. I think it's time to put a little more effort into your school work—especially your Sunday school work."

"It's OK to dream of being a treasure hunter," added Mother, "as long as you find the treasure of wisdom first."

HOW ABOUT YOU? Do you search for wisdom? Are you growing in Bible knowledge and Christian living? Nothing can be compared to the treasure of wisdom, and it begins with learning what God wants to teach you from His Word. □ V.R.

TO MEMORIZE: *Wisdom is better than rubies, and all the things one may desire cannot be compared with her.* Proverbs 8:11, NKJV

10

Holy Holly

"I KNOW I should keep inviting Missy to Sunday school," Holly told her mother as they walked to the grocery store, "but I don't really want to anymore. I don't see how I could ever be her friend, anyway. Sometimes she swears at me or even hits me. But the worst thing is that she always says, 'Holy Holly. Holy Holly. Ho! Ho! Ho!' when she sees me. I hate that! I don't think God is going to use me to get her to Sunday school."

When they were almost to the store, Holly asked if she could run ahead. "I'll wait for you just inside the store," she promised.

"Oh, I don't know," said Mother. "Actually, I'm surprised you want to go into the store at all."

"Why?" asked Holly in surprise. "I always do."

"But the door is in the way," Mother pointed out.

Holly eyed her mother suspiciously. "What of it? Besides, it swings open by itself—almost like magic!"

"But how do you know it's going to open for you? These electric doors can fail, you know," persisted Mother.

"They never have before," replied Holly. "The store keeps them fixed."

"Aha!" Mother chuckled. "It sounds to me like someone has more faith in that store to keep their door in working order than in an all-powerful God to open doors He tells her to go through."

"What do you mean by that?" asked Holly.

"Just that if God wants you to do something, He'll make a way!" replied Mother. "He'll 'open the door' to make it possible. Holly, we both know God wants you to keep reaching out to Missy, don't we?"

"You're right, Mom," admitted Holly. "I know I should keep trying and that God will help me if I do. And I guess 'Holy Holly' isn't such a bad name after all!"

HOW ABOUT YOU? Are you discouraged and ready to give up doing something God wants you to do? Don't quit. Pray about it and trust God to open doors at just the right time. □ S.N.

TO MEMORIZE: *Praying also for us, that God would open to us a door for the word, to speak the mystery of Christ, for which I am also in chains.* Colossians 4:3, NKJV

FROM THE BIBLE:
Continue earnestly in prayer, being vigilant in it with thanksgiving; meanwhile praying also for us, that God would open to us a door for the word, to speak the mystery of Christ, for which I am also in chains, that I may make it manifest, as I ought to speak. Walk in wisdom toward those who are outside, redeeming the time. Let your speech always be with grace, seasoned with salt, that you may know how you ought to answer each one.
Colossians 4:2-6, NKJV

Trust God to open doors

11

Soap in a Pillow

FROM THE BIBLE:

"The kingdom of heaven will be like ten virgins who took their lamps and went out to meet the bridegroom. Five of them were foolish and five were wise. The foolish ones took their lamps but did not take any oil with them. The wise, however, took oil in jars along with their lamps. The bridegroom was a long time in coming. . . . At midnight the cry rang out: 'Here's the bridegroom! Come out to meet him!' . . . The foolish ones said to the wise, 'Give us some of your oil; our lamps are going out.' 'No,' they replied, 'there may not be enough for both us and you. Instead, go to those who sell oil and buy some for yourselves.' But while they were on their way to buy the oil, the bridegroom arrived. The virgins who were ready went in with him to the wedding banquet. And the door was shut. Later the others also came. 'Sir! Sir!' they said. 'Open the door for us!' But he replied, 'I tell you the truth, I don't know you.' Therefore keep watch, because you do not know the day or the hour."

Matthew 25:1-13, NIV

Be ready when Jesus comes

MOTHER AND CINDY finished arranging the folds of the freshly-laundered curtains in the guest room. "They look so pretty," remarked Cindy. "I'm glad Grandma's coming for a long visit."

Mother smiled as she unwrapped a bar of delicately scented soap. "So am I, Cindy." She handed the soap to Cindy. "Tuck this between the pillows," she said.

"Mother, why are we putting soap in Grandma's bed?" asked Cindy. She sniffed the bar before tucking it in.

"That scented soap will make the pillows smell sweet and fresh for as long as we leave it there." replied Mother. "We're not quite sure just when Grandma will arrive, but we can have the bed ready ahead of time, and the soap will make it seem 'same-day' fresh."

"Oh," said Cindy. "Just like getting ready for Jesus."

Mother looked puzzled. "What do you mean?" she asked.

"Pastor Bank said in his sermon last Sunday that Jesus is coming back someday—nobody knows quite when. If we want to go to heaven, we need to get ready now, because when He comes there will be no time to get ready then," explained Cindy. She grinned. "And I bet you thought I didn't listen!"

Mother smiled back. "And do you know how we get ready for the Lord's return?" she asked. "A bar of soap won't help."

"No," agreed Cindy. "We need to invite Jesus into our lives and be saved."

Mother nodded. "Good," she said. "No one needs to be left behind when Jesus comes."

"I'm ready for Grandma 'cause I put soap in her bed," said Cindy. "Better yet, I'm ready for Jesus because I have Christ in my heart."

HOW ABOUT YOU? If Jesus comes back today, will you go to heaven to be with Him forever, or will you be left behind in the world of confusion, without a Savior? Ready or not, He'll come someday. The foolish virgins in today's Scripture missed a marriage because they weren't ready. Don't miss heaven because you're not ready. Invite Jesus into your heart and let His presence sweeten your life. □ L.A.T.

TO MEMORIZE: *"Keep watch, because you do not know the day or the hour."* Matthew 25:13, NIV

JIM THREW his books on the counter, took an apple from the fruit bowl, and looked over to the corner where a small dog lay in a basket. "How's Alpha, Mom?" he asked.

Alpha was a little dog that looked like a mop with no handle, and she had developed some distressing symptoms. First she had a cough, then a lack of appetite, then a lump on her neck, and finally a nasty sore.

"I took her to the vet," Mother answered Jim. "He gave me some medicine for the sore, but he said we shouldn't get our hopes up, Son."

Several days later, Jim's mother called from the kitchen. "Come and see what I've found." Jim and the rest of the family arrived just in time to see Mother pull a sewing needle, with a bit of thread attached, from poor Alpha's neck. "Alpha must have swallowed this needle, and it lodged in her throat," said Mother. "If it hadn't worked itself out, it could have been the end of her!"

"Aha!" exclaimed Dad. "Now we know the cause of all those symptoms."

Jim gently patted the whimpering dog. "Now you'll get better, Alpha," he said encouragingly.

Before many days, Alpha was recovered. "That dog reminds me of people," said Dad as he watched her romp in the yard. "Her symptoms were not her real problem. The needle was her problem. Once that was removed, she got well. People have symptoms, too, such as acts of pride, envy, and anger—all a result of a sinful heart. They often try to reverse the symptoms or cover them up with good works. But the only real cure is to remove the problem—to remove the sin in their hearts. And the only way to do that is through the Lord Jesus Christ."

HOW ABOUT YOU? Is your life filled with the symptoms of sin—such as discontent, the inability to behave properly, or lack of friendliness? Do you know what the cure is? It's found in God's "medical dictionary," His Word. Come to Jesus and let Him wash away your sins—the real cause of your symptoms. □ P.R.

TO MEMORIZE: *"Though your sins are like scarlet, they shall be as white as snow; though they are red as crimson, they shall be like wool."* Isaiah 1:18, NIV

12
Symptoms

FROM THE BIBLE:
"Wash and make yourselves clean. Take your evil deeds out of my sight! Stop doing wrong, learn to do right! Seek justice, encourage the oppressed. Defend the cause of the fatherless, plead the case of the widow. Come now, let us reason together," says the Lord. *"Though your sins are like scarlet, they shall be as white as snow; though they are red as crimson, they shall be like wool. If you are willing and obedient, you will eat the best from the land."* Isaiah 1:16-19, NIV

Have sins washed away

13

The Rooster Lays an Egg

FROM THE BIBLE:

Evil men and false teachers will become worse and worse, deceiving many, they themselves having been deceived by Satan. But you must keep on believing the things you have been taught. You know they are true for you know that you can trust those of us who have taught you. You know how, when you were a small child, you were taught the holy Scriptures; and it is these that make you wise to accept God's salvation by trusting in Christ Jesus. The whole Bible was given to us by inspiration from God and is useful to teach us what is true and to make us realize what is wrong in our lives; it straightens us out and helps us do what is right. It is God's way of making us well prepared at every point, fully equipped to do good to everyone.
2 Timothy 3:13-17, TLB

Check the book (the Bible)

"WHY DON'T ROOSTERS lay eggs?" asked Martin as he watched his aunt and his cousin, Lynne, stuff a big Rhode Island Red rooster.

Lynne laughed. "Oh, but they do," she said. "Marty, will you please get out the meat thermometer from that cupboard behind you?" she asked. Martin found the thermometer, and when he turned back again, Lynne withdrew her hand from inside the bird. "I found an egg!" she exclaimed. "Look!" Martin could hardly believe his eyes as Lynne held out a big egg.

Aunt Marcia hid a smile. "Martin," she said, "I think Lynne is playing a joke on you. Go take a look at the book on the coffee table—it tells a lot about birds."

Martin went to see. As he paged through the book, he read, "The male fowl does not lay eggs." He ran to show his aunt and cousin.

"While you were getting the meat thermometer, I put an egg in the old rooster just for fun," Lynne chuckled. "I guess I didn't really expect you to believe me."

"Your joke reminded me of something serious," said Aunt Marcia. "It reminded me that we need to watch out for deceivers who purposely give out false information. Satan is like that—he wants to deceive us, and he's not doing it just for fun like Lynne did with the egg. Can you think of some ways he tries to fool us?"

"He wants us to think that we're good kids and have no need of a Savior," suggested Lynne.

"Yeah," agreed Martin, "and he wants us to think we don't need to go to Sunday school or church."

Aunt Marcia nodded. "And just like Martin checked a book to learn the truth about chickens, you must keep checking God's Book, the Bible, so you will not be fooled."

HOW ABOUT YOU? Have you ever felt foolish over being deceived? It's not so serious when someone fools you just to tease, but don't let Satan deceive you. He may try to convince you that it's okay to tell a "little" lie. He may say it's all right to cheat sometimes. He may encourage you to disobey your parents. He tries many ways to deceive you, so keep checking the Book! □ P.R.

TO MEMORIZE: *He must hold firmly to the trustworthy message as it has been taught, so that he can encourage others by sound doctrine and refute those who oppose it.* Titus 1:9, NIV

DAWN COUGHED uncontrollably and then put her head back down on the pillow. This cold, or flu, or whatever it was, made her feel terrible. "What makes you get the flu?" Dawn asked, looking up at her mother.

Mother smiled. "A virus, I guess," she replied. "At least that's what they think."

"What does a virus look like?" Dawn asked.

Mother shook her head. "You can't see a virus," she answered, "unless you're looking through a microscope."

"If a virus is that small," Dawn countered, "how can it make a person feel so awful?"

"Because once it gets into your system, it grows and fights until you aren't strong enough to overcome its power," replied Mother. "It wins, and you get sick."

Dawn's father, who had just stepped into the room, agreed. "That's a good illustration of the way sin works in our lives," he said. "When we become careless in our Christian lives," Dad explained, "sin gets in and takes control. If we don't confess our sin and ask Jesus to cleanse us, sin grows. Soon we allow it to lead us into other sinful things."

"That's why it's so important to confess our sin when we know we've done something that is not pleasing to God," added Mother. "We must ask His forgiveness before sin grows and develops into something even more serious."

Dawn sat up and coughed again. She felt lousy! She wished her virus had been stopped before it developed into the illness she had now. If sin grew like that, she'd have to agree that it had better be taken care of right away. As Dawn remembered the unkind words she'd exchanged with Kelli, she closed her eyes and asked Jesus to forgive her. As soon as she felt better, she'd call Kelli and ask her to forgive her, too. She sure didn't want that "sin virus" to develop into a full-scale quarrel.

HOW ABOUT YOU? Have you told any "little" lies lately? Have you sneaked a couple of cookies when Mom wasn't looking? Were there some unkind words, or thoughts directed toward a friend? Whatever "little" sin there may be in your life, it needs to be taken care of before it develops and grows. Confess it today. □ R.J.

TO MEMORIZE: *If we confess our sins, He is faithful and just to forgive us our sins and to cleanse us from all unrighteousness.* 1 John 1:9, NKJV

FEBRUARY
14

Virus Doesn't Show

FROM THE BIBLE:
This is the message which we have heard from Him and declare to you, that God is light and in Him is no darkness at all. If we say that we have fellowship with Him, and walk in darkness, we lie and do not practice the truth. But if we walk in the light as He is in the light, we have fellowship with one another, and the blood of Jesus Christ His Son cleanses us from all sin. If we say that we have no sin, we deceive ourselves, and the truth is not in us. If we confess our sins, He is faithful and just to forgive us our sins and to cleanse us from all unrighteousness.
1 John 1:5-9, NKJV

Confess "little" sins

15

The Umbrella

FROM THE BIBLE:

The law of the Lord is perfect, converting the soul; the testimony of the Lord is sure, making wise the simple; the statutes of the Lord are right, rejoicing the heart; the commandment of the Lord is pure, enlightening the eyes; the fear of the Lord is clean, enduring forever; the judgments of the Lord are true and righteous altogether. More to be desired are they than gold, yea, than much fine gold; sweeter also than honey and the honeycomb. Moreover by them Your servant is warned, and in keeping them there is great reward.
Psalm 19:7-11, NKJV

Open your Bible and read

MOMMY, I WANT that 'brella," pleaded four-year-old Missi, pointing to a brightly colored umbrella on display in the children's department.

Mother laughed. "Well," she said, "the way it's been raining lately, it might be a good idea for you to have your own umbrella. We'll see how much it is." The price was right, and the saleslady showed Missi how she could carry it by a strap over her wrist when it wasn't raining. Missi walked proudly from the store, merrily swinging the umbrella back and forth.

The next day, to Missi's delight, it rained. "Can I go outdoors with my 'brella? Please, Mommy?" she begged.

Mother smiled at her eager little daughter. "All right," she agreed. "Just for a little while."

When Mother looked out the window a little later, she saw Missi hurrying up the front walk, her new umbrella swinging on her arm while the rain pelted down on her head. Mother hurried to the door. "My 'brella don't work good," complained Missi. "I'm all wet!"

"The umbrella works all right," Mother replied, drawing Missi inside, "but you have to open it and hold it over your head if you want it to do its job." She helped Missi change into dry clothes and then allowed her to go out once more, this time with the umbrella opened and held high. That evening, the rest of the family laughed when they heard the story, but Missi pouted.

"It's OK, Sweetheart," Dad told her, reaching for the Bible he used in family devotions. "Sometimes we all act a lot like you did."

Missi's face brightened. "You do?"

"Yep," said Dad, nodding. "You left your umbrella closed, and too often we leave this Book closed." He held up the Bible. "God's Word helps us understand His plan for us, and teaches us about Him. It also keeps us from sin. Just as you needed to open your umbrella to get any use from it, we need to open our Bibles. Let's do that right now."

HOW ABOUT YOU? Do you open your Bible and read something from God's Word every day? You should. It can't help you if you leave it closed. □ H.M.

TO MEMORIZE: *The law of the Lord is perfect, converting the soul; the testimony of the Lord is sure, making wise the simple.* Psalm 19:7, NKJV

"I HATE YOU!" Julie screamed as she ran out of the house. She was glad to see the school bus coming around the corner. She climbed on quickly before her mother had a chance to call her back, but she knew she would have to answer for her words when she got home from school.

Later, Julie's anger began to go away, but she didn't want to lose it. When she felt it weakening, she would feed it bitter thoughts. *Why does she always say no? Why can't she be like Connie's mother? Her mom lets her do what she wants to do.*

At lunchtime Julie scowled. Thanking God for her food didn't fit her mood, so she skipped it. Feeling guilty, she pulled her favorite sandwich from her lunchbox. Tucked in the sandwich bag was a note, "Julie, I love you. Mother." Julie felt a bit ashamed, but not too much. *She's just feeling guilty for not letting me go to Lana's party,* she reminded herself.

By the time school was dismissed, Julie had made a long list of complaints to present to her mother. She had to have something to justify her angry words that morning. She was thinking about them when she heard sirens scream, and a fire engine roared past the bus. The kids watched and talked excitedly as the bus followed slowly. When Julie saw the lights flashing in front of her house, terror gripped her. She stumbled from the bus and ran wildly up the street. Was her house on fire? Where was her mother?

Frantically, she searched the crowd. Oh, there was Mother, standing on the edge of the crowd, watching the firemen pour water onto the burning storage building behind the house. Sobbing, Julie ran into her mother's arms, "Oh, Mama," she whispered, "I'm sorry! I love you!"

HOW ABOUT YOU? Do you ever leave home with sharp words hanging between you and your family? Do you feed those feelings of anger with bitter thoughts? Right now, make up your mind to stop. Determine to say only words you would not regret if you knew they were the last words you would ever say to that person. □ B.W.

TO MEMORIZE: *In the multitude of words sin is not lacking, but he who restrains his lips is wise.* Proverbs 10:19, NKJV

16

The Last Words

FROM THE BIBLE:
But how can I ever know what sins are lurking in my heart? Cleanse me from these hidden faults. And keep me from deliberate wrongs; help me to stop doing them. Only then can I be free of guilt and innocent of some great crime. May my spoken words and unspoken thoughts be pleasing even to you, O Lord my Rock and my Redeemer.
Psalm 19:12-14, NIV

Watch your words

FEBRUARY

17

The Most Important Call

FROM THE BIBLE:

Then the Lord called Samuel. Samuel answered, "Here I am." And he ran to Eli and said, "Here I am; you called me." But Eli said, "I did not call; go back and lie down." So he went and lay down. Again the Lord called, "Samuel!" And Samuel got up and went to Eli and said, "Here I am; you called me." "My son," Eli said, "I did not call; go back and lie down." Now Samuel did not yet know the Lord: The word of the Lord had not yet been revealed to him. The Lord called Samuel a third time, and Samuel got up and went to Eli and said, "Here I am; you called me." Then Eli realized that the Lord was calling the boy. So Eli told Samuel, "Go and lie down, and if he calls you, say, 'Speak, Lord, for your servant is listening.' " So Samuel went and lay down in his place. The Lord came and stood there, calling as at the other times, "Samuel! Samuel!" Then Samuel said, "Speak, for your servant is listening."

1 Samuel 3:3-10, NIV

God still calls today

THE TELEPHONE RANG and Mary ran to answer it. It was her friend Clair, and they talked for a long time, even though they had just seen each other at school. Soon after they hung up, the phone rang again. This time it was a very important long distance call for her father. After a third call came that evening, Mary laughed. "It's a good thing we have a telephone," she said, and everyone agreed.

Nothing more was said about the telephone calls until evening devotional time. Then Mary's dad brought up the subject. "You know, those phone calls remind me that God often calls, and He expects us to listen and obey."

Mary laughed ever so slightly. "But God doesn't have a telephone," she replied.

"No," Dad agreed. "But He has other ways to call us."

"How?" Mary wanted to know.

"Well," began Mother, "there's that still small voice He uses sometimes. That's the way he called Samuel. Remember? And He also talked to Elijah that way."

Mary nodded. She had heard the stories many times.

"Today He uses His Word to call us," Dad added. "He uses it to show us things that are wrong in our lives. Other times He tells us things to do. And sometimes He just wants to talk with us."

"Like when Clair called me today," Mary spoke up. "We just wanted to talk to each other."

"That's right," her father said. "Your call was pleasure, and my call was business. The important thing is that we were here so we could listen to the caller."

Mary thought abut that for a minute. "And that's what God wants us to do, too?" she asked. "Be where He can call us and make us listen?" Her mother and father both nodded. That was it. That was important. In fact, that was most important!

HOW ABOUT YOU? Are you living where God can speak to you? Or do you let your daily activities crowd out His call? Sometimes you need to take time off from your "busyness" and spend extra time with God's Word. You need to be quiet so you can hear Him speak. □ R.J.

TO MEMORIZE: *The Lord had called us to preach the gospel to them.* Acts 16:10, NKJV

JERRY RINSED the soap suds from the hood of the car and moved the hose to the driver's side. He picked up his portable radio and moved it, too. When he set it down again, it suddenly went dead. As he shook it, his father came outside. "Got a problem?" Dad asked.

Jerry nodded. "Maybe this radio needs new batteries, but it was playing fine till I moved it."

"Try turning it in a circle," suggested Dad.

Jerry didn't think that was very good advice, but he tried it. Amazingly, the radio began to play again! But when he set it beside a tree, once more it quit. "I give up!" cried Jerry.

Dad walked over. He picked up the radio and slowly moved it. The music blared! "You're using that old radio of mine, and it helps to turn the antenna toward the broadcasting tower," he said.

"Oh, I see!" This was beginning to make sense. "When I moved it, I turned it away from the station's signal."

"Right!" Dad looked at the little radio. "Maybe I could use this in my Sunday school class this week."

Jerry began to wash the car door. "What does the radio have to do with the Bible?" he asked.

"Our lesson is going to be about the help God gives us when we look to Him," explained Dad.

Jerry wiped his hands and picked up his radio, slowly turning it. The station went off and came back on. "I get it!" he said. "We're like my radio. We have to be turned in the right direction. When we trust God rather than other people or things, He gives us the help we need and the power to live for Him."

HOW ABOUT YOU? Do you wonder why God hasn't helped you with a particular problem? Are you sure you're turned toward Him? Have you prayed about your problem? Have you looked into His Word to see if He wants to use it to guide you? Are you really trusting Him to help you? He'll do His part. Your part is to completely trust in Him and allow Him to direct your life. Then you'll find that you can do things you thought impossible. God has a plan for you. Stay tuned in to Him! □ M.S.

TO MEMORIZE: *I lift up my eyes to you, to you whose throne is in heaven.* Psalm 123:1, NIV

FEBRUARY

18

The Portable Radio

FROM THE BIBLE:
I lift up my eyes to the hills—
where does my help come from?
My help comes from the Lord,
the Maker of heaven and earth.
He will not let your foot slip—he
who watches over you will not
slumber; indeed, he who
watches over Israel will neither
slumber nor sleep.
Psalm 121:1-4, NIV

I lift up my eyes to you, to you
whose throne is in heaven. As
the eyes of slaves look to the
hand of their master, as the eyes
of a maid look to the hand of
her mistress, so our eyes look to
the Lord our God, till he shows
us his mercy.
Psalm 123:1-2, NIV

Turn to God for help

19

The Boss's Boss

FROM THE BIBLE:

You slaves must always obey your earthly masters, not only trying to please them when they are watching you but all the time; obey them willingly because of your love for the Lord and because you want to please him. Work hard and cheerfully at all you do, just as though you were working for the Lord and not merely for your masters, remembering that it is the Lord Christ who is going to pay you, giving you your full portion of all he owns. He is the one you are really working for. And if you don't do your best for him, he will pay you in a way that you won't like—for he has no special favorites who can get away with shirking.

Colossians 3:22-25, TLB

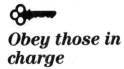

Obey those in charge

"SOMEONE'S ALWAYS BOSSING me around," griped Tim. "My teacher said I had to quit talking in class. My dad said I had to clean the garage. My mom said I had to make my bed each morning. My Sunday school teacher said that I have to learn my Bible verses. My pastor said . . ."

"That's quite a list of bosses," Grandpa Hill teased.

"My pastor said that I have to obey all these people!" added Tim.

"And you do," Grandpa agreed.

"I'll be glad when I grow up. Then I'll be my own boss," sighed Tim.

Grandpa chuckled. "That's just what I thought when I was eleven, but now I have more bosses than ever."

"You do?" asked Tim. "Who's your boss?"

It was Grandpa's turn to count. "First, there is God. Second, your pastor is my pastor, too. Remember?"

"But does Pastor Green tell you what to do?"

"He certainly does! Oh, he doesn't say, 'Sweep the floor,' 'Pay your tithes,' 'Visit the nursing home.' But lots of times he has preached sermons that told me what I needed to do. God placed him in the church to lead me."

"Who else tells you what to do?" Tim questioned.

"My employer gives me orders at work. The city council tells me if I can build a new house and if I can keep chickens. The police tell me where I can park my car."

Tim sighed. "I guess you're right. You sure take the fun out of growing up."

"Homer!" Grandma called. "Please come and take out this trash."

Grandpa stood up. "I'm coming, Sarah." He grinned at Tim as he spoke. "Even your grandmother tells me what to do," he joked, and Tim laughed. "But really, it's not so bad having a boss," added Grandpa. "Saves you the trouble of having to figure it out for yourself."

HOW ABOUT YOU? Sure you get tired of being bossed around! But remember, God has placed people in authority over you to save you a lot of heartache. You will never be sorry for being obedient. □ B.W.

TO MEMORIZE: *Obey those who rule over you, and be submissive, for they watch out for your souls.* Hebrews 13:17, NKJV

CARRIE COULD HARDLY believe what her English teacher was saying. "We're going to give speeches next week," said Miss Thompson. "Pick any topic in which you're interested, and be prepared to talk about it for three minutes."

Carrie was so upset she could hardly wait to speak to her teacher about it after class. As soon as the other students had left, she approached Miss Thompson. "Please don't make me give a speech, Miss Thompson," she pleaded in a shaking voice. "I just can't talk in front of people! I know I'll make a mistake, and the other kids will laugh at me!"

Her teacher smiled kindly. "Part of being a good speaker is learning to forget about yourself and to concentrate on your subject matter. Don't worry so much about what others will think. Just be yourself. I'm sure you'll do fine."

During the next few days, Carrie often thought and prayed about her speech. When her turn finally came, she swallowed hard and walked up to the front of the room. "My topic for today," she said in a nervous, squeaky voice, "is 'stage fright.' It's something I really feel like an expert on." The kids laughed, and Carrie began to feel better. She talked about the causes of stage fright and about some famous people who had problems with it. She shared some of what she had learned from Miss Thompson, and she ended by saying, "A verse in the Bible has really helped me this week. It's Philippians 4:13: 'I can do all things through Christ who strengthens me.' "

As Carrie went back to her seat she thought, *That wasn't so bad, after all. I don't think I'd want to make another speech right away, but if I had to, I'm sure God would help me again!*

HOW ABOUT YOU? Does it make you nervous to have to talk in front of a group of people? It's true that some people are just naturally more shy than others. But it will help if you are honest about your nervousness and if you stop worrying about what others will think of you. Pick a subject about which you feel strongly, and use the opportunity as a witness to God's help and power. If He wants you to speak, either privately or publicly, He will help you find the right words to say. □ S.K.

TO MEMORIZE: *"Now therefore, go, and I will be with your mouth and teach you what you shall say."* Exodus 4:12, NKJV

20

Stage Fright

FROM THE BIBLE:
Moses said to the Lord, "O my Lord, I am not eloquent, neither before nor since You have spoken to Your servant; but I am slow of speech and slow of tongue." So the Lord said to him, "Who has made man's mouth? Or who makes the mute, the deaf, the seeing, or the blind? Have not I, the Lord? Now therefore, go, and I will be with your mouth and teach you what you shall say." But he said, "O my Lord, please send by the hand of whomever else You may send." So the anger of the Lord was kindled against Moses, and He said: "Is not Aaron the Levite your brother? I know that he can speak well. And look, he is also coming out to meet you. When he sees you, he will be glad in his heart. Now you shall speak to him and put the words in his mouth. And I will be with your mouth and with his mouth, and I will teach you what you shall do." Exodus 4:10-15, NKJV

God helps his children

21

The Christian Thing to Do

FROM THE BIBLE:

As they continued onward toward Jerusalem, they reached the border between Galilee and Samaria, and as they entered a village there, ten lepers stood at a distance, crying out, "Jesus, sir, have mercy on us!" He looked at them and said, "Go to the Jewish priest and show him that you are healed!" And as they were going, their leprosy disappeared. One of them came back to Jesus, shouting, "Glory to God, I'm healed!" He fell flat on the ground in front of Jesus, face downward in the dust, thanking him for what he had done. This man was a despised Samaritan. Jesus asked, "Didn't I heal ten men? Where are the nine? Does only this foreigner return to give glory to God?" And Jesus said to the man, "Stand up and go; your faith has made you well."
Luke 17:11-19, TLB

Express thanks to others

BILLY HAD JUST received a birthday present from his grandmother—a large erector set. "Wow! Just what I wanted!" he exclaimed in delight. Dumping the blocks on the floor, he began building a space station like the picture on the box cover.

"Before you get too busy, why not write Grandma a thank-you note?" his mother suggested. "Let her know how much you appreciate her gift."

"Aw, Mom, do I have to?" objected Billy. "I want to play with this now. Besides, I can thank her when she comes to visit us next month."

"Billy, your grandmother loves you very much," Mother answered. "She went to a lot of trouble to find the exact blocks you wanted. I happen to know she had to spend an entire afternoon going from store to store before she found the right ones. The least you can do is spend fifteen minutes writing her a thank-you note."

Billy knew his mother was right. He knew that, as a Christian, he should be thankful for all things, and he should also be courteous. In this case, he needed to let his grandmother know that he thought she was a very special lady and that he loved her very much. It was the Christian thing to do. He put the blocks back in the box. They could wait. Right now he had a job to do!

HOW ABOUT YOU? Do you think writing thank-you notes is a boring job? Do you sometimes forget to write them? When Jesus was on earth, He noticed who said thank you and who didn't. Don't assume that everyone knows how thankful you are. Say it. Write it when necessary. Express it to other people, and to God as well. □ L.W.

TO MEMORIZE: *Let the peace of God rule in your hearts, to which also you were called in one body; and be thankful.* Colossians 3:15, NKJV

Ah-CHOO!" sneezed Pete Benson as he wandered into the kitchen. He gave a loud sniff and then scowled. "Aw, Mom, why do I have to have a cold? It's Saturday, and Dad promised to take me fishing with him!"

"Your dad would have enjoyed taking you," said his mother, "but it's too chilly to go out with that cold."

"I even prayed about it," Pete moaned, "but it didn't help. Now I'm stuck at home with nothing to do except watch TV and eat." He opened the cupboard and peered inside. "Hey, Mom!" he exclaimed. "Did you notice these bananas in here?" He pulled out some shriveled, brownish-black pieces of fruit and was ready to drop them into the wastebasket.

"Oh, don't throw those away!" Mother said quickly. "I'm saving them for banana bread. They're just about right."

Pete made a face. He could hardly believe it. "You mean you wanted these bananas to turn rotten?"

Mother smiled. "Maybe 'ripe' would be a better word," she said. "I've found that soft, dark, mushy bananas make the best banana bread."

"That sounds crazy to me," said Pete, "but I do like your banana bread!"

"You know," said his mother, "in a way, your cold is like these bananas. You can't see anything good about it, but God can still use it for His purposes."

Pete sniffed and thought about what his mother had said. "I did get some extra homework done this morning," he told her. "And since I had some free time, I talked to Kevin on the phone for a while. I invited him to go to church with us tomorrow, and I think he's going to come!"

"I hope you'll feel better by then," said Mother, "but we'll have to wait until God thinks the time is 'ripe.' You can trust the Lord to turn bad situations into good!"

HOW ABOUT YOU? Have you ever been in a situation that seemed to keep getting worse and worse? Perhaps you've even prayed about it, but God didn't seem to answer. Maybe He was using this situation in your life in a way you never realized. Keep trusting God. Thank Him for "bad bananas!" □
S.K.

TO MEMORIZE: *It is God who arms me with strength and makes my way perfect.* Psalm 18:32, NIV

Bad Bananas?

FROM THE BIBLE:
As for God, his way is perfect; the word of the Lord is flawless. He is a shield for all who take refuge in him. For who is God besides the Lord? And who is the Rock except our God? It is God who arms me with strength and makes my way perfect. Psalm 18:30-32, NIV

Trust God in all things

23

Be Ready

FROM THE BIBLE:

"Blessed are those servants whom the master, when he comes, will find watching. Assuredly, I say to you that he will gird himself and have them sit down to eat, and will come and serve them. And if he should come in the second watch, or come in the third watch, and find them so, blessed are those servants. But know this, that if the master of the house had known what hour the thief would come, he would have watched and not allowed his house to be broken into. Therefore you also be ready, for the Son of Man is coming at an hour you do not expect." Then Peter said to Him, "Lord, do You speak this parable only to us, or to all people?" And the Lord said, "Who then is that faithful and wise steward, whom his master will make ruler over his household, to give them their portion of food in due season? Blessed is that servant whom his master will find so doing when he comes."

Luke 12:37-43, NKJV

Be ready for Jesus

KELLY AND SHAWN were excited. Dad had promised that if they had their rooms cleaned by the time he got home, he would take them to the carnival for the rest of the day.

"Let's watch cartoons and then clean our rooms," suggested Shawn after Dad left. "We've got plenty of time." Mother started to speak but changed her mind.

The two planned to start on their work right after the program. But Shawn's friend Neil came over to play, and Kelly got a phone call. Before they knew it, it was lunchtime. "Let's go over to the Ice Cream Shoppe after lunch," suggested Kelly, and Shawn quickly agreed. By the time they got home, it was almost three o'clock. "I guess we'd better get started on our rooms," sighed Shawn. "Mine is really a mess."

"Mine too," agreed Kelly. "Dad would really be upset if he saw all that junk in my closet." They were just about to go to their rooms when they heard the door open. Their father had come home!

"Dad!" Shawn exclaimed in dismay. "You're back early! We figured you'd be gone at least another hour or so. We were just going to clean our rooms."

"You mean you two haven't even started on your rooms yet?" asked Dad in a stern voice. Kelly and Shawn hung their heads. "I'm sorry, kids, but we'll have to forget our trip to the carnival."

"But, Dad," said Kelly, "if we'd only known what time you were going to get back, we'd have been ready for you."

Dad smiled. "That reminds me of a story in the Bible," he said. "Jesus warned us that we should be ready for His return, for we don't know just when that will be."

"Boy, I'd hate to be caught unprepared when *He* comes," Shawn said. "There's a lot I want to do for Him first."

"Me too," agreed Kelly. "We'd better get busy."

HOW ABOUT YOU? Would you be ready if Jesus came back today? Do you know Him as your Savior? If so, are you busy serving Him and obeying His commandments? Don't be taken by surprise. Be ready! □ S.K.

TO MEMORIZE: *"Therefore you also be ready, for the Son of Man is coming at an hour you do not expect."* Luke 12:40, NKJV

"Wow, STEVE, I can't believe all the books you borrowed from the library!" exclaimed Barry as his brother came into the house and put a stack of reading material on the table. "You must like to read a lot better than I do."

Mother entered the kitchen. "There's nothing wrong with reading," she observed. "It's a good way to learn about other countries, animals, or any number of things."

"Right," Steve agreed. "You can learn how to do things, too. Last year Dad built Rover's dog house from plans he found in a wood project book."

"And where would I be if I had to cook without my recipe books?" asked Mother.

"Well, I like reading some books," Barry admitted. "I like to read adventure stories, and I like those books we have about science experiments."

"How about the Bible?" Mother suggested.

Steve nodded. "I like reading about the miracles Jesus did—especially the one where He used a little boy's lunch to feed five thousand people."

"You know," added Barry, "if we couldn't read the Bible, we wouldn't be able to learn about God."

"Did you know that the Bible only tells us a few things that Christ did?" asked Mother. "In fact, it tells us that the world can't even contain all the books that would have to be written if everything that Jesus did was recorded!"

"What a fantastic library we would have then!" Steve exclaimed.

"Yeah," agreed Barry. "That would keep you happy for a long, long time!"

HOW ABOUT YOU? Do you like to read books? Reading can be fun. Reading the Bible is most important because that is how you learn about God, the Lord Jesus, and the plan of salvation. There's so much to know that even the oldest Christian will tell you he is still learning as he continues to read and study the Bible. □ L.W.

TO MEMORIZE: *Jesus did many other things as well. If every one of them were written down, I suppose that even the whole world would not have room for the books that would be written.* John 21:25, NIV

24

Bundles of Books!

FROM THE BIBLE:
A huge crowd, many of them pilgrims on their way to Jerusalem for the annual Passover celebration, were following him wherever he went, to watch him heal the sick. . . . He soon saw a great multitude of people climbing the hill, looking for him. Turning to Philip he asked, "Philip, where can we buy bread to feed all these people?" . . . Philip replied, "It would take a fortune to begin to do it!" Then Andrew, Simon Peter's brother, spoke up. "There's a youngster here with five barley loaves and a couple of fish! But what good is that with all this mob?" "Tell everyone to sit down," Jesus ordered. And all of them—the approximate count of the men only was 5,000—sat down on the grassy slopes. Then Jesus took the loaves and gave thanks to God and passed them out to the people. Afterwards he did the same with the fish. And everyone ate until full! "Now gather the scraps," Jesus told his disciples, "so that nothing is wasted." And twelve baskets were filled with the leftovers!
John 6:5-13, TLB

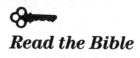

Read the Bible

25

Depend on Me!

FROM THE BIBLE:

Lord! Help! Godly men are fast disappearing. Where in all the world can dependable men be found? Everyone deceives and flatters and lies. There is no sincerity left. But the Lord will not deal gently with people who act like that; he will destroy those proud liars who say, "We will lie to our hearts' content. Our lips are our own; who can stop us?" The Lord replies, "I will arise and defend the oppressed, the poor, the needy. I will rescue them as they have longed for me to do." The Lord's promise is sure. He speaks no careless word; all he says is purest truth, like silver seven times refined. O Lord, we know that you will forever preserve your own from the reach of evil men, although they prowl on every side and vileness is praised throughout the land. Psalm 12, TLB

Be dependable

"BOBBY, YOU LOOK discouraged," said Mother as Bobby came into the kitchen after school.

"I am, Mom." Bobby dropped his books down on the table. "Today Ryan told me he'd wait for me after class so we could go to lunch together. I was supposed to meet him by my locker, but he wasn't there. When I saw him in the lunchroom later, he was with some older boys, and he just ignored me."

"Well, that's too bad," said Mother, "but you do have other friends."

"I know," said Bobby, reaching for an apple. "It wasn't so important that I eat with Ryan, but the thing that bothers me is that he says he's a Christian. He lied to me, Mom! I would expect that from one of my unsaved friends, but not from a Christian!"

"That happens, though, Bobby—and not just with children," replied Mother. "Often grown-ups disappoint one another, too. Try to be patient when that happens. And remember there's one Friend who is totally dependable—the Lord Jesus."

Bobby signed. "It's still discouraging when someone you trust lets you down," he said.

"Yes, it is," nodded Mother, "but each time it happens, let it also be a lesson to you." She put her arm around her son. "Remember, Bobby, others are watching you! They know you're a Christian. Be sure that you don't discourage someone else by the way you act!"

HOW ABOUT YOU? Do you get discouraged when a friend lets you down? Can you think of a time when you may have discouraged someone else? It does happen once in a while. You need to be sensitive to other people—to be kind to them. If you tell a friend you will do something, you should mean what you are saying and do it. If you know the Lord, people should be able to depend on you. □ L.W.

TO MEMORIZE: *They claim to know God, but by their actions they deny him.* Titus 1:16, NIV

REACHING HER THIRTEENTH birthday had seemed like the most important thing in Rozanne's life. "How come you want to be thirteen?" asked Julie, her little sister.

"Because now that I'm thirteen, people will think of me as grown-up—or almost," Rozanne replied.

Julie still didn't understand. "You mean that last night, when you were twelve, you were just a kid, and now, today, you're a grown-up?"

Before Rozanne could answer, Mother came into the room. "Rozanne, your father just called from Boston. He's not going to get home in time for your birthday party, and that means we won't have a car to pick up the cake we ordered at the bakery."

Something inside of Rozanne flashed, and before she knew what she was doing, she shouted at her mother about people not caring how important this day was to her and spoiling it for her. Without giving her mother a chance to make any suggestions for getting the cake, she blurted out angry things she did not mean to say.

Julie looked at her. "Are you being thirteen or twelve?" she asked innocently.

The words struck Rozanne's heart. She sighed. "I'm thirteen in numbers but only twelve in my actions, I guess. I'm sorry," she apologized, turning toward her mother. "I've still got a lot to learn about being thirteen—and about being a good Christian, too."

Mother smiled at her. "Why don't you take your bike and get the cake," she suggested. "I think your bike basket is big enough."

"But I'm too old to run errands on my bike," Rozanne began. Suddenly she stopped and whispered a prayer for help. "Dear Lord," she said sincerely, "I think You're going to have to help me be thirteen."

HOW ABOUT YOU? Are you eager to be older? Do you think being "grown-up" happens automatically at a certain age? It doesn't. It's a gradual process, just as growing physically is a process. Growing in the Lord takes time, too. We need to pray for help to become more mature every day—more like our Savior. Start now! □ R.J.

TO MEMORIZE: *Grow in the grace and knowledge of our Lord and Savior Jesus Christ.* 2 Peter 3:18, NIV

FEBRUARY

26

Finally Thirteen

FROM THE BIBLE:
Since everything will be destroyed in this way, what kind of people ought you to be? You ought to live holy and godly lives as you look forward to the day of God and speed its coming. That day will bring about the destruction of the heavens by fire, and the elements will melt in the heat. But in keeping with his promise we are looking forward to a new heaven and a new earth, the home of righteousness. So then, dear friends, since you are looking forward to this, make every effort to be found spotless, blameless and at peace with him. . . . But grow in the grace and knowledge of our Lord and Savior Jesus Christ.
2 Peter 3:11-14, 18, NIV

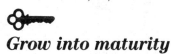

Grow into maturity

27

Sharing the Best

FROM THE BIBLE:

We must bear the "burden" of being considerate of the doubts and fears of others—of those who feel these things are wrong. Let's please the other fellow, not ourselves, and do what is for his good and thus build him up in the Lord. Christ didn't please himself. As the Psalmist said, "He came for the very purpose of suffering under the insults of those who were against the Lord." These things that were written in the Scriptures so long ago are to teach us patience and to encourage us, so that we will look forward expectantly to the time when God will conquer sin and death. May God who gives patience, steadiness, and encouragement help you to live in complete harmony with each other—each with the attitude of Christ toward the other. And then all of us can praise the Lord together with one voice, giving glory to God, the Father of our Lord Jesus Christ. So, warmly welcome each other into the church, just as Christ has warmly welcomed you; then God will be glorified.
Romans 15:1-7, TLB

Care by sharing

I HOPE YOU made a lot of those," Steve said when he saw the fresh cinnamon rolls on the kitchen table.

"I did," Mother replied. "I even baked a dozen for the Carlsons."

"The Carlsons?" Steve questioned. "What for?"

"Because they don't have money for such things," she answered, "and I thought they might enjoy some."

"Can't you give them bread or potatoes or something?" grumbled Steve. As soon as he spoke, he knew he had said the wrong thing. He was being selfish, and both he and his mother knew it. He blushed with embarrassment.

"The Bible tells us to bear one another's burdens," Mother replied, quoting a Scripture that Steve had memorized. He did not answer immediately. He didn't really mind helping a family like the Carlsons, but did his mother have to give away something that he liked as much as her homemade cinnamon rolls?

Mother broke into his thoughts just as though she knew what he was thinking. "You know," she said, "when God the Father saw the need of people, He gave His very best." She paused significantly. "Is it too much for us to give a needy family something that we like?"

Steve had no answer for his mother's question. He was a Christian, and he knew that selfishness was not to be part of the Christian life. "You're right," he said finally. "But then, you usually are."

There was a smile on his face as he picked up the plate of cinnamon rolls and made his way to the Carlsons' house. With every step, he took a deep breath, so as to inhale the good aroma of the rolls. The Carlsons would enjoy them; he was sure of that!

HOW ABOUT YOU? Are you willing to help someone in need even if it means giving something that is very special to you? God was! By sharing with others—sharing your time, your money, your things, your prayers—you can make their burden a little lighter. □ R.J.

TO MEMORIZE: *Bear one another's burdens, and so fulfill the law of Christ.* Galatians 6:2, NKJV

28

"Goody-Goody"

JON PUT HIS baseball glove on the table and went to get a glass of milk from the refrigerator. "Wow, what a day!" he said to his mom.

"What happened?" asked Mother.

"During recess a bunch of boys were playing kickball, and Chad King asked if he could play. A lot of boys make fun of Chad because of the way he acts, but it's a rule that you have to let anyone play that wants to, so the boys said he could. Well, Chad kicked the ball and took off running toward first base, except he tripped and fell flat on his face! You should've heard the boys tease him! I noticed he was actually hurt, so I went over, helped him to his feet and went to the nurse's office with him. When I came out again, the kids started calling me a 'goody-goody.' They were being pretty mean about it, too!"

"Then what?" Mother was giving Jon her full attention.

"Well, they stopped when the bell rang," explained Jon, "but two of the boys followed me home, kidding me and calling me 'Mr. Goody-Goody' all the way home."

"It's hard to be called names as a result of kindness, isn't it?" asked Mother sympathetically.

Jon nodded. "Yes," he admitted, "it sure is."

"You have to remember, Jon, that there's nothing wrong with being good," Mother told him. "As a Christian, you have the responsibility of being kind to others. But we can't expect everyone to understand. The apostle Paul wrote that the gospel is foolishness to those who don't believe in Christ. Because unbelievers choose to think the Bible is foolishness, they are also going to think we are foolish for following God's guidelines."

Jon nodded. "Those kids didn't understand how I could be friendly to Chad, but I'm glad I was. Chad needs friends!"

HOW ABOUT YOU? Is it hard for your non-Christian friends to understand why you won't join them in cheating, swearing, or treating someone unkindly? Do you get teased for doing what is right? God says it's better to suffer for well-doing than for evil-doing. Continue to follow His way, even when your friends don't understand. □ L.W.

TO MEMORIZE: *The message of the cross is foolishness to those who are perishing, but to us who are being saved it is the power of God.* 1 Corinthians 1:18, NKJV

FROM THE BIBLE:
The Lord is watching his children, listening to their prayers; but the Lord's face is hard against those who do evil. Usually no one will hurt you for wanting to do good. But even if they should, you are to be envied, for God will reward you for it. Quietly trust yourself to Christ your Lord and if anybody asks why you believe as you do, be ready to tell him, and do it in a gentle and respectful way. Do what is right; then if men speak against you, calling you evil names, they will become ashamed of themselves for falsely accusing you when you have only done what is good. Remember, if God wants you to suffer, it is better to suffer for doing good than for doing wrong!
1 Peter 3:12-17, TLB

God's way is best

29

I Blew It Already

FROM THE BIBLE:

What I want to do I do not do,
but what I hate I do. And if I do
what I do not want to do, I
agree that the law is good. As it
is, it is no longer I myself who
do it, but it is sin living in me. I
know that nothing good lives in
me, that is, in my sinful nature.
For I have the desire to do what
is good, but I cannot carry it
out. . . . Now if I do what I do
not want to do, it is no longer I
who do it, but it is sin living in
me that does it. So I find this
law at work: When I want to do
good, evil is right there with me.
For in my inner being I delight
in God's law; but I see another
law at work in the members of
my body, . . . making me a
prisoner of the law of sin at
work within my members. What
a wretched man I am! Who will
rescue me from this body of
death? Thanks be to God—
through Jesus Christ our Lord!
So then, I myself in my mind
am a slave to God's law, but in
the sinful nature a slave to the
law of sin.

Romans 7:15-25, NIV

Change comes
through the Lord

TAMMY TOOK her pen and wrote carefully on a piece of paper, "I resolve never to fight with my brother David again." Then she took a piece of tape and fastened the paper on the door so that she wouldn't forget what she had written. All went well for two hours, because David was at his friend's house, but then he came home. "You dummy!" he yelled at Tammy. "You were riding my bike, weren't you? There's a scratch on it!"

"I rode it," admitted Tammy, "but I didn't scratch it."

"You did, too," screamed David, and before Tammy knew what was happening, she and her brother were having still another fight.

Tammy was discouraged. "I promised myself never to fight with David again, and already I broke my promise," she told Mother. "It'll never work, so why bother trying?"

"You sound like the apostle Paul," said Mother. "In Romans 7, he wrote that he often did things he knew were wrong and didn't do things he knew were right. He recognized that it was because his old sin nature was still active within him."

"What did Paul do about it?" Tammy asked.

"He understood that righteousness, or doing right, comes only through Christ," Mother replied. "It's not something we can do by ourselves. You see, Honey, there are ways you can improve your relationship with David, but saying that you will never fight with him again doesn't work if you try to do it in your own strength. You and David are both human. Instead of saying, 'I will never fight with my brother,' why not try doing something nice for him each day? I think the end result would be less fighting as well."

HOW ABOUT YOU? Do you set impossible goals for yourself, such as "I'll never be bad again"? You see, we all have a sin nature within us. We are human. Even Christians do not do what is perfectly right all the time. Recognize that you cannot make a change in your life without the Lord's help. Be positive in your goals, make sure they are reasonable, and rely on Jesus to help you achieve them. □ L.W.

TO MEMORIZE: *There is therefore now no condemnation to those who are in Christ Jesus, who do not walk according to the flesh, but according to the Spirit.* Romans 8:1, NKJV

CINDY WAS AFRAID of the dark and of being alone. Sometimes her brother, Dave, would deliberately play tricks on her—tricks he knew would frighten her. *She's got to get over being afraid,* he thought, *and she will if I tease her about it.* But Cindy's continuing screams indicated that it wasn't working.

One day, after one of Dave's tricks, Dad asked him if he was afraid of anything. "Well, hornets, I guess," Dave answered.

"Do you think you'll get over your fears if someone sends hornets at you until you stop screaming?" asked Dad.

"But Dad, hornets can hurt you," David defended himself. "The dark can't!"

"Then tell Cindy that the dark won't hurt her. Don't terrify her!" said Dad. He turned to Cindy. "Real courage comes from God. When we're in real danger, we must trust God to take care of us, and He will help us face it."

As Mother tucked her in bed that night, Cindy asked, "Will you stay with me for a while?"

"Yes," agreed Mother. "I will." Ten minutes after the light was turned out, Mother asked, "Are you asleep?"

"No," murmured Cindy.

"Are you afraid?" asked Mother.

"No."

"Why not?"

"Because you're here," said Cindy.

"You can't see me in the dark, so how did you know I was here?" asked Mother.

"You said you would stay," explained Cindy, "so I knew you would."

"You know, Cindy," said Mother, "you accepted Jesus as your Savior, and He said not to be afraid because He will never leave you. He doesn't lie. Even when we can't see Him, we can believe Him. We can know He is with us—just because He said He would be."

HOW ABOUT YOU? Do you trust God to take care of you? There are many verses in the Bible that tell you not to be afraid. Learn some of these verses and believe them when something frightens you. □ A.L.

TO MEMORIZE: *Do not fear, for I am with you; do not be dismayed, for I am your God.* Isaiah 41:10, NIV

Be Not Afraid

FROM THE BIBLE:
All who rage against you will surely be ashamed and disgraced; those who oppose you will be as nothing and perish. Though you search for your enemies, you will not find them. Those who wage war against you will be as nothing at all. For I am the Lord, your God, who takes hold of your right hand and says to you, Do not fear; I will help you.
Isaiah 41:11-13, NIV

God is with you

Behind the Wheel

FROM THE BIBLE:

I know how to be abased, and I know how to abound. Everywhere and in all things I have learned both to be full and to be hungry, both to abound and to suffer need. I can do all things through Christ who strengthens me. . . . And my God shall supply all your need according to His riches in glory by Christ Jesus.
Philippians 4:12-13, 19, NKJV

God will help with hard things

"HI, GRANDMA," called Karen. "Where's Mom?"

"She had some errands to do, so she asked me to pick you up from practice," replied Grandma. "Get in, Dear."

Karen climbed into the front seat of Grandma's car. She put her books beside her and buckled in. Then she sighed deeply. "Oh, Grandma," she said, "I don't know how Sandy and I will ever be ready to sing in church next week. I've memorized the song, but I still keep forgetting the words. I don't think I can sing in front of so many people."

"Sounds like butterflies to me," said Grandma, "but God has given you a lovely voice, and I'm sure you'll do fine."

"I'm too scared," Karen insisted. Her voice trembled.

Grandma stopped at a red light. She looked at Karen. "You're a Christian, Honey," she said, "and you can do whatever God gives you to do." She turned her eyes back to the flow of traffic and moved forward as she continued, "Do you remember when Grandpa died? I was all alone and lived miles from anyone—and I had never driven a car."

"You hadn't?" asked Karen. "I didn't know that. You drive all the time now."

"Yes," said Grandma, "but at first I was so terrified of driving that I thought I'd never learn. Then one day I realized that the Lord was right there with me. I began to trust Him to help me, and after that it became easier and easier. Even now, I never get into this car without first thanking God that He's here with me in the driver's seat." She paused, then added, "With Him 'behind the wheel'—in any area of my life—I can go anywhere. And so can you."

Grandma pulled up to the curb in front of Karen's house. Karen smiled at her grandmother before opening the car door. "I guess I haven't been asking for God's help," she admitted, "but when we practice again, I will. And when we get up to sing, I especially will. Maybe I'm too scared to sing, but if God helps me, I know I can do it."

HOW ABOUT YOU? Is it hard for you to pray in public? To meet new people? To give your testimony? When you have to do something you find hard to do, who is "behind the wheel"? Do you turn to God and seek His help? He'll help you do anything He wants you to do. Just ask Him. □ G.L.J.

TO MEMORIZE: *I can do all things through Christ who strengthens me.* Philippians 4:13, NKJV

"DAD, ARE YOU in here?" Joel's voice sailed over the top of the roses, carnations, and daffodils in the greenhouse.

"Back here with the orchids, Joel," Dad responded. Joel plodded to the back of the greenhouse where his father was patting down the soil in a flower pot. "Well, how was your first day at Mr. Callaway's store?" asked Dad.

"Just terrible," grumbled Joel. "I stocked, I swept, I painted. Still all Mr. Callaway said was, 'You can stack those cans better. You missed some dirt. You didn't put enough paint on your brush.' It made me so mad."

"Hmmm," murmured Dad. "Well, I know he can be gruff, but I hope you were polite anyway. You can be a testimony for the Lord by your attitude as well as your words." He paused, and Joel just looked glum. "You can be like the *Rhizanthella gardneri*," added Dad.

"The what?" gasped Joel.

Dad chuckled. "*Rhizanthella gardneri* is the scientific name for an all-white orchid from Australia. The orchid spends its entire life underground, except when it pokes its pod above the ground to disperse its seeds." He took the flower pot he had been working with and motioned for Joel to follow him into a dark room. Digging carefully, Joel's father revealed a small white flower under the soil.

"Neat!" Joel exclaimed. "But how does my working for Mr. Callaway compare to that flower?"

"You can be like the white orchid by poking your head above Mr. Callaway's gruffness and spreading Christian 'seeds' of kindness, patience, and love," explained Dad. "You can serve the Lord by serving Mr. Callaway. In time, he's almost sure to notice. Even more importantly, God sees. He's the One who really matters."

HOW ABOUT YOU? Do you remain kind, loving, and thoughtful even when it seems you're not appreciated? Your actions and attitudes are an important part of your testimony for the Lord. Don't look for the praise of man. Instead, look for God's future praise of, "Well done, good and faithful servant." □ D.A.L.

TO MEMORIZE: *Let your light so shine before men, that they may see your good works and glorify your Father in heaven.* Matthew 5:16, NKJV

3

Rhizanthella Gardneri

FROM THE BIBLE:
Apollos and I should be looked upon as Christ's servants who distribute God's blessings by explaining God's secrets. Now the most important thing about a servant is that he does just what his master tells him to. What about me? Have I been a good servant? Well, I don't worry over what you think about this, or what anyone else thinks. I don't even trust my own judgment on this point. My conscience is clear, but even that isn't final proof. It is the Lord himself who must examine me and decide. So be careful not to jump to conclusions before the Lord returns as to whether someone is a good servant or not. When the Lord comes, he will turn on the light so that everyone can see exactly what each one of us is really like, deep down in our hearts. Then everyone will know why we have been doing the Lord's work. At that time God will give to each one whatever praise is coming to him.
1 Corinthians 4:1-5, TLB

Witness through your attitude

Out of Control

FROM THE BIBLE:

Stop lying to each other; tell the truth, for we are parts of each other and when we lie to each other we are hurting ourselves. If you are angry, don't sin by nursing your grudge. Don't let the sun go down with you still angry—get over it quickly; for when you are angry you give a mighty foothold to the devil. If anyone is stealing he must stop it and begin using those hands of his for honest work so he can give to others in need. Don't use bad language. Say only what is good and helpful to those you are talking to, and what will give them a blessing. Don't cause the Holy Spirit sorrow by the way you live. Remember, he is the one who marks you to be present on that day when salvation from sin will be complete. Stop being mean, bad-tempered and angry. Quarreling, harsh words, and dislike of others should have no place in your lives. Instead, be kind to each other, tender-hearted, forgiving one another, just as God has forgiven you because you belong to Christ.
Ephesians 4:25-32, TLB

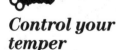

Control your temper

JASON, YOU DIDN'T take out the trash this morning," said Mother. "Please take care of it right now." Jason angrily threw down the newspaper, picked up the wastebasket, and stomped out of the room, slamming the door behind him. "Come back here!" ordered Mother. Jason came into the kitchen and stood scowling at his mother. "You go back out that door and close it right!"

A few minutes later, Mother heard Jason yell. She looked out the door. A neighbor's car was careening out of control down the street. Jason ran up on the porch. "Mrs. Wheeler left Donny in the car and went back in the house. I guess he must have put it into gear," he explained breathlessly. "Look at that car go!"

The car was gaining speed. "Oh, Lord," prayed Mother, "please stop it before it gets to the intersection." At that moment the car turned sharply, veered onto the curb, and ran into a tree. Jason and his mother quickly ran to the car. "Thank God!" Mother exclaimed. "Donny's not hurt."

When the excitement was over, Jason returned to his reading. "Look at this article in the newspaper," he said. "It says, 'Man shoots neighbor in fit of anger over dog.' That was a stupid thing to do."

"Yes," Mother agreed. "Most fits of anger are stupid—and dangerous." She looked at Jason thoughtfully. "An uncontrolled temper is like a car out of control," she added. "No doubt this man's problem started when he was a boy who slammed doors and threw temper tantrums."

Jason frowned. "Just because someone slams a door doesn't mean he's going to be a murderer," he objected.

"Just because a car careens down a street out of control doesn't mean it will kill anyone, either, but it could," replied Mother. "It's a dangerous situation. As your mother, I intend for you to learn now to control your temper. If you don't put on the brakes, I'll do it for you."

Jason didn't want to grin, but he couldn't help it. "OK, Mom," he said, "I get the point."

HOW ABOUT YOU? Do you have trouble controlling your temper? When you feel angry, ask the Lord to help you control the way you act and to give you more patience. □ B.W.

TO MEMORIZE: *Whoever has no rule over his own spirit is like a city broken down, without walls.* Proverbs 25:28, NKJV

MOLLY WAS READY for Sunday school—at least she thought she was. "Oh, no," she said with a sigh. "How did I get that?" She'd caught a glimpse of herself in the hallway mirror. There was a black smudge across her forehead.

As Molly went to wash off the smudge, three-year-old Kara stopped her. "Molly, help me, please." Kara had managed to get her shoes on, but she couldn't buckle them. So Molly helped her sister, and the smudge was forgotten.

On the way to church, they passed the home of Barb, a new girl in the neighborhood. Molly felt guilty. Recently she had been memorizing verses about winning others to Jesus, and all week she had felt she should invite Barb to Sunday school, but she had not done so. *Oh, well,* she thought, *she probably wouldn't come anyway.*

When Molly walked into her classroom, her friend Jean laughed. "You should see yourself," said Jean. "You look like you forgot to take a bath this morning." Suddenly Molly remembered the smudge on her forehead. She hurried out to wash it off.

When Molly returned, the Scripture reading caught her attention. It was about a man who looked in a mirror, but when he left the mirror, he forgot what he'd seen. *That's like me this morning,* Molly thought, stifling a giggle.

"When you learn what God wants you to do, but you don't do anything about it," the teacher said, "you're like that man. You're a hearer but not a doer of God's Word."

Why, she's talking about me! Molly thought. It wasn't the smudge on her forehead that came to mind now. It was a smudge in her life—something she knew God wanted her to do but she hadn't done. She would go see Barb that very afternoon.

HOW ABOUT YOU? Do you have any forgotten "smudges" in your life? Has God shown you from His Word that you should not lie? Cheat? Lose your temper? Has He shown you that you should be friendly? Helpful? Obedient? It's wonderful that you are learning how God wants you to live. But if you don't do anything about what you learn, He isn't pleased. Look in the mirror of God's Word, and don't forget what you see there. □ K.R.A.

TO MEMORIZE: *Be doers of the word, and not hearers only.* James 1:22, NKJV

The Forgotten Smudge

FROM THE BIBLE:
Be doers of the word, and not hearers only, deceiving yourselves. For if anyone is a hearer of the word and not a doer, he is like a man observing his natural face in a mirror; for he observes himself, goes away, and immediately forgets what kind of man he was. But he who looks into the perfect law of liberty and continues in it, and is not a forgetful hearer but a doer of the work, this one will be blessed in what he does. If anyone among you thinks he is religious, and does not bridle his tongue but deceives his own heart, this one's religion is useless. Pure and undefiled religion before God and the Father is this: to visit orphans and widows in their trouble, and to keep oneself unspotted from the world.
James 1:22-27, NKJV

Do what God says

Fire!

FROM THE BIBLE:

The tongue is a little member and boasts great things. See how great a forest a little fire kindles! And the tongue is a fire, a world of iniquity. The tongue is so set among our members that it defiles the whole body, and sets on fire the course of nature; and it is set on fire by hell. For every kind of beast and bird, of reptile and creature of the sea, is tamed and has been tamed by mankind. But no man can tame the tongue. It is an unruly evil, full of deadly poison. With it we bless our God and Father, and with it we curse men, who have been made in the similitude of God. Out of the same mouth proceed blessing and cursing. My brethren, these things ought not to be so. James 3:5-10, NKJV

Don't spread rumors

MINDY AND HER mother watched in horror as fire swept through the wheat field. "How did it start, Mother?" Mindy sobbed.

"We can't be certain, Mindy," answered Mother. "It could have been someone driving by who was careless with a cigarette, or it could have been started by a spark from the combine. A little spark is all it takes to start a fire."

The wheat crop was lost. "I'm just thankful we were able to keep the fire from spreading to any other fields or buildings," said Dad that evening.

Just then the phone rang, and Mindy answered it. It was her friend Rachel, and the girls talked for a while. After Mindy had hung up, Mother looked at her thoughtfully.

"The fire this afternoon was not nearly as destructive as some of those fires you just started," she said.

"What?" Mindy was shocked. "I never in my whole life started a fire. What are you talking about?"

"I'm talking about the rumors I heard you sharing with Rachel about the new girl in school," Mother replied.

"Rhonda? Well, if she didn't cheat, how could she get such a good grade on her first day at school?" Mindy defended herself. "Stacy told me some things about Rhonda. I was only warning Rachel."

"Mindy, you said some very unkind things about a girl you don't even know. You had no right to do that," scolded Mother. "You can't be certain that any of those rumors are true, but they'll spread like a fire and ruin that girl's reputation. I think you ought to have the courage to stop the fire instead of spreading it."

"But, Mom," Mindy protested. "I was just—"

"You were just starting a fire," Mother finished. "I hope you'll call Rachel and make an effort to put out the fire you helped start. Be more cautious from now on."

HOW ABOUT YOU? Do you ever say unkind words? Do you help spread gossip and rumors that will hurt other people? God says that a mouth which is used to bless and praise Him should not be used to hurt others. How will you use your tongue? □ B.D.

TO MEMORIZE: *The tongue is a fire, a world of iniquity.* James 3:6, NKJV

AND THE MEAN old wolf blew down the house of the first little pig, because it was made of straw." Joanie was telling her family about the story she'd read in school. "And he blew down the house of the second little pig, 'cause it was made of sticks. But even though he huffed and he puffed, he couldn't blow down the house of the third little pig. It was make of bricks." Joanie looked proudly around the table.

"Pooh," scoffed her brother, Matt. "You've known that story ever since you were little."

"Yes, but now she can read it all by herself," said Dad, smiling at his little daughter. "Good for you, Little Pig."

"Daddy!" protested Joanie. "I'm not a pig."

"No, you're not," agreed Dad. "I called you that because the little pigs were builders, and you are, too."

"Me?" asked Joanie. "I'm not building a house."

Dad smiled. "No," he said, "but you're building your life. We all are. We add a little to it every day by the things we do or say and the places we go. Sometimes we add 'straw' or 'sticks'—the Bible calls it 'wood, hay, or straw.' Sometimes we add something even better than brick—the Bible refers to 'gold, silver, and costly stones.' They're the only things that will last."

"What do you think are some of the 'wood, hay, and straw' things we do?" asked Mother.

"Cheating and lying and disobeying are all bad things," said Matt promptly. "They're wood, hay, and straw."

"Yes," agreed Dad, "and so are the good works that we do with the wrong attitude."

"Like helping, but being mad about it?" asked Joanie.

Dad nodded. "Now, what are some things that will last?"

"Inviting a friend to Sunday school," suggested Matt.

"Running errands for Grandma," said Joanie.

"Good," nodded Dad. "As we build our 'life-houses,' let's be careful to use materials that last."

HOW ABOUT YOU? What are you using to build your "life-house"? Will you use "wood, hay, or straw" today? Or will you build with materials that will last for all eternity—with actions and attitudes that please God? □ H.M.

TO MEMORIZE: *If what he has built survives, he will receive his reward.* 1 Corinthians 3:14, NIV

Foolish Pigs and People

FROM THE BIBLE:
No one can lay any foundation other than the one already laid, which is Jesus Christ. If any man builds on this foundation using gold, silver, costly stones, wood, hay or straw, his work will be shown for what it is, because the Day will bring it to light. It will be revealed with fire, and the fire will test the quality of each man's work. If what he has built survives, he will receive his reward. If it is burned up, he will suffer loss; he himself will be saved, but only as one escaping through the flames.
1 Corinthians 3:11-15, NIV

Build with good works

Foolish Pigs and People

(Continued from yesterday)

FROM THE BIBLE:
"All who listen to my instructions and follow them are wise, like a man who builds his house on solid rock. Though the rain comes in torrents, and the floods rise and the storm winds beat against his house, it won't collapse, for it is built on rock. But those who hear my instructions and ignore them are foolish, like a man who builds his house on sand. For when the rains and floods come, and storm winds beat against his house, it will fall with a mighty crash."
Matthew 7:24-27, TLB

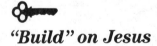

"Build" on Jesus

JOANIE CLIMBED into the car after Sunday school, eager to share her lesson with her family. "My teacher talked about the three little pigs today," she said.

Matt scowled. "Aw, she didn't, either."

"Did too," insisted Joanie. "She said the Bible tells us about a builder who was even more foolish than the first two little pigs. Bet you don't know who he was." Matt thought for a few minutes before giving up. "He was the man who built his house on the sand," stated Joanie. "When the storms came, his house fell."

"Well, I don't see how he was more foolish than the little pigs. Their houses fell, too," argued Matt.

Joanie couldn't think of an answer for a moment. "Well, he was more foolish because they were just pigs," she decided. "The wolf ate them and that was the end of them. But the man who built on the sand is like people who don't follow what Jesus says and don't accept Him as Savior. So then they don't go to heaven—they're lost forever." Matt had to admit that this was worse than what happened to the pigs.

"Now tell us the good part of the story," suggested Dad.

"Another man—a wise man—built his house on the rock," said Joanie, "and it stood through even the worst storms. He's like people who hear and believe what Jesus says. They accept Him as Savior, so they live forever in heaven."

HOW ABOUT YOU? Where are you building—on the sand or on the Rock, Jesus Christ? All the good things you do won't last unless you are building your life on the right foundation—unless you've accepted Jesus as your Savior. □ H.M.

TO MEMORIZE: *No one can lay any foundation other than the one already laid, which is Jesus Christ.* 1 Corinthians 3:11, NIV

A S THE TYLERS' car edged up the mountain road, Jeff pouted in the back seat. "Going on a picnic is boring for a kid my age," he grumbled. "Why couldn't I stay with Lane instead?"

Mother sighed. "We already told you—Uncle Lee and Aunt Sue are out of town, and we don't think you should be over there while they're gone."

Jeff frowned. "You treat me like a little kid."

Suddenly, six-year-old Jessica squealed as she looked out the car window to the valley below. "Be careful, Daddy!" Her nose was pressed hard against the car window. "It's a long way to the bottom."

Dad laughed. "I'll be careful. But if I should happen to slip off the road, the guardrail will keep us from going over the edge."

"Before they put up the guardrail, a car did go over the edge," said Mother. "I remember that it was three days before they found it."

When they reached the picnic area at the top of the mountain, Jeff's spirits lifted. He couldn't stay mad.

The trip home was quiet. After again being assured that the guardrail would protect them, Jessica went to sleep. Even Jeff and Mother dozed.

"Wake up, everyone!" called Dad as he drove into the yard and turned off the engine. "Oh, I hear the telephone ringing." He ran into the house.

Jeff and Mother were unloading the picnic supplies when Dad came back out. "I have bad news. Your cousin Lane had an accident this afternoon on his dirt bike." Jeff stared at Dad in horror.

Later, as they returned from visiting Lane at the hospital, Jeff voiced what they had all been thinking. "If I had stayed with Lane, it could have been me," he said.

Dad nodded. "Uncle Lee told Lane not to ride that bike while he and Aunt Sue were gone, but Lane didn't listen."

"Parents are like guardrails," Jeff said thoughtfully. "They keep us from danger . . . if we obey them."

HOW ABOUT YOU? Do you obey your parents? You need their guidance, and God commands you to obey them. Next time you're tempted to disobey, remember that he often uses parents to guard you from danger. □ B.W.

TO MEMORIZE: *"Honor your father and mother,"* *which is the first commandment with promise: "that* *it may be well with you and you may live long on* *the earth."* Ephesians 6:2-3, NKJV

The Guardrail

FROM THE BIBLE:
Young men, listen to me as you *would to your father. Listen,* *and grow wise, for I speak the* *truth—don't turn away. For I,* *too, was once a son, tenderly* *loved by my mother as an only* *child, and the companion of my* *father. He told me never to forget* *his words. "If you follow them,"* *he said, "you will have a long* *and happy life. Learn to be* *wise," he said, "and develop* *good judgment and common* *sense! I cannot overemphasize* *this point." Cling to wisdom—* *she will protect you. Love* *her—she will guard you.* *Getting wisdom is the most* *important thing you can do!* *And with your wisdom, develop* *common sense and good* *judgment. If you exalt wisdom,* *she will exalt you. Hold her fast* *and she will lead you to great* *honor; she will place a beautiful* *crown upon your head. My son,* *listen to me and do as I say, and* *you will have a long, good life.* Proverbs 4:1-10, TLB

Obey your parents

10

The Band-Aid Kid

FROM THE BIBLE:

What happiness for those whose guilt has been forgiven! What joys when sins are covered over! What relief for those who have confessed their sins and God has cleared their record. There was a time when I wouldn't admit what a sinner I was. But my dishonesty made me miserable and filled my days with frustration. All day and all night your hand was heavy on me. My strength evaporated like water on a sunny day until I finally admitted all my sins to you and stopped trying to hide them. I said to myself, "I will confess them to the Lord." And you forgave me! All my guilt is gone.

Psalm 32:1-5, TLB

Confess and forsake sin

DAD SIGHED AS he arrived home and saw Monty sweeping the garage. When Monty did work without being asked, it usually meant he'd done something wrong. However, Dad went into the house without questioning his son. "Hi," he greeted his wife. "Anything happen today?"

"Travis has chicken pox," she announced, "and Monty shot Mr. White's dog with Kyle Roe's BB gun."

Dad frowned. "I've told him over and over not to play with Kyle's gun! Did he hurt the dog?"

"No—just scared him and made Mr. White angry," replied Mother. "He's coming over this evening."

"Look at me! Look, Daddy!" interrupted three-year-old Travis. Mother's mouth fell open, and Dad roared with laughter when he saw Travis. "I got the chicken poxes. See? I put Band-Aids on them."

"How dumb can you get!" grumbled Monty as he entered the room and saw his brother. "You can't cure chicken pox by covering up the spots!"

"That's true," agreed Dad. "And neither can you cover up sin with good deeds."

Monty hung his head in shame.

"I've noticed that whenever you do something wrong, you try to cover it up by doing something good," continued Dad. "When you disobeyed me, you raked the leaves. When you disobeyed your mother, you washed dishes. Now you've been sweeping the garage as if that would make up for what you did this afternoon."

"Kyle dared me, and he said—" Monty stopped.

"When you do something wrong, Monty, don't blame it on anyone else. Be big enough to admit it," Dad said sternly. "Don't try to cover up your sins with 'Band-Aids' of good deeds, either. The only cure for sin is repentence."

Tears filled Monty's eyes. "I'm sorry, Dad. Do you suppose Mr. White will forgive me?"

Dad sighed. "I surely hope so. You also owe the Lord Jesus an apology, Monty. When you wrong someone, you sin against the Lord, too."

Monty gulped. "I'll go talk to the Lord now."

HOW ABOUT YOU? Are you a "Band-Aid" kid? Don't try to cover your sins with good deeds or excuses. You need to repent, and you need to do it now. □ B.W.

TO MEMORIZE: *He who conceals his sins does not prosper, but whoever confesses and renounces them finds mercy.* Proverbs 28:13, NIV

THANKS FOR INVITING me to go to church with you next Sunday, Uncle Al." Keith and his uncle were on their way to Bonny Lake. They had heard it was great fishing there. "I don't want to hurt your feelings," continued Keith, "but I'm not sure I want to get into this religious stuff."

"Oh?" asked Uncle Al in surprise. "You sounded quite interested last week. You even said the gospel was beginning to make sense to you."

"Yeah, but since then I've done a lot of thinking," Keith said slowly. "I don't think I feel like getting 'saved' right now. The crowd I hang around with at school might not understand, and I like being with them. Someday I'll start going to church, but I think I'll just go on the way I am for a while. I know I'm not perfect, but I'm not so bad, either."

Keith's uncle drove on silently for a few minutes. "Oh, no!" he exclaimed as they passed a road sign. "I missed the turnoff. We should have gotten off this road five miles back."

"Guess we'll have to turn around and go back now, huh?" asked Keith.

But Uncle Al shook his head. "I don't feel like turning around right now," he said. "I guess we'll just keep going this way. I kinda like this road."

Keith looked at his uncle in amazement. "But we have to turn around to get to Bonny Lake," he protested, "and the longer we keep going this way, the longer it will take to get back. If we wait too long to turn around, we might not even get there in time to fish."

Uncle Al smiled at Keith as he slowed down for the next turn. "You're right," he said, "and what you said just now is exactly what I've been trying to tell you about your spiritual life—that when you're travelling down the wrong road, the sooner you turn around, the better. If you wait too long, you might never get to your goal—heaven."

HOW ABOUT YOU? Do you need to "turn around and go in a different direction" to get to heaven? You do if you've never accepted Jesus as Savior. Don't let habits, the opinions of others, or even your own feelings of laziness keep you from taking the right road. Don't wait until it's too late to turn to Jesus. □ S.K.

TO MEMORIZE: *Repent! Turn away from all your offenses; then sin will not be your downfall.* Ezekiel 18:30, NIV

The Long Way Home

FROM THE BIBLE:
O house of Israel, I will judge you, each one according to his ways, declares the Sovereign Lord. Repent! Turn away from all your offenses; then sin will not be your downfall. Rid yourselves of all the offenses you have committed, and get a new heart and a new spirit. Why will you die, O house of Israel? For I take no pleasure in the death of anyone, declares the Sovereign Lord. Repent and live!
Ezekiel 18:30-32, NIV

Turn to Jesus

MARCH

12

To Talk or Not to Talk

FROM THE BIBLE:
Praise be to you, O Lord; teach me your decrees. With my lips I recount all the laws that come from your mouth. I rejoice in following your statutes as one rejoices in great riches. I meditate on your precepts and consider your ways. I delight in your decrees; I will not neglect your word.
Psalm 119:12-16, NIV

Talk about Jesus

CARL AND SUSIE were having fun looking through some old trunks in Grandpa and Grandma's attic. "Aren't these old clothes funny?"

"Yeah," agreed Carl as he tried on one of Grandpa's old hats. "Hey, look at this trunk! It's full of army stuff. There's a uniform, pictures of soldiers, even some medals!"

Susie came over to look. "I wonder what this means?" She held up a poster with these words: *Loose Lips Sink Ships.* It had a picture of a sinking ship above the words.

"Let's go ask Grandpa," suggested Carl. "Maybe it was some kind of a joke."

They climbed down the narrow stairs, clutching the old poster. When they asked Grandpa about it, his face grew serious. "No, it was no joke," he said. "These signs were posted in areas where military secrets were discussed. 'Loose lips' are lips that talk a lot, so these signs were a reminder that talking about such things could be disastrous. Enemy spies were anxious to discover what our plans were. If someone carelessly gave out that information, it might mean death to hundreds of American sailors or soldiers."

"Wow!" exclaimed Carl. "Just think—hundreds of lives depended on whether or not you happened to say a few words to the wrong person!"

Grandpa held up the old poster and thoughtfully gazed at it. "You know, 'loose lips' aren't always bad," he said. "In fact, sometimes we need to loosen up our lips in order to save lives."

"What do you mean by that?" asked Susie in surprise.

"God has entrusted a very special message to us—the gospel," explained Grandpa, "but He doesn't want us to hide it. He expects us to share it so that many lives may be saved from the fires of hell."

HOW ABOUT YOU? Are you tight-lipped when it comes to telling others about Jesus? Do you think it's enough that your life-style pleases the Lord— that you're honest, kind, helpful, cheerful? That's good, but God also wants to use your lips to spread His message. Don't be afraid to talk about Him. □ S.K.

TO MEMORIZE: *With my lips I recount all the laws that come from your mouth.* Psalm 119:13, NIV

E_D SCOOPED UP a large spoonful of cookie dough and began shaping it. Mother laughed. "Hold on there!" she said. "I know that's the size cookie you like to eat, but we're going to make them a little smaller. Here, let me make a model for you." She scooped up some dough and made it into a round ball. "There! Check the amount of dough you take to see if it's this size before you flatten it. I'll be back after I get Susie out of her crib."

When Mother returned, she looked at the pan of cookies Ed had made. Some were the size of half dollars, some much larger. "I tried, Mom," Ed said. "They just didn't come out right."

"Did you compare your pieces of dough with the piece I made for you?" asked Mother.

"Well, I did for a while," replied Ed, "but then I started to judge them by the last one I had made. If the piece of dough was too big, I made it smaller. If it was too small, I made it bigger."

"I see," said Mother. "So your standard changed for each cookie. No wonder they're all different sizes." She set to work, making the cookies closer to the same size. "This reminds me that Christians have an unchanging standard for life," she added. "Do you know what that standard is?"

"I think it's God's Word, the Bible," said Ed. "That's the only thing I know of that gives us good rules for living."

"Right," approved Mother. "Actually, His standard is Himself, and He is revealed to us in His Word. Remember these cookies, Ed—and remember to judge each decision of your life on what is pleasing to God as He teaches you through His Word. Then your life will shape up nicely."

HOW ABOUT YOU? Do you think it's old-fashioned to stick to old standards? Do you think Christians should keep up with the times and be free to do things if they 'sound right' or 'feel good'? Times do change, it's true—and it's okay to change some things. But when it comes to what God has taught in His Word, that never changes. The commandments He has given (don't lie, steal, covet, etc.) must always be obeyed. □ C.R.

TO MEMORIZE: *I am the Lord, I do not change.* Malachi 3:6, NKJV

An Unchanging Standard

FROM THE BIBLE:
Whatever is good and perfect comes to us from God, the Creator of all light, and he shines forever without change or shadow. . . . Dear brothers, don't ever forget that it is best to listen much, speak little, and not become angry; for anger doesn't make us good, as God demands that we must be. So get rid of all that is wrong in your life, both inside and outside, and humbly be glad for the wonderful message we have received, for it is able to save our souls as it takes hold of our hearts. And remember, it is a message to obey, not just to listen to. So don't fool yourselves. For if a person just listens and doesn't obey, he is like a man looking at his face in a mirror; as soon as he walks away, he can't see himself anymore or remember what he looks like. But if anyone keeps looking steadily into God's law for free men, he will not only remember it but he will do what it says, and God will greatly bless him in everything he does.
James 1:17-25, TLB

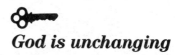

God is unchanging

14

Trace It

FROM THE BIBLE:

To this you were called, because Christ suffered for you, leaving you an example, that you should follow in his steps. "He committed no sin, and no deceit was found in his mouth." When they hurled their insults at him, he did not retaliate; when he suffered, he made no threats. Instead, he entrusted himself to him who judges justly. He himself bore our sins in his body on the tree, so that we might die to sins and live for righteousness; by his wounds you have been healed. For you were like sheep going astray, but now you have returned to the Shepherd and Overseer of your souls.
1 Peter 2:21-25, NIV

Live close to Jesus

I DON'T SEE why it's so important to read the Bible every single day," observed Bette as she sat down on the couch. She picked up a book with colorful illustrations of birds and flowers. "If we go to church and Sunday school every week, that should be enough." She studied a picture of a beautiful red cardinal. "I'd sure like this picture for my bird project at school," she said.

"Well, why don't you trace it?" suggested Mother.

"Good idea." Bette jumped up and got some paper.

Mother watched as Bette worked. "Why do you put the paper right on top of the picture?" asked Mother.

"So I can see the picture through the paper," replied Bette, surprised at Mother's question.

"But you just saw the picture a minute ago," argued Mother, "and you can look at it every now and then."

"I'm tracing it, not copying it," said Bette. "When you trace, your paper has to touch the picture." She looked at her mother suspiciously. "I'm sure you know that. And since you're the one who suggested I trace it, I have an idea you're asking those questions for a reason. Right?"

"You're right," admitted Mother. "You see, the Bible says that our lives should be like Christ's—that we should follow in His steps. Just as you need to touch the picture with your paper in order for you to trace it, we need to 'touch' Jesus—to live close enough to Him so our lives are copies of His. We do that through constant contact with Him in prayer and Bible reading as well as through church and Sunday school."

Bette lifted her paper and looked at the picture she had made of the cardinal. "Before I color this, I'm going to have my devotions," she decided. "It's important."

HOW ABOUT YOU? Do you realize that you should spend time each day with God? You can't expect to live the way He did if you think about Him only occasionally. Constant contact with the Lord is important. □ H.M.

TO MEMORIZE: *To this you were called, because Christ suffered for you, leaving you an example, that you should follow in his steps.* 1 Peter 2:21, NIV

BOBBY SHRIEKED IN protest as his mother got up to lead him into the doctor's examining room. Bobby's sister Lisa looked at him sympathetically. "Don't cry yet, Bobby!" she said. "You haven't even gotten your shot yet!"

"I don't wanna get shot!" screeched the little boy.

While the nurse swabbed Bobby's arm with antiseptic, he screamed and wiggled. "This will prick a little bit," she said kindly, "but it will be over soon." Sure enough, almost before Bobby could draw a breath to give another yell, the nurse had finished. As they walked out to their car, Bobby wore a big smile and admired the little toy car the nurse had given him.

"That wasn't so bad, was it?" asked Lisa.

Bobby shook his head. "Not so bad," he murmured, "but I still don't like shots. They hurt!"

"We know, Honey," said Mother soothingly, "but the hurt lasts only a little while, and the medicine in the shot helps you stay healthy. If you didn't get shots, you might get a sickness that would hurt far worse than a shot."

"Bobby's too little to understand," remarked Lisa as she watched her brother play with his car. "But someday he'll be glad he got 'hurt' today, won't he, Mom?"

"I'm sure he will," smiled Mother. "And you know, that could serve as a lesson for you and me. When we're going through hard times, we may wonder whether or not God really cares about us. But everything He allows us to experience—even moments of pain and sadness—are for our good and His glory. If we could see things from His point of view, we'd think about our earthly trials in a completely different way."

HOW ABOUT YOU? Is it hard to be patient when you're not feeling well? When you have to go to a new school? When things just aren't going well? Perhaps God wants to teach you something, or to allow you to be an example of His grace. Maybe He wants to cleanse you of some sin in your life, or to protect you from an even greater danger in the future. Whatever His purposes are, you will find peace and joy when you fully submit to Him. He knows best! □ S.K.

TO MEMORIZE: *We know that all things work together for good to those who love God, to those who are the called according to His purpose.* Romans 8:28, NKJV

The Hurt That Helps

FROM THE BIBLE:
The sufferings of this present time are not worthy to be compared with the glory which shall be revealed in us. For the earnest expectation of the creation eagerly waits for the revealing of the sons of God. For the creation was subjected to futility, not willingly, but because of Him who subjected it in hope; because the creation itself also will be delivered from the bondage of corruption into the glorious liberty of the children of God. For we know that the whole creation groans and labors with birth pangs together until now. And not only they, but we also who have the firstfruits of the Spirit, even we ourselves groan within ourselves, eagerly waiting for the adoption, the redemption of our body. . . . And we know that all things work together for good to those who love God, to those who are the called according to His purpose.
Romans 8:18-23, 28, NKJV

Trust God in all situations

16

The Monkey Trap

FROM THE BIBLE:
A rich man had a fertile farm that produced fine crops. In fact, his barns were full to overflowing—he couldn't get everything in. He thought about his problem, and finally exclaimed, "I know—I'll tear down my barns and build bigger ones! Then I'll have room enough. And I'll sit back and say to myself, 'Friend, you have enough stored away for years to come. Now take it easy! Wine, women, and song for you!'" But God said to him, "Fool! Tonight you die. Then who will get it all?" Yes, every man is a fool who gets rich on earth but not in heaven.
Luke 12:16-21, TLB

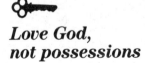

Love God, not possessions

JORDAN'S PARENTS WERE serving as missionaries in Africa, and he was learning many new things. One day his friend Paul helped him make a trap to catch a monkey. "It's easy," said Paul, handing Jordan a gourd. "First, make a hole in this gourd, just big enough for a monkey to put his hand through." He supervised while Jordan worked. "There," Paul said, "that's big enough. The gourd is hollow, so now we'll put some nuts and fruit in it. Then we'll fasten it to a branch of a tree at the edge of the village."

"I don't get it," said Jordan as the boys walked to the tree Paul had selected. "How will this work? I can see that a monkey might reach into the gourd to get the food out, but what will keep him from getting away with it?"

"When he has nuts in his fist, his hand won't go through the hole," explained Paul. "If he'd just let them go, he could get away. But he won't. He hangs on even though it means he gets caught." Paul helped Jordan attach the gourd to a tree. "There. By tomorrow morning, you'll probably have a monkey."

When he returned home, Jordan told his mother about the monkeys. Mother nodded. "They certainly are silly," she agreed. "But do you know I was just as foolish myself once? I wanted certain things," she explained. "A nice home, pretty clothes, a nice car, a grassy lawn. I wanted to hang on to them. I didn't want to give them up and come to the mission field. But the Lord showed me that by following His will, I wasn't really giving up anything important. I was just letting those things go for something better. I've never been as happy as I've been here in Africa, bringing the message of salvation to these people."

HOW ABOUT YOU? What things do you want very badly? What goals do you have for your life? Good grades? Money? Fun? Pretty clothes? A big car? Don't set your heart on the things of this world. Don't let them trap you into missing what God intends for you. It may be that He has those things in His plan for you, but you need to be willing to let them go. If they are not in His plan, you can be sure He has something even better. □ H.M.

TO MEMORIZE: *Set your minds on things above, not on earthly things.* Colossians 3:2, NIV

BOBBY GAZED at his friend Adam, uncertain what to say. Adam had asked a simple enough question, but for a moment, Bobby was stumped for an answer. "Why do I go to church?" Bobby repeated the question, stalling for time to think of a good answer to give his friend.

"Yeah," nodded Adam, sounding as though he really wanted to know. "Why do you and your family always go to church?"

Bobby wasn't sure what his answer should be. "Because it's Sunday," he said finally.

Adam looked at him quizzically. "That's a stupid answer," he said, a smirk on the corners of his mouth. "That's like saying, 'I go to school because it's Monday or Friday.' "

Bobby knew his answer had not been a good one. He thought about it as he headed for home. Why did he go to church? Was it because his folks had taken him there as a little baby, and he had never questioned going as he grew older? Or was it because it was part of their family life, and his folks made him go? He talked with his father about it when he reached the house.

"That's a question you need to answer for yourself," his father said. "I go to worship the Lord."

"Can't you worship Him at home or out in the field," interrupted Bobby, "or some place other than church?"

Dad nodded. "Yes, you can worship the Lord any time and any place. But if you don't go to church, you'll miss the fellowship you need to have with other Christians. The Bible tells us that we should assemble together with others who believe like we do."

Bobby thought about that. When the people of his church got together, it was actually a time to praise the Lord through singing and preaching. When the pastor brought the message, Bobby almost always got something new and special from it—something he probably couldn't learn from the Bible by himself. "I'm going down to talk with Adam again," he called to his parents. "I think I can give him the right answer now."

HOW ABOUT YOU? Do you attend church just out of habit? It's a good habit to have, but you should also go to worship the Lord, to sing praises to Him, to hear His Word, and to fellowship with other Christians. □ R.J.

TO MEMORIZE: *I rejoiced with those who said to me, "Let us go to the house of the Lord."* Psalm 122:1, NIV

Why Go to Church?

FROM THE BIBLE:
All the earth shall worship you and sing of your glories. Come, see the glorious things God has done. What marvelous miracles happen to his people! He made a dry road through the sea for them. They went across on foot. What excitement and joy there was that day! Because of his great power he rules forever. He watches every movement of the nations. O rebel lands, he will deflate your pride. Let everyone bless God and sing his praises, for he holds our lives in his hands. And he holds our feet to the path. You have purified us with fire, O Lord, like silver in a crucible. You captured us in your net and laid great burdens on our backs. You sent troops to ride across our broken bodies. We went through fire and flood. But in the end, you brought us into wealth and great abundance. Now I have come to your Temple with burnt offerings to pay my vows.
Psalm 66:4-13, TLB

Worship God in church

18

Spice in Your Life

FROM THE BIBLE:

Do not get drunk on wine, which leads to debauchery. Instead, be filled with the Spirit. Speak to one another with psalms, hymns and spiritual songs. Sing and make music in your heart to the Lord, always giving thanks to God the Father for everything, in the name of our Lord Jesus Christ. Submit to one another out of reverence for Christ.

Ephesians 5:18-21, NIV

All God sends is good

JENNY PILED HER taco shell with all the things her father had prepared—meat, cheese, lettuce, tomatoes, and his own special taco sauce. Between bites Jenny managed to say, "There's something in this sauce that makes it different from the ones in the restaurant. What is it?"

"Well, Jenny, I double the amount of ground cumin in my sauce recipe," said Dad with a smile. "I also add a little sweet red pepper along with the green. But it's the cumin that gives Mexican-style foods their unique flavor."

The memory of that special supper stayed with Jenny. Then, as she was filling a salt shaker one day, she noticed the bottle of ground cumin in the spice drawer. She opened the bottle, and the smell reminded her of those delicious tacos. She shook a little of the powder into her hand and licked it. "Oh, yuk!" she gasped, nearly choking. She ran to the sink, spitting and sputtering, and rinsed her mouth with water three times.

When Jenny told her father what had happened, she asked, "Why doesn't that spice taste good? It sure makes the tacos good."

"I think this is an example of having too much of a good thing," said Dad, laughing. "Have you ever heard anyone refer to something as the 'spice of life', Jenny? They're usually talking about one of the fun things they enjoy—vacations, holidays, and so on. Sometimes we think we'd like those kinds of things all the time. But if we had parties all the time, soon they would mean nothing. It would be like having too much of a good spice. The hard times God allows to come our way are needed, too. They help us see the value of the good times."

"Hmmmm," said Jenny with a smile. "Whoever thought life as a Christian would be like eating tacos?"

HOW ABOUT YOU? Do you think it would be nice to play all the time and never work? Just as there are many kinds of spices—hot, sweet, bitter, and fragrant—that lend their special touch to foods, God sends you many kinds of experiences to make your life rich. He knows just what good times and hard times you need to help you live life at its best. □ C.R.

TO MEMORIZE: *Submit to one another out of reverence for Christ.* Ephesians 5:21, NIV

HEY, RODNEY," whispered Max. "Look over there by the bushes."

"Wow!" Rodney whispered back. "Mr. Jones must have a new dog. He's big, but he looks harmless."

"I think we can still take our regular shortcut through his backyard," said Max a little bit louder.

"But look, Max." Rodney pointed to a sign on a tree. "It says, 'Beware of the Dog.' "

"Sure! Just look at that baby face!" exclaimed Max as he slowly walked toward the dog. The dog began to growl. "Nice doggy, nice doggy," repeated Max.

"Hey, Max," warned Rodney, "maybe we better not go any closer. That chain looks pretty long!"

"He's as gentle as a lamb. You'll see," Max assured him. "You just have to have a way with animals, Rodney."

Suddenly, the dog lunged towards Max. "Help!" yelled Max as he frantically tried to free his pant leg from the dog's teeth.

The boys heard a shout. "What are you doing in my backyard?" Mr. Jones asked angrily as he walked towards the snarling dog. "Come here, Dude!" Dude wagged his tail and trotted to his master. "You boys should read signs more carefully." Mr. Jones spoke firmly. "You were trespassing. See that it doesn't happen again. Dude may look gentle, and most of the time he is, but he's been known to scare a few people. Warnings are given for a reason. Obey them."

Max and Rodney were quiet as they walked home. "Max," Rodney broke the silence, "Mr. Jones sounded a lot like Rev. Parker."

Max nodded. "Yeah." They were remembering Sunday's evening message. "Sin may look attractive," Rev. Parker had said. "It may look harmless. But God warns against all sin. Heed this warning. Say no when Satan tempts you."

HOW ABOUT YOU? Would you like to be like "everybody else" once in a while? Do you think it wouldn't hurt you to go where they go and do what they do, even though you know it wouldn't please the Lord? You're wrong. God warns that sin has dreadful consequences. Heed His warning and live for Him. □ V.R.

TO MEMORIZE: *After desire has conceived, it gives birth to sin; and sin, when it is full-grown, gives birth to death.* James 1:15, NIV

Beware!

FROM THE BIBLE:
When tempted, no one should say, "God is tempting me." For God cannot be tempted by evil, nor does he tempt anyone; but each one is tempted when, by his own evil desire, he is dragged away and enticed. Then, after desire has conceived, it gives birth to sin; and sin, when it is full-grown, gives birth to death. James 1:13-15, NIV

Beware of sin

20

Two Boys, Two Fathers

FROM THE BIBLE:
Be careful not to jump to conclusions before the Lord returns as to whether someone is a good servant or not. When the Lord comes, he will turn on the light so that everyone can see exactly what each one of us is really like, deep down in our hearts. Then everyone will know why we have been doing the Lord's work. At that time God will give to each one whatever praise is coming to him. . . . You must not be proud of one of God's teachers more than another. What are you so puffed up about? What do you have that God hasn't given you? And if all you have is from God, why act as though you are so great, and as though you have accomplished something on your own? You seem to think you already have all the spiritual food you need. You are full and spiritually contented, rich kings on your thrones, leaving us far behind! I wish you really were already on your thrones, for when that time comes you can be sure that we will be there, too, reigning with you.
1 Corinthians 4:5-8, TLB

Don't look down on others

JEFF BLAIR WAS proud of his dad. He was a police officer, and often the kids at school would say, "I saw your dad on the news last night," or, "That was your dad's name in the paper again, wasn't it, Jeff?"

One night Jeff's dad helped capture a dangerous criminal. The next day, newspaper headlines proclaimed that Officer Blair was a hero. Jeff eagerly read the whole account. He laughed a little over the name of the man his dad had captured—Percy J. Crane! *If I were a dangerous criminal, I'd be embarrassed to have a name like Percy,* Jeff thought.

About a week later, Jeff's teacher introduced a new class member. Smiling, Mrs. Townsend turned to a tall, thin, sad-faced boy. "This is Percy J. Crane, Jr.," she said. Jeff could hardly believe what he was hearing. This must be the son of the criminal his dad had caught! "He's from Illinois," continued Mrs. Townsend. "He's been in our town only a short time, and I'd like each of you to make him welcome." The teacher's bright, cheerful voice made Jeff think that she was unaware of what had happened to Percy's dad.

Jeff looked at Percy J. Crane, Jr. He was standing quietly, head down, eyes fixed on the floor. Jeff thought about Percy's dad. *What would it be like to feel ashamed of your dad?* He remembered that his own father had once said, "Don't ever be proud, Son. Anyone can be tempted to sin. Remember to ask God to keep you on the right path, and thank Him for His protection every day." Jeff shivered a little as he realized that it could be him—Jeff Blair—instead of Percy Crane standing there.

"Mrs. Townsend, I'll show Perk around school, and he can eat lunch with the guys and me," offered Jeff.

HOW ABOUT YOU? Do you know someone who has reason to be ashamed of his parents? Do you tend to "look down" on that person—to consider yourself better than him? Don't be proud. It's only because of God's grace to you that you're not in his position and he in yours. Thank God for what He's done for you. Then love others as God does. □ P.K.

TO MEMORIZE: *Though the Lord is on high, he looks upon the lowly, but the proud he knows from afar.* Psalm 138:6, NIV

W OW!" BRENT'S eyes were wide. His parents had just been explaining to Brent and his little brother Sammy that the doctors had decided that Grandpa should have a heart transplant as soon as a donor could be found. "Wow!" repeated Brent. "That's neat!"

"It's amazing what doctors have learned to do," agreed Dad. "We must remember, though, that it's a very dangerous operation and not always successful. Let's trust the Lord for the outcome."

"But what if Grandpa has the heart transplant and then dies anyway?" Sammy asked anxiously. "He wouldn't go to heaven."

Everyone turned and looked at Sammy curiously. "Why do you say that?" asked Mother. "Of course Grandpa would go to heaven. He has been a Christian for many years."

"But my Sunday school teacher said we won't go to heaven unless we've asked Jesus to come into our hearts," replied Sammy, "so if Grandpa has a different heart, he won't be a Christian anymore, will he?"

"Oh, I see your problem," said Dad thoughtfully. "I'm afraid you've been confused by the terms we've used. You see, I can say that you have a big place in my heart, Sammy. But, of course, I don't mean you actually are inside my physical heart. What do you think I mean?"

Sammy thought for a moment. "I guess you mean that you love me a whole lot."

Dad nodded. "Right. I love you very much and you are a big part of my life. When we say we ask Jesus to come into our hearts, we don't mean our physical hearts either. What we mean is that we love Jesus very much, too—so much that we ask Him to come into our lives and control us. No matter what physical heart is inside Grandpa's body, Grandpa loves Jesus and belongs to Him."

Sammy looked relieved.

HOW ABOUT YOU? Have you wondered just what it means to ask Jesus to come into your heart? The word *heart* often does not refer to the physical organ in your body. Instead, it refers to your innermost being, your "self"—not your physical body, but the real you. It's the part of you that goes on living after the body dies. It's the part that sins and needs to be saved. Have you asked Jesus to take those sins away? □ H.M.

TO MEMORIZE: *Christ may dwell in your hearts through faith.* Ephesians 3:17, NIV

A New Heart

FROM THE BIBLE:
O loving and kind God, have mercy. Have pity upon me and take away the awful stain of my transgressions. Oh, wash me, cleanse me from this guilt. Let me be pure again. For I admit my shameful deed—it haunts me day and night. It is against you and you alone I sinned, and did this terrible thing. You saw it all, and your sentence against me is just. But I was born a sinner, yes, from the moment my mother conceived me. You deserve honesty from the heart; yes, utter sincerity and truthfulness. Oh, give me this wisdom. Sprinkle me with the cleansing blood and I shall be clean again. Wash me and I shall be whiter than snow. And after you have punished me, give me back my joy again. Don't keep looking at my sins—erase them from your sight. Create in me a new, clean heart, O God, filled with clean thoughts and right desires.
Psalm 51:1-10, TLB

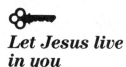

Let Jesus live in you

22

Daily Care Needed

FROM THE BIBLE:

To you, O Lord, I pray. Don't fail me, Lord, for I am trusting you. Don't let my enemies succeed. Don't give them victory over me. None of those who have faith in God will ever be disgraced for trusting him. But all who harm the innocent shall be defeated. Show me the path where I should go, O Lord; point out the right road for me to walk. Lead me; teach me; for you are the God who gives me salvation. I have no hope except in you. Overlook my youthful sins, O Lord! Look at me instead through eyes of mercy and forgiveness, through eyes of everlasting love and kindness. Psalm 25:1-6, TLB

Read God's Word daily

CARLA WAS DELIGHTED when her grandmother gave her a plant for her birthday. "If you take good care of this and water it according to the instructions I'm giving you, you'll soon have a lovely plant with beautiful red flowers," Grandmother said.

At first Carla followed the directions carefully. But as time passed, she found it a little boring to care for her plant, and she didn't water it regularly. From time to time she checked it for buds, but there were only stems and leaves. They seemed to be turning brown.

One day, Grandmother came to visit. Immediately she asked how the plant was doing. "Are there buds on it yet?" she wanted to know.

Carla shook her head. "No, in fact my plant looks like it's dying," she confessed.

Grandmother followed her into her room to check it out. "Oh, my," she remarked. "This poor plant is drowning in water!"

Carla nodded. "Yeah. I sometimes forget to water it, so whenever I remember I just give it twice as much."

Grandmother smiled in spite of her disappointment. "How would you like it if your mother forgot to fix dinner for about three days, and then when she remembered she made you eat enough for all the meals she had forgotten?"

"I wouldn't like it," Carla laughed. "I guess I'd get just as sick as this plant is."

As they turned to leave the room, Grandmother noticed the Bible on Carla's dresser. "I see you have your Bible handy."

Carla nodded and picked it up. "This is one thing I haven't forgotten, Grandma," she said. "When you gave it to me you told me to read it every day, and that's what I've been doing."

Grandmother smiled. "Well, I'm glad to see you're getting a regular diet of spiritual food."

HOW ABOUT YOU? Do you forget to read your Bible, or even purposely neglect it, and then suddenly try to "catch up" by reading faster or more often? That doesn't work well. The Bible is your spiritual food, and you need some of it every day. Set up a regular schedule for Bible reading. You'll see growth in your Christian life. □ R.J.

TO MEMORIZE: *Look in the scroll of the Lord and read.* Isaiah 34:16, NIV

THE SUNDAY SCHOOL lesson had been about sharing Christ with others. During class, the children had talked about different ways they could witness to their friends. Mike, however, hadn't participated in the discussion. When class was over, he waited until the others had left so that he could talk to Mrs. Winfield privately. "What is it, Mike?" she asked gently. "You were very quiet today."

"It's my family," Mike told her. "I'm the only one who believes in Christ. I come to church with my neighbors. My parents are the ones I really want most to witness to. But my dad is always telling me that church is crazy, and my mother laughs when I try to tell her about the Bible. The other kids in the class all come from Christian homes. They don't know how good they have it!"

"It is hard to be the only Christian in the family," agreed Mrs. Winfield. "I know, because I started attending church with a friend, too, and it was at church I accepted the Lord. I prayed for my parents daily, yet they seemed to grow angry about what I was learning."

"What did you do?" Mike asked.

"What I did was talk to *my* Sunday school teacher, and she reminded me that the Lord understood my situation and the problems I was having in a non-Christian home. Then she showed me a verse I hadn't seen before." Mrs. Winfield opened her Bible. "Did you know, Mike, that the Lord's own brothers didn't believe in Him? Look at John 7:1-6."

"I never knew that before," Mike said thoughtfully. "The Lord does understand my problem, doesn't He?"

"He sure does, Mike," agreed the teacher. "Remember that truth as you pray for your parents, and live each day so that they can see Christ in you."

HOW ABOUT YOU? Are you the only Christian in your family? Do your parents or brothers and sisters think it's silly to believe the Bible? The Lord does understand. He knows you are in a tough situation. There was a time when His own brothers did not believe in Him. Talk to the Lord about your feelings. He will help you. □ L. W.

TO MEMORIZE: *He came to that which was his own, but his own did not receive him. Yet to all who received him, to those who believed in his name, he gave the right to become children of God.* John 1:11-12, NIV

23

A Hard Job for Mike

FROM THE BIBLE:
After this, Jesus went to Galilee, going from village to village, for he wanted to stay out of Judea where the Jewish leaders were plotting his death. But soon it was time for the Tabernacle Ceremonies, one of the annual Jewish holidays, and Jesus' brothers urged him to go to Judea for the celebration. "Go where more people can see your miracles!" they scoffed. "You can't be famous when you hide like this! If you're so great, prove it to the world!" For even his brothers didn't believe in him. John 7:1-5, TLB

Pray about unsaved relatives

24

The Honor Roll

FROM THE BIBLE:
Happy are those who are persecuted because they are good, for the Kingdom of Heaven is theirs. When you are reviled and persecuted and lied about because you are my followers—wonderful! Be happy about it! Be very glad! for a tremendous reward awaits you up in heaven. And remember, the ancient prophets were persecuted too.
Matthew 5:10-12, TLB

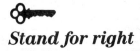

Stand for right

AMY CURLED UP in her favorite chair with a new book, but before long her forehead wrinkled tighter and tighter. She slammed the book shut. It was not a good book. In fact, it was dirty! But she had to read it for one of her classes! Or did she? She took it to her mother. "Mrs. Rogers assigned this book." Amy handed it to Mother. "It's terrible. I'm going to ask if I can read a different one."

Mother scanned the first few pages. "I'm glad you decided that," she said, smiling.

But Mrs. Rogers would not assign another book to Amy. "This is a very real book. It tells it like it is. You can't hide from life behind your cloak of religion, Amy."

"But the words they use are gutter talk. And the things they do are terrible," Amy protested.

"It is real life," Mrs. Rogers insisted. "Those are words you hear every day."

"But I don't have to *read* them," objected Amy. "I try to keep my mind clean by thinking clean thoughts."

"You'll read that book or take a zero!" said Mrs. Rogers.

Amy blinked back the tears. She had worked hard for an *A* and a zero would bring her grade down. It could keep her from making the honor roll. "I guess I'll have to take a zero," Amy said softly as she left the room.

Three weeks later Amy burst into the house, sobbing. "It's not fair! She's so hateful! She gave me a *C* and made me miss the honor roll."

Mother didn't have to ask what Amy was talking about. She knew. Gathering her sobbing daughter into her arms, she said gently, "Never mind, Honey. Don't be bitter toward Mrs. Rogers. Just pray for her. You may have missed the honor roll at Clayton Middle School, but I think you've made the one in heaven."

HOW ABOUT YOU? Have you ever taken a stand for your convictions? Have you said no to an invitation to smoke? Have you refused to listen to dirty jokes? Have you spoken up for the Lord when evolution was taught? Taking a stand is not easy, and the immediate results are not always pleasant. But remember, the testing time will soon pass, and your reward for doing right will be eternal. □ B.W.

TO MEMORIZE: *Our light and momentary troubles are achieving for us an eternal glory that far outweighs them all.* 2 Corinthians 4:17, NIV

WHAT CAN YOU do to serve Jesus, boys and girls?" asked Mr. Jim, the leader of Children's Church.

Good question, thought Mary Lou. She wanted to be used by God, but she didn't see any way the Lord could possibly use her. Some kids brought money to Sunday school, but she didn't have any money of her own to give. Some kids sang in the children's choir, but Mary Lou was sure she didn't have a good voice. Some kids always gave testimonies on Sunday nights, but she just knew she would stutter if she tried to do that.

Just then Mr. Jim asked, "Are you smarter than a donkey?" All the kids laughed. "Then," continued Mr. Jim, "you can serve Jesus." He went on to read Luke 19:28-35, and then he explained how a donkey was once a perfect picture of a servant. "First of all," said Mr. Jim, "he was where God wanted him to be. He was available."

Hmmm, thought Mary Lou. *At least I qualify on that point, because I want God to be able to use me.*

"Second," added Mr. Jim, "he was loosed, as Jesus said he should be. This makes me think that maybe you're afraid to try to serve Jesus. Maybe you need to let Him untie your fears." Now Mary Lou knew that this lesson was just for her. She had to admit that she was afraid to try to sing or witness for Jesus.

"Also, the donkey was controlled," Mr. Jim continued. He explained how, even though this donkey had never been ridden before, he didn't buck in fright when Jesus sat on him. He just let Jesus control him. "Have you truly let Jesus control you, or have you been stubborn?" asked Mr. Jim. Mary Lou began to feel uncomfortable. She knew she had been thinking only about how she felt and what she would like to do. She hadn't asked Jesus to control her life and actions.

When Mr. Jim asked the children to bow their heads for prayer, Mary Lou asked God to take control of her life. She asked Him to loosen her tongue and untie all her fear of failure. "Let me be a servant just like the little donkey," she prayed.

HOW ABOUT YOU? Are you afraid to try to speak out for Jesus? Are you afraid that if you try to sing a song or play an instrument to serve Him, you will make a mistake? Take a lesson from the donkey. Be available. Be loosed. And be controlled. The Lord needs you! □ R.P.

TO MEMORIZE: *They replied, "The Lord needs it."* Luke 19:34, NIV

25

Like a Donkey

FROM THE BIBLE:
As he approached Bethphage and Bethany at the hill called the Mount of Olives, he sent two of his disciples, saying to them, "Go to the village ahead of you, and as you enter it, you will find a colt tied there, which no one has ever ridden. Untie it and bring it here. If anyone asks you, 'Why are you untying it?' tell him, 'The Lord needs it.'" Those who were sent ahead went and found it just as he had told them. As they were untying the colt, its owners asked them, "Why are you untying the colt?" They replied, "The Lord needs it." They brought it to Jesus, threw their cloaks on the colt and put Jesus on it.
Luke 19:29-35, NIV

Be a servant

26

Two "Tents"

FROM THE BIBLE:

Be anxious for nothing, but in everything by prayer and supplication, with thanksgiving, let your requests be made known to God; and the peace of God, which surpasses all understanding, will guard your hearts and minds through Christ Jesus. Finally, brethren, whatever things are true, whatever things are noble, whatever things are just, whatever things are pure, whatever things are lovely, whatever things are of good report, if there is any virtue and if there is anything praiseworthy—meditate on these things. The things which you learned and received and heard and saw in me, these do, and the God of peace will be with you. But I rejoiced in the Lord greatly that now at last your care for me has flourished again; though you surely did care, but you lacked opportunity. Not that I speak in regard to need, for I have learned in whatever state I am, to be content.

Philippians 4:6-11, NKJV

Be content

I WISH MY dad had time to spend with us like yours does," Sonya complained. "He's always so busy!"

Bethany looked at the beautiful furnishings in Sonya's home. "Well, you sure have lots of nice things," she sighed. "At our house we have lots of time, but no money."

After listening to the girls complain for several minutes, Sonya's mother persuaded them to join her in making some visits for the church welcoming committee. At the first stop, a young mother invited them in. "You'll have to excuse this house," she sighed. "The children are about to drive me crazy. I'll be glad when they're all in school. Then maybe I'll have some peace and quiet." Motioning them to sit down, she continued, "It's so lonesome here. Everyone is so unfriendly." For thirty minutes Mrs. Marshall continued her tirade.

When they finally left, Bethany whistled. "Wow! I wonder if she's happy about anything."

Reluctantly, the girls followed Mother up the steps of another house. A smiling lady answered the door. "We're so happy here," Mrs. Perry bubbled to her guests. "We're thankful we found a loving church family so quickly."

On the way home, Mother spoke quietly. "There are two tents in which we can live. One is con*tent*ment, and the other is discon*tent*ment. Mrs. Marshall and Mrs. Perry moved to town about the same time. Their husbands work for the same company. They live in the same neighborhood and attend the same church. Mrs. Marshall has chosen to live in discon*tent*ment, but Mrs. Perry lives in con*tent*ment." Mother smiled, then continued, "It's not how much time or money you have that determines how happy you are. It's whether you choose to live in contentment or discontentment."

Remembering their earlier conversation, Sonya grinned sheepishly at her friend. "Well, Beth, it looks like we need to move. We've been camping in the wrong tent!"

HOW ABOUT YOU? Where do you live? Do you find yourself complaining about what you don't have instead of counting your blessings? If so, now is the time to move out of that state of discontentment. Determine to be content whatever your circumstances. □ B.W.

TO MEMORIZE: *I have learned in whatever state I am, to be content.* Philippians 4:11, NKJV

OOOHHH, MOTHER, isn't he sweet?" Lisa cuddled the puppy in her arms. "Can I keep him? Mrs. Johnson said I could have him—free! Please, Mother!"

Mother looked down at four pleading eyes. "Very well, but remember, he's your responsibility. You'll have to take care of him, and you'll have to use your allowance to buy food and supplies for him."

"Oh, that's OK. Thank you!" Lisa jumped to her feet and held up the puppy. "Give Mother a kiss, Taffy."

Mother laughed and backed away. "No, thank you. I can do without puppy love."

In the following days, Lisa found that she had to quite often give up something she had hoped to buy for herself in order to have money for puppy food, flea powder, a collar, and dog shampoo. Sometimes she had to leave her play or a favorite book to go and care for her dog.

One day when Lisa's friend Denise was visiting, Mother said, "Lisa, don't forget that Taffy needs a bath today."

"Will you give him one, Mother?" pleaded Lisa.

"Oh, I'll help you, Lisa," Denise offered as Mother shook her head. "It'll be fun." Later, Mother heard the girls talking as they worked. "I wish I had a puppy like Taffy. How much did he cost?" Denise asked.

"Oh, he was free," Lisa replied, "but he sure has cost me a lot since we got him. He's lots of work, too. But he's worth it, really. I sure do love him."

HOW ABOUT YOU? Salvation is a free gift from God, but with it comes responsibilities. If you have been saved from sin, you have the responsibility of being a Christian witness, of living for God, of keeping His commandments. Every blessing comes with responsibility attached. Are you using your good mind, your voice, or your ability to make friends for the Lord? Are you giving Him your time and your money? Thank God for your blessings, use them for Him, and He will continue to bless you. □ B.W.

TO MEMORIZE: *My son, do not forget my law, but let your heart keep my commands; for length of days and long life and peace they will add to you.* Proverbs 3:1-2, NKJV

27

Not Quite Free

FROM THE BIBLE:
If you fully obey the Lord your God and carefully follow all his commands I give you today, the Lord your God will set you high above all the nations on earth. . . . The Lord your God will bless you in the land he is giving you. The Lord will establish you as his holy people, as he promised you on oath, if you keep the commands of the Lord your God and walk in his ways. Then all the peoples on earth will see that you are called by the name of the Lord, and they will fear you. The Lord will grant you abundant prosperity— in the fruit of your womb, the young of your livestock and the crops of your ground—in the land he swore to your forefathers to give you. The Lord will open the heavens, the storehouse of his bounty, to send rain on your land in season and to bless all the work of your hands. . . . If you pay attention to the commands of the Lord your God that I give you this day and carefully follow them, you will always be at the top, never at the bottom.
Deuteronomy 28:1, 8-13, NIV

Use blessings for God

28

Who's Ashamed?

FROM THE BIBLE:

He called the crowd to him along with his disciples and said: "If anyone would come after me, he must deny himself and take up his cross and follow me. For whoever wants to save his life will lose it, but whoever loses his life for me and for the gospel will save it. What good is it for a man to gain the whole world, yet forfeit his soul? Or what can a man give in exchange for his soul? If anyone is ashamed of me and my words in this adulterous and sinful generation, the Son of Man will be ashamed of him when he comes in his Father's glory with the holy angels."

Mark 8:34-38, NIV

Don't be ashamed of Jesus

DENNIS, IF YOU'LL watch Bonnie for me, I can get my groceries in a jiffy," suggested Mother. "Then I'll drop you off at the game."

"Oh, all right," Dennis agreed reluctantly. "Come on, Bonnie. Let's take a walk."

"Thanks. I'll meet you at the checkout counter in about fifteen minutes," Mother said. "Keep a good eye on Bonnie."

"Don't touch anything, Bonnie," Dennis warned as they strolled down the aisle. "Let's go this way."

As they reached the end of the aisle, they met Brad, one of Dennis's friends. The two boys had been chatting a few minutes, when, *crash!* Dennis whirled around to see Bonnie sitting in the middle of the tomato sauce display. Cans were rolling everywhere! "Bonnie!" Dennis wailed. "I told you not to touch!"

Bonnie began to cry, and Dennis tried to restack the cans. A stock boy relieved him of the task, so Dennis grabbed Bonnie and rushed to find Mother. That night, Dennis told the story to his dad. "I was so embarrassed. I wanted to hide. I didn't want anyone to know Bonnie was my sister!"

Dad laughed and hugged Bonnie. "Did you really do that?"

"Yes, Daddy," Bonnie admitted. "But Dennis yelled real loud. I was 'shamed of him, too. He made me cry."

"So you were each ashamed of the other," mused Dad. "That reminds me of some verses in Mark."

"How, Dad?" Dennis asked.

"So often Christians act ashamed of their relationship to Jesus Christ," Dad explained. "We're afraid of what people will think if they know that we're Christians. But someday Jesus may be ashamed of us! He's coming back to earth in blazing glory, and then we'll want to be claimed by Him. Meanwhile, we should be glad to identify ourselves as His followers, no matter what it costs."

HOW ABOUT YOU? Do your actions or words indicate that you're ashamed of Jesus? Are you embarrassed to be known as a Christian? Remember, some day Jesus will come as King. Then, who will be ashamed of whom? □ B.D.

TO MEMORIZE: *If anyone is ashamed of me and my words in this adulterous and sinful generation, the Son of Man will be ashamed of him when he comes in his Father's glory with the holy angels.* Mark 8:38, NIV

STEVEN WAITED patiently as the food was put on the table and his father offered a prayer of thanks. Then he spoke up. "Please pass the sodium chloride."

Dad laughed. "I know what you're talking about, but where did you hear that?"

Steven laughed, too. "In school today," he said. "We had a lesson on salt."

"Well, if you were trying to impress us," Mother said, "you did."

"Salt's important," Steven informed them. "Our teacher said that it's used in science and medicine."

Dad agreed. "Well, she's right. Chemical compounds of sodium are used in those things, and in photography and industry, too."

"Not to mention the way we use salt right here in our home," Mother added. "Salt is used to flavor food and also to keep it from spoiling."

"Did you know that sodium chloride is mentioned in the Bible?" asked Dad.

"Aw, c'mon, Dad," protested Steven. "In the Bible?"

"Well, not by that name," chuckled Dad, "but it does talk about salt. It tells us that Christians are the salt of the earth. Christians can help preserve and flavor the earth. Unless—" he stopped abruptly.

"Unless what?" Steven asked.

"Unless the salt has lost its flavor. The Bible says that if the salt doesn't have the power to flavor anything, then it's actually good for nothing except to step on."

"So a Christian has to be careful to live in such a way that he has the power of Christ in his life and can help people," Mother added. "Christians are to be like salt, helping, preserving, and being useful—being a good influence on those they meet."

Steven was quiet for a long time. At last he spoke. "I wonder if my teacher can tell I'm part of the sodium chloride of the earth. I hope so."

HOW ABOUT YOU? Are you being a "good flavor" to your schoolmates? To your family? Jesus didn't say you could be like salt if you wanted to be. No, He said you *are* the salt of the earth. Live that way. □ R.J.

TO MEMORIZE: *You are the salt of the earth.* Matthew 5:13, NIV

29

The Sodium Chloride of the Earth

FROM THE BIBLE:

You are the salt of the earth. But if the salt loses its saltiness, how can it be made salty again? It is no longer good for anything, except to be thrown out and trampled by men. You are the light of the world. A city on a hill cannot be hidden. Neither do people light a lamp and put it under a bowl. Instead they put it on its stand, and it gives light to everyone in the house. In the same way, let your light shine before men, that they may see your good deeds and praise your Father in heaven.

Matthew 5:13-16, NIV

Be a useful Christian

MARCH

30

A Disappointing Birthday

FROM THE BIBLE:

Now on his way to Jerusalem, Jesus traveled along the border between Samaria and Galilee. As he was going into a village, ten men who had leprosy met him. They stood at a distance and called out in a loud voice, "Jesus, Master, have pity on us!" When he saw them, he said, "Go, show yourselves to the priests." And as they went, they were cleansed. One of them, when he saw he was healed, came back, praising God in a loud voice. He threw himself at Jesus' feet and thanked him—and he was a Samaritan. Jesus asked, "Were not all ten cleansed? Where are the other nine? Was no one found to return and give praise to God except this foreigner?" Then he said to him, "Rise and go; your faith has made you well."

Luke 17:11-19, NIV

Express thankfulness

WHEN LAURIE'S birthday arrived, she found an envelope for her in the mailbox. She clapped her hands. She had known it would be there. Every year Aunt Joy sent twenty dollars, and Laurie could buy whatever she wanted with it. Quickly, she tore the envelope open and found a beautiful card from Aunt Joy. Laurie opened the card, expecting twenty dollars inside, but there was no money. The card was signed, "All my love, Aunt Joy."

"I can't believe this!" Laurie exclaimed, disappointed. "Mom, I got a birthday card from Aunt Joy, but there's no money in it!"

"I know you're disappointed," Mom said gently. "Aunt Joy told me she was going to leave it out this year."

"But why?" asked Laurie.

"Last year you never wrote to thank her for it," answered Mom. Laurie blushed. She remembered the many times Mom had reminded her, but she had never gotten around to writing. Mom continued. "Aunt Joy loves you very much, and she cares what kind of person you become. She doesn't want you to be an ungrateful person. Do you remember the story of the ten lepers Jesus healed? It seems to me they must all have been delighted to be healed, yet only one came back to tell Jesus how he felt. Jesus was pleased with that one. It's not enough just to be grateful for a gift. You must *show* that gratefulness."

Laurie was very sober as she thought it over. "I was wrong not to write Aunt Joy," she said finally. "From now on, I'm going to be thoughtful enough to thank people for things they do for me."

HOW ABOUT YOU? Do you remember to thank others when they do something for you? How about thanking your parents for all the washing, cooking, shopping, and errands they do for you? How about thanking them for providing a home for you? Think of other people who do things for you and thank them. It takes practice to become a grateful and thoughtful person, but that's the kind of person God wants you to be. □ C.Y.

TO MEMORIZE: *Jesus asked, "Were not all ten cleansed? Where are the other nine?"* Luke 17:17, NIV

31

Broken Eggs

"LET'S MAKE some colored Easter eggs, Grandma," suggested Beth, who was spending Easter vacation at Grandma Bell's house.

Grandma laughed. "You know that colored eggs don't have a thing to do with Easter," she answered, "but I guess if you want to color some just for fun, we could do that."

Grandma helped boil eggs. Then Beth dyed them a rainbow of colors. How pretty they looked! Each egg was special. Now they were sitting on the kitchen counter to cool and dry.

Beth sat down to read a book, and Grandma's big tomcat, Smokey, snuggled down into her lap. Smokey purred in appreciation as Beth stroked his soft fur. Suddenly some dogs began to bark outside the window. Smokey was frightened. Quick as a flash, he leaped out of Beth's lap, ran to the kitchen, and jumped on the counter to get away from the noise. *Crash!* Beth's eggs rolled one by one off the counter and onto the floor. Cracks zigzagged across the colored shells.

"Smokey! Look what you've done!" Beth cried in dismay. "You've ruined the eggs! You bad, bad cat!"

Grandma carefully picked up the cracked eggs. "Get me your colored markers," she ordered. When Beth brought them, Grandma reached for a pink one. She sketched in some pink flowers, using the large cracks for some of the lines. Then she drew in leaves with a light shade of green. She used a bright purple to make violets on another egg. On some she used the crack lines to make interesting designs. Soon Beth was designing eggs, too.

"Grandma, they're more beautiful than before," Beth whispered.

"Beth, this reminds me that God works miracles," Grandma said with a joyous glow. "We just rescued some cracked eggs, but God rescues broken people—people ruined by sin. God sent His Son, Jesus, to die for them. Broken people need Jesus, and once they accept Him as Savior, they're more beautiful than before."

HOW ABOUT YOU? Have you realized you are a broken person—broken by sin? You don't need to stay that way. Jesus died for you. Ask Him to be your Savior. He'll make you a new person. □ J.H.

TO MEMORIZE: *If anyone is in Christ, he is a new creation; the old has gone, the new has come!* 2 Corinthians 5:17, NIV

FROM THE BIBLE:

When we were utterly helpless with no way of escape, Christ came at just the right time and died for us sinners who had no use for him. Even if we were good, we really wouldn't expect anyone to die for us, though, of course, that might be barely possible. But God showed his great love for us by sending Christ to die for us while we were still sinners. And since by his blood he did all this for us as sinners, how much more will he do for us now that he has declared us not guilty? Now he will save us from all of God's wrath to come. And since, when we were his enemies, we were brought back to God by the death of his Son, what blessings he must have for us now that we are his friends, and he is living within us! Now we rejoice in our wonderful new relationship with God—all because of what our Lord Jesus Christ has done in dying for our sins—making us friends of God.

Romans 5:6-11, TLB

Christ makes you new

1

Mature Tastes

FROM THE BIBLE:

However, as it is written: "No eye has seen, no ear has heard, no mind has conceived what God has prepared for those who love him"—but God has revealed it to us by his Spirit. The Spirit searches all things, even the deep things of God. For who among men knows the thoughts of a man except the man's spirit within him? In the same way no one knows the thoughts of God except the Spirit of God. We have not received the spirit of the world but the Spirit who is from God, that we may understand what God has freely given us.

1 Corinthians 2:9-12, NIV

All of the Bible is important

MOM, CAN I get a Bible-story book like Cathy's?" asked Tina one day. "It's the kind that's full of short Bible stories and has lots of pictures. All the Bibles we have around here are too hard to read."

"Considering you got an *A* in reading last semester, I think you're exaggerating," said Mother as they began making lunches.

"Well, Cathy's Bible is easier to read—and more fun—without those parts that are hard to understand," insisted Tina. Then she frowned. "We have something besides white bread, don't we? You know I like whole wheat."

"Sorry. I wasn't thinking," said Mother. She got out the wheat bread. Then she smiled. "Remember when you were little, and all you would eat was white bread?"

Tina nodded. "Back then I didn't like anything that had a strong flavor or was hard to chew," she said.

"Right." Mother grinned. "I'm glad your tastes have matured. Natural foods like this whole wheat bread are so much better for you. I think the same principle applies to God's Word, Honey. When you were little, we read the Bible out loud to you and changed all the hard words. We skipped the doctrinal passages and stuck to stories like Daniel in the lions' den."

"I know," said Tina.

"I'm sure there are still many things about them that you haven't learned yet," said Mother, "but now you're ready for other things, too. When you read only the 'easy' parts of the Bible, you miss a lot of important truths God has for you. The simple parts may be easier to 'chew'—like white bread—but if that's all you read, you'll miss a lot of the nourishment God has for you in His Word."

"I guess my own Bible is just fine," said Tina.

HOW ABOUT YOU? Do you complain about hard words or hard ideas in the Bible? Some of the Bible is not easy to understand, but all of it is important. Be patient, and you'll develop a taste for the challenging parts of God's Word. □ S.K.

TO MEMORIZE: *God has revealed it to us by his Spirit. The Spirit searches all things, even the deep things of God.* 1 Corinthians 2:10, NIV

AS THE WRIGHT family waited for their lunch, Dad studied the map. "How would you like to include a visit to an old battlefield on this family trip?" he asked.

"Yeah!" agreed the twins, Josh and Jonathan. "Where is it?"

"Right here." Dad pointed at a dot on the map. "And here's where we are now," he said, pointing to another dot.

Soon they were on their way. "I hope they have some literature I can take back to my history class," said Jonathan a little later. "It might help my grade. Mr. Grant's a hard teacher. He doesn't believe the Bible. He says his grandmother did, and that she was already expecting Jesus to come back to earth when she was a little girl. Now she's dead, and Jesus still hasn't come."

Josh pressed his nose against the window. "Aren't we about there, Dad?"

Dad glanced at the odometer. "About twenty-five more miles, Son."

"Twenty-five!" exclaimed Josh. "It looked like such a little way on the map."

Mother smiled. "The map is drawn to scale," she said. "One-fourth of an inch represents ten miles. If we forget that, the distance will seem long to us even though it looks short on the map."

Dad nodded. "The Bible is our map to heaven," he said, "and it tells us Jesus is coming again. It seems to men that they have been waiting forever for the Lord to return. But on God's scale of time, it hasn't been long at all."

Jonathan wiggled and turned. "How close are we to the battlefield now, Dad?" he asked.

Dad chuckled. "About two miles closer than we were the last time someone asked."

HOW ABOUT YOU? Do you sometimes wonder if the Lord Jesus will ever come? What sounds like "just a little while" in the Bible may actually be many years, but compared to eternity it is "just a little while." So don't fret about it; just be ready. Jesus could come any day. □ B.W.

TO MEMORIZE: *Keep watch, because you do not know on what day your Lord will come.* Matthew 24:42, NIV

APRIL

2

Visit to a Battlefield

FROM THE BIBLE:

In the last days there will come scoffers who will do every wrong they can think of, and laugh at the truth. This will be their line of argument: "So Jesus promised to come back, did he? Then where is he? He'll never come! Why, as far back as anyone can remember everything has remained exactly as it was since the first day of creation." They deliberately forget this fact: that God did destroy the world with a mighty flood. . . . And God has commanded that the earth and the heavens be stored away for a great bonfire at the judgment day, when all ungodly men will perish. But don't forget this, dear friends, that a day or a thousand years from now is like tomorrow to the Lord. He isn't really being slow about his promised return, even though it sometimes seems that way. But he is waiting, for the good reason that he is not willing that any should perish, and he is giving more time for sinners to repent.

2 Peter 3:3-11, TLB

Jesus is coming again

APRIL

3

Visit to a Battlefield

(Continued from yesterday)

FROM THE BIBLE:

This is what the Lord himself has said about his Table, and I have passed it on to you before: That on the night when Judas betrayed him, the Lord Jesus took bread, and when he had given thanks to God for it, he broke it and gave it to his disciples and said, "Take this and eat it. This is my body, which is given for you. Do this to remember me." In the same way, he took the cup of wine after supper, saying, "This cup is the new agreement between God and you that has been established and set in motion by my blood. Do this in remembrance of me whenever you drink it." For every time you eat this bread and drink this cup you are retelling the message of the Lord's death, that he has died for you. Do this until he comes again.

1 Corinthians 11:23-26, TLB

Be thankful for freedom

WHEN THE WRIGHTS pulled into the parking lot at the battlefield, the twins tumbled out of the car and followed their parents through the gate. Jonathan looked puzzled. "Where's the guns?" he asked. "Awfully quiet here."

"This is a cemetery!" grumbled Josh. "I thought we were going to a battlefield!"

"Yeah," agreed Josh. "The only soldier around here is a concrete one in the middle of the graves."

"That's a memorial," said Dad as they moved toward the statue. "In fact, the whole battlefield is a memorial."

"What's a memorial?" asked Jonathan.

"Well, it could be a monument or a holiday or a service designed to remind us of someone or something," explained Dad.

Josh's eyes brightened. "That's why we have 'Memorial Day,' because we remember people who have died," he said.

Mother nodded. "Right," she agreed. "We especially remember those who died while fighting for our freedom, like the soldiers buried in this cemetery."

"Hey!" Jonathan called. "Look here. Here's a guy with the same name as me. Jonathan Wright. Born 1760. Died 1778. Then that means he was only . . ." Jonathan counted on his fingers, "eighteen years old when he died."

"Jesus was only thirty-three when He died," Josh remembered. "Why don't we have a memorial day for Jesus?"

"We do have a memorial service," Dad replied. "Every time we take the Lord's Supper at church, we remember the Lord's death and the sacrifice he made that we might be free from sin."

The twins skipped beside their mother as they started for the gate. "And we have a memorial day for Jesus," she added, "but it's to remember His Resurrection, not His death."

"Easter!" the boys sang out. Mother smiled and nodded.

HOW ABOUT YOU? People have died to give you freedom to worship God. Jesus died to give you freedom from sin. Remember this often. Give thanks for the sacrifices which were made so you can be free. □ B.W.

TO MEMORIZE: *He took bread, gave thanks and broke it, and gave it to them, saying, "This is my body given for you; do this in remembrance of me."* Luke 22:19, NIV

KENNY SIMMONS had worked hard all morning. First he had to get out the ladder. Then he climbed up the ladder to wash a window, rinse it, and dry it with a clean soft rag. Next he had to climb down the ladder and move it to the next window. He was glad when it was finished. His mother had been baking oatmeal cookies, and when Kenny came in to tell her the windows were done, she gave him four huge cookies and a big glass of milk. He really felt good about himself.

It had been a dreary, gray morning, but the afternoon became beautiful when the sun finally came out. Kenny was jumping on his bike to go to a friend's house when Mother called from the living room. "Kenneth Eugene Simmons, get in here!" Kenny knew that whenever Mother used his full name, he was in trouble. So he ran inside.

"Kenny, you'll have to wash the windows all over again."

As Kenny looked at the picture window, he couldn't believe his eyes! Now, with the sun shining so brightly on the glass, he saw big streaks all over. "But, Mom, I couldn't see the streaks before!"

"Oh, Kenny," Mother replied, "don't you remember I warned you about that? You can't see the streaks until the sun hits the window. In the same way, you can't see the dirt in a room unless you turn on a light."

As Kenny got the ladder out of the garage to rewash the window, he was reminded of how his heart used to be dark with sin. Until he began to learn about Jesus, he had not even known that he was a sinner who needed to be saved. *It's just like the window,* Kenny thought. *I didn't see the streaks till the sunshine was on it, and I didn't see the dirt of sin in my heart until God's Son shined His light on it.* As Kenny worked carefully to wash the streaks away, he thanked God for the blood of Jesus which had washed away the sin from his heart.

HOW ABOUT YOU? Has the light of Christ shined into your heart? Have you seen the sin that is there? If so, confess your sin. Ask God to forgive you, and receive the "light of life." □ R.P.

TO MEMORIZE: *Those doing right come gladly to the Light to let everyone see that they are doing what God wants them to.* John 3:21, TLB

Streaks on the Windows

FROM THE BIBLE:
"Their sentence is based on this fact: that the Light from heaven came into the world, but they loved the darkness more than the Light, for their deeds were evil. They hated the heavenly Light because they wanted to sin in the darkness. They stayed away from that Light for fear their sins would be exposed and they would be punished. But those doing right come gladly to the Light to let everyone see that they are doing what God wants them to."
John 3:19-21, TLB

Jesus is the light

5

Discovering the Wind

FROM THE BIBLE:

Who else but God goes back and forth to heaven? Who else holds the wind in his fists, and wraps up the oceans in his cloak? Who but God has created the world? If there is any other, what is his name—and his Son's name—if you know it?
Proverbs 30:4, TLB

He who forms the mountains, creates the wind, and reveals his thoughts to man, he who turns dawn to darkness, and treads the high places of the earth—the Lord God Almighty is his name.
Amos 4:13, NIV

God controls nature

JERRY LOVED the windy weather that spring brought, for one of Jerry's favorite things was kite-flying. To watch a kite soar high above the earth gave him the feeling of freedom that the birds must feel. And when the kite came to the end of the string, Jerry got a feeling of power. All he had to do was move the hand that held the string a few inches, and the kite would move several feet.

One day Jerry and his friend Ted were flying kites together. "Sure is windy today!" yelled Ted.

"Sure is," Jerry replied. He added thoughtfully, "When I'm flying a kite, I get to wondering—you know, about scientific stuff!"

Ted knew, as everyone did, how much Jerry loved science. "OK, Einstein," he laughed, "what great theory are you devising today?"

Jerry laughed, too. "It's just that I often wonder what causes wind," he said. "I know about high pressure cells of air and low pressure cells and collisions of air masses and all that. But that doesn't explain why some days there's not enough air moving to cause a ripple in the bay while other days, like today, the waves are probably ten feet high."

Ted shrugged. "Why don't you look it up in one of your science journals at home?"

"I already have," replied Jerry. "I talked to my science teacher about it, too, but no one can really explain what makes it all happen."

"I bet I know a book you never tried," said Ted.

In a few short minutes, the boys had reeled in their kites and pedaled their bikes to Ted's house. Ted looked in the concordance in the back of his Bible. As they looked up verses with the word *wind* in them, Jerry discovered his answer: God controls the wind. He also discovered that this same God who controls all of nature loved him. That was the best discovery he made.

HOW ABOUT YOU? Have you ever wondered what causes wind, or rain, or snow, or any other happenings of nature? The Bible teaches that God is in control of all things. The next time you hear the wind blow, experience a thunderstorm, or hear a tornado warning, thank God that He is in control. □ R.P.

TO MEMORIZE: *Mightier than the thunder of the great waters, mightier than the breakers of the sea—the Lord on high is mighty.* Psalm 93:4, NIV

JOSH FROWNED when his little brother asked to take some eggs to school for show-and-tell. "You mean the green eggs from my Araucanas hens?" Josh asked. "I'm selling those eggs to earn money for Wilderness Camp. But I guess you can take a couple."

"Oh, goody!" exclaimed Nathan. "I've told all the kids about your green eggs, but they don't believe me."

After school, Paul called Josh. "Going to the football game tonight?" he wanted to know.

"No, we're having a special meeting at our church, and I'm going there. Wanta come?"

"No way! Not me! I can't see that church really makes any difference anyway," said Paul.

That night, the pastor mentioned the spring dinner in two weeks when they would be collecting food and money for the needy. "We all have something we can give," said Pastor Allen. "Even boys and girls do. Think about it."

Josh did think about it. He was thankful, but he had nothing to give. Suddenly he remembered his eggs! Oh, no! He couldn't give them up! That was his camp money!

The night of the dinner, Josh thought about the fun he'd have at camp, but he also thought about the many people out of work and facing hard times. He saw all the gifts others had brought, and he had nothing. Suddenly he knew what to do. He would give his egg money to help the needy. Wilderness Camp could wait for another year.

Later, Josh told Paul about it. "Why did you do a crazy thing like that?" Paul asked.

"Well, it's kind of like my little brother's show-and-tell," Josh explained. "I always tell God I'm thankful, but I decided it was time I showed Him that I really meant it. So to show thanks for all I have, I gave money to help those who have less than I do."

Paul was quiet. Finally he said, "I never thought believing in God made much difference. You've told me, but now you've showed me, too. Guess maybe I'll go to church with you sometime."

HOW ABOUT YOU? Do you just tell God you're thankful, or do you also show thanks? By obeying His Word, doing things with a right attitude, and helping others, you show your thanks to God—and you tell the world He's great! □ J.H.

TO MEMORIZE: *You are a chosen people, a royal priesthood, a holy nation, a people belonging to God.* 1 Peter 2:9, NIV

Show-and-Tell

FROM THE BIBLE:
The man who had been demon-possessed begged to go too, but Jesus said no. "Go back to your family," he told him, "and tell them what a wonderful thing God has done for you." So he went all through the city telling everyone about Jesus' mighty miracle. On the other side of the lake the crowds received him with open arms, for they had been waiting for him.
Luke 8:38-40, TLB

Show God you're thankful

7

Don't Blame the Helps

FROM THE BIBLE:

The law of the Lord is perfect, reviving the soul. The statutes of the Lord are trustworthy, making wise the simple. The precepts of the Lord are right, giving joy to the heart. The commands of the Lord are radiant, giving light to the eyes. The fear of the Lord is pure, enduring forever. The ordinances of the Lord are sure and altogether righteous. They are more precious than gold, than much pure gold; they are sweeter than honey, than honey from the comb. By them is your servant warned; in keeping them there is great reward. Who can discern his errors? Forgive my hidden faults. Keep your servant also from willful sins; may they not rule over me. Then will I be blameless, innocent of great transgression. May the words of my mouth and the meditation of my heart be pleasing in your sight, O Lord, my Rock and my Redeemer.

Psalm 19:7-14, NIV

Learn from all God's Word

J OHN BENSON TOOK his crutch and threw it across the room. Ever since he had broken his leg, he needed to wear a heavy cast and walk with crutches. Under these conditions he could only watch as his friends played baseball and soccer, his two favorite sports. There wasn't a chance in the world that he could join them.

Mother came into the room when she heard the noise. "What's going on here?" she asked curiously.

"If it weren't for these dumb things," grumbled John, "I could be out there playing just like everyone else."

John's mother shook her head. "Oh, no, John," she corrected. "It's not because of the cast or the crutches that you can't play. It's because of the broken leg."

John thought about his mother's words, but said nothing.

"You see, Son," Mother continued. "The cast is there to protect your leg. It's holding things together and assisting in the healing process. And the crutches are to help you get around while the leg is mending."

John knew that his mother was right. The cast and the crutches were helping, not hindering, him. Grinning sheepishly, he hopped over to pick up his crutch. "Right!" he exclaimed. Waving the crutches, he added, "My friends here and I are going out to cheer the boys on to victory."

HOW ABOUT YOU? Do you sometimes act like John? When God's Word pierces your heart and reminds you that you're a sinner, do you want to blame God or the Bible? Do you feel angry because you think the Bible keeps you from some activities that are wrong? The Bible is not to blame. Like the cast and the crutches, it helps you by showing you what is wrong and what needs to be done to change your life. □ R.J.

TO MEMORIZE: *By them is your servant warned; in keeping them there is great reward.* Psalm 19:11, NIV

DARK, THREATENING CLOUDS rolled overhead as the Martin family drove home from church. "Jesus is coming in the clouds," five-year-old Mark said as he intently watched the sky. "Do you think He's coming today?"

"He could," Mother replied.

"I've heard that all my life," fifteen-year-old Merri sneered. "I think preachers just say that to scare people into living right."

"Why, Merri!" Mother was shocked. "Surely you—"

Her words were drowned out by the thin, piercing wail of a siren. The wind began to blow fiercely, and large drops of rain pelted the car.

"Oh, a tornado!" Merri cried above the noise.

"Keep calm," Dad answered, peering through the blinding rain. "We're almost home."

"Maybe Jesus is coming," Mark said excitedly.

"Don't say that!" Merri cried. "Hurry, Daddy!"

"Calm down, Merri," Dad repeated as he turned the car into the driveway. Hail began to salt the ground as the Martins ran for the storm cellar in their backyard. Next door, Mr. Carson stood on his porch, watching the clouds.

"Better come to the cellar with us, Mr. Carson," Mother invited as they ran past him.

Mr. Carson laughed. "No thanks," he said. "They blow that tornado siren every time a little cloud comes up. No need to hide in a dark hole in the ground." As the cellar door closed behind the Martin family, a loud roar filled the air.

About half an hour later Dad left the cellar to see what happened. When he returned, his face was grim. "It was a tornado. It took only part of the roof off our house, but Mr. Carson's house was demolished."

"What about Mr. Carson?" Merri asked.

"He's on his way to the hospital," answered Dad sadly.

Mother looked at her trembling daughter. "Merri," she said, "don't be foolish like Mr. Carson. Do you see now why preachers are sounding the warning? Jesus might not come today, but He is coming, and we need to be ready."

HOW ABOUT YOU? Everywhere there are signs that warn us that Jesus is coming soon. It will be a wonderful day for those who are ready, but a day of destruction for those who are not. Don't be foolish and ignore the warnings. □ B.W.

TO MEMORIZE: *A prudent man foresees evil and hides himself, but the simple pass on and are punished.* Proverbs 22:3, NKJV

Listen to the Warning

FROM THE BIBLE:
Another time when he appeared to them, they asked him, "Lord, are you going to free Israel now and restore us as an independent nation?" "The Father sets those dates," he replied, "and they are not for you to know. But when the Holy Spirit has come upon you, you will receive power to testify about me with great effect, to the people in Jerusalem, throughout Judea, in Samaria, and to the ends of the earth, about my death and resurrection." It was not long afterwards that he rose into the sky and disappeared into a cloud, leaving them staring after him. As they were straining their eyes for another glimpse, suddenly two white-robed men were standing there among them, and said, "Men of Galilee, why are you standing here staring at the sky? Jesus has gone away to heaven, and some day, just as he went, he will return!"
Acts 1:6-11, TLB

Be ready for Christ's return

The Wrong Bulbs

FROM THE BIBLE:

You He made alive, who were dead in trespasses and sins, in which you once walked according to the course of this world, according to the prince of the power of the air, the spirit who now works in the sons of disobedience, among whom also we all once conducted ourselves in the lusts of our flesh, fulfilling the desires of the flesh and of the mind, and were by nature children of wrath, just as the others. But God, who is rich in mercy, because of His great love with which He loved us, even when we were dead in trespasses, made us alive together with Christ (by grace you have been saved), and raised us up together, and made us sit together in the heavenly places in Christ Jesus, that in the ages to come He might show the exceeding riches of His grace in His kindness toward us in Christ Jesus. For by grace you have been saved through faith, and that not of yourselves; it is the gift of God, not of works, lest anyone should boast. For we are His workmanship, created in Christ Jesus for good works. Ephesians 2:1-10, NKJV

Jesus gives life

SIX-YEAR-OLD Nadine pointed to a picture of flowers in the seed catalog. "Can we get seed for these?" she asked.

Mother looked at the picture. "Those are tulips, and they grow from bulbs," she replied.

"Bulbs?" asked Nadine, looking perplexed.

Mother nodded. "Some flowers grow from seeds, but others grow from bulbs," she explained.

A couple of days later, Nadine showed her mother a spot near the back fence. "I planted some bulbs here. Mr. Jenks, next door, was throwing them away," she said.

Every day Nadine checked to see if the flowers were coming up. When the dirt became dry, she carefully watered it. Several weeks later, she stood looking sadly at the bare spot on the ground. "Nothing's growing," she said.

"Well, let's see if they've started sprouting at all," suggested Mother. She took a trowel and dug into the dirt. To her amazement, she uncovered two Christmas tree light bulbs. "Are these the bulbs you planted?" she asked. Nadine nodded. "Oh, Honey!" Mother gave her a hug. "These are *light* bulbs, not *flower* bulbs. There's no life in these. They never will sprout. I'll tell you what— we'll go buy some flower bulbs, and you can try again."

That evening, Nadine told her father about the bulbs that wouldn't grow, and she showed him where she planted the new bulbs. "The man at the store said these will really grow," she told him.

"When there's life, there should be growth," nodded Dad.

"That's what my Sunday school teacher said, too," replied Nadine. "She said Jesus gives us life and we're supposed to grow as Christians."

"That's right," agreed Dad. "Sometimes we expect people to grow when there's no life there— when they've never accepted Jesus as Savior. They struggle to do good, but they're dead in sin—as dead as those light bulbs you planted. They need the life only Jesus can give."

HOW ABOUT YOU? Are you "growing in the Lord"— developing the characteristics He wants to see in you, such as love, kindness, helpfulness, honesty, and a desire to serve Him? If not, search your heart—you can't "grow in Jesus" unless you have His life "planted" there. □ H.M.

TO MEMORIZE: *You He made alive, who were dead in trespasses and sins.* Ephesians 2:1, NKJV

10

Worth the Wait

"LET ME DRIVE, Dad—please!" Craig begged as Dad turned the car onto a country road leading to Grandfather's farm. "There's not much traffic here."

Dad shook his head. "You're not old enough, Son."

"I'm fourteen. Next year I can get my permit," Craig pleaded. "Besides, Steve's dad lets him drive all the time." Immediately, Craig knew he had said the wrong thing. His father was never impressed by what Steve's dad did. When Dad did not respond, Craig knew the subject was closed. Dad was a stickler for obeying the Bible and "the laws of the land."

When they arrived at the farm, they found Grandpa in the garden, planting potatoes. Craig's little brother Tyson squatted down on the ground and began digging. "I wantta make a garden, too," he said.

Craig headed for the barn. "I'm going to ride Princess. At least I don't need a license to ride a horse!" he mumbled.

As they prepared to leave later that afternoon, Tyson was nowhere to be found. They searched all over, calling his name. Even Dad was beginning to look worried. Then Grandpa came across the yard carrying a tired little boy. "Found him in the garden sound asleep," Grandpa explained as he put Tyson in his father's arms.

Dad smiled. "What were you doing in the garden?"

"Waitin' for the 'tatoes to come up," the little boy yawned. "But it took 'em so long, I went to sleep."

Dad and Craig were still chuckling as they drove onto the freeway. "Patience is a wonderful thing," said Dad. "It's something God wants all of us to learn. In time, Craig, you'll have your driver's license, and it will have been worth the wait. And in time, Tyson, we'll have our potatoes."

HOW ABOUT YOU? Do you try to "leap-frog" over time to get what you want before the "right season"? God knows the best time for everything. Waiting is hard, but it is important. When you are told to wait, don't fret and fuss. Be patient. □ B. W.

TO MEMORIZE: *He has made everything beautiful in its time.* Ecclesiastes 3:11, NIV

FROM THE BIBLE:
There is a time for everything, and a season for every activity under heaven: a time to be born and a time to die, a time to plant and a time to uproot, a time to kill and a time to heal, a time to tear down and a time to build, a time to weep and a time to laugh, a time to mourn and a time to dance, a time to scatter stones and a time to gather them, a time to embrace and a time to refrain, a time to search and a time to give up, a time to keep and a time to throw away, a time to tear and a time to mend, a time to be silent and a time to speak, a time to love and a time to hate, a time for war and a time for peace. . . . He has made everything beautiful in its time. He has also set eternity in the hearts of men; yet they cannot fathom what God has done from beginning to end. Ecclesiastes 3:1-11, NIV

Be patient

11

Remodeling Time

FROM THE BIBLE:

*My brethren, count it all joy
when you fall into various
trials, knowing that the testing
of your faith produces patience.
But let patience have its perfect
work, that you may be perfect
and complete, lacking nothing. . . . Let the lowly brother
glory in his exaltation, but the
rich in his humiliation, because
as a flower of the field he will
pass away. For no sooner has
the sun risen with a burning
heat than it withers the grass;
its flower falls, and its beautiful
appearance perishes. So the rich
man also will fade away in his
pursuits. Blessed is the man
who endures temptation; for
when he has been proved, he
will receive the crown of life
which the Lord has promised to
those who love Him.*
James 1:2-4, 9-12, NKJV

Let God "remodel" you

THE STORM HOWLED as Mr. Gordon stuffed an old towel under the door. "That ought to keep some of the water from leaking in," he said.

"I wish it hadn't rained," sighed Anne. "I wanted to go shopping with some of the girls."

"And I wanted to go down to the video arcade," scowled her brother, Tim.

"Well," said Mother, "at least the storm is keeping us together for an evening. It seems we hardly ever spend time as a family anymore." At that moment, there was a flash of lightning, followed by a sharp cracking sound. An instant later, there came a terrible crash! Anne screamed.

"Sounds like a tree fell through the roof!" Dad shouted over the roar of the wind as they all hurried to the kitchen. Sure enough, a large tree branch was poking through a dark, gaping hole overhead. Water was pouring over everything. "Grab anything of value and go over to the neighbor's," Dad instructed.

Soon the family was huddled in the Taylors' living room, while Mrs. Taylor fixed them some hot chocolate. "What a terrible night," Anne moaned.

"Don't feel too badly," Dad said. "At least no one was hurt, and we do have insurance." Then he grinned at Mother. "You'll finally get your kitchen remodeled!"

"I guess I will," said Mother. "I never expected it to take a storm to get the remodeling started." Then she looked thoughtful. "You know, I think God sometimes lets troubles come into our lives so He can do some 'remodeling work' on us. For example, we'll need to spend a lot of time together fixing up our house, and that will probably be good for all of us."

"When I heard that crash, it scared me," Anne said. "I thought, *What if the roof caves in, and I die?* I know I'm saved, but I sure haven't been living for God. It really makes you think."

"Yeah," Tim agreed. "I think I'll appreciate our family more. It even sounds good now to spend a quiet evening home together."

HOW ABOUT YOU? Are you going through a rough time right now? Trust God! He can work, even through situations that seem tragic to you, to "remodel" your life into something better than ever. Use this time to rethink your values, your habits, and your goals in the light of God's Word. □ S.K.

TO MEMORIZE: *Let patience have its perfect work, that you may be perfect and complete, lacking nothing.* James 1:4, NKJV

PASSENGER TRAINS had not stopped at Centerville for years, but for the city's anniversary celebration there was going to be a train with free rides for anyone! John had urged his dad to go with him, and together they climbed aboard. But it seemed as though the train would never start. "Shouldn't we be going pretty soon?" John asked.

"Maybe they're waiting for more people," suggested Dad. The car was not very full.

At that moment a man dressed as a conductor stepped into the car. "Guess you folks didn't read the sign," he said. "This car's not going anywhere."

John looked at the few people on the train and then at the conductor. "How come?" he asked, looking bewildered.

"'Cause this car's not hooked up to the engine," the man laughed. "It's on a second track. The train with the cars we're using will be back soon."

John and his father and the others got off the train to wait. "We had good intentions of taking that ride," Dad said, putting his hand on John's shoulder, "but good intentions didn't get us there."

"That sounds like a good sermon topic," John said, looking down the track to see if there was a train coming.

Dad agreed. "You're right. Some people think they're headed for heaven just because they attend church. But being in a church doesn't necessarily mean you're in Christ."

"Guess you have to be hooked up to the engine," John added. "If you haven't come to Christ, and confessed your sin and asked Him to be your Savior, you're just not on the right track."

When the train returned, John and his father were careful to board one of the cars right behind the engine. "I know we're going somewhere," John said as they sat waiting for the train to start. "This time I checked to see if this car is hooked up, and it is."

HOW ABOUT YOU? Some people do not check to see what the Bible says about the way to heaven. They think that whatever their church teaches must be right. God's Word says there is only one way to heaven, and Jesus is that way. Have you accepted Him as the way? You must if you expect to go to heaven. □ R.J.

TO MEMORIZE: *Jesus answered, "I am the way and the truth and the life. No one comes to the Father except through me." John 14:6,* NIV

The Right Track

FROM THE BIBLE:
"Do not let your hearts be troubled. Trust in God; trust also in me. In my Father's house are many rooms; if it were not so, I would have told you. I am going there to prepare a place for you. And if I go and prepare a place for you, I will come back and take you to be with me that you also may be where I am. You know the way to the place where I am going." Thomas said to him, "Lord, we don't know where you are going, so how can we know the way?" Jesus answered, "I am the way and the truth and the life. No one comes to the Father except through me."
John 14:1-6, NIV

Be sure you're saved

13

Poisoned Arrows

FROM THE BIBLE:

No human being can tame the tongue. It is always ready to pour out its deadly poison. Sometimes it praises our heavenly Father, and sometimes it breaks out into curses against men who are made like God. And so blessing and cursing come pouring out of the same mouth. Dear brothers, surely this is not right! Does a spring of water bubble out first with fresh water and then with bitter water? Can you pick olives from a fig tree, or figs from a grape vine? No, and you can't draw fresh water from a salty pool. If you are wise, live a life of steady goodness, so that only good deeds will pour forth. And if you don't brag about them, then you will be truly wise!
James 3:8-13, TLB

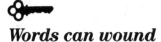

Words can wound

I DON'T KNOW why Dan had to invite Tony Blackwell to our boys' Bible club tomorrow. He's crazy like his mom," Josh raged as he hung up the phone. "She's in a mental institution, y'know. It will be just our luck that he'll decide to join our club."

"Shame on you, Josh," said Mrs. Parker with a frown. "I'm glad Dan invited Tony. As the club sponsor, your father's goal is to reach unsaved boys." Mrs. Parker sniffed. "Oh! My cookies!" She hurried from the room.

The next afternoon when Mr. Parker finished the Bible lesson, the boys went out in the backyard to play with Josh's new archery set. "Be careful," warned Mr. Parker.

The boys had a great time shooting at the target—and missing. "Your turn now, Tony." Dan handed the bow to him.

When Tony missed, the boys hooted. "I knew he'd miss. What a dumb shot!"

As Tony walked away from the boys, Mr. Parker followed him. "I'm glad you came today, Tony."

Tony shook his head. "I'm not. These guys don't want me."

Just then four-year-old Jodi ran across the lawn toward her dad. "Mom said the food is . . ."

"Jodi! Get out of the way!" screamed Josh. "Don't go over by the . . ." But it was too late! An arrow struck Jodi's forehead!

Later, Mr. and Mrs. Parker brought Jodi home from the emergency room. "The doctor put six stitches in her forehead," Mr. Parker told Josh, "but she'll be fine." Then he added, "I only wish Tony's wounds would heal as easily as Jodi's."

"Was Tony hurt?" asked Josh in surprise.

"Yes," replied Dad. "He was hurt today—and many times in the past, too. The Bible tells us that words can be like poisoned arrows shot out by the tongue, which wound and even kill."

Josh hung his head. "I'm sorry, Dad. I didn't realize we were shooting him with words. I'd better call him and apologize."

HOW ABOUT YOU? Have you been shooting poisoned arrows? Do you need to apologize to someone? Do it today. And if you know someone who is having family problems, be especially kind. □ B.W.

TO MEMORIZE: *A man who bears false witness against his neighbor is like a club, a sword, and a sharp arrow.* Proverbs 25:18, NKJV

CHAD SIGHED as he began his homework. What a lousy day it had been! Nothing had gone the way he wanted. As he opened a book, the lights went out—not just in his room, but in the whole house! "Hey!" Chad called. "What happened?"

"It must be a power blackout," his dad said, coming up from the basement where he had been working. "The street light out front is off, too."

Mother came in from the kitchen with a lighted candle, and that helped a little bit. "Tell you what," suggested Dad. "Let's build a fire in the fireplace. You boys can get your sleeping bags and put them in front of the fire."

"Yeah!" Chad exclaimed. "That will be almost like camping out!"

"We could roast some marshmallows, too," added his brother, Peter.

After the family was settled in the living room, Dad and Mom told stories about things they had done when they were younger. Mom remembered one time the power was out on their farm for over three days. "We had to do many chores by the light of kerosene lamps," she said.

Chad spoke up. "You know, when the lights first went out, I figured it was just another bad thing to happen today. But this has turned out to be fun."

"It sure has," agreed Peter, pulling a marshmallow off a weiner fork.

"You know," said Dad, "when troubles come, we can either get scared, or worried, or impatient—or we can turn the problem into an adventure. We know that God is always with us, but we can also help ourselves by having a good attitude and by looking for ways to turn troubles into happy times."

HOW ABOUT YOU? When something happens that seems like trouble, do you start to worry or complain? Next time, look for ways to turn that trouble into an adventure. Ask the Lord to help you have a happy attitude even when things go wrong. □ C.V.M.

TO MEMORIZE: *In all these things we are more than conquerors through Him who loved us.* Romans 8:37, NKJV

14

Power Blackout

FROM THE BIBLE:

Who shall separate us from the love of Christ? Shall tribulation, or distress, or persecution, or famine, or nakedness, or peril, or sword? As it is written: "For Your sake we are killed all day long; we are accounted as sheep for the slaughter." Yet in all these things we are more than conquerors through Him who loved us. For I am persuaded that neither death nor life, nor angels nor principalities nor powers, nor things present nor things to come, nor height nor depth, nor any other created thing, shall be able to separate us from the love of God which is in Christ Jesus our Lord.
Romans 8:35-39, NKJV

Turn trouble into triumph

15

God-given Reins

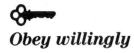

Obey willingly

AIMEE WAS HAVING a wonderful time at her aunt and uncle's farm. Every day she went for a ride on her favorite pony, Socks. She loved to trot through the fields and wander through the shady woods. However, she did not like all the work that went along with riding Socks.

"Did you remember to clean out your pony's stall this morning, Aimee?" asked Uncle Rob at lunch one day.

Aimee frowned. "Well, I did it yesterday, and it really didn't look very dirty yet," she explained.

"I see." Uncle Rob didn't look very pleased. "Does Socks have plenty of hay and water?"

"She has water, but she needs some hay," said Aimee.

"Aimee," said Uncle Rob thoughtfully, "God has given us animals to enjoy, but it's also our respon-sibility to make sure they are well taken care of. Tell me, why do you like to ride Socks so much?"

"Because she does what I tell her to without fussing," replied Aimee promptly. "I don't have to pull hard on the reins to get her to stop or turn—she listens really good."

Uncle Rob nodded. "You know," he said, "in some ways, we're like horses. Nobody likes a horse that doesn't listen well. It wouldn't be any fun to ride. In the same way, a Christian who doesn't listen well to God's instructions is not a Christian He can use." Aimee looked at her uncle uncer-tainly, not sure what he was getting at. "Part of God's instructions are to obey those in authority over us," added Uncle Rob. "When you came to spend the week with us, we gave you both the pleasure *and* the responsibility of having a horse."

"You mean I should take better care of Socks?" Aimee asked.

"Yes," said Uncle Rob. "When you only do the things you want to do, you're being selfish instead of obeying instructions—you're fighting the 'reins' God has given."

"I'm sorry, Uncle Rob," apologized Aimee. "I'll go feed Socks right now!"

HOW ABOUT YOU? Do you listen well and quickly obey those whom God has placed over you? Or do you listen to some instructions and ignore others? You need to obey in all areas. Remember, God is pleased with Christians who listen well and obey quickly. □ D.M.

TO MEMORIZE: *If you are willing and obedient, you shall eat the good of the land.* Isaiah 1:19, NKJV

LISA AND her friend Shawna sat at the table talking. Little Jimmy sat on the floor nearby, playing with his new building blocks. "Did you see Rachel today?" asked Lisa. "She got her hair all chopped off, and it looks just awful!"

"If she were smart, she'd dye it," said Shawna with a laugh. "I'm so glad I don't have hair the color of hers."

"Did you know that Mona dyes her hair?" asked Lisa.

"No!" Shawna gasped. "No wonder it's so blonde. Well, she's so fat, she may as well do something to try to improve herself." She nibbled on a cookie.

Mother, who was listening, began to speak, but just then a horn sounded outside. "There's my mom," said Shawna, getting up quickly. "Bye, everybody." As she headed for the door, her long coat brushed against the tall block building Jimmy had just finished, knocking it over. "Mommy," he moaned, "Shawna tore my building down."

"I know, Honey," sympathized Mother, "but it was an accident. Why don't you go build it back up again? It will make you feel better." As Jimmy got busy, Mother looked at Lisa and added, "I'm afraid Shawna's not the only one who knocked down in a moment what it took a long time to build. I'm afraid you've done the same thing."

"Me?" asked Lisa. "I didn't touch Jimmy's blocks."

"No," said Mother, "but you girls tore apart half your friends. I think that's even more serious than knocking down a few blocks, don't you?"

Lisa stared down at the table. "I guess so."

"People are a little like Jimmy's building," said Mother. "They need to be built up by compliments and kind words, not torn down by criticism. If you have knocked them down, you'll feel a lot better about yourself when you build them back up again."

Lisa nodded. "But how do I do that?" she asked.

"From now on, when you hear a criticism of another person, try to replace it with a compliment," suggested Mother. "Why not begin by calling Shawna and telling her something nice about each person you knocked down?"

HOW ABOUT YOU? Do you compliment or criticize? The Bible says to speak evil of no one. Don't tear down—build up instead. □ V.R.

TO MEMORIZE: *Let all bitterness, wrath, anger, clamor, and evil speaking be put away from you, with all malice.* Ephesians 4:31, NKJV

16

Building Blocks

FROM THE BIBLE:
Encourage each other to build each other up, just as you are already doing. Dear brothers, honor the officers of your church who work hard among you and warn you against all that is wrong. Think highly of them and give them your wholehearted love because they are straining to help you. And remember, no quarreling among yourselves. Dear brothers, warn those who are lazy; comfort those who are frightened; take tender care of those who are weak; and be patient with everyone. See that no one pays back evil for evil, but always try to do good to each other and to everyone else.
1 Thessalonians 5:11-15, TLB

Don't criticize

17

A Welcome Message

FROM THE BIBLE:

But you must keep on believing the things you have been taught. You know they are true for you know that you can trust those of us who have taught you. You know how, when you were a small child, you were taught the holy Scriptures; and it is these that make you wise to accept God's salvation by trusting in Christ Jesus. The whole Bible was given to us by inspiration from God and is useful to teach us what is true and to make us realize what is wrong in our lives; it straightens us out and helps us do what is right. It is God's way of making us well prepared at every point, fully equipped to do good to everyone.
2 Timothy 3:14-17, TLB

Don't vacation from God

"GRANDMA, I'M glad Mom and Dad went to that convention. Staying with you will be a vacation for me," Megan said happily after her parents had left her at Grandma's.

That morning Grandma gave Megan all her attention as the two of them played Megan's favorite board games. For lunch, they had ham sandwiches and chips—Megan's favorite. Then Grandma took out her Bible.

"This is when I usually have my daily Bible reading," she said. "I thought we could take turns reading to each other. I've looked forward to us sharing God's Word."

"Oh, Grandma, I'm on vacation," protested Megan. "I don't want to read anything. I just want to have fun." Grandma looked disappointed, but she let Megan run outside and climb the apple tree.

As Megan got ready for bed that night, she thought about what a nice day she had spent. But then she began thinking of her parents and feeling a little lonely. "I wish Mom and Dad were here to tuck me in," she told Grandma.

Grandma smiled and said, "Your mom knew you'd be a little lonesome tonight. She asked me to give you this." She pulled an envelope from her pocket. Megan opened it eagerly and read the note her parents had left her. She felt much better after reading their words of love and assurance.

"Some people are so important to us that we never want to take a vacation from them. Aren't you glad your parents left that message for you to read?" Grandma asked, and Megan nodded. "Someone else had a message for you today, but you wanted to take a vacation from Him," added Grandma.

Megan knew Grandma was talking about God. As she thought about it, she knew she had missed reading about His love and assurance today. "Grandma, can we read your Bible together before I go to sleep?" she asked.

HOW ABOUT YOU? When you're on vacation, do you also take a vacation from God's Word? You sometimes need a rest from your normal routine, but you need to hear from God every day no matter where you are. Be sure to give Him an opportunity to speak to you through His Word—with no vacations. □ K.R.A.

TO MEMORIZE: *I run in the path of your commands, for you have set my heart free.* Psalm 119:32, NIV

"I WISH I had enough money to buy that new game I've been wanting," said Tony to his friend Jacob. "If only there were some way I could make extra cash." Tony thought a minute. "I know! You wanted to buy the tires from my old bike, and Dad said it would be okay. So I'll sell them both to you for ten dollars."

"My dad okayed it, too, so it's a deal," Jacob agreed.

Tony took part of the money he received and bought the game. It was lots of fun, and the boys enjoyed it nearly every day.

When the weather turned sunnier, Tony and Jacob began taking long bike rides—until one day when Tony ran over a broken bottle and slashed his front tire. "Now I wish I had kept those old bike tires I sold to you," he groaned.

"Well, I only used one, so I'll sell the other back to you," offered Jacob.

"It's a deal," agreed Tony. The boys got the tire and went to Tony's house to fix his bike.

"I thought you sold those tires to Jacob," said Tony's dad when he saw the boys at work.

"I bought this one back," Tony explained.

Dad smiled. "You redeemed it."

"*Redeemed* it?" asked Tony. "Isn't that a Bible word?"

Dad nodded. "Yes, it's used many times in the Bible. What you did with the bike tire is a good example of the meaning of the word. *Redeemed* simply means 'bought back.' God wanted to buy us back from the slavery of sin. He knew we were sinful people and that the only way we could be redeemed was for His Son to die. We weren't redeemed by money, but rather by the blood of the Lord Jesus Christ."

"Wow!" said Tony. "Now when I hear that word I'll know what it means."

HOW ABOUT YOU? Have you been redeemed? If you are not a Christian, you are a slave to sin. This sin separates you from God. He had to pay the price to redeem you—to buy you out of sin and back to Himself. No amount of money can do that. It's only through the precious blood of the Lord Jesus Christ that you can be redeemed from sin. Accept what Jesus has done for you. □ L. W.

TO MEMORIZE: *You were not redeemed with corruptible things, like silver or gold, from your aimless conduct received by tradition from your fathers, but with the precious blood of Christ.* 1 Peter 1:18-19, NKJV

18

The Good Deal!

FROM THE BIBLE:
. . . always thankful to the Father who has made us fit to share all the wonderful things that belong to those who live in the Kingdom of light. For he has rescued us out of the darkness and gloom of Satan's kingdom and brought us into the Kingdom of his dear Son, who bought our freedom with his blood and forgave us all our sins.
Colossians 1:12-14, TLB

Be redeemed by Jesus' blood

19
Spring Cleanup

FROM THE BIBLE:

Rid yourselves of all such things as these: anger, rage, malice, slander, and filthy language from your lips. Do not lie to each other, since you have taken off your old self with its practices and have put on the new self, which is being renewed in knowledge in the image of its Creator. . . . Therefore, as God's chosen people, holy and dearly loved, clothe yourselves with compassion, kindness, humility, gentleness and patience. Bear with each other and forgive whatever grievances you may have against one another. Forgive as the Lord forgave you. And over all these virtues put on love, which binds them all together in perfect unity. Let the peace of Christ rule in your hearts, since as members of one body you were called to peace. And be thankful. Let the word of Christ dwell in you richly as you teach and admonish one another with all wisdom, and as you sing psalms, hymns and spiritual songs with gratitude in your hearts to God.
Colossians 3:8-16, NIV

Throw out bad habits

"MOM, WHATEVER are you doing?" asked Tiffany as she walked in the front door. Piles of old clothes, jewelry, and broken furniture were scattered around the living room.

"It's spring cleanup time, and I decided to clean things out," Mother replied. "Why keep clothes or jewelry I never wear or furniture that I'll never get around to repairing?"

"Good point, Mom," said Tiffany as she began climbing the stairs to her bedroom.

"Hey, Honey," Mother called after her, "why don't you go through some of your things, too?"

"But I use everything I have," Tiffany protested. A short time later, however, she brought a big box downstairs. "Hey, Mom, check it out," she said with a grin. She pulled out an old, stuffed animal. "Look at this—hardly any stuffing left inside. And look at this old sweatshirt. It's ten sizes too small."

Mother smiled and nodded. "You know," she began thoughtfully, "this reminds me of when I was saved."

"How's that, Mom?" asked Tiffany. "Were you having a spring cleanup then, too?"

Mother laughed. "Well, in a way. After I was saved, I had to get rid of a lot of old, bad habits and replace them with new, good ones like church attendance and prayer. I had no use for my sinful garbage any longer."

"Well, I was saved when I was just a little girl," replied Tiffany. "I didn't really have any bad habits to get rid of."

"No?" Mother's brows went up. "I seem to remember that you used to tell a lot of lies."

"Oh, yeah," Tiffany blushed. "I forgot about that. I used to get mad quickly, too, didn't I? I guess I did have some garbage to get rid of—I still do sometimes."

"We all need to check our lives daily to see if they please the Lord," said Mother. "When we belong to Him we're 'new creatures' and want our lives to show that."

HOW ABOUT YOU? Are there bad habits you should throw away? Smoking? Alcohol? Drugs? Cheating? Selfishness? Get rid of bad habits and make room for new, good ones. Live as a "new creature" in Christ. □ V.R.

TO MEMORIZE: *As God's chosen people, holy and dearly loved, clothe yourselves with compassion, kindness, humility, gentleness and patience.* Colossians 3:12, NIV

As JERRY CLIMBED into Grandpa's car, he held out a tin can. "Look! I dug some worms for bait yesterday."

Grandpa smiled. "You can try them," he replied, "but I've heard that what the fish are really going for are salmon eggs. I brought some along."

Later, as Jerry and Grandpa sat on the pier, Grandpa asked, "How is your friend Alex? Have you been able to witness to him?"

"I've tried, Grandpa," Jerry sighed. "Like last week—I saw him smoking, so I told him smoking was a sin. He just looked at me funny and walked away. And the other day he told me he had gone to church with his uncle. I told him his uncle's church doesn't preach the gospel, and that our church is better. He just got mad," said Jerry. "I don't think he'll ever want to know about Jesus." He frowned as he added, "And I don't think I'll ever catch any fish. You've caught two big ones so far, and I haven't had a nibble."

"Now don't get discouraged," Grandpa began. Then he shouted, "Whoa! I think I've got one!" Sure enough, he reeled in a large salmon and caught it up with his net. "Sure you don't want to try some of my bait?" asked Grandpa.

"I guess I will," decided Jerry. "I thought all fish liked worms, but I guess they don't."

Grandpa shook his head. "A real fisherman learns about the fish he's trying to catch," he said, "and uses the kind of bait that type of fish likes—whether it's worms, minnows, or something else. And you know, Jerry, the principle of using the right bait applies to witnessing for the Lord, too. Some people will respond to a simple straightforward approach. Others need a gentler touch and must be won with soft words and acts of kindness."

"You mean I should try that with Alex, don't you?" asked Jerry thoughtfully. "I guess you're right. If I start using the right bait, maybe I'll catch both kinds of 'fish'!"

HOW ABOUT YOU? Are you unsure about how to witness to your friends? Take time to really get to know them. Find out more about their backgrounds, what they believe, and what their needs are. Then ask God to show you how to present Christ to them in the best way possible. □ S.K.

TO MEMORIZE: *To the weak I became as weak, that I might win the weak. I have become all things to all men, that I might by all means save some.* 1 Corinthians 9:22, NKJV

20

The Right Approach

FROM THE BIBLE:
Woe is me if I do not preach the gospel! For if I do this willingly, I have a reward; but if against my will, I have been entrusted with a stewardship. What is my reward then? That when I preach the gospel, I may present the gospel of Christ without charge, that I may not abuse my authority in the gospel. For though I am free from all men, I have made myself a servant to all, that I might win the more; and to the Jews I became as a Jew, that I might win Jews; to those who are under the law, as under the law, that I might win those who are under the law; to those who are without law, as without law (not being without law toward God, but under law toward Christ), that I might win those who are without law; to the weak I became as weak, that I might win the weak. I have become all things to all men, that I might by all means save some.

1 Corinthians 9:16-22, NKJV

Witness with care

21

Leader Needed

FROM THE BIBLE:

Then Jesus said to the disciples, "If anyone wants to be a follower of mine, let him deny himself and take up his cross and follow me. For anyone who keeps his life for himself shall lose it; and anyone who loses his life for me shall find it again. What profit is there if you gain the whole world—and lose eternal life? What can be compared with the value of eternal life? For I, the Son of Mankind, shall come with my angels in the glory of my Father and judge each person according to his deeds. And some of you standing right here now will certainly live to see me coming in my Kingdom."

Matthew 16:24-28, TLB

Follow Jesus

JOHN AND TIM were on a camping trip with their Sunday school class. The first thing they did was take a group hike through the woods. Mr. Ward, their teacher, led the way. After a while, John saw a side path he wanted to explore. "Come on!" he said to Tim. "Let's see where this goes."

"But then we'll lose the rest of the group," said Tim.

John shrugged. "So what?" he said. "We don't have to stay with them. We can make it on our own. We'll just come back to this main path and follow it to the camp when we're ready. Think about the story we could tell the guys tonight about how we went exploring on our own."

Hesitantly, Tim agreed, and the two boys wandered down the side path, stopping to look at things along the way. Quite a while later, Tim looked at his watch. "John, look what time it is!" he exclaimed. "We'd better get going if we want to make it to camp before dark."

The boys hurried back the way they had come. When they reached a fork in the path, they stopped. "Now where do we go?" puffed Tim, trying to catch his breath.

John looked down each path carefully. "I don't know," he admitted finally.

Just then, they heard a shout. "Tim! John!" It was Mr. Ward. And it was with very relieved minds that the two boys followed their teacher down the trail.

Around the campfire that night, Mr. Ward spoke to the group. "When Tim and John got lost today," he said, "it reminded me of people who think they can find their own way through life. Even Christians sometimes go their own way rather than depending on God to show them how to live. Boys, it's important for you to follow Jesus. He's the only true leader for you."

HOW ABOUT YOU? Do you want to do something your own way instead of doing what you know is right? Jesus wants to help you and lead you. But you have to be willing to follow where He takes you. He knows the way you should go. □ D.M.

TO MEMORIZE: *Whoever serves me must follow me; and where I am, my servant also will be. My Father will honor the one who serves me.* John 12:26, NIV

22

Just a Lamb's Keeper?

"GOOD MORNING, Hendrick," William greeted his lamb as he entered the fenced enclosure. "You're going to win that blue ribbon at the fair in a couple of months." He then groomed Hendrick until Mother called him for lunch.

"Hendrick is going to win that blue ribbon, Mom. I just know he is," William said.

Mother smiled. "He just might," she agreed. "By the way, have you called Kevin to see if he'll be going to church with us tomorrow?"

"No." William shook his head. "But it doesn't matter, because he got saved last week." William walked over to the door. "I'm going to see what Hendrick's up to."

When William reached the enclosure, he discovered that he had left the gate open, and the lamb was gone. Quickly he ran to the house, calling for his mother. She helped William search for his lamb, and before long they found him in a field—right in the middle of nettles and spiny flowers which caught and stuck in his coat.

"Oh, Hendrick, you naughty lamb," William moaned. "I had you all cleaned and brushed. Now look at you!"

Mother stood and eyed the lamb. "We wouldn't want this to happen to your friend Kevin, would we?" she said.

"Kevin?" William was puzzled. "What do you mean?"

"Hendrick needs guidance and restrictions even after he has been brushed and fed. Left to himself, he gets all messed up again," explained Mother. "And Kevin—even after he's saved—needs guidance, too. He needs to be around people of God, who can guide him in the way he should go. God not only wants you to be your lamb's keeper, but also your brother's keeper."

William nodded slowly. "I get it," he said. "I'll ride over to Kevin's and ask him to go to church with us—as soon as I get this naughty lamb locked up."

HOW ABOUT YOU? Do you think a newly saved person should take care of himself? All Christians need help and guidance, especially those who are new converts. You can help them. Jesus' advice to Peter is good advice for you, too. ☐ D.A.L.

TO MEMORIZE: *When you have turned back, strengthen your brothers.* Luke 22:32, NIV

FROM THE BIBLE:

Jesus said to them, "The kings of the Gentiles lord it over them; and those who exercise authority over them call themselves Benefactors. But you are not to be like that. Instead, the greatest among you should be like the youngest, and the one who rules like the one who serves. For who is greater, the one who is at the table or the one who serves? Is it not the one who is at the table? But I am among you as one who serves. You are those who have stood by me in my trials. And I confer on you a kingdom, just as my Father conferred one on me, so that you may eat and drink at my table in my kingdom and sit on thrones, judging the twelve tribes of Israel. Simon, Simon, Satan has asked to sift you as wheat. But I have prayed for you, Simon, that your faith may not fail. And when you have turned back, strengthen your brothers."

Luke 22:25-32, NIV

Strengthen new Christians

23

Who Gets the Credit?

FROM THE BIBLE:

I, brethren, could not speak to you as to spiritual people but as to carnal, as to babes in Christ. I fed you with milk and not with solid food; for until now you were not able to receive it, and even now you are still not able; for you are still carnal. For where there are envy, strife, and divisions among you, are you not carnal and behaving like mere men? For when one says, "I am of Paul," and another, "I am of Apollos," are you not carnal? Who then is Paul, and who is Apollos, but ministers through whom you believed, as the Lord gave to each one? I planted, Apollos watered, but God gave the increase. So then neither he who plants is anything, nor he who waters, but God who gives the increase. Now he who plants and he who waters are one, and each one will receive his own reward according to his own labor. For we are God's fellow workers; you are God's field, you are God's building.

1 Corinthians 3:1-10, NKJV

Work together for Christ

L AURA GRAHAM was at our Sunday school party today," announced Lindsey. "What a bummer!"

"Why, I thought you wanted her to go," said Mother. "Didn't you invite her?"

"That's just the point," said Lindsey. "I've invited her for three years in a row, and she always said no. Then today she shows up with Bonnie."

"Well, I'm sure Mr. Paterson had a good Bible message, just as he always does," observed Mother. "I should think you'd be happy Laura came." She was interrupted by the doorbell. "That must be Grandma with those marigold plants she said she'd bring over."

After Grandma had left, Lindsey and her mom decided to plant the marigolds right away.

"You know something, Honey?" Mother handed Lindsey a trowel. "These plants remind me of you and Laura."

"Of me and Laura?" exclaimed Lindsey. "How?"

Mother dug in the dirt as she explained. "Well, Grandma started these plants and nursed them along until they developed healthy roots," she said. "Now we must back up Grandma's efforts and care for these plants. And, in a way, you 'started' Laura—you first invited her. Then Bonnie backed up your efforts by inviting her, too. Right?"

"I guess so," said Lindsey. "But why couldn't Laura have come when I invited her?"

Mother shook her head. "I don't know," she said, "but sharing Christ is not a competition. When we tell someone about the Lord, we don't always see the final result. God is using both you and Bonnie to help Laura spiritually, just as Grandma, you, and I are helping these plants physically."

HOW ABOUT YOU? Have you ever been upset because someone else received credit for bringing your friend to church? Did that seem more important to you than the fact that your friend would hear about the Lord? You need to work together with other Christians in winning others to Jesus. Paul understood this. He knew the Lord was using himself *and* Apollos to further the Gospel. Witnessing is not a competition where one person wins and another loses. Instead, it's a responsibility that Christians share. □ L. W.

TO MEMORIZE: *I planted, Apollos watered, but God gave the increase.* I Corinthians 3:6, NKJV

KEVIN WATCHED as his little brother Gary, wearing dark glasses as usual, pedaled his tricycle full speed down the driveway. It was getting dark out, but Gary insisted on wearing sunglasses in rain or shine, light or dark.

Then it happened. *Crash! Bang!* Gary plowed into a skateboard left on the concrete. Shaking his head, Kevin went to help. "If you'd take off those sunglasses you could see where you're going," he scolded.

Gary brushed himself off. "I'm not taking 'em off," he said stubbornly. "I need 'em to be a motorcycle driver!" Kevin threw up his hands in disgust and left for his boys' club meeting at church.

The lesson that day was about heaven. "Can you imagine never having a stomachache or never feeling sad?" asked Mr. Potts, the leader. "In heaven there will be no sickness nor sorrow. And in heaven, no one will ever sin—or even want to sin. There will be nothing to destroy the beauty of heaven." Kevin tried hard to think of a life that would be perfect.

"We can't fully know what heaven is like," continued Mr. Potts, "although God has given us some clues in the Bible. It's a little as if we're wearing dark glasses right now. We can see just enough to give us an idea of how wonderful it will be, but a good deal of our vision of heaven is not clear. Some great day we'll experience it completely."

Wearing dark glasses rang a bell with Kevin. He thought of Gary pedaling down the driveway, barely able to see in the dusk. *It'll be great to see heaven without dark glasses*, he thought. *I'm looking forward to that.*

HOW ABOUT YOU? Have you wondered what heaven will be like? There are all sorts of wrong ideas about it. One is that everyone will float on a cloud and have nothing to do except play a little harp. Such ideas aren't from the Bible, but God does tell us some of the good things that are in store for those who have believed on his Son, Jesus. There will be only good—no bad. Heaven is beautiful in every way, and we'll be fully happy. □ C. Y.

TO MEMORIZE: *Now we see but a poor reflection; then we shall see face to face. Now I know in part; then I shall know fully, even as I am fully known.* I Corinthians 13:12, NIV

Dark Glasses

FROM THE BIBLE:
We know in part and we prophesy in part, but when perfection comes, the imperfect disappears. When I was a child, I talked like a child, I thought like a child, I reasoned like a child. When I became a man, I put childish ways behind me. Now we see but a poor reflection as in a mirror; then we shall see face to face. Now I know in part; then I shall know fully, even as I am fully known.
1 Corinthians 13:9-12, NIV

Heaven is wonderful

APRIL

25

Part of the Furniture

FROM THE BIBLE:
Who can discern his errors?
Forgive my hidden faults. Keep
your servant also from willful
sins; may they not rule over me.
Then will I be blameless,
innocent of great transgression.
May the words of my mouth and
the meditation of my heart be
pleasing in your sight, O Lord,
my Rock and my Redeemer.
Psalm 19:12-14, NIV

Houseclean your life

I AM NOT a slob!" shouted Becky to her brother, Ted.

"You are, too," replied Ted. "Everywhere you go, you leave things a mess!"

Just then, Mother walked in. "Now, Ted, let's not be name-calling!" she said. Then she added, "I'll admit, Becky, your housekeeping habits do leave something to be desired. Have you looked at your room lately?"

"Of course I've looked at it. I sleep there, don't I?" pouted Becky. "Sure, it's a little messy, but it's not that terrible. You two just like to pick on me." With that, she stormed into her bedroom and slammed the door.

Imagine Ted calling me a slob, she thought. *I can keep things neat when I want to!* Suddenly she stopped. For the first time in weeks she took a good look around her room. Books and half-done homework papers lay scattered across the floor. Clothes, both clean and dirty, were piled in one corner. Crumbs and trash covered the carpet, and her blankets and bedspread were all wadded up. Then she gave a shout of laughter. On a paper plate atop her desk sat a dried-out bologna sandwich—complete with lettuce and cheese!

I must have brought that in here when I was studying last week and forgot about it, Becky thought. *It was there so long that I didn't even notice it anymore—it was just like part of the furniture.* She quickly emptied the plate into the trash and then started to pick up some papers. It was time to do some housecleaning.

HOW ABOUT YOU? Have you taken a good look at yourself lately? Sometimes lives, as well as rooms, need "housecleaning." Perhaps there are some sins in your life that have been there so long you've gotten used to them. They've become "part of the furniture." You may need to ask someone else to point out the "messy spots." Do some housecleaning today. □ S.K.

TO MEMORIZE: *Who can discern his errors? Forgive my hidden faults.* Psalm 19:12, NIV

"BECKY! BRIAN!" called Mrs. Swanson. "Time to get ready for church!"

"Oh, Mom!" grumbled Brian from the family room. "Do we have to? We just started playing our new video game."

"Yeah!" agreed Becky. "It's neat, Mom! It's lots more fun than Sunday school. Can't we stay home, just once?"

"I'm surprised at you children," said Mother. "You both know that studying God's Word is more important than playing a game. Now, go and get dressed!"

After church, the Swansons came home to a delicious dinner of roast turkey with dressing, mashed potatoes, corn, and apple pie. But Becky just picked at her food. When her parents asked her why, she looked embarrassed.

"Well," she admitted, "my Sunday school teacher brought cupcakes for us today. She had three left, and she said I could bring them home, but I ate them instead."

"So that's what spoiled your appetite!" said her mother. "You know, kids, this reminds me of our conversation this morning. Remember when you said you'd rather play that video game than go to Sunday school?"

"Yeah, we remember," Brian said.

"I think the excitement of that game made you 'lose your appetite' for spiritual things," continued Mother. "The world's pleasures can't nourish our souls any more than cupcakes can give us all the vitamins we need for our bodies. True happiness can only come as we serve the Lord and 'feed' on the Word of God!"

HOW ABOUT YOU? Is there something you'd rather be doing than going to church or reading the Bible? That activity may not be bad in itself, but it is bad if it takes you away from what you should be doing for the Lord. If you want to be a healthy, growing Christian, don't spoil your appetite! □ S.K.

TO MEMORIZE: *Do not love the world or the things in the world. If anyone loves the world, the love of the Father is not in him.* I John 2:15, NKJV

APRIL

26

Spoiled Appetite

FROM THE BIBLE:

Do not love the world or the things in the world. If anyone loves the world, the love of the Father is not in him. For all that is in the world—the lust of the flesh, the lust of the eyes, and the pride of life—is not of the Father but is of the world. And the world is passing away, and the lust of it; but he who does the will of God abides forever.

1 John 2:15-17, NKJV

Give Jesus first place

27

Acknowledge It

FROM THE BIBLE:

That man is a fool who says to himself, "There is no God!" Anyone who talks like that is warped and evil and cannot really be a good person at all. The Lord looks down from heaven on all mankind to see if there are any who are wise, who want to please God. But no, all have strayed away; all are rotten with sin. Not one is good, not one!

Psalm 14:1-3, TLB

Confess and believe

ROBIN WAS STUNNED. Her mother had cancer.

"I think we need to talk about it," Robin's father said one evening. "We will have to make some adjustments in our home, and it will involve all of us."

Robin shook her head. "No, I don't want to talk about it."

"But, Honey," Dad persisted, "we must talk about it. This is something real, and we have to face it."

"I don't want to face it," Robin snapped back. She knew most people with cancer suffered a great deal. She just wasn't going to think about it. And that was final! For several days, Robin made all kinds of excuses for not staying home.

One Sunday morning, the family got into the car and headed for church. "Now," said Mother, "we're all together, and I want us to talk about my illness."

"No," Robin answered. "I don't want to talk about it!"

"Robin," Mother said sternly, "refusing to talk about it isn't going to change anything."

"Robin, do you remember when you accepted Jesus as your Savior?" Dad asked.

"Yes," sighed Robin.

"What was the first thing necessary before you became a Christian?" he pressed.

"Tell Jesus that I knew I was a sinner," replied Robin.

"That's right," agreed Dad. "You had to acknowledge the fact before anything could be changed."

Suddenly Robin saw what her father was trying to tell her. A person must accept the fact that he is a sinner before Jesus can take away his sin. And Robin had to accept the fact that her mother had cancer before she could deal with the problem of living with her mother's illness. "OK, Mom," she said finally. "Let's talk about it."

HOW ABOUT YOU? Have you admitted your sinful condition? If not, this is the first step for you to take. Acknowledge it, and ask Jesus to cleanse you and make you His child. □ R.J.

TO MEMORIZE: *I know my transgressions, and my sin is always before me.* Psalm 51:3, NIV

PHIL EVANS WASN'T really listening to the Scripture his father was reading. He had something else on his mind—Jim Kardon. Phil had invited Jim to church and Sunday school three different times, but Jim wanted no part of it. Phil was ready to give up. After they finished their devotional time, he spoke of his feelings. "I'm never going to invite Jim to church again," he said bluntly.

"Why not?" Dad wanted to know.

"Because he always turns me down," Phil said emphatically.

Phil's father was quiet for a time. "Did you notice what tonight's Scripture lesson was about?" he asked finally. Phil admitted that his thoughts were elsewhere, so Dad added, "It was about the growth of the early church. The early Christians were 'steadfast,' and God added souls to the church. We need to be steadfast, too. By the way, how long has it been since you accepted Jesus as your Savior?"

Phil looked up at this father in surprise. "About a year," he replied. "Why?"

"And how long before you made your decision did you hear the gospel from church and Sunday school—and from your mother and me?" asked Dad.

Phil shrugged. "Seems like I heard it over and over all my life." He stopped suddenly. He was beginning to see what his father was trying to tell him. If Dad and Mom or his pastor and Sunday school teachers had only talked with him three times about the Lord and then quit, maybe he wouldn't be a Christian now. Suddenly he knew what it meant to be steadfast. It meant to keep on even when things got hard or people didn't respond right away.

"I guess I'm giving up too quickly," he said finally. "I'll ask Jim again this week."

HOW ABOUT YOU? Do you know someone who needs Jesus as Savior? Have you talked with him about it? How many times? How often? Learn to be steadfast in witnessing and praying for your friends, then leave the results to the Lord. □ R.J.

TO MEMORIZE: *Always give yourselves fully to the work of the Lord, because you know that your labor in the Lord is not in vain.* 1 Corinthians 15:58, NIV

28

Being Steadfast

FROM THE BIBLE:
And those who believed Peter were baptized—about 3,000 in all! They joined with the other believers in regular attendance at the apostles' teaching sessions and at the Communion services and prayer meetings. A deep sense of awe was on them all, and the apostles did many miracles. And all the believers met together constantly and shared everything with each other, selling their possessions and dividing with those in need. They worshiped together regularly at the Temple each day, met in small groups in homes for Communion, and shared their meals with great joy and thankfulness, praising God. The whole city was favorable to them, and each day God added to them all who were being saved.
Acts 2:41-47, TLB

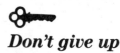

Don't give up

29

Don't Go to Sleep

FROM THE BIBLE:

Since you don't know when it will happen, stay alert. Be on the watch [for my return]. My coming can be compared with that of a man who went on a trip to another country. He laid out his employees' work for them to do while he was gone, and told the gatekeeper to watch for his return. Keep a sharp lookout! For you do not know when I will come, at evening, at midnight, early dawn or late daybreak. Don't let me find you sleeping. Watch for my return! This is my message to you and to everyone else.

Mark 13:33-37, TLB

Be spiritually alert

"WHAT'S THE MATTER with Kimberly?" Grandmother asked. "She's stumbling around like she's half-asleep."

Kimberly's mother looked up from her sewing. "I don't know. I—"

"Come quickly, Linda," Grandmother interrupted. "I think Kimberly has been in Stanley's medicine."

The concerned mother and grandmother counted the little pills spilled on the coffee table. "Only one missing," sighed Mother. "That shouldn't hurt her too much."

Grandmother frowned as the two-year-old staggered into the table. "I'm not so sure. They are very powerful. We'd better call the doctor."

Following the doctor's orders, Kimberly was taken to the emergency room at the hospital. "I think she will be all right," Dr. Burns said after he had examined her. "But just to be safe, we'll keep her here for several hours. One of you should stay with her and keep her awake. Whatever you do, don't let her go to sleep!"

Both Mother and Grandmother stayed, and the next few hours were a nightmare for them. Kimberly was so sleepy! Mother played games with her, tickled her, washed her face. Then Grandmother walked the little girl up and down the hall, played games with her, and washed her face again and again. The minutes dragged by. Mother and Grandmother were getting tired.

"This is a switch." Mother smiled faintly. "Usually I have trouble getting her to go to sleep."

Finally, the danger period passed, and Kimberly was allowed to curl up and sleep.

"I am exhausted," Grandmother said. "Who would have thought one little pill could have caused so much trouble?"

HOW ABOUT YOU? Satan would like to give you one "little pill." It could be the drug of "busyness" so that you don't have time for God. Or maybe it's an attitude of indifference—not caring about God and His Word. The Lord is saying to you, "Wake up. Watch and pray. I am coming soon." Don't let the enemy drug your soul. □ B.W.

TO MEMORIZE: *Let us not be like others, who are asleep, but let us be alert and self-controlled.* 1 Thessalonians 5:6, NIV

SHARON WENT WITH her mother to the pharmacy and then to Mrs. Engel's house. Mother visited the elderly widow often, bringing cookies or some other thing she had baked, but today she was bringing medicine.

"But I don't have money to pay for that right now," Mrs. Engel confessed as Mother handed her the bottle.

Mother smiled. "I know. That's why Sharon and I got it today—so we could bring it to you as a small gift."

The elderly woman shook her head. "Oh, no," she argued. "I refuse to accept it unless I can pay for it."

Mother was quiet for a short time. When she spoke, her voice was soft and kindly. "Mrs. Engel," she said, "there are two reasons why we want to give this to you. First, because we love you and want to see you get well again."

As mother paused, the elderly woman looked up at her. "And what's the second reason?" she asked.

"To use it as an illustration," answered Mother. "We've talked with you about receiving Christ as your Savior, but we don't know if you've ever done it."

The sick woman shook her head. "No," she managed, "I haven't. I never felt like I had anything to offer God."

"We can only offer ourselves," Mother answered. "Salvation is free."

"Free?" Mrs. Engel repeated. "But I think it should cost something."

"It did! It cost Jesus His life," explained Mother. "He died willingly because He loves us, but He also rose again. Now He's offering free salvation to all who will accept it."

Sharon could not be quiet any longer. "It's just like the medicine," she said excitedly. "If you'll just accept it as our gift, that's all you have to do. It's free to you."

"Sharon's right," Mother continued. "Will you accept both our gift—and God's?"

HOW ABOUT YOU? Salvation was provided by Jesus Christ. It cost Him His life. But He offers it to anyone who will accept it, and there is no charge. It's free! □ R.J.

TO MEMORIZE: *To the man who does not work but trusts God who justifies the wicked, his faith is credited as righteousness.* Romans 4:5, NIV

30
Costly but Free

FROM THE BIBLE:
In those days when you were slaves of sin you didn't bother much with goodness. And what was the result? Evidently not good, since you are ashamed now even to think about those things you used to do, for all of them end in eternal doom. But now you are free from the power of sin and are slaves of God, and his benefits to you include holiness and everlasting life. For the wages of sin is death, but the free gift of God is eternal life through Jesus Christ our Lord. Romans 6:20-23, TLB

Jesus paid for sin

1

Sing a Song

FROM THE BIBLE:

*Sing a new song to the Lord
telling about his mighty deeds!
For he has won a mighty victory
by his power and holiness. He
has announced this victory and
revealed it to every nation by
fulfilling his promise to be kind
to Israel. The whole earth has
seen God's salvation of his
people. That is why the earth
breaks out in praise to God, and
sings for utter joy! Sing your
praise accompanied by music
from the harp. Let the cornets
and trumpets shout! Make a
joyful symphony before the Lord,
the King! Let the sea in all its
vastness roar with praise! Let
the earth and all those living on
it shout, "Glory to the Lord."
Let the waves clap their hands
in glee, and the hills sing out
their songs of joy before the
Lord, for he is coming to judge
the world with perfect justice.*
Psalm 90, TLB

Sing to God

THE HARPER TWINS were grounded—Gayle for telling a lie, and Greg for refusing to cooperate with the junior choir director. During practice he would often whisper and poke the other boys, and he would not sing.

"This is stupid!" growled Greg. "Just 'cuz I don't like to sing I have to sit home!"

"Look at the bright side. At least we can play checkers or something since we're both grounded," advised Gayle.

"Easy for you to say," grumbled her brother. "After all, you're grounded for a better reason than I am."

"Am not!" she flashed back defensively.

"Are too!"

"Am not!"

Mother, hearing voices raised, had come to see what was causing the problem. "Perhaps your father and I didn't make it perfectly clear why you're grounded, Greg," she said. "First of all, when your behavior in junior choir is so bad that the director complains to us, it's time to do something about it. Second, I've noticed lately that you not only refuse to sing in junior choir, but you also don't sing in church. I've learned that you goof off during song time in Sunday school, too, and you distract some of the other children." Mother paused for a moment, then continued. "Many times in God's Word, especially in the Psalms, we are told to sing unto the Lord."

Greg looked ashamed. Just then they heard a baby's cry, and Greg jumped up and headed for his brother's room. "I'll get Tommy back to sleep," he told his mother with a grin. "I'll sing him a lullabye!"

HOW ABOUT YOU? Do you hate to sing? Do you feel you can't sing well? You can still make a "joyful noise" unto God. You need not sing a solo, but you do need to sing unto the Lord. □ H.M.

TO MEMORIZE: *Sing to the Lord, you saints of his; praise his holy name.* Psalm 30:4, NIV

FOR THE TENTH time in a half an hour, Janie pushed the button on the call box lying on her hospital bed. Soon a nurse came into the room. "What is it this time?" she asked patiently.

"I'm tired of having this needle in my arm all the time," whined Janie. "Why do I have to be so sick?"

"But you're getting a little better every day, and it will be taken out soon," the nurse replied. Janie was ready to complain about something else, but the nurse smiled and added, "I have many sick patients to care for. Please try to be patient and not call again unless it's really necessary."

Pouting, Janie turned to her roommate, Beth. "She's a mean nurse, isn't she?" Janie sniffed. "My back is getting sore from lying down. Isn't yours?"

"Yes," nodded Beth, "but the back rubs the nurses give help a lot. And my mom tells me to think about pleasant things to keep my mind off my problems. She says it's good medicine. So I've been saying Psalm 23 over and over in my mind. That helps, too."

Just then another nurse bustled into the room with Beth's medicine. "Here you are, my dear." She smiled at Beth. "I never hear a word of complaint from you. It's a joy to take care of you. Can I get you anything else?" she asked, as she handed Beth a glass of water.

Janie was quiet after the nurse left. Finally, she said, "Beth, I've been thinking about what you said. I guess I need to think of better things than how I'm feeling. Shall we say Psalm 23 together?"

Beth smiled. "Sure, that'll be fun. First let's say the whole thing together, then the next time I'll say one verse and you say the next. Maybe we could learn some new verses, too."

Janie was surprised at how fast the time passed that afternoon!

HOW ABOUT YOU? When you're sick or in trouble, do you concentrate on that and complain about it? Practice being cheerful. Put good things in your mind, and God will give you peace. □ C.Y.

TO MEMORIZE: *Why are you downcast, O my soul? Why so disturbed within me? Put your hope in God, for I will yet praise him.* Psalm 42:5, NIV

MAY

2

Good Medicine

FROM THE BIBLE:

Why are you downcast, O my soul? Why so disturbed within me? Put your hope in God, for I will yet praise him, my Savior and my God. My soul is downcast within me; therefore I will remember you from the land of the Jordan, the heights of Hermon—from Mount Mizar. Deep calls to deep in the roar of your waterfalls; all your waves and breakers have swept over me. By day the Lord directs his love, at night his song is with me—a prayer to the God of my life. I say to God my Rock, "Why have you forgotten me? Why must I go about mourning, oppressed by the enemy?" My bones suffer mortal agony as my foes taunt me, saying to me all day long, "Where is your God?" Why are you downcast, O my soul? Why so disturbed within me? Put your hope in God, for I will yet praise him, my Savior and my God.

Psalm 42:5-11, NIV

Think about good things

3

Labeled

FROM THE BIBLE:

A new commandment I give to you, that you love one another; as I have loved you, that you also love one another. By this all will know that you are My disciples, if you have love for one another.
John 13:34-35, NKJV

Love one another

BACK SO SOON?" asked Mother as Peggy came in with a grocery sack. "Did you find the tomato sauce all right?"

"Sure did. And look what else I bought," said Peggy, taking several cans from the bag. "These were really cheap because the labels are gone. I saved lots of money for you."

"But we don't know what they are!" frowned Mother. Then she laughed. "Very well," she said, "choose one for dinner tonight. Whatever it turns out to be, you'll have to eat some, okay? You bought it—you eat it!"

Peggy agreed. She looked over the array of un-labeled cans, finally setting one aside for dinner. "I think it's corn," she guessed.

At the dinner table that evening, Peggy's brother Todd wrinkled his nose as Mother brought in the food. "What's that strange smell?" he asked.

Mother set a bowl on the table. "It's sauerkraut. Peggy chose it for us tonight," she said. "I hope you like it. You go first, Peggy. Not too small a serving!"

Dad laughed when he heard the story of the unlabeled cans, and he took a large serving of the sauerkraut. "Well, I'm glad you bought this," he said. "I haven't had it for years. I like it! It's good."

But Peggy and Todd didn't agree. "I wonder what else I bought," said Peggy in a worried tone. "I see now why they sold that stuff so cheap. Labels are important."

For family devotions that night, Dad handed each of the children a Bible. "As we've learned, labels are important," he said, "and as Christians, we have a label, too. Do you know what it is? It's found in John 13:34-35."

Peggy and Todd scrambled to see who could find it first. "Oh! I've got it!" exclaimed Peggy. "It's love."

"Right," nodded Dad. "People should be able to see by our label of 'love' that we are Christians. Let's make sure others can see our label."

HOW ABOUT YOU? Can others tell by your label that you're a Christian? Do they see love in your words? In your actions? They should not only see you display love toward the unsaved, but especially toward other Christians. Check your actions today. Make sure the label of "love" is there for everyone to see. □ H.M.

TO MEMORIZE: *By this all will know that you are My disciples, if you have love for one another."* John 13:35, NKJV

"Hey, MARCIA!" called Kent from the living room. "Did you see this article in the paper about the man who was killed when his car skidded off a bridge? Here's a picture. It's pretty gruesome."

"Oooh, let me see," said Marcia. "Look! Do you suppose that's blood on the ground?"

At that moment, Mother spoke up. "Don't you two have anything better to do?"

"Sure," Kent replied. "Let's watch television. They're doing a rerun of that shark movie tonight. You know, the one where that shark attacks the girl and—"

"No, let's watch boxing," said Marcia. "Last week a boxer got a cut over his eye. Wasn't that neat?"

This time, it was Dad's turn to speak up. "What's so 'neat' about injury and suffering?"

"Oh, Dad," Kent scowled. "Why take it so seriously? After all, these things happen every day."

Dad nodded. "Yes, because of Adam's sin, sickness and injury and death are part of life. But they're not good things, and it's wrong to take pleasure in thinking about them. I've been reading a book about ancient Rome. A popular entertainment was to watch Christians being thrown to the lions. You children remind me of the Roman spectators."

Marcia was horrified. "Oh, Dad!" she exclaimed. "That would be gross!"

"I'm sure it was," Mother said, "but many people came to watch anyway. Is what you're doing so different? I don't think the Roman spectators, or you, ever really considered how terrible it was for the people involved. The hearts of the spectators had become so hard that they were fascinated by suffering instead of hating it. You children seem to like watching people suffer, too. Instead of enjoying the pain of others we should do all we can to help them."

HOW ABOUT YOU? If you or someone you love were hurt, how would you want others to react? Would you like it if they seemed to enjoy your suffering? Or would you want them to respond with kindness and compassion? Remember, suffering isn't fun. □ S.K.

TO MEMORIZE: *Be of one mind, having compassion for one another.* I Peter 3:8, NKJV

Suffering Isn't Fun

FROM THE BIBLE:
Your hands are stained with blood, your fingers with guilt. Your lips have spoken lies, and your tongue mutters wicked things. No one calls for justice; no one pleads his case with integrity. They rely on empty arguments and speak lies; they conceive trouble and give birth to evil. They hatch the eggs of vipers and spin a spider's web. Whoever eats their eggs will die, and when one is broken, an adder is hatched. Their cobwebs are useless for clothing; they cannot cover themselves with what they make. Their deeds are evil deeds, and acts of violence are in their hands. Their feet rush into sin; they are swift to shed innocent blood. Their thoughts are evil thoughts; ruin and destruction mark their ways. The way of peace they do not know; there is no justice in their paths. They have turned them into crooked roads; no one who walks in them will know peace.
Isaiah 59:3-8, NIV

Be compassionate

5

Make It Shine

FROM THE BIBLE:

I thank God, whom I serve with a pure conscience, as my forefathers did, as without ceasing I remember you in my prayers night and day, greatly desiring to see you, being mindful of your tears, that I may be filled with joy, when I call to remembrance the genuine faith that is in you, which dwelt first in your grandmother Lois and your mother Eunice, and I am persuaded is in you also. Therefore I remind you to stir up the gift of God which is in you through the laying on of my hands. For God has not given us a spirit of fear, but of power and of love and of a sound mind. Therefore do not be ashamed of the testimony of our Lord, nor of me His prisoner, but share with me in the sufferings for the gospel according to the power of God.
2 Timothy 1:3-8, NKJV

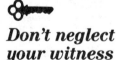

Don't neglect your witness

THE MUSTY, DUSTY smell of the attic tickled Shawn's nose, and he sneezed. "Some of this stuff looks like it hasn't been touched in years!" he exclaimed. Shawn was helping his mother sort out things in Grandmother's attic. They worked in silence for several minutes before Shawn cried out, "Look, Mother! Here's an old Bible!"

"It's my grandmother's family Bible," Mother said softly. "Look at all the markings in it, Shawn. It has been well used. What a treasure!" Shawn knew that he came from a long line of Christians, but lately he had become weary of religion. He often skipped private devotions, and he made excuses to stay home from church as much as possible.

Next, Shawn opened a large, dust-covered trunk. On the top lay a flat velvet box. He opened it. "Here's some dingy old silverware, Mother. Do you want it for your garage sale?"

Mother looked up and gasped. "I'll say not! That silver was given to my mother as a wedding present. It's very valuable!"

As she began counting knives, forks, and spoons, Shawn sniffed. "Doesn't look valuable to me. It looks grubby!"

Mother set down the box of silverware. "I'll be right back," she said as she left the room. Soon she returned with a cloth and a bottle. "Watch," she instructed, and she began cleaning one of the spoons. The dark, dingy silver began to sparkle. "This silver was once beautiful, but it has been neglected." She rubbed harder. "Silver is something like our Christian witness," she continued. "It must be used and cared for, or it will lose its shine. Our witness will become tarnished, too, if it's neglected. It will lose its shine, and the Christian life may even seem dull."

Shawn shook his head and grinned, "Mother, you could get an object lesson out of anything. I get the point."

HOW ABOUT YOU? Have you been neglecting your Christian witness? Have you become slack about praying, reading your Bible, or attending church? In today's reading Paul tells Timothy to "stir up the gift" that is in him. This may be good advice for you, too. The Christian life should be exciting, not dull. Use God's power to make it shine. □ B.W.

TO MEMORIZE: *God has not given us a spirit of fear, but of power and of love and of a sound mind.* 2 Timothy 1:7, NKJV

THE CHURCH that Pete and Julie attended was going to collect a special offering for their missionaries in South America. As the family talked about it, Pete said, "I promised God I'd put half of my allowance in the missionary offering next week. That's a whole fifty cents!"

"I will, too," nodded Julie.

But when the offering plate was passed the following week, Peter put in only a dime, and Julie put in a nickel. Mother noticed, but said nothing.

Later that day, Pete's friend Jack came over with his new book about space exploration. "I want to be an astronaut when I grow up," said Jack.

"Me, too," Pete agreed. Julie overheard them and commented, "Not me. I want to be a fashion model. They make lots of money."

After Jack left, Mother spoke. "I thought you both told your Sunday school teacher that you were going to be missionaries," she said.

"Well, uh, I guess we forgot," said Pete.

"What difference does it make?" asked Julie. "Is it wrong for a Christian to be an astronaut or a model?"

"Not necessarily. And it's not necessarily wrong to put a nickel or dime in the offering plate, either," said Mother. "But if you make a promise to God and then break it, that's wrong. You both promised God half of your allowance. If you're unable to keep a promise through no fault of your own, that's one thing. But if you keep changing your mind whenever you feel like it, that's sin. It's better not to make a promise than to make one and not keep it."

Pete's face was red. "I think I'll have to be more careful about the promises I make—and about keeping them, too."

"Me, too," agreed his sister. "I'm going to put the rest of the money I promised in the offering tonight."

HOW ABOUT YOU? Are you quick to make promises to God—or to others—but reluctant to carry them out? God always does what He says He will do. You should, too. If keeping your promise means doing something hard or inconvenient, do it anyway. Think before you promise! □ S.K.

TO MEMORIZE: *When you make a vow to God, do not delay in fulfilling it. He has no pleasure in fools; fulfill your vow.* Ecclesiastes 5:4, NIV

6

What Did You Promise?

FROM THE BIBLE:
Guard your steps when you go to the house of God. Go near to listen rather than to offer the sacrifice of fools, who do not know that they do wrong. Do not be quick with your mouth, do not be hasty in your heart to utter anything before God. God is in heaven and you are on earth, so let your words be few. As a dream comes when there are many cares, so the speech of a fool when there are many words. When you make a vow to God, do not delay in fulfilling it. He has no pleasure in fools; fulfill your vow. It is better not to vow than to make a vow and not fulfill it. Do not let your mouth lead you into sin. And do not protest to the temple messenger, "My vow was a mistake." Why should God be angry at what you say and destroy the work of your hands? Much dreaming and many words are meaningless. Therefore stand in awe of God.
Ecclesiastes 5:1-7, NIV

Keep your promises

7

The Scrawl

FROM THE BIBLE:

We are not our own bosses to live or die as we ourselves might choose. Living or dying we follow the Lord. Either way we are his. Christ died and rose again for this very purpose, so that he can be our Lord both while we live and when we die. You have no right to criticize your brother or look down on him. Remember, each of us will stand personally before the Judgment Seat of God. For it is written, "As I live," says the Lord, "every knee shall bow to me and every tongue confess to God." Yes, each of us will give an account of himself to God.
Romans 14:7-12, TLB

Sin brings shame

"MOM, LOOK at this!" called Brad from his bedroom. He had decided to rearrange his furniture—but when he moved the dresser, he saw that the wallpaper behind it was covered with ugly crayon marks.

"This is awful!" Brad said as his mother walked in. "Tricia must have done it. It looks terrible!"

Mother smiled. "Don't blame your little sister," she said. "I happen to know that those marks were made long before she was born."

"But if Tricia didn't do it, who did?" asked Brad.

"You did!" Mother answered. "You were about two years old when you marched into the kitchen, holding a crayon, and tugged at my skirt. I followed you in here, and this is what I found. I tried to wash the marks off, but they wouldn't budge. So, I moved the dresser in front of it."

"Wow!" exclaimed Brad. "Did you spank me?"

"Of course!" replied Mother. "I had warned you several times about staying out of the drawer where the crayons were kept. Yet you eagerly showed me what you had done. Apparently you thought I'd praise you for your fine art work instead of punishing you for disobeying."

Brad looked at the scrawl and laughed. "Some art work!" he said. "It's funny how things seem different when you get older. I suppose I was proud of this drawing at the time."

"I wonder how many other things in life are like that," said his mother. "Probably quite a few. When I was a girl, I did a lot of things just to make myself seem older or more important. I followed the crowd in many ways. Now I wish I could go back and undo those foolish things, but I can't. You still have your life ahead of you, Son. Be careful not to do things you'll be ashamed of later."

HOW ABOUT YOU? Do you "live for today," doing whatever seems like the most fun at the moment? If you live in sin, you'll regret it someday—at the Judgment, if not before. Obey God's Word and serve Him. Then you'll look back on your life with gladness, not with shame! □ S.K.

TO MEMORIZE: *What benefit did you reap at that time from the things you are now ashamed of? Those things result in death!* Romans 6:21, NIV

"MAY I HAVE more mashed potatoes?" asked Matt.

"Yes, but share them with Mike," replied Mother without even noticing there were only a few spoonfuls left.

Later, Matt watched an animal program he enjoyed, but soon he heard an all too familiar request. "Matt," Dad said, "Mike wants to watch Circus Hour." Why not let him watch it?"

Leaving the TV to Mike, Matt decided to try an experiment with his new beginner's science lab set. But soon there was a knock at the door. "I thought you wanted to see Circus Hour, Mike," Matt said as Mike came in.

"I did, but now I want to do science." replied Mike.

"You can't," Matt told him. Mike ran out of the room. Soon Mother brought him back. Before Matt could explain that Mike was too young to understand the science experiment, she said, "Matt, can't you be kind and share your things with your younger brother?"

Later, Mother said, "Boys, it's bedtime," and both the children were sent to get ready for bed. When Matt went to kiss his parents good night, Dad noticed tears in his eyes. He gently questioned him about it, and the boy finally began to talk. "Oh, Dad," he sobbed, "I love Mike, but to me it just doesn't seem fair!"

"What do you mean, Son?" asked Dad.

"Well, Mike gets his own way just because he's the youngest! Last Christmas he wouldn't even touch his own gifts, and everyone kept telling me to share my things with him. He played with my stuff more than I did! And it says right on my new science kit that it's for children eight years and older! But I have to let him do it with me, even though he messes things up. And I . . ." Matt couldn't go on because he was crying too hard.

Dad folded him into his arms and soothed his feelings. "You've put the Golden Rule into action many times, Son," Dad said. "I'm proud of you, and I know God has been pleased, too. Go to sleep now, and we'll talk about it again tomorrow."

HOW ABOUT YOU? Today's verse is called the Golden Rule. Do you practice it? Do you treat others the way you would like to be treated even if it doesn't seem fair to you? Jesus gave us this rule. Honor Him by obeying it. □ R.P.

TO MEMORIZE: *Do to others as you would have them do to you.* Luke 6:31, NIV

MAY 8

The Youngest

FROM THE BIBLE:
Love your enemies, do good to those who hate you, bless those who curse you, pray for those who mistreat you. If someone strikes you on one cheek, turn to him the other also. If someone takes your cloak, do not stop him from taking your tunic. Give to everyone who asks you, and if anyone takes what belongs to you, do not demand it back. Do to others as you would have them do to you.
Luke 6:27-31, NIV

Practice the golden rule

The Youngest

(Continued from yesterday)

FROM THE BIBLE:
You children must always obey your fathers and mothers, for that pleases the Lord. Fathers, don't scold your children so much that they become discouraged and quit trying.
Colossians 3:20-21, TLB

And be kind to one another, tenderhearted, forgiving one another, just as God in Christ also forgave you.
Ephesians 4:32, NIV

Talk with your parents

THE NEXT MORNING at breakfast, Dad told the boys he wanted to talk to them. "Matt and Mike, last night Mother and I realized that we haven't been treating you fairly, and we want to apologize," he said.

"What do you mean, Daddy?" asked Matt, while Mike just glanced at him and began to eat his cereal.

"Well," Dad answered, "after you and Mike were in bed, Mother and I talked about the things you told me. We realized we were always telling you to give in to your brother, to share your things with him, and to let him do everything you do because he is younger. We were always quoting Ephesians 4:32 to you."

"I know that verse," piped up little Mike. "Be kind to one another."

"That's right, Mike," nodded Dad, "and that verse applies just as much to you as it does to your older brother. From now on we want you to be as kind to him as he has always been to you. Sometimes being kind means allowing Matt to do his nine-year-old activities with no interference from a five-year-old. We realized last night that we have been guilty of 'provoking Matt to anger' like it says in Colossians 3:21, and we're sorry. Now let's have prayer together."

As the boys left the table, Mother gave them each a hug as she said, "Oh, yes, one more thing. From now on Matt's bedtime is nine o'clock. Mike, when you are nine years old, your bedtime will change, too. OK?"

Both boys grinned as they said, "OK."

HOW ABOUT YOU? Do you ever feel that you're being treated unfairly by your parents? Perhaps if you would talk over the problem with them in a calm way—not angrily—something could be worked out. Apply the Bible verse to all family situations whether you are the youngest or oldest child. □ R.P.

TO MEMORIZE: *Be kind to one another, tenderhearted, forgiving one another, just as God in Christ also forgave you.* Ephesians 4:32, NKJV

Marty's uncle Rick was visiting them while he was on furlough from the military service, and Marty had lots of questions to ask. He had never talked to any soldiers, and he wasn't even sure what they did in the army.

"Do you have a job?" Marty asked bluntly.

"I sure do," Uncle Rick replied. "I work on jeeps, just like I did before I entered the service."

"Do you have a boss?" Marty pressed.

"Yes," Uncle Rick replied again, "my commanding officer is my boss."

"What do you do for him?" Marty persisted.

"Well, I follow every order he gives me."

And so the question-and-answer session continued. Marty really enjoyed it, and he hoped his uncle didn't mind. One Sunday evening, Uncle Rick was asked to give his testimony at church. He wore his uniform, and Marty listened proudly as Uncle Rick spoke. He started by telling the people about some of Marty's questions.

"When Marty asked me what I did for my commanding officer, it reminded me of my spiritual Commanding Officer, Jesus Christ. I wonder if I'm as careful about obeying His orders as I am about obeying the orders given to me in the army," Uncle Rick said. "God has commanded us to 'go into all the world and preach the gospel.' He has also commanded us to 'love one another' just as He loved us."

Marty's thoughts became very serious as he listened to his uncle talk about other commands given by God. Silently Marty prayed, asking God to help him to be obedient to the commands in the Bible. He was going to follow all the orders from his Commanding Officer, the Lord Jesus.

HOW ABOUT YOU? Have you read today's Scripture? It lists just a few of the commands God has given. If you're a Christian, He expects you to obey them. Read them again. After each one, ask yourself, "Am I obeying this command?" Good soldiers don't question their orders; they just obey them. □ R.J.

TO MEMORIZE: *Go and make disciples of all nations, baptizing them in the name of the Father and of the Son and of the Holy Spirit, and teaching them to obey everything I have commanded you.* Matthew 28:19-20, NIV

10

Your Commanding Officer

FROM THE BIBLE:

Stop lying to each other; tell the truth, for we are parts of each other and when we lie to each other we are hurting ourselves. If you are angry, don't sin by nursing your grudge. Don't let the sun go down with you still angry—get over it quickly; for when you are angry you give a mighty foothold to the devil. . . . Don't use bad language. Say only what is good and helpful to those you are talking to, and what will give them a blessing. . . . Stop being mean, bad-tempered and angry. Quarreling, harsh words, and dislike of others should have no place in your lives. Instead, be kind to each other, tenderhearted, forgiving one another, just as God has forgiven you because you belong to Christ. Follow God's example in everything you do just as a much loved child imitates his father. Be full of love for others, following the example of Christ who loved you and gave himself to God as a sacrifice to take away your sins.

Ephesians 4:25—5:2, TLB

Follow God's orders

11
The Pottery Lesson

FROM THE BIBLE:

This is the word that came to Jeremiah from the Lord: "Go down to the potter's house, and there I will give you my message." So I went down to the potter's house, and I saw him working at the wheel. But the pot he was shaping from the clay was marred in his hands; so the potter formed it into another pot, shaping it as seemed best to him. Then the word of the Lord came to me: "O house of Israel, can I not do with you as this potter does?" declares the Lord. "Like clay in the hand of the potter, so are you in my hand, O house of Israel."
Jeremiah 18:1-6, NIV

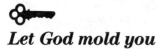

Let God mold you

JOAN AND THE others in her ceramics class watched as her mother poured a liquid into a mold. All the girls were interested in seeing how something so runny could get hard enough to become a lovely vase. Then Mother brought out a piece that had been molded a few days ago.

"Is that one done?" asked one of the girls.

"Oh, no," replied Joan's mother. "As soon as it's dry enough to handle, it needs to be rubbed and cleaned and scraped, and then it will be put into the fire."

The girls watched again as Joan's mother worked on the piece of pottery. With a knife, she scraped away the excess clay. Then, with a piece of sandpaper, she smoothed the pottery. Finally, she rubbed it with a soft sponge.

"All that work?" Joan said.

"That's just the beginning," Mother answered. "After it has gone through one firing, a colorful glaze will be applied. Then it will be put into the fire again. You know, girls, this reminds me of our lives. God works on Christians, scraping off our bad habits, smoothing us out to become more like Him, and finally making us beautiful and shiny by putting us through the fire."

"But I don't think I'd like to be put through all those things," remarked one girl.

"Neither would I," Joan agreed.

"If we're not willing to let God work on us—taking away bad habits, sinful thoughts, angry words and stubborn attitudes—then our lives will not shine for Jesus," Joan's mother replied. "It's part of His plan to make us more like Him."

HOW ABOUT YOU? Has God been scraping off the bad habits and sinful deeds in your life? Has He sent punishment when you lie, cheat, or talk back? Has He taught you patience through illness or through doing without something you really want? When He works in your life do you object? Or do you know that He cares so much about you that He wants to make you one of His shining witnesses? □ R.J.

TO MEMORIZE: *Does not the potter have the right to make out of the same lump of clay some pottery for noble purposes and some for common use?* Romans 9:21, NIV

PETER WAS UPSET! He was settled in front of the TV to watch his favorite program. He had been looking forward to it all week, because last time it had ended at a very exciting place with the words "To be continued." Peter could hardly wait to see what would happen to the hero tonight. But now the words "Special Bulletin" had come on the screen. Then an announcer's voice said, "All regular programming is being preempted tonight by a special message on the economy by our President."

"Oh, Mom!" Peter whined. "I don't want to hear the President. I don't even understand what the economy is."

"Well, I'm sorry," said Mother, "but there's nothing I can do about it. Evidently the networks think this speech is pretty important. Now be quiet so I can hear." Peter disgustedly went to his room and spent the evening playing with his train set.

At Sunday school, Mr. Wilson had the boys read Colossians 1:16-19. When they got to verse 18, Chad asked Mr. Wilson what the word *preeminence* meant. As he often did, Mr. Wilson asked if anyone could help with the meaning of the word.

Peter hesitantly raised his hand. "I'm not sure, but it sounds something like the word *preempt*. On TV this week they preempted my favorite program for the President. Mom said it was because what he had to say was important. Does preeminence mean 'importance', or maybe to give something first place?"

Mr. Wilson seemed very pleased. "That's right, Peter. This verse means that Christ should have first place over everything else in our lives." After more discussion, Mr. Wilson concluded by saying, "Let's pray now and tell God we want Him to have the preeminence in our lives, shall we?"

HOW ABOUT YOU? Does Christ have first place in your life, or is He crowded out by other things like hobbies, sports, TV, or friends? Let Him preempt those things in your life rather than allowing them to preempt Him. You shouldn't let anything come between you and your Savior! □ R.P.

TO MEMORIZE: *He is the head of the body, the church; he is the beginning and the firstborn from among the dead, so that in everything he might have the supremacy.* Colossians 1:18, NIV

12

Pre-eminence

FROM THE BIBLE:

By him all things were created: things in heaven and on earth, visible and invisible, whether thrones or powers or rulers or authorities; all things were created by him and for him. He is before all things, and in him all things hold together. And he is the head of the body, the church; he is the beginning and the firstborn from among the dead, so that in everything he might have the supremacy. For God was pleased to have all his fullness dwell in him. Colossians 1:16-19, NIV

Put Jesus first

MAY

13

Wear the Label

Let Christ be seen in you

THE YOUTH PASTOR at the church had just gotten married, and Josh was in charge of planning a surprise party for him and his new wife. Josh had thought of all sorts of games and tricks. He finally decided on a food shower. "Everybody bring a couple cans of food," he instructed the youth group, "but change the labels. Either exchange the label on the can with something else or leave the label off altogether."

The group thought it would be a good joke to pull on their youth pastor. When Josh's mother heard about it, she wasn't so sure. "How will that poor bride know what she's getting into when she starts to fix their meal?" she asked.

Josh laughed uproariously. "That's the whole point." He stopped and grinned broadly as he thought about his clever idea. "I'd like to be a little bird, looking in," he said.

On the night of the party each one presented Pastor Loren and his wife with one or more cans of food. Some had labels, others had none. Amid much laughter, Pastor Loren thanked each one for their kindness. "You've reminded me of something tonight," he said after the group had settled down. "Each of us wears a label, too. If we're born again, our label is 'Christian.' But sometimes Christians are afraid or ashamed to wear that label. Sometimes people believe one thing but let their outward actions show something else. They're not ready to stand up for what they really believe."

Josh thought seriously about Pastor Loren's message. It seemed to describe him right to the letter. He was sure he was a Christian, but he wasn't sure that his actions always labeled him as one. In fact, he was afraid that sometimes he wore one label and sometimes another. No wonder the kids at school didn't know where he stood.

When Pastor Loren closed the evening's activities with prayer, Josh bowed his head and sincerely asked God to help him let everyone know exactly what he believed.

HOW ABOUT YOU? Do you wear the label of Christian? Can your friends tell by your words and actions that you belong to Christ? Or are you a big question mark to those who see you? Stand up for what you believe! □ R.J.

TO MEMORIZE: *Do not be ashamed to testify about our Lord, or ashamed of me his prisoner. But join with me in suffering for the gospel, by the power of God.* 2 Timothy 1:8, NIV

As KURT TURNED his bike into the driveway, he skidded on some gravel and fell, scraping his elbow. "It doesn't hurt," he said as Mother bandaged it. Actually, his arm hurt quite a bit, but Kurt would never admit it. He felt that he had to be brave and not show his feelings.

"Come on," said Mother. "Let's see if the TV news has anything about that house fire this afternoon." As they watched, they saw a film clip of Kurt's father, a fireman, climbing a tall ladder to help a woman escape the burning house. "Boy, did you see that?" asked Kurt. "Dad is sure brave. He's a real man!"

Kurt was excited when his father arrived home, dirty and smelling like smoke. "Hey, Dad, we saw you on TV!" Kurt began, but his father didn't smile. Instead, he slumped down in a chair, put his face in his hands, and started to cry. Kurt was horrified!

"What's wrong, Honey?" asked Kurt's mother.

Dad wiped his eyes. "I'm all right. But the man we rescued from the burning house died in the hospital. His wife is terribly upset and frightened. I just feel so sorry for her!"

Kurt grew quiet and went to his room. A short time later, his father came in to see him. "Are you all right, Son?" Dad asked.

Kurt looked away. "Well," he mumbled, "I thought that men never—at least, a fireman wouldn't—well, I never thought *you* would."

Dad smiled kindly. "You mean you thought men never cried, right?" Kurt nodded, and his father continued. "I know that I don't usually seem very emotional, but I wouldn't make a very good fireman if I didn't care about people—or a good Christian, either. Jesus cried when His friend Lazarus died, remember? You don't think He was a sissy, do you?"

"No," Kurt replied slowly. "He was brave enough to go to the cross and die for us. I guess I've got a lot to learn about being a 'real man,' haven't I?"

HOW ABOUT YOU? Do you think that men should be tough—that they should hide their feelings to prove how brave they are? Jesus didn't hide His feelings, but He was no weakling either. He accomplished the difficult through the power of God. You can do the same, whether you're a young man or a young woman. □ S.K.

TO MEMORIZE: *Jesus wept. Then the Jews said, "See how he loved him!"* John 11:35-36, NIV

A Real Man

FROM THE BIBLE:
When Mary reached the place where Jesus was and saw him, she fell at his feet and said, "Lord, if you had been here, my brother would not have died." When Jesus saw her weeping, and the Jews who had come along with her also weeping, he was deeply moved in spirit and troubled. "Where have you laid him?" he asked. "Come and see, Lord," they replied. Jesus wept. Then the Jews said, "See how he loved him!"
John 11:32-36, NIV

"Real men" have feelings

15

Favorite Son

FROM THE BIBLE:

In the beginning was the Word, and the Word was with God, and the Word was God. He was with God in the beginning. Through him all things were made; without him nothing was made that has been made. In him was life, and that life was the light of men. The light shines in the darkness, but the darkness has not understood it. There came a man who was sent from God; his name was John. He came as a witness to testify concerning that light, so that through him all men might believe. He himself was not the light; he came only as a witness to the light. The true light that gives light to every man was coming into the world. He was in the world, and though the world was made through him, the world did not recognize him. He came to that which was his own, but his own did not receive him. Yet to all who received him, to those who believed in his name, he gave the right to become children of God.
John 1:1-12, NIV

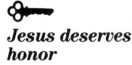

Jesus deserves honor

AS THEY TRAVELED with their parents, Billy and Jenny played a game to see who could spot the biggest variety of license plates. Before long Billy had seen seven different kinds, and Jenny had seen five. Then Jenny said, "Look, there's another one! I saw it first! It says 'Ill-i-noise, Land of Lincoln.' "

"That's pronounced 'Illi-*noy*,' " corrected Mother with a smile. "And it's called 'Land of Lincoln' because that's where Abraham Lincoln completed his education, was married, was elected to Congress and finally, to the presidency. Folks in Illinois are proud of old Abe."

"Abraham Lincoln is my favorite President," said Jenny. "It must have been neat to grow up in the same state with him and know that one of your own 'neighbors' had become President."

"I'm sure you're right," agreed Dad. "When a person earns the respect of his neighbors by doing some great thing, he is often called the 'Favorite Son' of that city or state. But let me ask you something. What would you think if the people of Illinois today refused to acknowledge him—if they were ashamed to even mention his name?"

"That would be crazy," said Billy.

"It's hard to believe that anyone would do that," agreed Dad, "but that's exactly what happened when Jesus came to His own people, the Jews. In fact, to this day the majority of Jewish people do not recognize Jesus as their Messiah."

"That's too bad," said Jenny. "It seems strange, doesn't it? He should be their 'Favorite Son.' "

"Yes," answered Dad. "It's sad, too, that some people tend to look down on the Jews because of the way they treated Jesus. But these same people fail to recognize Jesus as the Savior of the world, and they, too, 'receive him not.' "

HOW ABOUT YOU? How does today's memory verse apply to you? You may not be Jewish, but Jesus still deserves your honor and obedience, because He created you and died to save you. □ S.K.

TO MEMORIZE: *He came to that which was his own, but his own did not receive him.* John 1:11, NIV

"YOU'RE UNUSUALLY QUIET this evening, Misty. Is something bothering you?" Mother asked.

"Oh, Mom," Misty choked, "I just can't do it. I've tried!"

"Tried what?" Mother probed as Misty set the table.

"Tried acting like a Christian," Misty blurted out. "I told a lie today. Christians don't tell lies. Last week I lost my tempter. Christians don't lose their tempers. I might as well give up!"

Mother frowned. "Misty, you aren't a Christian because you don't tell lies or lose your temper. You're a Christian because you have been born again."

"Then why can't I act like a Christian?" Misty asked.

"Living the Christian life is a growing process," Mother explained. "Sometimes we lose a battle, but we have to keep fighting."

"Well, I can't do it," Misty declared stubbornly, "and I'm tired of trying to be something I'm not. I'm just a big flop!"

After Dad gave thanks for the food, Misty watched in surprise as her mother heaped her plate full. "Mother! I thought you were on a diet." Misty had been so proud of her mother as she had lost pound after pound.

"I was," Mother responded, "but today I ate a piece of cake. I cheated on my diet. It's too hard! I just can't do it! I'm tired of dieting."

"But Mother, you were doing so good! You look so much better," Misty protested.

Mother shook her head. "But I can't do it. I've tried and tried, and I'm tired of trying. I'm just a big flop."

"No, you're not, Mother. You . . . " Misty's mouth fell open. She stared at her mother for several seconds, then grinned. "OK, I get the point. You're not a flop because you cheated on your diet, and I'm not a flop because I told a lie. We both lost a battle, but we haven't lost the war."

HOW ABOUT YOU? Have you ever been tempted to quit living for Jesus because you made a mistake? Maybe you've decided that being a Christian is too hard. Don't be discouraged if you lose a battle with sin occasionally. Confess your sin. God will forgive you. Victory is sure in Jesus! □ B.W.

TO MEMORIZE: *If we confess our sins, He is faithful and just to forgive us our sins and to cleanse us from all unrighteousness.* 1 John 1:9, NKJV

FROM THE BIBLE:
God is light and in Him is no darkness at all. If we say that we have fellowship with Him, and walk in darkness, we lie and do not practice the truth. But if we walk in the light as He is in the light, we have fellowship with one another, and the blood of Jesus Christ His Son cleanses us from all sin. If we say that we have no sin, we deceive ourselves, and the truth is not in us. If we confess our sins, He is faithful and just to forgive us our sins and to cleanse us from all unrighteousness. If we say that we have not sinned, we make Him a liar, and His word is not in us.
1 John 1:4-10, NKJV

Keep fighting sin

17

No More Troubles

FROM THE BIBLE:

We have this treasure in jars of clay to show that this all-surpassing power is from God and not from us. We are hard pressed on every side, but not crushed; perplexed, but not in despair; persecuted, but not abandoned; struck down, but not destroyed. We always carry around in our body the death of Jesus, so that the life of Jesus may also be revealed in our body.
2 Corinthians 4:7-10, NIV

Grow through trouble

THE MAN ON TV waved his arms as he spoke. "Do you have health problems? Money problems? Family problems? Do you want to get rid of your troubles? Just follow Jesus," he shouted.

Turning off the TV, Mary went outside. She looked up when she heard the tap of a cane. It was old Mrs. Koning, who could see only dimly. As she approached with her white cane, Mary skipped up to her and put her small hand in the wrinkled palm of the old lady.

"Guess what I just heard a man on TV say," she said.

"I can't guess, Mary," chuckled Mrs. Koning.

"A preacher said all your troubles will be gone if you follow Jesus." She paused, peering in curiosity at Mrs. Koning. "You follow Jesus, don't you?"

Mrs. Koning smiled. "I certainly do, Mary."

"Then why doesn't God help you see again?" asked Mary.

"God could do that," Mrs. Koning told her. "He's powerful enough to make the blind see. But He never promised that all my troubles would go away if I follow Jesus. Instead, He promised He'd be with me in times of trouble, take care of all my needs, and be my friend."

"But the preacher said you could be well," protested Mary, "and rich, too—if you trust Jesus."

"In a way, he may be right," chuckled Mrs. Koning. "My sins are taken away, so my soul is very healthy. I'm rich in love for God and others." She squeezed Mary's hand. "Never try to use Christianity as a means of obtaining smooth sailing through life," she advised. "Christians experience troubles, too. The difference is that they have God to help them through those troubles."

"I see," said Mary slowly. "Following Jesus does make you healthy and rich—but not in the way you might think at first."

HOW ABOUT YOU? Have you gotten the idea, from books you've read or messages you've heard, that God wants all Christians to have lots of money, beautiful clothes, and perfect physical health? This may be God's plan for you, or it may be His plan that, through troubles, you will come to know Him in a special way. God knows what you need to best serve Him. □ C.Y.

TO MEMORIZE: *He said to me, "My grace is sufficient for you, for my power is made perfect in weakness."* 2 Corinthians 12:9, NIV

As PART OF a community awareness program in Molly's town, all the newspaper carriers checked up on the senior citizens who were on their routes. At first, Molly resented the extra time it took, especially with Mrs. Deaton, an old lady on her route who talked and talked while Molly impatiently wished she were at home, playing.

One day, Mrs. Deaton got out a faded photograph album. "Who are these?" Molly asked, pointing to a picture of four little girls sitting on a log.

"Oh," replied Mrs. Deaton, "those are my children."

"How come they never visit you or take care of you, now that you're old?" Molly blurted out without thinking.

"The children all died during a smallpox epidemic many years ago," Mrs. Deaton explained. "Then it was just George and me until he died about twenty years ago." Molly fidgeted when she heard that. "Now don't fret," Mrs. Deaton added. "The Lord gives, and the Lord takes away, but He never forsakes! He's been with me all these years."

One day not long after that, Mrs. Deaton didn't come to the door even though Molly pounded loudly. Peering through a window, Molly saw that Mrs. Deaton was slumped over the table. "Oh, no!" Molly cried in alarm, but just then Mrs. Deaton's head jerked up. Seeing Molly's frightened face at the window, she quickly came to the door.

"Land sakes, child," she said, "I was so busy, I didn't even hear you." She smiled as Molly looked questioningly at her. "I was praying for the missionaries from my church."

Later, Molly told her mother what had happened. "I thought Mrs. Deaton was a worthless old lady," she said, "but I was wrong. I've learned a lot from her. She really knows what it means to trust God! If I live to be as old as she is, I hope I'll be as active in my faith."

HOW ABOUT YOU? How do you feel about older people? Do you respect them? Do you spend time with them and listen to what they have to say? You'll find that older Christians can teach valuable lessons from the experiences they've faced. □ J.H.

TO MEMORIZE: *Even when I am old and gray, do not forsake me, O God, till I declare your power to the next generation, your might to all who are to come.* Psalm 71:18, NIV

18
Not Worthless

FROM THE BIBLE:
Do not cast me away when I am old; do not forsake me when my strength is gone. For my enemies speak against me; those who wait to kill me conspire together. They say, "God has forsaken him; pursue him and seize him, for no one will rescue him." Be not far from me, O God; come quickly, O my God, to help me. May my accusers perish in shame; may those who want to harm me be covered with scorn and disgrace. But as for me, I will always have hope; I will praise you more and more. My mouth will tell of your righteousness, of your salvation all day long, though I know not its measure. I will come and proclaim your mighty acts, O Sovereign Lord; . . . Since my youth, O God, you have taught me, and to this day I declare your marvelous deeds. Even when I am old and gray, do not forsake me, O God, till I declare your power to the next generation, your might to all who are to come.
Psalm 71:9-18, NIV

Learn from older Christians

19

Brand Names

FROM THE BIBLE:

Put on the new man which was created according to God, in righteousness and true holiness. Therefore, putting away lying, each one speak truth with his neighbor, for we are members of one another. "Be angry, and do not sin": do not let the sun go down on your wrath, nor give place to the devil. Let him who stole steal no longer, but rather let him labor, working with his hands what is good, that he may have something to give him who has need. Let no corrupt communication proceed out of your mouth, but what is good for necessary edification, that it may impart grace to the hearers. And do not grieve the Holy Spirit of God, by whom you were sealed for the day of redemption. Let all bitterness, wrath, anger, clamor, and evil speaking be put away from you, with all malice. And be kind to one another, tenderhearted, forgiving one another, just as God in Christ also forgave you.

Ephesians 4:24-32, NKJV

"Christian" is your label

MARGE AND HER friend Valerie ran to the window display of a clothing store in the mall. "Mom, hurry!" Marge pleaded impatiently. "Look at that neat outfit! Could I have that for my birthday?"

"I don't know," Mother answered doubtfully. "I'm afraid it's a bit expensive. And really, Marge, I think it's sloppy looking."

"I love it!" Marge exclaimed. "It's the latest fashion. Everyone's wearing sweatshirts like that."

"The jeans are so neat, too," Valerie added.

"Yeah," agreed Marge. "All the kids wear that brand. Oh, please, Mom!"

Mother frowned. "I've seen jeans at the discount store that look just as nice."

"Aw, Mom," Marge wailed, "I don't want to wear those. Everyone would know they were the cheap kind."

"Well," said Mother wearily, "the stores are closing, so we won't be getting any jeans today." Reluctantly the girls nodded, and they all went out to the car. "You know, girls," said Mother as they drove home, "brand names seem so important to you. Yet you wear a name much more important than that on any jeans."

Marge and Valerie looked puzzled. "What do you mean, Mom?" asked Marge.

"When you trusted in Christ you were sealed by the Holy Spirit," Mother explained. "You wear Christ's name—the name 'Christian.' Brand names are really advertisements, and our lives should 'advertise' for Jesus. I wonder, girls, can your friends tell that you wear Christ's name?"

"Wow!" Marge exclaimed. "I don't know. I never thought about it in that way before."

"Me, either," Valerie agreed. "That's a neat idea. Just think—we wear the most important name of all!"

HOW ABOUT YOU? Have you trusted Jesus Christ as your Lord and Savior? If so, you bear the mark or seal of the Lord. You belong to Him. You bear His name. Let others see by your words and actions that you belong to God. Let your life be a pleasing "advertisement" for Christ. □ B.D.

TO MEMORIZE: *Do not grieve the Holy Spirit of God, by whom you were sealed for the day of redemption.* Ephesians 4:30, NKJV

JACK'S COUSIN Neil had come for a visit. It had been two years since the boys had been together, and they were excited to see one another. They spent the afternoon playing and talking about various things they would like to do during Neil's stay. "You have a skating rink in town, don't you?" asked Neil. "Maybe we could go skating."

"We could ask," agreed Jack, but he looked doubtful.

As expected, Dad shook his head when they asked about it. "It would be fine if they played decent music," he said, "but you know they play only hard rock. Your mother and I prefer that you don't go." Just then, Mother called them for dinner.

"Spaghetti and meatballs!" exclaimed Jack as they sat down to eat. "My favorite!"

"Mine, too!" agreed Neil. The boys ate heartily and then went outside to play. But soon Neil began to feel sick. He sat down on the porch while Jack went to get his mother. "I don't know what's wrong," Neil said. "My skin itches, and it's hard for me to breathe. I'm allergic to eggs, and I feel like I do when I've eaten them. But I didn't eat any eggs."

"Yes, you did!" gasped Mother. "I always put eggs in my meatballs, and you ate quite a few. We'd better call the doctor right away!"

Later that night, after Dad had bought some medicine for Neil, he came up to talk to the two boys. "I'm sorry you had this trouble, Neil," he said. "You know, this incident reminds me of the request to go roller skating. Sometimes we want to do something so badly that we're tempted to overlook the parts of that activity that could hurt us. But if we must 'swallow poison' in order to participate, then it's just not worth it."

"I'll say!" agreed Neil as he rubbed his itchy skin.

HOW ABOUT YOU? Are there some things you'd like to do, but can't because they contain one element of sin? Today's memory verse says a little "leaven" (yeast) affects the whole batch of dough. In the Bible, leaven is a symbol of sin. Just a little sin affects your whole life. Remember, God made Christians to be 'allergic' to sin. Always check out an activity carefully before you get involved. Even a 'little bit' of sin can be poison! □ S.K.

TO MEMORIZE: *Do you not know that a little leaven leavens the whole lump?* 1 Corinthians 5:6, NKJV

20

Poisoned Meatballs

FROM THE BIBLE:
Your glorying is not good. Do you not know that a little leaven leavens the whole lump? Therefore purge out the old leaven, that you may be a new lump, since you truly are unleavened. For indeed Christ, our Passover, was sacrificed for us. Therefore let us keep the feast, not with old leaven, nor with the leaven of malice and wickedness, but with the unleavened bread of sincerity and truth.

1 Corinthians 5:6-8, NKJV

Sin is poison

21

Not Ashamed

FROM THE BIBLE:

As Peter was sitting in the courtyard a girl came over and said to him, "You were with Jesus, for both of you are from Galilee." But Peter denied it loudly. "I don't even know what you are talking about," he angrily declared. Later, out by the gate, another girl noticed him and said to those standing around, "This man was with Jesus—from Nazareth." Again Peter denied it, this time with an oath. "I don't even know the man," he said. But after a while the men who had been standing there came over to him and said, "We know you are one of his disciples, for we can tell by your Galilean accent." Peter began to curse and swear. "I don't even know the man," he said. And immediately the cock crowed. Then Peter remembered what Jesus had said, "Before the cock crows, you will deny me three times." And he went away, crying bitterly.

Matthew 26:69, TLB

Don't be ashamed of Christ

"HEY, MATT!" called Billy from the other side of the playground. "Where were you last night? I called your house at least six times, but you weren't home. I wanted to know if you could go to the video arcade."

"Oh, well, we were out," Matt stammered. He didn't want to tell Billy he had been at church. They were having a missionary conference, and Matt enjoyed the speakers. But Billy wouldn't understand! He'd only laugh.

"How about tonight?" Billy asked. "They've got a new game. I tried it a couple of times, and it's a blast!"

"Well, we're going to be busy again tonight," Matt said. The conference lasted all week, and Matt's family was going to attend each night.

"Tomorrow night?"

"No."

"What does your family do every night?" asked Billy. "No one goes out that much!"

Again Matt hesitated. Then it hit him: here he was, going to a missionary conference and praying for the missionaries to reach more people for the Lord, yet he didn't even have the courage to admit to one of his closest friends that he was going to church! Something was wrong, but Matt knew he could correct it!

"Billy," he began, "we're having a missionary conference at church, and our entire family enjoys the meetings. In fact, maybe you'd like to come, too?"

HOW ABOUT YOU? Are you ashamed to tell your friends you go to church? Are you ashamed to tell them about Christ? Do you deny that you love Him by your actions if not by your words? Should you, like Peter, "weep bitterly" because you've denied the Lord Jesus Christ? Don't feel embarrassed to talk about Him. Look for opportunities to tell your friends about your relationship with the Lord. □ L.W.

TO MEMORIZE: *I am not ashamed of the gospel, because it is the power of God for the salvation of everyone who believes: first for the Jew, then for the Gentile.* Romans 1:16, NIV

22

Guess Who's Coming?

"GUESS WHO'S coming to our house?" Cathy asked as she skipped down the street with her friend Julie. Her eyes were bright with excitement.

"I don't know. Who?" Julie asked. "It must be someone important. You're so excited."

"Oh, Julie," squealed Cathy. "Remember when we read that book at school about the orange elephant?"

Julie nodded. "Sure, I remember. That was a good book! Now tell me who's coming to your house—the orange elephant?"

"Almost!" laughed Cathy. "No, it's Martha Briggs—the lady who wrote the book! See, my mom knew Mrs. Briggs in college, except her name was Martha Alberg then, since she wasn't married yet. My mom didn't realize it was the same Martha! But now she . . ."

"Wait a minute," Julie interrupted. "Slow down, Cathy. You mean the author of *The Orange Elephant* is coming to your house?"

"That's right," bubbled Cathy, "and you could come over and meet her while she's here!"

Julie had to admit that Cathy had reason to be excited. "I wish I knew an author personally," she said to her mother later.

Mother smiled. "You do, Julie—an author who is more important than Mrs. Briggs."

"I do?" Julie couldn't believe it! "Who?"

"You're a Christian, a child of God," Mother told her, "and God is the author of the Bible."

"That's right, Mom!" agreed Julie. She giggled. "I can tell Cathy that I know an author, too!"

HOW ABOUT YOU? Do you know any authors? You do if the Lord Jesus Christ is your Savior! Through the Holy Spirit, God told men (such as John, Paul, and Moses) what to write in the Bible, so it is God rather than man who is the author of the Bible. And He wrote it especially for you! □ L. W.

TO MEMORIZE: *Prophecy never had its origin in the will of man, but men spoke from God as they were carried along by the Holy Spirit.* 2 Peter 1:21, NIV

FROM THE BIBLE:
We did not follow cleverly invented stories when we told you about the power and coming of our Lord Jesus Christ, but we were eyewitnesses of his majesty. For he received honor and glory from God the Father when the voice came to him from the Majestic Glory, saying, "This is my Son, whom I love; with him I am well pleased." We ourselves heard this voice that came from heaven when we were with him on the sacred mountain. And we have the word of the prophets made more certain, and you will do well to pay attention to it, as to a light shining in a dark place, until the day dawns and the morning star rises in your hearts. Above all, you must understand that no prophecy of Scripture came about by the prophet's own interpretation. For prophecy never had its origin in the will of man, but men spoke from God as they were carried along by the Holy Spirit.

2 Peter 1:16-21, NIV

God wrote the Bible

23

A Pouting King

FROM THE BIBLE:

Ahab went home, sullen and angry because Naboth the Jezreelite had said, "I will not give you the inheritance of my fathers." He lay on his bed sulking and refused to eat. His wife Jezebel came in and asked him, "Why are you so sullen? Why won't you eat?" He answered her, "Because I said to Naboth the Jezreelite, 'Sell me your vineyard; or if you prefer, I will give you another vineyard in its place.' But he said, 'I will not give you my vineyard.' " Jezebel his wife said, "Is this how you act as king over Israel? Get up and eat! Cheer up. I'll get you the vineyard of Naboth the Jezreelite." So she wrote letters in Ahab's name, placed his seal on them, and sent them to the elders and nobles who lived in Naboth's city with him. In those letters she wrote: "Proclaim a day of fasting and seat Naboth in a prominent place among the people. But seat two scoundrels opposite him and have them testify that he has cursed both God and the king. Then take him out and stone him to death."

1 Kings 21:4-10, NIV

Don't pout

THERE WAS SOMETHING about the Bible story that made Tami uncomfortable. Her Sunday school teacher was telling about an Old Testament king who acted like a spoiled child. When he didn't get his own way, he refused to eat, ran to his bedroom, threw himself on his bed, and began to pout.

Tami squirmed uneasily in her seat as she remembered what happened at home just that morning. She had wanted to wear her new slacks to Sunday school, but her mother insisted that she wear a dress. Like the king, Tami had thrown herself on the bed. She had waited for her mother to come up and tell her she could wear anything she wanted, but that didn't happen. Tami had grudgingly put on a dress, but she continued to pout all the way to church and avoided even speaking to her mother.

Although pouting didn't work for her, it had seemed to work for King Ahab. His wife, wicked Queen Jezebel, told him, "You're the king. You should be able to have anything you want. If you can't get it, I'll get it for you." Then she arranged for the man who had displeased the king to be killed, and Ahab could now have the thing he had wanted! But wait! Tami's teacher was now pointing out verses from the Bible that said God was displeased with Jezebel and Ahab. He told them He would punish both of them. King Ahab's pouting had not paid off after all.

As Tami left the Sunday school room that morning, she made a very important decision. First, she would tell her mother that she was sorry for the way she had acted. Then she would try, with God's help to accept her parents' decisions even when it meant she would not get her own way.

HOW ABOUT YOU? Do you pout when parents or teachers don't allow you to have your own way? When your friends don't want to play what you want to play? If you allow yourself to pout in self-pity, it may result in unkind actions against the person you're "mad at." God is not pleased when you pout. Don't insist on your own way. Please God by pleasing others. □ R.J.

TO MEMORIZE: *Each of us should please his neighbor for his good, to build him up.* Romans 15:2, NIV

SANDRA WALKED briskly into the house, slamming the door. "I'm never going to talk to Candy again. Never!"

Her mother put down her sewing. "Never is a long time, Honey," she said. "I thought Candy was your best friend."

"That's right," Sandra retorted. "She *was* my best friend, but not anymore. She's been going around telling all kinds of stories about me."

"And are any of them true?" Mother asked.

"No, they're not true!" Sandra snapped. "Candy's just being mean and hateful, that's all. I told her off good, and I'm not going to have anything to do with her ever again!"

"And what about Sunday?" asked Mother. "You girls are in the same Sunday school class, you know."

"I'll sit on the other side of the room." Sandra tossed her head.

"Honey," Mother said, "maybe Candy hurt you by talking the way she did. But you're a Christian, and your reactions must not be unkind. The Bible tells us to be loving and forgiving."

Sandra thought about that for a moment. "I can't forgive her," she said at last.

"No, not in your own strength," her mother agreed. "But the Bible tells us that we can do all things through Christ. He gives us the strength to do what's right."

Her mother was right. Sandra knew that. She knew what the Bible said about loving and forgiving even your enemies. And Candy really wasn't an enemy; she was a friend. That was all the more reason to forgive her.

"I'll try," Sandra said. "I'll ask Jesus to help me."

HOW ABOUT YOU? It's easy to be nice to someone who is nice to you, isn't it? The Bible says even sinners do that. But is there someone who has been mean to you? Are you nice to that person, too? If you're a Christian, God says you should show love even to those who are mean to you. When you see that person at school or church this week, give him or her a smile. God will help you. □ R.J.

TO MEMORIZE: *But love your enemies, do good, and lend, hoping for nothing in return; and your reward will be great, and you will be sons of the Highest. For He is kind to the unthankful and evil.* Luke 6:35, NKJV

Love for Hate

FROM THE BIBLE:
Love your enemies, do good to those who hate you, bless those who curse you, and pray for those who spitefully use you. To him who strikes you on the one cheek, offer the other also. And from him who takes away your cloak, do not withhold your tunic either. Give to everyone who asks of you. And from him who takes away your goods do not ask them back. And just as you want men to do to you, you also do to them likewise. But if you love those who love you, what credit is that to you? For even sinners love those who love them. And if you do good to those who do good to you, what credit is that to you? For even sinners do the same. But love your enemies, do good, and lend, hoping for nothing in return; and your reward will be great, and you will be sons of the Highest. For He is kind to the unthankful and evil. Therefore be merciful, just as your Father also is merciful. Luke 6:27-36, NKJV

Repay evil with good

25

Too Far

FROM THE BIBLE:

Let us draw near to God with a sincere heart in full assurance of faith, having our hearts sprinkled to cleanse us from a guilty conscience and having our bodies washed with pure water. Let us hold unswervingly to the hope we profess, for he who promised is faithful. And let us consider how we may spur one another on toward love and good deeds. Let us not give up meeting together, as some are in the habit of doing, but let us encourage one another—and all the more as you see the Day approaching.

Hebrews 10:22-25, NIV

Stay close to spiritual help

RON'S RADIO-CONTROLLED CAR zipped down the driveway. Just as it reached the road, Ron pushed the lever on the control box to the right, guiding the car back up the driveway. "Ready, Dad?" he asked as his father stepped out the front door, with another car in his hand. "Let's hit the parking lot!"

When they reached the nearby parking lot, Ron and his father found a couple of boys already there. "That's OK. There's room for all of us," said Dad as he and Ron went to the far end.

They had a good time. Dad made his Chevy model jump off the curb, flipping it back onto its tires. Ron skidded his Turbo through some sand, turning it sharply to catch up with Dad's car. "Look! My car is going crazy!" Ron exclaimed. "It won't follow my directions!"

Dad watched for a moment. "I think it's too far away to receive your signals," he observed. "Look—it's too close to those other boys and must be on the same frequency as one of their cars. I think it's following the directions one of them is giving."

Just then one of the boys looked up. He laughed and waved. "I'll send it back to you," he called.

Soon Ron's car was again under his control.

On the way home, Ron and Dad talked about what had happened. "It reminds me of how important it is for us, as Christians, to say close to the right source to guide us," Dad said. "If we get too far away—for example, if we skip Bible reading and prayer or miss Christian fellowship at church—we may not get the spiritual guidance we need. We also place ourselves in a position to be easily influenced in the wrong direction by unbelieving friends." Ron looked at his car. "I'll remember that," he said. "I don't want to be controlled by wrong influences."

HOW ABOUT YOU? Do you find yourself "going along with the crowd?" Are you easily influenced to join in when friends are trying to get you to do something that isn't right? Perhaps it's because you've gotten too far from the Lord. Remember that steady Christian fellowship, Bible reading, and prayer will help you live as a Christian should. Ask Him for strength against the influence of the world. □ N.E.K.

TO MEMORIZE: *Let us hold unswervingly to the hope we profess, for he who promised is faithful.* Hebrews 10:23, NIV

J ANET AND HER friends Kathy and Alice stopped at Janet's driveway to finish the discussion they'd been having on the way home from school. "My cousin was killed last year because of a drunk driver," said Alice, "so my parents decided to quit drinking. They told us kids never to start. I doubt I'll ever take a drink." Kathy nodded in agreement.

Janet had been waiting for an opportunity to witness to her friends, and now seemed like a good time. "You know, the Bible says drinking is dangerous," she began. "There are some verses in Proverbs that talk about it."

Kathy and Alice looked at Janet strangely. "Yeah. Well, I've got to get home," Kathy said. "See ya later."

Alice nodded. "Me, too."

Janet told her mother about the discussion. "They both think drinking is bad, so why did it bother them that I mentioned some Bible verses?" Janet asked. Just then, her little brother walked into the room. Janet laughed when she saw him. "Alex, your shirt's on backward," she said. "The tag goes in the back."

Alex grinned at them. "I ripped the tag out," he said. "Now it doesn't matter how I wear it."

"The shirt looks just as wrong when it's on backward, whether the tag is still there or not!" Mother told him. She turned to Janet. "You know, this reminds me of the problem you had with your friends. Many people don't like to think that there's an absolute standard of right and wrong, or that it's found in the Bible. They don't want to accept the Bible as a standard for right behavior because then they'd have to apply it to other areas of their lives, too."

"Oh. So should I just forget about telling them what the Bible says?" asked Janet.

"No!" said Mother firmly. "Whether they like it or not, the standard is still there. Pray that God will open their hearts to accept His Word instead of trying to ignore it."

HOW ABOUT YOU? Would you sometimes rather not know what God says about a particular sin? His standards remain the same, and they're always right! He says, "Don't lie. Don't cheat. Be Kind. Love one another. Love God." Search out His rules. Don't ever try to ignore them. □ S.K.

TO MEMORIZE: *The word of God is living and powerful, and sharper than any two-edged sword.* Hebrews 4:12, NKJV

The Unchanging Standard

FROM THE BIBLE:

The king sent Jehudi to get the scroll, and Jehudi brought it from the room of Elishama the secretary and read it to the king and all the officials standing beside him. It was the ninth month and the king was sitting in the winter apartment, with a fire burning in the firepot in front of him. Whenever Jehudi had read three or four columns of the scroll, the king cut them off with a scribe's knife and threw them into the firepot, until the entire scroll was burned in the fire . . . . After the king burned the scroll containing the words that Baruch had written at Jeremiah's dictation, the word of the Lord came to Jeremiah:
. . . "I will punish him and his children and his attendants for their wickedness; I will bring on them and those living in Jerusalem and the people of Judah every disaster I pronounced against them, because they have not listened."
Jeremiah 36:21-23, 27, 31, NIV

God's standards are right

27

Not a Taurus

You have trusted in your wickedness and have said, "No one sees me." Your wisdom and knowledge mislead you when you say to yourself, "I am, and there is none besides me." Disaster will come upon you, and you will not know how to conjure it away. A calamity will fall upon you that you cannot ward off with a ransom; a catastrophe you cannot foresee will suddenly come upon you. Keep on, then, with your magic spells and with your many sorceries, which you have labored at since childhood. Perhaps you will succeed, perhaps you will cause terror. All the counsel you have received has only worn you out! Let your astrologers come forward, those stargazers who make predictions month by month, let them save you from what is coming upon you. Surely they are like stubble; the fire will burn them up. They cannot even save themselves from the power of the flame. Here are no coals to warm anyone; here is no fire to sit by. Isaiah 47:1-14, NIV

Don't trust superstitions

M OTHER, LINDA TOLD me I'm a Taurus!" exclaimed Jenny as she burst through the front door. "Her mother says the stars can tell us all about ourselves and advise us about what we should do according to what day we were born. She says we can read the horoscope in the paper every day to find out what the stars say."

Jenny's mother looked up. "And does it make sense to you to believe that the stars have power over a person's life?" she asked. "Does it make sense for people to have to wait until the newspaper arrives to find out what the stars advise them to do that day?"

Jenny thought about that. She remembered a girl at summer camp who'd always worn a rabbit's foot on her belt, even to go swimming. She had believed it would bring her luck, until another little girl had asked, "How much luck can a foot bring? Look what happened to the rabbit, and he had four of them!" Believing in the power of the stars to direct her life, Jenny decided, made about as much sense as believing in a rabbit's foot.

Jenny glanced at the family Bible lying on a nearby shelf. "Linda may say I was born under the sign of Taurus," she said, "but I've been born again." She smiled at her mother. "I'm a Christian, not a Taurus. I have Jesus in my life. He's more powerful than any star—He made them! And I don't have to wait for the newspaper. I have God's Word to tell me how to live!"

HOW ABOUT YOU? Do you ever find yourself avoiding the cracks in the sidewalk? Crossing the street to dodge a black cat? Reading the horoscope section of the paper? Astrology and superstition have no place in Christianity. Rid your life of these things. God hates them! □ L.B.M.

TO MEMORIZE: *Turn to me and be saved, all you ends of the earth; for I am God, and there is no other.* Isaiah 45:22, NIV

STACY EAGERLY welcomed her friends to her birthday party. But as the afternoon went on, she insisted on being first in every game. She grabbed the biggest piece of cake at the table. And as the girls were eating ice cream, she said, "Please hurry! I want to open my presents." After she had torn open the nicely wrapped packages, Stacy sighed, "Well, I guess that's all."

"Wait!" cried Stacy's little sister Kim. "You forgot mine. See? I wrapped it myself!" She held out a crumpled-looking package, and the girls laughed. Stacy was sure the gift was a sloppy, homemade item. But when she tore open the wrapping, she was surprised to find a beautiful transistor radio. "Mommy said I could use the money Grandma gave me," Kim announced with a smile.

After everyone had left, Stacy looked at the radio.

"What a fun party!" she said to her mother. "The food and games were great, and I got some neat presents—especially this radio from Kim. The wrapping was so messy, I never thought there could be anything very nice inside." Then she added, "I even remembered to give the girls the tracts we got in Sunday school last week. I hope they read them!"

Mother looked at Stacy seriously. "I hope they read them, too," she said, "but I'm afraid they may be discouraged by the sloppy way you wrapped them."

"What?" asked Stacy, confused. "I didn't wrap them."

"I'm talking about the poor manners you displayed while the girls were here." Mother frowned. "You see, our lives show what the gospel of Christ really means to us. If people see that we are greedy, selfish, and unthankful, they're not likely to take our message very seriously."

Stacy blushed. She knew she had been a poor example of a Christian. "I'll call the girls and apologize," she said finally. "Kim's 'messy present' taught me a good lesson!"

HOW ABOUT YOU? Do you try to witness to your unsaved friends? You should! But remember—the way you live will determine how seriously they take your message. The gospel is very precious, and it has power to change lives and bring people to heaven. So be sure to "wrap it right!" □ S.K.

TO MEMORIZE: *In every way . . . make the teaching about God our Savior attractive.* Titus 2:10, NIV

MAY

28

Wrap It Right!

FROM THE BIBLE:
In everything set them an example by doing what is good. In your teaching show integrity, seriousness and soundness of speech that cannot be condemned, so that those who oppose you may be ashamed because they have nothing bad to say about us. Teach slaves to be subject to their masters in everything, to try to please them, not to talk back to them, and not to steal from them, but to show that they can be fully trusted, so that in every way they will make the teaching about God our Savior attractive. For the grace of God that brings salvation has appeared to all men. It teaches us to say "No" to ungodliness and worldly passions, and to live self-controlled, upright and godly lives in this present age, while we wait for the blessed hope—the glorious appearing of our great God and Savior, Jesus Christ, who gave himself for us to redeem us from all wickedness and to purify for himself a people that are his very own, eager to do what is good.
Titus 2:7-14, NIV

Witness with words and actions

29

No Throwaway Friends

FROM THE BIBLE:

Love is very patient and kind, never jealous or envious, never boastful or proud, never haughty or selfish or rude. Love does not demand its own way. It is not irritable or touchy. It does not hold grudges and will hardly even notice when others do it wrong. It is never glad about injustice, but rejoices whenever truth wins out. If you love someone you will be loyal to him no matter what the cost. You will always believe in him, always expect the best of him, and always stand your ground in defending him. All the special gifts and powers from God will someday come to an end, but love goes on forever.

1 Corinthians 1:4-8, TLB

Be a faithful friend

"DOREEN, DON'T FORGET that you promised to clean your closet," reminded Mother as Doreen finished a snack after school. But her closet was the last thing on Doreen's mind.

"I'm never going to speak to Katy Carter again," Doreen stated as she put her empty glass in the sink. "She's always saying mean things, and she gets mad for no good reason. No one likes her anymore. She told Amy that I looked like I'd used an eggbeater to comb my hair this morning."

"That wasn't a nice comment," agreed Mother, "but I hardly think it deserves ending your friendship. After all, you've been friends since kindergarten. It sounds to me like something's bothering Katy. I think she needs a friend now more than ever."

"Well, it's not going to be me," declared Doreen, and she stomped off to clean her closet.

When Doreen returned, she was clutching something furry in her arms. "Look what I found in the closet," she said, holding out her old Teddy bear to show her mother.

Mother smiled and patted the bear. "That old thing," she said fondly. "You used to take him everywhere."

"Teddy was my best friend," Doreen recalled.

Mother took Teddy from Doreen's arms. "Look at him now," she said. "The color is rubbed off his nose, the fur is gone from the back of his head. I think it's time to throw him away."

"No, Mom!" Doreen cried, reaching for the bear. "He's my friend, and I won't throw him away."

Mother stopped. "Well, all right," she agreed, "but you'll have to clean him up a bit," She looked into Doreen's eyes as she added, "We shouldn't throw our friends away, should we?"

Doreen hugged Teddy to her tightly. "I know you mean Katy," she said. "I guess you're right. I won't throw her away, either."

HOW ABOUT YOU? Have you been tempted to "throw away" one of your friends? Perhaps someone has been mean to you, or maybe an old friend is cross or gloomy lately. God didn't throw you away—He loved you while you were still unsaved, and He continues to love you always. He wants you to love others even when they're unpleasant and hard to love. Don't throw anyone away. □ K.R.A.

TO MEMORIZE: *Accept one another, then, just as Christ accepted you, in order to bring praise to God.* Romans 15:7, NIV

RUSTY JUMPED DOWN from his stilts. "You try these now, Jeremy," he said. He held the stilts while his young cousin climbed up on the picnic table to get on them. "You have to use your arms to help your legs take steps," instructed Rusty. "It's a bit like being a marionette and pulling your own strings." He helped Jeremy get started.

When Rusty let go of the stilts, they went flying from under Jeremy's feet. One crashed sideways, smacking Rusty hard on the side of the head. Several swear words exploded from his mouth.

Jeremy looked suspiciously at his cousin. "I thought you said you asked Jesus to be your Savior and take away your sins," he said.

"I did," Rusty said with a sigh as he helped Jeremy up onto the stilts again, "but I've got some bad habits. I've got to learn to live a whole new way. I shouldn't have lost my temper and said those things. I'm sorry."

Jeremy wobbled dangerously when Rusty let go of the stilts again. "I have to learn to walk on these stilts," said Jeremy, "and you have to learn to walk as a Christian."

"Hey! That's right!" exclaimed Rusty. "You have to go carefully and think about each step until you learn that new skill. Otherwise you'll fall. And I have to go carefully and think about my steps as a Christian. When I'm not careful, I fall back into old habits."

Just then Jeremy tipped sideways, and the stilts fell toward Rusty again. He grabbed them just in time to keep from getting another bruise. "I'm sorry," apologized Jeremy. "I didn't mean to hurt you."

Rusty laughed. "I know you didn't," he said. "I'll forgive you for falling with the stilts, if you'll forgive me for taking that fall in my Christian life a few minutes ago."

HOW ABOUT YOU? Are you patient with new Christians? Perhaps you grew up in a Christian home and never learned to swear or be violent. But there are those who have learned to walk the world's way, and now they need to learn to walk as a Christian. Forgive and pray for the Christian who is trying to learn to walk as he should. □ C.R.

TO MEMORIZE: *Live a life worthy of the calling you have received. Be completely humble and gentle; be patient, bearing with one another in love.* Ephesians 4:1-2, NIV

New Way to Walk

FROM THE BIBLE:
So I tell you this, and insist on it in the Lord, that you must no longer live as the Gentiles do, in the futility of their thinking. They are darkened in their understanding and separated from the life of God because of the ignorance that is in them due to the hardening of their hearts. Having lost all sensitivity, they have given themselves over to sensuality so as to indulge in every kind of impurity, with a continual lust for more. You, however, did not come to know Christ that way. Surely you heard of him and were taught in him in accordance with the truth that is in Jesus. You were taught, with regard to your former way of life, to put off your old self, which is being corrupted by its deceitful desires; to be made new in the attitude of your minds; and to put on the new self, created to be like God in true righteousness and holiness. Ephesians 4:17-24, NIV

Encourage new Christians

31
The Penny Drive

FROM THE BIBLE:

Notice among yourselves, dear brothers, that few of you who follow Christ have big names or power or wealth. Instead, God has deliberately chosen to use ideas the world considers foolish and of little worth in order to shame those people considered by the world as wise and great. He has chosen a plan despised by the world, counted as nothing at all, and used it to bring down to nothing those the world considers great, so that no one anywhere can ever brag in the presence of God. For it is from God alone that you have your life through Christ Jesus. He showed us God's plan of salvation; he was the one who made us acceptable to God; he made us pure and holy and gave himself to purchase our salvation. As it says in the Scriptures, "If anyone is going to boast, let him boast only of what the Lord has done."
1 Corinthians 1:26-31, TLB

Look for God's values

LISTEN TO THIS," said Jody's mother as she came into the room holding a newspaper. "The writer of this article says that the use of the penny should be discontinued in our money system. It says, 'Nothing can be purchased for a penny. The nickel should be the smallest valued coin in our system.' What do you think?"

"I agree," stated Dad. "Pennies are a nuisance. I have a whole jar of them on my dresser. I dump them in there because I don't like to be bothered by so much change."

Just then Todd came charging into the house after his youth club meeting at church. "Guess what!" he said. "We're going to have a penny drive to get money for our missionaries. The money will help pay for sending all their stuff to Europe. We can only bring pennies! Will you help me? There's a prize for bringing the most."

Mother laughed. "I guess the person who wrote this article didn't know about missionaries," she said. "Sure, we'll all help."

The Johnsons dug pennies out of the sofa and from underneath the washing machine. Dad contributed the jar of pennies from his dresser. Each day they all cleaned out pockets and purses and gathered in the pennies.

"I've got $9.68 all together," said Todd the following Sunday. "That will help a lot."

"Pennies seem so worthless by themselves," observed Jody, "but they can add up in a hurry, can't they?"

Dad nodded. "God often takes something for which the world has no use and turns it into something valuable. We changed our way of thinking about the pennies. Perhaps there are other areas where we need to change our way of thinking."

"You're right," agreed Mother. "I think that's especially true when it comes to people. We often fail to recognize that all people are of great value to God—and that we should value them, too."

HOW ABOUT YOU? Have you ever taken an object that someone threw away and made it into something useful? Or bought something no one else wanted, because it was just right for you? Perhaps you know a person who seems worthless to others because of a handicap or annoying habit. Learn to see value in all kinds of people as God does. □ C.R.

TO MEMORIZE: *Even the very hairs of your head are all numbered.* Matthew 10:30, NIV

ROXIE SAT curled up on the couch with Mittens, her cat, purring on her lap. "Mittens, things will never be the same," she told the cat sadly. "We're moving, and I'll never see my friends again."

"Mittens, you're not going to like moving." Roxie was surprised to hear Dad's voice behind her. "As far as you know, this apartment is all there is to the world, but we're going to take you out of it," continued Dad. He sat down next to Roxie. She stared at him curiously as he went on talking to the cat. "Mittens, you're going to be scared when we put you in the pet carrier and put it on the plane. You're going to think your life will never be the same." Dad paused. "Maybe we should just leave you here," he added.

"But, Dad," protested Roxie, "you said that Mittens will be able to climb trees and chase mice at our new house. She'll do lots of things she's never done before. She might not like moving, but she'll like it after she gets there."

"Think so?" asked Dad. "Well, I guess you're right. Since you're not a cat, you see things from a different point of view than Mittens does, don't you? You know that when Mittens gets to her new home in the country, she'll be happy there. And Roxie, just as you see the cat's future from a different point of view than she does, God sees your future from a different point of view than you do. He knows you'll hurt for a while, but He also sees past that to the wonderful things He has in store for you in our new home. If you let Him, He'll help you get over the hurt so you can enjoy that wonderful future."

Roxie sniffed as she stroked the cat. "Well, Mittens, maybe there's a different world out there for both of us," she said finally. "We might even find a tree to climb together." Roxie smiled as she gave the cat a squeeze.

HOW ABOUT YOU? Is there a circumstance in your life that is so hard you feel you'll never get over it? God doesn't let you see into the future, but He sees what's there. You must live by faith, trusting Him to use even the hard things to work for good in your life. □ K.R.A.

TO MEMORIZE: *We live by faith, not by sight.* 2 Corinthians 5:7, NIV

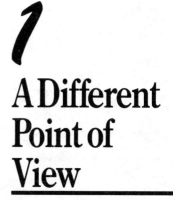

JUNE

1

A Different Point of View

FROM THE BIBLE:
"My thoughts are not your thoughts, nor are your ways My ways," says the Lord. "For as the heavens are higher than the earth, so are My ways higher than your ways, and My thoughts than your thoughts." Isaiah 55:8-9, NKJV

Trust God's plan

2

Somebody's Watching

FROM THE BIBLE:

God is closely watching you, and he weighs carefully everything you do. The wicked man is doomed by his own sins; they are ropes that catch and hold him.

Proverbs 5:21-22, TLB

It will become as evident as yeast in dough. Whatever they have said in the dark shall be heard in the light, and what you have whispered in the inner rooms shall be broadcast from the housetops for all to hear!

Luke 12:2-3, TLB

God sees all you do

OH, BOY!" exclaimed Jeff when his little sister walked into the living room. Her mouth was circled with something which looked like mashed strawberries. "Wait until Mom sees you, Kristy!" scolded Jeff. "You're going to get it!"

As Kristy wandered away, Jeff watched a news flash that interrupted the ballgame he'd been watching. Several well-dressed men were being escorted by police officers into waiting police cars. The announcer gave a quick report of a successful FBI crackdown on a large spy ring. "Did you hear that, Dad?" Jeff asked as his father came into the room. "I wonder how the cops find out about guys like that."

"Well, God's Word teaches clearly that nobody can do wrong and get away with it," Dad stated positively. "God always knows what's going on, and He often uses human government to bring lawbreakers to justice. It's true that some seem to get away with wrongdoing for a very long time. But the day will come when they will stand before God and answer for the deeds they have done."

Mom's voice interrupted from the kitchen. "Who spilled my strawberries? Somebody made a real mess out of tonight's shortcake! Where's the dog? Was he in here?" Then in a softer tone, Jeff and Dad heard, "Kristy! Naughty girl! Look at you!"

Dad exchanged an amused glance with Jeff. "See, Son," he said, "sometimes the evidence is so plain there's no denying it. Kristy probably thought no one would know what she did, but it was obvious to Mother. And those fellows on TV probably thought no one would ever catch them, but it was plain to the Lord."

"Too bad no one ever told those guys that God is watching," Jeff said. Then he added thoughtfully, "Unless someone did, and they just didn't listen."

HOW ABOUT YOU? Are you aware that God sees all you do? If you've done something wrong, God knows all about it. A day of reckoning will come. If you're not a Christian, the first thing you need to do is receive Jesus into your life. If you are saved, you need to ask God to forgive you and help you make things right again. □ P.K.

TO MEMORIZE: *The eyes of the Lord are everywhere, keeping watch on the wicked and the good.* Proverbs 15:3, NIV

SHE IS SO my aunt!" insisted Ellie indignantly. She was trying to convince the other campers that she was the niece of the well-known author whose books were displayed on the book table. But no one would believer her!

"If she's your aunt," asked Sherri, "how come you can't tell us which one of these books is your favorite?"

"Yeah," nodded Donna. She picked up a book and held it before Ellie. "What's this book about?" she asked. "If this author is your aunt, like you say, and if you have copies of all her books, you should be able to tell us what's in them."

Ellie bit her lower lip. "I can't," she confessed at last. "I've never finished reading most of them." She paused, not sure how to explain. "I used to read them when she first started sending me books. But I don't really care a lot about reading, so after a while I'd just look at the cover and then file it away with the others."

"But, Ellie, don't you love your aunt?" asked Donna.

Ellie was embarrassed. "Of course, I love my aunt and I'm very proud of her, but—"

"But you don't bother to read what she—" Donna stopped as Miss Patti, their cabin counselor, walked up.

"I overheard a bit of this conversation," Miss Patti told them as she picked up one of the books. "I was just thinking that most of us are like Ellie. God has given us a Book—a most important Book—and we don't read it as often as we should." She paused briefly. "In fact, we read it so seldom that we might have trouble convincing anyone that we love the Author, or even know Him." She glanced around as she laid the book back on the table.

After Miss Patti left, not another word was said to Ellie about her neglect of her aunt's books. Ellie touched the one Miss Patti had put down. "When I get back home," she said determinedly, "I'm going to read these books. And I'm going to read God's Book, too."

HOW ABOUT YOU? Do you know the Author of the Bible? Do you have a copy of His Book in your home? It's intended to be read, but are you reading it regularly? Pick it up and read at least a few verses every day. □ R.J.

TO MEMORIZE: *Your testimonies I have taken as a heritage forever, for they are the rejoicing of my heart.* Psalm 119:111, NKJV

JUNE

3

Meant to Be Read

FROM THE BIBLE:
My son, never forget the things I've taught you. If you want a long and satisfying life, closely follow my instructions. Never tire of loyalty and kindness. Hold these virtues tightly. Write them deep within your heart. If you want favor with both God and man, and a reputation for good judgment and common sense, then trust the Lord completely; don't ever trust yourself. In everything you do, put God first, and he will direct you and crown your efforts with success.

Proverbs 3:1-6, TLB

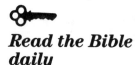

Read the Bible daily

JUNE

4

Cut Down

FROM THE BIBLE:
*Great men have persecuted me,
though they have no reason to,
but I stand in awe of only your
words. I rejoice in your laws
like one who finds a great
treasure. How I hate all falsehood but how I love your laws. I
will praise you seven times a day
because of your wonderful laws.
Those who love your laws have
great peace of heart and mind
and do not stumble. I long for
your salvation, Lord, and so I
have obeyed your laws. I have
looked for your commandments
and I love them very much; yes,
I have searched for them. You
know this because everything I
do is known to you.*
Psalm 119:161-168, TLB

Don't stay down

STOP, BRAD!" Mother's cries were drowned out by the roar of the lawn mower. "Oh, no!" she moaned. "He's cut down my rose bush."

When Brad apologized later, Mother sighed. "It was a small bush, and I know you didn't see it," she said. "Let's forget it."

A few weeks later, when Brad came in from mowing Mr. Johnson's lawn, he had tears in his eyes. "Why, Brad, what's the matter? Did you hurt yourself?" Mother asked.

"No." Brad choked down a sob, "but Mr. Johnson is so hateful!"

"Didn't your work please him?" Mother handed Brad a tissue.

"I do my best, but it's never good enough." Brad blew his nose loudly. "He's always cutting me down, saying I'm too slow or too sloppy or charge too much. Said in his day folks did things for their neighbors without charging. Said he could be dead a week and wouldn't even be missed until someone came wanting some money."

"Poor old man," Mother said softly.

"He's not poor!" Brad snorted. "He's got more money than anyone I know, and he intends to keep it, too. No wonder he doesn't have any friends."

"I feel sorry for him. It's sad to be old and lonely and rich. Even when people try to help him, he thinks they're after his money. Don't let what he says get to you," Mother comforted. "Now, how about mowing our lawn?"

Several minutes later Brad called, "Mom, come out here. I want to show you something." Mother found him pointing at the ground. "Remember the rose bush I cut down? There it is, sprouting out again from the roots."

Mother smiled as she knelt and pulled grass from around the bush. "We can do the same thing, Brad. When people cut us down, we can sprout again. If our roots are in the Word of God, His love will cause us to spring up."

HOW ABOUT YOU? Do you know someone who seems to delight in "cutting you down?" Don't stay down. Get up! You can do this by (1) praying for those who have hurt you, (2) refusing to think about what they did or said, (3) meditating on the Word of God. Get your roots in God's Word. □ B. W.

TO MEMORIZE: *Though I have fallen, I will rise. Though I sit in darkness, the Lord will be my light.* Micah 7:8, NIV

JANE'S HANDS skillfully slid the skin off a peach. Then she passed the fruit to her mother who slit it with a knife, broke it apart, and removed the pit.

"Too bad peaches don't grow all year long," sighed Jane. "Then we wouldn't have to do all this canning."

"That would be nice," agreed Mother as she cut another peach in half. "But just thinking of the enjoyment we'll get from eating these peaches throughout the winter makes the job more pleasant. We'll have enough peaches stored up to last till after the cold weather is gone."

"That thought does help—a little," said Jane as she slid the skin from another peach.

"Did you know that Jesus talked about storing up things?" asked Mother.

"Oh, Mom," giggled Jane, "Jesus didn't do any canning."

"I'm sure He didn't," replied Mother with a smile. "He was talking about storing up things in our hearts."

"Like Bible verses maybe?" asked Jane.

"Yes," agreed Mother. "He also talked about the thoughts and feelings we store up. Jesus said you can tell what a person has stored in his heart by the way that person talks. Good thoughts and feelings about people and about God will bring out kind words. It's as though our mouths overflow with whatever is stored up in us."

Jane reached over to pick up a shriveled peach, and showed it to her mother. "Storing up bad thoughts would be like canning rotten peaches," she said. "Yuk! Who would want to eat rotten peaches?"

HOW ABOUT YOU? What do people hear from your storehouse of thoughts? Thinking of God's goodness and greatness, thinking of Bible verses, and thinking kind thoughts of others will help you store up good things in your heart. □ C.Y.

TO MEMORIZE: *The good man brings good things out of the good stored up in his heart, and the evil man brings evil things out of the evil stored up in his heart.* Luke 6:45, NIV

Storing Up

FROM THE BIBLE:
No good tree bears bad fruit, nor does a bad tree bear good fruit. Each tree is recognized by its own fruit. People do not pick figs from thornbushes, or grapes from briars. The good man brings good things out of the good stored up in his heart, and the evil man brings evil things out of the evil stored up in his heart. For out of the overflow of his heart his mouth speaks. Luke 6:43-45, NIV

Store up good thoughts

6

Always Tuned In

FROM THE BIBLE:

Bend down and hear my prayer, O Lord, and answer me, for I am deep in trouble. Protect me from death, for I try to follow all your laws. Save me, for I am serving you and trusting you. Be merciful, O Lord, for I am looking up to you in constant hope. Give me happiness, O Lord, for I worship only you. O Lord, you are so good and kind, so ready to forgive; so full of mercy for all who ask your aid. Listen closely to my prayer, O God. Hear my urgent cry. I will call to you whenever trouble strikes, and you will help me. Psalm 86:1-7, TLB

God is tuned in to you

DAVID LOOKED AROUND at all the people lying on the beach. Many others were swimming in the ocean waters. It seemed that everyone was laughing and shouting and making noise of some kind. Suddenly a lifeguard jumped down from his high position and ran into the water. With quick strokes, he swam out into the deep water. In a few minutes a crowd gathered nearby and watched as the lifeguard rescued a drowning girl.

"Hey, Dad," David asked later, "how did the lifeguard know that girl was drowning? There was so much noise all around. I was standing right here, and I didn't hear her call for help."

"That's because your ears and eyes weren't tuned to hear or see that she was drowning," David's father replied.

"You mean lifeguards learn to hear and see those things?" the boy asked.

Dad nodded. "First they have to take a life-saving course," he explained. "Once they are put on duty, they keep very alert so they can both see when someone is in trouble and hear his call for help!"

David was quiet for a time. Finally he spoke. "Isn't there a verse in the Bible that tells us that God always hears us when we call?"

"Yes, there are several," replied Dad.

David began to think about some of the verses he had learned in church and Sunday school. "Call unto me and I will answer," he said aloud.

"That's one," Dad agreed. "Another one says, 'In my distress I called upon the Lord, and he heard me.' "

On and on David and his father quoted verses that told about God's care and concern. David was glad that God was always "tuned in" and ready to hear him.

HOW ABOUT YOU? Can you think of some verses that assure you that God's eyes and ears are tuned in your direction? Learn the one below and see how many more you can find in your Bible. Then don't forget to thank Him for His love and care. □ R.J.

TO MEMORIZE: *Call to Me, and I will answer you, and show you great and mighty things.* Jeremiah 33:3, NKJV

MARK'S UNCLE JEFF was scheduled to have surgery on his back. "It's a funny thing," Dad told the family. "The doctor says it's an old injury that's causing the trouble. I had forgotten that Jeff was butted by a goat years ago."

"Butted by a goat?" echoed Mark. "How'd that happen?"

"Our uncle always kept animals—among them a mean old billy boat," said Dad. "Uncle Ted warned Jeff and me not to go into the stall where the goat was, but Jeff did anyway. When he tried to get out, the goat got him."

"Was he hurt bad?" Lisa asked.

"Pretty bad, but he never told anyone what happened because he was afraid he'd be punished," answered Dad. "He pretended he fell. He was really stiff for a long time, and he had a big bruise. Now that spot is giving him a lot of trouble."

"Then he really didn't get away with it," said Mother.

"No," agreed Dad. "It took a while, but he's paying for his disobedience. Perhaps if he had confessed it, a doctor could have prevented what's happening now."

The next week, Dad and Mark came home with a shrub Mother had been wanting. She came out to watch as Dad started to dig a hole, and Mark suddenly remembered something! A few months ago he had tossed a ball in the house and had broken his mother's best vase. He had buried the pieces in this very spot. Sure enough, in a few minutes, Dad turned up some broken pieces of pottery.

"Oh," Mark said sorrowfully, "I guess I'm just like Uncle Jeff." Then Mark told his story and apologized. "I'm sorry, Mom. I'm so ashamed."

"Oh, Mark, I would have forgiven you the day it happened if you had told me," Mother answered. "All sins are uncovered sometime, and it's always unpleasant. Actually, it's easiest to confess what you did wrong at the time you did it."

HOW ABOUT YOU? Are you hiding some sins, thinking they will never be found out? Do you think you are getting away with something? God knows all about it. Confess your sins, take the consequences, and receive forgiveness. □ A.L.

TO MEMORIZE: *I the Lord search the heart and examine the mind, to reward a man according to his conduct, according to what his deeds deserve.* Jeremiah 17:10, NIV

Delayed Action

FROM THE BIBLE:
Because the sentence against an evil work is not executed speedily, therefore the heart of the sons of men is fully set in them to do evil. Though a sinner does evil a hundred times, and his days are prolonged, yet I surely know that it will be well with those who fear God, who fear before Him. But it will not be well with the wicked; nor will he prolong his days, which are as a shadow, because he does not fear before God.
Ecclesiastes 8:11-13, NKJV

Confess right away

JUNE

8

Baloney Sandwiches

FROM THE BIBLE:

As for the work this man of rebellion and hell will do when he comes, it is already going on, but he himself will not come until the one who is holding him back steps out of the way. Then this wicked one will appear, whom the Lord Jesus will burn up with the breath of his mouth and destroy by his presence when he returns. This man of sin will come as Satan's tool, full of satanic power, and will trick everyone with strange demonstrations, and will do great miracles. He will completely fool those who are on their way to hell because they have said "no" to the Truth; they have refused to believe it and love it, and let it save them, so God will allow them to believe lies with all their hearts, and all of them will be justly judged for believing falsehood, refusing the Truth, and enjoying their sins.
2 Thessalonians 2:7-12, TLB

Don't believe lies!

As THE Wilson family was enjoying their lunch out on the picnic table, Tim took a large bite of his sandwich. "Boy, food tastes good out here!" he remarked.

Mother, who had been sipping her iced tea, coughed and started to laugh. "I'm glad you like it," she grinned. "That little black ant you just ate must have added extra flavor."

"What!" shouted Tim, making a face. Everyone laughed as he hurriedly drank his tea and carefully searched through the rest of his sandwich.

"Don't worry, Tim. I'm sure that one little ant won't make you sick," Dad assured him. "It's not so serious. It reminds me of something the devil likes to do, though—something that *is* serious."

"The devil?" exclaimed Tim. "What about him?"

"Well," replied Dad, "Satan likes to trick people with his favorite 'sandwich'—truth on the outside, 'baloney' in the middle. He often deceives people by mixing a little truth with his lies, so that they don't see what they're swallowing until it's too late."

"I don't get it," said Tim. "Like what?"

"Well, there are some religions that teach love for our fellow man and doing good works," explained Dad. "Now, it's true that we should love others and do good things. But these same religions teach that Christ was just a good man and that the Bible is not really the Word of God."

"But I don't understand," said Tim. "Why would Satan want to tell us anything good? Why wouldn't he just try to teach us lies?"

"Let me ask you a question. Would you have taken a bite if your whole sandwich was full of ants?" asked Dad.

Tim shuddered. "Of course not," he said. "I only ate it because it looked good. I didn't even notice the ant."

"And that's what Satan is counting on—that people will believe the good things they hear without noticing the bad," said his father.

"OK, Dad," Tim replied. "I'll try to be more careful about what I swallow!"

HOW ABOUT YOU? Do you think that something is true because it sounds good? Watch out! Satan often mixes truth with his lies. Compare everything people say, do, or write, with what the Bible says. Don't swallow a lie! □ S.K.

TO MEMORIZE: *The simple believes every word, but the prudent man considers well his steps.* Proverbs 14:15, NKJV

TIM CAME BURSTING into the house early one evening. "Dad, can I go fishing with Jerry? His dad is taking him, and they asked if I'd like to go? Can I? Please?" He waited breathlessly.

Dad laughed. "Sounds like fun," he said. "When do they plan to go?"

"Early Sunday morning," replied Tim. He hurried on as he saw Dad's frown. "He says if I go fishing with him in the morning, he'll come to church with me in the evening."

"But, Tim," Mother objected, "you know it wouldn't be right to go fishing instead of going to Sunday school!"

"It's only this once," coaxed Tim, "and it's for a good reason. Why, just think! I might even be able to witness to him! And his dad will be there, and maybe I could witness to him, too. I might not get another chance."

Dad laid aside his newspaper. "I think you've swallowed another baloney sandwich," he said.

Tim looked at him in surprise.

"Remember the sandwiches Satan likes to feed us," Dad asked, "those made up of truth, mixed with lies? It's true that you might get a chance to witness, and yes, it would be good for Jerry to come to church with you in the evening. But the lie Satan wants you to believe is that it's OK to neglect church and Sunday school on Sunday morning."

Tim hung his head. "I forgot what we talked about," he admitted.

"The Bible says to seek God first," Mother told him. "Do that, and I'm sure you'll have opportunities to witness to Jerry, too."

Tim nodded and thought about it. A twinkle came to his eyes. "Dad," he asked, "will you take Jerry and me fishing next Saturday morning? Maybe we'll get a chance to witness while we fish. Maybe he'll even agree to come to Sunday school and church on Sunday morning."

HOW ABOUT YOU? Do you think it's OK to tell a little "white" lie if it's for a "good reason?" Is it all right to copy from your friend's paper so that you'll have more time to study Bible verses? The Bible never teaches that it's right to do something wrong in the hope that good will result from it. □
S.K.

TO MEMORIZE: *If anyone competes as an athlete, he does not receive the victor's crown unless he competes according to the rules.* 2 Timothy 2:5, NIV

Baloney Sandwiches

(Continued from yesterday)

FROM THE BIBLE:
Samuel said [to Saul], "When you were little in your own eyes, were you not head of the tribes of Israel? And did not the Lord anoint you king over Israel? Now the Lord sent you on a mission, and said, 'Go, and utterly destroy the sinners, the Amalekites, and fight against them until they are consumed.' Why then did you not obey the voice of the Lord? Why did you swoop down on the spoil, and do evil in the sight of the Lord?" And Saul said to Samuel, "But I have obeyed the voice of the Lord, and gone on the mission on which the Lord sent me, and brought back Agag king of Amalek; I have utterly destroyed the Amalekites. But the people took of the plunder, sheep and oxen, the best of the things which should have been utterly destroyed, to sacrifice to the Lord your God in Gilgal." Then Samuel said: "Has the Lord as great delight in burnt offerings and sacrifices, as in obeying the voice of the Lord? Behold, to obey is better than sacrifice, and to heed than the fat of rams."
1 Samuel 15:16-22, NKJV

Sin is never right

10

A T-Shirt Christian

FROM THE BIBLE:

Out of the same mouth come praise and cursing. My brothers, this should not be. Can both fresh water and salt water flow from the same spring? My brothers, can a fig tree bear olives, or a grapevine bear figs? Neither can a salt spring produce fresh water. Who is wise and understanding among you? Let him show it by his good life, by deeds done in the humility that comes from wisdom. But if you harbor bitter envy and selfish ambition in your hearts, do not boast about it or deny the truth. Such "wisdom" does not come down from heaven but is earthly, unspiritual, of the devil. For where you have envy and selfish ambition, there you find disorder and every evil practice. But the wisdom that comes from heaven is first of all pure; then peace-loving, considerate, submissive, full of mercy and good fruit, impartial and sincere. Peacemakers who sow in peace raise a harvest of righteousness.

James 3:10-18, NIV

Witness with actions

IT'S NOT MY turn anyway. Make Cindi do it!" Brad yelled over his shoulder as he slammed the door behind him.

"Hi, Brad. You mad about something?" a voice called.

Brad looked up to see Nathan, his new neighbor, leaning against the gate, grinning. "I sure am!" exclaimed Brad. "You would be, too, if your mother was always on your back."

"Oh, she is," Nathan replied, "but I just let it go in one ear and out the other. Say, that's a neat T-shirt you're wearing. But isn't 'I am a King's Kid' a little misleading? Your dad's a plumber."

"That's talking about God," Brad scowled. "I'm a child of God."

Nathan shrugged, "Well, if you say so."

Brad picked up his bat and glove. "I'm going to the park to play ball with the gang. You want to go?"

All the way to the park Nathan bragged about what a good pitcher he was. When the boys chose teams, Brad chose Nathan. "Let me pitch, Brad. We'll wipe 'em out," Nathan whispered.

After Nathan had walked the first three batters, Brad began to have doubts about Nathan's pitching ability. By the end of the second inning, Brad's team was behind six to one and Brad was angry. He told Nathan what he thought about his pitching and replaced him with Clint.

That evening, he told his parents about Nathan. "He's just a bunch of talk. He couldn't hit the side of the barn, and he wouldn't know a good pitcher if he saw one."

Mother raised her eyebrows. "I heard you talking to Nathan this afternoon, Brad."

Brad shrugged, "So?"

"So, Nathan claimed to be a pitcher, but you think he's a poor one. You claim to be a Christian, but I wonder just what kind of Christian Nathan thinks you are—especially after your little exhibition this afternoon. You said Nathan wouldn't recognize a good pitcher if he saw one. I just wonder if he would recognize a good Christian."

HOW ABOUT YOU? Do your works match your words? While you claim to be a Christian, do your actions deny it? Being a Christian is more than T-shirt advertising. □ B.W.

TO MEMORIZE: *Who is wise and understanding among you? Let him show it by his good life, by deeds done in the humility that comes from wisdom.* James 3:13, NIV

SHARI WATCHED as Jamie took a cigarette out of the pack in his hand. He placed it on the picnic table along with a match. Other kids in the neighborhood had tried smoking that afternoon, but Shari had refused to join them. "You're just scared to try it," Jamie teased.

"I'm not scared," she retorted unconvincingly. "I just think it's dumb to smoke, that's all."

But her answer didn't satisfy Jamie. "I'll leave one right here," he said. "Maybe you'll want to try it when nobody's looking."

Shari watched Jamie go into his house next door, and then she looked again at the cigarette on the table. If she could just show him a partly smoked cigarette, maybe he'd quit bugging her about it. She picked it up and rolled it around in her fingers. Suddenly there was a strong urge to take just one small puff. Just then her mother came out of the back door. "Shari, what are you doing out here?"

"Nothing," Shari replied, slipping the cigarette and match into her pocket. Quickly she skipped back to the house and walked briskly into the bathroom. Nervously she pulled the cigarette out of her pocket, lit it, and took a short puff. Ugh! It was awful! Just as quickly, she put it out. Then she heard the back door open and close.

"Shari?" It was her mother's voice. "Are you smoking?"

Mother was waiting, a hurt look in her eyes. Suddenly Shari broke into tears. She explained how Jamie had tempted her and teased her until she gave in.

Shari's mother shook her head. "No, Honey, Jamie's teasing isn't why you gave in. You gave in because you didn't run from temptation. You looked at the cigarette, maybe even took it in your fingers to see how it would feel, and finally gave in and smoked it. If you had turned and left it, the temptation would not have overtaken you. Temptations will come. When they do, run away from them."

HOW ABOUT YOU? Do your friends sometimes coax you to go along to see a dirty movie? Smoke? Look at indecent pictures? When you are tempted by these or other sins, don't stand around and think about them. Turn and run. Ask Jesus to help you. He will. □ R.J.

TO MEMORIZE: *Flee also youthful lusts; but pursue righteousness, faith, love, peace with those who call on the Lord out of a pure heart.* 2 Timothy 2:22, NKJV

Turn and Run

FROM THE BIBLE:
Oh, the joys of those who do not follow evil men's advice, who do not hang around with sinners, scoffing at the things of God: But they delight in doing everything God wants them to, and day and night are always meditating on his laws and thinking about ways to follow him more closely. They are like trees along a river bank bearing luscious fruit each season without fail. Their leaves shall never wither, and all they do shall prosper. But for sinners, what a different story! They blow away like chaff before the wind. They are not safe on Judgment Day; they shall not stand among the godly. For the Lord watches over all the plans and paths of godly men, but the paths of the godless lead to doom.
Psalm 1:1-6, TLB

Run when tempted

12

The Guiding Hand

FROM THE BIBLE:

In You, O Lord, I put my trust; let me never be ashamed; deliver me in Your righteousness. Bow down Your ear to me, deliver me speedily; be my rock of refuge, a fortress of defense to save me. For You are my rock and my fortress; therefore, for Your name's sake, lead me and guide me. Pull me out of the net which they have secretly laid for me, for You are my strength. Into Your hand I commit my spirit; You have redeemed me, O Lord God of truth.
Psalm 31:1-5, NKJV

Let God guide you

NINE-YEAR-OLD Tim watched as his father guided the aluminum fishing boat across the lake. The wind was strong, and the waves were high! Dad had to fight to keep the small boat on course, and Tim was intrigued by it all.

"This is fun," he cried out. "Can I steer for a while?"

"The lake is pretty rough," Dad said, raising his voice to be heard above the motor sound. "I'm afraid you can't handle it alone."

"You can help me," Tim insisted. He still wanted to guide the boat across the lake to the spot where he and his father were to spend the day fishing. "When you see I'm not doing it right, you can help me."

Carefully Tim and his dad changed places in the boat, and Tim began to guide it across the rough waters. "This is easy!" he called out. Suddenly a big wave stood before them, and Tim turned the boat with a jerk. The boat began to zigzag back and forth until Dad came to the rescue. Placing his hand over Tim's, he guided the fishing craft until things were once again under control.

"Boy," Tim said with relief in his voice, "I guess it's a good thing you were there to take over."

His father smiled and nodded. "This is a good example of our Christian life, Son. We sometimes think we can handle the problems of the world by ourselves, and God lets us try. Then just about the time things seem to be completely out of hand, God puts His hand over ours and guides us through the situation."

HOW ABOUT YOU? When things seem to be going well, do you forget that you need God? Do you think you can handle that math test alone? That you don't need help with your paper route? When you try to get along without God's help, sooner or later you'll run into trouble. God wants to help you. Let Him. □ R.J.

TO MEMORIZE: *You are my rock and my fortress; therefore, for Your name's sake, lead me and guide me.* Psalm 31:3, NKJV

JERRY STOPPED WORKING and wiped sweat from his face. Grandpa stopped, too. "Gardening is hard work," said Grandpa. "Maybe we should take a break."

Jerry dropped his hoe. "That sounds good to me."

They walked around the garden. A single row of peas was sprouting where Grandpa had planted them two weeks earlier. Otherwise, the garden was still full of weeds. "It takes work to plant a garden," said Grandpa, "but weeds grow easily, don't they?"

"Yeah," said Jerry. "Why did God make weeds, anyway?"

"Well, they're the result of sin," said Grandpa. "Since they're here, we might as well learn a lesson from them. Just as farmers need to destroy weeds to keep them from spoiling their crops, we have to tend to the sinful things in our lives, so they don't take over."

"What do you mean?" asked Jerry. "I don't get it."

Grandpa stooped to pull a tall weed. "I get angry sometimes when things don't go the way I'd like them to," he said. "In a way, my temper is like this weed. It has tough roots and grows fast. It could take over my life and cause me to spend a lot of time being angry at people."

"Oh, I see," said Jerry. He thought for a minute. "Sometimes I'm not very nice to Jenny," he confessed. "That's like a weed, too, isn't it?" Grandpa nodded. "So what can I do about it?" asked Jerry.

"First confess it to God," advised Grandpa. "Ask Him to forgive you and help you to be the kind of brother He wants you to be." Grandpa sat down on a bench near the garden. "You may need to ask Jenny to forgive you, too."

Jerry sat down next to him. "That's hard," he said slowly. "Almost harder than asking God to forgive me." He sighed. "But I know you're right. If I really mean it when I tell God I'm sorry and ask for His help, He'll help me apologize, too."

HOW ABOUT YOU? Is there a "weed" that you need to remove from your life? Do you have a bad temper? A habit of disobeying? Whatever it is, seek God's forgiveness first. Then show your sincerity by also asking forgiveness of anyone you've hurt. □ G.L.J.

TO MEMORIZE: *Do not let sin reign in your mortal body so that you obey its evil desires.* Romans 6:12, NIV

JUNE

13

Taking Root

FROM THE BIBLE:
What shall we say, then? Shall we go on sinning so that grace may increase? By no means! We died to sin; how can we live in it any longer? . . . In the same way, count yourselves dead to sin but alive to God in Christ Jesus. Therefore do not let sin reign in your mortal body so that you obey its evil desires. Do not offer the parts of your body to sin, as instruments of wickedness, but rather offer yourselves to God, as those who have been brought from death to life; and offer the parts of your body to him as instruments of righteousness. For sin shall not be your master, because you are not under law, but under grace. Romans 6:1-2, 11-14, NIV

Confess sin

175

14

Just One Sting

FROM THE BIBLE:

When the perishable has been clothed with the imperishable, and the mortal with immortality, then the saying that is written will come true: "Death has been swallowed up in victory."
"Where, O death, is your victory? Where, O death, is your sting?" The sting of death is sin, and the power of sin is the law. But thanks be to God! He gives us the victory through our Lord Jesus Christ.

1 Corinthians 15:54-57, NIV

Jesus took your punishment

GET AWAY! Get away!" Joanie swung her arms wildly as a bee buzzed round and round her head. "Mother!" she screamed. "He's going to get me!" She dashed toward her mother who was working in the flower garden. Mother held out her arms, and Joanie rushed into them and hid her face in Mother's skirt. The angry bee followed.

Mother stood still, waiting for the bee to leave, but the excited insect seemed determined to find a victim. As Mother brushed the bee away from Joanie, it landed on her own bare arm. "Ow!" Mother exclaimed with a gasp. Then she said quietly, "Look, Honey. You don't need to be afraid of this bee anymore. It has stung me." Fearfully, Joanie lifted her head and looked at her mother's arm. She drew back as she saw the bee still crawling there. "It can't hurt you now," Mother assured her. "It has only one sting."

"Oh, Mother! Does it hurt awfully?" Joanie asked as the bee tumbled to the ground. "You took the sting for me!"

"I'm glad I was there to do it," said Mother.

As Mother treated the sting, Joanie spoke shyly. "Last Sunday, my teacher said that Jesus took the punishment for our sins," she said. "I didn't quite understand it then, but now I do. Just like you're suffering for me, He did, too—only more. I'd like to ask Him to save me now."

The bee sting was forgotten while Joanie and Mother knelt together beside the couch.

HOW ABOUT YOU? Do you understand that Jesus took the punishment you deserve? Because He died for you, you no longer need to fear death. When you accept Him as your Savior, He removes the "sting." If you've never acknowledged what He did for you and asked Him to save you, won't you do that right now? □ H.M.

TO MEMORIZE: *Thanks be to God! He gives us the victory through our Lord Jesus Christ.* 1 Corinthians 15:57, NIV

"DADDY," CALLED KAREN as her father worked in the garden, "Mom wants eight ears of corn for supper." She watched eagerly as her father laid his hoe aside and began checking the ears of corn. She could almost taste the corn dripping with butter, and she could hardly wait.

"When I was a boy," said Dad as he picked off an ear, "we used to have large fields of sweet corn."

In her mind, Karen pictured row after row of corn rustling in a summer breeze. "I bet you had corn on the cob at every meal!" she exclaimed.

Dad smiled. "You can do a lot more with corn than just eat it," he said. "The cobs can be turned into charcoal; the leaves and husks are used for toys; the entire plant is used to feed hogs and cattle. Every part of the corn plant can be used!"

As she and her father walked to the house with the corn, Karen said, "Daddy, I asked Jimmy Eldon to church."

"Good! What did he say?" asked Dad.

Karen sighed. "He laughed and said he didn't want any part of 'corny Christians.' I was kind of hurt."

"Remember what I just told you about corn?" asked Dad.

"You said you can use all of it," Karen replied.

Dad had another question. "When you gave your life to Jesus, how much of yourself did you give Him?"

"All!" declared Karen.

Dad nodded. "And every part of you—your heart, hands, lips, feet, and mind—can be used to serve God."

Karen grinned. "So I guess when Jimmy called me a 'corny Christian,' he gave me a compliment and didn't even know it!"

HOW ABOUT YOU? Are you giving your "all" to God or are you holding back because someone might tease you? Don't be afraid to speak up for Jesus. Ask for God's guidance and help. Then rejoice in the bountiful harvest of blessings that will surely result when you make a total commitment to the Lord! □ M.S.

TO MEMORIZE: *"You shall love the Lord your God with all your heart, with all your soul, with all your strength, and with all your mind," and "your neighbor as yourself."* Luke 10:27, NKJV

15

A "Corny" Christian

FROM THE BIBLE:
A certain lawyer stood up and tested Him, saying, "Teacher, what shall I do to inherit eternal life?" He said to him, "What is written in the law? What is your reading of it?" So he answered and said, " 'You shall love the Lord your God with all your heart, with all your soul, with all your strength, and with all your mind,' and 'your neighbor as yourself.' " And He said to him, "You have answered rightly; do this and you will live."
Luke 10:25-28, NKJV

Give God your all

16

Beneath the Problem

FROM THE BIBLE:

Don't worry about anything; instead, pray about everything; tell God your needs and don't forget to thank him for his answers. If you do this you will experience God's peace, which is far more wonderful than the human mind can understand. His peace will keep your thoughts and your hearts quiet and at rest as you trust in Christ Jesus. And now, brothers, as I close this letter let me say this one more thing: Fix your thoughts on what is true and good and right. Think about things that are pure and lovely, and dwell on the fine, good things in others. Think about all you can praise God for and be glad about. Keep putting into practice all you learned from me and saw me doing, and the God of peace will be with you.
Philippians 4:6-9, TLB

Look for God's workings

THE LONG MONTHS in casts had finally come to an end, but Jenni's legs were still very weak. She was anxious to get started with physical therapy to strengthen them again, so she greeted Jan, her therapist, with a grin. Jan smiled back as she held out a swimsuit. "Get into this," she instructed. "Your first session will be in the pool."

"Oh, no!" Jenni cried. "I'm scared of water. And with my legs so weak, I just know my face will go under! Couldn't we do it some other way?"

But all her coaxing and pleading was useless, for working with the legs under water was the prescribed treatment. Into the pool Jenni went, but she craned her neck and kept pulling herself up high on the edge of the pool. Finally Jan spoke firmly. "Jenni, your muscles are all very tense. The therapy will be useless unless you relax. Try not to worry about the water. Look down, through the water, at your legs. Think about the good that is being accomplished in the water." Nodding fearfully, Jenni tried it. She watched Jan exercise her legs under the water. To her surprise, the therapy was much easier after that.

On the way home, Jenni told her mother how Jan's idea had calmed her. Mom smiled. "Jenni, this reminds me of the way I felt seven months ago when that drunk driver hit you," she said. "All I could think about at first was anger toward him. Then I realized that the Bible says God will keep us in perfect peace if we keep our minds on Him. When I quit looking *at* the problem and looked *through* the problem to God, I found peace. Now I pray for the driver, and I thank God for how well you're doing."

Jenni grinned. "I guess it's all according to what your mind is set on," she said.

HOW ABOUT YOU? Are there problems in your life that seem to be more than you can handle? Perhaps trouble at school, divorce in your family, illness, or even death? Look through the problem and try to see God working all things out for good. God promises peace if we keep our minds on Him. □ R.P.

TO MEMORIZE: *You will keep in perfect peace him whose mind is steadfast, because he trusts in you.* Isaiah 26:3, NIV

L ET'S GO FOR a hike," Mandy suggested after the big meal at the family reunion. "Let's take one of those nature trails." Soon several of the children found their way to the trail where a large map was posted beside the path. Though some glanced at it, no one stopped to study it.

After walking a while, they came to a place where the trail divided. "Let's take the path to the left," said Mandy. "It doesn't look as steep as the other one."

"Sissy! I'm going to take the trail that goes up the mountain and around the lake," declared George.

The girls hesitated. "How long is it?" asked Carolyn.

"And where does it end?" asked Mandy.

Len shrugged. "I'd guess it circles back to the road. C'mon. Let's go." He led the way.

It was fun at first, but after nearly an hour, many were getting tired. "How much farther?" asked Joyce.

"How should we know?" George snapped.

"Didn't you read the map?"

"Sorta," he replied. "Didn't you?"

Joyce shook her head. "I thought you guys did."

"We only glanced at it," Len told her. "But this trail is bound to lead back to the road—sooner or later."

Mandy stood still. "Well, I'm exhausted," she said. "I'm going back the way we came." The others agreed.

Although there was some grumbling, soon everyone was heading back down the trail. When they came to the map much later, they stopped to look at it. Len laughed. "I can just hear what Granny Williams will say when she hears about this."

Mandy shook her finger at the group. "You're just like all those people who try to get through life without reading the Bible," she said in her best "Granny voice."

"And don't depend on someone else to lead you," Joyce added in quavering tones. "Read the map for yourself."

HOW ABOUT YOU? Are you studying God's "map"— the Bible—or are you depending on someone else to tell you what God says? Good teachers who love the Lord can be a great help, but you need to read the Bible for yourself, too. □ B.W.

TO MEMORIZE: *Show me your ways, O Lord, teach me your paths.* Psalm 25:4, NIV

The Hike

FROM THE BIBLE:

Just tell me what to do and I will do it, Lord. As long as I live I'll wholeheartedly obey. Make me walk along the right paths for I know how delightful they really are. Help me to prefer obedience to making money! Turn me away from wanting any other plan than yours. Revive my heart toward you. Reassure me that your promises are for me, for I trust and revere you. How I dread being mocked for obeying, for your laws are right and good. I long to obey them! Therefore in fairness renew my life, for this was your promise—yes, Lord, to save me! Now spare me by your kindness and your love. Then I will have an answer for those who taunt me, for I trust your promises. Psalm 119:33-40, TLB

Read your Bible

18

Surprise Party

FROM THE BIBLE:

Dear friends, let us practice loving each other, for love comes from God and those who are loving and kind show that they are the children of God, and that they are getting to know him better. But if a person isn't loving and kind, it shows that he doesn't know God—for God is love. God showed how much he loved us by sending his only Son into this wicked world to bring to us eternal life through his death. In this act we see what real love is: it is not our love for God, but his love for us when he sent his Son to satisfy God's anger against our sins. Dear friends, since God loved us as much as that, we surely ought to love each other too. For though we have never yet seen God, when we love each other God lives in us and his love within us grows ever stronger.
1 John 4:7-12, TLB

Show love with actions

WHAT'S BETH'S PROBLEM?" asked Brian as his sister left the room. "She was acting awful gloomy."

"This is the day her friends leave for summer camp," sighed Mother. "Beth was fortunate to get a job, and she can't afford to quit—but she loves camp so much!"

"We ought to do something special for her so she won't be so mopey." Brian wrinkled his brow. Then he snapped his fingers. "Let's have a party— a surprise family party."

"A 'You're Special to Us' party?" asked Mother. "All right. I'll fix her favorite dinner, and you can decorate the dining room."

"What about presents?" asked Brian.

Mother thought for a minute. "Why don't we make 'love coupons?' I'll make one with a promise to make her bed and clean up her room every day this week. Then she can sleep later. You could wash the dishes when it's her turn," suggested Mother.

Brian groaned. "Let's not get carried away. We do want to make her feel better, but there's a limit!"

Mother laughed and gave him a quick hug. "This is a lovely idea, Son. God says we should show love to one another, and you're doing that today."

When Beth came in from work, she stood in the doorway and stared. On the dining room wall was a big banner—"We love you, Beth." The table was set with the best china, and there were streamers and balloons everywhere.

After dinner, Beth looked around at her family. "I love all of you," she said. Looking at the dirty dishes, she winked at Brian. "Especially you, little brother. I hope you don't get dishpan hands this week!"

HOW ABOUT YOU? Does someone in your family need a "pick-me-up"? As you remember all that God did to show His great love for you, will you, in turn, go out of your way to show love to that downhearted person? Maybe you can plan a party, do more than your share of the chores, or help in some special way. You'll be surprised to find how much it will lift everyone's spirits. □ B.W.

TO MEMORIZE: *Dear friends, since God loved us as much as that, we surely ought to love each other too.* 1 John 4:11, TLB

JAMES LOOKED DOWN at the biggest turtle he had ever seen. His family had moved to a new home way out in the country, and now here was a huge turtle, right in their very own backyard!

James bent down and tried to get the turtle to eat some food he had brought for it. But instead of eating, the turtle turned slowly and headed for the woods. Both James and his father tried to stand in the way so the turtle wouldn't leave, but the big turtle only went in another direction, away from the food. "Why won't he take it?" James asked.

"He must have thought we would hurt him," Dad replied. "I guess he just misunderstood our actions."

"Well, that's dumb," James retorted.

A smile began to appear on Dad's face. "You know what this reminds me of?" he asked, putting his hand on James' shoulder. "Christians."

"Christians?" James retorted. "How?"

"Well, sometimes when God is trying to help us by leading us in a certain direction, we misunderstand and insist on following the path we've laid out for ourselves," explained Dad. "Other times, we grumble about the circumstances He allows in our lives."

James had to agree that he didn't always understand how God led people. He thought of the time Aunt Jennifer got sick. When he asked her why God would treat a good missionary that way, she told him that God was teaching her some lessons she might not have learned if she had not been bedridden. "When you're flat on your back," she had said, "there's only one direction to look. And that's up. God knew I had been so busy working for Him that I needed some time just to listen to Him."

James watched as the turtle disappeared into the wooded area near the swamp. "Come again," he called, "and thanks for the lesson."

HOW ABOUT YOU? When things don't go the way you want them to, do you get angry or irritable? Do you question God's judgment? Maybe He's trying to teach you a lesson you haven't been willing to learn before. Listen when God uses your parents, your teachers, or even some trying experience to get you to obey His will for your life. □ R.J.

TO MEMORIZE: *As the heavens are higher than the earth, so are my ways higher than your ways and my thoughts than your thoughts.* Isaiah 55:9, NIV

Taught by a Turtle

FROM THE BIBLE:
I will say this: because these experiences I had were so tremendous, God was afraid I might be puffed up by them; so I was given a physical condition which has been a thorn in my flesh, a messenger from Satan to hurt and bother me, and prick my pride. Three different times I begged God to make me well again. Each time he said, "No. But I am with you; that is all you need. My power shows up best in weak people." Now I am glad to boast about how weak I am; I am glad to be a living demonstration of Christ's power, instead of showing off my own power and abilities. Since I know it is all for Christ's good, I am quite happy about "the thorn," and about insults and hardships, persecutions and difficulties; for when I am weak, then I am strong—the less I have, the more I depend on him.
2 Corinthians 12:7-10, TLB

Learn God's lessons

20

A Miserable Week

FROM THE BIBLE:

The whole Israelite community set out from Elim and came to the Desert of Sin, which is between Elim and Sinai, on the fifteenth day of the second month after they had come out of Egypt. In the desert the whole community grumbled against Moses and Aaron. The Israelites said to them, "If only we had died by the Lord's hand in Egypt! There we sat around pots of meat and ate all the food we wanted, but you have brought us out into this desert to starve this entire assembly to death." Then the Lord said to Moses, "I will rain down bread from heaven for you. The people are to go out each day and gather enough for that day. In this way I will test them and see whether they will follow my instructions. On the sixth day they are to prepare what they bring in, and that is to be twice as much as they gather on the other days." So Moses and Aaron said to all the Israelites, "In the evening you will know that it was the Lord who brought you out of Egypt."

Exodus 16:1-6, NIV

Be friendly to others

THE SIGN READ "Camp Joy—Christ-centered fun for girls and boys."

"Wow," Nicholas said to himself as he scuffed into the dining hall, "if this is fun, I'd hate to see something that isn't fun!"

Nicholas didn't like camp. He didn't like the kids in his cabin, and he didn't like the food. He usually ate, though, because he wouldn't have to talk to anyone if his mouth was full of food. During rest time, he stretched out on his bunk and ignored the talking that went on around him.

Mr. Dave, his counselor, stopped him as he walked reluctantly toward the softball field one afternoon. "Nicholas, you don't look as if you're having much fun."

"I'm not," grumbled Nicholas. "I don't like this camp. None of the kids are friendly to me."

"Oh, I see," murmured Mr. Dave. "Have you been friendly to them?"

"Well, . . ."

"The Bible tells us that if we show friendliness to others, they will be friendly to us," encouraged Mr. Dave. "We have to make that effort, though. Go over there and get excited about that ball game. Talk to the other kids. You might be surprised at how much fun you can have."

Nicholas didn't really believe his counselor, but he supposed he could give it a try. He ran over to the backstop where the camp director was assigning teams. He laughed at a joke told by one of the campers, and then surprised himself by telling a joke of his own. When he was up to bat or catching a ball in right field, he did his very best. Suddenly he realized that what his counselor said was right—he *was* having fun!

HOW ABOUT YOU? When you're in a new situation, do you wait for others to be friendly to you, or do you make an effort to talk to those around you? Do you pout and complain that you aren't having fun, or do you enter into the activities and do your best to be an asset to your team? Over and over in the Bible, we read that we are to love others, be friendly, and get along with those around us. □ L.W.

TO MEMORIZE: *A man of many companions may come to ruin, but there is a friend who sticks closer than a brother.* Proverbs 18:24, NIV

RANDY BOUNCED ALONGSIDE of Grandpa in the pickup truck. They stopped at the vineyard, and Grandpa got out the long-handled clippers. "I'm going to do some pruning," he said as he began to clip.

"Are those *prune* vines?" asked Randy.

"Oh, no," chuckled Grandpa. "These are grapevines. Prunes are dried plums, and plums grow on trees. But the grapevines need pruning. That just means I take out some of the vines."

"How do you know which branches to cut off?" Randy asked.

"The ones that are attached to the main vine are the branches that I leave," answered Grandpa. "They're the strongest and will grow nice, fat grapes. The branches that only grow from other branches, not right from the main vine, won't grow good grapes, so I cut those off." Grandpa showed Randy how he followed a branch to its beginning to see whether or not it was attached to the main vine. "Whenever I prune the grapevines, I'm reminded of what Jesus said about them," said Grandpa.

"Jesus talked about grapevines?" Randy asked.

"Sure," nodded Grandpa. "Jesus compared Himself to the main vine of a grapevine, and He said people are like the branches. Some are the true branches attached to the vine and will be fruitful, and others are just secondary branches to be cut off."

"Which people are the true branches?" asked Randy.

"Those who trust in Jesus as the way to heaven," answered Grandpa. "The other branches are those who try to get there on their own."

"I've asked Jesus to forgive my sins, and I love Him. So I'm a true branch, right?" Randy asked.

"Right you are," said Grandpa while he cut another branch.

HOW ABOUT YOU? Are you attached to Jesus, the Vine? Or are you attached to your church membership, your baptism, or your good works? There is only one way to get to heaven, and that is to trust Jesus to forgive your sins. If you do that, you'll be like a fruitful branch attached to the vine. If you've never asked Jesus to be your Savior, do it now. Don't be cast away like an unfruitful branch. □ C.Y.

TO MEMORIZE: *If anyone does not remain in me, he is like a branch that is thrown away and withers; such branches are picked up, thrown into the fire and burned.* John 15:6, NIV

Fruitful Branches

FROM THE BIBLE:
I am the true vine, and my Father is the gardener. He cuts off every branch in me that bears no fruit, while every branch that does bear fruit he prunes so that it will be even more fruitful. You are already clean because of the word I have spoken to you. Remain in me, and I will remain in you. No branch can bear fruit by itself; it must remain in the vine. Neither can you bear fruit unless you remain in me. I am the vine; you are the branches. If a man remains in me and I in him, he will bear much fruit; apart from me you can do nothing. If anyone does not remain in me, he is like a branch that is thrown away and withers; such branches are picked up, thrown into the fire and burned. If you remain in me and my words remain in you, ask whatever you wish, and it will be given you. This is to my Father's glory, that you bear much fruit, showing yourselves to be my disciples.
John 15:1-8, NIV

Be attached to Jesus

JUNE

22

Protected

FROM THE BIBLE:

*My sheep hear My voice, and I
know them, and they follow Me.
And I give them eternal life,
and they shall never perish;
neither shall anyone snatch
them out of My hand. My
Father, who has given them to
Me, is greater than all; and no
one is able to snatch them out of
My Father's hand. I and My
Father are one.*
John 10:27-30, NKJV

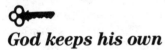

God keeps his own

CINDY AND her Aunt Joy strolled through the
field. It was a balmy summer day, and everything
seemed fresh and new after the rain of the evening
before. "Oh, smell the air!" said Cindy.

Aunt Joy took several deep breaths, "God is
good to let us live in such a beautiful world," she
commented.

Then Cindy spotted a brightly colored flower.
She sprinted forward and with a cry of delight
bent down to pick it. "No!" shouted Aunt Joy.
"Don't pick it!"

Cindy straightened up and with a puzzled look
asked, "Why not?"

"It's a protected flower," answered Aunt Joy.
"It's so rare that there's a state law that forbids
picking it."

"Oh, I didn't know." said Cindy. She knelt down
to examine it.

"I guess you could say we're like protected flowers to God," mused Aunt Joy as they walked on
again.

Cindy giggled. "What do you mean by that?"

"Well," replied Aunt Joy, "that protected flower
made me think of something Jesus said—'no man
is able to pluck them out of my hand.' "

"What does 'pluck them out' mean?" asked
Cindy.

"It means that when you belong to Jesus, He
won't let anyone pick, or 'pluck,' you away from
Him. You're like a protected flower that no one is
allowed to pick."

Cindy skipped along through the sweet-smelling
grass. "That makes me feel safe," she said.

"We are safe," answered Aunt Joy. "Much safer
than the flowers, in fact. It would be possible for
us to pick them in spite of the law that forbids it.
But when Jesus promises to protect us, He'll
do it."

HOW ABOUT YOU? When you've been mean to someone, told a lie, cheated in school, or sinned some
other way, do you wonder if Jesus still loves you?
Do you wonder if you're still saved? If you have
received Jesus as your Savior from sin, He promised never to leave you. When you sin, you must
confess it and give it up before you can have real
fellowship with Jesus. But you're still under Jesus'
protection. No one can ever take that away from
you. □ C.Y.

TO MEMORIZE: *I give them eternal life, and they
shall never perish; neither shall anyone snatch them
out of My hand.* John 10:28, NKJV

IT HAD BEEN a busy day for Jeremy, who was on a week's camping trip with his Uncle Bob and cousin Eric. As the sun went down, two tired boys stretched out beside the campfire. "That was the best fish I ever ate," declared Jeremy.

Uncle Bob nodded in agreement. "Now let's have some spiritual food before we turn in for the night," he said. "I hope you boys remembered your Bibles."

Eric nodded, but Jeremy shook his head. "I always think the Bible is something for weak people who can't think for themselves," he said. "I don't need it."

Uncle Bob raised his eyebrows questioningly. "The Word of God is a very important part of my life, Jeremy," he said. "Listen to what God says about it—He calls it a light." Taking the Bible Eric handed him, Uncle Bob turned to Psalm 119. The boys listened quietly as he read several verses and then led in prayer.

As the boys were unrolling their sleeping bags a bit later, Jeremy groaned. "The mosquitoes are terrible! Where's the insect repellent?"

"It's in the glove compartment of the car," said Uncle Bob. He picked up the flashlight. "I'll get it."

"Let's go with him, Jeremy," suggested Eric. "Maybe we'll see a bear!"

As they headed into the darkness, Jeremy stumbled over a log, and down he went. As he got to his feet, he saw Uncle Bob bump into an overhanging branch. "Why don't you turn on the flashlight, Uncle Bob?" he asked. "I can't see where I'm going."

"Flashlights are OK for weak people who can't see in the dark," Uncle Bob replied carelessly, "but I don't think I need it."

Jeremy chuckled. "OK, Uncle Bob, I get the point—we need light in the dark, and we need the Bible to give us light in our lives. Now, would you please turn on that flashlight?"

HOW ABOUT YOU? It's foolish to stumble along and not use the light that's available, isn't it? Only the light of God's Word will keep you from stumbling into sin. Are you using it? □ B.W.

TO MEMORIZE: *For the commandment is a lamp, and the law is light; reproofs of instruction are the way of life.* Proverbs 6:23, NKJV

Unused Light

FROM THE BIBLE:

Oh, how I love them. I think about them all day long. They make me wiser than my enemies, because they are my constant guide. Yes, wiser than my teachers, for I am ever thinking of your rules. They make me even wiser than the aged. I have refused to walk the paths of evil for I will remain obedient to your Word. No, I haven't turned away from what you taught me; your words are sweeter than honey. And since only your rules can give me wisdom and understanding, no wonder I hate every false teaching. Your words are a flashlight to light the path ahead of me, and keep me from stumbling.
Psalm 119:97-105, TLB

Read your Bible

24

Neglected Letter

FROM THE BIBLE:

*Teach me, O Lord, to follow
your decrees; then I will keep
them to the end. Give me
understanding, and I will keep
your law and obey it with all my
heart. Direct me in the path of
your commands, for there I find
delight. Turn my heart toward
your statutes and not toward
selfish gain. Turn my eyes away
from worthless things; preserve
my life according to your word.
Fulfill your promise to your
servant, so that you may be
feared. Take away the disgrace I
dread, for your laws are good.
How I long for your precepts!
Preserve my life in your righteousness.*

Psalm 119:33-40, NIV

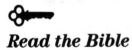

Read the Bible

J IM MATTHEW picked up his baseball mitt and ran outside. At the same moment, the mail carrier arrived and started up the porch steps. "Hey, slow down there, young fellow," he said, "and I'll give you a letter from your friend in Clarksville."

"Just leave it in the box with the rest of the mail," Jim called out and went quickly on his way. The mailman scratched his head in surprise. Not too many weeks ago Jim had stopped him every day asking if there was a letter from Clarksville. Now he hardly seemed to care at all.

Jim's mom and dad had noticed the change in him, too. All of a sudden he seemed to have found new friends and had almost no interest in his old ones. His parents were also concerned because he seemed so restless and impatient when they had family devotions. He was just in a hurry to be finished and get back to his friends.

When they gathered for devotions that evening, the letter from Clarksville still lay unopened on the coffee table. Dad placed the Bible beside it. "You've been neglecting your letters lately, haven't you?" he observed.

"Letters?" asked Jim. "Oh, you mean the one that came today. I'll read it pretty soon."

"I mean that one," said Dad, picking it up, "and this one, too." He also picked up the Bible. "You used to like to discuss things you read in the Bible, but lately, your new friends seem to take all your time and attention. Letters from old friends—even God's letter to you—have had to take second place, or maybe even third or fourth place."

Jim thought about that. Yes, not only had he shoved aside his friends' letters, reading them only if it was convenient, but he had done the same with God's letter—the Bible. Silently he bowed his head and asked God to give him a new love for the Word of God and for the Lord Jesus Christ. "Thanks, Lord," he prayed, "for being such a good Friend." As he finished his prayer, Jim thought about his friend in Clarksville. He would read that letter right away and answer it soon.

HOW ABOUT YOU? If you wrote a letter to someone, you would want him to read it, wouldn't you? God does, too. Is reading His letter, the Bible, a regular part of your day's schedule? □ R.J.

TO MEMORIZE: *I delight in your decrees; I will not neglect your word.* Psalm 119:16, NIV

DON WALKED INTO the house and headed straight for the telephone. Some of the guys on the baseball team had told him what Jeremy Carlson was saying about him. They had encouraged Don to call Jeremy on the phone and give him a piece of his mind. "That's the only way you'll get him to stop telling stuff like that. Let him have it," they said. Don couldn't agree with them more.

But one thing bothered him. He was a Christian, and Jeremy was not. On several occasions, he had talked with Jeremy about the Lord. A couple of times Jeremy had seemed to be ready to come along to Sunday school, but then he had walked away, ignoring everything Don tried to tell him. Well, he wasn't going to walk away this time!

As Don picked up the phone, a Bible verse came to his mind. "Father, forgive them for they know not what they do." That's how Jesus had reacted when people treated Him wrong. But Don wasn't Jesus, and he couldn't take it anymore! He dialed the number, but no one answered.

As Don slammed down the phone, his sister Julie walked toward him. "You look angry," she said.

"I am angry," Don responded bitterly. "I'm sick and tired of this guy talking about me, and I'm going to give him a piece of my mind!"

"You mean like a tornado tongue?" Julie asked. "The damage is done in a matter of seconds, but it usually takes years to rebuild the damaged area."

Don thought about his sister's words. If he talked to Jeremy the way he planned, he knew it probably would do all kinds of damage that would take years to correct. The more he thought about it, the more he knew he could not be guilty of a "tornado tongue." He would still talk to Jeremy and ask him not to tell untrue stories about him, but he would ask the Lord to help him do it in a way that would show Jeremy that Christians truly are different.

HOW ABOUT YOU? When someone makes you angry, do you give him or her "a piece of your mind" before thinking about the damage you might be doing? Like a tornado, your tongue can do a lot of damage in a few seconds, but it might take years to repair the situation. □ R.J.

TO MEMORIZE: *Set a guard over my mouth, O Lord; keep watch over the door of my lips.* Psalm 141:3, NIV

25

Tornado Tongue

FROM THE BIBLE:
Don't be too eager to tell others their faults, for we all make many mistakes; and when we teachers of religion, who should know better, do wrong, our punishment will be greater than it would be for others. If anyone can control his tongue, it proves that he has perfect control over himself in every other way. We can make a large horse turn around and go wherever we want by means of a small bit in his mouth. And a tiny rudder makes a huge ship turn wherever the pilot wants it to go, even though the winds are strong. So also the tongue is a small thing, but what enormous damage it can do. . . . It is full of wickedness, and poisons every part of the body. And the tongue is set on fire by hell itself, and can turn our whole lives into a blazing flame of destruction and disaster. Men have trained, or can train, every kind of animal or bird that lives and every kind of reptile and fish, but no human being can tame the tongue. It is always ready to pour out its deadly poison.
James 3:2-8, TLB

Control your tongue

26
The Perfect Roommate

FROM THE BIBLE:

Don't criticize, and then you won't be criticized. For others will treat you as you treat them. And why worry about a speck in the eye of a brother when you have a board in your own? Should you say, "Friend, let me help you get that speck out of your eye," when you can't even see because of the board in your own? Hypocrite! First get rid of the board. Then you can see to help your brother.

Matthew 7:1-5, TLB

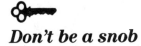

Don't be a snob

"WHO DID YOU get for a roommate?" Jody asked her friend Kim as they stood in the girls' dormitory at their church youth conference.

"Oh, Jody, it's dreadful," moaned Kim. "Her name is Mandy, and she goes to a slow learners' class. She has this children's Bible with big print, and she was reading it aloud and missing half the words. She asked me to pray with her." Kim sighed. "I wish you and I could be roommates."

"Girls from the same church can't be roommates," replied Jody as they went into her room and sat down. "They want us to make new friends and get new ideas. But you know what? Shawna—that girl who sang at our opening meeting—has the room next door. She told me her roommate cancelled."

Kim jumped out of her chair. "Do you think maybe I could switch to her room?"

In a matter of seconds the girls were knocking on the door of Room 17. Shawna opened the door. "Hi, I'm Kim, a friend of Jody's," said Kim. "Jody said your roomie didn't show. I thought maybe we could be roommates."

"Maybe." Shawna hesitated. "Do you sing?"

"No," Kim answered.

"Can you play the piano or organ?" Kim shook her head. "I didn't think so." Shawna tossed her long hair back over her shoulder. "I'm afraid we don't have much in common." She quickly closed the door.

"Just because I don't play the piano or sing she thinks I'm not good enough to be her roommate. She didn't even give me a chance," sputtered Kim. "What a snob."

"It takes one to know one," Jody said thoughtfully.

"Hey, I'm not like that," protested Kim.

Suddenly she stopped. "Oh," she said, "I guess I am. I didn't give Mandy a chance." She paused at Jody's door. "I'll see you later," she added. "I'm going to find Mandy. I may never be the perfect roommate, but with God's help I can be a better one than I have been so far."

HOW ABOUT YOU? Do you give people a chance to show you what they're like? Do you consider yourself superior to those who have learning problems or those whose clothes are not as nice as yours? God looks on the heart. Ask Him to help you see them through His eyes. □ R.M.

TO MEMORIZE: *Stop judging by mere appearances, and make a right judgment.* John 7:24, NIV

I HATE HAVING to be nice to Sue," said Kathy. "She's never nice to me."

"Well, it's a church picnic, so you have to do it," replied Amy. "Just pretend."

Mother frowned as she looked at her daughters in the rearview mirror. "Who said you should pretend to like someone just because you're at a church function?"

"Isn't that the Christian thing to do?" asked Amy.

"Hmmm," said Mother as she tapped her finger against the steering wheel. "Do you remember last summer, when you wanted to paint that old desk?"

"Sure," said Amy.

"Yeah. You wanted to just paint over the old paint," said Kathy, "but Dad made you sand it first."

"Right," said Mother, "and why was that?"

"He said if I didn't, the new paint would eventually chip off and the old paint would show through," replied Amy.

"Pretending to like someone is like painting over old, chipped paint," said Mother. "All the old feelings are still under the surface, and sooner or later, they'll show through."

"So should we just not bother to be nice to Sue at all then?" asked Amy.

Mother shook her head. "You didn't 'just not paint' the old desk," she said. "You sanded and got rid of the rough spots. You need to get rid of the old feelings, too."

"But how?" asked Kathy.

"It isn't easy," admitted Mother, "but a good place to start is with prayer. It's hard to dislike someone you're praying for." She handed Kathy a picnic basket. "Before we get out, shall we ask the Lord to help you love Sue as He does?" The girls nodded, and they bowed their heads.

As they got out of the car, they saw that Sue was just arriving, too. "Shall we go and talk to Sue?" asked Amy.

"Yes," said Kathy. "Let's go."

HOW ABOUT YOU? Do you ever just pretend to like someone? Why not ask God right now to teach you to love somebody you find it difficult to like. He loves that person. Ask Him to fill you heart with His love. □ G.L.J.

TO MEMORIZE: *My command is this: Love each other as I have loved you.* John 15:12, NIV

JUNE

27
Under the Surface

FROM THE BIBLE:

One of the teachers of religion who was standing there listening to the discussion realized that Jesus had answered well. So he asked, "Of all the commandments, which is the most important?" Jesus replied, "The one that says, 'Hear, O Israel! The Lord our God is the one and only God. And you must love him with all your heart and soul and mind and strength.' The second is: 'You must love others as much as yourself.' No other commandments are greater than these." The teacher of religion replied, "Sir, you have spoken a true word in saying that there is only one God and no other. And I know it is far more important to love him with all my heart and understanding and strength, and to love others as myself, than to offer all kinds of sacrifices on the altar of the Temple."

Mark 12:28-33, TLB

Learn to love others

28
Rainy Day Riddle

FROM THE BIBLE:

Are not two sparrows sold for a penny? Yet not one of them will fall to the ground apart from the will of your Father. And even the very hairs of your head are all numbered. So don't be afraid; you are worth more than many sparrows.

Matthew 10:29-31, NIV

God cares for you

SAM WAS BORED. "Grandpa, this rain has ruined our fishing," he complained. "What can I do now?"

Grandpa settled back in his rocker. "Know any good riddles?" he asked.

Sam thought for a minute. "What is black and white and red all over?"

Grandpa snapped his finger. "A newspaper," he said.

"Nope." Sam grinned as he shook his head. "It's an embarrassed zebra." Grandpa laughed. "I know another one," said Sam. "What happens to a blue shoe that is thrown into the Red Sea?"

"I guess it turns purple," suggested Grandpa.

"No, it gets wet," said Sam. They laughed together, and then Sam asked, "Do you know any riddles, Grandpa?"

"Well, let's see." Grandpa reached into his pocket, pulled out his hand, and held out a closed fist. "In my hand there is something no one on earth has ever seen," he said. "The farmer who grew it, the grocer who sold it, your grandma who bought it—none of them has seen it. I have it in my hand, but I've never seen it."

"Aw, that can't be!" protested Sam. Grandpa opened his hand. "A peanut!" yelled Sam. "Lots of people saw that."

"Who has ever seen the peanut inside the shell?" asked Grandpa. Sam hadn't thought of that. "There is one Person who knows exactly what this peanut looks like, though," added Grandpa. "Do you know who that is, Sam?"

"God!" answered Sam promptly. "He knows everything, doesn't He?"

Grandpa nodded. "He sure does. He even knows what you're feeling and thinking. God loves you, and His love is very, very special because He knows you so well."

"He knows I needed a riddle to laugh about on a rainy day like this," agreed Sam. He eyed the peanut. "And He knows I'm hungry."

Grandpa laughed and tossed him the peanut.

HOW ABOUT YOU? Do you ever feel alone and disappointed, as though no one understands your problems? God does. He knows you better than anyone. He knows and shares your happy times, and He also feels your pain and your loneliness. He cares when you hurt. Aren't you glad you can always count on Him? □ M.S.

TO MEMORIZE: *So don't be afraid; you are worth more than many sparrows.* Matthew 10:31, NIV

NATHAN HADN'T been very happy lately. His father's work had moved the family from the Midwest to the South, and Nathan missed his friends and the happy times they had together. He was sure he never could be happy here. There was just no use to even try.

One day, the family took a trip to the beach. They all went swimming, but Nathan refused to admit it was fun. Later, the family hunted for shells on the beach. Nathan found a starfish, but two of its arms were broken off. He was about to throw it away when Dad spoke up. "Let me see it," said Dad holding out his hand. Nathan handed the starfish to him, and Dad turned it over. "See the little moving feet?"

"You mean it's alive?" Nathan asked in surprise. Dad nodded. "But it's gonna die," continued Nathan. "It only has three arms instead of five."

Dad nodded. "Yes, but it will survive. Starfish can regenerate."

"What does that mean?"

"In time, the starfish will grow new arms to replace the old ones," Dad explained.

"And I thought it was useless," Nathan said thoughtfully.

"Nathan, right now you're something like that starfish. You've been cut off from your old friends and associations, and you're hurting. It's scary to begin again, but with God's help, you can make new friends and develop new interests," encouraged Dad.

Nathan looked at the starfish and smiled. "If he can begin again, I guess I can, too."

HOW ABOUT YOU? How do you face new situations? Do you accept them as a challenge to learn and grow? Or do you look at them with discouragement and refuse to try again? Perhaps a loved one has died, a friend has moved away, or you've gained a new stepparent, and things seem so uncertain for you. Ask God for strength to accept your new situation. Then look for ways you can reach out and be friendly to those around you. □ J.H.

TO MEMORIZE: *His compassions fail not. They are new every morning; great is Your faithfulness.* Lamentations 3:22-23, NKJV

A New Beginning

FROM THE BIBLE:
I said, "My strength and my hope have perished from the Lord." Remember my affliction and roaming, the wormwood and the gall. My soul still remembers and sinks within me. This I recall to my mind, therefore I have hope. Through the Lord's mercies we are not consumed, because His compassions fail not. They are new every morning; great is Your faithfulness. "The Lord is my portion," says my soul, "Therefore I hope in Him!" The Lord is good to those who wait for Him, to the soul who seeks Him. It is good that one should hope and wait quietly for the salvation of the Lord.
Lamentations 3:18-26, NKJV

Accept new situations

30

For His Glory

FROM THE BIBLE:

When I look up into the night skies and see the work of your fingers—the moon and the stars you have made: I cannot understand how you can bother with mere puny man, to pay any attention to him! And yet you have made him only a little lower than the angels, and placed a crown of glory and honor upon his head. You have put him in charge of everything you made; everything is put under his authority: all sheep and oxen, and wild animals too, the birds and fish, and all the life in the sea. O Jehovah, our Lord, the majesty and glory of your name fills the earth.
Psalm 8:3-9, TLB

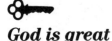

God is great

CRICKETS CHIRPED and June bugs buzzed. Mike and his friend Steve lay in their sleeping bags, looking up at the star-filled sky. They were camping out in Mike's backyard. "I wonder how many stars there are," said Mike softly. "I'll bet we could count about a thousand up there if we tried."

"Yeah, and that's just the ones that are close enough for us to see without a telescope," Steve replied. "My science teacher says there are hundreds of millions of galaxies, and each galaxy has about ten billion stars. Just think how big this universe must be."

Mike was silent for a moment. "There's something I don't understand," he said slowly. "I can see why God created the earth and sun and moon—maybe even the other planets in our solar system, because we might be able to visit them someday. But why did He make the rest of the universe? I mean, what's the use of making something so great and wonderful if no one's ever going to see it?"

"Yeah," agreed Steve. "That reminds me of what I told my mom when I cleaned my room yesterday. I told her I didn't see why I had to clean under my bed, since nobody would see it anyway."

"What did she say?" asked Mike.

"Well," said Steve, "she said that having it clean was important to her even if it wasn't important to me. She says she likes order and beauty, and that God does, too."

"I guess all mothers are like that," said Mike. "Maybe God didn't make the universe just for us," he added, "but for Himself. I guess it's silly for us to think that the universe is wasted just because we can't see all of it."

"Besides, all those stars help us realize how great He really is," added Steve. "Makes me feel kind of small."

HOW ABOUT YOU? When you think about the greatness of the universe, does it make you feel small and unimportant? Does it make you realize the vast difference between God and mere human beings? You can never fully comprehend His greatness or all the things He has done. All you can do is worship Him with praise and thanksgiving. □ S.K.

TO MEMORIZE: *The heavens declare the glory of God; the skies proclaim the work of his hands.* Psalm 19:1, NIV

As MIKE AND STEVE ate breakfast the morning after their campout, they told Mike's mother that they had talked about the stars and the vast universe. "It made us feel kind of small and unimportant," said Mike.

Mother smiled. "God is interested in little things, too," she said. "Mike, have you shown Steve the microscope you got for your birthday?"

"Yeah, he did. It's neat!" exclaimed Steve. "Let's go use it, Mike."

"OK," agreed Mike. "I've got something on a slide to show you." The boys hurried off.

As Steve peered through the lens, he saw what appeared to be a giant, horned monster. "Yuck!" he exclaimed. "What's that thing?"

"It's just a flea," Mike laughed. "I got if off my dog."

Steve took another look. "I didn't know fleas had all those horns and claws," he said. "Let's find some other things to look at." Soon the boys had examined an ant, a leaf stem, a worm, and part of a flower.

Then the boys looked at a drop of water they had taken from a puddle. They were amazed at all the tiny things they found swimming in it. "I can't believe it," said Mike, moving over so Steve could peer into the lens. "There must be millions and billions of these things all over the world, and we never even see them."

"Even though no one sees these little creatures, each one of them was created by God in a special way." Mother's voice came from the doorway. She smiled at the boys. "I'm glad He's interested in little things as well as in big things," said Mike. "That means He's interested in us, too. It's nice to know we're important to God."

HOW ABOUT YOU? Do you realize that God cares about you—that you are important to Him? He created you and has a purpose for your life. You could not even live if it were not for His loving care, protecting and sustaining you every minute of every day. Don't you think you should be able to trust Him completely? □ S.K.

TO MEMORIZE: *You open your hand and satisfy the desires of every living thing.* Psalm 145:16, NIV

For His Glory

(Continued from yesterday)

FROM THE BIBLE:
Praise the Lord, O heavens!
Praise him from the skies!
Praise him, all his angels, all
the armies of heaven. Praise
him, sun and moon, and all
you twinkling stars. Praise
him, skies above. Praise him,
vapors high above the clouds.
Let everything he has made give
praise to him. For he issued his
command, and they came into
being; he established them
forever and forever. His orders
will never be revoked. And
praise him down here on earth,
you creatures of the ocean
depths. Let fire and hail, snow,
rain, wind and weather, all
obey. Let the mountains and
hills, the fruit trees and cedars,
the wild animals and cattle, the
snakes and birds, the kings and
all the people with their rulers
and their judges, young men
and maidens, old men and
children: all praise the Lord
together. For he alone is worthy.
His glory is far greater than all
of earth and heaven.
Psalm 148:1-13, TLB

God cares about small things

2

A Higher View

FROM THE BIBLE:

In all things God works for the good of those who love him, who have been called according to his purpose. For those God foreknew he also predestined to be conformed to the likeness of his Son, that he might be the firstborn among many brothers. And those he predestined, he also called; those he called, he also justified; those he justified, he also glorified. What, then, shall we say in response to this? If God is for us, who can be against us? He who did not spare his own Son, but gave him up for us all—how will he not also, along with him, graciously give us all things?
Romans 8:28-32, NIV

God's ways are good

KATIE AND DERRICK grinned at one another as their family rode the elevator to the observation deck of the Sears Tower in Chicago. Their ears popped as they whizzed by floor after floor, going higher and higher. Getting off the elevator, the children ran to the window to look out at the view below.

"Everything looks so tiny!" Katie exclaimed. "The cars look like toys."

Mother nodded. "You surely can see a long way from here. See the boats on the lake?"

"Look way ahead, over to your right," Dad instructed.

"Traffic's stopped there."

"Yes, but look right below us," Derrick said. "See that red car? It keeps changing lanes, trying to get ahead of everyone else."

"Probably in a hurry," Katie suggested.

"Probably," agreed Dad. "That guy is in such a hurry he's foolishly and dangerously passing everyone. But he's going to be slowed down because it looks like there's a roadblock up ahead. That will stop him."

"Too bad he can't see the roadblock like we can," Katie said. "Then he wouldn't be in such a hurry."

"You know," said Dad, "as Christians, we sometimes act a lot like that fellow. God has a plan mapped out for each of our lives, but we often try to hurry ahead of His ways. We complain when we have to wait, but we don't stop to think that there is a purpose for the delay."

Mother nodded. "The higher view is better, isn't it?"

HOW ABOUT YOU? Do you fret when your plans are changed? Do you grumble when someone gets sick or hurt, making it necessary to cancel an activity? Changes aren't always pleasant, but they can be good for you. Trust God to work through your interrupted plans. □ J.H.

TO MEMORIZE: *If God is for us, who can be against us?* Romans 8:31, NIV

G ET A move-on, Josh," grumbled Jeff loudly. "You're just being lazy."

"Am not!"

"Are too!"

Jeff and Josh were at it again. Mother reluctantly headed for the kitchen to try to solve this one. "I'm tired of the constant bickering that goes on between you boys," she scolded. "You are brothers, and you ought to show love for one another."

"Love? Who could love him?" Jeff asked angrily. "Every time we do dishes, Josh just drags his feet, so I end up doing most of the work."

"Do not!" Josh shot back. "He always picks on me!"

"That does it!" exclaimed Mother. "You boys need to work off some extra steam. When these dishes are done, we'll all go out to the garden and pull crabgrass. I'll give you each the same number of rows to do, so nobody needs to complain about doing the most. And if anybody 'drags his feet,' it will just take him longer."

Soon they were all busy in the garden. By the time they took a lemonade break, the boys were hot, dusty, and too tired to quarrel. Mother sat back on the dirt. "You know, this makes me think of a verse in the Bible that talks about a 'root of bitterness' springing up," she said. "I can see that such a root is springing up between you boys. It has been destroying your friendship much the same way this crabgrass is destroying our strawberry patch. Let's tackle both of them. Let's talk about the things that are bugging you and see if you can get rid of that bitterness."

The boys looked at each other and nodded. They bowed their heads as Mother led them in prayer, asking God's guidance.

HOW ABOUT YOU? Are you feeling bitter toward somebody? Has someone been unfair to you? Do you feel more and more angry as the days go by? Ask God to show you if there is anyone with whom you should "talk things out." If He brings someone to your mind, go to that person and discuss the problem. Ask God to help you pull bitterness out by the roots. □ P.R.

TO MEMORIZE: *See to it that no one misses the grace of God and that no bitter root grows up to cause trouble and defile many.* Hebrews 12:15, NIV

3

Root of Bitterness

FROM THE BIBLE:

No discipline seems pleasant at the time, but painful. Later on, however, it produces a harvest of righteousness and peace for those who have been trained by it. Therefore, strengthen your feeble arms and weak knees. "Make level paths for your feet," so that the lame may not be disabled, but rather healed. Make every effort to live in peace with all men and to be holy; without holiness no one will see the Lord. See to it that no one misses the grace of God and that no bitter root grows up to cause trouble and defile many. Hebrews 12:11-15, NIV

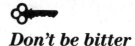

Don't be bitter

Closer to the Light

FROM THE BIBLE:
Your laws are wonderful; no wonder I obey them. As your plan unfolds, even the simple can understand it. No wonder I wait expectantly for each of your commands. Come and have mercy on me as is your way with those who love you. Guide me with your laws so that I will not be overcome by evil. Rescue me from the oppression of evil men; then I can obey you. Look down in love upon me and teach me all your laws.
Psalm 119:129-135, TLB

Spend time alone with God

BRIAN AND HIS family went to visit his grandparents' farm. Brian loved seeing the animals, climbing on the haystacks, swinging on the rope in the barn, and fishing and wading in the creek. "This sure is a neat place!" he exclaimed as he washed up for supper one evening.

Mother smiled. "You seem to be enjoying yourself in spite of no playgrounds or ice cream stores out here, or even a TV."

"Yeah, it's kind of nice to have it quiet—a guy has a chance to think out here."

After a hearty supper, Dad looked over at Brian. "Your Grandpa and I have a surprise for you, Son. We thought you might enjoy camping out in the woods with us tonight."

Three hours later, they sat contentedly by the smoldering campfire. "Time for devotions," Grandpa announced as he pulled out his Bible.

As Brian reached in his duffle bag for his own Bible, he glanced upward. "Wow! Look at all those stars!" he cried. "We sure can't see this many at our house. They must be a lot closer here."

Dad and Grandpa laughed. "No, the stars aren't any closer," Dad replied, "but we're out in the country now, away from all the city lights, which tend to blot out the smaller lights of the stars."

"I think there's a spiritual lesson here," Grandpa said thoughtfully as he leafed through his Bible. "Just as the glaring lights of the city blot out the stars, so the busyness of everyday activities can make it hard to see how God is working in our lives. That's why it's good to draw apart to a quiet place—a place where you can be alone and concentrate on God's Word and your relationship to Him."

"I'll try to remember that," Brian said. He listened very carefully as Grandpa read from the Bible.

HOW ABOUT YOU? Is your time so filled with school activities and recreation that you hardly ever think about God or the Bible? Be careful! If you don't set aside "quiet times" to be alone with God, you'll miss many of the wonderful blessings the Lord has planned for you. □ S.K.

TO MEMORIZE: *After he had dismissed them, he went up on a mountainside by himself to pray. When evening came, he was there alone.* Matthew 14:23, NIV

THE CARR FAMILY was on vacation, and one of the places they visited was Jewel Cave. Ryan was excited about being in a cave. He listened carefully as Peter, their tour guide, led them down the narrow paths. He was fascinated by the different rock formations and was interested in hearing about the people who first explored the cave.

"Now," Peter said, as they stopped in a small opening, "I'm going to turn off the lights so you can see what it means to be truly in the dark." Peter was certainly right about it being dark. Ryan couldn't see a thing! He could not even see his fingers, though he put them right in front of his face. It was darker than night. At night Ryan could at least see shadows.

Peter made a joke about leaving the people in the darkness while he went on a coffee break. Everyone laughed, but it made Ryan think. He knew the Bible described people who didn't know Jesus as Savior as being lost in darkness. Now that he was in the dark, he realized that it was a scary place to be.

Of course, Peter was just joking about leaving the tour group in the dark cave, but Ryan knew the Lord wasn't joking when he talked about the darkness of sin. He remembered, too, that Jesus spoke of being the Light of the world, and He was thankful he knew Jesus as Savior.

HOW ABOUT YOU? Are you still in darkness—the darkness of sin? Jesus is called the Light of the world, and He is willing to take away the darkness from those who trust in Him. Won't you ask Him to do that today? □ L.W.

TO MEMORIZE: *I am the light of the world. Whoever follows me will never walk in darkness, but will have the light of life.* John 8:12, NIV

A Trip to Jewel Cave

FROM THE BIBLE:
For God loved the world so much that he gave his only Son so that anyone who believes in him shall not perish but have eternal life. God did not send his Son into the world to condemn it, but to save it. There is no eternal doom awaiting those who trust him to save them. But those who don't trust him have already been tried and condemned for not believing in the only Son of God. Their sentence is based on this fact: that the Light from heaven came into the world, but they loved the darkness more than the Light, for their deeds were evil. They hated the heavenly Light because they wanted to sin in the darkness. They stayed away from that Light for fear their sins would be exposed and they would be punished. But those doing right come gladly to the Light to let everyone see that they are doing what God wants them to.
John 3:16-21, TLB

Jesus is the light of the world

6

Happy Birthday

FROM THE BIBLE:

I will praise you, O Lord, with all my heart; before the "gods" I will sing your praise. I will bow down toward your holy temple and will praise your name for your love and your faithfulness, for you have exalted above all things your name and your word. When I called, you answered me; you made me bold and stouthearted. May all the kings of the earth praise you, O Lord, when they hear the words of your mouth. May they sing of the ways of the Lord, for the glory of the Lord is great. Though the Lord is on high, he looks upon the lowly, but the proud he knows from afar. Though I walk in the midst of trouble, you preserve my life; you stretch out your hand against the anger of my foes, with your right hand you save me. The Lord will fulfill his purpose for me; your love, O Lord, endures forever—do not abandon the works of your hands.

Psalm 138, NIV

Make the best of situations

DAVID FROWNED when he looked outside. "It can't rain today," he grumbled. "It will spoil everything!" It was David's birthday and his grandparents were coming for a picnic.

Just then the phone rang, and Mother went to the kitchen to answer it. "Grandma wants to talk to you, David," she called a little later.

"Some birthday," David muttered when he had finished talking with his grandmother. "Grandpa hurt his back and has to stay in bed. They'll try to come next week instead of today. It's going to be a lonely day!"

Mother hugged David. "I'm sorry things aren't working out the way we planned. But we'll do something else today, and we'll celebrate your birthday next week."

"I have an idea," said Dad. "Who else might be lonely today?"

"Maybe Jeff," said David. "His father died a couple of months ago."

"Call him up," suggested Dad, "and see if he can come over."

Jeff was delighted with the invitation, and he and David had a great time together. David was surprised to find that the two of them had many things in common.

Before bedtime, David and his dad had a talk. "I expected my birthday to be perfect," David said, "and then everything went wrong. But I found out that things don't have to happen just one certain way in order to have a good time."

"I'm glad to hear that," said Dad. "You know, some Christians figure that once they accept Christ as Savior, everything will be perfect, and they won't have troubles or trials. But it just isn't so. Jesus doesn't guarantee an easy, happy life, but He does promise to be with us. And if we'll allow Him, He'll use what seem like trials to bring us a blessing."

"That should make us happy every day," David murmured sleepily. "G'night, Dad."

HOW ABOUT YOU? Have you found that things don't always work out the way you hope? Remember, happiness comes from Jesus, not from circumstances. So when your plans go astray, cheerfully look to see what other plans He may have for you. □ J.H.

TO MEMORIZE: *The Lord will fulfill his purpose for me; your love, O Lord, endures forever.* Psalm 138:8, NIV

"MOTHER," called Danny. "Is it OK if Dad and I take a little hike before supper?"

"All right," Mother agreed, "but don't be too long."

So off they went, just the two "men" of the family. They were spending a week at Lake Michigan, and Danny loved those hikes with his dad. Today he had an important question. "Can people tell just by looking at you that you're a Christian?" he asked. "We talked about it in Sunday school, and my teacher said something about people looking at our lives."

"Good question," approved Dad, glancing around. "See that sand dune with all the trees growing on it? Does any one tree catch your eye?"

"Hmmmm," said Danny. "Oh, that one over there, growing sideways on the slope! It stands out from all the rest."

Dad nodded. "You picked out that tree because it was different. When people look at the way you live your life, they should be able to see that you're different."

"But how?" asked Danny. "What can I do? I'm only twelve."

"Take another look at that tree," answered Dad. "It isn't very big, but it's special. You might not be so big, but every day you see a lot of people at school. Maybe you hear kids using bad language. Or maybe your friends want you to go along with them to a dirty movie. God doesn't want you to do those things. He wants you to be different."

"Oh, I get it!" exclaimed Danny. "If I'm careful about the things I do, then people will notice."

"That's right, but even if everyone doesn't notice, remember that you're pleasing God, and that's most important."

HOW ABOUT YOU? Can people tell by looking at your life that you're a Christian? They can't if they see cheating, bad language, disobedience, or lying. Instead, let them see honesty, kindness, love, and consideration. Let them see that you are "different" for Jesus. □ D.M.

TO MEMORIZE: *Come out from among them and be separate, says the Lord.* 2 Corinthians 6:17, NKJV

JULY

7

Like the Tree

FROM THE BIBLE:

God's truth stands firm like a great rock, and nothing can shake it. It is a foundation stone with these words written on it: "The Lord knows those who are really his," and "A person who calls himself a Christian should not be doing things that are wrong." In a wealthy home there are dishes made of gold and silver as well as some made from wood and clay. The expensive dishes are used for guests, and the cheap ones are used in the kitchen or to put garbage in. If you stay away from sin you will be like one of these dishes made of purest gold—the very best in the house—so that Christ himself can use you for his highest purposes. Run from anything that gives you the evil thoughts that young men often have, but stay close to anything that makes you want to do right. Have faith and love, and enjoy the companionship of those who love the Lord and have pure hearts.

2 Timothy 2:19-22, TLB

Be different for Jesus

JULY

8

What You See

FROM THE BIBLE:
*Rejoice in the Lord always.
Again I will say, rejoice! Let
your gentleness be known to all
men. The Lord is at hand. Be
anxious for nothing, but in
everything by prayer and
supplication, with thanksgiving,
let your requests be made known
to God; and the peace of God,
which surpasses all understanding, will guard your hearts and
minds through Christ Jesus.
Finally, brethren, whatever
things are true, whatever things
are noble, whatever things are
just, whatever things are pure,
whatever things are lovely,
whatever things are of good
report, if there is any virtue and
if there is anything praiseworthy—meditate on these things.
The things which you learned
and received and heard and saw
in me, these do, and the God of
peace will be with you.*
Philippians 4:4-9, NKJV

See the good in others

THIS YEAR I'M going to have a garden of my own," Brenda announced to her younger sister, Diane. Then she scowled. "Hey, are you biting your nails again, Diane? I can't stand it when you do that." Brenda was always after Diane about one thing or another.

Brenda did get to plant her own garden, and it grew well. The weeds irked her, though. "They grow faster than the plants," she complained one day as she showed her Aunt Joy the garden.

"But the flowers are so beautiful!" Aunt Joy exclaimed. "And look! Your sweet corn already has ears."

"Yeah, but look at the weeds growing beside the flowers," grumbled Brenda, "and there by the corn, too. Hey!" Brenda turned to Diane who had followed them. "Get your big feet out of here before you step on a plant," she commanded. As Diane turned and slowly walked toward the house, Brenda turned her attention back to the garden and Aunt Joy. "I do hate the weeds," she sighed.

"I can see that you do," said Aunt Joy. "But you become so irritated about each little weed, that you don't enjoy the good plants."

Brenda thoughtfully picked a leaf. "You're right," she admitted. "I'll concentrate on my plants rather than on the weeds."

Aunt Joy nodded. "And one more thing—could you do the same with Diane?"

"Diane?" Brenda exclaimed. "She's not a plant!"

"Well, no," Aunt Joy smiled, "but you're doing the same thing with your sister that you've done in your garden. The Lord has given you a sister to love, and He's given her many good qualities which you could enjoy. But you keep noticing all the little things she does wrong and letting them irritate you. Instead, think of all the good things Diane does."

It was a new thought to Brenda, but she knew her aunt was right. "I'll try," she promised.

HOW ABOUT YOU? Is it easy for you to see the faults instead of the good points in others? That seems to come naturally, but you can train yourself to concentrate on what you like about others. Ask God to help you love others as He does. □ C.Y.

TO MEMORIZE: *If there is any virtue and if there is anything praiseworthy—meditate on these things.*
Philippians 4:8, NKJV

AMANDA AND JOELLE were enjoying a vacation with their parents. There were new things to see every day. "What are we going to see tomorrow?" asked Amanda when they stopped at a motel on Saturday night.

"Tomorrow we're going to church," answered Mother, "just like we do when we're at home."

"Oh, Mom, do we have to? I'll feel so out of place in a strange church," complained Amanda.

Dad smiled. "I think we can find one where we'll feel at home," he assured her. "Mom and I will look over the church list in this town and maybe even make a few phone calls. I think we can find a good church to attend."

Sure enough, early Sunday morning Mother woke Amanda and Joelle and told them to put on their very best clothes. After breakfast, they headed for the church they had chosen. When they arrived, they were met at the door by a friendly couple who took them to their Sunday school classes. The pianist was playing a song as Amanda and Joelle entered the Sunday school room. "We know that song," Amanda whispered.

As the morning passed, the girls were surprised to find many things similar to their own church. Even the pastor's message sounded like a message they might hear in their church at home. They were glad they had come.

"Sometimes," said Dad as they got back into their car, "we think we're the only Christians in the world—but that's not true. There are people everywhere who love the Lord."

"And it's fun to meet other Christians," Joelle decided.

"I think so, too," agreed Amanda. "After all, we all belong to God's family!"

HOW ABOUT YOU? Have you ever visited a church in another town? Was it a lot like the one you regularly attend? Christians have much in common—especially their love for the Lord. When you're on vacation over a weekend, you'll find that it's a good time to meet other Christians and fellowship with them. □ L. W.

TO MEMORIZE: *I am a friend to all who fear you, to all who follow your precepts.* Psalm 119:63, NIV

Just like Us

FROM THE BIBLE:
Now you are no longer strangers to God and foreigners to heaven, but you are members of God's very own family, citizens of God's country, and you belong in God's household with every other Christian. What a foundation you stand on now: the apostles and the prophets; and the cornerstone of the building is Jesus Christ himself! We who believe are carefully joined together with Christ as parts of a beautiful, constantly growing temple for God. And you also are joined with him and with each other by the Spirit, and are part of this dwelling place of God.
Ephesians 2:19-22, TLB

Christians have much in common

10

Roses and Roots

FROM THE BIBLE:

I want you to know what a great conflict I have for you and those in Laodicea, and for as many as have not seen my face in the flesh, that their hearts may be encouraged, being knit together in love, and attaining to all riches of the full assurance of understanding, to the knowledge of the mystery of God, both of the Father and of Christ, in whom are hidden all the treasures of wisdom and knowledge. Now this I say lest anyone should deceive you with persuasive words. For though I am absent in the flesh, yet I am with you in spirit, rejoicing to see your good order and the steadfastness of your faith in Christ. As you have therefore received Christ Jesus the Lord, so walk in Him, rooted and built up in Him and established in the faith, as you have been taught, abounding in it with thanksgiving.
Colossians 2:1-7, NKJV

Be rooted in Christ

"CAN I GO play at Dave's house now?" asked Bryce.

Mother looked up from the rose bush she was pruning. "Is your Sunday school lesson finished?" she asked. Bryce nodded. "Say your verse to me then," said Mother.

"Aw, Mom," protested Bryce, but he went to his room to learn the verse. After a while, he found Mother in the kitchen and handed his book to her. "Here," he said. "I know the verse now—but I don't understand it." Mother listened while Bryce recited Colossians 2:7.

As Bryce finished, the screen door slammed and Bryce's little sister, Mindy, came in. "It died," she wailed. "My rose died." She pulled on Mother's hand and led her out to the flower bed. Bryce followed. Mindy pointed to a limp, wilted rose sticking out of the ground. "I picked that rose and planted it," she said. "Why did it die? Your roses grew and made more roses. Why didn't mine?"

"Oh, Honey," replied Mother, "there's a great difference between the roses I planted and the one you planted. When you pick them, they don't have roots." She knelt down and explained to the little girl how roses must have roots to grow. "Next time I plant roses, you can help," she promised. Standing up, she looked at Bryce. "You see, Son," she said, "just as plants need to be rooted in the soil to give them stability and to take in food and water, we, as Christians, need to be rooted in the Lord. As we study His Word and learn more about Him—and as we pray—we're taking in spiritual nourishment and developing stronger, deeper roots so that when troubles come we're able to stand and grow."

"That's what my verse means, huh?" Bryce grinned at his mother. "And the last part of it means I should be thankful when you make me study my lesson before I play."

HOW ABOUT YOU? Do you take advantage of opportunities to be rooted in the Lord? Do you study your Bible? Listen in church? Take time to pray? You need to do those things. You need to be firmly rooted and established in your faith in Christ. □ H.M.

TO MEMORIZE: *Rooted and built up in Him and established in the faith, as you have been taught, abounding in it with thanksgiving.* Colossians 2:7, NKJV

GENTLY DAD SHOOK Todd's shoulder. "Time to go," he whispered. "Fishing is best in early morning, you know."

Todd groaned but rolled out of bed. Before long, he and Dad were pushing off in a rowboat. Todd yawned as he pulled at the oars. "We can't even see where we're going," he complained.

"What happened to all the enthusiasm that you had yesterday?" asked Dad. "I heard you tell your friends you were going to catch the most fish."

"Yeah, and I am, too," Todd boasted.

Dad was the first to reel in a good-sized bass, and then he caught several others. Todd snagged a small sunfish which he threw back into the water. After a few hours, in which he caught little, Todd was discouraged.

"I'm ready to quit," he grumbled. "I've gotta call Bill. We're gonna toss a few balls before our game today." He looked at his father. "Are you coming to the ball game? We're really going to beat those guys. I'm gonna knock one right out of the ball park!"

Dad laughed. "I want to be there to see that," he said, "but you'd better be careful about what you say. Not long ago you were going to catch the most fish. Now you're going to be the best ball player. It's a little embarrassing when you boast like that and then come up empty-handed."

"That's for sure," Todd admitted, glancing at the few small fish he had caught.

"The Bible warns against boasting about plans without considering God's will," said Dad. "We can't be sure what will happen today or tomorrow, you know. We need to live each day with a desire to do God's will instead of bragging about our own plans."

HOW ABOUT YOU? Do you have plans for today? For tomorrow? For next week? Do you make plans without considering God's will for you? He is in control of all that happens, and your plans will come to pass only as He allows them to. Make all your plans with that knowledge in mind. □ B.D.

TO MEMORIZE: *What is your life? It is even a vapor that appears for a little time and then vanishes away.* James 4:14, NKJV

Why Boast?

FROM THE BIBLE:
Come now, you who say, "Today or tomorrow we will go to such and such a city, spend a year there, buy and sell, and make a profit" whereas you do not know what will happen tomorrow. For what is your life? It is even a vapor that appears for a little time and then vanishes away. Instead you ought to say, "If the Lord wills, we shall live and do this or that." But now you boast in your arrogance. All such boasting is evil. Therefore, to him who knows to do good and does not do it, to him it is sin. James 4:13-17, NKJV

Plan— seeking God's will

12

The Hero

FROM THE BIBLE:
*You call me "Master" and
"Lord," and you do well to say
it, for it is true. And since I, the
Lord and Teacher, have washed
your feet, you ought to wash
each other's feet. I have given
you an example to follow: do as
I have done to you. How true it
is that a servant is not greater
than his master. Nor is the
messenger more important than
the one who sends him. You
know these things—now do
them! That is the path of
blessing.*
John 13:13-17, TLB

Let Jesus be your hero

"DID YOU SEE the way Greg hit that last ball?"
asked Chad excitedly as his father started the car.
"It went so far I bet the other team hasn't found
it yet! I want to be just like him when I get to
high school."

"Me, too! Greg's the best player we have."
Chad's friend Travis continued the hero worship.

"Can we stop at this next restaurant, Dad?"
asked Chad. "The team's going to eat here."

The three of them were just starting to enjoy
their food when the team burst loudly through the
restaurant entrance. Chad and Travis were delighted when Greg and three of the other players
took a table near their booth. But as the boys
watched, they saw the team members—led by
Greg—blow the paper from their straws onto the
floor, throw food at the busboy, and shout rude
statements until the coach threatened to make
them get back on the bus. They heard Greg swear.
They saw him behave rudely toward the waitress.
Both Chad and Travis felt disappointed as they
realized their hero's behavior was not something
to be admired.

As the boys returned silently to the car, they
tried to forget what they'd heard, but it was impossible. "How can such a neat ball player be such a
rotten person?" asked Chad.

"You can still admire Greg's athletic ability," Dad
said, "but it's not a good idea to make people into
idols. Sooner or later they always let you down.
Jesus is the One you should choose for your role
model. He'll never let you down."

HOW ABOUT YOU? Has that sports figure you admire
been found guilty of bribery or taking drugs? Does
the television personality you like use foul language
and brag about an immoral lifestyle? Beware of
making people into idols. Only Jesus is perfect.
Choose Him for your hero. □ R.M.

TO MEMORIZE: *Dear children, keep yourselves from
idols.* 1 John 5:21, NIV

"LOOK AT THIS odd plant," called Scott as he and his fellow campers made their way around the swamp. As the boys crowded around, they saw a cluster of green, pitcher-shaped leaves.

"Hmmmm," murmured Mr. Pete, the counselor. "A pitcher plant! That's an insect-eating plant."

"What are all those flies doing down there?" asked one of the boys as he peered into the largest "pitcher."

"The plant has caught them for food," explained Mr. Pete. "It uses a nectar-like substance to attract them. They easily enter the opening at the top of the leaves, but the sides are slippery, and the insects can't get back out."

"So they drown in that pool at the bottom, I guess," remarked Scott. "What stupid flies."

"They were foolish, weren't they?" said Mr. Pete. "The way the nectar in this plant draws flies to their doom reminds me of how drugs pull so many young people down. They think they're getting something good, but instead they get caught."

Scott looked thoughtful. "A kid gave my brother free samples of drugs, so he tried them," he said. "Before he even stopped to think about it, he was hooked pretty bad."

"What happened then, Scott?" asked one of the boys.

"Mom and Dad sent him to a drug rehabilitation center. I can't even send him a bag of potato chips or cheese curls, because the people are afraid someone might try to sneak him some drugs that way," explained Scott. "I'm never going to try drugs, not even for free."

"I hope not," said Mr. Pete. "It's a very foolish thing to do." He looked at the boys. "Let's remember to pray for Scott's brother. And as we do, let's be sure to ask the Lord each day to keep us from ever acting like one of those foolish flies and giving in to the temptation to try drugs."

As the boys nodded solemnly, they heard a buzzing sound. A fly was circling the pitcher plant, drawing a little closer with each pass.

HOW ABOUT YOU? Are you attracted by the drug culture? By its music? By its way of dressing? Keep your distance! The closer you get, the harder it will be to turn back. Ask the Lord to keep you safe from its evil influence. □ L.B.M.

TO MEMORIZE: *Do not get drunk on wine, which leads to debauchery. Instead, be filled with the Spirit.* Ephesians 5:18, NIV

The Foolish Flies

FROM THE BIBLE:
Whose heart is filled with anguish and sorrow? Who is always fighting and quarreling? Who is the man with bloodshot eyes and many wounds? It is the one who spends long hours in the taverns, trying out new mixtures. Don't let the sparkle and the smooth taste of strong wine deceive you. For in the end it bites like a poisonous serpent; it stings like an adder. You will see hallucinations and have delirium tremens, and you will say foolish, silly things that would embarrass you no end when sober. You will stagger like a sailor tossed at sea, clinging to a swaying mast. And afterwards you will say, "I didn't even know it when they beat me up. Let's go and have another drink!"
Proverbs 23:29-35, TLB

Steer clear of drugs

14

The Brightest Star

FROM THE BIBLE:

I am coming quickly, and My reward is with Me, to give to each one according to his work. I am the Alpha and the Omega, the Beginning and the End, the First and the Last. Blessed are those who do His command-ments, that they may have the right to the tree of life, and may enter in through the gates into the city. But outside are dogs and sorcerers and sexually immoral and murderers and idolaters, and whoever loves and practices a lie. I, Jesus, have sent My angel to testify to you these things in the churches. I am the Root and the Offspring of David, the Bright and Morning Star. And the Spirit and the bride say, "Come!" And let him who hears say, "Come!" And let him who thirsts come. And whoever desires, let him take the water of life freely. Revelation 22:12-17, NKJV

Accept Jesus as Savior

I KNOW WHAT let's do," said Jeff one hot sum-mer evening as he and his sister, Jill, stretched out on the grass beneath the starry sky. "Let's see who can find the brightest star. The loser has to pay for ice cream tomorrow."

Jill didn't think much of the idea. "How are we going to prove which one is the brightest anyway?" she asked grumpily. But she suddenly pointed to the north. "That one's mine! That real bright one up there."

Jeff squinted. "I think I see the one you mean, but I see a brighter one," he said, pointing in another direction. "See, right in the middle of that cluster of stars. That one's brighter than the one you found."

"Uh-uh!" protested Jill. They continued to search the heavens as they argued about which star was brighter. When Dad came out to tell them it was bedtime, they asked him to be the judge.

"Hmmmm," murmured Dad as they pointed out the stars they had chosen. "As judge, I declare that neither of those is the brightest star of all. In fact, I think the two of you should buy me a treat, because I know the brightest star personally. And I hope you do, too. It's important."

"What do you mean, you know a star?" asked Jill. "We're not talking about football or baseball stars. Besides, I can get along fine without know-ing any of them."

Dad laughed. "I'm not talking about them, but I'm not talking about a star in the sky, either," he admitted. "I'm talking about the Lord Jesus. He's called the 'Bright and Morning Star.' I'd say that's the brightest star of all, wouldn't you? And it's very important to know Him."

"OK, Dad." Jeff grinned at his father as he got up to go in. "But no treat. You weren't in on the deal."

"Right," agreed Jill. She glanced once more at the sky. "I wonder what my friends would say if I told them I know a star," she added.

HOW ABOUT YOU? Do you know Jesus, the "Bright and Morning Star"? God wants you to know Him. Even in the final chapter of the Bible, God invites you to come to Him. But one day it will be too late to do that. Don't wait. Accept Him today. □ H.M.

TO MEMORIZE: *I am the Root and the Offspring of David, the Bright and Morning Star.* Revelation 22:16, NKJV

As JEFFREY CRAWLED into bed, his mind was made up. He was going to stop praying for Uncle Carl and spend his prayer time on someone else—someone for whom it would do more good. Uncle Carl was a hopeless case.

When Jeffrey came in from school the next afternoon, Mother met him at the door. "I want you to run over to Gramp Nelson's," she said. "He has fresh tomatoes for us."

Quick as a wink, Jeffrey was on his bicycle. At Gramp Nelson's house, he knocked loudly. No answer. He knocked again, louder. Still no answer. "Must not be home," he mumbled as he jumped on his bike and pedaled home.

As Jeffrey came into the kitchen, Mother was on the telephone. "Oh, here he is now," she said. "Thanks for calling." She hung up the receiver.

"Gramps wasn't home," Jeffrey announced.

"Yes, he was," Mother answered. "He was on the patio. By the time he got to the door, you had left. He wants you to come back."

"Ohhhh, no." Jeffrey plopped down on the couch. "Let me catch my breath first."

Mother picked up the mail. "Here's a letter from Uncle Carl," she said. Quickly, she opened it. As she read, a broad smile spread over her face. "Listen to what he writes. 'I am so unhappy. I'm going to have to change my life-style. Keep praying for me.'" She folded the letter. "Sometimes we're tempted to quit praying just before the answer comes," she added.

Jeffrey felt guilty as he remembered last night's decision. Then he nodded. "Just like I quit knocking before Gramps got to the door," he said, jumping up. "Guess I'll go try again. This time I'll keep knocking until I get an answer." As he left, he made up his mind to pray for Uncle Carl again, too.

HOW ABOUT YOU? Have you been praying for something or someone for a long time? Are you about ready to give up? Don't! Keep knocking. The answer is on the way. □ B.W.

TO MEMORIZE: *Ask, and it will be given to you; seek, and you fill find; knock and it will be opened to you.* Matthew 7:7, NKJV

JULY

15

Keep Knocking

FROM THE BIBLE:
Jesus told his disciples a story to illustrate their need for constant prayer and to show them that they must keep praying until the answer comes. "There was a city judge," he said, "a very godless man who had great contempt for everyone. A widow of that city came to him frequently to appeal for justice against a man who had harmed her. The judge ignored her for a while, but eventually she got on his nerves. " 'I fear neither God nor man,' he said to himself, 'but this woman bothers me. I'm going to see that she gets justice, for she is wearing me out with her constant coming!' " Then the Lord said, "If even an evil judge can be worn down like that, don't you think that God will surely give justice to his people who plead with him day and night? Yes! He will answer them quickly!"
Luke 18:1-8, TLB

Keep on praying

16

Give It Back

"Will a man rob God? Yet you rob me. But you ask, 'How do we rob you?' In tithes and offerings. You are under a curse—the whole nation of you—because you are robbing me. Bring the whole tithe into the storehouse, that there may be food in my house. Test me in this," says the Lord Almighty, "and see if I will not throw open the floodgates of heaven and pour out so much blessing that you will not have room enough for it. I will prevent pests from devouring your crops, and the vines in your fields will not cast their fruit," says the Lord Almighty. "Then all the nations will call you blessed, for yours will be a delightful land," says the Lord Almighty. Malachi 3:8-12, NIV

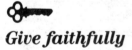

Give faithfully

As CHURCH BEGAN, Janice was thinking about how she had finally earned enough for a whole week at Bible camp, plus a few dollars for crafts and treats. Her thoughts were interrupted by a nudge on her elbow. The offering was being taken, and it made her feel a little guilty. For weeks she had been putting every cent she earned into the bank. She hadn't put anything into the offering. *After all,* she reasoned, *it's for camp where I'll be learning more about the Lord, so in a way, it's for Him.*

After church, Janice went to her Sunday school teacher's home for a picnic lunch. As they ate, Janice told Mrs. Harper about her decision not to tithe while she was saving for camp.

"It doesn't seem like it's wrong since the money is all going for something good, but I do have a funny feeling about not giving," Janice admitted. "The problem is, I won't have enough for camp if I give ten percent of the money. Maybe I could just give a dollar."

"Watch this," Mrs. Harper said, throwing a ball far across the lawn. Pixie, her little dog, appeared as if by magic, burrowed under the bushes to find the ball, and ran back to drop it into Mrs. Harper's hand. Each time Mrs. Harper threw the ball, Pixie got it and brought it back.

"This game wasn't much fun for either Pixie or me at first," said Mrs. Harper. "She didn't know me very well or trust me very much. When I threw the ball, she would grab it and hold it. Then she learned to bring it back, but she wouldn't let go. She was afraid the game would be over. Now she knows that if there is to be a game of catch, she has to give up the ball."

Mrs. Harper turned to Janice. "God has commanded us to give back to Him a part of everything He gives to us. Trust Him, Janice. The more we give, the more we are blessed, just like a game of catch. If we hold on, we only cheat ourselves."

HOW ABOUT YOU? Have you been giving God part of all the money that comes to you? God doesn't use only large offerings. He also uses the pennies, nickels, and dimes of boys and girls. Giving to God is exciting and rewarding. See how much you can give, not how much you can keep. □ C.R.

TO MEMORIZE: *Give, and it will be given to you.* Luke 6:38, NKJV

"MOTHER, WHAT'S WRONG with these ice cubes?" asked Janice. "They're all brown!"

Mother glanced at the dark cubes and grinned. "I used iced tea to make those," she explained. "I made them for Grandpa. You know how he loves good, strong iced tea on hot summer days."

Janice nodded and smiled at her grandfather, who was sitting at the kitchen table. She knew he disliked his tea watery and weak, the way it became when too many ice cubes melted in it. She popped several of the brown cubes into tall glasses and poured fresh iced tea over them. "Here you are, Grandpa. Pure tea, undiluted by ordinary ice cubes."

Grandpa took the tea and thanked Janice politely. "Just the way I like it," he said. "This reminds me of a Scripture passage that urges Christians to be pure and undiluted by the world." Mother and Janice exchanged knowing glances. Grandpa could make a spiritual lesson out of anything. "It tells us to come away from sinful things and be separated unto God," continued Grandpa. "We're not to have anything to do with sinful things, because righteousness and unrighteousness don't belong together. Iced tea becomes weak and tasteless when ice melts into it, and our lives become weak and ineffective when we allow worldliness to come into them."

Mother nodded. "There's so much pressure to dress, act, talk, and think like the world," she said. "If we're not careful, we forget that we belong to Jesus and should live to please Him. When Christians let the world dilute their testimony, it pollutes their effectiveness!"

Janice chuckled. "Now there are two in the family making up spiritual lessons!" she teased. But she knew they were right.

HOW ABOUT YOU? Are such things as selfishness, bad TV, or foul language diluting your testimony? Do you try to dress like and act like the "trendy" kids you know, even if their ways are displeasing to God? Don't pollute your life with impure things. Ask God to keep you true to Him. □ L.A.T.

TO MEMORIZE: *Do not be yoked together with unbelievers. For what do righteousness and wickedness have in common?* 2 Corinthians 6:14, NIV

Diluted or Pure?

FROM THE BIBLE:
Do not be yoked together with unbelievers. For what do righteousness and wickedness have in common? Or what fellowship can light have with darkness? What harmony is there between Christ and Belial? What does a believer have in common with an unbeliever? What agreement is there between the temple of God and idols? For we are the temple of the living God. As God has said: "I will live with them and walk among them, and I will be their God, and they will be my people. Therefore come out from them and be separate," says the Lord. "Touch no unclean thing, and I will receive you. I will be a Father to you, and you will be my sons and daughters," says the Lord Almighty.
2 Corinthians 6:14-18, NIV

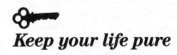

Keep your life pure

JULY

18

Wrong Way

FROM THE BIBLE:

Be strong in the Lord and in the power of His might. Put on the whole armor of God, that you may be able to stand against the wiles of the devil. For we do not wrestle against flesh and blood, but against principalities, against powers, against the rulers of the darkness of this age, against spiritual hosts of wickedness in the heavenly places. Therefore take up the whole armor of God, that you may be able to withstand in the evil day, and having done all, to stand. Stand therefore, having girded your waist with truth, having put on the breastplate of righteousness, and having shod your feet with the preparation of the gospel of peace; above all, taking the shield of faith with which you will be able to quench all the fiery darts of the wicked one. And take the helmet of salvation, and the sword of the Spirit, which is the word of God; praying always with all prayer and supplication in the Spirit, being watchful to this end with all perseverance and supplication for all the saints.

Ephesians 6:10-18, NKJV

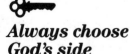

Always choose God's side

STEVEN LOOKED UP when he heard his father's voice. Dad didn't sound very happy. "I told you to mow the lawn," said Dad. "Instead, I find you playing ball. In our discussion last night about the way a Christian should live, I believe it was you who said obeying your parents was one of the most important things you could do. Now, today, you disobey."

Steven took off his baseball mitt. "I'm really sorry. I'll get the lawn mower out right now."

"It's time to leave now," said Dad. "As soon as we come home, however, I want that lawn mowed."

Soon Steven and his whole family were on their way to see six-year-old Sammy's very first soccer game. "Keep the ball in front of you and run fast!" advised Dad.

The game began, but it wasn't until the beginning of the second period that the ball came to Sammy. Then he kept it in front of him and ran as fast as he could, just as his father had told him. "Oh, no!" moaned his family. Sammy had done everything exactly right, only he had kicked the ball through his own team's goal!"

On the way home, Sammy's family did their best to comfort him. "It's only your first game. You'll learn," said Dad as they drove into their yard. Dad looked at the unmowed lawn and then at Steven. "And I hope you learn which side you're on, too, Steven." Steven knew just what Dad meant. "A Christian is on the Lord's side," added Dad, "and he should not act as though he were on the world's side, even for a while."

Steven nodded. He knew he had done that when he had failed to obey his father. He jumped out of the car and went to get the lawn mower.

HOW ABOUT YOU? Are you living as though you're on the world's side or on the Lord's side? The world teaches you to do whatever "feels good" to you. God says, "Be holy as I am holy." The world teaches you to disobey and to be disrespectful to your parents. God says, "Honor your father and mother." Don't listen to the world's view or be swayed to their side in any area of your life. Be strong in the Lord. □ L.W.

TO MEMORIZE: *Be strong in the Lord and in the power of His might.* Ephesians 6:10, NKJV

O̲H, NO!" Kayla moaned. "I have to turn in my Bible reading chart this morning, and it's blank—I forgot to have devotions this week! Do I *have* to go to Sunday school this morning?"

"Why, Kayla, what a question!" Mother was shocked.

Later, as the junior choir sang, Kayla had a solo. "Oh, how I love Jesus because He first loved me," she sang. When the choir had finished, she slipped into the seat beside her mother. Kayla waited expectantly. Mother always complimented her singing. But Mother didn't say one word. So Kayla reached for her mother's hand and squeezed it. Still Mother didn't respond. Kayla frowned. What was wrong?

As Mother prepared Sunday dinner, Kayla chattered happily, but Mother was unusually quiet. Finally, Mother said, "Kayla, why don't you go into the living room until dinner is ready?" Kayla could not believe her ears. Her mother didn't want to talk to her!

After lunch, Kayla went to her room and wrote a note to her mother, telling her how much she loved her. She slipped into the bathroom and taped it to the mirror. But Mother didn't even open it!

Kayla's eyes filled with tears. What had she done? Why was Mother upset with her? Didn't she love her anymore? Just then, she felt her mother's arm around her shoulders.

"I know what's bothering you, Kayla," Mother said softly. "I didn't *want* to hurt your feelings. I do love you, Honey, but you needed to know how it feels to be neglected by someone you love."

"But why?" cried Kayla.

"Because Jesus loves you, and you have been neglecting Him. This morning you grumbled because you had to go to His house. You admitted you hadn't talked to Him or read His book all week. Then at church you sang, 'Oh, how I love Jesus.' Love is more than telling. It's telling and showing."

"I know you're right," Kayla sniffed, "and I'm sorry. I do love Him."

HOW ABOUT YOU? Do you say you love Jesus? Do your actions prove it? It's not enough to say you love Him; you must show your love. If you love Him, you will want to go to His house, read His Word, and talk to Him. □ B. W.

TO MEMORIZE: *Dear children, let us not love with words or tongue but with actions and in truth.* 1 John 3:18, NIV

Tell and Show

FROM THE BIBLE:
A lawyer spoke up: "Sir, which is the most important command in the laws of Moses?" Jesus replied, " 'Love the Lord your God with all your heart, soul, and mind.' This is the first and greatest commandment. The second most important is similar: 'Love your neighbor as much as you love yourself.' All the other commandments and all the demands of the prophets stem from these two laws and are fulfilled if you obey them. Keep only these and you will find that you are obeying all the others."
Matthew 22:35-40, TLB

Show Jesus you love him

JULY

20

Part of the Family

FROM THE BIBLE:

(If by the one man's offense many died, much more the grace of God and the gift by the grace of the one Man, Jesus Christ, abounded to many. And the gift is not like that which came through the one who sinned. For the judgment which came from one offense resulted in condemnation, but the free gift which came from many offenses resulted in justification. For if by the one man's offense death reigned through the one, much more those who receive abundance of grace and of the gift of righteousness will reign in life through the One, Jesus Christ.) Therefore, as through one man's offense judgment came to all men, resulting in condemnation, even so through one Man's righteous act the free gift came to all men, resulting in justification of life. For as by one man's disobedience many were made sinners, so also by one Man's obedience many will be made righteous.

Romans 5:15-19, NKJV

Salvation is a choice

GREG'S UNCLE DAN and Aunt Judy, missionaries to Africa, were returning to the United States for their first furlough. Everyone was eager to see them and their little son, now almost two years old, who had been born in Africa. There was much excitement as they watched the plane taxi to a stop at the gate. Greg watched while the grownups hugged and kissed one another. Finally Uncle Dan turned toward him. "And this must be little Greg," Uncle Dan said, "for he's got his father's eyes. But you're not so little anymore, are you?"

"No, I'm eight years old," Greg said proudly. "Is that your baby?" He pointed to the little boy his mother was holding.

"Yes, that's our Benjamin," answered Uncle Dan.

"He looks just like your Uncle Dan," Mother told Greg.

"Yes," Uncle Dan laughed joyfully, "he's my boy!"

Driving home that night, Greg was full of questions. "How did I get Dad's eyes, and why does Benjamin look like Uncle Dan?" he asked.

"Children inherit certain characteristics—size or shape or color of hair and eyes—from their ancestors," replied Mother. "Benjamin inherited his father's looks, and you inherited your father's eye color."

"That's right," nodded Dad. "But we inherit more than just physical traits from our ancestors."

"What do your mean?" Greg asked.

"The Bible tells us we are all descendants of Adam, the first man God created. Adam sinned against God, and everyone inherits his sinful nature," explained Dad. "But we don't have to remain in our sin. If we accept Jesus as Savior, we become children of God. And God's family is the best family to be a part of!"

HOW ABOUT YOU? Did you know that Adam is your ancestor and through him you inherited a sinful nature? Even though God created you, you are not automatically His child. Your sinful nature is inherited, but salvation is a definite choice. Have you chosen Christ as your Savior? If not, do so today, and you'll be part of God's family forever! □ J.H.

TO MEMORIZE: *For as by one man's disobedience many were made sinners, so also by one Man's obedience many will be made righteous.* Romans 5:19, NKJV

FOR WEEKS, Alyce had promised her grandfather that she would make time to take daily walks with him, and finally the day came when she decided she must begin. To her surprise she enjoyed the brisk walk. "I should have started this long ago," she said as they walked together one day. "I always figured walking would be good for me and that being with you would be fun, but it was so difficult getting started. Now I see that I missed something great."

"I know what you mean," nodded her grandfather. "That's just the way I used to be about reading my Bible."

Alyce stopped and looked at the man beside her. "Reading your Bible?" she asked in disbelief. "You've read your Bible every day as long as you've lived with us!"

"That's true," Grandfather smiled. "But I had a hard time getting myself to do it with regularity, though I've always believed I *should* read it. One day someone told me that if I would make it a regular part of my day's activities, it would soon be a natural part of my life—almost like breathing or eating."

Alyce knew what her grandfather was trying to tell her. She hadn't been very faithful in reading the Bible he had given her last Christmas. She *planned* to read it and had even started once or twice, but soon she had forgotten all about it. She confessed that fact to her grandfather.

"How did you read it?" he asked. "Did you try to see how many chapters you could read at one sitting? Or did you take a bit at a time to see what you could get out of it?" Alyce admitted that she had tried to read as much as her brother, so he would not get ahead of her. "In this case, a slow start is probably best," her grandfather suggested. "It's like walking or jogging. You don't walk three miles the first day. You start slowly, do it regularly, and add the miles gradually."

HOW ABOUT YOU? Have you tried and failed to establish a period of time each day for reading the Bible? When you do read, do you simply try to get through as fast as you can? God's Word should be read regularly, but it ought to be read to get help for the Christian walk. Make God's Word a natural part of your life. □ R.J.

TO MEMORIZE: *Let us walk in the light of the Lord.* Isaiah 2:5, NIV

21

A Slow Start

FROM THE BIBLE:
Forever, O Lord, your Word stands firm in heaven. Your faithfulness extends to every generation, like the earth you created; it endures by your decree, for everything serves your plans. I would have despaired and perished unless your laws had been my deepest delight. I will never lay aside your laws, for you have used them to restore my joy and health. I am yours! Save me! For I have tried to live according to your desires. Though the wicked hide along the way to kill me, I will quietly keep my mind upon your promises. Nothing is perfect except your words.
Psalm 119:89-96, TLB

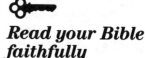

Read your Bible faithfully

22

Welcome to My Room

FROM THE BIBLE:

They are traveling for the Lord, and take neither food, clothing, shelter, nor money from those who are not Christians, even though they have preached to them. So we ourselves should take care of them in order that we may become partners with them in the Lord's work. I sent a brief letter to the church about this, but proud Diotrephes, who loves to push himself forward as the leader of the Christians there, does not admit my authority over him and refuses to listen to me. When I come I will tell you some of the things he is doing and what wicked things he is saying about me and what insulting language he is using. He not only refuses to welcome the missionary travelers himself, but tells others not to, and when they do he tries to put them out of the church. Dear friend, don't let this bad example influence you. Follow only what is good. Remember that those who do what is right prove that they are God's children; and those who continue in evil prove that they are far from God.

3 John 6-11, TLB

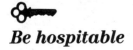

Be hospitable

"I TOLD Pastor Blake we would be glad to have the Whitlocks stay with us," said Mother on the way home from church. "I always enjoy entertaining missionaries."

"That's good news and bad news," Cathy piped up. "It's good news that the Whitlocks are coming, but it's bad news because I'll have to clean my room." Cathy's room turned into the guest room when the family had company.

"That'll take at least ten years," her brother Ken teased.

All that week, Cathy worked in her room after she got home from school—cleaning her closet, dresser drawers, and desk. On Saturday morning, her mom helped her put clean sheets on the bed, wash the windows, and dust. "True hospitality is thinking about the little things that will make your guests comfortable," her mother told her, so Cathy decided to pick some flowers and bake some cookies for the guests.

By late afternoon the room was ready. Cathy made a "Welcome to the Whitlocks" sign with her markers, and then wearily fell asleep on the couch in the family room.

Soon after supper, the Whitlocks arrived, and they spent the next three nights in Cathy's home. The visit went fine, and when they left, Cathy had a special surprise. On her bed was a beautiful Indian necklace and a note. Cathy read, "Thank you for your hospitality. It's a good habit to learn early in life, and you have a special gift of making guests feel welcome. Love, Mr. and Mrs. Whitlock."

"Hey! Next time I think I'll insist they stay in my room," teased Ken.

Cathy grinned at him. "I don't think this necklace would look very good on you," she retorted. "I do love it, but I'd have been glad to give them my room anyway. Having them here was worth all the work, even without the necklace."

HOW ABOUT YOU? When your parents ask guests to come to your house, do you complain because it means extra work? The next time company is coming, remember that hospitality is one of the gifts given by the Lord. Practice showing Christian love by doing everything you can to welcome the guests. □ L. W.

TO MEMORIZE: *Distributing to the needs of the saints, given to hospitality.* Romans 12:13, NKJV

MARTIN DIDN'T understand why his mother had to have the accident! Oh, he knew the roads were wet and slippery, but other cars had been driven safely that day. So why did God let it happen? Why did Mom have the wreck?

One day during hospital visiting hours, Mother seemed to sense Martin's feelings. "Martin," she said, "don't be angry and question why God let this happen. I really believe it's working for my good—that He's refining me to make me more like Jesus. You see, Son, I was so busy that I was drifting away from a close walk with the Lord. Now that I'm lying here flat on my back, I have to look up to God." Martin nodded, but he wasn't quite sure what she meant.

Later that week, Martin's class took a field trip to a nearby silver refining plant. The refining process was very complicated, involving the use of chemicals and all sorts of sophisticated equipment. At the end of the tour they saw a small, primitive-looking furnace. Their guide explained that they kept this old furnace to remind themselves of how far the silver industry had come. "Years ago, silver refiners heated the ore in furnaces like this, cooled it, reheated it, and so forth," he said. "It was a very long process before the impurities were finally worked out."

"How did they know when the silver was pure?" one of the children asked.

The guide smiled. "We're told that when the refiner could see a good clear image of himself in the silver, he turned off the furnace and knew his job was done."

That evening, Martin thought again about what Mother had said. Perhaps Jesus had allowed her to be put in the "furnace" of suffering so He could see a clearer reflection of Himself in her life.

HOW ABOUT YOU? Do you ever wonder why someone has to suffer? Sometimes God allows an experience which seems to be a tragedy just to get our attention and make us better people. Don't rebel when God works out the impurities in you. Just as purified silver shows a clear reflection of the refiner, so your life should show a clear reflection of Jesus. □ R.P.

TO MEMORIZE: *When he has tested me, I will come forth as gold.* Job 23:10, NIV

Refined Silver

FROM THE BIBLE:
He knows the way that I take; when he has tested me, I will come forth as gold. My feet have closely followed his steps; I have kept to his way without turning aside. I have not departed from the commands of his lips; I have treasured the words of his mouth more than my daily bread. But he stands alone, and who can oppose him? He does whatever he pleases. He carries out his decree against me, and many such plans he still has in store.

Job 23:10-14, NIV

Let God refine you

24

Another Bible

FROM THE BIBLE:

Let the thirsty one come—anyone who wants to; let him come and drink the Water of Life without charge. And I solemnly declare to everyone who reads this book: If anyone adds anything to what is written here, God shall add to him the plagues described in this book. And if anyone subtracts any part of these prophecies, God shall take away his share in the Tree of Life, and in the Holy City just described. He who has said all these things declares: Yes, I am coming soon! Amen! Come, Lord Jesus!
Revelation 22:18-21, TLB

Follow the holy Bible

SEE WHAT LARRY loaned me?" Martin handed a book to his father. "They use it in his church—it's their Bible. It reads almost like ours, except there are a few things in it that aren't in ours."

Dad flipped through the pages. "There certainly are."

"But there are lots of things that are the same as our Bible," Martin continued. "It's interesting."

"Yes, but very dangerous," Dad warned.

"Dangerous?" Martin snorted. "How could it be dangerous? It teaches a lot of the same things the Holy Bible teaches—things like loving one another and not stealing or lying. If a person followed all the teachings in this book, he would be a good person."

"Good in the sight of man, but being a 'good' person won't save anyone," Dad reminded. "There is only one way to heaven—Jesus."

"Well, yeah, but, . . ." Martin hesitated. "I still don't see anything so wrong with this book."

Dad explained. "This book is portrayed as God's revelation to man, yet it doesn't acknowledge Jesus as the only way to heaven. When people accept it as the Word of God, they get off course. I saw a chart yesterday that would interest you. It showed what would happen if a rocket fired at the moon were off course by five degrees."

"What did it say?" Anything regarding space exploration fascinated Martin.

"If a rocket fired toward the moon were five degrees off course at blastoff, it would be 13,579 miles off target by the time it reached the moon," said Dad. "In fact, it wouldn't reach the moon—it would bypass it completely."

"Wow!" Martin raised his eyebrows.

"Being just a little bit 'off course' on our journey to heaven means missing heaven completely," continued Dad. "The Holy Bible is our chart. We must follow it and not be side-tracked by other so-called 'bibles' which seem to be 'almost' right."

HOW ABOUT YOU? The Holy Bible is the Book which will show you the way to heaven. Other books may explain how you can be sure of heaven, but they must always refer to, and agree with, what God says in the Bible. If they don't, you must not believe them. Stay with the Word of God. □ B. W.

TO MEMORIZE: *Forever, O Lord, Your word is settled in heaven.* Psalm 119:89, NKJV

"IF GOD LOVED us, He wouldn't let us have all this trouble," Keith argued with his big brother, Mark. "What good does it do to pray? I asked God to heal Grandma Davis, and she died. I asked Him to give Dad a job, but He hasn't. And don't start preaching at me either, just 'cuz you're going to seminary now."

Mark shrugged and sighed, "Very well. Have it your way. Nothing I say seems to help. But your attitude sure is making it hard on Dad. Isn't it bad enough that he's lost his job without you acting like a spoiled brat? So what if you won't get a new bike for your birthday? You'll live."

"That's easy for you to say!" Keith ran out of the house, slamming the door behind him.

Later, Keith went downstairs where Dad and Mark were using Mark's new weight-lifting equipment. After watching a while he grinned. "What's the matter, Dad? You getting soft in your old age?" he teased as his father strained to lift the weights.

Dad laughed, "Been sitting at a desk too long, I guess. I didn't realize I was so out of shape."

"You need to spend some time working out every day, Dad." Keith grinned as he took a turn at the weights. "I'm not nearly as big as you, and I can lift these."

"You're not nearly as old as I am, either." Dad playfully took a jab at Keith.

"It's not age nor size," Keith replied. "It's keeping fit."

"And that's also why it's important to keep in touch with God every day," Mark told his brother. "So your spiritual muscles won't become flabby. If you were in good spiritual shape, Keith, your attitude about our problems would be a lot different," Mark answered pointedly. "You would trust God instead of pouting. You would wait for a bike without complaining."

HOW ABOUT YOU? Are you out of shape spiritually? Have you been skipping daily prayer and Bible reading? If so, your attitude probably shows it. Don't allow your spiritual muscles of faith to become flabby. Determine now to "work out" spiritually every day. □ B. W.

TO MEMORIZE: *I will sing praise to Your name forever, that I may daily perform my vows.* Psalm 61:8, NKJV

Keeping Fit

FROM THE BIBLE:
That night the Christians hurried Paul and Silas to Berea, and, as usual, they went to the synagogue to preach. But the people of Berea were more open-minded than those in Thessalonica, and gladly listened to the message. They searched the Scriptures day by day to check up on Paul and Silas' statements to see if they were really so. As a result, many of them believed.
Acts 17:10-12, TLB

Develop spiritual muscles

26

Dried and Difficult

FROM THE BIBLE:

Remember your Creator in the days of your youth, before the days of trouble come and the years approach when you will say, "I find no pleasure in them"—before the sun and the light and the moon and the stars grow dark, and the clouds return after the rain; when the keepers of the house tremble, and the strong men stoop, when the grinders cease because they are few, and those looking through the windows grow dim; when the doors to the street are closed and the sound of grinding fades; when men rise up at the sound of birds, but all their songs grow faint; when men are afraid of heights and of dangers in the streets; when the almond tree blossoms and the grasshopper drags himself along and desire no longer is stirred. Then man goes to his eternal home and mourners go about the streets.

Ecclesiastes 12:1-5, NIV

Don't put off salvation

CARRIE'S MOTHER HAD gone to buy groceries, and Carrie was all alone in the house. As she sat reading a new book, she suddenly remembered that Mother had told her to clean up the kitchen before she got back. Now it was almost noon, so Carrie hurried to the kitchen and tackled the stack of dishes she had left on the counter. But egg yolk had dried on the plates, and it didn't seem to wash off. She had to scrub each one with the scouring cloth.

As Carrie continued to work, she heard the car pull up in the driveway. When Mother walked into the kitchen, Carrie was still scrubbing the plates. She began to explain why the job was taking such a long time. "I forgot all about it," she confessed. "I thought I'd be done before you got here, but this stuff doesn't want to come off!"

Carrie's mother nodded. "There's nothing harder to wash off than a dried egg yolk," she agreed. Suddenly her eyes brightened. "Would you mind if I used this as an illustration in my class next Sunday?"

"Illustration?" Carrie asked. "How?"

"I've been telling my girls that it's important to make their decision for Christ right now. Delay only makes it more difficult. The egg on these plates demonstrates that. If you had done the dishes right away, the egg yolk would have washed right off. But once it was set, it was very difficult to remove. In the same way, as people grow older and become set in their ways, they often find it difficult to come to Christ."

Carrie got the point. "If I had washed those dishes right after you left," she said, "I could have saved myself a lot of trouble."

"And if my girls would put their faith and trust in Jesus Christ now while they're young, it could save them a lot of trouble." Mother smiled at Carrie.

HOW ABOUT YOU? Have you put off giving your heart and life to Jesus? Remember, as a rule, the older people get, the harder it is for them to confess their sinful ways. You will probably be no exception to that rule. The Lord Jesus is waiting for you to come now to confess your sin and believe in Him. □ R.J.

TO MEMORIZE: *Remember your Creator in the days of your youth, before the days of trouble come.* Ecclesiastes 12:1, NIV

B ECKY, WOULD YOU share your testimony next week?" Mr. Helton asked after the Bible club meeting.

"Ohhh, I don't know," Becky responded dejectedly. "I don't really have anything to share."

"Why, Becky, I thought you asked Jesus to save you at one of our meetings last year," answered the teacher.

"Yes, but every time I hear people give testimonies, they tell about all the bad things they did before Jesus came into their hearts. They have a lot to thank Jesus for since He saved them from all these things," Becky said. "I didn't do a lot of horrid things before I was saved."

Mr. Helton smiled. He knew Becky was remembering the rally to which he had taken his Bible club. First a pro football player had told about his life as a drug addict before he'd been born again. Then a lady had shared her testimony as to how she had been in the very act of committing suicide when a friend stopped in and won her to the Lord. "Becky, perhaps you have *more* to thank God for than any of the people you've heard giving testimonies," suggested Mr. Helton. "You see, since you accepted Jesus into your heart at a young age, the Lord has protected you from ever getting involved in some of the horrible sin which might have entered your life as you grew older. You can express thanks to God for this."

"But do you think anyone is interested in hearing what I have to say?" Becky wondered.

"Oh, yes," Mr. Helton assured her. "Many others in our Bible club may feel just as you do— that they have little to testify about. Hearing what you have to say may help them realize how blessed they are, too. And some who are not saved may see the value of accepting Jesus now, while they are young."

Becky smiled and nodded. "Plan on my testimony next week," she said.

HOW ABOUT YOU? Are you one of those who accepted Jesus as Savior before you ever got deeply involved in a life of sin? If so, never be sorry that you have not experienced some of the evil in the world. Instead, thank the Lord for protecting you. □ R.P.

TO MEMORIZE: *Let the redeemed of the Lord say so.* Psalm 107:2, NKJV

The Sooner the Better

FROM THE BIBLE:
Oh, give thanks to the Lord, for He is good! For His mercy endures forever. Let the redeemed of the Lord say so, whom He has redeemed from the hand of the enemy, and gathered out of the lands, from the east and from the west, from the north and from the south. They wandered in the wilderness in a desolate way; they found no city to dwell in. Hungry and thirsty, their soul fainted in them. Then they cried out to the Lord in their trouble, and He delivered them out of their distresses. And He led them forth by the right way, that they might go to a city for habitation. Oh, that men would give thanks to the Lord for His goodness, and for His wonderful works to the children of men!
Psalm 107:1-8, NKJV

All Christians have a testimony

28

A Fresh Lump

FROM THE BIBLE:

Don't you know that a little yeast works through the whole batch of dough? Get rid of the old yeast that you may be a new batch without yeast—as you really are. For Christ, our Passover lamb, has been sacrificed. Therefore let us keep the Festival, not with the old yeast, the yeast of malice and wickedness, but with bread without yeast, the bread of sincerity and truth.

1 Corinthians 5:6-8, NIV

Clean out sin

MOTHER, THOSE LOAVES of bread look so little," said Janice as she watched Mother baking bread. "Shouldn't you put more dough in the pans?"

Mother laughed. "Come and look at them in about an hour," she said.

Janice forgot about the baking as she played house with her friend Audrey. They wore some of Mother's old dresses and high heels and pretended to be grand ladies. As Janice teetered through the hall, she noticed a small bottle of perfume on Mother's dresser. She knew she wasn't supposed to touch Mother's things, but after all, grand ladies should have some perfume. They would use only a very little. She opened the bottle and put a tiny bit on her wrist.

A little later Mother called her. "Come have a look at these loaves now, Janice," she said. "They're ready for the oven." Janice was surprised to see that the loaves now were raised over the top of the pans.

Mother sniffed. "What do I smell?" she asked. "Did you use my perfume?" Janice was startled. "N–no," she stammered. Just then her little sister came into the kitchen. "Smell me!" she exclaimed. She held a half-empty perfume bottle. As Mother began to scold her, tears filled her eyes, and she turned to Janice. "Janny used it," she said, "so I thought I could too." Mother looked at Janice, and soon she heard the whole story. She pointed to the loaves of bread. "You see what happened to the bread dough," she said. "It contains a small amount of yeast which grows and makes the loaves big. Sin is like yeast—it grows, too. Your sin of disobedience grew and caused you to lie to me. It also spread to others. Your sister followed your example."

"I'm sorry, Mother," Janice said. "I guess there isn't any such thing as a little sin because it grows fast."

"That's right," agreed Mother. "That's why the Bible says we need to get rid of the 'yeast,' or sin, in our lives. We do this by confessing and forsaking it. Then God will forgive us, and we can have a new start."

HOW ABOUT YOU? Are you tempted to do something you know isn't right? Be very careful. Clean out that "yeast," or sin, before it can grow. □ H.M.

TO MEMORIZE: *Get rid of the old yeast that you may be a new batch without yeast—as you really are.* 1 Corinthians 5:7, NIV

O H, SHUT UP!" Terri yelled at Lynn, as she shoved her aside. As soon as she said the words, she regretted it. As a Christian, she knew this wasn't the way she should act, but sometimes Lynn could be so exasperating!

That night she shared her frustrations with her dad. "We often say wrong things, because we are thinking the wrong things," he told her. "Unfortunately, the combination of wrong thoughts and wrong words often leads to wrong actions. Terri, do you know what an acrostic is?"

"A what?" Terri wanted to know.

"I'll show you what I mean," Dad answered. On a sheet of paper, he wrote the following, and showed it to Terri.

W—ords
A—ctions
T—houghts
C—ompanions
H—abits

"You see that the first letters of these words spell the word *watch,*" Dad explained. "Each letter stands for something you should watch! You learned today that wrong words and actions can slip out pretty easily as a result of wrong thoughts. As for companions, I think you're finding that Lynn is not really the kind of person you want for a close companion. She just doesn't bring out the best in you and doesn't help you to grow as a Christian should. If wrong thoughts, words, and actions come often enough, they produce some bad habits."

"You know what, Dad?" Terri said with a grin. "You would make a good preacher. I'm going to remember your little outline, and it will help me make right choices."

HOW ABOUT YOU? Ask the Lord to help you in each of these five areas of your life. Develop good habits that will be pleasing to the Lord. □ C.V.M.

TO MEMORIZE: *May the words of my mouth and the meditation of my heart be pleasing in your sight, O Lord, my Rock and my Redeemer.* Psalm 19:14, NIV

Watch It

FROM THE BIBLE:
The law of the Lord is perfect, reviving the soul. The statutes of the Lord are trustworthy, making wise the simple. The precepts of the Lord are right, giving joy to the heart. The commands of the Lord are radiant, giving light to the eyes. The fear of the Lord is pure, enduring forever. The ordinances of the Lord are sure and altogether righteous. They are more precious than gold, than much pure gold; they are sweeter than honey, than honey from the comb. By them is your servant warned; in keeping them there is great reward. Who can discern his errors? Forgive my hidden faults. Keep your servant also from willful sins; may they not rule over me. Then will I be blameless, innocent of great transgression. May the words of my mouth and the meditation of my heart be pleasing in your sight, O Lord, my Rock and my Redeemer.
Psalm 19:7-14, NIV

Live to please God

30

My Little Light

FROM THE BIBLE:

Love the Lord your God with all your heart and with all your soul and with all your strength. These commandments that I give you today are to be upon your hearts. Impress them on your children. Talk about them when you sit at home and when you walk along the road, when you lie down and when you get up.

Deuteronomy 6:5-7, NIV

Study the Bible with others

"THIS LITTLE LIGHT of mine, I'm gonna let it shine," sang the kids around the campfire at their retreat. "For our special fun time tonight, we're going to have a treasure hunt," said Mr. Scott, the retreat director. "The first team to find all the clues will win. Take your flashlights with you, and be sure you don't lose your treasure hunt list."

Soon Johnny and the other members of his team were headed through the dark woods, looking for the clues listed on the treasure hunt paper. They were making good progress when suddenly a gust of wind blew the all-important paper out of their hands. Before they could catch it, the wind had whisked it out of sight. With a cry of dismay, Johnny plunged off the path in the direction it had gone. He shined his light all around, but no paper came into view. "Come and help," he called. "Add your lights to mine. Unless we find that paper we can't even finish the treasure hunt." The others joined him, and with all of their lights searching the area, the paper was soon discovered caught on the branch of a tree. They held on tight after that—and won!

Johnny and the others told Mr. Scott about almost losing the paper. They told him how they combined their lights to find it.

"Well, there's a good lesson to be learned from your experience," said Mr. Scott with a grin. "We could compare the treasure hunt list to the Bible. There's no way you can successfully make it through life without God's guidebook, the Bible. There's another lesson here, too. Sometimes we're stumped about the meaning of a verse. We can't seem to understand it until others join us, and we begin talking about it and discussing it. By combining our efforts, we can often understand more about the Bible than we do by just studying it on our own."

HOW ABOUT YOU? Have you learned to find your way through life by following the instructions in the Word of God? And when you are "stumped" by what some verses mean, have you ever tried talking it over with other Christians and studying it together? Try it! □ C.V.M.

TO MEMORIZE: *Impress them on your children. Talk about them when you sit at home and when you walk along the road, when you lie down and when you get up.* Deuteronomy 6:7, NIV

EIGHT-YEAR-OLD Mitch was excited as he put an *X* on the corner spot of the tic-tac-toe game. He was finally going to win against his big sister Marcia. He laughed out loud because on the next move, he could win two different ways. It didn't matter where she put her *O* to block him! But his laughter stopped suddenly as Marcia marked an *O* and went on to draw a line through three *O's* in a row! She had won again!

"I hate you!" he shrieked as he threw his pencil across the room and stomped out. A little later Mother found him lying on his bed.

"Marcia told me what happened," she said. "You lost two things—the game and your temper. And you lost both of them for the same reason. It was because you didn't watch your opponent."

Mitch sat up straight and looked at her, a question in his eyes. "That's right," she said. "Marcia was your opponent in the game, but you were so concerned about how you would win that you forgot to think about how *she* would play. You also have another opponent, a more serious one. The Bible says that the devil is our adversary, or opponent. We need to be alert and not allow him to get the best of us. You weren't watching out for him when you lost your temper."

Mitch nodded sadly. "I guess not," he said. Then he brightened. "But Jesus will forgive me, won't He? I'll ask Him, and Marcia, too. And I'll ask God to help me not to do it again."

HOW ABOUT YOU? Do you sometimes forget to watch out for Satan? He loves to see you lose your temper. He's happy when you cheat. It pleases him if you disobey Mother or Dad. He likes to hear you gossip. Whenever you sin, Satan is glad. But you don't have to lose to him. Resist him, and God will give you victory. □ H.M.

TO MEMORIZE: *Submit to God. Resist the devil and he will flee from you.* James 4:7, NKJV

Watch Your Opponent

FROM THE BIBLE:
If you will humble yourselves under the mighty hand of God, in his good time he will lift you up. Let him have all your worries and cares, for he is always thinking about you and watching everything that concerns you. Be careful— watch out for attacks from Satan, your great enemy. He prowls around like a hungry, roaring lion, looking for some victim to tear apart. Stand firm when he attacks. Trust the Lord; and remember that other Christians all around the world are going through these sufferings too.
1 Peter 5:6-9, NIV

Resist Satan

1

Getting the Credit

FROM THE BIBLE:

*Honor goes to kind and gracious
women, mere money to cruel
men. Your own soul is nourished
when you are kind; it is destroyed when you are cruel. The
evil man gets rich for the
moment, but the good man's
reward lasts forever. The good
man finds life; the evil man,
death. The Lord hates the
stubborn but delights in those
who are good. You can be very
sure the evil man will not go
unpunished forever. And you
can also be very sure God will
rescue the children of the godly.*
Proverbs 11:16-21, TLB

Don't look for praise

AFTER SUNDAY SCHOOL, Angela and Diane caught up with Allison in the hall. The three girls had just been appointed to the food committee for the class picnic, with Allison as chairman. "When shall we meet?" Diane asked.

"Not today. I'm going home with Shelly," Allison called over her shoulder as she hurried away.

Later that week, the committee finally got together. "What do we want to eat?" Allison asked.

Diane had been thinking about it, and she handed Allison a copy of the menu she had planned. Allison glanced at it. "Looks OK. Who brings what?"

Diane handed her another list. Allison glanced at it, too.

"I suppose this will do," she said. "I don't have time to plan a better one. Why don't you and Angela tell everyone what to bring?" She handed the second list back to Diane. "I'd better keep this first list so I can show Miss Wilson the menu. See you later."

The picnic was a success. "We didn't forget a thing," Angela remarked as she and Diane cleared the table. Allison was playing games.

As everyone prepared to leave, Diane saw Miss Wilson pat Allison's shoulder. "You did a great job, Allison," said the teacher. "It's nice to have someone I can depend upon."

Allison smiled sweetly. "I enjoyed helping, Miss Wilson."

A dark red flush spread over Diane's face. "Did you hear that, Angela? Allison didn't do one thing, and she's taking the credit for our hard work!"

Angela laughed. "Oh, well, I know better, and you know better. In fact, most of the kids know who did the work. I'm not going to let Allison's attitude spoil my day. We had fun doing it, and we did a good job. That's the important thing. Besides, my dad always says God doesn't settle His accounts immediately, but pay day is coming."

HOW ABOUT YOU? Have you ever worked hard, done a good job, and then had someone else get the credit for your work? The reward for a job well done is not always praise and honor from others. The satisfaction of knowing you've done your best is more important than praise. Ask God to help you do all things as unto Him. His approval is most important. □ B.W.

TO MEMORIZE: *Be strong and do not give up, for your work will be rewarded.* 2 Chronicles 15:7, NIV

WHEN TONY ARRIVED at Sunday school, he was surprised to see a beautiful radio on the table in front of his teacher, Mr. Brock. In fact, it was more than just a radio. It also held a cassette deck. "Whew!" whistled Tony. "That's really neat. What's it for?"

Mr. Brock smiled. "It is pretty nice-looking, isn't it?" he agreed. The boys all crowded around as he pointed out various attractive features of the set. He showed them how the cassette was inserted and which buttons controlled it. He pointed out that they could either listen or record; he showed them where the speakers were located. He indicated the controls for the radio and demonstrated how the aerial was used. When one of the boys suggested that they listen to it, Mr. Brock nodded agreeably and turned the radio on. But all remained silent. Mr. Brock looked at the class.

"Say, can anyone tell me why there is no sound coming from the radio?" he asked.

"Is it plugged in?" asked one of the boys.

"Aha!" said Mr. Brock, "that's exactly the problem. It needs to be plugged in." He took the plug and inserted it into the electrical outlet behind him. Immediately the room was filled with music.

"I brought the radio for an object lesson, boys," said Mr. Brock. "Our lives are much like this radio. We may look good to those who see us. We may even look good to ourselves. But that is just our outward appearance. We don't look good to God, who sees our hearts. Without Him, our lives are hollow. We have no power. Before we can amount to anything, we have to be 'plugged in' to the right source of power. That power is God Himself, and we come to God only through Jesus Christ, God's Son. I want to challenge each of you boys to accept Jesus as your Savior."

HOW ABOUT YOU? Do you read the Bible? Pray? Go to church? Do good deeds? All these are fine things to do, but by themselves, they accomplish nothing. You must first be "plugged in" to the source of power. You must trust Christ as your own personal Savior. Have you done that? Why not do it right now. □ C.V.M.

TO MEMORIZE: *The Lord does not look at the things man looks at. Man looks at the outward appearance, but the Lord looks at the heart.* 1 Samuel 16:7, NIV

Source of Power

FROM THE BIBLE:
Woe to you, Pharisees, and you religious leaders—hypocrites! You are so careful to polish the outside of the cup, but the inside is foul with extortion and greed. Blind Pharisees! First cleanse the inside of the cup, and then the whole cup will be clean. Woe to you, Pharisees, and you religious leaders! You are like beautiful mausoleums—full of dead men's bones, and of foulness and corruption. You try to look like saintly men, but underneath those pious robes of yours are hearts besmirched with every sort of hypocrisy and sin.
Matthew 23:25-28, TLB

"Plug in" to God's power

3

Big or Small?

FROM THE BIBLE:

If you really fulfill the royal law according to the Scripture, "You shall love your neighbor as yourself," you do well; but if you show partiality, you commit sin, and are convicted by the law as transgressors. For whoever shall keep the whole law, and yet stumble in one point, he is guilty of all. For He who said, "Do not commit adultery," also said, "Do not murder." Now if you do not commit adultery, but you do murder, you have become a transgressor of the law.

James 2:8-11, NKJV

Sin is sin

"HAVE YOU FINISHED cleaning your room already?" asked Mom as Jeff joined her on the front porch. Jeff nodded, but he avoided his mother's eyes as he seated himself on the porch swing. He had not cleaned his room at all, but he would be sure to get it done before she checked later that afternoon.

"You know, Mom," he said, "I'm glad I'm not as bad as Rick." He waved at the neighbor boy.

"Oh?" Mom gave Jeff a questioning glance.

"Rick does such bad things all the time," explained Jeff. "He cheats sometimes when we play games, and he can tell the biggest lies! I've heard him swear, too."

"I'm glad to hear that you don't do those things," replied Mom, "but I assume you do sin sometimes. Right?"

"Oh, sure." Jeff remembered the lie he had just told his mother. But it was such a little one.

"Well, don't think that your sins are less important in God's eyes than Rick's are," Mom continued.

"What do you mean?" asked Jeff.

"I mean that God looks at sin and sees it for what it is. There are no big sins or small sins from God's point of view," explained Mom. "It's all just plain sin to Him."

"Does that mean I might as well do the things Rick does because it's all the same to God anyway?" asked Jeff.

"Of course not," replied Mom. "It means that when people do things like that, we shouldn't think we're so much better than they are. We commit sin, too, so instead of pointing a finger at others, we should confess our own sin to God."

Jeff was quiet for a moment. Suddenly he jumped up. "I didn't really clean my room," he confessed as he headed for the door. "I'm sorry. I'm going to do it now. And I'll think twice before I start saying that I'm better than somebody else!" he added.

HOW ABOUT YOU? Do you know somebody who cheats, lies, steals, or does other things you wouldn't think of doing? Don't have a "holier than thou" attitude. Remember that you do wrong things, too. God can't stand sin of any kind. Ask God's forgiveness, and ask Him to help you be less critical of others. □ D.M.

TO MEMORIZE: *Whoever shall keep the whole law, and yet stumble in one point, he is guilty of all.* James 2:10, NKJV

ALEX RAN to the car as Dad drove up in front of his school. "Have a good day?" Dad asked as Alex got in. Alex shrugged. "Are you unhappy with me for not letting you go to the movie with the others?" Dad asked softly.

Alex shook his head. "No. I'm glad you said no. It's not the kind of movie I should see," he said, truly grateful for a Christian dad.

"I'll bet your friends gave you a hard time, didn't they?" asked Dad.

"Yeah. Even Ben thought I should tell you I was going somewhere else and then go to the movie with them." Alex sighed. Ben was his friend from church.

When they got home, Dad took an empty pop can out of a carton standing in the garage. He handed it to Alex. "Crush this can," Dad said. Surprised, Alex started to ask a question, but then he shrugged. He set the can on the floor and easily smashed it with a stomp of his foot.

"Now crush this can," Dad said, handing Alex a full can of pop.

Alex stared at Dad. "I can't," he replied.

"Why not?" asked Dad.

"Because it's full," answered Alex.

"Which can are you like?" asked Dad. "Are you empty or full?" Alex frowned, trying to figure out what Dad was getting at. "I bet you had an empty feeling when your friends made fun of you, didn't you?" asked Dad. Alex nodded. "But you're not actually empty," continued Dad. "God's Holy Spirit came into your life when you became a Christian. He gives you strength so that no one can 'crush' you—no one can defeat you—no matter what happens."

Alex gave Dad a little smile. It wasn't easy having others against him, but God would help him do the right thing.

HOW ABOUT YOU? Are you discouraged as you live your life for Jesus? Does it bother you when others—especially other Christians—try to get you to do things you believe are wrong? Do you feel "down" when someone makes fun of you for doing right? Remember, if you're a Christian, God is living in you. You are uncrushable. □ K.R.A.

TO MEMORIZE: *We are hard pressed on every side, but not crushed; perplexed, but not in despair; persecuted, but not abandoned; struck down, but not destroyed.* 2 Corinthians 4:8-9, NIV

The Uncrushable Can

FROM THE BIBLE:
Dear friends, don't be bewildered or surprised when you go through the fiery trials ahead, for this is no strange, unusual thing that is going to happen to you. Instead, be really glad—because these trials will make you partners with Christ in his suffering, and afterwards you will have the wonderful joy of sharing his glory in that coming day when it will be displayed. Be happy if you are cursed and insulted for being a Christian, for when that happens the Spirit of God will come upon you with great glory. Don't let me hear of your suffering for murdering or stealing or making trouble or being a busybody and prying into other people's affairs. But it is no shame to suffer for being a Christian. Praise God for the privilege of being in Christ's family and being called by his wonderful name!
1 Peter 4:12-16, TLB

Don't be discouraged

5

Salty Songs

FROM THE BIBLE:

Don't be weary in prayer; keep at it; watch for God's answers and remember to be thankful when they come. Don't forget to pray for us too, that God will give us many chances to preach the Good News of Christ for which I am here in jail. Pray that I will be bold enough to tell it freely and fully, and make it plain, as, of course, I should. Make the most of your chances to tell others the Good News. Be wise in all your contacts with them. Let your conversation be gracious as well as sensible, for then you will have the right answer for everyone.
Colossians 4:2-6, TLB

Be a "salty" Christian

MANY OF JANET'S classmates had gone to a rock concert. Janet had stayed home because she knew that the words of many of the songs the group sang were not pleasing to God.

For several days after the concert, the kids sang some of the songs they'd heard. Soon Janet knew the words, too, but she didn't sing along. A Bible verse she had learned in Sunday school kept running through her mind, and it kept her from joining in. The verse was, "You are the salt of the earth," and Janet recalled her Sunday school teacher's words. "When Christians do wrong things just because others are doing them," Mrs. Drake had said, "they've lost their 'saltiness'—their usefulness."

After a week or so, the kids lost interest in the concert songs and turned to other subjects.

One afternoon Janet hummed a tune as she walked home. Sue, a classmate, heard her. "That's a pretty song you're humming. What is it?" asked Sue.

"It's 'God is So Good,'" said Janet. "We sing it a lot in Sunday school."

Sue shook her head. "I've never heard it before."

"It's real easy to learn. Sing along with me." suggested Janet. Sue did, and the girls sang many verses to the same tune, including the words "Christ died for me."

"What does that mean?" asked Sue.

Janet smiled and explained how Christ came to take everyone's punishment for sin, so all who believe can go to heaven. After reaching Janet's house, the girls sat on the front steps and talked a while longer. Janet was pleased when Sue agreed to go to church and Sunday school the next weekend. How glad she was that her song had been "salty!"

HOW ABOUT YOU? If you love Jesus, you can be "salty" in many ways, even in the songs you sing. Although some songs used by popular groups are all right, many are not. You can show your love for Jesus by not singing words that displease Him. Whenever possible, sing salty songs. □ C.Y.

TO MEMORIZE: *You are the salt of the earth; but if the salt loses its flavor, how shall it be seasoned?* Matthew 5:13, NKJV

D ADDY!" WAILED SHANA. "My flashlight won't work! I just put in new batteries, but it still doesn't light."

"Let me have a look," replied Dad. He removed the batteries. "I think I see the problem, Shana." Shana peered more closely at the batteries in Dad's hand. "Here on the end of the battery—the place where it must contact, or touch, the second battery—is a piece of clear plastic," continued Dad. "See? You didn't peel away all the packaging, and that ruined the contact." Dad deftly removed the plastic and wiped the contact points clean. Then he replaced the batteries in their proper position. "Now try it," he said, handing the flashlight to Shana. She flicked the switch, and the light shone brightly. Shana smiled happily as she thanked Dad for fixing the flashlight.

"You know, Shana," said Dad, "your flashlight is going to make a good illustration for the Sunday school lesson I'm teaching this week. Just as that piece of plastic came between the batteries and stopped their power, sin in our lives comes between us and God's power to work in us. It ruins our fellowship with God. When His power is cut off, we can't shine for Him."

Shana nodded. "Sin and plastic sure can make a big power failure, can't they?"

HOW ABOUT YOU? Are you shining brightly for Jesus every day? Or is there sin in your life which hinders God's power? Such things as lying, cheating, swearing, stealing, gossip, jealousy, selfishness, and disobedience are sins which spoil your fellowship with God. Confess your sin to Him, and let God's power light up your life. Be sure there's no sin between you and the Lord. □ L.A.T.

TO MEMORIZE: *Your iniquities have separated you from your God; your sins have hidden his face from you, so that he will not hear.* Isaiah 59:2, NIV

6

Power Failure

FROM THE BIBLE:
Surely the arm of the Lord is not too short to save, nor his ear too dull to hear. But your iniquities have separated you from your God; your sins have hidden his face from you, so that he will not hear. For your hands are stained with blood, your fingers with guilt. Your lips have spoken lies, and your tongue mutters wicked things. No one calls for justice; no one pleads his case with integrity. They rely on empty arguments and speak lies; they conceive trouble and give birth to evil. Isaiah 59:1-4, NIV

Shine today for Jesus

7

That's Ridiculous

FROM THE BIBLE:

Beloved, let us love one another, for love is of God; and everyone who loves is born of God and knows God. He who does not love does not know God, for God is love. In this the love of God was manifested toward us, that God has sent His only begotten Son into the world, that we might live through Him. In this is love, not that we loved God, but that He loved us and sent His Son to be the propitiation for our sins. Beloved, if God so loved us, we also ought to love one another.
1 John 4:7-11, NKJV

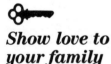

Show love to your family

IT WAS THE most ridiculous thing Shelly had ever heard! "Let your brothers and sisters know you love them," Mrs. Johnson, Shelly's Sunday school teacher, had said. "And don't just tell them—show them, too." Well, obviously Mrs. Johnson didn't know Todd, Shelly's brother. He was a pain! Even her folks were often mad at him.

When Shelly got home, Moppet, her dog, looked up from his basket. "Hi, Baby," crooned Shelly. As she sat down to pet him, Todd walked through the kitchen. Moppet promptly jumped from his basket and followed Todd outside. Shelly glared after him. "Hey," she complained, "you belong to me, you know." Shelly went to her room to change her clothes.

Later that evening, Shelly saw her brother sitting in the living room, watching TV. She could tell that he wasn't very interested in the program. She hadn't thought about it before, but Todd didn't have many friends. And he didn't spend much time talking to her parents. Neither of them did, because Mom and Dad were always too busy. Shelly never talked to Todd much, either, except to fight with him. She always kept busy with her own friends.

As Shelly thought about it, she remembered how she felt when Moppet chose to follow Todd instead of her. It annoyed her, but it made her feel kind of sad, too. *Is that how Todd feels?* she thought. *Sad, and maybe lonely?* She thought of Mrs. Johnson's words. Actually, she did love Todd, even though she didn't always get along with him.

Shelly went to the kitchen and got a Coke. She took it to the living room and handed it to her brother. He looked up in surprise. "Todd," she said softly as she sat down next to him, "I . . . I just want you to know that I . . . I love you."

Todd gave her a funny look. "At least somebody cares," he mumbled.

It wasn't much, but it was a start.

HOW ABOUT YOU? Do your brothers or sisters know you care about them? Sometimes it's harder to get along with family members than with anyone else, but it's important that you do so. Ask the Lord to help you be a good testimony to your family. □ L. W.

TO MEMORIZE: *And this commandment we have from Him: that he who loves God must love his brother also.* 1 John 4:21, NKJV

AMY AND HER new friend Sara chatted happily in the back seat as Dad drove them to the youth banquet at church. It was a dress-up event, and both girls had new dresses for the occasion. "I'm so glad you could come with me tonight," Amy told Sara. "Your dress looks so nice."

"Well, I'm glad you invited me," replied Sara. "I don't see the inside of a church very often, you know. How come you go all the time?"

"Well," said Amy, "I go to worship God and to learn more about Him. I'm a Christian. I've asked Jesus to save me and I love Him and want to learn how to live in a way that pleases Him."

"What do you mean—'save' you?" asked Sara, as Amy's dad drove up to the church and stopped.

"Well, we're all sinners," explained Amy, climbing out of the car, "and Jesus paid the price for our sins." Their conversation was interrupted as other kids arrived, so they waved good-bye to Dad and went up the church steps.

Just as Amy walked into the church, she glanced down at her feet. She froze in place. "Oh, no," she gasped. "Oh, Sara, look! I'm still wearing my sneakers. Oh, why didn't you tell me?"

"I never noticed," replied Sara, laughing. "They do look pretty funny with that dress."

"Well, I'm not going in there like this," declared Amy. She introduced Sara to a friend, and then left them to make a quick phone call to her mother. She waited at the church door for Dad to bring her good shoes.

"And I thought you had just the right shoes," Dad said when he finally came.

"You liked these sneakers?" asked Amy.

"Oh, I didn't notice them," laughed Dad, "but I did notice that you were ready with an answer when Sara questioned you about your salvation. According to the Bible, you had your 'feet shod with the preparation of the gospel of peace.' That's so much more important than wearing dressy shoes with your new outfit."

HOW ABOUT YOU? Are you ready at any time to tell others about Jesus—to be a witness for Him? That may mean talking to someone about Him. It also means living in such a way that others can see that you belong to Him. □ H.M.

TO MEMORIZE: *Stand therefore, having girded your waist with truth, having put on the breastplate of righteousness, and having shod your feet with the preparation of the gospel of peace.* Ephesians 6:14-15, NKJV

Amy's Shoes

FROM THE BIBLE:
Stand therefore, having girded your waist with truth, having put on the breastplate of righteousness, and having shod your feet with the preparation of the gospel of peace; above all, taking the shield of faith with which you will be able to quench all the fiery darts of the wicked one. And take the helmet of salvation, and the sword of the Spirit, which is the word of God; praying always with all prayer and supplication in the Spirit, being watchful to this end with all perseverance and supplication for all the saints—and for me, that utterance may be given to me, that I may open my mouth boldly to make known the mystery of the gospel, for which I am an ambassador in chains; that in it I may speak boldly, as I ought to speak.
Ephesians 6:14-20, NKJV

Be ready to witness

Torn Friendship

FROM THE BIBLE:
I have loved you even as the Father has loved me. Live within my love. When you obey me you are living in my love, just as I obey my Father and live in his love. I have told you this so that you will be filled with my joy. Yes, your cup of joy will overflow! I demand that you love each other as much as I love you. And here is how to measure it—the greatest love is shown when a person lays down his life for his friends; and you are my friends if you obey me. I no longer call you slaves, for a master doesn't confide in his slaves; now you are my friends, proved by the fact that I have told you everything the Father told me. You didn't choose me! I chose you! I appointed you to go and produce lovely fruit always, so that no matter what you ask for from the Father, using my name, he will give it to you. I demand that you love each other.
John 15:9-17, TLB

Love one another

DENNY, GET AWAY!" stormed Janice as her brother hopped and jumped through the hopscotch squares she and her friend Martha were using. Denny laughed and moved on down the street.

"He's an awful pest, isn't he?" asked Martha. Janice nodded as the girls resumed the game. "I don't know when I've seen such an awful kid," continued Martha.

"He's not all that bad," replied Janice.

"He should have a good whipping or something to keep him in line," grumbled Martha.

"Oh, he just likes to tease." Janice quickly came to the defense of her brother. "He's a good kid, really. Besides, your brother's no angel, either!"

"Well, Denny's much worse," insisted Martha. When she continued to criticize, Janice decided she'd heard enough. She left the game and went into the house to read.

As Janice opened one of her favorite books, she noticed a torn page. She found some tape and asked Mother to help her mend the page. As they worked, Janice told Mother about Martha's unkind words. "She's obnoxious!" fumed Janice. "She's not my friend anymore."

"Why did you stand up for your brother?" asked Mother. "You often criticize him yourself, you know." When Janice shrugged, Mother continued, "I think it's because you actually do love him." She pointed to the page they had just mended. "See how the tape holds the edges together and covers up the tear, making the paper strong again? Love is something like that. The Bible says it covers a 'multitude of sins.' I'm glad you defended Denny, but don't be too angry with Martha. She's part of your family, too, since you're both Christians. She's your sister in the Lord. That doesn't mean you have to stand around and listen to her criticize your brother, but it does mean you should be patient and willing to overlook some of her faults. Let love mend the tear in your friendship."

HOW ABOUT YOU? Has someone hurt you? God loves you and has graciously forgiven you. Will you love and forgive as He does? Be willing to overlook differences of opinion. Be tolerant of different ways of thinking. Love others as God has commanded. □ H.M.

TO MEMORIZE: *Above all, love each other deeply, because love covers over a multitude of sins.* 1 Peter 4:8, NIV

MARK MANEUVERED his skateboard up the front walk of his new home. He positioned it near the place where his dad was working and sat on it, looking rather unhappy. "Hey, Pal, haven't you gotten to know any of our new neighbors yet?" asked Dad. "What about that boy . . . uh . . . uh . . . ?"

"Chad," said Mark. "His name is Chad. I was just over at his house, and we played for a while. I told him we want to find a good church to go to around here and asked him if he knows of one. Do you know what he said, Dad? He said he didn't even believe in God! He said, 'If there really is a God, why does He let so many bad things happen? If God created people, how come He lets them suffer for no reason?' "

"Hmmmm," murmured Dad. "Suffering is due to sin in the world, but I'm not just sure how you can best show that to Chad or convince him of God's existence. I'll pray that God will show you how to answer him."

A few days later, Chad came over to Mark's house. Chad's leg was bandaged, and he was on crutches. "My sister pushed me over on my bike, and I hurt my leg," he explained. "Boy, was Dad mad. She really got it!"

Mark began to sympathize. Then he thought of something. "Your dad?" he asked. "You mean you have a dad, and he let you hurt your leg?"

"What do you mean, he 'let' me?" asked Chad. "It's not his fault. It's my sister's."

"Well, that's funny," observed Mark. "You blame God when bad things happen to people, but you don't blame your dad for what happened to you."

For once, Chad found nothing to say.

HOW ABOUT YOU? Have you ever felt like blaming God for the terrible things that happen in the world? God is not powerless to prevent such things, but He has given man his own will so that he can either obey or disobey God's laws. From the beginning of time, man chose to disobey, and the result is suffering. Terrible things do happen in the world—not because God is powerless, but because mankind chose to disobey the God who created him. Some day God will remove His children from this sinful world. If you're a Christian, you can look forward to that time. □ P.R.

TO MEMORIZE: *Know that the Lord, He is God; it is He who has made us, and not we ourselves; we are His people and the sheep of His pasture.* Psalm 100:3, NKJV

10

Who's to Blame?

FROM THE BIBLE:
The Lord God said to the serpent, "Because you have done this, cursed are you above all the livestock and all the wild animals! . . . And I will put enmity between you and the woman, and between your offspring and hers; he will crush his head, and you will strike his heel." To the woman he said, "I will greatly increase your pains in childbearing; with pain you will give birth to children. Your desire will be for your husband, and he will rule over you." To Adam he said, "Because you listened to your wife and ate from the tree about which I commanded you, 'You must not eat of it,' cursed is the ground because of you; through painful toil you will eat of it all the days of your life. It will produce thorns and thistles for you, and you will eat the plants of the field. By the sweat of your brow you will eat your food until you return to the ground, since from it you were taken; for dust you are and to dust you will return."
Genesis 3:14-19, NIV

Suffering is due to sin

11

The Storm

FROM THE BIBLE:

I bless the Lord: O Lord my God, how great you are! You are robed with honor and with majesty and light! You stretched out the starry curtain of the heavens, and hollowed out the surface of the earth to form the seas. The clouds are his chariots. He rides upon the wings of the wind. The angels are his messengers—his servants of fire! You bound the world together so that it would never fall apart.

Psalm 104:1-5, TLB

When the people saw the thunder and lightning and heard the trumpet and saw the mountain in smoke, they trembled with fear. They stayed at a distance and said to Moses, "Speak to us yourself and we will listen. But do not have God speak to us or we will die." Moses said to the people, "Do not be afraid. God has come to test you, so that the fear of God will be with you to keep you from sinning." The people remained at a distance, while Moses approached the thick darkness where God was.

Exodus 20:18-21, NIV

God is in charge of storms

KIM HUDDLED in her bed as a brilliant flash of lightning lit her room with an eerie white color. With thumping heart, she waited in dread for the next flash of light and loud crash of thunder. It didn't take long. The piercing light cracked the black darkness, and a frightening boom almost made her heart stop. Shaking, Kim reached for her bedside lamp, but when she pushed the switch, nothing happened. Dad came in with a flashlight. "The power is out," he said. "Come to the living room until the storm is over."

Mom lit some candles, and the three of them sat on the couch waiting for the worst of the storm to pass. "Why does it have to be so dark and the lightning so bright and the thunder so loud?" moaned Kim.

Dad gave her a hug. "I was just thinking," he said, "of how the Israelites were so afraid of the thunder and lightning and smoke from Sinai at the time God gave His Law. Of course, that was not an ordinary storm, but it does illustrate that God is in charge of the thunder and lightning and darkness. You know, when Moses met God in the darkness, he talked with Him. That's one of the best things to do when you're afraid. Let's do that right now so we'll remember that God is here with us in the storm and darkness, just as He was with Moses so long ago—and just as He's with us all the time."

Mom and Dad each prayed a short prayer, and then Kim prayed. "Dear God," she said, "I know You're right here in the stormy darkness with me. Please help me remember that, so I won't be so afraid." After her prayer, she suggested in a brave voice, "Why don't we have some milk and cookies while we're waiting for the storm to pass?"

"Great idea," agreed Mom. And they all headed for the kitchen by the light of the flashlight's beam.

HOW ABOUT YOU? Are you afraid of thunder and lightning? Many people of all ages and in all countries have been—and are—afraid of storms. But God is in the stormy darkness and the thunder and lightning just as He's in the sunshine. He'll take care of you. Talk with Him and tell Him about your fears. Praise Him for His care for you in storms. □ C.Y.

TO MEMORIZE: *Moses approached the thick darkness where God was.* Exodus 20:21, NIV

"MOM, LOOK AT this old mirror!" Carrie exclaimed, her voice echoing off the attic ceiling. She giggled at her short, squat reflection. "It makes me look so funny."

Mom came up behind her and looked. "That's very old," she said with a laugh. "It was your great-grandmother's."

"Can we take it down to show everybody?" asked Carrie.

"Sure," agreed Mom, "they'd like to see it, too. But first let's take the things for the garage sale downstairs."

That evening, the Stevens family laughed together over their reflections in the antique mirror. "It's fun to look in that old mirror, but I sure am glad we have better ones to use now," said Carrie as they ate their supper.

"Oh?" asked Dad. "Why is that?"

Carrie giggled. "Because that old one doesn't reflect me the way I really am," she said. "It makes me look all squashed."

"Yeah," agreed her brother, Gary. "A good mirror shows you just as you are."

"I wonder how well all our mirrors are working," said Mom as she cut the apple pie.

"What do you mean?" asked Carrie. "They're fine."

Mom smiled. "I don't mean the mirrors on the walls or dressers," she explained. "I mean us."

"Us! We're people, not mirrors," said Gary.

"We are also mirrors," said Mom. "As Christians we should reflect Christ in everything we say and do."

"And when we do, we should reflect a true image," added Dad. "People should see Christ living in us, the way He really is—not a 'squashed' reflection."

HOW ABOUT YOU? Do you reflect Christ's love in your life when you talk with your friends or when you play? Or is your reflection of Him marred by mean and hateful actions? Yield to Christ each moment of the day so your life can be a true reflection of His love. □ J.B.

TO MEMORIZE: *Just as he who called you is holy, so be holy in all you do.* 1 Peter 1:15, NIV

AUGUST

12

The Antique Mirror

FROM THE BIBLE:

To this you were called, because Christ suffered for you, leaving you an example, that you should follow in his steps. "He committed no sin, and no deceit was found in his mouth." When they hurled their insults at him, he did not retaliate; when he suffered, he made no threats. Instead, he entrusted himself to him who judges justly. He himself bore our sins in his body on the tree, so that we might die to sins and live for righteousness; by his wounds you have been healed.

1 Peter 2:21-24, NIV

Reflect Christ's love

13

Member of the Band

FROM THE BIBLE:

Giving thanks to the Father who has qualified us to be partakers of the inheritance of the saints in the light. He has delivered us from the power of darkness and translated us into the kingdom of the Son of His love, in whom we have redemption through His blood, the forgiveness of sins. He is the image of the invisible God, the firstborn over all creation. For by Him all things were created that are in heaven and that are on earth, visible and invisible, whether thrones or dominions or principalities or powers. All things were created through Him and for Him. And He is before all things, and in Him all things consist. And He is the head of the body, the church, who is the beginning, the firstborn from the dead, that in all things He may have the preeminence.
Colossians 1:12-18, NKJV

Become a member of the church

MOM!" TOM burst into the house, his eyes glistening with excitement. "Guess what! Jeffrey is moving, and he plays the French horn, and so now there's a French horn available, and Mr. Potter said I could use it and be in the band."

"Slow down, slow down!" said Mother. She smiled at her son's eager face. "I'm glad that worked out for you. When do you start?"

"Tomorrow," replied Tom. "I get my uniform then, too. It's neat."

That evening when Dad heard the big news, he grinned at Tom. "So you'll be in the band?" he said. "That's great."

But Gretchen, Tom's little sister, frowned. "I want to be in the band, too," she said with a pout.

"You can't. You're too small," Tom told her.

Dad smiled at Gretchen. "Tell me, what do you need to become a member of a band?" he asked.

"A horn," said Gretchen promptly.

"And a uniform," said Tom.

"And you have to be big enough," added Gretchen sadly.

Dad nodded. "But do you know," he asked, "that there's a band anyone may join?" Gretchen smiled at that news, but Tom looked doubtful. "It's not a musical band—it's a different kind of band," said Dad. "It's the band of Christians, called the church. Do you know what you need to become a member of that band?"

"You need Christ," said Tom promptly.

Again Dad nodded. "Good," he said. "That's exactly right. And anyone, big or small, may receive Him."

HOW ABOUT YOU? Do you belong to the band of Christians—the church? This does not mean the local congregation which you attend on Sundays. It means the whole group of believers throughout the world. The invitation is open for you to become a member of this group by receiving Jesus as your Savior. Become a part of the church, the body of Christ. □ H.M.

TO MEMORIZE: *We have redemption through His blood, the forgiveness of sins.* Colossians 1:14, NIV

Tom WAS PRACTICING his horn again, and Gretchen put her hands over her ears. She was tired of hearing it.

Tom was tired of it, too. He had decided to try to make "first chair"—to be the very best French horn player in the band—and so he had to practice at home every day. He had to go over and over the pieces that had been assigned. Playing in the band had been fun for a while, but now it seemed more like work.

"How's your band music coming along?" Dad asked one evening. "Have you made first chair yet?"

Tom shook his head. "It's too hard," he said. "I think I'll give up that idea. I don't feel like practicing anymore."

"Well," said Dad, "there's nothing wrong with not being first chair, but there is something wrong with not practicing. No matter what chair you have, you need to do the best you can, and that takes practice."

Gretchen grinned. "I'm glad I don't have to practice."

"Oh, but you do!" declared Dad.

Gretchen looked at her father. "I don't play in the band," she said.

Dad smiled. "Remember that we talked about how we could all belong to a different band—the band of Christians, called the church? Have you become a part of that band?" Gretchen nodded. "Well, then," continued Dad, "there are things you need to practice as a member of God's church. In His Word, the Bible, God tells us of many characteristics we should have. He describes the kind of people we should be, and He teaches us the kind of things we should do."

"Sometimes we get tired of doing the things we should," added Mother, "just like Tom gets tired of practicing. But we're told not to be 'weary in well doing.' We need to keep on practicing."

HOW ABOUT YOU? Were you once excited about being a Christian and learning to be like Jesus? Are you still faithfully practicing the things God teaches—things such as loving others, being honest, respecting authority, obeying parents, and giving cheerfully? God wants you to keep on. Do as He says. □ H.M.

TO MEMORIZE: *And as for you, brothers, never tire of doing what is right.* 2 Thessalonians 3:13, NIV

Member of the Band

(Continued from yesterday)

FROM THE BIBLE:
When you follow your own wrong inclinations your lives will produce these evil results: impure thoughts, eagerness for lustful pleasure, idolatry, spiritism (that is, encouraging the activity of demons), hatred and fighting, jealousy and anger, constant effort to get the best for yourself, complaints and criticisms, the feeling that everyone else is wrong except those in your own little group— and there will be wrong doctrine, envy, murder, drunkenness, wild parties, and all that sort of thing. Let me tell you again as I have before, that anyone living that sort of life will not inherit the Kingdom of God. But when the Holy Spirit controls our lives he will produce this kind of fruit in us: love, joy, peace, patience, kindness, goodness, faithfulness, gentleness and self-control; and here there is no conflict with Jewish laws.
Galatians 5:19-23, TLB

Practice Christian virtues

15

Member of the Band

(Continued from yesterday)

FROM THE BIBLE:
Be imitators of God, therefore, as dearly loved children and live a life of love, just as Christ loved us and gave himself up for us as a fragrant offering and sacrifice to God. But among you there must not be even a hint of sexual immorality, or of any kind of impurity, or of greed, because these are improper for God's holy people. Nor should there be obscenity, foolish talk or coarse joking, which are out of place, but rather thanksgiving.
Ephesians 5:1-4, NIV

Follow Jesus

YOU AND DAD are coming to the band concert tonight, aren't you?" asked Tom at breakfast one day. "I've been practicing so much, I think I know our pieces backwards!" He was especially looking forward to playing a special number with a smaller group, a brass ensemble.

Mother smiled. "We'll be there," she assured him. "We wouldn't miss it."

When it was time to get ready for the concert that evening, Tom was a bit nervous. "The timing on our piece is tricky," he said. "What if I make a mistake? I'd feel so dumb."

"Just watch your conductor carefully and you'll do fine, Son," said Dad.

Tom grinned. "Mr. Potter stopped us in the middle of a piece the other day," he said. "Pete, one of the drummers, was really going at it, and he wasn't watching. He played half a line before he realized that nobody else was playing. Everybody laughed, but Mr. Potter really yelled at him for that." He paused, then added, "I really like Mr. Potter, though. He's a good band leader."

"Mine's better," said Tom's little sister, Gretchen.

"You don't have one," said Tom. "You're not in a band."

"Am too," said Gretchen. "I'm a Christian, so I'm in God's band. You forgot." She looked accusingly at her brother.

"Good for you," cheered Dad. "And who is the leader you have to follow?"

"Jesus," said Gretchen positively. "And He's the best leader of all."

HOW ABOUT YOU? As a Christian, are you carefully following your leader? Do all your activities please the Lord? Are the places you go the kind of places He would feel comfortable? Are your close friends the kind of kids He would want you to spend a lot of time with? If not, you may find yourself in trouble. You are apt to fall into all kinds of sin. Don't get caught in such things. Follow Jesus. □ H.M.

TO MEMORIZE: *Be imitators of God, therefore, as dearly loved children.* Ephesians 5:1, NIV

IT WAS AT her Grandma Blair's house that Patty first heard about Jesus and how much He loved her. One special day when she was eleven years old, Patty knelt by Grandma's rocking chair and thanked Jesus for coming to die for her. "Please forgive my sins, Jesus, and help me to live for You," she prayed.

Grandma's sweet voice whispered, "Amen," and then Grandma gave Patty a warm hug. "Now you'll always have a friend close beside you, Honey," said Grandma. "You won't see Him, but He is real and He's there. Talk to Him in prayer each day. And when you read the Bible, ask Him to help you understand what He's saying to you."

For a long moment Patty sat with a faraway look in her eyes. Then she asked a strange question. "Grandma, do you remember Dayken Geehouse?"

"Dayken Geehouse!" Grandma exclaimed with a laugh. "You mean the little imaginary friend you had when you were three years old?"

"Oh, good! You didn't forget her! I'm glad," Patty said happily. "Dayken was my best friend, even if she was 'just pretend.' I couldn't see her, but I really felt like there was someone for me to play with all day long. Because of Dayken, I was never lonely."

"I remember asking you about your little companion's funny name," said Grandma. "Your reply was so solemn. You said, 'Grandma, Dayken told me her name.' "

With a little embarrassed smile, Patty said wistfully, "Sometimes I sorta miss Dayken now that I'm grown up."

"Well, Dear, you'll never grow up too much or get too old for your new friend, Jesus," Grandma assured her. "He'll be the best friend you've ever had—much better than an imaginary one. And He has promised that some day you'll truly see Him, too."

HOW ABOUT YOU? Are you sometimes lonely? Perhaps you've had an imaginary friend. That can be fun for a while, but it's only make-believe. Jesus wants to be your best friend. Have you asked Him to come into your heart? If not, do that today. Then you'll have a real friend with whom you may talk at any time. Even better, you'll meet Him face to face someday. □ P.K.

TO MEMORIZE: *I have called you friends, for every-thing that I learned from my Father I have made known to you.* John 15:15, NIV

No More Pretending

FROM THE BIBLE:

As the Father has loved me, so have I loved you. Now remain in my love. If you obey my commands, you will remain in my love, just as I have obeyed my Father's commands and remain in his love. I have told you this so that my joy may be in you and that your joy may be complete. My command is this: Love each other as I have loved you. Greater love has no one than this, that he lay down his life for his friends. You are my friends if you do what I command. I no longer call you servants, because a servant does not know his master's business. Instead, I have called you friends, for everything that I learned from my Father I have made known to you.
John 15:9-15, NIV

Jesus will be your friend

AUGUST

17

God's Handiwork

FROM THE BIBLE:

God said, "Let us make man in our image, in our likeness, and let them rule over the fish of the sea and the birds of the air, over the livestock, over all the earth, and over all the creatures that move along the ground." So God created man in his own image, in the image of God he created him; male and female he created them.
Genesis 1:26-27, NIV

Don't make fun of others

JUST LOOK AT Sally's hair," Marcia whispered to Stacy. "It must have been made with leftover straw from Farmer Brown's hay loft." The girls snickered and then quieted down as their Sunday school teacher entered the room.

"I'm happy to see each of you today," said Miss Ruth. "I'm especially glad you're back, Sally. We hope you'll become a regular member of our class, don't we, girls?" As a few girls weakly murmured, "Yes," Marcia rolled her eyes back in her head.

Soon the girls were involved in the activities of the lesson. "Today we're going to draw numbers and divide into teams to make a mural of the story of the prodigal son," Miss Ruth instructed.

Each girl drew a slip of paper. Marcia drew a six, and so did Sally. "Anyone want to trade?" asked Marcia loudly. When Miss Ruth looked shocked, Marcia mumbled, "Never mind." She turned to Sally. "Come on, Sally," she ordered. "You draw the pig pen. I'll draw the prodigal son and the pigs." Marcia soon discovered that Sally was a very good artist, but she didn't tell her so.

"Boy, that's good drawing," said Stacy, pointing to the pig pen, "really good!" Then she giggled. "Is that a two-legged pig or a four-legged man there in the middle?" Everyone laughed— everyone except Marcia and Miss Ruth. Marcia felt like she'd been hit in the stomach.

When the dismissal bell rang, Marcia darted for the door, but Miss Ruth called her back. After everyone had left, Miss Ruth put her arm around the girl's shoulders. "It hurt you when the girls laughed at your picture, didn't it?"

Marcia sniffed. "That was mean," she said.

Miss Ruth nodded. "Yes," she agreed, "but I wonder if the way you feel is something like the way God feels when we make fun of His handiwork. You created the picture, so it hurt you when the girls laughed at it. God created Sally, and it must hurt Him when you laugh at her."

HOW ABOUT YOU? Are you guilty of making fun of God's creation? Not only do you hurt others when you laugh at them, but you laugh at their Creator. God made man in His image. You wouldn't laugh at God, would you? □ B.W.

TO MEMORIZE: *He who mocks the poor reproaches his Maker; he who is glad at calamity will not go unpunished.* Proverbs 17:5, NKJV

Joel's Machine

IT'S A GREAT machine, huh, Dad?" Joel watched admiringly as his father polished the hood of their new car. It stood glistening in the sunshine, the dark red interior contrasting sharply with the gleaming white paint.

"Yes, Joel, it sure is," agreed Dad, putting the cleaning rags away. He walked into the garage and returned with a large hammer. He held it out to his son. "Here. Slam this into the windshield!" he urged. "Just for the fun of it."

"Dad!" Joel gasped in astonishment. He put his hands behind him and backed up a step or two. "You've gotta be kidding! What would I do that for?"

"I'm glad you have better sense than to do that," said Dad with a smile. "Let's talk a minute," He set the hammer down and put his arm around the boy's shoulders. "When you were born, God gave you a beautiful, precision-built 'machine,' your body," said Dad. "He asks that you treat it well. That's not expecting too much, is it?" Joel shook his head, smiling at the comparison, and Dad continued. "You've seen the TV ads showing young men and women who have drug problems, haven't you?"

Joel nodded. "Yes, Dad, I've seen them," he said.

"Well, Son," continued Dad, "please remember that there may come a time when some friend of yours will suggest that you try it just once, 'just for kicks,' he may say, or maybe to prove you're not 'chicken.' But just as it would be crazy for you to slam that hammer into our sharp new car," Dad nodded toward the driveway, "it would be even crazier to deliberately do something destructive to the wonderful 'machine' of your body."

Joel nodded. "You can trust me to keep my 'machine' in good shape," he said. Then he added, "And thanks for talking about this. I'll remember."

HOW ABOUT YOU? Have you been asked by friends to do something you know is wrong? It may happen, and if it does, "just say no." If you're a Christian, your body is the temple of the Holy Spirit. Use it to glorify God. □ P.K.

TO MEMORIZE: *My son, if sinners entice you, do not consent.* Proverbs 1:10, NKJV

FROM THE BIBLE:
Haven't you yet learned that your body is the home of the Holy Spirit God gave you, and that he lives within you? Your own body does not belong to you. For God has bought you with a great price. So use every part of your body to give glory back to God, because he owns it. 1 Corinthians 6:19-20, TLB

Keep your body pure

19

Some Bright Morning

FROM THE BIBLE:
Now we look forward with confidence to our heavenly bodies, realizing that every moment we spend in these earthly bodies is time spent away from our eternal home in heaven with Jesus. We know these things are true by believing, not by seeing. And we are not afraid, but are quite content to die, for then we will be at home with the Lord. So our aim is to please him always in everything we do, whether we are here in this body or away from this body and with him in heaven.
2 Corinthians 5:6-9, TLB

Christians live forever in heaven

THE LONG PROCESSION of cars moved slowly from the school auditorium to the cemetery. There, standing between her parents, Laura held a damp, wadded hanky and struggled to keep her tears from overflowing again as some final words were spoken.

"Even now, Kim is in the presence of Jesus," said Pastor Drew. "She sees His kind face and hears His gentle voice. All her pain and sorrow are already forgotten. Kim is able to run and laugh now. And God's Word says that those who belong to Jesus will see her again some bright morning in heaven." The minister's thoughtful words were stated with positive assurance as he spoke to the family and friends who had assembled after Kim's funeral service.

For as long as Laura could remember, she and Kim had gone to school and Sunday school together. They had learned about Jesus when they were little, and each had accepted Him as Savior. Laura couldn't think of life without her friend. But now Kim was gone, and Laura's heart was sad and lonely. A breeze brushed the faces of Kim's listening classmates. Each carried a brightly colored balloon.

The minister's quiet words broke into Laura's thoughts. "These balloons are to picture for you the freedom of Kim's spirit today. The Bible tells us that the body is laid to rest in the earth, but the spirit of the one who believes in Jesus goes to be with Him until the Resurrection. Kim's spirit is already at home with Jesus."

The pastor lifted a pink balloon and held it a moment. "Let's release our balloons together in celebration of Kim's new happiness," he said. In an instant, as all eyes were raised skyward, a cloud of vividly colored circles danced in the summer breeze.

"Goodbye, Kim," Laura whispered. She smiled through her tears. "I'll see you in the morning."

HOW ABOUT YOU? Have you known someone your own age who had died? Perhaps you wonder what it would be like to die. It's natural to be afraid of the unknown. But Jesus has promised to take Christians to heaven when they die. They live forever with Him there. The Bible says that for a Christian, being "absent from the body" is being "present with the Lord." □ P.K.

TO MEMORIZE: *We will be with the Lord forever.*
1 Thessalonians 4:17, NIV

A LIENS!"

"There go the aliens!"

Ginny and her friend Alicia cringed as the taunting cries followed them. They had once again refused to join the activities of a certain group of classmates. They had so often separated themselves from the bad behavior of other kids that they had been dubbed "aliens" by the other children. Ginny signed. "My mother keeps reminding me not to give in to the temptation to be like those kids," she remarked, "but I don't think she knows what it's like for kids in school these days."

"Yeah," agreed Alicia. "My mom keeps saying I should 'just say no' to drugs, but nobody has asked me to say yes yet. I don't think it would be so hard to say no anyway. I don't want any part of them. But sometimes I feel like giving in to some of the other stuff—like looking at the magazines the kids are passing around. Then maybe they wouldn't call us names all the time."

At home that evening, Ginny told her mother about what happened. "They call Alicia and me aliens because we don't do the things they do," she complained.

Mother nodded. "I can understand how you feel," she said. "But I guess it's not so strange they call you that. You really are aliens, you know."

"Mom," said Ginny, "we are not!"

Mother smiled. "Yes," she insisted, "you are. You girls have both accepted Jesus as Savior, so now your citizenship is really in heaven. You're different, because you live for Christ . . . you're not of this world, which lives for the devil. You're just passing through it."

"Then I guess it's not so bad to be called 'aliens' after all, is it?" said Ginny with a sigh. "I'll have to tell Alicia."

HOW ABOUT YOU? Do other boys and girls pressure you to join them in some ungodly ways? Do they tease you when you refuse? Perhaps you don't find it hard to say no to such things as smoking, drinking, or doing drugs, but you're tempted to laugh at dirty jokes, show disrespect to a teacher, or do some other thing you really know is wrong. Don't do it. If you belong to Jesus, you don't really belong to this world. Act the way a citizen of heaven should act. □ N.E.K.

TO MEMORIZE: *Our citizenship is in heaven, from which we also eagerly wait for the Savior, the Lord Jesus Christ.* Philippians 3:20, NKJV

Aliens

FROM THE BIBLE:
Our citizenship is in heaven, from which we also eagerly wait for the Savior, the Lord Jesus Christ, who will transform our lowly body that it may be conformed to His glorious body, according to the working by which He is able even to subdue all things to Himself. Therefore, my beloved and longed-for brethren, my joy and crown, so stand fast in the Lord, beloved. Philippians 3:20—4:1, NKJV

Christians are citizens of heaven

21

Not Sticky Enough

FROM THE BIBLE:
*Love is very patient and kind,
never jealous or envious, never
boastful or proud, never haughty
or selfish or rude. Love does not
demand its own way. It is not
irritable or touchy. It does not
hold grudges and will hardly
even notice when others do it
wrong. It is never glad about
injustice, but rejoices whenever
truth wins out. If you love
someone you will be loyal to him
no matter what the cost. You
will always believe in him,
always expect the best of him,
and always stand your ground
in defending him.*
1 Corinthians 13:4-7, TLB

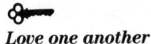

Love one another

As KIP AND his sister Margie drove home after a shopping trip with Mother, they saw a couple walking along, holding hands. "There go Mr. and Mrs. Glue," said Kip. "They're so sticky."

"Mr. and Mrs. Glue?" asked Mother.

Margie nodded. "That's what the kids call them because they're so stuck on each other," she said. "Yvonne thinks everything Clay says is so cute. And she's always running her fingers through his hair."

"Yuck!" responded Kip. Just then he spotted someone else. "Oh, and there goes Mr. Know-It-All," he added.

Margie looked. "That's Bud," she said. "He's OK. You just don't like him because he's smarter than you."

"Nobody likes him," retorted Kip.

"Brenda does, and that makes you mad, because you like Brenda," taunted Margie, as Mother pulled into their driveway. "I don't see why you like her. She's a snob." Kip made a face at his sister as they got out of the car.

In the kitchen, Margie pulled a big bottle of glue from a bag. "I really need this for my science project," she said. "Snobby Brenda used up half of my last bottle."

"She's not a snob," said Kip. "She's pretty and you're just jealous."

Mother sighed. "I have no doubt that the couple we saw earlier are too sticky, as you put it," she said, "but I get the feeling that the two of you are not sticky enough. I think you need a little more 'glue' in your lives." Margie looked at the bottle she held in her hand. "Not that kind," continued Mother. "But tell me—what does glue do?"

"It hold things together," replied Kip.

Mother nodded. "And the best glue—the best thing for holding people together—is love. God says we're to love each other. Were you two displaying God's love when you talked about your classmates? Were you showing love by fighting with each other? Think about it!"

HOW ABOUT YOU? Is there plenty of "glue"—plenty of love—displayed in your life? Are your words and thoughts loving and kind? Obey God's command. Display His love in your life. □ H.M.

TO MEMORIZE: *A new command I give you: Love one another. As I have loved you, so you must love one another.* John 13:34, NIV

22

Healing Tears

OOOHHH!!" MARK SCREAMED as his bike flipped through the air. A searing pain ripped through his palms and knees. Angrily, he brushed away his tears. "I will not cry!" he said aloud. Picking up his bike, he hobbled home.

Mark's hands and knees ached almost as much as his heart did. Ever since Grandpa had died two weeks ago, tears had been hiding right behind his eyelids.

Mark limped into the kitchen. "Oh, you're hurt!" Mother exclaimed. "Come into the bathroom and let me take care of you." Mark obediently followed her. Gently, she washed away the dirt and poured disinfectant into the wounds. Mark gritted his teeth as the medicine bubbled and fizzed. "I know it stings a bit," Mother sympathized, "but it's cleansing the wounds so they can heal."

Mark took a deep gulp of air and sniffed. Mother put her arm around his shoulders and drew him to her. Mark stiffened and drew away. *I will not cry,* he said to himself. *Eleven-year-old boys do not cry.*

Mother seemed to know what he was thinking. "Honey," she said, "it's OK to cry when you hurt." Mark shook his head angrily. "But it is," Mother insisted. "Don't you know that your daddy cried when Grandpa died?"

Mark looked startled. "I didn't think men cried," he stammered.

"But they do," Mother assured him. "Even Jesus cried. Tears are like the disinfectant I put on your wounds. Tears help wash out grief and speed the healing process." Mother put her hands on his shoulders. "Look at me, Son," she ordered softly. "God knows we hurt sometimes," she said. "He gave us tears to help us. If you'd let yourself cry, your broken heart would heal much faster."

Then Mother pulled him into her arms. Mark's shoulders heaved. As the tears he had been fighting rolled down his cheeks, he relaxed. It was such a relief to cry. Already he felt better.

HOW ABOUT YOU? God gave us laughter and tears. Both are like medicine that cleanses our hurts. Even men and boys can cry. Jesus did. When you need to cry, don't try to be big and tough. Let the tears flow and the hurt heal. □ B.W.

TO MEMORIZE: *Weeping may endure for a night, but joy comes in the morning.* Psalm 30:5, NKJV

FROM THE BIBLE:
When Mary arrived where Jesus was, she fell down at his feet, saying, "Sir, if you had been here, my brother would still be alive." When Jesus saw her weeping and the Jewish leaders wailing with her, he was moved with indignation and deeply troubled. "Where is he buried?" he asked them. They told him, "Come and see." Tears came to Jesus' eyes. "They were close friends," the Jewish leaders said. "See how much he loved him."
John 11:32-36, TLB

Tears heal our hurts

23

Only a Game

FROM THE BIBLE:

When you enter the land the Lord your God is giving you, do not learn to imitate the detestable ways of the nations there. Let no one be found among you who sacrifices his son or daughter in the fire, who practices divination or sorcery, interprets omens, engages in witchcraft, or casts spells, or who is a medium or spiritist or who consults the dead. Anyone who does these things is detestable to the Lord, and because of these detestable practices the Lord your God will drive out those nations before you. You must be blameless before the Lord your God. The nations you will dispossess listen to those who practice sorcery or divination. But as for you, the Lord your God has not permitted you to do so.

Deuteronomy 18:9-14, NIV

Trust only God for your future

ALL THE GIRLS at the slumber party giggled as one of them read their horoscopes from a magazine on astrology, but Candy felt uncomfortable. People used horoscopes to try to find out what would happen in the future, and she knew that only God knows what will happen.

Next, the girl who was giving the party got out her Ouija board, and the other girls gathered around. This was another thing used for fortune-telling. Candy sat apart from the group and self-consciously leafed through a magazine.

Candy was relieved when they went on to games she could play without feeling uncomfortable. Then she had a really good time. Her favorite was the "blind walk." Each girl was blindfolded while her partner led her around an obstacle course. If the blindfolded person was caught peeking, they lost points for their team. Candy found that it felt strange trusting her partner not to run her into the wall. But she really wanted to win, so she moved quickly ahead and never peeked at all. It paid off—they won.

When Candy's father picked her up the next day, she told him all about the party and the games they had played, including the activities that had bothered her. Dad nodded. "You were right to avoid those," he said. "The Bible teaches that 'divination,' or practices that seek to foresee the future, are wrong."

"Even if they're only a game?" asked Candy.

"Yes," said Dad. "Satan can use such activities to trick you into trusting your future to something other than God." He paused. "Your future is like the 'blind walk' game you played," he added. "God holds your hand, and you need to just let Him lead the way. He doesn't want you to have any part in something that encourages you to do otherwise."

HOW ABOUT YOU? Do you read your horoscope or participate in fortune-telling activities? Although these may seem like harmless fun, God's Word clearly speaks against them. When you try to find out your future in these ways, you are showing God you don't trust Him. □ K.R.A.

TO MEMORIZE: *O Lord Almighty, blessed is the man who trusts in you.* Psalm 84:12, NIV

"THIS IS A familiar story," Deana's father said before he began reading a passage for family devotions one morning, "but you may not know it as well as you think. Just because a story is familiar doesn't mean you can't learn new lessons from it. Sometimes it's good to try to read a familiar story as though you're reading it for the first time. God often blesses you with thoughts about it that you've never had before." Deana shrugged off Dad's advice and let her mind wander to her plans for the day.

That evening at youth choir practice, Mrs. Bell had the young people turn to a familiar song in the hymnbook. "Pastor Evans would like us to sing this song next Sunday, because it goes along with his sermon," explained Mrs. Bell. "Do you think we can learn it by then?"

"No problem. We've been singing this song our whole lives," someone said, and they all agreed.

But halfway through the song, Mrs. Bell stopped the choir. "I'm afraid that wasn't right," she said. "I know we've always sung it like that in church, but that isn't the way it's written." Mrs. Bell sang the song correctly to demonstrate. The timing, and even part of the tune, was quite different from the way Deana remembered it. "You don't know this song as well as you think," Mrs. Bell added.

Deana had heard those same words recently. Dad had said the same thing about familiar Bible stories. Maybe he was right!

"Mrs. Bell, maybe we should read the music more carefully—as though it were the first time we've seen it," Deana suggested, borrowing Dad's advice.

"That's right," agreed Mrs. Bell. "Forget that you've ever heard this song before. Read the music and think about the words."

As she began singing once again, Deana decided to also read a certain Bible story carefully when she got home.

HOW ABOUT YOU? Do you sometimes stop listening when you hear parts of the Bible you think you already know? Do you skim over some verses because they're so familiar to you? Never take for granted that you know everything about any part of the Bible. Allow God to speak to you through His Word each time you read or hear it. □ K.R.A.

TO MEMORIZE: *Do your best to present yourself to God as one approved, a workman who does not need to be ashamed and who correctly handles the word of truth.* 2 Timothy 2:15, NIV

Songs and Stories

FROM THE BIBLE:
Just tell me what to do and I will do it, Lord. As long as I live I'll wholeheartedly obey. Make me walk along the right paths for I know how delightful they really are. Help me to prefer obedience to making money! Turn me away from wanting any other plan than yours. Revive my heart toward you. Reassure me that your promises are for me, for I trust and revere you. How I dread being mocked for obeying, for your laws are right and good. I long to obey them! Therefore in fairness renew my life, for this was your promise—yes, Lord, to save me! Now spare me by your kindness and your love. Then I will have an answer for those who taunt me, for I trust your promises. Psalm 119:33-40, TLB

Pay attention to God's Word

25

The Crooked Arrow

FROM THE BIBLE:

Unless the Lord builds a house, the builders' work is useless. Unless the Lord protects a city, sentries do no good. It is senseless for you to work so hard from early morning until late at night, fearing you will starve to death; for God wants his loved ones to get their proper rest. Children are a gift from God; they are his reward. Children born to a young man are like sharp arrows to defend him. Happy is the man who has his quiver full of them. That man shall have the help he needs when arguing with his enemies. Psalm 127, TLB

Thank God for correction

SCOTT SHUFFLED ALONG half-heartedly as he and his father went out to practice with their new bow and arrows. He was angry because he had been grounded for going to the arcade instead of doing homework at a friend's house.

Dad shot first. His arrow sliced gracefully through the air, but it completely missed the target. Scott didn't bother to hide his snickers. "OK, Hotshot," Dad said with a laugh, "let's see you do better!"

Scott took careful aim. He gave his father a superior smile as he hit the bottom corner of the target. After several more tries, both of them could hit the target with a fair amount of accuracy. Then Dad saw a bent arrow. "I wonder what happened to this one," he murmured. "Why don't you try it, Scott? Let's just see what happens."

Scott tried it. The crooked arrow flew in a crazy arc and was lost in a tangle of prickly blackberry bushes. "I'm not going after *that* one!" exclaimed Scott as they rounded up the other wayward arrows.

"We'll leave it," agreed Dad. "Crooked arrows aren't much good. That's why I don't want you to be one."

Scott frowned. "What are you talking about?" he asked.

"Well," said Dad, "In Psalm 127, God says that children are like arrows in the hand of a mighty man. God gives parents the job of keeping those arrows nice and straight. This is so important, because when we send you off on your own, you must be able to 'hit the target' by living a life that is pleasing to God. If we don't straighten you out when you head in the wrong direction, you'll find yourself in some pretty thorny situations."

As they finished collecting the arrows, Scott began to feel almost glad about having been punished. After all, Dad was just obeying God. And Scott definitely did not want to grow up "crooked."

HOW ABOUT YOU? Do you submit to your parents when they punish you? Even when you feel they are too severe? God had given them the tremendously important job of raising you properly. They need to "straighten" you out when you start down the "crooked" path of sin. □ E.O.

TO MEMORIZE: *Folly is bound up in the heart of a child, but the rod of discipline will drive it far from him.* Proverbs 22:15, NIV

JASON POINTED a long stick at a clump of bushes. The imaginary enemy was just behind it, ready to take over Jason's territory!

"Winning the war again?" asked Dad, who had been in a real war. "You know I don't like you to even pretend to shoot anyone, Son."

"I hope I get to be a real hero some day," said Jason.

"I know how you feel," said Dad, "but I hope you get to be a hero some other way than by being in a war. Tell me, what would you like to be when you get older?"

"Somebody important," said Jason promptly. "Like David in the Bible. He killed Goliath and got to be king."

"How about being as important as Adino the Eznite?" asked Dad. Jason looked puzzled, and Dad laughed. "We'll talk about him later," he promised. "Right now I hear Mother calling for help in unloading the groceries."

Soon the whole family was working as Mother sent some groceries to the basement, some to the pantry, some to the kitchen. "She's like a general in the army," Jason muttered. "I don't like taking orders. I want to be the boss."

At family devotions Dad said, "We're going to read about Adino the Eznite." He read 2 Samuel 23:8 to introduce his family to Adino, one of David's mighty men.

"He was only famous because he served with King David," observed Jason when Dad had finished.

"Think so?" asked Dad. "Or could it be possible that King David was famous because he had mighty men like Adino?" Dad closed his Bible and looked at his family. "For every general, there are thousands of soldiers. They carry out his plans, and he becomes famous. We have one Lord— Jesus Christ—and it's our responsibility to glorify Him, not to make a name for ourselves. I'd be happy to be an 'Adino the Eznite' in God's army."

HOW ABOUT YOU? Does serving Jesus and others seem dull? Do you perform your chores routinely, just waiting for the time when you can be independent and not have to take orders anymore? Jesus instructed His people to serve. Forget about your own dreams of fame and get busy serving the Lord. That's the way to true greatness. □ C.R.

TO MEMORIZE: *Yet it shall not be so among you; but whoever desires to become great among you, let him be your servant.* Matthew 20:26, NKJV

Adino the Eznite

FROM THE BIBLE:
Jesus called them to Himself and said, "You know that the rulers of the Gentiles lord it over them, and those who are great exercise authority over them. Yet it shall not be so among you; but whoever desires to become great among you, let him be your servant. And whoever desires to be first among you, let him be your slave—just as the Son of Man did not come to be served, but to serve, and to give His life a ransom for many."
Matthew 20:25-28, NKJV

Be a servant

AUGUST

27

A Home for Caryn

FROM THE BIBLE:

"Do not let your hearts be troubled. Trust in God; trust also in me. In my Father's house are many rooms; if it were not so, I would have told you. I am going there to prepare a place for you. And if I go and prepare a place for you, I will come back and take you to be with me that you also may be where I am. You know the way to the place where I am going." Thomas said to him, "Lord, we don't know where you are going, so how can we know the way?" Jesus answered, "I am the way and the truth and the life. No one comes to the Father except through me."

John 14:1-6, NIV

Heaven is the best home

CARYN GAZED LONGINGLY at the miniature castle in the Chicago museum. How she wished she had a miniature house of her own to furnish with the little things she'd collected over the years. But she knew they were very expensive and she'd just have to get along with cardboard boxes, as she had in the past.

A couple months later, it was Caryn's birthday, but she didn't even dare to hope for a doll house. She expected she'd get something useful just as she had other years. Sure enough, when she opened her package, there was a blouse and a skirt. She was grateful, but she would have liked to have a miniature house!

"Now, close your eyes until I say you may open them," commanded Dad. The "birthday person" always had to close his eyes while the cake was brought in. But this time, when Dad finally said, "You may open your eyes," there stood a beautiful little house with tiny rooms to decorate and furnish.

"Dad! Dad! I love it," Caryn squealed, throwing herself into her father's arms.

Dad's eyes beamed with pleasure. "I worked on it every night while you were in bed," he told her. "I'm sure I had as much fun building the house as you'll have decorating it. All the time I was working on it, I thought about the wonderful home Jesus Christ is making for those who have believed on Him," added Dad. He gave Caryn one more hug. "If you think this is beautiful, just wait till you see what He's preparing. It's going to be perfect, much better than this house I built."

"And best of all, Jesus Himself will be there," added Mother. Smiling, Caryn nodded.

HOW ABOUT YOU? Do you enjoy the home God has provided for you here? Do you have good times with your family and friends? That's great, but think about the fact that Jesus is preparing a far more wonderful place for those who love Him. There will be no crying, sadness, or sickness in that perfect place. If you're a Christian, you can look forward to your home in heaven. □ C.Y.

TO MEMORIZE: *In my Father's house are many rooms; if it were not so, I would have told you. I am going there to prepare a place for you.* John 14:2, NIV

"HALF OF THESE nuts aren't any good," complained Kathy, who had been cracking nuts for the dessert her mother was making. "They're black and dried up on the inside." She picked up a nut and showed it to Mother.

"Use the good ones," advised her brother, Karl, who had just come into the kitchen.

Kathy scowled at him. "You can't tell which ones are good," she said. "They all look fine on the outside."

"I bet I can tell," insisted Karl, shaking one. "This one's good." Kathy took it and cracked it open. Sure enough, it was good. "See," said Karl gleefully. "I'll pick them for you." He chose another one. "This one's good too." Kathy cracked it open. No, it was dried up. Karl frowned and handed her another nut. It, too, was no good.

"You can't tell any better than I can," declared Kathy, cracking one Karl had rejected. It was good.

"Let's choose every other one," suggested Karl. "Let's see who can find the most good ones." They made a game of it, and soon the job was done.

As the family ate the nutty dessert that evening, Kathy told Dad about the trouble with the nuts. "They sound like some people I know," observed Dad.

Karl's eyes twinkled. "You know some nutty people?"

Dad smiled. "I know some people who look good on the outside, but I'm not sure what we'd see if we could look on the inside—at their hearts," he said. "Jesus said the scribes and Pharisees were like that. They appeared to be good, but they really were hypocrites."

"I wonder how many people are like that today— even among church members," added Mother. "They all look good to us. We really can't tell for sure who has accepted Jesus as Savior, but God knows. He sees through the 'shell' and knows what each person is like on the inside."

Kathy nodded. "We can't fool God, can we?" she said.

HOW ABOUT YOU? Are you fooling people? Do you go to church, say your memory verses, and look good to others? Your parents and teachers may think you're a Christian, but are you really? Have you truly trusted Jesus as Savior? If you haven't done so, accept Him today. Be clean and whole inside as well as outside. □ H.M.

TO MEMORIZE: *On the outside you appear to people as righteous but on the inside you are full of hypocrisy and wickedness.* Matthew 23:28, NIV

Inside the Shell

FROM THE BIBLE:
Woe to you, teachers of the law and Pharisees, you hypocrites! You give a tenth of your spices— mint, dill and cummin. But you have neglected the more important matters of the law—justice, mercy and faithfulness. You should have practiced the latter, without neglecting the former. You blind guides! You strain out a gnat but swallow a camel. Woe to you, teachers of the law and Pharisees, you hypocrites! You clean the outside of the cup and dish, but inside they are full of greed and self-indulgence. Blind Pharisee! First clean the inside of the cup and dish, and then the outside also will be clean. Woe to you, teachers of the law and Pharisees, you hypocrites! You are like whitewashed tombs, which look beautiful on the outside but on the inside are full of dead men's bones and everything unclean. In the same way, on the outside you appear to people as righteous but on the inside you are full of hypocrisy and wickedness. Matthew 23:23-28, NIV

Be clean inside

29

Let's Not Find Out

FROM THE BIBLE:

Prepare your minds for action; be self-controlled; set your hope fully on the grace to be given you when Jesus Christ is revealed. As obedient children, do not conform to the evil desires you had when you lived in ignorance. But just as he who called you is holy, so be holy in all you do; for it is written: "Be holy, because I am holy." Since you call on a Father who judges each man's work impartially, live your lives as strangers here in reverent fear. For you know that it was not with perishable things such as silver or gold that you were redeemed from the empty way of life handed down to you from your forefathers, but with the precious blood of Christ, a lamb without blemish or defect.

1 Peter 1:13-19, NIV

Don't use harmful substances

IT SMELLS SMOKY in here," April said, holding her nose. She waved her arms around her aunt's apartment.

"A friend of mine who smokes visited this afternoon," Aunt Mindy explained. "I didn't open the windows, because there are no screens on them, but I did leave the door open a while this evening, hoping it would air out before you arrived for the weekend."

April plopped onto the couch. "Aunt Mindy, did you ever try smoking?" she asked.

"No," Aunt Mindy said. "I never wanted to."

"Not even when you were a kid?" April challenged. "Didn't you wonder what it would be like?" She thought about the times that kids at school tried to persuade her to smoke. Sometimes she was curious to find out what it was like. "Just trying it wouldn't hurt, would it?" she added.

Aunt Mindy frowned. "Why don't you open the windows after all?" she suggested. "I'd like some fresh air in here."

"But bugs will come in, especially with the lights on now," protested April in surprise. "You said you didn't have screens."

"Maybe it wouldn't be so bad to have a few bugs in here," replied Aunt Mindy. "Maybe they wouldn't even come in much. I haven't tried it before. Why don't we find out?"

"Let's not find out!" objected April. "Mosquitoes always eat me up."

"Hmmm. I think maybe you're right. It would be better not to find out. Bugs don't belong in here." Aunt Mindy paused. "It isn't worth finding out what cigarette smoking is like, either," she added positively. "The contents in cigarettes don't belong in our bodies. We should be even more determined to keep harmful substances out of our bodies than we are to keep bugs out of the apartment."

HOW ABOUT YOU? Have you been tempted to use drugs, cigarettes, or alcohol? God did not make your body for those harmful things. When temptation comes, remember that His Spirit lives within you and keep yourself clean. □ N.E.K.

TO MEMORIZE: *As obedient children, do not conform to the evil desires you had when you lived in ignorance.* 1 Peter 1:14, NIV

MOM, GUESS WHAT? Carl's got chicken pox!" called Luke as he ran into the house. Luke had been the first in his class to get chicken pox, and now others were coming down with it.

Mother held up her hand and continued her phone conversation. As Luke listened, he figured out that their friends, the Taylors, were going to move to Texas.

"Don't tell anyone about this," Mom said when she hung up. "Mr. Taylor's boss is on vacation, and Mr. Taylor hasn't had a chance to tell him yet. Now, who did you say has the chicken pox?" Luke repeated his news about Carl.

As Mother had suggested, Luke didn't tell anyone about the Taylor's—until Sunday morning. Then it slipped out when he told his friend Eric that they would soon have a new Sunday school teacher. "But don't tell anyone," he added. And Eric didn't—at least not for a few hours. Then he told his older sister, who told her friend Karen.

By the end of that week, several more children in Luke's class had the chicken pox. Also by the end of the week, several more people knew that the Taylors were moving. Karen didn't know it was a secret, so she passed the news on to her parents, and they mentioned it at a committee meeting. After someone told the Taylors they would be missed when they moved to Texas, Mrs. Taylor told Luke's mother that the "news was out."

"Luke," said Mother that afternoon, "I didn't tell anyone about the Taylors. Did you?

"Well, just Eric. But I told him not to tell."

"Mr. Taylor wanted to tell his boss before he hears it from someone else, but now the news is all over town," said Mother. "News spreads fast."

"Like the chicken pox?" asked Luke.

"Something like that," agreed Mother. "Once you exposed your friends to the chicken pox, there was nothing you could do to stop it. And when you tell a 'secret,' the story is sure to spread."

Luke knew he had been wrong. He would apologize to the Taylors and tell the Lord he was sorry, too.

HOW ABOUT YOU? Are you a good friend? A good friend knows how to keep a secret. That means not telling even one person. When you're taken into someone's confidence, talk about it only to the Lord. □ L.W.

TO MEMORIZE: *The tongue of the wise commends knowledge, but the mouth of the fool gushes folly.* Proverbs 15:2, NIV

Don't Tell

FROM THE BIBLE:
A gentle answer turns away wrath, but a harsh word stirs up anger. The tongue of the wise commends knowledge, but the mouth of the fool gushes folly. The eyes of the Lord are everywhere, keeping watch on the wicked and the good. The tongue that brings healing is a tree of life, but a deceitful tongue crushes the spirit. A fool spurns his father's discipline, but whoever heeds correction shows prudence. The house of the righteous contains great treasure, but the income of the wicked brings them trouble. The lips of the wise spread knowledge; not so the hearts of fools. The Lord detests the sacrifice of the wicked, but the prayer of the upright pleases him. The Lord detests the way of the wicked but he loves those who pursue righteousness.
Proverbs 15:1-9, NIV

Control your tongue

31

Keep the Light On

FROM THE BIBLE:

Oh, how I love your law! I meditate on it all day long. Your commands make me wiser than my enemies, for they are ever with me. I have more insight than all my teachers, for I meditate on your statutes. I have more understanding than the elders, for I obey your precepts. I have kept my feet from every evil path so that I might obey your word. I have not departed from your laws, for you yourself have taught me. How sweet are your words to my taste, sweeter than honey to my mouth! I gain understanding from your precepts; therefore I hate every wrong path. Your word is a lamp to my feet and a light for my path.
Psalm 119:97-105, NIV

Read God's Word daily

SON, COME HERE, please," Mom called from Pete's room.

"What is it, Mom?" Pete asked as he skidded to a halt in front of her.

"This." Mother was holding up Pete's Bible. "It's all covered with dust."

"Sorry, Mom," said Pete. "I keep forgetting to dust that shelf by the bed."

"That's not what I meant," explained Mom. "Pete, how long has it been since you've read your Bible?"

Pete shrugged carelessly. "I need a Bible for Sunday school, but then I use the one I keep in the den downstairs. Anyhow, since we go to church on Sundays—twice—I hear enough about God then to last me through the week."

Mom followed Pete to his room at bedtime, switched on the light, and then shut it right back off. "Mom!" exclaimed Pete as the room once again became dark. "I can't see what I'm doing or where I am."

"But the light was on for a minute," said Mom, "and I'm sure you can remember where things are. Can't you just make do with the light you got then?"

"Don't be silly," grumbled Peter as he reached for the switch and turned the light back on. "Once it's off, it doesn't do anything for me. So don't turn it off, OK?"

"But, Pete," said Mom softly, "isn't that what you've been trying to do with God? You told me that by going to church twice on Sundays, you learn enough about God to be able to skip reading your Bible during the week. But it doesn't work that way. You need to make constant use of God's Word in order to grow as a Christian."

"By not reading my Bible, I 'turn off the light' on myself, huh?" asked Pete. "Well, can I leave my light on extra long tonight?" I want to 'turn on' my other 'light,' too."

HOW ABOUT YOU? Do you think that by going to church you can get through the rest of the week without bothering with daily devotions? That isn't true. Every day you need to "turn on" the light of God's Word for spiritual direction. □ D.M.

TO MEMORIZE: *The unfolding of your words gives light; it gives understanding to the simple.* Psalm 119:130, NIV

MATT FELT a little nervous. He was on his way to Pastor Stoner's house to deliver some books for his dad. Matt's family had just started attending Parkville Community church, and Matt had never talked to Pastor Stoner. He had shaken hands with him a couple of times, but now he would have to talk to him! What would he say to the pastor?

Matt parked his bike in the parsonage driveway and slowly walked to the door. Timidly he rang the bell. "Why, hello, Matt! Come on in," Pastor Stoner greeted him, taking the books. "My wife just took some of her famous chocolate chip cookies from the oven. Are you hungry?"

Matt never could turn down a chocolate chip cookie! As he entered the kitchen and greeted Mrs. Stoner, he was surprised to hear the radio turned to a ball game—the same game he had been listening to when he left home. "You listen to baseball games?" Matt asked in surprise.

Pastor Stoner laughed. "Sure. I've been a baseball fan ever since I was your age." Pastor Stoner picked up a small pail. "I was just going to pick some raspberries when I heard the doorbell. Why not come out to the berry patch with me and pick some for your mom? Maybe she'll make a raspberry pie." And that's how Matt found himself in the parsonage berry patch, talking to Pastor Stoner about school and ball games and all kinds of things.

"I didn't know pastors did regular things," Matt said after a while. "I thought you just read the Bible."

"A lot of people seem to think that," Pastor Stoner said with a smile. "In order to be able to teach God's Word to the congregation, pastors do have to study. But we're really just like anybody else."

The next Sunday, Matt listened to the sermon more attentively than usual. Knowing that Pastor Stoner liked baseball and chocolate chip cookies and gardens made it easier to listen.

HOW ABOUT YOU? Do you sometimes wonder what a pastor does when he's not preaching? Ask him. He'll be glad to talk to you. □ L.W.

TO MEMORIZE: *If a man wants to be a pastor he has a good ambition.* 1 Timothy 3:1, TLB

Just like Anybody!

FROM THE BIBLE:
If a man wants to be a pastor he has a good ambition. For a pastor must be a good man whose life cannot be spoken against. He must have only one wife, and he must be hard working and thoughtful, orderly, and full of good deeds. He must enjoy having guests in his home, and must be a good Bible teacher. He must not be a drinker or quarrelsome, but he must be gentle and kind, and not be one who loves money. He must have a well-behaved family, with children who obey quickly and quietly. For if a man can't make his own little family behave, how can he help the whole church? The pastor must not be a new Christian, because he might be proud of being chosen so soon, and pride comes before a fall. (Satan's downfall is an example.) Also, he must be well spoken of by people outside the church—those who aren't Christians—so that Satan can't trap him with many accusations, and leave him without freedom to lead his flock.
1 Timothy 3:1-7, TLB

Get to know your pastor

2

Running to Win

FROM THE BIBLE:

In a race, everyone runs but only one person gets first prize. So run your race to win. To win the contest you must deny yourselves many things that would keep you from doing your best. An athlete goes to all this trouble just to win a blue ribbon or a silver cup, but we do it for a heavenly reward that never disappears. So I run straight to the goal with purpose in every step. I fight to win. I'm not just shadow-boxing or playing around. Like an athlete I punish my body, treating it roughly, training it to do what it should, not what it wants to. Otherwise I fear that after enlisting others for the race, I myself might be declared unfit and ordered to stand aside.
1 Corinthians 9:24-27, TLB

"Run" for Jesus

AS THE CHEERLEADERS waved their pom-poms they chanted loudly, "John, John, he's our man! If he can't do it, no one can!"

After the pep rally, many students came up to congratulate John. He was the first person from his small Christian school to have qualified for the state track meet, and they were sure he'd win. "Hello, Champ," said Brad as he gave John a slap on the back.

"I haven't won yet," John reminded him, "but I'll sure do my best."

"How about celebrating with a banana split?" suggested Pat. "My treat."

"No, I'd better not." John shook his head. "I'm watching my diet. You have to do that when you're a runner."

"Listen to this guy," Pat mocked. "He's the one who always used to like to stuff his mouth and just sit and read."

"I was like that," John admitted, "but I've changed."

"Sounds like you have to make a big sacrifice to run," Brad commented. "I don't know if I'd like that."

"Running is hard work," John agreed, "but it feels good to stretch my legs and see God's creation, too."

"You're beginning to sound like a cross between a preacher and a health nut," Brad teased.

"That's OK if it makes him a champion for our school," exclaimed Pat. "Give it all you got, John."

"I will," John promised. He glanced at his watch. "Say, I'd better go."

John's mind was centered on the coming track meet as he drifted off to sleep that night. He thought the kids were right—he'd win the race. He had done his best preparing for it. *Here comes the Champ,* he said to himself as his eyes closed in sleep.

HOW ABOUT YOU? Do you prepare for tests, sports, and contests by getting lots of practice, a balanced diet, exercise, and proper rest? That's what you should do in order to do your best. Today's Scripture compares the Christian life to a race. Just as you're willing to sacrifice and work hard to win in school competitions, you also should be willing to do the same for the Lord. Do whatever the Lord asks as you "run" for Him. □ J.H.

TO MEMORIZE: *Let us run with perseverance the race marked out for us.* Hebrews 12:1, NIV

THE STARTER'S shot split the air! The race had begun! John and the other runners charged off at a steady pace, but by the second lap, some had dropped far behind. Chet Johnson from Hillsdale had the lead. Calvin Potts from Lakeview was in second place, with John in third. Soon John edged ahead of Calvin and pulled into second place. With an added spurt of power, he surged ahead again and took first place from Chet. One more lap to go, but now Calvin was moving with new speed. As he pulled alongside, John gave it all he had. Sweat poured down his face! Pain stabbed his muscles! He gasped for air! Just inches to go! John pushed ahead, but Calvin kept coming! "He's done it!" the announcer shouted as the tape across the finish line broke. "Our new state champion for this event is Calvin Potts!" The crowd roared.

A disappointed John joined his parents after the closing ceremonies. "Good race," his dad said.

"Who're you kidding?" John burst out. "I lost."

"But you gave it all you had, John. You did your best. I call that winning even if you didn't win the championship. I'm proud of you."

"But I let everyone down! I'm a failure," moaned John. "I'll never run a race again."

"Failing to win first place doesn't make you a failure," said Dad, "but giving up and quitting might. That would really be letting everyone down—including the Lord. Quitting because you lost would be a poor testimony. On the other hand, learning from your failure, being thankful for doing as well as you did, and continuing with God's help to do your best, would be a fine Christian example to your friends."

John still dreaded going home and facing his friends. But when he got there, he saw a large banner hanging in front of the school. "Welcome home, John! We're proud of you!" John was relieved. He wasn't a state champion, but his friends knew he had done his best.

HOW ABOUT YOU? Have you failed at something? That *doesn't* make you a failure! Don't give up, but try again! Do you think you've failed in your Christian race? Have you failed to witness? Told a lie? Done a poor job? Don't keep thinking about your failure. Ask for the Lord's help and try again. □ J.H.

TO MEMORIZE: *One thing I do: Forgetting what is behind and straining toward what is ahead.* Philippians 3:13, NIV

3

Running to Win

(Continued from yesterday)

FROM THE BIBLE:
I consider everything a loss compared to the surpassing greatness of knowing Christ Jesus my Lord, for whose sake I have lost all things. I consider them rubbish, that I may gain Christ and be found in him, not having a righteousness of my own that comes from the law, but that which is through faith in Christ—the righteousness that comes from God and is by faith. I want to know Christ and the power of his resurrection and the fellowship of sharing in his sufferings, becoming like him in his death, and so, somehow, to attain to the resurrection from the dead. Not that I have already obtained all this, or have already been made perfect, but I press on to take hold of that for which Christ Jesus took hold of me. Brothers, I do not consider myself yet to have taken hold of it. But one thing I do: Forgetting what is behind and straining toward what is ahead, I press on toward the goal to win the prize for which God has called me heavenward in Christ Jesus. Philippians 3:8-14, NIV

Learn from "failure"

4

Trees Need Leaves

FROM THE BIBLE:

I am the true vine, and my Father is the gardener. He cuts off every branch in me that bears no fruit, while every branch that does bear fruit he prunes so that it will be even more fruitful. You are already clean because of the word I have spoken to you. Remain in me, and I will remain in you. No branch can bear fruit by itself; it must remain in the vine. Neither can you bear fruit unless you remain in me. I am the vine; you are the branches. If a man remains in me and I in him, he will bear much fruit; apart from me you can do nothing. If anyone does not remain in me, he is like a branch that is thrown away and withers; such branches are picked up, thrown into the fire and burned. If you remain in me and my words remain in you, ask whatever you wish, and it will be given you.

John 15:1-7, NIV

Live in the Son-shine

ONCE A YEAR, Todd visited his uncle and aunt who lived in another state. There he had a great time playing with his cousins and helping in his uncle's big apple orchard. One day, after Todd had helped pick apples for a couple hours, he was resting beneath one of the trees when Uncle Mike came and sat next to him. "Ahhh!" exclaimed Uncle Mike, stretching. "A few minutes of rest sure sounds like a good idea. Here, how about having an apple?"

"No thanks, Uncle Mike," Todd replied. "I've been eating so many apples today, I can't look at another one. I've just been sitting here thinking. Why does a tree grow leaves as well as apples? You can't eat the leaves, and if there weren't leaves, there'd be more room for apples."

"Oh, but Todd, without the leaves there would be no apples," Uncle Mike stated.

"Really? I didn't know that! Are you sure?" Todd wanted to know.

"Oh, yes. Very sure," came his uncle's reply. "You see, Todd, the leaves absorb the sunshine and the rain, which then flow through the leaves, into the branch, and out into the fruit."

"How about that!" Todd exclaimed. "I probably heard that in school, but I'd forgotten it."

"Here's something else that's important," Todd's uncle continued. "Just as leaves soak up the sun, spelled s-u-n, in order to bear fruit, we need the Son, S-o-n, if we are to produce any fruit in our lives."

"Now you lost me, Uncle Mike. What do you mean?"

"Many people try their best to live good lives and do good things," explained Uncle Mike, "but without Jesus, the Son of God, their 'fruit'—or good living—is worthless. Jesus told His disciples that without Him they could do nothing. We need Jesus Christ living in our hearts and lives. That's why it's important to accept Him as Savior while we're young and then learn all we can about Him as we grow up. He can help us live the way we ought to."

HOW ABOUT YOU? Do you think you can get along without the Son of God? Do you try to produce fruit, or good deeds, in your own strength? You can do nothing good by yourself. You need God's Son, Jesus. □ C.V.M.

TO MEMORIZE: *I am the vine; you are the branches.* John 15:5, NIV

"THERE!" ELAINE looked at the string she had just tied around her finger. "That should help me remember to ask Tina to bring my sweater along to school tomorrow. My teacher says a string around your finger makes a good reminder when you need to remember something."

"Fine," smiled her mother. "Now I hope you're ready to go to church. It's almost time for Sunday school."

When Elaine arrived at church, she looked for Tina, but Tina wasn't there. So Elaine decided to leave the string on her finger until after church when she could call Tina.

"Please turn to 1 Corinthians 11," said Pastor Gates during the morning service. "The Lord knows we are a forgetful people," he continued. "He gave us a special way to remind us of what He's done for us—we call it the Lord's Supper. The pieces of bread eaten during the Lord's Supper remind us of Jesus' body and how He suffered for us on the cross. The grape juice is a reminder of His blood which was shed for us." Elaine twisted the string on her finger as Pastor Gates read the Scripture passage and continued his message.

When Elaine arrived home from church, she called Tina to tell her she missed her in Sunday school and to remind her to bring the sweater the next day. "I told her to put a string around her finger," Elaine said, "but I'm glad I can take this one off now. I'm tired of wearing it." She paused, then added, "I'm glad God planned such a nice way to remind us of what Jesus did for us. The Lord's Supper is lots nicer than wearing a string around our fingers, don't you think so?"

HOW ABOUT YOU? When Communion, or the Lord's Supper, is observed in your church, what do you think about? Are you reminded of all Jesus did for you and that He's coming again? You should be. If you're a Christian, you have the privilege of taking part of this service, but it is a serious thing. Don't whisper or daydream. It should be a happy time, but it should also be a serious time of remembering. Use it as God intended. □ H.M.

TO MEMORIZE: *This is my body, which is for you; do this in remembrance of me.* 1 Corinthians 11:24, NIV

SEPTEMBER
5

Tie a String

FROM THE BIBLE:

I received from the Lord what I also passed on to you: The Lord Jesus, on the night he was betrayed, took bread, and when he had given thanks, he broke it and said, "This is my body, which is for you; do this in remembrance of me." In the same way, after supper he took the cup, saying, "This cup is the new covenant in my blood; do this, whenever you drink it, in remembrance of me." For whenever you eat this bread and drink this cup, you proclaim the Lord's death until he comes. Therefore, whoever eats the bread or drinks the cup of the Lord in an unworthy manner will be guilty of sinning against the body and blood of the Lord. A man ought to examine himself before he eats of the bread and drinks of the cup. For anyone who eats and drinks without recognizing the body of the Lord eats and drinks judgment on himself.

1 Corinthians 11:23-29, NIV

Be serious about communion

6

Satisfied Customer

FROM THE BIBLE:

My mouth will tell of your righteousness, of your salvation all day long, though I know not its measure. I will come and proclaim your mighty acts, O Sovereign Lord; I will proclaim your righteousness, yours alone. Since my youth, O God, you have taught me, and to this day I declare your marvelous deeds.
Psalm 71:15-17, NIV

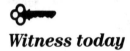

Witness today

"IT'S SO EASY to decide to witness when you hear a message like we heard this morning," observed Dad as the Dixon family drove home from church. "But we so often forget all about it the next day. Let's each think of one person to whom we could witness this week."

"Good idea," agreed Mother quickly. "I'll pick Mrs. Jellson. I've put off witnessing to her long enough."

"I'll talk to a salesman at my business dinner tomorrow," said Dad. He turned to Tom. "How about you, Son?"

Tom hesitated. "Well, I can see why we need to go to countries where people don't know about Jesus—I might do that some day. But doesn't everybody know about God here? Anybody who wants to know how to be saved can find out easily enough."

Dad was silent, then he pointed to a picture of a bicycle on a billboard at the side of the road. "Maybe you should get a Fly-Away bike," he said. "They look really great."

"No, I want a Speedster," Tom answered promptly, a little relieved that Dad was changing the subject.

"A Fly-Away would cost less," added Mother. "I saw a full-page ad in the paper last night."

Tom shook his head. "I've seen the ads and heard them on the radio, too. But Joel's big brother had a Speedster, and now Joel's got one. He says they'll outlast any other kind, and they roll better, too."

"So you'll take the word of a satisfied customer over the word of a salesman or an advertisement," observed Dad. He paused, then added, "We need to speak to others as 'satisfied customers' of the Lord."

Tom was startled. He hadn't thought of it like that before. "I think I'll witness to Joel this week," he said after a moment.

HOW ABOUT YOU? Do you tell your friends when you've bought something you really like? Do you also tell them about what the Lord has done for you? Or do you feel it's not necessary because they have plenty of opportunity to hear about Him? Businesses often report that satisfied customers are their best advertisement. You should be "advertising" for the Lord. □ H.M.

TO MEMORIZE: *My mouth will tell of your righteousness, of your salvation all day long.* Psalm 71:15, NIV

"TOM, TURN OFF that horrid music!" exclaimed Mother as Tom was watching television after school one day. "I've told you before—you are not to listen to that kind of music in this house!"

Tom laughed. "It's a commercial," he said. "It says that Kleaner King is the 'king of all cleaners.' Don't you want to get some, Mom?"

"No way," scowled Mother. "After a commercial such as that, I wouldn't use the stuff even if they were giving it away!" Dad walked into the room as Mother went on. "I can think of a couple of other products I wouldn't buy because I can't stand their ads."

"This conversation reminds me of our discussion yesterday about how we should advertise for the Lord," said Dad. "You bring up a good point. A commercial or advertisement should be a credit to what is being advertised. It should draw people to the product, not cause them to turn away. As 'satisfied customers' of the Lord, we want to attract people to Him."

"How can we be sure to do that?" asked Tom.

"Well, let's think about some ways," suggested Mother. "I'd say a neat appearance would help. What else?"

"We shouldn't be grumpy," said Tom, "or nobody will want to listen to us."

"Right," agreed Dad. "A happy smile is more attractive than a gloomy look. And how about our language? Good grammar would be a plus, I should think."

"And we shouldn't use foul language," added Tom, "or swear and use God's name."

Mother nodded. "Let's be careful always to live in a way that will draw people to the Lord and not push them away."

HOW ABOUT YOU? Does your life back up your witness for the Lord? People are impressed by the places you go, the friends you keep, and the way you look and talk, as well as by what you say. When they watch you, will they be attracted to the One who changed your life, or will they turn away? Ask the Lord to help you live, as well as speak, for Him. □ H.M.

TO MEMORIZE: *You are our epistle written in our hearts, known and read by all men.* 2 Corinthians 3:2, NKJV

Satisfied Customer

(Continued from yesterday)

FROM THE BIBLE:
Do we begin again to commend ourselves? Or do we need, as some others, epistles of commendation to you or letters of commendation from you? You are our epistle written in our hearts, known and read by all men; you are manifestly an epistle of Christ, ministered by us, written not with ink but by the Spirit of the living God, not on tablets of stone but on tablets of flesh, that is, of the heart. And we have such trust through Christ toward God. Not that we are sufficient of ourselves to think of anything as being from ourselves, but our sufficiency is from God, who also made us sufficient as ministers of the new covenant, not of the letter but of the Spirit; for the letter kills, but the Spirit gives life. 2 Corinthians 3:1-6, NKJV

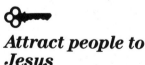

Attract people to Jesus

8

Close-up
Christian

FROM THE BIBLE:

*How can I ever know what sins
are lurking in my heart?
Cleanse me from these hidden
faults. And keep me from
deliberate wrongs; help me to
stop doing them. Only then can
I be free of guilt and innocent of
some great crime. May my
spoken words and unspoken
thoughts be pleasing even to
you, O Lord my Rock and my
Redeemer.*
Psalm 19:12-14, TLB

Be nice at home

Hello, MRS. RODGERS." Lisa smiled
sweetly at a lady picking out some oranges in the
produce department at the grocery store. "This
is my mother," Lisa continued. "Mother, this is
Mrs. Rodgers, my art teacher."

"You have a wonderful daughter," Mrs. Rodgers
told Lisa's mother. "She's so polite and helpful—
such a happy, cheerful child."

After Mrs. Rodgers went on her way, Lisa
turned to her mother. "Are you about done?" she
asked. "I'm sick of grocery shopping. I don't see
why I had to come along." Mother sighed, but
soon they were on their way home.

At home, Lisa grumbled when she had to help
put away the groceries. Then she picked a quarrel
with her brother, Craig. Finally she announced,
"I'm starved. Can I have a pear?"

Mother nodded. "There are just two left. You
and Craig can each have one."

"I get the biggest," said Lisa quickly. She
snatched the larger piece of fruit from the bowl
while Craig took what was left. Lisa was about to
take a bite when she let out a wail. "Oh, no fair!
This one's no good. Look!"

Mother looked at the pear Lisa held out. At
first glance, it looked fine, but when she looked
closely, she could see that it was actually bruised.
"This pear reminds me of you," Mother said.

Lisa scowled. "What's that supposed to mean?"

"Judging from what Mrs. Rodgers said this
morning, your life must look good from a distance—just like this pear," explained Mother. "But
from close up . . . well, if you'll think about it,
you'll have to admit there's been a lot of complaining
and grumbling. I haven't seen much of the 'helpful,
cheerful' person Mrs. Rodgers believes you to be."
Lisa was silent. "Your family sees you closeup at
home," continued Mother, "and the Lord does,
too. It's as important to look good close-up as it
is from a distance."

HOW ABOUT YOU? Do you talk sweetly at church
and then grumble when you get home? Are you
eager to help your teachers and unwilling to help
your mother? Please God by living for Him all the
time, at home as well as at church or at school.
□ H.M.

TO MEMORIZE: *May our Lord Jesus Christ himself
and God our Father, who loved us and by his grace
gave us eternal encouragement and good hope, encourage your hearts and strengthen you in every
good deed and word.* 2 Thessalonians 2:16-17, NIV

GENE AND HIS father were taking advantage of a lovely fall afternoon for one last fishing trip before winter, and they were having a serious discussion. "I know we're supposed to love everyone," said Gene as he stared at the river, "but to tell you the truth, I don't think I'll ever love Bruce. He's such a bully, and he makes me so mad. How can I love someone who acts the way he does?"

Dad was thoughtful as he reeled in his line. "Say, Gene," he said, taking out his pocket knife, "what do you think will happen if I toss this knife in the water?"

Gene took the knife from Dad's hand and examined it before handing it back. "It will sink like a rock, of course."

"I disagree," said Dad. "I think it will stay right at the top—I'll show you. Just watch."

"Don't throw it in the water," protested Gene. "You'll lose it. Give it to me if you don't want it anymore. It won't do anybody any good on the bottom of the river."

But Dad had turned to his tackle box. Taking out the biggest cork bobber he could find, he tied it to his fishing line. Just above it, he attached the knife. Gene watched as Dad threw the whole assembly into the river. It sank beneath the water, then began to float.

"Oh, no fair," protested Gene. "The cork is floating and the knife is just riding along."

"Well, I didn't say it would float by itself," replied Dad, reeling it in. "It would be impossible for it to do that. But with the help of the cork, it's carried along at the top of the water. It reminds me that with God, nothing is impossible. God gives many commands which I can't carry out by myself, but when I trust Him to help me, He just 'holds me up and carries me along'—even when it's against my natural instincts."

"I get the point, Dad," grinned Gene. "I'll ask God to help me love Bruce. I really will."

HOW ABOUT YOU? Is it unnatural for you to witness for Jesus? To quit complaining? To be cheerful? To be unselfish? God gives many commands that go against your natural inclinations. By yourself, you can't obey them—but with His help, you can. □ H.M.

TO MEMORIZE: *I can do all things through Christ who strengthens me.* Philippians 4:13, NKJV

The Floating Knife

FROM THE BIBLE:
Whatever God says to us is full of living power: it is sharper than the sharpest dagger, cutting swift and deep into our innermost thoughts and desires with all their parts, exposing us for what we really are. He knows about everyone, everywhere. Everything about us is bare and wide open to the all-seeing eyes of our living God; nothing can be hidden from him to whom we must explain all that we have done. But Jesus the Son of God is our great High Priest who has gone to heaven itself to help us; therefore let us never stop trusting him. This High Priest of ours understands our weaknesses, since he had the same temptations we do, though he never once gave way to them and sinned. So let us come boldly to the very throne of God and stay there to receive his mercy and to find grace to help us in our times of need. Hebrews 4:12-16, TLB

God can do the "impossible"

Pay Attention!

FROM THE BIBLE:

There was a man named Ananias (with his wife Sapphira) who sold some property, and brought only part of the money, claiming it was the full price. (His wife had agreed to this deception.) But Peter said, "Ananias, Satan has filled your heart. When you claimed this was the full price, you were lying to the Holy Spirit. The property was yours to sell or not, as you wished. And after selling it, it was yours to decide how much to give. How could you do a thing like this? You weren't lying to us, but to God." As soon as Ananias heard these words, he fell to the floor, dead! . . . About three hours later his wife came in, not knowing what had happened. Peter asked her, "Did you people sell your land for such and such a price?" "Yes," she replied. Peter said, "How could you and your husband even think of doing a thing like this—conspiring together to test the Spirit of God's ability to know what is going on? Just outside that door are the young men who buried your husband, and they will carry you out too." Instantly she fell to the floor, dead.
Acts 5:1-11, TLB

Learn from others

I'LL GET IT!" David jumped up as the teakettle started to whistle. He had been waiting for the water to boil so he could fix himself a cup of hot chocolate.

"Careful!" called Mother. "That handle gets very, very hot. Better use a potholder."

But David wasn't paying attention. He put a scoop of hot chocolate mix into a cup and then reached out to pick up the teakettle. "Ouch!" He dropped the kettle almost as soon as he touched it. "Oh, that burns!" He ran cold water over his hand as Mother came to help.

"I tried to warn you, because I've gotten burned on that teakettle, too," said Mother as she checked his hand. "Too bad you couldn't learn from my experience."

At school the next day, David's teacher called him up to her desk and showed him a baseball mitt. "You said you lost your mitt," said Miss Wiley, "and this one was found out on the playground. Is it yours?"

The mitt Miss Wiley held out was just like David's, only his was more worn. *Should I say it's mine, anyway?* he wondered. He felt guilty even thinking about it. Just the night before, he'd read about the lies Ananias and Sapphira had told. Still, well, he was sure God wouldn't strike him dead for telling a little lie. As David took the mitt, he felt a bit of pain in his burned palm. *I didn't learn from Mother's experience, but I am going to learn from Ananias and Sapphira*, he thought. He handed the mitt back to Miss Wiley. "It's like mine," he said, "but mine isn't this new."

As David walked back to his seat, he felt happy inside. He didn't have a mitt, but he had a clear conscience, and that was even better.

HOW ABOUT YOU? Do you learn from the examples and experiences of others? Do you learn from things written in God's Word? The Bible gives many examples from which you should learn. Read about these in the Bible. Pay attention to what happened to them and profit from their experiences. □ H.M.

TO MEMORIZE: *These things happened to them as examples and were written down as warnings for us, on whom the fulfillment of the ages has come.* 1 Corinthians 10:11, NIV

"DAD, CAN WE hike that trail?" asked Kim, pointing to a path a few feet from their campsite. "The sign says it's only a thirty-minute walk."

"It's OK with me if your mother doesn't mind waiting with little Timmy for half an hour," said Dad.

Mother laughed. "Go!" she ordered. "Timmy's sound asleep, and I have a good book to read."

Kim and her father began their hike enthusiastically, talking as they walked. Kim told her dad all about the problems she was having at school. "Sometimes Jane is so friendly and even seems interested in coming to Sunday school," she said. "At other times, she acts like she doesn't even know me. She and some other kids snickered right out loud when I prayed before I ate my lunch yesterday. Sometimes I wonder if it does any good to try to witness."

Soon the trail became more difficult. They climbed hills, fought branches, swatted at bugs, and stumbled over rocks. After a while Kim stopped to rest. "Tired?" asked Dad as he sank down beside her on a fallen log.

Kim nodded. "This trail seemed easy at first, but now it's really tough! I didn't realize there were so many little hills and valleys to go through. I feel like giving up!"

"You know, Kim, the Christian walk is a little like this," observed Dad. "There are sometimes rough trails to follow, and we get weary and discouraged. It's very tempting at times to stop and give up. Life has a lot of ups and downs—hills and valleys, you might say. But the Bible says we must run with patience."

"I suppose you're right, as usual!" agreed Kim with a grin. She scrambled to her feet. "I'm not going to give up in my Christian witness or on this hike. Let's go!"

HOW ABOUT YOU? Are you weary and discouraged in your Christian walk? Do kids at school laugh at you because you live for the Lord? Are you tempted to stop and give up? Remember that your Christian walk will have both lows and highs. Don't give up now! □ V.R.

TO MEMORIZE: *Be strong and take heart, all you who hope in the Lord.* Psalm 31:24, NIV

11

The Trail

FROM THE BIBLE:

How great is your goodness, which you have stored up for those who fear you, which you bestow in the sight of men on those who take refuge in you. In the shelter of your presence you hide them from the intrigues of men; in your dwelling you keep them safe from accusing tongues. Praise be to the Lord, for he showed his wonderful love to me when I was in a besieged city. In my alarm I said, "I am cut off from your sight!" Yet you heard my cry for mercy when I called to you for help. Love the Lord, all his saints! The Lord preserves the faithful, but the proud he pays back in full. Be strong and take heart, all you who hope in the Lord. Psalm 31:19-24, NIV

Don't give up!

SEPTEMBER

I Mean It

FROM THE BIBLE:

*Lord! Help! Godly men are fast
disappearing. Where in all the
world can dependable men be
found? Everyone deceives and
flatters and lies. There is no
sincerity left. But the Lord will
not deal gently with people who
act like that; he will destroy
those proud liars who say, "We
will lie to our hearts' content.
Our lips are our own; who can
stop us?" The Lord replies, "I
will arise and defend the
oppressed, the poor, the needy. I
will rescue them as they have
longed for me to do." The Lord's
promise is sure. He speaks no
careless word; all he says is
purest truth, like silver seven
times refined. O Lord, we know
that you will forever preserve
your own from the reach of evil
men, although they prowl on
every side and vileness is
praised throughout the land.*
Psalm 12, TLB

Give honest compliments

SOMETHING KIND OF funny happened in Nature Club today," Katy told her mother as she set the table for supper. "I sat down in my usual seat, and Sue Brown hurried over to me like we were best friends! I hardly know her at all. Anyhow, she told me how nice I looked in my green sweater and asked if it was new."

"Really?" asked Mother. "You've had that sweater a long time, and you wear it almost every week."

"I know," nodded Katy. "Then Sue went on to say how much she admired my math grades. I really got suspicious when she told me how she always liked to be around me!"

"She must have been in a good mood today," Mother commented.

"Well, after she got done telling me all those things, she went over to another girl and gave her the same treatment!" said Katy.

Mother looked thoughtful. "Maybe she's trying to make some new friends."

"You're right," laughed Katy, "and she wanted them in a hurry. I figured it out after the club meeting started. We were electing officers, and Sue was one of the three nominated for president. She thought she could get our votes by giving us compliments. I had already decided Greg would be the best president, and I guess most of the other kids agreed, because Greg won. After club, I said 'good-bye' to Sue, but she just ignored me."

"I'm glad you weren't taken in by her compliments," Mother said. "It's sad when someone tries to control others through flattery. Even the Bible says that flattering lips are wrong."

"I'm going to be careful to really mean what I'm saying when I give someone a compliment," declared Katy.

HOW ABOUT YOU? Have you ever complimented someone because you wanted him to do something for you? Insincere compliments are called 'flattery,' but, actually, they are lies. God's Word refers to flattery a number of times, but never favorably. It's nice to give a compliment when you really mean it, but it's wrong to give a compliment just to make someone like you. □ L.W.

TO MEMORIZE: *A man who flatters his neighbor spreads a net for his feet.* Proverbs 29:5, NKJV

"THIS IS THE life," said Stan as he sat with his back propped against an old log. He and his cousin, Steve, were on a camping trip with their grandfather.

"I feel close to God out here," remarked Grandpa.

Steve nodded. "I've been thinking about something our youth leader said about God."

"What's that?" asked Stan.

"He said God is one God, but yet three persons. There's God the Father, God the Son, and God the Holy Spirit," said Steve. "I just can't imagine how that can be."

"I don't really understand it either," shrugged Stan. "But I'm getting hungry! Let's start dinner, Grandpa. Shall we get some water from the spring?"

Grandpa walked over to the ice chest. "Just this once let's use some ice for cooking water," he said, dropping several ice cubes into a pan which he set on a rack over the campfire. "I think it might help us understand something." The boys watched as the ice began melting into water. Soon the water was steaming.

"Did you notice," asked Grandpa, "that first there was ice, then it melted into water, and then some of that water turned into steam? It's the same substance, but in three different forms."

"Hey, that's right!" exclaimed Steve. He looked at Grandpa. "And that's a little like God, right? He's one God, but He has three different forms."

Grandpa nodded. "Of course, God is much greater than water. He made it, and He made the freezing and boiling point laws. But seeing water in these three different forms can help us understand God in three persons."

The boys agreed. "It's good to think about God and His greatness," added Stan. He grinned. "And now I'd like to change some food to a different form. I'm still hungry!"

HOW ABOUT YOU? Do you find the Trinity hard to understand? God does not ask you to understand it perfectly. Just remember that we serve one God, not three—but He does have three forms. Give thanks for a great God—a God whose knowledge and understanding is far greater than your own. □ C.Y.

TO MEMORIZE: *For there are three who bear witness in heaven: the Father, the Word, and the Holy Spirit; and these three are one. 1 John 5:7, NKJV*

Ice, Water, and Steam

FROM THE BIBLE:
Who is he who overcomes the world, but he who believes that Jesus is the Son of God? This is He who came by water and blood—Jesus Christ; not only by water, but by water and blood. And it is the Spirit who bears witness, because the Spirit is truth. For there are three who bear witness in heaven: the Father, the Word, and the Holy Spirit; and these three are one. 1 John 5:5-7, NKJV

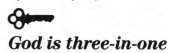

God is three-in-one

14

The Fishing Is Fine!

FROM THE BIBLE:

As Jesus was walking beside the Sea of Galilee, he saw two brothers, Simon called Peter and his brother Andrew. They were casting a net into the lake, for they were fishermen. "Come, follow me," Jesus said, "and I will make you fishers of men." At once they left their nets and followed him. Going on from there, he saw two other brothers, James son of Zebedee and his brother John. They were in a boat with their father Zebedee, preparing their nets. Jesus called them, and immediately they left the boat and their father and followed him.

Matthew 4:18-22, NIV

Be a fisher of men

THOUGH THE DAYS were getting chilly, Johnny sat on the front steps singing a song. Johnny liked to sing, and he sang a chorus he had often sung in Sunday school. "I will make you fishers of men . . . if you follow Me." Just as he finished the song, his mother came outside with a cup of hot chocolate.

"Here, Johnny," she said, "I thought you might like this to warm you up. What was the song I heard you singing just now?"

"Thanks for the chocolate, Mom! I was singing 'Fishers of Men.' Want to hear it?"

"Sure," said Mom. After Johnny had sung it again, she asked, "Do you know what that means?"

"Sure," Johnny answered, but he looked a bit startled. After Mother went back inside, he sipped the steaming hot chocolate and thought about Mother's question. Long ago his Sunday school teacher had explained that instead of fishing for fish, Jesus wants Christians to go fishing for people—to help others come to know Him.

Suddenly Johnny jumped off the step, and ran to Dick's house. "Hi, Dick," he said. "Want to go to Bible club on Thursday with me?"

"Bible Club? What do you do there?" Dick asked.

"Oh, it's neat, answered Johnny. "We play games, sing songs, and learn things from the Bible. How about going with me?" Johnny was pleased when Dick agreed to go. "Great!" he said. "Hey, let's go and ask Jim if he wants to go, too!" They did, and Jim agreed to join them.

As Johnny was getting ready for bed that night, he told his mother about his "fishing trip" that afternoon. "Well, Johnny, I see you really did learn the meaning of that song," she smiled. "I hope you'll be a 'fisherman' for Jesus as long as you live."

HOW ABOUT YOU? Are you trying to win your friends to Jesus? If you're a Christian, you should be doing this by your actions and your words. Lots of kids get excited about fishing for fish. Get excited about "fishing" for people, too! □ C.V.M.

TO MEMORIZE: *"Come, follow me," Jesus said, "and I will make you fishers of men."* Matthew 4:19, NIV

O H, NO!" Ted exclaimed. "I left my coat at Uncle Don's house. I wore it when we went fishing Saturday. Then it got hot, so I took it off and put it in Uncle Don's truck."

"Well, Ted," said Dad, "I guess I can't scold you. I left some research books at their house— the ones I took along to study during our visit there. I knew I should have put them in the car as soon as I was done with them! Good thing Aunt Jane and Uncle Don are planning on visiting us in a couple of weeks. They can bring the coat and books then."

"We'd better write them a letter and remind them, though," suggested Ted.

Mother walked into the room, laughing. "I overheard all that," she told them. "I have an idea. Just send them a postcard with the message '2 Timothy 4:13.' "

Ted looked puzzled. "What do you mean by that, Mom?"

"Look it up and see!"

Ted turned to 2 Timothy 4. Ted grinned. "I wonder if Uncle Don would understand."

"Probably," said Mother. "I always liked that verse. Sometimes we think the people in the Bible were different from us—that they weren't really human with human needs and problems. To me, this passage shows us the human side of Paul. He discusses things that are happening much as we would. He needed his coat and his books just like you need your coat and Dad needs his books. Paul was just an ordinary man, but God used him in an extraordinary way. God can use you, too, Ted."

Ted thought about what his mother had said as he went to find a postcard and a pen.

HOW ABOUT YOU? Do you sometimes think that people in the Bible were very different from you? Maybe you think Bible characters had unique personalities or abilities so God could use them in a special way. The people in the Bible were just ordinary men and women (and children) who were willing to let the Lord work in their lives. You can be that kind of person, too. □ L.W.

TO MEMORIZE: *God chose the foolish things of the world to shame the wise; God chose the weak things of the world to shame the strong.* 1 Corinthians 1:27, NIV

15

The Unique Letter

FROM THE BIBLE:
Please come as soon as you can, for Demas has left me. He loved the good things of this life and went to Thessalonica. Crescens has gone to Galatia, Titus to Dalmatia. Only Luke is with me. Bring Mark with you when you come, for I need him. (Tychicus is gone too, as I sent him to Ephesus.) When you come, be sure to bring the coat I left at Troas with Brother Carpus, and also the books, but especially the parchments. Alexander the coppersmith has done me much harm. The Lord will punish him, but be careful of him, for he fought against everything we said. The first time I was brought before the judge no one was here to help me. Everyone had run away. I hope that they will not be blamed for it. But the Lord stood with me and gave me the opportunity to boldly preach a whole sermon for all the world to hear. And he saved me from being thrown to the lions.
2 Timothy 4:9-17, TLB

God can use you

16

It's Not Fair

FROM THE BIBLE:

*A mob was quickly formed
against Paul and Silas, and the
judges ordered them stripped
and beaten with wooden whips.
Again and again the rods
slashed down across their bared
backs; and afterwards they were
thrown into prison. . . . Around
midnight, as Paul and Silas
were praying and singing hymns
to the Lord—and the other
prisoners were listening:
suddenly there was a great
earthquake; the prison was
shaken to its foundations, all
the doors flew open—and the
chains of every prisoner fell off!
The jailer wakened to see the
prison doors wide open, and
assuming the prisoners had
escaped, he drew his sword to
kill himself. But Paul yelled to
him, "Don't do it! We are all
here!" Trembling with fear, the
jailer called for lights and ran to
the dungeon and fell down
before Paul and Silas. He
brought them out and begged
them, "Sirs, what must I do to
be saved?" They replied, "Believe
on the Lord Jesus and you will
be saved, and your entire
household."*
Acts 16:22-32, TLB

**Grow through
unfair situations**

I DIDN'T MAKE the basketball team, Mom."
Joe slumped down in a chair as he came in from
school one day. "I'm not bragging or anything, but
I do play basketball well."

"Yes, you do, Son," agreed Mother, "but there
were only two openings on the team, and the coach
had to choose, didn't he? Who did make it?"

"Kevin, which we all expected. Kevin is good!
Then they chose Randy for the other opening. In
the try-outs, I made more baskets than he did,
and I dribbled the ball longer. But his dad is a
teacher at school, and I think that's why he made
it," Joe concluded bitterly.

Mother was quiet for a few minutes. She knew
there had been other times when Randy was chosen for something because his dad was a teacher.
She sighed. "I suppose that may be possible. If
you really believe that, perhaps you should ask
the coach about it," she suggested, "but do be
careful not to make accusations you can't prove.
And, Joe, you must learn that life isn't always fair.
Another thing you must learn is to maintain a
Christ-like attitude no matter what happens."

"Aw, Mom," Joe whined.

"Think of Paul and Silas. It wasn't fair that they
were thrown in jail for preaching about the Lord,"
continued Mother, "and yet they sang! They
weren't going to let the unfair actions of others
get them down. I know this experience is hard for
you, but you can learn something from it. Be challenged. Ask the Lord to help you handle the situation. You will come out of it a stronger and more
mature Christian."

Joe sighed. He knew his mom was right. It
wasn't going to help to be upset. He would ask
the Lord to help him turn a bad experience into
a growing experience.

HOW ABOUT YOU? Are you ever treated unfairly? It
happens to everyone. The next time you're faced
with an unfair situation that you can't change, remember Paul and Silas. Instead of complaining,
they sang! God used them through that experience, and He can also use you. Maintain a good
attitude. Grow through what has happened. □ L.W.

TO MEMORIZE: *He is the Rock, his works are perfect,
and all his ways are just. A faithful God who does
no wrong, upright and just is he.* Deuteronomy
32:4, NIV

THE TWINS, Paul and Polly, were spending the weekend with their grandparents. As they sat before the fire, popping corn with the old-fashioned, long-handled basket, Polly told her grandparents what they had discussed in school that day. "You know our teacher is a Christian," said Polly, "and she says that a person needs faith to live in this world as well as to become a Christian. She says that almost everything we do takes faith."

"Yeah," nodded Paul, "but then the bell rang, and she didn't have time to explain it. Sounds kind of silly to me." He took the corn popper and moved closer to the fireplace. Thrusting it over the hot coals, he shook it vigorously. Soon the kernels were turning into white puff balls. As they finished popping, he pulled the basket from the fire. "Where's the potholder?" he asked.

"What makes you think you need that?" asked Grandpa.

Paul stared unbelievingly. "I'll burn my hand on the basket. Fire is hot, and so is the basket."

"Perhaps so," said Grandpa. "At least fire always has been hot. Now, if you don't have faith that what was true in the past is still true, you might as well grab hold of that basket and open it up. Of course, if you do have faith, maybe you'd like this potholder."

Paul laughed. "I have faith," he declared, taking the potholder. "I guess Miss Wilson's right. We do use faith for lots of things we do."

Grandpa nodded his head. "Seeing that we exercise faith in the ordinary things we do should help us to see what it means to have faith in God, too. It's simply believing that what He says is true—even though we may not understand it."

HOW ABOUT YOU? Do you have faith? Do you ride in a bus or a plane or even a car without checking out the driver? That takes faith—a belief that those people will get you where you want to go. You'll find that you have faith in many other people, too. Then certainly you can have faith in God. Others can make errors, but not God. □ G.W.

TO MEMORIZE: *Without faith it is impossible to please Him.* Hebrews 11:6, NKJV

17

Fire Is Hot

FROM THE BIBLE:
Faith is the substance of things hoped for, the evidence of things not seen. For by it the elders obtained a good testimony. By faith we understand that the worlds were framed by the word of God, so that the things which are seen were not made of things which are visible. By faith Abel offered to God a more excellent sacrifice than Cain, through which he obtained witness that he was righteous, God testifying of his gifts; and through it he being dead still speaks. By faith Enoch was translated so that he did not see death, "and was not found because God had translated him" for before his translation he had this testimony, that he pleased God. But without faith it is impossible to please Him, for he who comes to God must believe that He is, and that He is a rewarder of those who diligently seek Him.
Hebrews 11:1-6, NKJV

Have faith in God

Just Camping

FROM THE BIBLE:

We know that if our earthly house, this tent, is destroyed, we have a building from God, a house not made with hands, eternal in the heavens. For in this we groan, earnestly desiring to be clothed with our habitation which is from heaven, if indeed, having been clothed, we shall not be found naked. For we who are in this tent groan, being burdened, not because we want to be unclothed, but further clothed, that mortality may be swallowed up by life. Now He who has prepared us for this very thing is God, who also has given us the Spirit as a guarantee. Therefore we are always confident, knowing that while we are at home in the body we are absent from the Lord. For we walk by faith, not by sight. We are confident, yes, well pleased rather to be absent from the body and to be present with the Lord. Therefore we make it our aim, whether present or absent, to be well pleasing to Him.

2 Corinthians 5:1-9, NKJV

Heaven is home

"I MISS Uncle Dick," said Jenny with a sigh. She watched her father pound a tent stake into the ground. "I know he's in heaven, but he always loved camping in the mountains with us, and now he can't share that. It doesn't seem right."

Of course, Jenny remembered how sick Uncle Dick had been for months, and how he had grown thin and weak. He had often talked about heaven and how good it would be to finally get "home," as he called it. It had made Jenny feel bad that he didn't seem sad to leave all of them behind.

A fews days later, Jenny woke up feeling cold and a little stiff. She pulled on a heavy sweater and went out to stand by the fire her father had built. "I have to admit I wouldn't want to sleep in a sleeping bag every night," she said. "I love camping, but being comfortable is pretty nice, too." She looked at the big pot of water Dad had placed over the fire. "A hot shower would feel good," she added.

"So you're getting tired of camping?" teased Dad. Then he became serious. "I think Uncle Dick was tired of camping, too, Jenny," he said. "He felt a lot like you do. He loved being here on earth—seeing all the wonderful things God was doing in people's lives and spending time with people he loved. He liked that kind of 'camping,' but 'home' is so much better for Uncle Dick. When you go home and sleep in your own bed and take hot showers again, it won't take away the joy of this trip, but your pain will be gone. You'll be where you belong. You won't be a stranger just passing through, as we are on camping trips."

As Jenny put her sleeping bag away, she thought about what Dad had said. She knew she would miss her uncle for a long time, but she understood a little better that he was safe and happy in his real home.

HOW ABOUT YOU? Does heaven seem strange and a bit scary to you? Is it hard to see how you can be happy for eternity without the things that you enjoy so much in this life? Though we don't know all about heaven, we can believe Jesus' promise that it will be wonderful. If you're a Christian, you'll find that it's where you belong. □ C.R.

TO MEMORIZE: *We are confident, yes, well pleased rather to be absent from the body and to be present with the Lord.* 2 Corinthians 5:8, NKJV

AARON WAS EXCITED as he and his father took their places on the tree stand. It was the first time Dad had taken him bow hunting. As Aaron squinted into the low sun, he noticed rows of standing corn in the field nearby. Glancing around, his gaze froze on something large and black. Black? Deer are tan, so what was this thing? Aaron shivered with something close to fear. He nudged his father, and whispered, "Dad, there's something out there, and it's coming this way!"

Just then the animal stood on its hind legs, revealing itself to be a large black bear. He raised his head and sniffed the air. Aaron and Dad stood still in shocked amazement. This was a rare sight in that area. Still sniffing, the bear cautiously moved to the edge of the woods. Checking for danger, he sat on his haunches where field and woods met, gazing longingly at the luscious corn. After several minutes of checking and smelling, the bear ventured cautiously toward the field. Soon, however, he returned to the safety of the woods.

Driving home later, Dad and Aaron talked about the bear's interesting behavior. "Did you see how much he wanted to get that corn?" asked Aaron.

"Yes, but apparently he sensed danger, and he was too smart to take a chance by staying out in the open," replied Dad. "We could take a lesson from him." Then he quoted Ephesians 5:15.

"What does that mean, Dad?" asked Aaron.

"Well, it means that, as Christians, we are to be very careful how we live and where we go—looking all around and being alert to every temptation—so we don't get trapped by some sin or trick of the devil," explained Dad.

When they got home, Mother asked about their hunting trip. "Don't make up some big story about hundreds of deer," she joked. "Just tell me the bare facts."

Dad grinned and winked at Aaron. "That's what we'll tell you," he replied. "Just the 'bear' facts."

HOW ABOUT YOU? Are you foolish about the way you live, or are you careful in all that you do? Do you stay away from places where you might be tempted to do wrong? Do you avoid people who encourage you to sin? Be careful to live as God wants you to live. Be wise. □ L.A.T.

TO MEMORIZE: *Be very careful, then, how you live—not as unwise but as wise.* Ephesians 5:15, NIV

The "Bear" Facts

FROM THE BIBLE:
Everything exposed by the light becomes visible, for it is light that makes everything visible. This is why it is said: "Wake up, O sleeper, rise from the dead, and Christ will shine on you." Be very careful, then, how you live—not as unwise but as wise, making the most of every opportunity, because the days are evil. Therefore do not be foolish, but understand what the Lord's will is. Do not get drunk on wine, which leads to debauchery. Instead, be filled with the Spirit. Speak to one another with psalms, hymns and spiritual songs. Sing and make music in your heart to the Lord, always giving thanks to God the Father for everything, in the name of our Lord Jesus Christ. Submit to one another out of reverence for Christ.
Ephesians 5:14-21, NIV

Walk carefully

20

An Early Frost

FROM THE BIBLE:
Woe to those who rise early in the morning to run after their drinks, who stay up late at night till they are inflamed with wine. They have harps and lyres at their banquets, tambourines and flutes and wine, but they have no regard for the deeds of the Lord, no respect for the work of his hands. Therefore my people will go into exile for lack of understanding; their men of rank will die of hunger and their masses will be parched with thirst. Therefore the grave enlarges its appetite and opens its mouth without limit; into it will descend their nobles and masses with all their brawlers and revelers. So man will be brought low and mankind humbled, the eyes of the arrogant humbled.
Isaiah 5:11-15, NIV

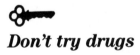

Don't try drugs

THE LEAVES ARE so pretty already, and it's only August!" exclaimed Rhonda as she and her grandfather walked to church together. She picked up a few leaves.

Grandpa, whom she was visiting for the week, nodded. "Jack Frost arrived a bit early this year," he said. "Some people say that means we're going to have a hard winter." He looked at the house they were passing and added, "This is where the Burmonts live. They're good friends of ours, but their oldest son, Craig, got involved with drugs. He's never gotten over it."

Rhonda remembered Craig—a good-looking boy who liked to draw. So he had used drugs! She felt a little guilty, because she had been wondering about trying some herself. She would be starting high school next year, and she was concerned about what kind of impression she would make. She felt she needed some experience to make her more worldly-wise, to give her a bit of color! She had thought using drugs might do that.

"In some ways this early frost we've had reminds me of what happens when young people use drugs," said Grandpa.

"What do you mean?" asked Rhonda.

"The frost resulted in beautiful leaves. And when kids take drugs, they usually feel good about themselves at first," explained Grandpa. "But just as the deadly effects of the frost will soon be seen, the effects of drugs also become apparent. Sometimes drugs actually kill young people. Craig Burmont might have been a great artist if he'd developed his talent through steady practice and study at a good art school. Instead he tried to take a shortcut with drugs. What a shame that he's very likely reached the end of his career!"

As Rhonda walked, she kicked some leaves that had already turned brown and dry. She wondered if God had sent this early frost just for her, as a warning against trying to live her life too quickly.

HOW ABOUT YOU? Have you been tempted to try drugs for the sake of being popular? It's far better to stand alone than to risk your health and your future by taking drugs. Pray that God will help you not to take any foolhardy risks. □ L.B.M.

TO MEMORIZE: *There is a way that seems right to a man, but in the end it leads to death.* Proverbs 14:12, NIV

"STACI, THIS IS the last time I'm going to tell you to turn out your light!" Mother called down the hall. "You know we have to get up early to go to the farm." Hurriedly, Staci stuffed the magazine she was reading under the mattress as she heard Mother's footsteps.

The next day at her grandparents' farm, time passed quickly. As they were preparing to leave, Grandma Walker handed Staci's father a paper sack. "Victor, will you fill this with potatoes from the smokehouse? Get some onions, too. But be careful. Last week Grandpa killed a black widow spider out there."

The following week Staci spent more and more time in her room reading the magazines Denise loaned her. She was very careful to keep them hidden in her notebook, for she knew her parents would not approve of them. Friday afternoon, just as she reached for a magazine, her mother screamed. Staci dropped her notebook and ran to the kitchen.

Mother was leaning against the cupboard. "There's a black widow spider in there!" She pointed at the open potato bin. "I was reaching in to get potatoes for dinner when I saw it!"

At that moment, Dad walked through the door. How glad they were to see him! When the spider was dead and the potato bin emptied, searched, and refilled, Mother took a deep breath. "Just think, I've put my hand in there several times this week."

Dad grinned wryly. "And I put the potatoes, spider and all, in the sack." Staci shivered.

After dinner and devotions, she excused herself—to do homework, she said. As she shut the door and reached for the magazine in her notebook, she remembered the hidden spider. Sharply, she drew back her hand. She could no more touch that magazine than she could have touched the spider. No one had said a word, but Staci knew the Spirit of the Lord was convicting her. *Tomorrow,* she promised herself, *I'll return it, and I'll tell Denise not to bring me any more.*

HOW ABOUT YOU? Is there hidden sin in your life? It may be hidden to people, but God knows all about it. Get rid of it before God has to judge and punish as He did Achan. Don't play with sin. It's far more dangerous than spiders. □ B.W.

TO MEMORIZE: *Be sure that your sin will find you out.* Numbers 32:23, NIV

21

The Black Widow

FROM THE BIBLE:

Early the next morning Joshua had Israel come forward by tribes, and Judah was taken. . . . Joshua had his family come forward man by man, and Achan son of Carmi, the son of Zimri, the son of Zerah, of the tribe of Judah, was taken. Then Joshua said to Achan, "My son, give glory to the Lord, the God of Israel, and give him the praise. Tell me what you have done; do not hide it from me." Achan replied, "It is true! I have sinned against the Lord, the God of Israel. This is what I have done: When I saw in the plunder a beautiful robe from Babylonia, two hundred shekels of silver and a wedge of gold weighing fifty shekels, I coveted them and took them. They are hidden in the ground inside my tent, with the silver underneath." So Joshua sent messengers, and they ran to the tent, and there it was, hidden in his tent, with the silver underneath. . . . Joshua said, "Why have you brought this trouble on us? The Lord will bring trouble on you today." Then all Israel stoned him, and after they had stoned the rest, they burned them.

Joshua 7:16-26, NIV

Don't try to hide sin

275

22

The Rules of the Game

FROM THE BIBLE:

Everyone should be quick to listen, slow to speak and slow to become angry, for man's anger does not bring about the righteous life that God desires. Therefore, get rid of all moral filth and the evil that is so prevalent and humbly accept the word planted in you, which can save you. Do not merely listen to the word, and so deceive yourselves. Do what it says. Anyone who listens to the word but does not do what it says is like a man who looks at his face in a mirror and, after looking at himself, goes away and immediately forgets what he looks like. But the man who looks intently into the perfect law that gives freedom, and continues to do this, not forgetting what he has heard, but doing it—he will be blessed in what he does.

James 1:19-25, NIV

Follow God's rules

YOU CAN'T do that!" exclaimed Larry as his friend Dennis moved his marker on the gameboard. "Don't you know the rules?"

Dennis looked up. "Yeah, but we always play it this way at home," he said as Mark, another friend, took a turn.

Then Dale took a turn. He landed on a space that said, "You lose ten points." Dale was scorekeeper, but he didn't subtract any points from his score. He just nudged Larry and said, "Your turn."

Mark frowned. "You have to subtract ten points," he said.

Dale shrugged. "We just skip those penalty points."

"This is no fun," declared Larry. "Everybody plays by his own rules. We might as well quit."

"Or play by the rules of the person who made up the game in the first place," suggested Mother, who had just come in. "There's a rule sheet right there in the box."

Larry and his friends looked at one another. "Good idea," they agreed. Soon the game was again in progress, with frequent references being made to the rule sheet.

When Larry's father came home, he greeted Larry with a grin. "Well, what did you learn today, Son?" he asked.

Larry explained what had happened that afternoon. "I learned," he said, "that it's important to play by the rules."

"Well, that's a good lesson to learn," approved Dad. "I wish everybody would learn that."

"Not everybody plays games," Larry pointed out.

Dad raised his eyebrows. "Well, in a way they do," he said. "Everybody plays the 'Game of Life.' If we'd all follow the rules of the One who 'invented' it, this would be a happier world. Do you know who I'm talking about?"

Larry nodded. "God," he said. "He gave His rules in the Bible. Everybody ought to follow them."

HOW ABOUT YOU? Do you know God's rules? Do you follow them, or do you change them to suit yourself? You need to refer to His "rule sheet," the Bible, so you'll know what He says. But "knowing" isn't enough. You need to follow His rules—to do what He says—as well. □ H.M.

TO MEMORIZE: *Do not merely listen to the word, and so deceive yourselves.* James 1:22, NIV

RODNEY ROLLED A tiny piece of paper into a ball, took aim, and flicked it toward Jeremy in the row ahead. It hit its mark. Eric snickered.

Rodney turned toward Eric. He was glad Eric had come along to Sunday school today to hear the missionary speaker from Africa. Usually he refused to come, saying the Bible was too hard to understand.

Something Mr. Telsen, the missionary, was saying now caught Rodney's attention, but he didn't understand a word of it. Mr. Telsen was speaking in one of the tribal languages. "How many of you understood what I said?" he asked a moment later. When no one raised a hand, Mr. Telsen again spoke in the foreign tongue. This time Mrs. Telsen repeated his words in English.

"In Africa we are involved in translating," said Mr. Telsen a little later. "We translate the Bible into the African language so the people can read it. But many of our people cannot read, and even those who can often don't understand. So we translate God's message to them in another way—by our lives. You see, we not only tell them what it means to be a Christian. We show them by such things as helping them with their work, treating them fairly, sharing with them, and being kind to them."

Mr. Telsen looked around the group. "Maybe you have friends who don't understand the Bible. Maybe you need to translate to your friends what it means to be a Christian," continued Mr. Telsen. "How can you do that?"

Jeremy, in the row ahead, raised his hand. "By sharing our toys and stuff," he said.

"By bringing them to Sunday school and church," added Rodney.

But he gulped when he heard the next suggestion. "By sitting quietly in church so they won't be disturbed and can hear the message."

Mr. Telsen nodded. "Good!" he said. "Ask God to make all of us good translators of His Word."

HOW ABOUT YOU? What kind of "translator" are you? Are you kind? Forgiving? Willing to share? Obedient? Friendly? Do those around you get a correct idea of what it means to be a Christian? Think about it. □ H.M.

TO MEMORIZE: *You will receive power when the Holy Spirit comes on you; and you will be my witnesses in Jerusalem, and in all Judea and Samaria, and to the ends of the earth.* Acts 1:8, NIV

The Translators

FROM THE BIBLE:
"You are my witnesses," declares the Lord, "and my servant whom I have chosen, so that you may know and believe me and understand that I am he. Before me no god was formed, nor will there be one after me. I, even I, am the Lord, and apart from me there is no savior. I have revealed and saved and proclaimed—I, and not some foreign god among you. You are my witnesses," declares the Lord, "that I am God."
Isaiah 43:10-12, NIV

Witness by your life

24

Red Light

FROM THE BIBLE:
Put to death, therefore, whatever belongs to your earthly nature: sexual immorality, impurity, lust, evil desires and greed, which is idolatry. Because of these, the wrath of God is coming. You used to walk in these ways, in the life you once lived. But now you must rid yourselves of all such things as these: anger, rage, malice, slander, and filthy language from your lips. Do not lie to each other, since you have taken off your old self with its practices and have put on the new self, which is being renewed in knowledge in the image of its Creator.
Colossians 3:5-10, NIV

Obey God's "stoplights"

KEVIN GOT A tight, scared feeling in the pit of his stomach when he saw the flashing lights from a police car behind them. Mr. Casey, the neighbor with whom Kevin was riding, pulled over to the side of the road and rolled down his window. With lights still flashing, the police car stopped behind them. The police officer walked up to the car and asked for Mr. Casey's driver's license. "You went through that traffic light when it was red," stated the officer.

"I did?" Mr. Casey was startled. "I'm sorry," he said. "I didn't notice that it was red. I'll certainly be more careful after this." Soon they were on their way again, but Mr. Casey had received a ticket and would have to pay a fine.

"I don't think it was fair for the police officer to give Mr. Casey a ticket," protested Kevin when he told his folks what had happened. "He didn't run a red light on purpose."

"That may be true," agreed Dad, "but he did do it. The red light was there for him to see. It means 'stop,' and he didn't stop, so it is fair for him to pay the consequences."

"Actually, I'm sure he's glad to be getting off so easily," added Mother. "He might have had an accident instead."

"That's right," agreed Dad. "You know, this reminds me of Pastor Lee's message on Sunday when he said Christians must expect to pay the consequences of sin if they don't heed God's warnings. God tells us to stop doing many things. If we don't listen—or don't notice—we can expect to pay. The excuses we offer won't change the fact that we've disobeyed."

Kevin nodded. "I guess you're right," he said. "I'm going to listen to God's warnings."

HOW ABOUT YOU? Are you going through "red lights" that God has established? He says to stop lying, stop getting angry, stop using bad words, stop being disobedient, stop all the sins you committed before you were saved. When you're tempted to do some of those "old" things, ask God to help you say no. Obey his "stop light," and you won't have to pay the "fine." □ H.M.

TO MEMORIZE: *Do not lie to each other, since you have taken off your old self with its practices.* Colossians 3:9, NIV

"BYE, MOM." Kevin got on his bike to ride to town.

"Bye, Son. Be careful," called Mother. "Don't forget, you have to obey all the traffic signals, just like cars do."

That evening, Kevin had a story to tell. "Know what I did?" he asked. "When I came to the traffic light at the corner of Main and Pine, I remembered Mom's warning to obey traffic signals. The light was red, so I stopped and waited for it to change."

"Good for you," approved Dad.

"Yeah, but I started thinking about something else, and when I looked at the light, it was just turning red again." Kevin slapped his forehead. "I had to sit through that light, too, and wait for it to turn green. What a dummy!"

They all laughed, but Mother shook her head. "I'm afraid you really weren't thinking much better than Mr. Casey was when he ran the red light yesterday," she said. "After all, a green light means 'go,' and you didn't go."

"Well, the second time it was green I did. You can be sure of that," Kevin told them. He thought for a moment. "Does God have green lights for us, too?"

Dad nodded. "He surely does—lots of them. He says to 'go' and tell others about Him, to be kind, to love, forgive, and all sorts of things—even to obey the laws of our land."

"And just as we need God's help to obey the 'stops,' " added Mother, "we need His help to 'go' as He tells us."

HOW ABOUT YOU? Are you "going" when you should? Do your actions show that you love God? Are you witnessing for Jesus? Have you forgiven the person who hurt you? Don't "stop" when you should be "going." Do something positive today to show your love for God and for others. □ H.M.

TO MEMORIZE: *But above all these things put on love, which is the bond of perfection.* Colossians 3:14, NKJV

25

Red Light

(Continued from yesterday)

FROM THE BIBLE:

As the elect of God, holy and beloved, put on tender mercies, kindness, humbleness of mind, meekness, longsuffering; bearing with one another, and forgiving one another, if anyone has a complaint against another; even as Christ forgave you, so you also must do. But above all these things put on love, which is the bond of perfection. And let the peace of God rule in your hearts, to which also you were called in one body; and be thankful. Let the word of Christ dwell in you richly in all wisdom, teaching and admonishing one another in psalms and hymns and spiritual songs, singing with grace in your hearts to the Lord. And whatever you do in word or deed, do all in the name of the Lord Jesus, giving thanks to God the Father through Him.
Colossians 3:12-17, NKJV

"Go," showing God's love

26
Oh Boy!

FROM THE BIBLE:

"For my thoughts are not your thoughts, neither are your ways my ways," declares the Lord. "As the heavens are higher than the earth, so are my ways higher than your ways and my thoughts than your thoughts. As the rain and the snow come down from heaven, and do not return to it without watering the earth and making it bud and flourish, so that it yields seed for the sower and bread for the eater, so is my word that goes out from my mouth: It will not return to me empty, but will accomplish what I desire and achieve the purpose for which I sent it."
Isaiah 55:8-11, NIV

God knows best

OH, BOY! It's a boy, isn't it?" Jeremy was jumping around the kitchen while his grandmother talked on the phone to Jeremy's father at the hospital. He was so excited, he almost dropped the apple he was holding.

Grandma hung up the phone. "You now have a beautiful baby sister," she said gently. "Her name is Melissa."

"That can't be!" Jeremy dropped his apple. "I've been praying for months for a brother. It's not fair. Cory got a baby brother, and he didn't pray at all."

Grandma sat down in the chair by the coffee table. "I got out the album that has your baby pictures in it, Jeremy," she said. "You sure were a cute little fellow."

"That was a long time ago. I'm in school now and everything," said Jeremy proudly.

"I remember how happy your mom and dad were when they were expecting you," Grandma told him. "When people asked if they wanted a girl or a boy, they said they just wanted a healthy baby."

Jeremy picked his apple up from the floor. "I'm sure they were glad I turned out to be a boy."

"They were mighty proud of you, but I was disappointed. I wanted a granddaughter," confessed Grandma.

"Grandma!" Jeremy was shocked. "Don't you like me?"

"Oh, yes," Grandma assured him, "but I already had five grandsons. I thought it would be nice to have a girl in the family." She gave Jeremy a big hug. "But you know what? Now I couldn't love anybody more. You'll love your sister, too. You'll see. Thank God for her."

"I still don't think it was fair of you, Grandma, to wish I was a girl," Jeremy pouted.

Grandma's eyes twinkled. "Less fair than for you to wish your sister was a boy?" she asked.

Jeremy looked surprised. "I guess I'm unfair, too," he admitted. He bit into his apple. "When can Melissa come home?" he asked eagerly.

HOW ABOUT YOU? Do you blame God if He doesn't answer your prayers your way? Do you ask for things to satisfy your own selfish desires, or do you ask for God's will to be done? He has a purpose for everything. □ R.M.

TO MEMORIZE: *Give thanks in all circumstances, for this is God's will for you in Christ Jesus.* 1 Thessalonians 5:18, NIV

"JOSH, WOULD you open the trunk, please?" asked Mom. She pulled the keys from the ignition and held onto one as she handed them to him.

Nine-year-old Josh grabbed the ring and scrambled out the door in a flash. He ran around to the trunk and eagerly shoved in a key. The lock wouldn't budge. He fumbled with the jangling ring and selected another key that looked good. It wouldn't even go in. Frustrated, he yelled, "Mom! Which one?"

Mom's hand came down gently over his fingers as she took the key ring from him. "It was the one I was holding," she said. "I tried to tell you, but you bolted out of the car before I could finish." She held out a short silver key.

Sheepishly, Josh slid the key in and unlocked the trunk. He returned the ring with a grin. "I guess there's only one that will work, huh?"

Mom smiled as she loaded his arms with a grocery bag. "Yes, and do you know what? There are still many people, even adults, who don't use the right key."

Josh's face crinkled in puzzlement as he followed his mother into the house. "What do you mean?" he asked.

"God sacrificed His Son, Jesus, so that we may have eternal life. But instead of using that key to salvation, many people try their own imitations, even if they have heard of the right way." She turned to Josh and dangled the key ring in front of him. "Do you remember how you felt when you tried to use the wrong ones?"

Josh nodded. "I thought for sure they'd work. They all looked like they would."

"Other people think the same thing about heaven," said Mom. "They think their keys will work, just because they go to church or try to be good. What they are doing looks like the right thing to them, but Jesus is the only way to heaven."

HOW ABOUT YOU? Are you trying to get to heaven by being good, going to church, or giving money? Those are things God wants you to do, but they can't save you. You can enter heaven only through Christ. □ J.B.

TO MEMORIZE: *I am the way and the truth and the life. No one comes to the Father except through me.* John 14:6, NIV

27
The Right Key

FROM THE BIBLE:

Just as Moses lifted up the snake in the desert, so the Son of Man must be lifted up, that everyone who believes in him may have eternal life. For God so loved the world that he gave his one and only Son, that whoever believes in him shall not perish but have eternal life. For God did not send his Son into the world to condemn the world, but to save the world through him. Whoever believes in him is not condemned, but whoever does not believe stands condemned already because he has not believed in the name of God's one and only Son.
John 3:14-18, NIV

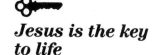

Jesus is the key to life

28

Cut Off

FROM THE BIBLE:

The body is a unit, though it is made up of many parts; and though all its parts are many, they form one body. So it is with Christ. For we were all baptized by one Spirit into one body— whether Jews or Greeks, slave or free—and we were all given the one Spirit to drink. Now the body is not made up of one part but of many. If the foot should say, "Because I am not a hand, I do not belong to the body," it would not for that reason cease to be part of the body. And if the ear should say, "Because I am not an eye, I do not belong to the body," it would not for that reason cease to be part of the body. If the whole body were an eye, where would the sense of hearing be? If the whole body were an ear, where would the sense of smell be? But in fact God has arranged the parts in the body, every one of them, just as he wanted them to be. If they were all one part, where would the body be? As it is, there are many parts, but one body.

1 Corinthians 12:12-20, NIV

We need one another

I JUST THINK it's silly, and I don't want to go!" As Tammy slammed down the phone, her mother looked up. "Where don't you want to go?"

"Oh, some kids in my Sunday school class are going to take cookies to the old folks' home." Tammy shrugged. "I wanted to take them to the day care center—but no, we have to do what Becky wants," she added sarcastically.

"Going to the nursing home sounds like a good idea to me," Mother replied. "That reminds me— your Sunday school teacher asked me why you didn't come to the class party. Why didn't you go?"

"I didn't want to," Tammy responded. "They play stupid games! Becky's always got to be the leader, and Regina thinks she's so cool because she has a boyfriend."

Mother raised her eyebrows as Tammy went out to get the newspaper from the front steps. A few minutes later, Tammy returned, pointing to an article and picture in the paper. "Listen! 'Local Boy's Hand Restored.' That's Eddie's picture!" she said excitedly. "I know him, Mother!"

Together they read about the accident in which the young boy's hand was severed from his arm. The doctors were able to sew his hand back on, and there was a good chance he'd be able to use it again.

After a restless evening, Tammy decided to go to bed. A little later Mother stopped at the door of her room. "What's the matter, Honey?" she asked gently. "You seemed unhappy all evening."

"I'm so lonesome," Tammy sobbed. "Why can't I get along with my friends anymore?"

Mother thought for a moment, then said, "You've cut yourself off from them, Tammy. If they don't do things your way, you refuse to have anything to do with them. Without Christian friends, you're like Eddie's hand—cut off and useless."

"Cut off—that's just how I feel," Tammy choked. Then she brightened. "But now I know what's wrong, and I know what to do about it. Good night, Mom. And thanks."

HOW ABOUT YOU? If things don't go your way, do you refuse to cooperate? Are your actions cutting you off from the fellowship of your friends? Christian friends are important, so ask God to forgive your selfishness. Be willing to sometimes do things someone else's way. □ B.W.

TO MEMORIZE: *The body is not made up of one part but of many.* 1 Corinthians 12:14, NIV

"I'M GOING TO climb the fence around the power station's transformer," Jason announced to this friend.

Michael's eyes widened. "Don't do it, Jason. Dad says it's dangerous. Why do you think the electric company put up that high fence with warning signs around it?"

"To keep out scaredy-cats like you," mocked Jason. "Well, have a good time playing with the girls."

I'd better stop him, Michael thought as he watched Jason leave. He jumped to his feet and ran toward the house. "I'll tell Mother."

As soon as Michael's mother heard about it, she called the electric company. Minutes later, she and Michael ran into the front yard when they heard sirens approaching. "Stay here," Mother ordered as she ran down the street.

When Mother returned, her eyes were red. She gave Michael a watery smile. "We were almost too late. Jason touched a high voltage wire just as the emergency squad arrived. They think he'll live, but he's badly burned. It will be a long time before he recovers."

"Jason said he wasn't afraid of anything," Michael told his mother.

Mother sighed. "It's good to fear some things," she said. "For instance, the Bible says that the 'fear of the Lord is the beginning of wisdom.'"

"Does that mean we're supposed to be afraid of God?" asked Michael.

"We are to fear God in the sense that we respect and obey Him," answered Mother.

"Like I respect and obey you and Dad?" Michael asked.

Mother nodded. "That shows wisdom. If you're smart, you fear many things, and it keeps you out of a lot of trouble."

"So that's what that verse means," Michael said.

HOW ABOUT YOU? Are you afraid of God? If you're a Christian, He's your heavenly Father. He loves you, but you do need to respect and obey Him. Do that, and you don't need to be afraid of Him. □ B.W.

TO MEMORIZE: *The fear of the Lord is the beginning of wisdom.* Psalm 111:10, NIV

Get Smart

FROM THE BIBLE:
O Israel, what does the Lord your God ask of you but to fear the Lord your God, to walk in all his ways, to love him, to serve the Lord your God with all your heart and with all your soul, and to observe the Lord's commands and decrees that I am giving you today for your own good? . . . For the Lord your God is God of gods and Lord of lords, the great God, mighty and awesome, who shows no partiality and accepts no bribes. He defends the cause of the fatherless and the widow, and loves the alien, giving him food and clothing. And you are to love those who are aliens, for you yourselves were aliens in Egypt. Fear the Lord your God and serve him. Hold fast to him and take your oaths in his name. He is your praise; he is your God, who performed for you those great and awesome wonders you saw with your own eyes.
Deuteronomy 10:12-13, 17-21, NIV

Fear God

30

Signed, Sealed, and Delivered

FROM THE BIBLE:

Now you can look forward soberly and intelligently to more of God's kindness to you when Jesus Christ returns. Obey God because you are his children; don't slip back into your old ways—doing evil because you knew no better. But be holy now in everything you do, just as the Lord is holy, who invited you to be his child. He himself has said, "You must be holy, for I am holy." And remember that your heavenly Father to whom you pray has no favorites when he judges. He will judge you with perfect justice for everything you do; so act in reverent fear of him from now on until you get to heaven.

1 Peter 1:13-17, TLB

Live each day carefully

TAMMY FUMED inside as she walked home from Katrina's house. The two friends had fought, and Tammy thought of some things she wished she had said to Katrina—not nice things, but she wished she had said them anyway. So as soon as she got home, she scribbled an angry note to her ex–best friend, marched down to the mailbox on the corner, and dropped it in. *That'll fix her!* she thought.

But as Tammy began to walk home again, the awfulness of what she had done began to sink in. Turning around, she saw that a mailman was just emptying the contents of the mailbox into a big sack. "Wait a minute!" she called as she ran back. "I need to get a letter out of there."

The mailman shook his head. "I'm sorry, but I can't allow anyone to handle this mail."

Tammy frowned. "It's my letter. I wrote it."

The mailman sighed. "It was your letter," he said, "up until the moment you dropped it into the mailbox. Then it became government property. It will have to be processed and delivered with the rest of the mail."

When Tammy got home, she told her mother what had happened. "Isn't that ridiculous?" she demanded.

"No one may interfere with the U.S. mail," Mother said. "You should have thought twice before you sent that letter." Then she added, "I see a spiritual side to this story, Tammy. God has given each of us a certain number of days in which to live our lives. We have a great deal of choice regarding the things we do, the thoughts we think, and the words we say. But once we do, think, or say them, we can't take them back again. Just as you couldn't get that letter back and rewrite it, we can't live any part of our lives over. That's why it's important to do the right thing—to do what Jesus wants us to—while we have the chance."

"I see," nodded Tammy. "I think I'll call Katrina and make up with her—while I still can."

HOW ABOUT YOU? Are you careless about the things you do or the words you say? Consider each day a gift from God. Live it carefully. You can't go back and change anything. You can, however, apologize to someone you may have hurt. Do that if you need to. Be able to look back on each day knowing you've done what you should. □ S.K.

TO MEMORIZE: *Teach us to number our days aright, that we may gain a heart of wisdom.* Psalm 90:12, NIV

LOOK AT THOSE slacks Kim has on today," snickered Beth to her friend MaryJo. "You'd think she'd know better than to wear those to Sunday school."

Just then Kim turned and looked at the girls. She seemed to know they were talking about her, but she just said "Hi" very quietly and took a seat.

Their teacher, Mrs. Newton, began the lesson with a question. "Someone once said this: A house divided against itself cannot stand. Who was it?"

Beth's hand shot up. "Abraham Lincoln. We just studied about the Civil War in school."

"Right," said Mrs. Newton. "Our country's people were fighting each other, and Abraham Lincoln wanted to teach Americans that they needed to be united if they wanted to be a strong country. But did you know that someone else said that long before Abraham Lincoln was born? Jesus is the one who first spoke almost those exact words." There were many looks of surprise as Mrs. Newton continued. "He was teaching a very important principle. You see, unity in our nation and unity in our homes is very important. But it is equally important to have unity among Christians and in the church." For the rest of the class time, Mrs. Newton used other Scriptures to teach the class how to show Christian unity in practical ways. "When we talk about others in an unfriendly way or do things that hurt other Christians rather than help them, we're dividing our own house," concluded Mrs. Newton.

Beth thought of her unkind words about Kim's clothes. She knew she had divided God's family instead of helping it grow strong. Silently she asked God to forgive her, and after class she went up to Kim. In a friendly way, she asked, "Would you like to come over this afternoon? I have a new game we could play."

Kim smiled shyly. "I'd like that," she said.

HOW ABOUT YOU? Do you sometimes say unkind things about other Christians? Do you think it will make *you* look better perhaps? Not so. You not only hurt that person, but you also hurt yourself and other Christians. When Christians are divided against each other, the whole church suffers. Work together, not against one another. □ C.Y.

TO MEMORIZE: *Every kingdom divided against itself is brought to desolation, and a house divided against a house falls.* Luke 11:17, NKJV

A House Divided

FROM THE BIBLE:
He was casting out a demon, and it was mute. So it was, when the demon had gone out, that the mute spoke; and the multitudes marveled. But some of them said, "He casts out demons by Beelzebub, the ruler of the demons." And others, testing Him, sought from Him a sign from heaven. But He, knowing their thoughts, said to them: "Every kingdom divided against itself is brought to desolation, and a house divided against a house falls. If Satan also is divided against himself, how will his kingdom stand? Because you say I cast out demons by Beelzebub. And if I cast out demons by Beelzebub, by whom do your sons cast them out? Therefore they will be your judges. But if I cast out demons with the finger of God, surely the kingdom of God has come upon you."
Luke 11:14-20, NKJV

Christians should be united

2

The Prodigal Brothers

FROM THE BIBLE:

A man had two sons. When the younger told his father, "I want my share of your estate now, instead of waiting until you die!" his father agreed to divide his wealth between his sons. . . . About the time his money was gone a great famine swept over the land, and he began to starve. He persuaded a local farmer to hire him to feed his pigs. The boy became so hungry that even the pods he was feeding the swine looked good to him. . . . When he finally came to his senses, he said to himself, "At home even the hired men have food enough. . . . I will go home to my father and say, 'Father, I have sinned against both heaven and you, and am no longer worthy of being called your son. Please take me on as a hired man.'" So he returned home to his father. . . . His father said to the slaves, "Quick! Bring the finest robe in the house and put it on him. . . . We must celebrate with a feast, for this son of mine was dead and has returned to life."

Luke 15:11-24, TLB

Don't be wasteful

JASON, HAVE YOU finished your homework?" Mother asked.

"Not quite, Mom." Jason looked up as he added, "I'm almost through."

"That's what you said thirty minutes ago. We leave in twenty-five minutes to go out for dinner. If your homework isn't finished, you stay home."

Exactly twenty-five minutes later, Jason dashed out of the house. He slid into the back seat beside Chad as his father started the motor. "Made it," he gasped.

"One of these days you're going to waste too much time and be left behind," Dad warned.

Later they all stood in line at the cafeteria. "Yummy! Everything looks so good!" Chad helped himself to many of the various dishes. Mother and Dad were talking to the couple behind them and didn't notice Chad's tray until the cashier had rung it all up.

"Chad," Mother scolded, "you'll never eat all that!"

When Mother, Dad, and Jason had finished eating, Chad had several untouched dishes.

"What a waste!" Dad scolded.

"Yeah, and think of all the money it cost. Wasting food is sinful," Jason added self-righteously.

Mother nodded, "Yes, it is." She looked at each of the boys. "We seem to have two prodigal sons."

"What do you mean?" asked Jason. "We didn't run away from home! We aren't prodigals."

"Yes, you are." Dad agreed with Mother. "The word *prodigal* means wasteful. Chad wastes food and money. Jason wastes time. One is as bad as the other."

"Now, Chad," said Mother, "you finish eating that meat. And from now on when we eat out, you make sure you order only as much as you can eat! It's time for the prodigals to change their ways."

HOW ABOUT YOU? The Scripture today is the story of the prodigal son. Are you a prodigal, too? Do you waste time? Money? Food? Luke 15:17 says the son came to his senses. He returned to his father, asking forgiveness and willing to be of service. If you're a prodigal, you need to change your ways, too. Ask forgiveness of God and of any others who have been affected by your wastefulness. □ B.W.

TO MEMORIZE: *One who is slack in his work is brother to one who destroys.* Proverbs 18:9, NIV

"YOU'LL BE LATE to school if you don't hurry, Anne," warned Mother. Anne gave her hair a final pat, smiled at herself one more time, and reluctantly turned away from the mirror. "OK, Mom, I'm leaving," she said, tucking her comb into her pocket. It was her first year in junior high, and that comb was her constant companion.

"Girls!" muttered her brother, Joey.

At dinner that evening, Anne talked excitedly about the Valentine party her Sunday school department was having the next evening. "I'll wear my new blouse," she announced. "It's just the right color for my hair. Gayle and I plan to go to the party together unless she has to baby-sit. Oh, I do hope she can go! I don't know what I'll do otherwise." She sighed dramatically.

"Can't you just go alone and meet everyone there?" asked Mother. "Or maybe you could go with Betty." Anne made a face. "Just what is that supposed to mean?" Mother wanted to know.

"Oh, Betty is so . . . plain, if you know what I mean."

Mother eyed Anne sternly. "I think appearance has become too important to you."

"But Betty is really homely," protested Anne.

"She looks all right to me," stated Joey.

"And she has beautiful feet," put in Dad. Anne looked at him in surprise. *Beautiful feet?*

The next evening Anne was again chattering at the dinner table. "Everyone just loves my hair this way," she said.

"Humph!" snorted Joey.

"Oh, and Gayle can go to the party! I'm so relieved," sighed Anne. "By the way, Dad, I looked at Betty's feet today. They look like ordinary feet. I didn't see anything so beautiful about them."

Dad smiled and reached for the Bible. "For devotions tonight, let's read Romans 10:13-15," he suggested. After reading, Dad spoke. "I can think of at least two people that Betty brought to church and Sunday school. And I know that she also witnessed to Mrs. Clark. The Bible says Betty has beautiful feet."

HOW ABOUT YOU? Do you have beautiful feet? You do if you are witnessing for Jesus. It's interesting to find that the Bible nowhere commends a beautiful face, but it speaks in praise of beautiful feet. And the wonderful part is that we can all have them. Start witnessing today! □ H.M.

TO MEMORIZE: *How beautiful are the feet of those who bring good news!* Romans 10:15, NIV

OCTOBER

3

What Beautiful Feet

FROM THE BIBLE:
"Everyone who calls on the name of the Lord will be saved." How, then, can they call on the one they have not believed in? And how can they believe in the one of whom they have not heard? And how can they hear without someone preaching to them? And how can they preach unless they are sent? As it is written, "How beautiful are the feet of those who bring good news!"
Romans 10:13-15, NIV

Witness for Jesus

Never Too Busy

FROM THE BIBLE:

My feet have not slipped from your paths. Why am I praying like this? Because I know you will answer me, O God! Yes, listen as I pray. Show me your strong love in wonderful ways, O Savior of all those seeking your help against their foes. Protect me as you would the pupil of your eye; hide me in the shadow of your wings as you hover over me.

Psalm 17:5-8, TLB

God always listens

DAD," SAID CRAIG, as he approached his father in the garage, "can I talk to you for a minute?"

"I'm sorry, Son," Dad replied, "but I was just leaving. I need to get an oil filter before the auto store closes."

Craig wandered into the kitchen where his mother was cooking. "Mom," he began, "today in math class, Ted Matthews said—"

"Can't it wait, Craig?" asked Mother impatiently. "I've got to make a few phone calls right now. We can talk while we're eating supper."

But during supper, Dad and Mom were busy talking about Dad's job and family finances, so Craig didn't interrupt. After supper he called his friend Bod on the phone. "Wait till you hear what Ted Matthews said today," Craig began. But Bob cut him short. "Sorry, Craig, I gotta go. My favorite TV program's on." Sadly, Craig hung up the phone. Didn't anyone have time to listen to him?

Later, as Craig was climbing into bed, his parents came in to say good night. "Did you want to talk about something?" asked Dad. Craig smiled. "Well, I did—but I don't anymore." Then he explained, "I wanted to tell you about Ted Matthews, a guy in my math class who always makes fun of me. But you and Mom were both busy, and Bob was, too. So I decided to talk to God about it! After I had prayed, I realized that Ted might be jealous because I get better grades than he does. I think tomorrow I'll offer to help him with his math."

Both Dad and Mom looked surprised and pleased. "I'm sorry we didn't listen before, Son," said Dad, "but it sounds like you learned a good lesson—that God is never too busy to listen to His children!"

HOW ABOUT YOU? Are your parents sometimes too busy to talk? Do you wish you had a friend who would always listen to what you have to say? Let Jesus be that friend. Talk to Him whenever you have a problem, or if you just feel lonely. He's never too busy! □ S.K.

TO MEMORIZE: *I will look to the Lord; I will wait for the God of my salvation; my God will hear me.* Micah 7:7, NKJV

GAIL WAS a Christian—and she let everybody at school know about it! But the things she did and said often made others angry. When Alice passed a note in class, Gail grabbed it and told the teacher. And when a few girls tried to be friendly and invited her to their party, Gail just looked shocked and said loudly, "Of course not! I'm a Christian!" The girls just shook their heads and walked away. Gail sighed. She certainly had to suffer a lot of persecution for the Lord!

One day she walked home with Tina. "Nobody likes me," groaned Gail, "and it's all because I'm a Christian!"

"I'm a Christian, too," said Tina quietly, "and I have a lot of friends. I've even been able to lead some of them to the Lord!"

"I don't understand it," Gail complained. "I witness like the Bible says, but nobody lets me talk about Jesus."

"Maybe it's your attitude," Tina suggested. "They get the impression that you think you're better than they are."

"But I am," replied Gail. "I don't smoke, or cheat, or tell dirty stories like most of the kids. You don't either!"

"Well, that's true," Tina smiled. "But I'm still not perfect. And if I didn't know Jesus, I'd probably be just like them—or worse. Don't forget, Gail, God loves them as much as He loves us. He wants them to be saved, too."

"But how can I witness to them?" asked Gail.

"Try being friendly to them," Tina said. "After all, Jesus was called 'The Friend of Sinners.' Don't always be putting the kids down, either. Let them know you love them and that God does, too. They'll be a lot more willing to listen to you then."

HOW ABOUT YOU? Have you experienced persecution for being a Christian? Be sure your attitude is right. Don't be afraid to witness for Christ, but do it out of love, not pride. Check to see if the qualities listed in today's Scripture can be seen in your witness. Don't be "pushy." □ S.K.

TO MEMORIZE: *It is better, if it is the will of God, to suffer for doing good than for doing evil.* 1 Peter 3:17, NKJV

5

Persecuted— or Pushy?

FROM THE BIBLE:
To obtain these gifts, you need more than faith; you must also work hard to be good, and even that is not enough. For then you must learn to know God better and discover what he wants you to do. Next, learn to put aside your own desires so that you will become patient and godly, gladly letting God have his way with you. This will make possible the next step, which is for you to enjoy other people and to like them, and finally you will grow to love them deeply. The more you go on in this way, the more you will grow strong spiritually and become fruitful and useful to our Lord Jesus Christ. But anyone who fails to go after these additions to faith is blind indeed, or at least very shortsighted, and has forgotten that God delivered him from the old life of sin so that now he can live a strong, good life for the Lord.
2 Peter 1:5-9, TLB

Be a loving witness

6

No Time to Eat

FROM THE BIBLE:

Get rid of your feelings of hatred. Don't just pretend to be good! Be done with dishonesty and jealousy and talking about others behind their backs. Now that you realize how kind the Lord has been to you, put away all evil, deception, envy, and fraud. Long to grow up into the fullness of your salvation; cry for this as a baby cries for his milk. Come to Christ, who is the living Foundation of Rock upon which God builds; though men have spurned him, he is very precious to God who has chosen him above all others. And now you have become living building-stones for God's use in building his house.

1 Peter 2:1-5, TLB

Eat spiritually

R ON GRABBED his school books and ran out the door. If he didn't hurry, he'd be late for class! It was that way every day—he'd sleep too long and then have to hurry to get ready on time. But no matter how late he was, he'd always take time for a big breakfast before rushing off to school.

One day a nutritionist, Mr. Pierson, came to speak to the youth group at church. He spoke about Ron's favorite subject—eating! "How many hours are there between breakfast and lunch?" Mr. Pierson asked one of the girls.

"About four or five," she replied.

"How many hours between lunch and supper?" he continued, turning to one of the boys.

"About the same," was the answer.

"And how many hours from suppertime until you eat again?" This time he pointed to Ron for an answer.

"Too many," moaned Ron, as he rubbed his stomach. Everyone laughed.

"Now let's ask those same questions about our spiritual intake," Mr. Pierson continued. "How long does your spiritual life have to wait for food from the Word of God?"

Ron was glad he did not have to answer that question out loud. Although he wouldn't think of missing meals, he hadn't been very faithful about having his spiritual food lately. Sometimes he'd go from one Sunday to the next without even opening his Bible.

"If you skip meals," the nutritionist was saying, "your physical body suffers. And if you do not regularly 'eat' from the Word of God, your spiritual life will suffer. Don't forget Peter's reminder to 'grow in grace and in the knowledge of our Lord and Savior Jesus Christ.' We can only grow when we eat."

As the youth meeting ended, Ron made a decision. He would get up early enough to have time for Bible reading and prayer to start the day with God. Then he would go down for breakfast.

HOW ABOUT YOU? Did you eat food today? Did you also "eat" from God's Word? It's important to take care of both your physical and spiritual needs on a daily basis. □ R.J.

TO MEMORIZE: *Blessed are those who hunger and thirst for righteousness, for they shall be filled.* Matthew 5:6, NKJV

CHURCH WAS OVER, and Tommy and his parents were heading for home. "You know," Dad said, "I've heard a lot of messages on doubting Thomas, but I believe the one this morning was the best I've ever heard."

Tommy's mother agreed. "It made me realize that I sometimes behave as Thomas did. I ask God for a sign that He's going to answer my prayers, when all I need is faith in my Lord."

"I sure can't figure out why Thomas wouldn't believe those other disciples when they told him they had seen Jesus," commented Tommy. "He should have known that they wouldn't lie about something like that."

Dad nodded his head. "You know, I think you've got a good point there." By this time they were home, and as Dad drove the car into the garage he looked at Tommy thoughtfully. Then he asked, "Do you think your mother and I would lie to you?"

Tommy looked at his father in surprise. "Well, no, of course not," he answered, a question still hanging in his voice. "Why do you ask?"

"I was thinking about the questions you have whenever you do your science homework," Dad replied. "You seem surprised that Thomas would not believe the word of Jesus' disciples, and still you do not seem to accept the word of your mother and me. More importantly, you don't accept the Word of God, Himself."

Tommy understood what his father was trying to say. Now that he had entered junior high school, doubts about God and His Word were beginning to crowd into his thoughts as he heard his teachers defend the theory of evolution. He was quiet for a long time. Finally he went to his room, picked up his Bible and began to read. "Lord, help me," he prayed silently. "I guess I'm just like Thomas." As he read, Tommy decided he wasn't going to doubt any longer!

HOW ABOUT YOU? Are you one who is blessed for believing on Jesus even though you have not seen Him physically? If not, won't you believe God's Word today and say with Thomas, "My Lord and my God?" When you hear teachings that do not agree with the instruction of the Bible, which do you believe? Don't be a doubting Thomas; believe that God's Word is absolutely true! □ R.J.

TO MEMORIZE: *Stop doubting and believe.* John 20:27, NIV

Believe It

FROM THE BIBLE:
Thomas (called Didymus), one of the Twelve, was not with the disciples when Jesus came. So the other disciples told him, "We have seen the Lord!" But he said to them, "Unless I see the nail marks in his hands and put my finger where the nails were, and put my hand into his side, I will not believe it." A week later his disciples were in the house again, and Thomas was with them. Though the doors were locked, Jesus came and stood among them and said, "Peace be with you!" Then he said to Thomas, "Put your finger here; see my hands. Reach out your hand and put it into my side. Stop doubting and believe." Thomas said to him, "My Lord and my God!"
John 20:24-28, NIV

God cannot lie

8

Broken Rules

FROM THE BIBLE:

*When they [the Pharisees]
heard that he had routed the
Sadducees with his reply, they
thought up a fresh question of
their own to ask him. One of
them, a lawyer, spoke up: "Sir,
which is the most important
command in the laws of Moses?"
Jesus replied, " 'Love the Lord
your God with all your heart,
soul, and mind.' This is the
first and greatest commandment. The second most important is similar: 'Love your
neighbor as much as you love
yourself.' All the other commandments and all the demands
of the prophets stem from these
two laws and are fulfilled if you
obey them. Keep only these and
you will find that you are
obeying all the others."*
Matthew 22:35-40, TLB

Obey the rules

I'M SICK of school," Lana said as she flung herself down on the couch. "There are too many rules.
Don't run in the halls. Don't slide on the banister.
Don't go too high in the swings. Don't, don't,
don't!"

"And what did you do that you weren't supposed
to do?" Mother asked. "Apparently you broke a
rule and got in trouble."

Lana looked at her mother out of the corner of
her eye. "All I did was run to get in front of the
line. I was thirsty. But Miss Marshall made me
go to the back of the line and stay in the rest of
recess. She's mean!"

"No, she isn't," Mother corrected. "How would
you like someone to cut in front of you in the line?"

Lana looked at her mother. "Oh, never mind!
Let's go play, Stephen." She followed her little
brother outside.

Soon Lana came bursting back into the house.
"Make Stephen play fair, Mother!" she exclaimed.
"It's my turn to hide, and he keeps peeking."

Lana's mother looked straight at her. "So?
Maybe he doesn't like rules, either."

"But, Mother, he has to obey the rules or we
can't play right," Lana cried.

"Lana, sit down," said Mother as she laid aside
her sewing. "Rules are things that we want
everyone else to obey, but we like to forget about
them ourselves. There are rules everywhere—at
home, at school, at church. God knew we had to
have rules to get along with one another. He has
rules, too."

"Like what?" Lana asked.

"There are many," replied Mother, "but the
most important one is that we love Him most of
all. Then we must love others as much as we love
ourselves. If we do this, it helps us obey other
rules."

"Ooooohhh, that's hard," Lana said, "but I guess
if I love God and the kids at school and Stephen
enough, I would do better at keeping rules." Then
she grinned. "Now will you come and teach
Stephen about obeying rules?"

HOW ABOUT YOU? Are there rules you don't like?
List three of them. Why do you think they are
needed? Can you see how loving God and others
will help you obey these rules? Pray for God's help
in obeying them. □ B.W.

TO MEMORIZE: *Love the Lord your God with all
your heart, soul and mind.* Matthew 22:37, TLB

As SOON AS he got home from school, Kevin went to his room and got out pencils, paints, and poster paper. The library was sponsoring an art contest, and Kevin wanted to win. Every afternoon that week, he hurried straight home and worked on his poster.

By Friday the poster was finished, and Mom drove him to the library. Kevin's heart beat heavily as he waited for the judges' decision. Finally, they nodded in agreement. Kevin watched while one of them put a third-prize ribbon on one of the posters. It wasn't Kevin's. The second-prize ribbon went on another poster, but it wasn't his, either. Finally, one of the judges picked up the first-prize ribbon, walked over to a poster, and attached it to the corner. Hot tears boiled up in Kevin's eyes. He had not won a prize.

When Dad came home from work that night, he asked, "How did the poster contest go, Kevin?"

"Terrible! I didn't win any prize, and I'm never going to enter a contest again," Kevin said bitterly.

Dad looked concerned. "I can understand your feelings," he said, reaching for a book. "Here's something that might interest you—did you know that Babe Ruth, the famous ball-player, struck out many times?"

"But I thought he was supposed to be so good," said Kevin.

"He was," Dad replied. "He was the first player to hit sixty home runs in a season. But he was a good player because he kept swinging that bat when others would have given up."

"I guess you're telling me I shouldn't give up in art," sighed Kevin.

Dad smiled. "You might say that. You may not have won a prize this time, but you enjoy art and you do have a talent for it. Besides, God doesn't bless quitters, but He does bless hard work. Even if you never win a prize, you'll become a better artist if you keep practicing."

"Well, . . . " Kevin hesitated. "The missions committee is sponsoring an art contest at church. I think I'll take a 'swing' at that."

HOW ABOUT YOU? Do you keep trying even though you're discouraged? If God has given you an interest in something, and a talent for it, keep on trying even if you're not the best in it, yet. Ask God to bless your efforts. □ C.Y.

TO MEMORIZE: *All hard work brings a profit, but mere talk leads only to poverty.* Proverbs 14:23, NIV

Keep On Swinging

FROM THE BIBLE:
All hard work brings a profit, but mere talk leads only to poverty. The wealth of the wise is their crown, but the folly of fools yields folly. A truthful witness saves lives, but a false witness is deceitful. He who fears the Lord has a secure fortress, and for his children it will be a refuge. The fear of the Lord is a fountain of life, turning a man from the snares of death.
Proverbs 14:23-27, NIV

Keep trying

10

Don't Make Excuses

FROM THE BIBLE:

Blessed is the man who endures temptation; for when he has been proved, he will receive the crown of life which the Lord has promised to those who love Him. Let no one say when he is tempted, "I am tempted by God" for God cannot be tempted by evil, nor does He Himself tempt anyone. But each one is tempted when he is drawn away by his own desires and enticed. Then, when desire has conceived, it gives birth to sin; and sin, when it is full-grown, brings forth death.

James 1:12-15, NKJV

Don't blame God for your sin

BARRY FELT GRUMPY. First he had to shut off the ball game on TV and do his homework—just because he'd gotten an *F* on his last history test. It wasn't his fault he'd been too busy to study. After all, he'd been working on a Sunday school project, so you'd think the Lord could have helped him with the exam!

Next, Mom got after him for leaving his things all over the house. He tried to tell her he couldn't help being messy—that was just his personality. It was the way God made him. But Mom made him pick up his things anyway.

And now she was fussing about his friends. "Oh, Mom," he complained. "You get so upset about nothing! So what if the guys use a little rough language? I don't use it, and there's nobody else to hang around with after school."

"Well, you've been staying out much too late," Mother answered, "and I'm not sure what kind of activities those boys might lead you into."

"Bring them home to play games," suggested Dad, "or invite them to your church activities."

"Hmph!" snorted Barry. "What for? I go, and I'm a Christian, but I wonder what difference it makes. I've prayed a long time for a job, but I never get one. If I had a job I wouldn't have to hang around with those guys."

"I see," Dad mused. "You blame God for your bad grades and for the way you leave things lying around. Now it seems you hold Him responsible for your bad companions. Your problems are all God's fault, right?"

Barry looked ashamed. "I didn't mean it that way," he mumbled. "I guess I just didn't want to take the blame myself." Soon he looked up and grinned. "You win. I know it's my fault. I'll ask the Lord to help me study and be neat. And I'll ask Him to help me find new friends or change the old ones."

HOW ABOUT YOU? When you get into trouble, do you blame God? When you do something wrong, do you really feel it's God's fault—or at least, not your own? Never blame God. Instead, ask Him to forgive and change you. □ H.M.

TO MEMORIZE: *Let no one say when he is tempted, "I am tempted by God"; for God cannot be tempted by evil, nor does He Himself tempt anyone.* James 1:13, NKJV

AFTER SCHOOL on Monday, Lynn bounced up the bus steps looking for Stacy, her best friend from church. She was thrilled that Stacy was transferring to her school. Of course, Stacy was a grade ahead of her, but she'd still see her at lunch and they would ride the same bus. "When I have a Christian friend at school, I'll witness like I should," Lynn promised herself.

Stacy hadn't been on the bus that morning, because her mother had taken her to school to enroll. Somehow Lynn had missed her at lunch, too, so now she was eager to hear about Stacy's day. But Stacy wasn't on the bus yet.

Soon Stacy and a couple of other girls boarded the bus. They were giggling and having a great time. "Stacy, I've saved you a seat by me," said Lynn as she scooted over.

"Oh, thanks, Lynn, but I'm with Beth and Amy. Beth's my cousin."

All the way home Lynn heard the happy chatter of the girls behind her. Tears welled up in her eyes, and sobs stuck in her throat. At her stop, she jumped off the bus and stumbled home. Once inside the house, the sobs burst from her.

"What's the matter?" Mother held her arms open wide.

Lynn hid her face on Mother's shoulder. "S-S-Stacy already has fr-friends at s-s-school. She's just my friend at ch-church."

"That's too bad," sympathized Mother when she had heard all about it. She sighed softly. "But isn't that just the way you've been treating your Best Friend?"

Lynn shook her head. "I'd never ignore her."

"Not 'her,' Lynn—'Him,' " Mother corrected. "I mean the Lord Jesus." Stacy had talked with her mother about her fear of witnessing.

"Oh!" Lynn gasped. "I never thought of it like that! You're right—I have hurt my Best Friend. I guess I only wanted Him for a part-time friend. I ignored Him when I was with kids who didn't know Him. I guess I've got some apologizing to do to my Friend, Jesus."

HOW ABOUT YOU? Are you a friend Jesus can depend on, or do you act as if you don't know Him when you're with people who aren't Christians? Are you a part-time friend to Jesus? Be a true friend to Him—show that you love Him at all times. Talk to Him and talk about Him. □ B.W.

TO MEMORIZE: *A friend loves at all times, and a brother is born for adversity.* Proverbs 17:17, NKJV

Part-Time Friend

FROM THE BIBLE:
My true disciples produce bountiful harvests. This brings great glory to my Father. I have loved you even as the Father has loved me. Live within my love. When you obey me you are living in my love, just as I obey my Father and live in his love. I have told you this so that you will be filled with my joy. Yes, your cup of joy will overflow! I demand that you love each other as much as I love you. And here is how to measure it—the greatest love is shown when a person lays down his life for his friends; and you are my friends if you obey me.
John 15:8-14, TLB

Be a true friend of Jesus

A Good Fuse

FROM THE BIBLE:
*Let him who thinks he stands
take heed lest he fall. No
temptation has overtaken you
except such as is common to
man; but God is faithful, who
will not allow you to be tempted
beyond what you are able, but
with the temptation will also
make the way of escape, that you
may be able to bear it. Therefore,
my beloved, flee from idolatry.*
1 Corinthians 10:12-14, NKJV

*You don't have
to sin*

WILL IT BE *so awful if I cheat a little just once?*
Jon thought as he walked home from school. *I
don't know why Mrs. Gray has that stupid rule
anyway.* The rule was that those who got a hundred
percent on a trial spelling test in the middle of the
week could go out early for recess on Friday while
the rest of the class repeated the test. Jon and
his friends seldom got out early, but this week
they figured out a way to "sneak a peek" at the
answers so they'd all get extra time to play.

Jon had agreed to the plan, but almost immediately his conscience started to bother him.
He was a Christian and knew it was wrong to
cheat. But now the others were counting on him.
He didn't know what to do.

As Mother was cleaning up after dinner that
evening, the lights suddenly went out. "Oh, no!"
she exclaimed. "I guess I blew a fuse by using too
many appliances at once."

Jon went to the basement with his father and
watched him replace the burned out fuse. "How
do those things work?" Jon asked.

"Well, it's a little complicated," said Dad. "You
see, there are wires running through the walls to
various switches and electrical outlets. If too many
things are turned on at once, it requires so much
electricity that the wires could get very hot and
even cause a fire. But the fuse will burn out and
stop the flow of electricity when there is too much
being used. The fuse won't let more electricity go
through the wires than is safe."

Jon and Dad started back up the stairs. "The
fuse reminds me of what God does for us," Dad
added. "He'll never let such a great temptation
come our way that we can't handle it. He stops it
before it can get that bad."

As Jon went to his room, he thought about the
things Dad had said. He knew he didn't have to
cheat. God would help him be honest. He took
out his list of words and began to study.

HOW ABOUT YOU? Do you sometimes feel that you
can't help doing something wrong? That the temptation is just too great? You're wrong. No matter
what the temptation, you can be sure that God
will help you overcome it if you are willing to let
Him do so. □ H.M.

TO MEMORIZE: *God is faithful, who will not allow
you to be tempted beyond what you are able, but
with the temptation will also make the way of escape,
that you may be able to bear it.* 1 Corinthians 10:13,
NKJV

DAVID'S MOM came into his room to check on his homework. "How's your report coming?" she asked.

"It's not," David barked, "and I don't want to do it anyway."

"You sound upset, David. Are you still fretting about yesterday?" Mom questioned.

David's eyes got misty. "I wanted to be class reporter for the school paper so bad," he said. "And what did Mrs. French say? 'You have a good imagination, but you don't check facts. A reporter must be accurate. Work on it, David. Maybe you can be a reporter next year.'"

"I know you're disappointed, David, but don't give up," encouraged Mom. "Now, what school report are you working on?"

"I have to write about some famous person," David muttered. "It can be anybody."

"I know who will be a real help to you! Come with me. Let's look in the encyclopedia." David's mother helped him find some books. Then she left to fold clothes.

When Mother returned, David looked up. "I can't believe it, Mom," he said. "Abraham Lincoln was one of our greatest presidents, but this book says he lost several important political races!"

"That's right," nodded Mom, "but he's remembered for his successes, not for his failures. Often it's easy to give up when we fail, but we don't grow that way. It's not what God would have us do either. He wants us to learn from our experiences and to try harder the next time. We must learn to depend on Him to help us turn failure into success."

David gave his mom a big hug. "Thanks, Mom," he said. "I see what you've been trying to tell me. I won't give up. I'll make this report so accurate that even Mrs. French would be proud of it."

HOW ABOUT YOU? What happens when you fail at something? Do you give up and quit trying? Don't get discouraged. Learn from your mistakes and realize that it takes time to learn to do things well. Depend on God to help you. □ J.H.

TO MEMORIZE: *We are hard pressed on every side, but not crushed; perplexed, but not in despair.* 2 Corinthians 4:8, NIV

13

Down, but Not Out

FROM THE BIBLE:
We do not preach ourselves, but Jesus Christ as Lord, and ourselves as your servants for Jesus' sake. For God, who said, "Let light shine out of darkness," made his light shine in our hearts to give us the light of the knowledge of the glory of God in the face of Christ. But we have this treasure in jars of clay to show that this all-surpassing power is from God and not from us. We are hard pressed on every side, but not crushed; perplexed, but not in despair; persecuted, but not abandoned; struck down, but not destroyed. We always carry around in our body the death of Jesus, so that the life of Jesus may also be revealed in our body.
2 Corinthians 4:5-10, NIV

Try again

14

Nobody's Perfect

FROM THE BIBLE:

Two men went to the Temple to pray. One was a proud, self-righteous Pharisee, and the other a cheating tax collector. The proud Pharisee "prayed" this prayer: "Thank God, I am not a sinner like everyone else, especially like that tax collector over there! For I never cheat, I don't commit adultery, I go without food twice a week, and I give to God a tenth of everything I earn." But the corrupt tax collector stood at a distance and dared not even lift his eyes to heaven as he prayed, but beat upon his chest in sorrow, exclaiming, "God, be merciful to me, a sinner." I tell you, this sinner, not the Pharisee, returned home forgiven! For the proud shall be humbled, but the humble shall be honored.
Luke 18:10-14, TLB

Sin cannot enter heaven

OH, WELL! Nobody's perfect!" laughed Jody as she missed the basket, and the other girls laughed with her. "Nobody's perfect" was one of Jody's favorite phrases, and the girls almost knew ahead of time when they would hear it again.

Later that day, Jody went with her friend Robin to an after-school Bible class. She enjoyed it, but she did not agree with what Mrs. Gates, the Bible teacher, said. "No matter how good you are," said Mrs. Gates, "you're not good enough for heaven. You're a sinner, but Jesus took the punishment for your sins. The only way you can get into heaven is to believe that and accept Jesus as your Savior."

Jody discussed it with Robin as the girls walked home. "She makes it sound like everybody's such a terrible sinner. I'm not all that bad!"

"You may be a pretty decent kid," replied Robin, "but you've done some things that are wrong. I remember the time you and I sneaked . . . "

Jody laughed. "But even that wasn't so awful bad. And what about people like my Uncle Joe? He's always helping others. He gives lots of money to places like the city mission—even the church. And last year when his neighbor's house was on fire, he rushed in himself to get the baby out." Suddenly she stopped. "Oh, I'm so busy talking, I'm not paying attention! We just passed my street, and I forgot to turn. How dumb can you be! Oh, well! Nobody's perfect!"

"You said it," laughed Robin. "I didn't. But you know what? God said it, too. He said we've all sinned, even the best of us, and no sin can enter heaven. No matter how much good you or your uncle do, you still have to get rid of your sin. Only Jesus can take it away. Think about that."

Jody did think about it as she turned and slowly headed back toward her own street.

HOW ABOUT YOU? Are you fit for heaven? No lying, disobedience, cheating, gossip—nor any other sin—is allowed to enter heaven. Today's Scripture tells of two men. One had done good things. The other admitted his sin and his need. Jesus says the one who asked for God's mercy is the one who was saved. Which of these men are you like? Confess your sin, and ask Jesus to forgive you and save you. □ H.M.

TO MEMORIZE: *Nothing impure will ever enter it, nor will anyone who does what is shameful or deceitful, but only those whose names are written in the Lamb's book of life.* Revelation 21:27, NIV

WE'VE GOT A new guy at school," Brad announced, "and he's a sissy! He wears big thick glasses. He doesn't play football. Guess what he does play—the piano!"

"How long have you known him?" Mother asked.

"Oh, I don't really know him," answered Brad. "He just started school today."

"Then you don't know he's a sissy. You just think he is," Dad corrected. "That reminds me of something I read. A couple was traveling through the country when they saw an old man sitting in a chair, hoeing his garden. 'That's the height of laziness,' the wife declared. 'No, it isn't,' argued her husband. 'Look closer.' When she did, she saw a pair of crutches beside the chair."

"He wasn't lazy. He was just the opposite," said Mother. "When we judge a situation or person too quickly, we're often wrong. God cautions us not to judge one another."

When Brad arrived at school the next day, the students were excitedly talking about a bus wreck. "Take your seats," Mrs. Harper said firmly. "We'll be getting information as soon as it's available."

It was almost noon before the announcement came from the principal. A lady had run a stop sign. Three students and the bus driver were in serious condition, but they were expected to recover. The others were being treated and released. "A new student, Dan Martin, has been credited with saving several lives," said the principal. "The bus caught fire, but Dan pulled the driver and two unconscious students to safety. In doing so, he was severely burned."

"Wow!" exclaimed Brad's friend, Nathan. "Who would have thought that guy had it in him? He sure looked like a sissy to me!"

Brad nodded. "I guess we've learned not to judge too quickly."

HOW ABOUT YOU? Are you guilty of judging those you don't know? Be careful. God doesn't want you to do that. Besides, you could be wrong. The Bible says the way you judge others is the way you will be judged. And, of course, you want fair judgment. Ask God to help you to be fair, too. □ B.W.

TO MEMORIZE: *Judge not, that you be not judged.* Matthew 7:1, NKJV

Too Quick to Judge

FROM THE BIBLE:
Judge not, that you be not judged. For with what judgment you judge, you will be judged; and with the same measure you use, it will be measured back to you. And why do you look at the speck in your brother's eye, but do not consider the plank in your own eye? Or how can you say to your brother, "Let me remove the speck out of your eye" and look, a plank is in your own eye? Hypocrite! First remove the plank from your own eye, and then you will see clearly to remove the speck out of your brother's eye.
Matthew 7:1-5, NKJV

Don't judge others

OCTOBER

16

Read and Obey

FROM THE BIBLE:
Continue in what you have learned and have become convinced of, because you know those from whom you learned it, and how from infancy you have known the holy Scriptures, which are able to make you wise for salvation through faith in Christ Jesus. All Scripture is God-breathed and is useful for teaching, rebuking, correcting and training in righteousness, so that the man of God may be thoroughly equipped for every good work.
2 Timothy 3:14-17, NIV

Follow God's directions

JOANNA SLIPPED QUIETLY through the kitchen, hoping to avoid her mom. She hung her jacket in the closet and tried to sneak to her bedroom, but Mother appeared in the doorway. "Hi, Honey," Mother greeted cheerfully. "I didn't hear you come in. How did you do on that math test?" Mother asked.

Joanna gulped. "Not so hot," she answered. "I studied so hard." She choked on her words. Taking the test from her notebook, she handed it to her mother.

"You didn't follow directions," Mother said. "Joanna, when are you going to learn to read the directions first?"

"I don't know," Joanna mumbled.

"Yesterday you attempted to make cupcakes. You didn't follow the directions in the recipe, and what happened?"

"I blew it," admitted Joanna, head down.

"And what about the time you helped me do laundry?" Mother reminded. "I told you exactly what to do, but you didn't follow directions."

Joanna giggled this time. "Yeah, and Dad ended up with pink underwear."

Mother smiled, too, but only briefly. "You know, Joanna," she sighed, "learning to follow directions is extremely important. Failure to follow directions could harm you—both physically and spiritually."

"What do you mean?" Joanna asked.

"God's Word is full of instructions for us. Often we neglect to follow those instructions, and we cause ourselves a lot of grief," Mother explained.

"Or sometimes we don't even bother to read the instructions at all," Joanna added thoughtfully. She couldn't remember the last time that she had read the Bible.

"Right," Mother agreed, "and unless you read them, you can't possibly obey them—on math tests or in life."

"Mom, I'm going to make a real effort to do better from now on. I don't want to fail any more tests!" Joanna said with determination.

HOW ABOUT YOU? When was the last time you read God's Word? The Bible contains many specific directions and many principles which you should follow in your daily life. Read it and follow the instructions God gives. □ B.D.

TO MEMORIZE: *All Scripture is God-breathed and is useful for teaching, rebuking, correcting and training in righteousness.* 2 Timothy 3:16, NIV

I T HAD BEEN a terrible day for Lanita! In the first place, Mother had said they were out of bread and Lanita would have to buy her lunch at school. Mother knew she hated to wait in line! Why hadn't she bought bread yesterday? Then Dad had refused to take her to school—it was only five miles out of his way—so she had to ride the bus.

Lanita was mad when she went to school, and she was madder when she came home, and she was maddest now! Why couldn't she stay up another thirty minutes? She was old enough to know when to go to bed without being sent there like a baby! She started to kneel, but changed her mind. She didn't feel like talking to God.

Lanita had just pulled the sheet over her head when there was a gentle knock on her door. She sighed heavily. *Here comes the scolding!* she thought.

Dad opened the door. Handing Lanita her robe, he said, "Put this on, Honey. There's something outside I want you to see." Lanita did as she was told, not daring to question. Outside, Dad pointed to the moon.

"It looks so big and close—almost like you could touch it," murmured Lanita.

Dad reached into his pocket. "Now hold this dime in front of you like this." He held it out from his face an arm's length. Then he handed it to Lanita. Puzzled, Lanita obeyed. "What do you see?" he asked.

"Just a dime," Lanita replied.

Dad nodded. "You can completely block out something as big and beautiful as the full moon with one little dime," he said. "And you can completely shut yourself off from a lot of beautiful things—love, friendship, happiness—when you make a big fuss about little things. Little things can even get between you and God."

Slowly Lanita handed her father his dime. Then she gave him a quick hug. "Thanks, Dad. I needed that."

HOW ABOUT YOU? Do you make a big fuss about little things? Do you know the most common cause of anger? It's selfishness, and it can ruin your day, your week—even your life. Make up your mind now not to let little things get between you and happiness—or between you and God. □ B.W.

TO MEMORIZE: *A little yeast works through the whole batch of dough.* Galatians 5:9, NIV

FROM THE BIBLE:
You must be a new and different person, holy and good. Clothe yourself with this new nature. Stop lying to each other; tell the truth, for we are parts of each other and when we lie to each other we are hurting ourselves. If you are angry, don't sin by nursing your grudge. Don't let the sun go down with you still angry—get over it quickly; for when you are angry you give a mighty foothold to the devil. If anyone is stealing he must stop it and begin using those hands of his for honest work so he can give to others in need. Don't use bad language. Say only what is good and helpful to those you are talking to, and what will give them a blessing. . . . Stop being mean, bad-tempered and angry. Quarreling, harsh words, and dislike of others should have no place in your lives. Instead, be kind to each other, tenderhearted, forgiving one another, just as God has forgiven you because you belong to Christ.
Ephesians 4:24-32, TLB

Don't fuss about little things

OCTOBER

18

Just an Old Poem

FROM THE BIBLE:

Dear friends, I urge you, as aliens and strangers in the world, to abstain from sinful desires, which war against your soul. Live such good lives among the pagans that, though they accuse you of doing wrong, they may see your good deeds and glorify God on the day he visits us. Submit yourselves for the Lord's sake to every authority instituted among men: whether to the king, as the supreme authority, or to governors, who are sent by him to punish those who do wrong and to commend those who do right. For it is God's will that by doing good you should silence the ignorant talk of foolish men. Live as free men, but do not use your freedom as a cover-up for evil; live as servants of God.

1 Peter 2:11-16, NIV

Be honest in your work

BRIAN SLUMPED DOWN in his chair and turned off the desk lamp. No matter how hard he tried, he couldn't seem to write a poem. It was due tomorrow, and if he didn't hand it in, Miss Collins was sure to send a note to his parents. Brian sighed. The only lines of poetry he could think of were, "There once was a big black cat, who chased a big black rat."

Then Brian remembered some old poetry books he had seen in the attic. He hurried up the attic stairs and looked through the books. Good! One of them was a book of children's poetry. Brian flipped through it until he came across a poem about a train. It sounded just like something Miss Collins would appreciate. Brian copied it quickly. His assignment was done!

When Brian went down for breakfast the next morning, Mother was waiting for him, the poem in her hand. "I happened to see your assignment on top of your math book," she said. "Your teacher may not realize you've stolen someone else's work, but God knows."

"Stolen!" Brian exclaimed. "I didn't steal anything! The man who wrote that book probably is dead!"

"That may be true," agreed Mother, "but the words on this paper still do not belong to you, Brian. It's not right for you to hand in this poem, pretending it's yours."

Brian hadn't known that copying someone else's poem was stealing, but now he knew it was true. He was pretending the poet's words were his. That certainly wasn't something the Lord would want him to do. "It's too late to write another poem," he said to his mother. "I'll have to tell Miss Collins what happened, but the next time I turn in a writing assignment, it'll be my own words!"

HOW ABOUT YOU? Have you ever copied someone else's work and claimed that it was yours? That is called "plagiarism." It means stealing something someone else has written and saying that you wrote it. The Bible says it's wrong to be dishonest and cheat. God says, "You shall not steal." That included stealing words. Be honest when you do an assignment. Do your own work. □ L.W.

TO MEMORIZE: *Live such good lives among the pagans that, though they accuse you of doing wrong, they may see your good deeds and glorify God on the day he visits us.* 1 Peter 2:12, NIV

TIM SCUFFED THE toe of his shoe in the playground dirt. He didn't feel very good inside. He didn't really think the words some of the boys were saying were very funny, and he knew they were wrong and did not honor God. But he didn't want to walk away, because he was afraid the other boys wouldn't let him play with them anymore if he did. He wanted to be like the other boys, and he wanted those boys to like him. So Tim stood in the small circle of boys, laughing at the words when the other boys laughed.

That night, as usual, Tim read his Bible before going to bed. He read from John 12. He came to verse 43 and read, "For they loved praise from men more than praise from God." Tim saw that he had done the very same thing on the playground. He had wanted praise from the other boys more than praise from God. Kneeling by his bed, he whispered, "Dear God, I'm sorry for laughing at words and jokes that are wrong. Help me to walk away the next time others are talking that way, no matter what they say about me."

A few days later the same boys stood together in a corner of the playground. The tallest boy began to use bad language. Everyone laughed—except Tim. He turned and began to walk away. "Hey, what's the matter, Tim?" someone jeered. "Can't you take it?"

Tim continued to walk away, each step becoming a little easier. He heard footsteps behind him, and then Bob was walking along with him. "I don't really like that kind of language either," said Bob.

"Hey, do you collect baseball cards?" asked Tim.

"I sure do," answered Bob, pulling some out of his pocket. "I've got some right here." That was just the beginning of a new friendship, and the two boys had many good times together. Tim found that he was much happier than when he was trying to make the other boys like him. He learned that when he pleased God, he also pleased himself.

HOW ABOUT YOU? Whose praise do you seek? Do you care more about what the kids at school will say than about what God will say? Do you dare to be a friend to an "odd" person? To not laugh at dirty jokes? To pray before you eat? Make sure that the words of today's verse can never be said about you! □ C.Y.

TO MEMORIZE: *They loved praise from men more than praise from God.* John 12:43, NIV

No Laughing Matter

FROM THE BIBLE:

Even after Jesus had done all these miraculous signs in their presence, they still would not believe in him. This was to fulfill the word of Isaiah the prophet: "Lord, who has believed our message and to whom has the arm of the Lord been revealed?" For this reason they could not believe, because, as Isaiah says elsewhere: "He has blinded their eyes and deadened their hearts, so they can neither see with their eyes, nor understand with their hearts, nor turn—and I would heal them." Isaiah said this because he saw Jesus' glory and spoke about him. Yet at the same time many even among the leaders believed in him. But because of the Pharisees they would not confess their faith for fear they would be put out of the synagogue; for they loved praise from men more than praise from God.

John 12:37-43, NIV

Seek God's praise

OCTOBER

20

The Problem

FROM THE BIBLE:

We can see and understand only a little about God now, as if we were peering at his reflection in a poor mirror; but someday we are going to see him in his completeness, face to face. Now all that I know is hazy and blurred, but then I will see everything clearly, just as clearly as God sees into my heart right now.

1 Corinthians 13:12, TLB

Open my eyes to see wonderful things in your Word.

Psalm 119:18, TLB

God's Word is without error

RICK WAS FRUSTRATED. No matter how hard he tried, he just couldn't get his math problem solved. "This book has to be wrong," he fumed. "This thing won't come out right no matter what I do!"

His father looked up from the newspaper. "What's your problem, Rick?"

"This stupid math book is the problem," complained Rick. "I don't care what the book says, the figures don't add up like they're supposed to."

Dad put aside the paper. "Let me take a look at it, Rick. Maybe we can solve the problem together."

Rick's father compared his son's work with the book's instructions. Then he studied the examples in the text. "I see what went wrong, Rick. You divided when you should have multiplied," he said, pointing to the mistake.

Rick studied it, "I guess you're right, Dad," he admitted, "but how come I didn't notice that?"

"You were so sure the book was wrong that you gave up trying to understand," Dad replied. "The problem wasn't the *book*. It was your lack of understanding."

"I heard that," announced Mother, coming into the room. "Do you know that some people treat the Bible the same way? Just because they have problems understanding all of God's Word, they claim the Bible is in error."

Dad nodded. "God's Word is true, but sometimes our understanding of it is faulty," he said. "I'll admit some things in the Bible might remain a mystery to us until we get to heaven, but that's OK. We don't need to understand all of it right now."

"I'm glad of that," Rick said with a grin. "I have a big enough problem understanding math!"

HOW ABOUT YOU? Do you excuse yourself from reading God's Word because you don't understand all of it? You don't need to understand everything to believe it's all true. Ask God to give you wisdom as you read it. Look up unfamiliar words in a dictionary. The more you read God's Word, the more you will understand it. □ J.H.

TO MEMORIZE: *Every word of God is flawless; he is a shield to those who take refuge in him.* Proverbs 30:5, NIV

SHARON CAUGHT UP with her brother. "Hey, Scott! I heard you had an oral quiz in math today. Brad told me you were pretty humiliated when you didn't know the answers."

"That's not the worst of it. I skipped a couple of homework assignments last week, too," Scott confessed. "Now Mr. Briggs is making me stay in every recess till I get my work caught up, and I've got to take this note home to Mom and Dad."

Sharon skimmed through the message. "Wow," she exclaimed. "You are in trouble!"

Scott's parents were greatly displeased when they read the note. "Did you hear Mr. Briggs assign those pages?" demanded Dad. Scott nodded. "Well, then did you forget to do them?" Dad asked.

"Not exactly," confessed Scott.

"What?" asked Mom. "Before you went to play, you told me your homework was finished."

"Uh, I guess I thought I'd get by without doing it," Scott admitted.

"Well, you'll be grounded for the rest of the week for lying to your mother," said Dad.

That evening, it was Sharon's turn to read the Bible aloud. "Well," said Dad, after she read James 1, "I think we all should make sure we do our homework assignments from God."

"From God?" asked Scott.

Dad nodded. "Mr. Briggs said, 'Do these pages,' but you didn't do your math homework. God says, 'Be doers of My Word.' When we don't do what He says, we've failed in the assignment He's given us. When you didn't do your math, Scott, you also failed God's assignment to obey those who have authority over you—your teacher and your parents. But I don't want to pick on you, Scott. I'm sure each of us can think of any area where we need to do the 'homework' assigned to us by the Lord."

HOW ABOUT YOU? As a Christian, do you hear God's Word being taught in Sunday school or at home? Have you heard such commands as "obey," "be kind," "be a friend," "pray," "love others"? Are you doing these assignments? Obedience to God's commands is important. Do your "spiritual homework." □ B.D.

TO MEMORIZE: *Anyone who listens to the word but does not do what it says is like a man who looks at his face in a mirror and, after looking at himself, goes away and immediately forgets what he looks like.* James 1:23-24, NIV

FROM THE BIBLE:
Get rid of all moral filth and the evil that is so prevalent and humbly accept the word planted in you, which can save you. Do not merely listen to the word, and so deceive yourselves. Do what it says. Anyone who listens to the word but does not do what it says is like a man who looks at his face in a mirror and, after looking at himself, goes away and immediately forgets what he looks like. But the man who looks intently into the perfect law that gives freedom, and continues to do this, not forgetting what he has heard, but doing it—he will be blessed in what he does.
James 1:21-25, NIV

Obey God's Word

OCTOBER

22

Perfect Teacher

FROM THE BIBLE:

Show me the path where I should go, O Lord; point out the right road for me to walk. Lead me; teach me; for you are the God who gives me salvation. I have no hope except in you. Overlook my youthful sins, O Lord! Look at me instead through eyes of mercy and forgiveness, through eyes of everlasting love and kindness. The Lord is good and glad to teach the proper path to all who go astray; he will teach the ways that are right and best to those who humbly turn to him. And when we obey him, every path he guides us on is fragrant with his lovingkindness and his truth. But Lord, my sins! How many they are. Oh, pardon them for the honor of your name. Where is the man who fears the Lord? God will teach him how to choose the best.

Psalm 25:4-12, TLB

God is a perfect teacher

KARI RAN INTO the house waving a paper she'd brought from school. "Guess what assignment Miss Beecher gave us to do," she puffed, out of breath with excitement. Mother smiled. She was used to hearing news about Kari's teacher. Kari liked Miss Beecher and talked about her constantly. "She gave us these pictures of birds, and we have to look them up in a book and color them," continued Kari. "Miss Beecher is wonderful. Her projects are always fun. She's a perfect teacher!"

Kari got out an encyclopedia and a book on birds. For some time she was busy coloring. But she was confused about one picture. The bird that Miss Beecher had labeled "blue jay" didn't look like the blue jay she found in the books. So she took the problem to Mother.

"I think Miss Beecher labeled this wrong," said Mother after looking at the picture. "I'm not sure what this bird is, but it's not a blue jay. Let's look in the books. Maybe we can find one that looks like this."

But Kari, nearly in tears, shook her head. "Miss Beecher knows birds," she insisted, "and she said this is a blue jay."

"Just leave it then," said Mother. "You can ask her about it tomorrow."

When Kari came home the next day, she again got out the bird books. "Miss Beecher wrote down the wrong name," she told Mother. "This is a blue*bird*, not a blue *jay*." She then added, "Maybe she's not perfect, but she's still a great teacher!"

Mother nodded. "Yes, she is," she agreed. "I'm glad you think so highly of Miss Beecher. But there is only one perfect teacher, you know. Only God never makes a mistake. When He teaches us something, we can know for sure it's right."

Kari thought that over as she worked. "I never thought of God as my teacher before," she said. "I guess He's the best teacher of all."

HOW ABOUT YOU? Even the best teachers occasionally make mistakes. But when God teaches you something, you can be sure that it's true. God is the beginning of all knowledge. When you read His Word, You can learn about His truths. □ C. Y.

TO MEMORIZE: *Teach me to do your will, for you are my God; may your good Spirit lead me on level ground.* Psalm 143:10, NIV

WHEN BOBBY CAME home from school, he was very hungry. He hadn't had an after-school snack, because he stayed for basketball practice. He peered into the pot of spaghetti sauce simmering on the stove. "Oh, good! My favorite!" He smacked his lips. "When do we eat?"

"In about fifteen minutes," answered Mother. "I have some chores for you to do first."

By the time Bobby finished several chores, he was ravenous. Mother had one last chore for him—taking out the garbage. Before handing it to him she said, "Wait a minute." Then taking a plate off the table, she carefully scooped some of the garbage from the bag onto the plate.

Bobby stared in disbelief at the peelings, coffee grounds, and leftovers heaped together in one soggy mess. "What in the world is that for?" he asked in surprise.

"This is your dinner, Bobby," said Mother.

"My dinner!" He stared at her in wonder. "I can't eat smelly garbage!"

"Why not?" asked Mother. "Garbage is what you're feeding your mind, so I figured we could feed garbage to your body, too." She took some magazines from the top of the refrigerator. "I found these under your blankets when I changed the sheets today. It upset me—and think how the Lord must feel about your reading these."

Bobby knew his mother was right. Those magazines with the dirty pictures in them were garbage, and his mind shouldn't feed on them. Ever since he'd bought them, he'd felt guilty and unhappy. "I'll throw them out right now, Mother," he said, "and I won't buy any more. Honest."

HOW ABOUT YOU? Do you refuse to look at pictures in magazines or on television that make your mind and heart "dirty"? If not, ask God to forgive you for feeding your mind on the world's garbage. Ask Him to help you think on pure, good things instead. □ M.N.

TO MEMORIZE: *I will set before my eyes no vile thing. The deeds of faithless men I hate; they will not cling to me.* Psalm 101:3, NIV

OCTOBER

23

Anyone for Garbage?

FROM THE BIBLE:
Always be full of joy in the Lord; I say it again, rejoice! Let everyone see that you are unselfish and considerate in all you do. Remember that the Lord is coming soon. Don't worry about anything; instead, pray about everything; tell God your needs and don't forget to thank him for his answers. If you do this you will experience God's peace, which is far more wonderful than the human mind can understand. His peace will keep your thoughts and your hearts quiet and at rest as you trust in Christ Jesus. And now, brothers, as I close this letter let me say this one more thing: Fix your thoughts on what is true and good and right. Think about things that are pure and lovely, and dwell on the fine, good things in others. Think about all you can praise God for and be glad about. Keep putting into practice all you learned from me and saw me doing, and the God of peace will be with you.
Philippians 4:4-9, TLB

Think about good things

OCTOBER

24

Dee and the Dandelions

FROM THE BIBLE:

How can I ever know what sins are lurking in my heart? Cleanse me from these hidden faults. And keep me from deliberate wrongs; help me to stop doing them. Only then can I be free of guilt and innocent of some great crime. May my spoken words and unspoken thoughts be pleasing even to you, O Lord, my Rock and my Redeemer.
Psalm 19:12-14, TLB

Speak kind words

"THERE GOES MELINDA—that new girl," said Dee to her friends at recess. "She wears funny clothes. And you should see her father! He has a big scar on his face and looks like a criminal."

"Do you think he's really a criminal?" asked Lois. "What do you suppose he did?"

Dee shrugged. "Who knows? Robbed a bank maybe."

As Dee slid into her seat, she heard Lois whisper to Pam, "Beware of Melinda—her dad's a bank robber."

The rumor flew and grew until everyone in the class was whispering about Melinda and avoiding her. A little voice in Dee's heart said, *Dee, what have you done?* but she tried not to listen.

Sprawling on the lawn after school to enjoy the sunshine, Dee picked a dandelion that had gone to seed. She blew on it, and the seeds floated off into the air like dozens of tiny parachutes.

"Oh dear!" said Mother, who had come out with a glass of lemonade for Dee. "Those little seeds are going to take root and become more pesky dandelions!"

"Oops!" said Dee. "Sorry, Mom."

Mother sat down in a lawn chair. "Well, if you hadn't blown them, the wind would have," she said. Then she added thoughtfully, "Those little seeds remind me of words. Those seeds are gone forever. There's no way you could gather them back. Words are like that. Once we've said them, they're gone. The good ones bring happiness and help to people, and the unkind ones bring sorrow."

Dee squirmed uncomfortably as she remembered her words about Melinda and her father. "Before we speak about anyone," continued Mother, "we should ask ourselves, 'Is what I'm about to say true? Is it kind? Would God be pleased to hear me say it?'"

Dee's conscience seemed to be shouting now. Her words about Melinda's father had certainly not been kind or pleasing to God. Probably they were not even true! "Mother," she said as she started for the house, "I've got some phone calls to make. I'll tell you all about it later."

HOW ABOUT YOU? What kind of words do you speak? Are they true? Kind? Pleasing to God? Do they build, or do they destroy? Ask God to help you watch your words. □ M.N.

TO MEMORIZE: *Set a guard over my mouth, O Lord; keep watch over the door of my lips.* Psalm 141:3, NIV

SANDRA BURST INTO the house after school. "Mom," she called, "something awful has happened. Lots of kids at school have lice! The school nurse inspected all our heads. She says I don't have them, but I think I do, because my head itches." Sandra was almost in tears. "I hate to think of bugs crawling on my head."

"Well, just to make sure, we'll scrub your head with some special soap that's made to kill those tiny creatures," Mother said comfortingly.

They took a trip to the store and returned with the soap. "I'm sure it's Lisa and her brother who brought the lice to our school," complained Sandra as Mother helped her scrub her head. "They live in a dumpy trailer down by the tracks and always come to school with greasy hair. Everybody is mad at them."

"I hope you're not," said Mother.

"Well, some kids say that lice spread diseases. I wouldn't want to get some awful disease!"

"Keeping clean is extremely important in the prevention of disease," said Mother as she ran clean water to rinse away the soap. "But it's even more important to keep our hearts clean from sin. Little bugs can cause a lot of trouble, and they cause us to shudder. But 'little' sins are even worse—we should also shudder over them. Things like unkind thoughts make our hearts dirty and lead to spiritual sickness."

"You mean like being mad at Lisa and her brother, don't you?" asked Sandra.

Mother nodded. "You don't really know that the lice started with them, do you?" she said. "And even if they did, how do you think God would want you to treat them?"

Sandra took the towel Mother offered her and began to dry her hair. She thought about Mother's words. "Please forgive my unkind thoughts, Father," she prayed silently. "And please help me be nice when I see Lisa tomorrow."

HOW ABOUT YOU? Is there some little sin that you should confess to God? Maybe you said something nasty, snubbed someone, or told a lie. Whatever it is, confess it right now and let God make your heart clean once again. □ M.N.

TO MEMORIZE: *Create in me a pure heart, O God, and renew a steadfast spirit within me.* Psalm 51:10, NIV

A Lesson from Lice

FROM THE BIBLE:
This is the message God has given us to pass on to you: that God is Light and in him is no darkness at all. So if we say we are his friends, but go on living in spiritual darkness and sin, we are lying. But if we are living in the light of God's presence, just as Christ does, then we have wonderful fellowship and joy with each other, and the blood of Jesus his Son cleanses us from every sin. If we say that we have no sin, we are only fooling ourselves, and refusing to accept the truth. But if we confess our sins to him, he can be depended on to forgive us and to cleanse us from every wrong. [And it is perfectly proper for God to do this for us because Christ died to wash away our sins.] If we claim we have not sinned, we are lying and calling God a liar, for he says we have sinned.
1 John 1:5-10, TLB

Confess even "little" sins

26

The New Friend

FROM THE BIBLE:

Is there any such thing as Christians cheering each other up? Do you love me enough to want to help me? Does it mean anything to you that we are brothers in the Lord, sharing the same Spirit? Are your hearts tender and sympathetic at all? Then make me truly happy by loving each other and agreeing wholeheartedly with each other, working together with one heart and mind and purpose. Don't be selfish; don't live to make a good impression on others. Be humble, thinking of others as better than yourself. Don't just think about your own affairs, but be interested in others, too, and in what they are doing. Philippians 2:1-4, TLB

Kindness comes back to you

PETE NOTICED an Oriental boy sitting by himself in the school cafeteria. *He's new here, and he must be lonely,* thought Pete, remembering how he had felt last year when he was the new boy at school. Pete started to go out to play with his friends, but at the door, he stopped and turned around.

Pete slid onto the bench across from the new boy. "Hi," he said. "I'm Pete. What's your name?"

"My name is Kim," said the boy.

"Where are you from?" asked Pete.

"Korea," answered the boy.

Pete wasn't sure what made him do it, but as they walked to class together, he invited Kim to come home with him after school. Kim looked pleased.

Playing with Kim turned out to be more fun than Pete expected. The boys played ping pong, darts, and marbles.

When Kim invited Pete over to meet his family, Pete went. They served him Korean food and taught him to eat with chopsticks. He also learned about Korea. Before long, Pete and Kim became good friends.

"I'm so glad I got to know Kim," Pete confided to his father one day. "I feel like I've had a trip to Korea every time I visit his home."

"He that waters shall be watered himself," quoted Dad with a smile.

"What does that mean?" asked Pete.

"It's from the Bible, and it means that your actions often work like a boomerang—they come back to you," replied Dad. "Kindness comes right back to the one who practices it. When you are kind to others, you are blessed yourself."

HOW ABOUT YOU? Are you kind to everyone, even those who may be different from you? Kindness always pays. Even if the person to whom you are kind should fail to respond in gratitude, God sees all, and He will repay you. But He works things out so that if you are kind to someone, you will not only make that person happy but you will become happy yourself! □ M.N.

TO MEMORIZE: *A generous man will prosper; he who refreshes others will himself be refreshed.* Proverbs 11:25, NIV

TEARS STREAMED DOWN Melanie's face as she came in the back door. "Nancy is having a birthday party on Saturday," she cried. "She invited all the girls in our room except me. Mom, why didn't she invite me? It's not fair."

Mother put her arms around Melanie and hugged her tightly. "I'm sorry, Honey," she said. "I know rejection hurts. We want our friends and family to accept us. When they don't, our hearts ache."

Melanie wiped her eyes and looked at Mother in surprise. "Have you felt rejected?"

"Do you remember when I wanted to work part-time at the school?" asked Mother. "They hired someone with more skills, and I didn't get the job. That was rejection, and it hurt." She smiled. "I got over it, though, and you will, too. Maybe it will help to remember that no one felt unloved more than Jesus did."

"Yeah, but Jesus' friends didn't reject Him. It was His enemies who crucified Him," Melanie pointed out.

"Let's read something," said Mother, getting a Bible. Together they read about one day when Jesus taught in the synagogue at Nazareth.

"Does this mean Jesus' friends didn't believe Him?" Melanie asked.

Mother nodded. "They ridiculed and rejected Him," she said. "Remember, it was one of His own disciples who betrayed Him. And the others all left Him when He was arrested."

"I guess He does know how I feel right now," decided Melanie.

"Yes," Mother assured her, "He understands and cares."

HOW ABOUT YOU? Do you feel rejected when someone says no to you or forgets you? Remember that Jesus knows the pain of rejection. He knows and cares how you feel. Let that comfort you, and then treat those who have hurt you the way you think Jesus would treat them. □ M.S.

TO MEMORIZE: *Cast all your anxiety on him because he cares for you.* 1 Peter 5:7, NIV

Rejected!

FROM THE BIBLE:
When Jesus had finished giving these illustrations, he returned to his home town, Nazareth in Galilee, and taught there in the synagogue and astonished everyone with his wisdom and his miracles. "How is this possible?" the people exclaimed. "He's just a carpenter's son, and we know Mary his mother and his brothers—James, Joseph, Simon, and Judas. And his sisters—they all live here. How can he be so great?" And they became angry with him! Then Jesus told them, "A prophet is honored everywhere except in his own country, and among his own people!" And so he did only a few great miracles there, because of their unbelief. Matthew 13:54-58, TLB

God understands

28

Gift or Garbage

FROM THE BIBLE:
*Warn those who are unruly,
comfort the fainthearted, uphold
the weak, be patient with all.
See that no one renders evil for
evil to anyone, but always
pursue what is good both for
yourselves and for all. Rejoice
always, pray without ceasing, in
everything give thanks; for this
is the will of God in Christ
Jesus for you. Do not quench the
Spirit. Do not despise prophecies.
Test all things; hold fast what is
good. Abstain from every form of
evil. Now may the God of peace
Himself sanctify you completely;
and may your whole spirit,
soul, and body be preserved
blameless at the coming of our
Lord Jesus Christ. He who calls
you is faithful, who also will do
it.*
1 Thessalonians 5:14-24, NKJV

Clothes send a message

ARE YOU GOING to wear *that* to school?" Mother's familiar question made Tammy sigh as she came into the kitchen. She said nothing, but sat down and poured herself some cereal, hoping the question would go away. "I want you to change," added Mom.

If Mom had her way, Tammy thought, *I'd be dressed like an old lady!* Aloud, she said, "I could wear the T-shirt Brenda gave me—the one that says—"

"No," her mother interrupted, "that's even worse."

"I thought what's on the inside of a person was what counted," muttered Tammy as she went to change. When she returned, she looked around the kitchen. "I'm going to Darcy's birthday party right after school, remember?" she said. "Did someone move the present I wrapped? I left it right here by the sink when I went to bed last night."

"What did it look like?" asked Mother.

"It's a little pearl necklace," replied Tammy. "I put it in a box, and then, for a joke, I wrapped it in newspaper and tied it with a string. Then I put it in one of those little yellow plastic bags you use for—"

"For garbage!" gasped Mother. "I thought it *was* garbage, and I put it out with the rest of the trash."

Tammy ran for the street and began lifting the lid on first one garbage can, then another. In the distance, she could hear the whine of the approaching garbage truck. At last she found the bag and ran back into the house.

As she changed clothes, Tammy realized that she had sent a message by wrapping the gift as garbage—a message that what was inside could not be very valuable. *Maybe my wrappings give a false message, too,* she thought as she checked her clothing, hair, and posture. *God can see inside of me, but nobody else can. I should dress like there's something worthwhile inside.*

HOW ABOUT YOU? What does your appearance say? Would Jesus approve of the clothes you wear? It's not necessarily wrong to wear what is popular, but be sure your clothes don't mark you as a person who belongs to the world. And don't forget that the perfect accessory for every outfit is a smile. □ C.R.

TO MEMORIZE: *Abstain from every form of evil.* 1 Thessalonians 5:22, NKJV

BETHANNE DIDN'T FEEL much like going on the class field trip to the rock quarry. She just wanted her lost kitten to come home. And she wanted her daddy to get his job back.

The quarry superintendent met their bus and handed out hard hats to the class of fourth-graders. "We're going to have a dynamite blast today to loosen and break the stone in the quarry," he said as they stood in the parking lot. A loud horn blared. A moment later, it sounded again. "The horn goes off three times as a warning before the blast," the superintendent explained. "We blow it one time after the blast to let everyone know it's safe to come near." The third horn blared. Then, *boom!* A loud explosion sounded while the children watched the side of the pit break up and rise into the air, sending dust and rocks flying in the distance. When the "all clear" horn sounded, the superintendent allowed the children to take a closer look at what had happened. They also saw the men who controlled the operation and set off the blasts.

As Bethanne told her mother about it when she got home, she picked up a picture of her cat. "It's almost like we've had a dynamite blast in our house," she said sadly. "Everything's fallen apart."

"Sometimes it does feel like our comfortable little world is blowing to pieces," Mother agreed. "But those men at the quarry who carefully prepare safe blasts remind me that God is in control of what happens to us. And just as the stone company profits from their explosions, we can profit from what seem like troubles in our lives. God will teach us needed lessons, and help us grow in our Christian lives as we trust him through the rough circumstances." She smiled at Bethanne. "The quarry's horn sounds to make sure everyone gets to a safe place. In our case, God is with us throughout every experience we face, so we are always safe in His loving arms."

HOW ABOUT YOU? Are you having a rough day? When difficult or sad things happen, remember that God is in complete control and will work through the hard situations to strengthen your life for Him. □ N.E.K.

TO MEMORIZE: *A righteous man may have many troubles, but the Lord delivers him from them all.* Psalm 34:19, NIV

The Dynamite Blast

FROM THE BIBLE:
The righteous cry out, and the Lord hears them; he delivers them from all their troubles. The Lord is close to the brokenhearted and saves those who are crushed in spirit. A righteous man may have many troubles, but the Lord delivers him from them all. Psalm 34:17-19, NIV

God is in control

30

So Embarrassed!

FROM THE BIBLE:

You know from watching me that I am not that kind of person. You know what I believe and the way I live and what I want. You know my faith in Christ and how I have suffered. You know my love for you, and my patience. You know how many troubles I have had as a result of my preaching the Good News. You know about all that was done to me while I was visiting in Antioch, Iconium and Lystra, but the Lord delivered me. Yes, and those who decide to please Christ Jesus by living godly lives will suffer at the hands of those who hate him. In fact, evil men and false teachers will become worse and worse, deceiving many, they themselves having been deceived by Satan. But you must keep on believing the things you have been taught. You know they are true for you know that you can trust those of us who have taught you.

2 Timothy 3:10-14, TLB

Thank God for concerned parents

DAVID LOOKED UP as his friend Jimmy sank down beside him on the school bus. "You see the paper this morning?" Jimmy asked. "Some crazy parents are getting all upset about sex education being taught in school." David just stared out the window. His father and mother were some of those "crazy" parents. They were upset with the lack of moral teaching in the books being used.

"My mom said those people are just a bunch of fanatics," Jimmy added. David opened his math book and pretended to be studying until the bus arrived at school.

That wasn't the end of the subject, however. It came up during science class, and his teacher said those who objected "weren't smart enough to know what they were talking about." David was embarrassed. When he got home, his mother was writing to the newspaper, and that meant the whole town would see her name. "Do you have to make a fuss about it?" he asked.

"I want the school board to know exactly how I feel," his mother replied.

Discouraged, David went into the family room and sat down with a sports magazine. Soon his mother came into the room to get a stamp from her desk. "Oh, dear," she said as she picked up a plant from the top of her desk, "This looks rather sick." David watched as a leaf fell to the floor. "I hope I can revive it," Mother continued. She looked at David thoughtfully. "I didn't drop this plant or feed it poison. I just ignored it because I've been busy."

"So?" David asked.

"Well, I could do the same with your education," explained Mother. "I could ignore what you're being taught, but the results might be even more sad than what's happened to this plant. Your mind could become weakened spiritually. Instead, because we love you, Dad and I have chosen to fight for what we know is right."

HOW ABOUT YOU? Have you ever been embarrassed because your parents protested something that was being taught at your school? Have you ever been ashamed of your parents' testimony? They care about you and want you to have the very best training there is. Thank them for their concern. □ L.W.

TO MEMORIZE: *If you suffer as a Christian, do not be ashamed, but praise God that you bear that name.* 1 Peter 4:16, NIV

"I GIVE UP!" Jodi slammed her books on the kitchen table. "I've tried, but I just can't do it. I give up."

"Can't do what?" Mother wanted to know.

"Can't be perfect. I tried all day. Then just before the last bell, I lost my temper. It seems the harder I try to be perfect, the more I goof up."

Mother smiled. "I know the feeling. But why this sudden interest in being perfect? Oh, I remember. Our verse this morning was about being perfect." Mother paused, then spoke again as Jodi opened the refrigerator door. "You don't have time for a snack, Jodi. We're going to Aunt Melody's to see the new baby."

Later, Jodi proudly held her new cousin. "Oh, she's beautiful," she gushed. "Crystal is perfect, isn't she?"

Mother curled the sleeping baby's fist around her finger. "Yes. She is a perfect baby."

Jodi wrinkled her brow. "Crystal is perfect. I wish I was."

"Perhaps you have the wrong definition of 'perfect', Jodi," suggested Aunt Melody. "When the Bible speaks of 'perfect', it often means 'mature'. Crystal can't walk or talk or eat meat, yet she is a perfect newborn infant. However, if she stays like this for six months, we will be worried. She would not be perfect anymore."

Jodi frowned. "I still don't understand."

"To be perfect is to be complete for your age," Aunt Melody continued. "You know more and can do more than Crystal because you're a ten-year-old. To be a 'perfect' Christian doesn't mean we never make mistakes. It means we grow, and overcome, and learn from them."

Mother nodded. "It doesn't mean you'll never lose your temper, but it does mean you will learn to say you're sorry when you do. Eventually, you'll become mature enough to control it. As Christians, we have to grow up."

The baby wiggled in Jodi's arms and puckered her lips. Aunt Melody laughed. "Better let me have that perfect baby, Jodi. She's about to lose her temper."

HOW ABOUT YOU? Are you growing in Christ? Do you learn from your mistakes? That's a sign of growth. Each day you should become a little more like Jesus. □ B.W.

TO MEMORIZE: *Perseverance must finish its work so that you may be mature and complete, not lacking anything.* James 1:4, NIV

31

Grow Up

FROM THE BIBLE:
You can look forward soberly and intelligently to more of God's kindness to you when Jesus Christ returns. Obey God because you are his children; don't slip back into your old ways—doing evil because you knew no better. But be holy now in everything you do, just as the Lord is holy, who invited you to be his child. He himself has said, "You must be holy, for I am holy."
1 Peter 1:13-16, TLB

Be perfect

1

Throw It Out

FROM THE BIBLE:

Do not go about spreading slander among your people. Do not do anything that endangers your neighbor's life. I am the Lord. Do not hate your brother in your heart. Rebuke your neighbor frankly so you will not share in his guilt. Do not seek revenge or bear a grudge against one of your people, but love your neighbor as yourself. I am the Lord.

Leviticus 19:16-18, NIV

Don't hold grudges

L ET'S GO TO the sidewalk sale, Mother," suggested Patty.

Mother sighed. "I'd love to, but look at this kitchen. We'll have to get it cleaned up first."

"OK." agreed Patty. "Shall I clean out the fridge?"

Mother nodded, and they worked several minutes in silence. Then Mother asked, "Would you like to invite Melissa to go with us?"

"No," Patty answered shortly as she unloaded the refrigerator shelves.

Mother looked surprised. "Why not?"

Patty shrugged. "She's probably doing something with Amy today. Melissa is Amy's friend now."

"Can't Melissa have more than one friend?" Mother asked. "You could invite Amy, too."

"No," snapped Patty. After a long silence, she added, "Melissa knows I can't stand Amy. Last year Amy said some really hateful things about me, and she—phew! What do I smell?"

Mother grimaced. "You must have uncovered something spoiled," she said.

Patty gingerly picked up a bowl. "It's this old tuna casserole. Phewweeee!"

Mother reached for it. "Let's get rid of it. There's no telling how long that's been in there."

After the casserole was disposed of and the kitchen was sprayed with air freshener, Mother said, "Patty, sometimes we keep old things in our hearts until they spoil and cause our attitudes to stink. For a year you have been carrying a grudge against Amy. It's beginning to stink."

"But, Mother," began Patty, "she said . . ."

"I know. You've told me at least twenty times," Mother reminded. "And you have said some pretty nasty things about her, too." Patty hadn't thought of that. "Don't you think it's time to throw that stinking grudge out?" Mother asked gently.

Patty took a deep breath. A few minutes later, she went to the telephone. Mother smiled as she heard Patty say, "Amy, would you and Melissa like to go shopping with my mom and me today?"

HOW ABOUT YOU? Are you carrying a nasty, stinking grudge? Ask God to help you get rid of it today. Ask Him to give you a sweet and forgiving spirit. □ B.W.

TO MEMORIZE: *Do not grumble against one another, brethren, lest you be condemned. Behold, the Judge is standing at the door!* James 5:9, NKJV

"THERE'S A For Sale sign at the house on the corner," called Margie as she burst through the door. "Can we look at it again, Mom? It's so neat!"

"It is lovely," agreed Mother, "but it was too expensive when we looked at it before, and I'm afraid it still is. God has provided well for us, however. I love this house, too."

"But that one is so much bigger!" said Margie.

Mother smiled. "I think the only way we could pay for that house would be to live on canned spaghetti and powdered milk for twenty or thirty years," she said. "How does that sound to you?"

Margie laughed. "Not so good." She sighed. "I wish we were richer. Couldn't you get a job maybe?"

"Margie," said her mother, "do you remember what happened when we tried to make a super-duper buffet lunch last week?"

"Yeah." Margie laughed. "We had the oven going, and every appliance we own was plugged in. And we blew one fuse after another, so we couldn't get anything done!"

"Yes," said Mother. "We ended up with a lot of half-cooked food because we tried to do too much. Can you see how we might learn something from that experience?"

"Sure." Margie giggled. "We learned that you need to get circuit breakers!"

Mother smiled. "I had in mind a more spiritual lesson."

"Well," said Margie thoughtfully, "do you mean that we could overload ourselves, like we overloaded the wiring?"

Mother nodded. "More possessions, along with more debt, might make us lose track of what really matters," she said. "Let's just thank the Lord for leading us to a safe and comfortable home we can afford."

HOW ABOUT YOU? Do you sometimes wish your parents were richer? Surprisingly, many rich people worry so much about their possessions that they can't enjoy them. Money provides physical comforts, but it cannot satisfy the hunger and thirst of the spirit. It's much better to be "rich toward God" than to be rich in the things of this world. Don't overburden yourself seeking riches that don't satisfy. □ L.B.M.

TO MEMORIZE: *Seek the kingdom of God, and all these things shall be added to you.* Luke 12:31, NKJV

2

Overload

FROM THE BIBLE:
He said to them, "Take heed and beware of covetousness, for one's life does not consist in the abundance of the things he possesses." Then He spoke a parable to them, saying: "The ground of a certain rich man yielded plentifully. And he thought within himself, saying, 'What shall I do, since I have no room to store my crops?' So he said, 'I will do this: I will pull down my barns and build greater, and there I will store all my crops and my goods. And I will say to my soul, "Soul, you have many goods laid up for many years; take your ease; eat, drink, and be merry." ' But God said to him, 'You fool! This night your soul will be required of you; then whose will those things be which you have provided?' So is he who lays up treasure for himself, and is not rich toward God."
Luke 12:15-21, NKJV

"Things" don't satisfy

3

"Lone Ranger" Christians

FROM THE BIBLE:

Now the body is not made up of one part but of many. If the foot should say, "Because I am not a hand, I do not belong to the body," it would not for that reason cease to be part of the body. And if the ear should say, "Because I am not an eye, I do not belong to the body," it would not for that reason cease to be part of the body. If the whole body were an eye, where would the sense of hearing be? . . . But in fact God has arranged the parts in the body, every one of them, just as he wanted them to be. If they were all one part, where would the body be? As it is, there are many parts, but one body. The eye cannot say to the hand, "I don't need you!" And the head cannot say to the feet, "I don't need you!" . . . If one part suffers, every part suffers with it; if one part is honored, every part rejoices with it. Now you are the body of Christ, and each one of you is a part of it.
1 Corinthians 12:14-17, NIV

Christians need one another

"MOM, CAN I stay over at Frank's house tonight?" asked Jerry. "I can go to church with his family tomorrow."

Mother looked up from her sewing. "That's a possibility," she said. "What church do they belong to?"

Jerry shrugged. "None, really," he replied. "His parents don't think it's good to be tied down to just one church. They visit lots of different churches."

Dad spoke up from his desk. "They sound a bit like 'Lone Ranger' Christians to me," he said.

Jerry gave Dad a funny look. "What do you mean? Isn't the Lone Ranger that guy in those old TV shows?"

"Yes." Dad smiled. "When I was a boy, I loved watching that show. The Lone Ranger was a lawman who wasn't associated with any official agency—he worked on his own. That idea was fine for a TV show, but real policemen don't work that way. They know a lot more can be accomplished through teamwork. And that principle applies to Christians, too."

"How?" asked Jerry.

"Well, when we accept Christ as Savior, we become members of His Body—the church," explained Dad. "Just as our eyes or hands or feet work together and need each other, Christians need each other, too. As Christians, we need the close association with other Christians, and can accomplish more for the Lord by working together."

"Right," agreed Mother. "Uniting with a good, Bible-believing local church enables us to use our gifts to help other Christians—and to be helped by them in return."

"I just got an idea," said Jerry with a grin. "How about if I ask Frank to stay at our house and go to church with us tomorrow?" Maybe he'll see how good it is not to be a 'Lone Ranger' Christian."

HOW ABOUT YOU? Do you have a personal relationship with Christ as your Savior? That's wonderful! But don't stop there. Jesus never meant for you to live the Christian life without the fellowship and help of other believers. Get involved in a good, Bible-teaching local church. Other Christians need you—and you need them. □ S.K.

TO MEMORIZE: *You are the body of Christ, and each one of you is a part of it.* 1 Corinthians 12:27, NIV

KALEEN LOOKED AT the pictures in her Bible story book. "Isn't this one pretty, Dad?"

Her father smiled. "Yes," he said. "That's a copy of *The Last Supper*. It was painted by Leonardo da Vinci nearly five hundred years ago."

"He was a good painter," Kaleen said.

Dad nodded. "He was, but I'm afraid if you saw the real painting today, it wouldn't look much like the one in that book. A TV program said that the original painting is badly damaged."

"That must be because it's so old," observed Kaleen.

Dad shook his head. "No—some much older paintings have survived well through the years. The artist himself was the cause of this painting's problems."

"He was?" asked Kaleen in surprise. "What did he do?"

"He did a wonderful job painting the picture—in fact, he worked on it for three years," said Dad. "The problem is, he decided to use a new, experimental painting technique because he thought it would work better than the usual one. Unfortunately, the painting done by the new method just couldn't stand the test of time. The paint peeled and flaked when it was exposed to sunlight, moisture, and dust. The end result is a dim shadow of what the artist intended."

"I'll bet if he could, he'd do it all over again the right way," Kaleen said thoughtfully.

"I'm sure he would," agreed Dad. "You know, Honey, it would be good for us to remember that everything we do will have to stand a test, too. It will be tested, or 'tried,' by the Lord. All the things we have done out of love for Christ will stand the test and be rewarded. But other works we have done will prove to be worthless, because we did them out of pride or a desire to impress others rather than out of sincere love for the Lord."

Kaleen nodded. "I'm going to try to do all I can for the Lord—and to do it in the right way so I won't be wishing I could do it over again."

HOW ABOUT YOU? Do you want to be a success? No matter how hard you work or how many "good" things you do, it will all come to nothing if it's not done for the Lord. Ask the Lord to guide you in all that you do. Only what's done for Christ will last! □ S.K.

TO MEMORIZE: *Let each one take heed how he builds on it.* 1 Corinthians 3:10, NKJV

Standing the Test

FROM THE BIBLE:

According to the grace of God which was given to me, as a wise master builder I have laid the foundation, and another builds on it. But let each one take heed how he builds on it. For no other foundation can anyone lay than that which is laid, which is Jesus Christ. Now if anyone builds on this foundation with gold, silver, precious stones, wood, hay, straw, each one's work will become manifest; for the Day will declare it, because it will be revealed by fire; and the fire will test each one's work, of what sort it is. If anyone's work which he has built on it endures, he will receive a reward. If anyone's work is burned, he will suffer loss; but he himself will be saved, yet so as through fire.
1 Corinthians 3:10-15, NKJV

Serve Christ with your life

NOVEMBER

5

The Monster's Face

FROM THE BIBLE:

It is God himself, in his mercy, who has given us this wonderful work [of telling his Good News to others], and so we never give up. We do not try to trick people into believing—we are not interested in fooling anyone. We never try to get anyone to believe that the Bible teaches what it doesn't. . . . We stand in the presence of God as we speak and so we tell the truth, as all who know us will agree. If the Good News we preach is hidden to anyone, it is hidden from the one who is on the road to eternal death. Satan, who is the god of this evil world, has made him blind, unable to see the glorious light of the Gospel that is shining upon him, or to understand the amazing message we preach about the glory of Christ, who is God. . . . For God, who said, "Let there be light in the darkness," has made us understand that it is the brightness of his glory that is seen in the face of Jesus Christ.
2 Corinthians 4:1-6, TLB

Beware of Satan's influence

WASN'T DR. FRANKLIN'S message scary last night?" asked Kathy with a shiver. She and her brother Kevin had heard a missionary speaker at their church tell about heathen practices of black magic, voodoo, and Satan worship.

"Yeah—creepy!" Kevin replied as they went out to play. I'd sure hate to meet one of those witch doctor guys in a dark alley."

Soon the children came bursting back into the house. "Dad! Dad!" shouted Kathy as her brother held out a stick with a large green caterpillar on it. "Look at this thing's great big eyes and ugly monster face!"

Dad looked up from his newspaper. He smiled as he examined the caterpillar. "He does look scary, doesn't he?" he said. "But don't let that 'monster face' fool you. Actually, it's not a face at all—just a pattern of markings designed to scare away any bird who might want to eat him. His real head is on the other end. See?"

"He sure fooled us." Kathy laughed as they peered at the caterpillar.

Dad said, "You know, Satan is like this caterpillar—he has two sides, too."

"What do you mean, Dad?" asked Kevin.

"Well, last night we heard about what we might call the 'scary' side of Satan, which influences people to commit sins like witchcraft and magic spells," Dad explained. "That side of Satan is very dangerous, and we sometimes tend to think that because those things may not be happening in our own neighborhood, we're safe from Satan's influence. But the main reason Satan is dangerous is because he tempts us to commit 'ordinary' sins, like lying, gossip, disobedience, pride, and unbelief. Don't be fooled, kids. A sin doesn't have to be 'scary' to be dangerous!"

HOW ABOUT YOU? Do you think that because you don't worship idols or practice witchcraft, you are safe from Satan's influence? Satan knows that even "ordinary" sins are enough to separate you from God and to keep you from doing His will. Don't be lulled into thinking that any sin is harmless. □ S.K.

TO MEMORIZE: *Be self-controlled and alert. Your enemy the devil prowls around like a roaring lion looking for someone to devour.* 1 Peter 5:8, NIV

AS PASTOR PAGE began his sermon, Debbie yawned and began scribbling a note on her bulletin. "Carol," she wrote, "Sorry I can't study at your house tomorrow night. My mom and I signed up for an exercise class at the YWCA. I think it will be fun!" Then she added, "Much more fun than sitting here for an hour. What a drag!"

Debbie folded the note and turned around to pass it, but she noticed Mother frowning at her. So she stuffed it into her purse and read her Sunday school paper instead.

As Debbie and her folks drove home from church, her mother said, "I wish you'd pay more attention during the sermon, Honey."

"Sermons are boring," Debbie grumbled.

"You're old enough to listen and take notes," said Dad. "If you'd do that, you'd get more out of the sermons."

The next night, Debbie excitedly went with her mother to the YWCA. She was impressed with all the exercise equipment, and she had a great time trying it out during the class.

"That sure was neat, Mom," Debbie said happily as they drove home. "I like the rowing machine, and it was fun lifting weights. Maybe we can try out the pool next time."

Mother yawned. "It sure made me tired," she said.

"I'm tired, too," agreed Debbie, "but it was fun. My muscles are a little sore, but I feel good. I know that working out makes me stronger."

Mother smiled. "I know what you mean," she said with a nod. "That's how I felt after my workout yesterday, too."

"Yesterday?" Debbie frowned. "You didn't exercise yesterday, Mom. We just went to church."

"Ah, but I got a spiritual workout yesterday," said Mother, "and I needed that. You missed it, though. You see, you can't just sit in church on Sundays and expect to grow spiritually. If you ever expect to become strong in the Lord, you need to exercise your faith, like you do your body."

HOW ABOUT YOU? Do you feel that church is a waste of time—that you don't get anything out of it? Church is not just a place to sit on Sunday mornings. It's a place where true believers in Christ meet to worship and serve God and to learn how to live for Him. Don't let church become a bore. Get involved. □ S.K.

TO MEMORIZE: *It is good for our hearts to be strengthened by grace.* Hebrews 13:9, NIV

Spiritual "Workout"

FROM THE BIBLE:
Remember your leaders, who spoke the word of God to you. Consider the outcome of their way of life and imitate their faith. Jesus Christ is the same yesterday and today and forever. Do not be carried away by all kinds of strange teachings. It is good for our hearts to be strengthened by grace, not by ceremonial foods, which are of no value to those who eat them. Through Jesus, therefore, let us continually offer to God a sacrifice of praise—the fruit of lips that confess his name. And do not forget to do good and to share with others, for with such sacrifices God is pleased. Obey your leaders and submit to their authority. They keep watch over you as men who must give an account. Obey them so that their work will be a joy, not a burden, for that would be of no advantage to you.
Hebrews 13:7-9, 15-17, NIV

Get involved in church

7

The Overdue Book

FROM THE BIBLE:

Remember that your heavenly Father to whom you pray has no favorites when he judges. He will judge you with perfect justice for everything you do; so act in reverent fear of him from now on until you get to heaven. God paid a ransom to save you from the impossible road to heaven which your fathers tried to take, and the ransom he paid was not mere gold or silver, as you very well know. But he paid for you with the precious lifeblood of Christ, the sinless, spotless Lamb of God. God chose him for this purpose long before the world began, but only recently was he brought into public view, in these last days, as a blessing to you. Because of this, your trust can be in God who raised Christ from the dead and gave him great glory. Now your faith and hope can rest in him alone.

1 Peter 1:17-21, TLB

Jesus paid your debt

AS CHRISTIE WAS cleaning out her closet, she found a library book tucked away in the corner. "Oh, no!" she groaned. "I took this book out ages ago. I'll never be able to pay the fine. Mom and Dad will be mad, too."

Christie hid the book under the pillow, but she continued to worry about it for days. Finally, just before family devotions one evening, she told her parents about the problem. "I'm really sorry I forgot to take it back," she said. "I don't want to go to the library until I've saved enough to pay the fine. But every day I wait, the fine gets bigger and bigger. What can I do?"

"Oh!" exclaimed her mother. "I guess I forgot to tell you. When I was at the library about a month ago, the librarian asked me about that book. It was already so long overdue that it was cheaper to buy it than to pay the fine, so that's what I did."

Christie breathed a sigh of relief. "Thanks a lot, Mom. Just think—I've been feeling so guilty and worried, and all the time the book was paid for!"

"What happened to you is similar to what happens to lots of people," said Dad. "People often feel guilty for years about things they've done wrong. Just as you were afraid to go back to the library, they wait to come to God, thinking that they'll first 'clean up' their lives. But they'll never be able to do that. They just keep on sinning more. They don't realize that Jesus paid the full price for all their sins on the cross, and all they have to do is accept His gift for it to take effect."

HOW ABOUT YOU? Do you feel guilty about things you have done? Are you trying to do better—to clean up your life? Perhaps you even try to do good things to "pay for" bad deeds of the past. Jesus already paid the price for all your sins. Confess them to Him and accept Him as your Savior. Then thank Him for purchasing your forgiveness. Don't feel guilty anymore—feel glad for what God did for you. □ S.K.

TO MEMORIZE: *You were bought at a price. Therefore honor God with your body.* 1 Corinthians 6:20, NIV

DEBBY AND HER mother were cleaning the attic when Debby found a small leather-bound volume. "Look! My old five-year diary!" she exclaimed. "I started writing in this when I was five." She pointed to the large, oddly shaped letters at the top of one page. "It's so sloppy, I can hardly read it," she said with a laugh. "And just look! I spelled *Grandma*, g-r-a-m-e."

Mother smiled. "Your writing improved through the years, though."

"Yeah, it keeps getting better and better," agreed Debby. Then she said, "But look at the bottom section. I wrote this two years ago, when I was nine. This writing looks almost like the way I write now."

"Yes, it does," said Mother, looking at it closely. "And your spelling hasn't changed much, either. You still spell *friend*, f-r-e-i-n-d, the way it is here."

Debby blushed. "I always did have trouble with that word."

Mother grew thoughtful. "Your diary makes me think of my Christian life," she said. "I remember the first couple of years after I was saved. It seemed I was constantly learning new things from God's Word and trying to live for Him in all areas of my life. But I guess I started losing enthusiasm after that. The changes and improvements started coming more slowly. I wonder how different my spiritual life is now from what it was five years ago."

"I was saved just three years ago," Debby said, "but I know what you mean, Mom. What do you think happened?"

"I think it's just easy to get lazy," said Mother. "I'm going to confess that to the Lord and work harder. There certainly is room for improvement in my life."

"Mine, too!" Debby agreed. "Let's start today."

HOW ABOUT YOU? Have you accepted Jesus as your Savior? If so, think back to that time. Were you more enthusiastic and committed to Him then than you are now? You should be growing as a Christian, not just growing older. Ask Him to renew your devotion to Him. Until you reach heaven, there will always be room for improvement. □ S.K.

TO MEMORIZE: *Remember therefore from where you have fallen; repent and do the first works, or else I will come to you quickly and remove your lampstand from its place—unless you repent.* Revelation 2:5, NKJV

Debby's Diary

FROM THE BIBLE:
We are looking forward to God's promise of new heavens and a new earth afterwards, where there will be only goodness. Dear friends, while you are waiting for these things to happen and for him to come, try hard to live without sinning; and be at peace with everyone so that he will be pleased with you when he returns. And remember why he is waiting. He is giving us time to get his message of salvation out to others. . . . Grow in spiritual strength and become better acquainted with our Lord and Savior Jesus Christ. To him be all glory and splendid honor, both now and forevermore. Good-bye. Peter
2 Peter 3:13-15, 18, TLB

Keep growing in Christ

New Father, New Rules

FROM THE BIBLE:

As the Father has loved me, so have I loved you. Now remain in my love. If you obey my commands, you will remain in my love, just as I have obeyed my Father's commands and remain in his love. I have told you this so that my joy may be in you and that your joy may be complete. My command is this: Love each other as I have loved you. Greater love has no one than this, that he lay down his life for his friends. You are my friends if you do what I command.

John 15:9-14, NIV

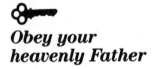

Obey your heavenly Father

MR. ARENDS HELD the adoption papers tightly in his hand as he hugged Alex. "Now you're really mine!" he said. "I'm so glad I finally got you for my son."

Alex hugged him back. "I'm glad you wanted me, Mr. Ar—I mean, *Dad*. I'm going to be the best kid in the whole world for you."

Alex meant what he said. He had already learned that he had to obey the rules in his new home. At first, coming straight home from school, attending church, hanging up his clothes, and doing his homework often annoyed Alex, but he soon got used to it. In fact, as he learned to love his new parents, he found that he wanted to do the things that pleased them. And it wasn't long after his adoption was final that he accepted the Lord Jesus as his Savior.

A few days later, Alex was writing with a new pen. "Where did you get that pen?" asked his father.

"It's Jerry Stern's," Alex answered. "He broke mine on purpose, so I took his from his desk."

Dad frowned. "Son," he said, "when you came into my family, I had some rules for you to follow. When you received Jesus as your Savior, you came into God's family. He also has rules for you to obey. One of them is, 'You shall not steal.' God wants you to give that pen back to Jerry."

"But, Dad, he broke mine!" protested Alex.

"You said yourself that the pen is Jerry's," Dad pointed out. Then he asked, "Alex, why have you tried so hard to obey my rules?"

"Because . . . well . . . because I love you, Dad, and you love me." Alex paused as he thought about his words. "I love God, too," he added slowly, "and I should also obey Him. OK, Dad. I'll give the pen back to Jerry."

HOW ABOUT YOU? Have you become a child of God by receiving the Lord Jesus as your Savior? Do you obey your Heavenly Father? His rules are in the Bible. If you love Him, you'll want to obey Him. □ A.L.

TO MEMORIZE: *If you love me, you will obey what I command.* John 14:15, NIV

At THE DEPARTMENT store, Scott met his friends, Jerry and Ken. "Hi," he said. "Whatcha doin'?"

"We're playing five finger discount," Jerry announced, holding up a small pocket knife.

"What's that?" asked Scott.

"You find something in the store that you can pick up with five fingers, and you hide it in your hand," whispered Jerry. "The discount is when you walk out of the store without paying for it."

"That's stealing," gasped Scott.

"Shhh," Ken signaled. "It's just a game. Sometimes you can't get what you want any other way."

Scott cupped his hand around a little car he had been looking at. For a long time he had wanted a car like that for his collection. It would be so easy to get the "five finger discount."

"Go on," his friends urged him. "It's easy."

Scott looked longingly at the car. "I'd better go," he said, putting down the car.

"Well, think about it," said Jerry. "You can come back for it tomorrow."

Dessert that night was Scott's favorite—chocolate fudge cake. Mother sat down and looked at her piece. Suddenly she got up and put it back on the cake plate. "When I take dessert, I take it because it tastes so good," she said. "Then when the doctor weighs me at the end of the week, I get upset that my diet isn't working. Sometimes it's hard to resist immediate pleasure regardless of what it will cost me in the long run."

Scott knew just what she meant. He had been tempted to do something wrong just for the immediate pleasure of having the little car. Even if he hadn't gotten caught the car would have cost him a guilty conscience. It would have cost him many uncomfortable moments. He was glad he had resisted.

HOW ABOUT YOU? Are there things you think you need right away just to please yourself? The immediate pleasure you'd receive isn't worth the long term results. Trust God to meet your needs in His own good time. □ N.E.K.

TO MEMORIZE: *We have renounced secret and shameful ways.* 2 Corinthians 4:2, NIV

10

Five Finger Discount

FROM THE BIBLE:
Listen, son of mine, to what I say. Listen carefully. Keep these thoughts ever in mind; let them penetrate deep within your heart, for they will mean real life for you, and radiant health. Above all else, guard your affections. For they influence everything else in your life. Spurn the careless kiss of a prostitute. Stay far from her. Look straight ahead; don't even turn your head to look. Watch your step. Stick to the path and be safe. Don't sidetrack; pull back your foot from danger.
Proverbs 4:20-27, TLB

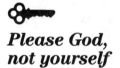

Please God, not yourself

11

Bad-tasting Medicine

FROM THE BIBLE:

You have forgotten that word of encouragement that addresses you as sons: "My son, do not make light of the Lord's discipline, and do not lose heart when he rebukes you, because the Lord disciplines those he loves, and he punishes everyone he accepts as a son." Endure hardship as discipline; God is treating you as sons. For what son is not disciplined by his father? If you are not disciplined (and everyone undergoes discipline), then you are illegitimate children and not true sons. Moreover, we have all had human fathers who disciplined us and we respected them for it. How much more should we submit to the Father of our spirits and live! Our fathers disciplined us for a little while as they thought best; but God disciplines us for our good, that we may share in his holiness. No discipline seems pleasant at the time, but painful. Later on, however, it produces a harvest of righteousness and peace for those who have been trained by it.
Hebrews 12:5-11, NIV

Be thankful for discipline

Oh!" YELLED DANNY. "Oh, ouch! That hurts!"

"I know, Son," said Dad. "Spankings do hurt, but that's the point. Maybe this will help you remember to obey next time." He patted Danny's shoulder. "We don't enjoy spanking you. We do it because we love you."

Later that day, Danny came down with a cough. It grew worse and worse, until finally Mother called the doctor's office. Soon Dad was on his way to pick up a prescription at the pharmacy. When he returned with a big bottle of dark brown medicine, Danny eyed the bottle warily. "Do I really have to take that stuff?" he asked. Mother nodded and poured out a big spoonful. Danny gulped it down. "Oh, yuck! It tastes terrible! I'm sure not going to take any more!" But that night, Danny woke up coughing again. His throat hurt, and he was glad when Mother came in, bringing the medicine bottle.

The next morning Danny felt better. "That medicine really helped," he admitted at breakfast. "It tasted awful, but I'm glad I took it."

"Good," said Dad, "because you'll need to take another dose after breakfast. "Neither spankings nor bad-tasting medicines are enjoyable. But both produce good results. It reminds me that God sometimes has to use unpleasant things to bring about good results in His children, too."

"That's right," agreed Mother. "Even when you're grown up, the Lord will sometimes use difficult circumstances to convict you of sin and help you grow in Him. Times of chastening are always hard, whether from parents or from God, but the results are worth it. Try to remember that and even be thankful for discipline." Danny nodded as he watched Mother pour out another spoonful of medicine.

HOW ABOUT YOU? Do you enjoy being disciplined? No one does! But the discipline you receive from your parents helps you grow into a mature, responsible adult. Even if you think your parents aren't always fair in their discipline, remember that God is in control, and His chastening is always "just right." Don't resent discipline—be glad someone cares. □ S.K.

TO MEMORIZE: *The Lord disciplines those he loves, and he punishes everyone he accepts as a son.* Hebrews 12:6, NIV

WHEN BILL'S MOTHER reminded him that he still hadn't studied his Sunday school lesson or learned the memory verse, he looked up from his work on an airplane model. "Aw, Mom, I know all that stuff," he argued. "I don't need to study. I go to church and Sunday school on Sundays, to Boys' Club on Wednesday, and to a Christian school every day." But when Dad gave him a stern look, he obediently worked on his lesson until bedtime.

The following morning, Bill worked on his airplane model until Mother told him to get ready for church. Again he protested that he already knew "all that stuff the pastor says." Unwillingly, he went to his room to change, but in a few minutes was back again. "Look at these pants!" he exclaimed. "They're so short on me."

Mom nodded. "So they are," she agreed. "You've grown right out of them. We'll look for a new pair this week."

The next day, Mom bought his new pants, and Bill tried them on later that evening. "They're a perfect fit, and you look great," Dad said with a big smile. Then he became serious. "But, Son, I'm concerned, because lately I get the feeling that you think God is like your old pair of pants."

Bill looked at Dad. "What do you mean?" he asked.

"Well, you've implied that you know all there is to know about God," explained Dad. "You seem to think you've outgrown Him. But it takes a whole lifetime to learn about God and His ways, and then you still can only know just a little. God is so great and His ways so wonderful, we'll never know all there is to know."

Bill looked down at his new pants. "I'll try to remember that next Sunday when I'm wearing these pants."

Sure enough, as he thought about the words of the songs and listened to the pastor and Sunday school teacher, he heard several things he hadn't thought of before. *I'm glad I'll never outgrow God like I did my old pants,* he thought.

HOW ABOUT YOU? Do you think your Bible lessons are dull and that you've heard all the stories before? Although it may seem that you know everything, you'll discover new things about God and His ways. You can never outgrow God. □ C.Y.

TO MEMORIZE: *Oh, the depth of the riches of the wisdom and knowledge of God!* Romans 11:33, NIV

Outgrown

FROM THE BIBLE:
Oh, the depth of the riches of the wisdom and knowledge of God! How unsearchable his judgments, and his paths beyond tracing out! "Who has known the mind of the Lord? Or who has been his counselor?" "Who has ever given to God, that God should repay him?" For from him and through him and to him are all things. To him be the glory forever! Amen.
Romans 11:33-36, NIV

You can't outgrow God

13

Nick's Prayer

FROM THE BIBLE:

Love your enemies. Do good to those who hate you. Pray for the happiness of those who curse you; implore God's blessing on those who hurt you. If someone slaps you on one cheek, let him slap the other too! . . . When things are taken away from you, don't worry about getting them back. Treat others as you want them to treat you. Do you think you deserve credit for merely loving those who love you? Even the godless do that! And if you do good only to those who do you good—is that so wonderful? Even sinners do that much! And if you lend money only to those who can repay you, what good is that? Even the most wicked will lend to their own kind for full return! Love your enemies! Do good to them! Lend to them! And don't be concerned about the fact that they won't repay. Then your reward from heaven will be very great, and you will truly be acting as sons of God: for he is kind to the unthankful and to those who are very wicked.

Luke 6:27-36, TLB

Pray for your enemies

NICK CAME RUNNING into the house as fast as he could. "Mom! It worked!" he shouted. "Pastor Dunn said that we should pray for our enemies, so all week I've been praying for Todd."

"Isn't he the boy who knocked you off the swing set at school a few weeks ago?" asked Mom.

Nick nodded. "He's mean. Nobody likes him. Anyway, I've been praying, and God answered my prayers. Today Todd had to go to the hospital to have his appendix out, and he won't be back in school for quite a while!"

"What has that got to do with your prayers?" asked Mom in surprise.

"I asked God to make something bad happen to Todd," explained Nick impatiently. "And God did it! Todd will be way behind in school now. Maybe he'll get so far behind that he'll flunk this year and have to stay back!"

"Hold on!" exclaimed Mom. "You prayed for something bad to happen to Todd?"

"Sure."

"Nick," said Mom, "when the Bible talks about praying for your enemy, it means you should ask God to help you be nice to that person and not hate him. You should also ask God to help you set a good Christian example for him and pray that he'll be saved, too."

"I guess I've been doing it all wrong," said Nick thoughtfully. "From now on I'm going to pray that God will help me love Todd, and that Todd will accept Jesus."

HOW ABOUT YOU? Do you know someone who doesn't like you, or who isn't very nice to anybody? Pray *for* them, and not *against* them. The Bible also says you should love them. It may not be easy at first, but after a while you may find that someone you thought was an enemy really isn't so bad after all. Try it! □ D.M.

TO MEMORIZE: *Love your enemies and pray for those who persecute you.* Matthew 5:44, NIV

14

Go, Little Bird

TOM POUNDED THE last nail in the bird trap he was building, then took it to the backyard to set it. He tilted the cage upward on its end and propped a stick under the raised end. Next he scattered bread crumbs, trailing them inside the cage. Finally, he unraveled a string attached to the stick and hid behind a bush, string in hand. "There!" he muttered to himself. "Hope some dumb bird falls for my trap."

Tom waited, almost motionless, for an unsuspecting, hungry bird. This project had kept his mind off a big problem he was having. But now, while waiting, he began to worry once more. *Swimming lessons again this afternoon*, he thought. *All the other kids can already swim, but I just stiffen up. What if I can't learn to swim?* Then Tom remembered something he'd heard on a children's radio program the day before. "Trust God for help" had been the theme of the lesson. *That's something I haven't done*, he thought.

Tom looked up and saw a little bird pecking at the bread crumbs, following the crumbs right into the trap. Tom yanked on the string, and the cage crashed down, trapping the bird inside. "I got one!" Tom yelled, running to get a closer look. The frightened little bird fluttered its wings wildly, trying to get free.

Tom gazed at the unhappy bird for a few minutes, then slowly lifted the cage while the bird hopped to freedom. "Go, little bird," he said, as the bird soared into the sky. "I'm bigger and more powerful than you are, so I can help you escape this cage. And God is bigger and more powerful than I am, so He can help me with my problems." Right then and there, Tom prayed that God would help him relax in the water.

HOW ABOUT YOU? Are you afraid of going to the doctor, the dentist, or a new school? Do you worry about school, parents, friends? Are your problems too hard for you to work out? They're not too hard for God. Don't spend needless time worrying about them. Worrying won't help. Praying and trusting God will. Take your problems to Him. □ C.Y.

TO MEMORIZE: *Our help is in the name of the Lord, the Maker of heaven and earth.* Psalm 124:8, NIV

FROM THE BIBLE:

If the Lord had not been on our side—let Israel say—if the Lord had not been on our side when men attacked us, when their anger flared against us, they would have swallowed us alive; the flood would have engulfed us, the torrent would have swept over us, the raging waters would have swept us away. Praise be to the Lord, who has not let us be torn by their teeth. We have escaped like a bird out of the fowler's snare; the snare has been broken, and we have escaped. Our help is in the name of the Lord, the Maker of heaven and earth.
Psalm 124, NIV

Trust God for help

15

A Matched Set

FROM THE BIBLE:

Gird up the loins of your mind, be sober, and rest your hope fully upon the grace that is to be brought to you at the revelation of Jesus Christ; as obedient children, not conforming yourselves to the former lusts, as in your ignorance; but as He who called you is holy, you also be holy in all your conduct, because it is written, "Be holy, for I am holy."

1 Peter 1:13-16, NKJV

Be like Jesus

HAS ANYONE seen my pearl ring?" asked Mary after she had hunted all over the house for it with no success.

Mother shook her head. "You'll have to find it later," she said. "It's time to leave for church now."

"But I don't like to wear my pearl necklace without the ring," objected Mary as she put on her coat.

"Big deal," said Mary's brother, Dan. "What's so terrible about that?"

Just then Mary spied the ring on the floor near the refrigerator. "I found it! Now I'm ready to go." They went out to the garage where Dad was already waiting in the car. Mary happily climbed in, too. "I'm so glad I found my ring," she declared as she admired it on her hand. "It's special because it matches the necklace."

"That's something like what God wants for His children," observed Dad as he started the engine. "The Bible tells us to be like Him, so in a sense we are to 'match' Him."

"Be like God!" Dan exploded from the back seat. "We couldn't hope to be as great as God."

"You're right, Dan," agreed Dad. "We could never be almighty like God. We can't control nature or do miracles. But there is a way we can match up at least a little with God. Jesus showed us how to do it."

"Do you mean become more kind and loving and things like that?" Mary asked, twisting her ring on her finger.

"That's it." Dad smiled at her. "Each day we should become a little more like Jesus. We want to match Him as closely as possible. If we pray for that, He'll help us do it."

HOW ABOUT YOU? Are you trying to "match" the example Jesus gave you? He was always loving, kind, and thoughtful of the needs of others. He treated people with respect. The more you act like this, the more you'll "match" Jesus. Ask God to help you. You can't do it alone. □ C.Y.

TO MEMORIZE: *It is written, "Be holy, for I am holy."* 1 Peter 1:16, NKJV

16

Spiritual Checkup

A S KEVIN ENTERED the waiting room, the office nurse smiled at him. "Your father's almost done for the day, Kevin," she said.

Soon Kevin and his father were in their car, headed for home. "Dad, when someone comes for a checkup, how do you tell whether they're sick or not?" Kevin asked.

Dr. Brown grinned at his son. "Well, when a patient comes in for an exam, I first ask if he has any complaints," he explained. "I also check height, weight, blood pressure, and heartbeat. I listen to the lungs, and I look at the ears, eyes, nose, and throat. If I suspect any illness, I sometimes take a blood sample or make some other tests. But normally, if the basic signs are all OK, the patient is healthy."

"That doesn't sound very complicated," exclaimed Kevin. "If that's all there is to a check up, it must not be very important."

"Oh, but it is!" replied his father. "If everyone would have an examination regularly, many illnesses could be prevented." Then he added, "There's another kind of checkup that's even more important—a spiritual one. And that's one we can give ourselves."

"How do we do that?" asked Kevin.

"By examining the 'vital signs' of our Christian life," said his father. "First, think about your prayer and Scripture reading habits. Have they become irregular? Also consider your church attendance and your general attitude toward spiritual things. If you have bad feelings towards anyone, make up your mind to repair the relationship as soon as possible. Ask God to reveal any areas of sin in your life. Finally, try to remember the last time you witnessed to someone or did any other work for the Lord."

"That doesn't sound too hard," said Kevin thoughtfully. "I think I'll give myself a checkup today."

HOW ABOUT YOU? When was the last time you gave yourself a spiritual checkup? You'd be surprised at how often a simple lapse in Bible reading, prayer, or church attendance can lead to big problems. God doesn't want your Christian life to be an unstable, unhappy experience. Be sure to take regular "checkups!" □ S.K.

TO MEMORIZE: *A man ought to examine himself before he eats of the bread and drinks of the cup.* 1 Corinthians 11:28, NIV

FROM THE BIBLE:
How can we be sure that we belong to him? By looking within ourselves: are we really trying to do what he wants us to? Someone may say, "I am a Christian; I am on my way to heaven; I belong to Christ." But if he doesn't do what Christ tells him to, he is a liar. . . . Anyone who says he is a Christian should live as Christ did. Dear brothers, I am not writing out a new rule for you to obey, for it is an old one you have always had, right from the start. You have heard it all before. Yet it is always new, and works for you just as it did for Christ; and as we obey this commandment, to love one another, the darkness in our lives disappears and the new light of life in Christ shines in. Anyone who says he is walking in the light of Christ but dislikes his fellow man, is still in darkness. But whoever loves his fellow man is "walking in the light" and can see his way without stumbling around in darkness and sin.
1 John 2:3-10, TLB

Examine your Christian life

17

The Mangled Slipper

FROM THE BIBLE:

Dear brothers, don't be too eager to tell others their faults, for we all make many mistakes; and when we teachers of religion, who should know better, do wrong, our punishment will be greater than it would be for others. If anyone can control his tongue, it proves that he has perfect control over himself in every other way. We can make a large horse turn around and go wherever we want by means of a small bit in his mouth. And a tiny rudder makes a huge ship turn wherever the pilot wants it to go, even though the winds are strong. So also the tongue is a small thing, but what enormous damage it can do. A great forest can be set on fire by one tiny spark. And the tongue is a flame of fire. It is full of wickedness, and poisons every part of the body. And the tongue is set on fire by hell itself, and can turn our whole lives into a blazing flame of destruction and disaster.

James 3:1-6, TLB

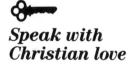

Speak with Christian love

"LOOK AT WHAT Scuffy did to my slipper!" cried Anne. The slipper she held looked soggy and torn. "I scolded Scuffy and put him outside."

"I'm sorry, Honey," said Dad as he took the mangled slipper.

Mother spoke from the doorway. "Anne, Jody is on the phone."

After a few words, Anne screeched, "You always want me to do all the work! You're awful!" And she banged down the phone.

"I thought Jody was your best friend," said Mother.

"She is." Anne hung her head. "She just caught me at a bad time."

"Did your sister catch you at a bad time, too?" asked Mother. "I heard you lash out at her this morning."

Anne blushed. "She bothers me when I'm tired. But I always tell her I'm sorry. I'll call Jody back and apologize."

Just then Scuffy whined at the door. "I think Scuffy wants to apologize, too," suggested Dad, handing the chewed-up slipper to Anne.

Anne looked at it. "I think he should stay out longer. After all, my slipper is ruined for good."

Dad nodded. "That's true," he agreed. He looked thoughtful, as he added, "You need to know, Anne, that feelings can be mangled just like your slipper, and once you've said a word it really can't be taken back. You can apologize, but the words have already hurt."

Anne looked startled. "I didn't realize how awful I've been," she said. "What should I do?"

"Well, you do need to apologize," said Mother. "And you need to try and control your tongue. Think before you speak. When you feel angry, count to ten before you say anything. Quickly ask God to help you say things that are loving and kind."

HOW ABOUT YOU? Do you say things you don't mean? Do you speak too quickly? It's so easy to do. The Bible has a lot to say about how much trouble your tongue can cause. The Bible also gives the cure—let the love of Christ control what you say. □ H.A.D.

TO MEMORIZE: *He who guards his mouth and his tongue keeps himself from calamity.* Proverbs 21:23, NIV

"LOOK, DAD!" Ken exclaimed one afternoon. "Smokie's playing dead, just like I taught him."

Dad laughed as he saw the dog stretched out on the porch. "I think he's just resting," he said. "Let's go for a walk and teach him to heel."

When they started out with Smokie on a leash, the dog plodded along willingly at first. Then he began to strain at the leash, trying to go out to the street. Ken scolded and tugged, but the dog paid no attention. Suddenly Smokie turned and ran in the direction Ken had been pulling. "Hey, look! He's minding me now!" Ken called.

When Smokie came to a trash can, he stopped short, sniffing at the contents. No amount of coaxing by Ken could get him to budge.

"I don't understand it," moaned Ken as Dad walked up. "Sometimes Smokie minds me, and sometimes he doesn't."

"I don't think he's obeying you at all," Dad remarked. "I think he does whatever he wants, and sometimes he just happens to want the same thing you do."

"You mean he's *accidentally* good?" asked Ken.

Dad laughed. "You could say that." Dad took the leash and showed Ken how to direct the dog, giving the leash a firm jerk every time Smokie went the wrong way.

"You know, people often behave the way Smokie did," observed Dad as they walked. "When they're in a good mood, they act kindly toward others. They go to church when they feel like it, and they contribute money or time if they feel generous. But that's not really obeying God. The true test of obedience is how we respond when we *don't* feel like obeying."

"I get it," Ken replied as he jerked the leash. "I'll try to remember that. I don't want to be just accidentally good."

HOW ABOUT YOU? Do you think you're a good person because you obey God's commandments sometimes—whenever you feel like it? That's not really obeying. It's still just doing what you want to do. You need to follow Jesus' example. He became a servant and was "obedient unto death—even the death of the cross." You need to obey Him in everything, regardless of how you feel or what it might cost you. □ S.K.

TO MEMORIZE: *Then Jesus said to his disciples, "If anyone would come after me, he must deny himself and take up his cross and follow me."* Matthew 16:24, NIV

18

Accidentally Good?

FROM THE BIBLE:
Your attitude should be the kind that was shown us by Jesus Christ, who, though he was God, did not demand and cling to his rights as God, but laid aside his mighty power and glory, taking the disguise of a slave and becoming like men. And he humbled himself even further, going so far as actually to die a criminal's death on a cross. Yet it was because of this that God raised him up to the heights of heaven and gave him a name which is above every other name.
Philippians 2:5-9, TLB

Obey God always

19

A Good Police Officer

FROM THE BIBLE:

"He will wipe away all tears from their eyes, and there shall be no more death, nor sorrow, nor crying, nor pain. All of that has gone forever." And the one sitting on the throne said, "See, I am making all things new!" And then he said to me, "Write this down, for what I tell you is trustworthy and true: It is finished! I am the A and the Z—the Beginning and the End. I will give to the thirsty the springs of the Water of Life—as a gift! Everyone who conquers will inherit all these blessings, and I will be his God and he will be my son. But cowards who turn back from following me, and those who are unfaithful to me, and the corrupt, and murderers, and the immoral, and those conversing with demons, and idol worshipers and all liars—their doom is in the Lake that burns with fire and sulfur. This is the Second Death."

Revelation 21:4-8, TLB

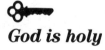

God is holy

IF GOD IS so loving, I don't think He would send anybody to hell," said Jerry firmly.

"Well," his friend Don began, praying for the right words to say, "The Bible—" A loud outburst of yelps from his dog interrupted the discussion. They boys rushed to the door just in time to see a boy ride off on Jerry's new bike. They ran after him, but soon realized it would do no good.

Jerry moaned, "Call your dad." Don's father was a police officer.

Don ran to the phone, and soon a squad car pulled up to the curb. Don's father emerged and led a young boy up to the house. Another officer lifted a mangled bike from the trunk. Jerry's jaw sagged as he recognized the bent frame, and he started shouting at the boy. Don's father held up his hand. "Calm down, Jerry," he said. "If that's your bike, this boy will have to pay for the damage."

Later that day, the boys resumed their discussion about whether God would send anyone to hell. When Jerry continued to insist that a loving God wouldn't do that, Don had an idea. "Hey, Jerry," he said, "why should the kid who took your bike today have to be punished for it?"

Jerry stared at him. "Because he stole it and ruined it!"

"But aren't you a loving person?" Don asked.

"Well, sure, but—" Jerry stopped. He saw where this conversation was going.

"What if my dad had seen that boy commit a crime but refused to do anything it?" Don continued.

"He wouldn't refuse," replied Jerry. "He's a police officer."

Don nodded. "It would be wrong for him to ignore crime," he agreed. Then he made his point. "God is holy and He can't ignore crime, either—the crime of sin. If He did, it would be wrong."

"I guess you're right," Jerry said. He knew he'd better give this matter more thought.

HOW ABOUT YOU? Do you find it hard to believe that a loving God could send someone to hell? Do you think that everyone will go to heaven, one way or another? Because God is loving, He provided a way to heaven through the blood of Jesus. Because He is holy, He demands that those who refuse His gift be punished eternally. That need not happen to you. Accept His gift today. □ J.B.

TO MEMORIZE: *The wicked shall be turned into hell, and all the nations that forget God.* Psalm 9:17, NKJV

20

The Surprise Party

"MOM, YOU WON'T believe what happened," Carrie said with disgust as she came into the room. "Scott didn't show up for his surprise party. We baked him a cake. We decorated Melissa's living room—everything."

"Where was he?" asked Mother.

"At his grandma's," said Carrie. "Kyle forgot to ask Scott's mom to keep him home, and when he went to pick him up, Scott was gone. And he won't be back for a week."

"Doesn't sound like much of a party," Mother observed.

"It wasn't," agreed Carrie. "We played some games and had refreshments, but it just wasn't much fun since it was supposed to be a party for Scott."

"Well, that's too bad," said Mother sympathetically, "but right now you'd better look over your Sunday school lesson. Tomorrow is Sunday, you know."

"Yeah. What a drag." Carrie clapped her hand over her mouth as she glanced quickly at Mother. "I'm sorry," she said, "but I haven't gotten much out of church services lately. The way the song leader drags out all those old hymns, it sounds like a funeral."

Mother said nothing for a while. "I've been thinking about your party for Scott," she said at last. "It's probably good that he didn't come. After all, no one yelled 'surprise.' No one sang 'Happy Birthday.' Everyone sat around talking about how the party wasn't any fun."

"Mother! If Scott had come, the party wouldn't have been like that," Carrie said impatiently. "It was for Scott, not us."

"In other words, if he had been there, you would have participated enthusiastically, right?" asked Mother. "Who is the church worship service for?"

Carrie paused, then nodded slowly. "For God," she said, "and He is there, isn't He?"

HOW ABOUT YOU? What do you think of when you're at church? Perhaps there are things about the service you don't like and you wonder if going to church is really for you. Next Sunday, go with the idea of giving praise and worship to God instead of worrying about what you might get out of it. □ K.R.A.

TO MEMORIZE: *Enter his gates with thanksgiving and his courts with praise.* Psalm 100:4, NIV

FROM THE BIBLE:
Shout for joy to the Lord, all the earth. Worship the Lord with gladness; come before him with joyful songs. Know that the Lord is God. It is he who made us, and we are his; we are his people, the sheep of his pasture. Enter his gates with thanksgiving and his courts with praise; give thanks to him and praise his name. For the Lord is good and his love endures forever; his faithfulness continues through all generations.
Psalm 100, NIV

Worship God in church

21
Under the Bed

FROM THE BIBLE:

Don't forget to do good and to share what you have with those in need, for such sacrifices are very pleasing to him. Obey your spiritual leaders and be willing to do what they say. For their work is to watch over your souls, and God will judge them on how well they do this. Give them reason to report joyfully about you to the Lord and not with sorrow, for then you will suffer for it too.

Hebrews 13:16-17, TLB

Live honestly

SUSAN FLICKED THE dust cloth over the window sill, took another quick swipe at the bedside table, and tugged the curtains so they hung neatly. She glanced approvingly around her room. Then she saw a telltale scrap of paper sticking out from under the edge of the ruffled bedskirt. Susan slid the offending piece out of sight with her toe.

"Dear Mom," she wrote on a note pad, "I finished my room. I'm at Julie's. Love ya." She signed her name, almost unable to believe she'd done that room in less than ten minutes.

When Susan returned home, Mother greeted her with a question. "Did you really clean your room?"

"Sure, Mom," Susan replied uneasily.

"It looked fine until I looked under the bed," Mother said. "Then I wondered about your integrity."

"My what?" asked Susan.

Mother answered with a question of her own. "Just suppose I swept all the dirt and crumbs under the table, piled last month's newspapers on top of them, and pretended they weren't there. What would you think?"

"We'd all see the mess," said Susan with a laugh, "so we'd know better."

"Well, what if I covered them up so you couldn't see them?" asked Mother. "Would it be dishonest to try to persuade you that the kitchen was clean?"

"Well, I guess so," said Susan hesitantly.

"I agree." said Mother. "Hiding the mess and pretending it's all cleaned up is like telling a lie about your work. When I ask you to do something, I expect you to do a good job. It will take longer, but you'll be happier with yourself, and I'll be able to trust you to accept responsibility honestly. That's integrity."

"I'll go finish my room right now—with integrity," said Susan.

HOW ABOUT YOU? Do you always act with integrity—with honesty? See how well you can do a job, rather than how quickly you can get it done. It pleases God when you respond to authority with integrity. It means you are responding to Him. □ P.K.

TO MEMORIZE: *Judge me, O Lord, according to my righteousness, according to my integrity.* Psalm 7:8, NIV

DANNY, WHILE you were gone, Michael called," Danny's mother told him. "He wants you to call him back."

Danny went to phone his friend. There was no answer. Then he remembered that Michael was out of town for the weekend. "Are you sure it was Michael *Burk?*" he asked.

"Oh, no, it was Michael *White,*" said Mother.

Just then Danny's older sister burst into the room. "Guess what! I'm finally going out with Michael!"

Danny and Mother looked at each other and burst out laughing. "*Which* Michael?" they said together.

That night, Danny looked at his list of prayer requests. One name on it was that of a boy at church who needed surgery for a serious heart condition. "Dear Lord, please bless Michael," Danny began. Then he paused. "You know, the one who needs heart surgery."

Suddenly, Danny thought about how many Michaels there were in the world and how many Dannys. There must be plenty of Joes and Janes and Pauls, too. Danny had always thought of God as his personal friend, but suddenly he felt small and unimportant and lonely.

A few days later, Dad, who was a doctor, called from the hospital. "Michael had his surgery today, and he's doing fine," he told Danny. "Guess what? There are three other Michaels on this floor! But don't worry. *Our* Michael's mother is the head nurse on this floor. Believe me, she knows which Michael belongs to her."

When Danny prayed for his friend that night, he knew he didn't have to remind God which Michael was being prayed for, or which Danny was doing the asking. Just as a mother knows her son, God knows each of His children.

HOW ABOUT YOU? Do you think God ever gets tired of caring for so many people? Do you ever wonder if He is too busy to hear your requests, fears, or problems? Don't worry! God knows each of His children, and each one is special to Him. □ C.R.

TO MEMORIZE: *Fear not, for I have redeemed you; I have summoned you by name; you are mine.* Isaiah 43:1, NIV

Too Many Michaels

FROM THE BIBLE:
O Lord our God, the majesty and glory of your name fills all the earth and overflows the heavens. You have taught the little children to praise you perfectly. May their example shame and silence your enemies! When I look up into the night skies and see the work of your fingers—the moon and the stars you have made: I cannot understand how you can bother with mere puny man, to pay any attention to him! And yet you have made him only a little lower than the angels, and placed a crown of glory and honor upon his head. You have put him in charge of everything you made; everything is put under his authority: all sheep and oxen, and wild animals too, the birds and fish, and all the life in the sea. O Jehovah, our Lord, the majesty and glory of your name fills the earth.
Psalm 8, TLB

God knows you

23

The Worst Pain of All

FROM THE BIBLE:

We have confidence before God and receive from him anything we ask, because we obey his commands and do what pleases him. And this is his command: to believe in the name of his Son, Jesus Christ, and to love one another as he commanded us. Those who obey his commands live in him, and he in them. And this is how we know that he lives in us: We know it by the Spirit he gave us.
1 John 3:21-24, NIV

Love others for Jesus' sake

ERIC SAVAGELY kicked a stone, sending it flying along the sidewalk. He heard someone coming up behind him and turned. It was Doug, one of the few people in his class at school who didn't make fun of Eric's bald head. "What's wrong?" Doug asked when he saw how upset Eric looked.

"Oh, not much," mumbled Eric. "It's just that the kids have been making fun of me again."

"Does having leukemia make your hair fall out?" Doug asked cautiously.

Eric shook his head. "That's caused by the treatments I have to take," he explained. He bit his lip, struggling not to show how much the teasing hurt. "Thanks for never teasing me, Doug," he added.

"Oh, that's all right," smiled Doug. "Want to come over and play with my race car set? You can call your mom from my house."

After getting permission from his mother, Eric followed Doug to the basement. As his little car sped around the track, Doug asked, "Does it hurt to have leukemia?"

"Some of the tests hurt, and the treatment makes me feel sick to my stomach. But for me, the worst part is that my hair falls out," said Eric, stopping his car. "I feel so ugly, and the teasing just makes it worse. If it weren't for you not joining them, I think I'd give up. How come you don't tease like the others?"

"Because Jesus wouldn't want me to," Doug said. "It's that simple."

"Wish the other kids knew more about Jesus then," said Eric. "I don't know much about Him, either."

Doug smiled. "Let's go upstairs and have some cookies and milk, and I'll tell you more about Him," he said.

HOW ABOUT YOU? Do you know someone who is teased because he or she looks different? You can make life easier for that person by refusing to join in teasing. It's a powerful witness to Jesus in your life when you refuse to join in cruelty. □ C.Y.

TO MEMORIZE: *This is his command: to believe in the name of his Son, Jesus Christ, and to love one another as he commanded us.* 1 John 3:23, NIV

As MIKE CLEANED his bike, his father was listening to a preacher on the radio. Mike heard snatches of the message—something about a very important book God keeps, called the "Book of Life." The preacher said that only people whose names were written in the book would be allowed in heaven. Mike wanted to be sure his name was there, so he decided he'd be very good.

When Mike started to tease his little sister later that day, he thought about that "Book of Life," and so he gave Susie a ride on his bike instead. He also took out the garbage without being asked, and he didn't fuss when his mother said he couldn't have a cookie so close to supper.

Mike made a list of all the good things he had done and showed it to his Sunday school teacher. "Do you think God will write my name in His book now?" he asked.

Miss Lewis put her arm around Mike. "Let me ask you something," she said. "Do you think I should write down your name as one of the winners in our Bible-Reading Rally because you have done all these good things?"

Mike looked puzzled as he shook his head. "I didn't read enough chapters yet," he said.

Miss Lewis nodded. "That's right," she agreed. "You have to meet the requirement to be a winner. It's that you read the assigned chapters, not that you be good. In the same way, you must meet God's requirement to get your name in His book— and it's not that you be good, either."

"Really?" Mike's spirits fell.

"God's requirement is that you trust Jesus to be your Savior. God knew that no one could ever be good enough to go to heaven," explained Miss Lewis. "We're all sinners, and heaven is a perfect place."

As they talked about it, Mike realized for the first time that He really was not good and that He needed Jesus to take his sins away. Mike bowed his head right there and told God how sorry he was that he had sinned, and he asked Jesus to come into his life. In his mind's eye, he could see Jesus writing in a big book in heaven: "Mike Roberts."

HOW ABOUT YOU? Is your name written in the Book of Life? If not, receive Jesus as your Savior. Then thank Him for writing your name in His book and preparing a place for you in heaven. □ M.N.

TO MEMORIZE: *Rejoice that your names are written in heaven.* Luke 10:20, NIV

The Important Book

FROM THE BIBLE:
The twelve gates were made of pearls—each gate from a single pearl! And the main street was pure, transparent gold, like glass. No temple could be seen in the city, for the Lord God Almighty and the Lamb are worshiped in it everywhere. And the city has no need of sun or moon to light it, for the glory of God and of the Lamb illuminate it. Its light will light the nations of the earth, and the rulers of the world will come and bring their glory to it. Its gates never close; they stay open all day long—and there is no night! And the glory and honor of all the nations shall be brought into it. Nothing evil will be permitted in it—no one immoral or dishonest—but only those whose names are written in the Lamb's Book of Life.
Revelation 21:21-27, TLB

Have your name written in heaven

25

The Stone Bracelet

FROM THE BIBLE:
Since we have been justified through faith, we have peace with God through our Lord Jesus Christ, through whom we have gained access by faith into this grace in which we now stand. And we rejoice in the hope of the glory of God. Not only so, but we also rejoice in our sufferings, because we know that suffering produces perseverance; perseverance, character; and character, hope. And hope does not disappoint us, because God has poured out his love into our hearts by the Holy Spirit, whom he has given us.
Romans 5:1-5, NIV

Learn from problems

"MOM! KAITLYN'S GOING to move in three weeks!" Abbie sat down looking very mournful. "Why does everything have to go wrong? First my kitten disappeared, then I ruined my favorite blouse, and now this."

"I'm sorry, Honey," soothed Mother. "Can you trust God to teach you through these things He's allowed to happen?"

"I don't want to learn," mumbled Abbie.

Mother looked at Abbie thoughtfully and then left the room. Soon she returned, carrying a box. "These are some stones your father and I picked up long ago when we were on a trip to the Black Hills," said Mother. "I thought maybe you'd be willing to trade your new bracelet for these."

Abbie looked at her bracelet, which was made of polished stones, and shook her head. "Why would I do that?" she asked. "The stones in this box are rough and dull and dirty. Mine are smooth and shiny. What are you getting at, Mom?"

Mother smiled. "Well," she said, "when we brought these home long ago, we intended to have them polished and made into jewelry, but we never got around to it. So they've just been lying around, enjoying an easy life. Now those used in your bracelet have been tumbled around with sand and other stones. The rough edges have been ground off, and they've been rubbed until they shine." Mother paused, then added, "Our lives are something like that. When difficult circumstances come to us, some of the rough edges get polished off. We learn lessons from our troubles. Although we may not like what's happening, we become more like Christ as we allow Him to 'polish' us."

"I don't see how," mumbled Abbie.

"Perhaps losing Whiskers helps you understand how others feel when they lose someone they love," suggested Mother. "I believe that ruining your blouse has taught you to be careful. Having your best friend move may help you be more friendly to children who don't have a best friend. Those things will make you a better person."

HOW ABOUT YOU? Do you feel like you're being bumped around by circumstances? Maybe the Lord wants to polish off a few more rough edges. What lesson can you learn from what is happening in your life? Thank God for patiently polishing you and making you more like Him. □ H.M.

TO MEMORIZE: *Not only so, but we also rejoice in our sufferings, because we know that suffering produces perseverance.* Romans 5:3, NIV

26

The X Ray

BILLY'S MOTHER TOOK him to the dentist for a checkup. Billy hopped up into the chair, leaned his head back, and opened his mouth wide so the dentist could examine his teeth. "Good," said the dentist after gently examining Billy's mouth with his special instruments. "I see only one small cavity. Now I'm going to take an X ray of your teeth, Billy."

"But why?" Billy asked.

"I want to see if it will show any problems that I can't see with my eyes alone," the dentist explained. "Now hold very still for the X ray, Billy, so the picture will be clear."

The X ray showed that Billy had one more cavity, and his mother made an appointment to have them filled. "I don't see why the dentist had to take that X ray," grumbled Billy on the way home. "Now I have to have two cavities filled instead of just one!"

"That's true," agreed Mom, "but on the other hand, it would have shown up some day in the future. By then it would have gotten much bigger, and you'd need a big filling instead of just a little one. So you see, it's a good thing he found it now."

That evening Billy told his Dad about the X ray and the cavities. "X rays can be a big help," said Dad. "In a way this reminds me of the Bible."

"How?" asked Billy, surprised.

"Well," replied Dad, "when we read God's Word, He uses it to examine our hearts—deep inside where we can't see. The Bible is given for 'doctrine, reproof, correction, and instruction in righteousness.' That means the Bible will point out sin in our lives. When we recognize our sin, we can go to God and ask for His forgiveness. He will take away our sin and help us forsake it with His power."

"Yeah," said Billy. "I'm glad God gave us the Bible—and dentists, too. I'll try to obey their instructions."

HOW ABOUT YOU? Do you read the Bible to see what it has to say to you? Is there a sin to avoid? Is there a commandment to obey? A lesson to learn? Study the Bible for your profit! □ J.H.

TO MEMORIZE: *For the word of God is living and active.* Hebrews 4:12, NIV

FROM THE BIBLE:

You must keep on believing the things you have been taught. You know they are true for you know that you can trust those of us who have taught you. You know how, when you were a small child, you were taught the holy Scriptures; and it is these that make you wise to accept God's salvation by trusting in Christ Jesus. The whole Bible was given to us by inspiration from God and is useful to teach us what is true and to make us realize what is wrong in our lives; it straightens us out and helps us do what is right. It is God's way of making us well prepared at every point, fully equipped to do good to everyone. 2 Timothy 3:14-17, TLB

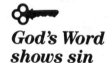

God's Word shows sin

27

Ten Feet Tall

FROM THE BIBLE:

Samuel did what the Lord said. When he arrived at Bethlehem, . . . he consecrated Jesse and his sons and invited them to the sacrifice. When they arrived, Samuel saw Eliab and thought, "Surely the Lord's anointed stands here before the Lord." But the Lord said to Samuel, "Do not consider his appearance or his height, for I have rejected him. The Lord does not look at the things man looks at. Man looks at the outward appearance, but the Lord looks at the heart." . . . Jesse had seven of his sons pass before Samuel, but Samuel said to him, "The Lord has not chosen these." So he asked Jesse, "Are these all the sons you have?" "There is still the youngest," Jesse answered, "but he is tending the sheep." Samuel said, "Send for him; we will not sit down until he arrives." So he sent and had him brought in. He was ruddy, with a fine appearance and handsome features. Then the Lord said, "Rise and anoint him; he is the one."

1 Samuel 16:4-13, NIV

Inner beauty counts

"MOTHER, WHY AM I so little?" asked Todd. He put down his pencil and scowled in disgust at his small hands.

"Well, Todd, you're only ten," his mother called from the kitchen. "You've got a lot of growing to do yet."

"I know, Mom, but while I'm growing, all my friends will be growing, too. They'll always be bigger than I am!" Todd grumbled. "Whenever we play baseball or football or anything, I'm the worst. I always get knocked over because I'm so small. Nobody ever wants me on their team."

"So you think that God made a mistake when He made you," observed Mother.

"Mother!" exclaimed Todd. "I never said anything like that!"

"Didn't you?" asked Mother. "You just said you didn't like being small. Isn't that the same as saying that God didn't make you to your liking?"

"Well," said Todd thoughtfully, "I hadn't thought about it that way."

"You should never be ashamed of the way you're made, Todd. God made you the way you are for a reason, and He loves you just as you are. It's how you look on the inside that counts, not the outside."

Todd sighed. "I suppose you're right, Mom." Suddenly he grinned. "I'll give up trying to be big on the outside and start trying to be big on the inside."

"How will you do that?" asked Mother, puzzled.

"I can work hard in school and get good grades." explained Todd. "And I can learn Bible verses and Bible stories so I'll know more about God, too."

"Todd," said Mother, smiling, "You've already got a good start on being grown up. And don't forget that your dad and I will always love you, no matter how small you are."

"Small?" said Todd. "Right now I feel about ten feet tall!"

HOW ABOUT YOU? Have you ever wished you were taller? Or prettier? Or had brown eyes instead of green or blue? God made you the way you are because He wanted you that way. He never makes mistakes. Don't worry so much about how you look on the outside. Work on growing and being beautiful on the inside. □ D.M.

TO MEMORIZE: *The Lord does not look at the things man looks at. Man looks at the outward appearance, but the Lord looks at the heart.* 1 Samuel 16:7, NIV

"WHAT ARE YOU doing, Mom?" asked Ann curiously.

Mother looked up from the paper she was studying. "I'm trying to organize our family tree, to figure out who our ancestors were," she answered. "I have records about our relatives back to the mid 1800s, but I can't seem to get any information from before that time."

"Is it important?" Ann wanted to know.

"Well, Ann, I guess it's more interesting than important," replied Mother. "I like knowing our heritage—what the men and women were like, and what they did for a living. For instance, did you know that your great-great-grandfather was governor of our state?"

"Really? That'll be something to tell in history class!" Ann was impressed. "What other kinds of things did our ancestors do?"

"Well," said Mother with a twinkle in her eye, "your great-great-great-Uncle Thaddeus was arrested for stealing pumpkins from a neighbor's farm."

"Wow," laughed Ann, "looking at our family tree is fun!"

"There's another family tree that's interesting," said Mother. "Do you remember the Bible story of Ruth?"

Ann nodded. "Sure. Ruth followed her mother-in-law from Moab to Bethlehem. It was a strange country to Ruth, and they were poor, but God worked things out for her, and she married Boaz."

"Good," approved Mother, "and Ruth and Boaz had a son named Obed. He was King David's grandfather." Ann looked a little puzzled, and Mother asked, "Can you think of the reason why that's important?"

Ann thought it over. Suddenly she smiled. "Oh, I know!" she exclaimed. "The Lord Jesus was born of the line of David, wasn't He? So Ruth and Boaz were part of Jesus' human family tree!" Mother smiled in agreement.

HOW ABOUT YOU? Have you ever read parts of the Bible that just list one name after another? Maybe you've thought it was boring to hear who "begat" whom, but historians find important information in these lists. Sometimes they contain information that's interesting even for boys and girls, as in today's Scripture passage. □ L.W.

TO MEMORIZE: *How sweet are your words to my taste, sweeter than honey to my mouth!* Psalm 119:103, NIV

FROM THE BIBLE:

Boaz took Ruth and she became his wife; and when he went in to her, the Lord gave her conception, and she bore a son. Then the women said to Naomi, "Blessed be the Lord, who has not left you this day without a near kinsman; and may his name be famous in Israel! And may he be to you a restorer of life and a nourisher of your old age; for your daughter-in-law, who loves you, who is better to you than seven sons, has borne him." Then Naomi took the child and laid him on her bosom, and became a nurse to him. Also the neighbor women gave him a name, saying, "There is a son born to Naomi." And they called his name Obed. He is the father of Jesse, the father of David. Now this is the genealogy of Perez: Perez begot Hezron; Hezron begot Ram, and Ram begot Amminadab; Amminadab begot Nahshon, and Nahshon begot Salmon; Salmon begot Boaz, and Boaz begot Obed; Obed begot Jesse, and Jesse begot David. Ruth 4:13-22, NKJV

Genealogies are important

29

Immunized!

FROM THE BIBLE:

If you tell others with your own mouth that Jesus Christ is your Lord, and believe in your own heart that God has raised him from the dead, you will be saved. For it is by believing in his heart that a man becomes right with God; and with his mouth he tells others of his faith, confirming his salvation. For the Scriptures tell us that no one who believes in Christ will ever be disappointed. Jew and Gentile are the same in this respect: they all have the same Lord who generously gives his riches to all those who ask him for them. Anyone who calls upon the name of the Lord will be saved.
Romans 10:9-13, TLB

Religion is not enough

RICKY SQUIRMED as the needle went into his arm. "Ow! that hurts!" he yelled. "Wish I didn't have to get these dumb old shots!"

"Oh, but they're very important," said the nurse as she wiped off the spot with cotton and applied a small bandage. "If you didn't get them, you might get a serious illness that could cripple you or even cost you your life. An immunization will protect you for years to come."

"They must use really strong medicine in those shots for it to last so long," observed Ricky.

The nurse smiled. "There's really no medicine at all in these shots," she said. "What we're putting into your body is a form of the germ that causes the disease."

Ricky gasped. "But that'll make me get sick!"

"No," said the nurse, "because what we put into you are weak, sickly germs which your body easily fights off. In doing so, it produces special weapons called antibodies. These continue to float through your bloodstream, fighting off new germs that try to get into your body. It's really a very good defense system."

During devotions that evening, Dad told the family about a conversation he had had with his boss. "Mr. Harper is a fine man," said Dad, "but he feels that he's all right just because he goes to church and listens to Christian music and mentions God's name occasionally. It's almost as if his religion acts like a shot to dull his senses to his needs."

Ricky's eyes lit up. "I got a shot today," he said, and he told his parents what the nurse had said. "I think Mr. Harper got 'immunized' in the wrong way," finished Ricky.

"I think you've given us an excellent illustration," nodded Dad. "A weak, halfhearted form of religion often seems to be enough to 'immunize' people against the real thing."

HOW ABOUT YOU? Do you think that doing religious things is enough to make you right with God? That's not true! You must come to Christ in repentance and allow His blood to wash away your sins. Simply being "religious" will never save you. Only Christ can do that. □ S.K.

TO MEMORIZE: *Having a form of godliness but denying its power.* 2 Timothy 3:5, NIV

JASON WHISTLED AS he rang the door bell of the big house on the hill.

"Hey! What do you want?" The door was jerked open, and Mr. Atkins stood there frowning.

"I'm Jason Parker, your new paper boy," Jason replied. "I'd like to collect for the paper, please. It's five dollars."

"I know how much it is! It's *too* much!" the old man snapped. "And I suppose you expect a tip for putting it on the porch. Well, you aren't going to get it!"

Jason stood quietly as Mr. Atkins counted out the exact amount. "Thank you, Sir," Jason said. The old man just slammed the door.

Jason wasn't whistling when he knocked on the door of the little house where Miss Patterson lived. "Yes? Oh, it's the new paper boy." A sweet voice came from a wrinkled face. "Just a minute. I'll get your money." Soon she was back with the money and a plastic bag. "I do so appreciate having the paper put on my porch. I'd like to give you a tip, but I don't have any extra money this month. However, I do have some homemade cookies."

Later Jason told his mother about Mr. Atkins. "Poor old man," was her response.

"Poor?" Jason snorted. "He's the richest man in town!"

"He's also one of the poorest men in town," replied Mother. "He was determined to make lots of money, and he did. But in the process, he turned his back on God and on his friends."

When Jason told his mother about Miss Patterson, she smiled. "Everyone loves her. She may not have much money, but she's what the Bible would call 'rich in good works.' She's also rich in friends. She's a good example of the way Christians ought to love and care for others."

"So Mr. Atkins is a poor rich man, and Miss Patterson is a rich poor lady," Jason reasoned.

HOW ABOUT YOU? Do you want to be rich? There's nothing wrong with having money if God has provided it, but a strong desire for lots of money is dangerous. Don't make the mistake of thinking money brings happiness. There is a better kind of "riches." Invest your time and efforts in making friends, in helping others, and in serving the Lord. □ B.W.

TO MEMORIZE: *Command them to do good, to be rich in good deeds, and to be generous and willing to share.* 1 Timothy 6:18, NIV

The Poor Rich Man

FROM THE BIBLE:
People who want to get rich fall into temptation and a trap and into many foolish and harmful desires that plunge men into ruin and destruction. For the love of money is a root of all kinds of evil. Some people, eager for money, have wandered from the faith and pierced themselves with many griefs. But you, man of God, flee from all this, and pursue righteousness, godliness, faith, love, endurance and gentleness. . . . Command those who are rich in this present world not to be arrogant nor to put their hope in wealth, which is so uncertain, but to put their hope in God, who richly provides us with everything for our enjoyment. Command them to do good, to be rich in good deeds, and to be generous and willing to share.

1 Timothy 6:9-18, NIV

Money doesn't bring happiness

1

The Sun Still Shines

FROM THE BIBLE:

Don't be weary in prayer; keep at it; watch for God's answers and remember to be thankful when they come. Don't forget to pray for us too, that God will give us many chances to preach the Good News of Christ for which I am here in jail. Pray that I will be bold enough to tell it freely and fully, and make it plain, as, of course, I should. Make the most of your chances to tell others the Good News. Be wise in all your contacts with them. Let your conversation be gracious as well as sensible, for then you will have the right answer for everyone.
Colossians 4:2-6, TLB

Be ready to witness

VIC MET HIS friend Matt before school one day. "Guess what my aunt gave me for my birthday!" exclaimed Matt scornfully. "A Bible! What would I want with a Bible?"

"You could read it," suggested Vic, who was a Christian.

"You've got to be kidding!" exclaimed Matt. "I could never understand it. I'm just an ordinary guy. Give me one good reason why I should read it."

"Well . . . well . . . the Bible tells us how to . . . uh . . . how to live," stammered Vic. He knew he should use this opportunity to witness to Matt, but he just couldn't think of what to say.

"How to live?" echoed Matt. "Man, I know how to live! Besides, how could an old book, written thousands of years ago, tell me how to live? Why, the Bible was written before there were cars or planes or telephones. It's an old-fashioned, outdated book. It's got to be."

"No, it isn't," disagreed Vic. "It's more up-to-date than the morning newspaper. My dad said so."

"Yeah? Well, my dad says it's old-fashioned. These are modern times! Besides, we can't understand it anyway, so I don't see how it could affect our lives. Hey, there's the bell. Let's run, or we'll be late!"

That evening, Vic told his dad what had happened. "I flubbed it," he confessed. "I was taken by surprise and couldn't think of a good answer."

"That's too bad," Dad said. "The Bible says we should always be ready to give an answer concerning our faith. You be sure to do your 'spiritual homework.' Study God's Word, meditate on it, pray each day—and I'll pray with you, that you may have another opportunity to witness to Matt. When that opportunity comes, speak, and God will give you the right words to use."

HOW ABOUT YOU? Are you ever caught off guard, so that you're not prepared to witness? Do you sometimes keep quiet when you know you should speak, because you just can't think of what to say? Read God's Word every day, talk with Him, and as opportunities come, do speak up, trusting God to use the words He gives you for His glory. He will do it. □ B.W.

TO MEMORIZE: *Always be prepared to give an answer to everyone who asks you to give the reason for the hope that you have.* 1 Peter 3:15, NIV

MATT'S UNCLE WAS building a new home, one with a solar energy system. With his uncle's permission, Matt invited Vic to go along to look it over. "Whew! Quite a layout," whistled Vic when he saw the house.

"Yeah! Look at that solar power unit!" answered Matt. "Most of the power for heating and cooling will come from the sun. That old sun's been around a long time. I wonder why men are just now thinking about using it for energy."

Suddenly Vic recalled their conversation about the Bible the day before, and he had an idea. "Using the sun for heating and cooling sounds silly to me!" he declared. "Like you said, the sun has been around a long, long time—it's so old, it's outdated. Something that old can't have much effect on my life. Your uncle should use something more modern and up-to-date."

"Have you gone bananas?" exclaimed Matt. "Solar energy is the most modern thing going."

"Yeah? What do you know about solar energy?" asked Vic. "What's that thing?" He pointed to a piece of equipment. "And that one?"

"Aw, Vic, I don't understand all about it," Matt admitted.

"There you go," Vic told him. "You don't understand solar energy, but you believe it. The sun is as old as creation, but you still believe it's useful." Vic paused a moment, then added, "If the old sun is useful and powerful even though you don't understand it, why can't that be true of the Bible, too?"

"Well. . . I. . ." stammered Matt in surprise.

"Besides, you've never tried to understand the Bible," Vic continued. "You need to read and study it and ask God to help you. The Bible can affect your life even more than the sun does."

Matt looked startled. "How do you know?" he asked.

"The Bible says so," answered Vic. "If you'd read it, you'd learn lots of things."

HOW ABOUT YOU? Have you felt that the Bible is outdated? The things it teaches are just as appropriate today as when they were first written down. Read it daily. It teaches many things (such as love, kindness, honesty, obedience) that you need in your daily life. Best of all, it teaches you how to get to heaven. □ B.W.

TO MEMORIZE: *Heaven and earth will pass away, but my word will never pass away.* Mark 13:31, NIV

FROM THE BIBLE:
You have a new life. It was not passed on to you from your parents, for the life they gave you will fade away. This new one will last forever, for it comes from Christ, God's ever-living Message to men. Yes, our natural lives will fade as grass does when it becomes all brown and dry. All our greatness is like a flower that droops and falls; but the Word of the Lord will last forever. And his message is the Good News that was preached to you.
1 Peter 1:23-25, TLB

The Bible is for today

3

The Prowler

FROM THE BIBLE:

Look upon your old sin nature as dead and unresponsive to sin, and instead be alive to God, alert to him, through Jesus Christ our Lord. Do not let sin control your puny body any longer; do not give in to its sinful desires. Do not let any part of your bodies become tools of wickedness, to be used for sinning; but give yourselves completely to God—every part of you—for you are back from death and you want to be tools in the hands of God, to be used for his good purposes. Sin need never again be your master, for now you are no longer tied to the law where sin enslaves you, but you are free under God's favor and mercy.

Romans 6:11-14, TLB

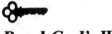

Read God's Word

DOUG SAT UP in bed with a start. Something woke him up. What was it? The floor creaked downstairs. Was somebody down there? Maybe he was just imagining things. Then he heard drawers opening and closing. Doug was scared now. He tiptoed across the hall and knocked lightly on his parents' bedroom door. "Dad! Dad!" he whispered.

Dad stumbled to the door. "Doug! It's the middle of the night," Dad began.

"I know," Doug replied, "but there's a prowler downstairs." Just then the outside doorknob clicked.

"Stay here," Dad cautioned, "and I'll investigate." Slowly he sneaked down the stairs. The outside door was open, and Dad tiptoed outside. He saw a shadow by the tree. Someone was walking away with a brown bag in his hand. Dad went after him, caught him, and then led him into the house and up the stairs.

"Doug, here's your prowler," Dad said. "Your brother Randy has been walking in his sleep. Go to bed now."

"I can't believe I could walk in my sleep last night and not know what I was doing," Randy said the next morning.

"You did," laughed Doug. "You looked funny. You were walking barefoot in the snow carrying a lunch."

"That's right," Dad said. "I guess you were on your way to school." Then his smile turned to a thoughtful gaze. "You know, Randy's walking in his sleep is sort of like sinners walking through life. They're moving along, going through the motions of living, but they're dead in their sins, unaware that they face eternal death without Christ. Going through the motions of living doesn't give eternal life. Only Christ can do that. We must wake them up with the truth of the gospel."

HOW ABOUT YOU? Do you go through the motions of being a Christian—being good, attending church, praying, reading your Bible—yet you have never trusted Christ as your own personal Savior? Going through the motions won't save you from your sins, but accepting Christ will. □ J.H.

TO MEMORIZE: *If one walks in the night, he stumbles, because the light is not in him.* John 11:10, NKJV

MARYANN SAT in her usual place in Sunday school, but she was not comfortable. Last week someone had suggested they organize a "Good Samaritan Club." To become a member, a person had to do something special for someone else. Now it was report time, and Maryann had nothing to report.

James was the first to tell what he had done. "On my way home from school I saw an old man trying to shovel the snow off his walk, so I did it for him."

Then it was Brenda's turn. "Our neighbor is in the hospital. Since she doesn't have any relatives living in this area, I decided to visit her."

Mrs. Peters, the teacher, nodded at both James and Brenda. "I'd say they deserve to become members of the Good Samaritan Club, wouldn't you?" Everyone agreed.

"Does anyone else have a report?" Mrs. Peters asked. "Maryann, did you do something special?"

Maryann shook her head, somewhat embarrassed. "I couldn't go any place," she replied. "My mother was sick in bed all week."

Mrs. Peters smiled sympathetically. "Oh, that's too bad! Who took care of your brother and made meals?"

"I did," Maryann said. "We didn't have very big meals. I just made sandwiches and salads and things like that."

Mrs. Peter nodded. "And did you stack the dishes in the sink?"

"Oh, no," Maryann replied. "I washed and wiped them. It didn't take long."

Mrs. Peters looked around. "All in favor of making Maryann a member of the Good Samaritan Club, raise your hand." Each one raised his hand. "The things you did, Maryann, were every bit as important as those done by the others," added Mrs. Peters. "You helped in the hardest place of all—home."

HOW ABOUT YOU? Is it more fun to help a neighbor or a friend than to help at home? Both kinds of help are needed. Think of ways you can be a "good samaritan" at home. There are many ways to help. Will you do it? □ R.J.

TO MEMORIZE: *Whatever you did for one of the least of these brothers of mine, you did for me.* Matthew 25:40, NIV

A Good, Good Samaritan

FROM THE BIBLE:
Jesus replied with an illustration: "A Jew going on a trip from Jerusalem to Jericho was attacked by bandits. They stripped him of his clothes and money and beat him up and left him lying half dead beside the road. By chance a Jewish priest came along; and when he saw the man lying there, he crossed to the other side of the road and passed him by. A Jewish Temple-assistant walked over and looked at him lying there, but then went on. But a despised Samaritan came along, and when he saw him, he felt deep pity. Kneeling beside him the Samaritan soothed his wounds with medicine and bandaged them. Then he put the man on his donkey and walked along beside him till they came to an inn, where he nursed him through the night. . . . Now which of these three would you say was a neighbor to the bandits' victim?" The man replied, "The one who showed him some pity." Then Jesus said, "Yes, now go and do the same."
Luke 10:30-37, TLB

Help at home

DECEMBER

5

A Mighty Weapon

FROM THE BIBLE:
Oh, how I love them [God's laws]. I think about them all day long. They make me wiser than my enemies, because they are my constant guide. Yes, wiser than my teachers, for I am ever thinking of your rules. They make me even wiser than the aged. I have refused to walk the paths of evil for I will remain obedient to your Word. No, I haven't turned away from what you taught me; your words are sweeter than honey. And since only your rules can give me wisdom and understanding, no wonder I hate every false teaching.
Psalm 119:97-104, TLB

Read God's Word

PHIL AND PENNY went to visit Gramps, who was well-known for quoting Scripture. "How do you remember so much?" Phil asked. "Penny and I learn a lot of verses for Bible club, but it's so hard to remember them all."

Gramps smiled. "Do you know your phone number?" he asked. "And what about your locker combination or your house number? Aren't those hard to remember?"

Phil shook his head. "They're easy 'cuz I use them a lot."

"Well," replied Gramps, "it's like that with the Word of God. We remember what's important to us—and what we use a lot." He sniffed the air. "Hey," he continued, "if my sniffer is still working, I smell fresh bread!"

Penny nodded. "Right! Mom sent this loaf for you."

"That was kind of her," said Gramps. Taking the bread, he set it on the table, next to the lamp. "It looks good there, don't you think?" he asked.

The children protested. "But Gramps, if you let it just sit there, it won't do you any good."

Gramps looked surprised. "What should I do with it?"

"Why, eat it, of course," Penny replied.

"I agree," Gramps told them, "but I was trying to teach you something. Just as we need bread or food each day for our bodies, so we need the Word of God each day for our souls. Bread doesn't do any good on the table, and God's Word doesn't do any good on the book shelf! We need to taste it by reading it, and digest it by memorizing it. We need to get it into our hearts so it can work in our lives." He picked up the loaf. "Thank your mother for this bread, and keep on learning your verses."

HOW ABOUT YOU? Where is your spiritual "bread"? Are you letting it just lie on the table, or are you "eating" it? □ J.H.

TO MEMORIZE: *Man shall not live by bread alone, but by every word that proceeds from the mouth of God.* Matthew 4:4, NKJV

NANCY RUSHED INTO the house. "Oh, Mother, Barbie has a new baby sister!" she exclaimed. "Her name is Tracy, and she's so cute!" Nancy was breathless. "Mother, how do people know what to name their babies?"

"Well," answered Mother, "some babies are named for a member of the family or for a person the parents like. And sometimes a name is chosen because of its meaning."

Nancy was surprised. "Names have meanings?"

"Some do," said Mother. "For instance, 'John' means 'God is gracious.' I have a book that tells the meaning of many names."

Nancy was fascinated. She took the book out on the front steps to look up the names of her friends. As she read, her pastor came along and asked about the book. "Names are interesting," said Pastor White after she explained. "Did you know the Bible says, 'A good name is rather to be chosen than great riches'?"

"But we don't choose our own names, Pastor White," protested Nancy.

Pastor White smiled. "No matter what we are named," he answered, "we can have a good name. Do you remember the Bible story of Dorcas?"

"Oh, yes," replied Nancy. "She did sewing for the poor people. Does the name 'Dorcas' have a meaning?"

"Yes," nodded Pastor White. "It means 'gazelle.' But do you think people thought of a gazelle when they thought of Dorcas?"

"No," said Nancy slowly, "they probably thought of all the nice things Dorcas did for them. Oh! I get it! A good name is like a good reputation—what you're known for."

"That's right," said Pastor White. "Your name should be well spoken of. Since you have accepted Jesus as Savior, you also have Christ's name— Christian. God wants you to live in a way that honors that name."

"Oh, that's right!" exclaimed Nancy. "If I do that, I'll always keep my good name."

HOW ABOUT YOU? Do you have the name "Christian"? You do if you've asked Jesus to be your Savior. Each day ask Him to help you do everything in a way that honors Him, and then you will truly have a good name. □ A.L.

TO MEMORIZE: *Whatever you do, whether in word or deed, do it all in the name of the Lord Jesus, giving thanks to God the Father through him.* Colossians 3:17, NIV

DECEMBER

What's In a Name?

FROM THE BIBLE:
In the city of Joppa there was a woman named Dorcas ("Gazelle"), a believer who was always doing kind things for others, especially for the poor. About this time she became ill and died. Her friends prepared her for burial and laid her in an upstairs room. But when they learned that Peter was nearby at Lydda, they sent two men to beg him to return with them to Joppa. This he did; as soon as he arrived, they took him upstairs where Dorcas lay. The room was filled with weeping widows who were showing one another the coats and other garments Dorcas had made for them. But Peter asked them all to leave the room; then he knelt and prayed. Turning to the body he said, "Get up, Dorcas," and she opened her eyes! And when she saw Peter, she sat up! He gave her his hand and helped her up and called in the believers and widows, presenting her to them. The news raced through the town, and many believed in the Lord.
Acts 9:36-42, TLB

Honor God's name

DECEMBER

7

Not Too Cold

FROM THE BIBLE:
Since we have confidence to enter the Most Holy Place by the blood of Jesus, by a new and living way opened for us through the curtain, that is, his body, and since we have a great priest over the house of God, let us draw near to God with a sincere heart in full assurance of faith, having our hearts sprinkled to cleanse us from a guilty conscience and having our bodies washed with pure water. Let us hold unswervingly to the hope we profess, for he who promised is faithful. And let us consider how we may spur one another on toward love and good deeds. Let us not give up meeting together, as some are in the habit of doing, but let us encourage one another—and all the more as you see the Day approaching.
Hebrews 10:19-25, NIV

Attend church regularly

IT'S SO COLD out," Tom said as he looked out the front window. "Do we really have to go to youth choir and church tonight? Can't we just stay home and keep warm?"

Dad smiled. "I don't think going to church will be that much of a sacrifice, Son. The car's warm, and the church is warm."

"Mike's not going," Tom said. "I just talked to him on the phone. He says he might get sick if he goes out in such cold weather. I don't want to catch a cold, either."

"How come you guys weren't worried about getting sick yesterday when you were at the hockey rink all afternoon?" asked Terry, Tom's older brother.

"It wasn't as cold yesterday," replied Tom weakly.

"It was almost as cold." Terry flipped on the TV. "Hey, look at this!"

The family turned toward the TV screen and saw a football game in progress. Snow was blowing across the field, but the people were still there, huddled together and cheering for their team.

"It's interesting," commented Dad, "that thousands of people will sit for hours in bad weather watching a football game, yet they'll use the same weather as an excuse for not attending church. Satan is delighted at how quickly people can find reasons for not learning more about the Lord. God's Word plainly tells us that we are not to 'forsake the assembling of ourselves together.' We need Christian fellowship as well as the study of God's Word."

"I see what you mean, Dad," Tom agreed. "Saying it's too cold to go to church is just a silly excuse."

HOW ABOUT YOU? Do you often think of excuses for not going to church? It's true that sometimes the weather is so bad that older people or those in poor health cannot go outside. But if you are able to go to a friend's house, to school, or to a game, don't use the excuse that it's too cold (or too hot) to go to church! You need the Christian fellowship and good Bible study that can be found there. □ L.W.

TO MEMORIZE: *Let us not give up meeting together, as some are in the habit of doing, but let us encourage one another.* Hebrews 10:25, NIV

"I PRAY TODAY," announced Ricky as the family sat around the breakfast table. Dad smiled his approval at the little boy, and they all bowed their heads. "Thank You, God, for bacon an' eggs an' milk an' toast an' flowers," said Ricky. He paused and peeked to see what else was on the table. "An' jam," he added, "Amen."

"Thank you, Ricky," said Dad. He frowned at Jesse and Suzanne, who were giggling at their little brother.

After breakfast, everyone went out to work in the yard. When it was time for lunch, Mother called them together around the picnic table. "We'll pray," she said, "and then you can all sit and relax while I grill some burgers and get the rest of the food on the table."

"I pray," announced Ricky again. Once more they all bowed their heads. "Thank You for . . ." Ricky hesitated. He paused a long moment as he looked at the table. There wasn't any food on it yet. ". . . for plates an' knives an' forks an' spoons an' cups an' napkins an' salt. Amen."

Jesse and Suzanne snickered. But Dad smiled at his younger son. "I'm glad you thanked God for all those things today," he said. "We usually take them for granted."

"That's right," agreed Mother as she got up. "Now, I don't need any help today—you've all been extra busy already. But while I get the food, maybe you can think of some other things we should remember to thank the Lord for but seldom do. You go first, Jesse."

"Uh . . ." murmured Jesse, "we should be thankful for our grill."

"Good," said Dad. "How about it, Suzanne?"

Suzanne was ready. "For pepper—Ricky forgot that."

"And for a picnic table," said Jesse.

"And picnic benches." They were really getting into the spirit of the game.

"And for a little child to teach us," added Mother with a smile. "Dig in."

HOW ABOUT YOU? Are you really thankful for everything? Look around you. How many things can you find that you take for granted day after day and never thank the Lord for? Take a few moments to thank Him right now. □ H.M.

TO MEMORIZE: *It is good to give thanks to the Lord.* Psalm 92:1, NKJV

All Things Great and Small

FROM THE BIBLE:
Shout with joy before the Lord, O earth! Obey him gladly; come before him, singing with joy. Try to realize what this means—the Lord is God! He made us—we are his people, the sheep of his pasture. Go through his open gates with great thanksgiving; enter his courts with praise. Give thanks to him and bless his name. For the Lord is always good. He is always loving and kind, and his faithfulness goes on and on to each succeeding generation.
Psalm 100, TLB

Give thanks for everything

Attic Adventure

FROM THE BIBLE:
The word of the Lord is right and true; he is faithful in all he does. The Lord loves righteousness and justice; the earth is full of his unfailing love. By the word of the Lord were the heavens made, their starry host by the breath of his mouth. He gathers the waters of the sea into jars; he puts the deep into storehouses. Let all the earth fear the Lord; let all the people of the world revere him. For he spoke, and it came to be; he commanded, and it stood firm. The Lord foils the plans of the nations; he thwarts the purposes of the peoples. But the plans of the Lord stand firm forever, the purposes of his heart through all generations. Blessed is the nation whose God is the Lord, the people he chose for his inheritance.
Psalm 33:4-12, NIV

God's ways don't change

COME ON, JENNY," called Mark. "Mom says we can play with the old clothes in the attic."

"Oh, goody!" exclaimed Jenny. "I love to wear those big hats."

The clatter of feet echoed through the house as Mark and Jenny climbed the steep steps to the attic of the old family home. Soon they had the wardrobes opened and were trying on clothes their grandmother and mother had saved through the years.

They trooped down the stairs, where they found both Mother and Dad in the kitchen. "I wore those old saddle shoes when I was a teenager," said Mother as she observed Jenny, "and that hat belonged to my great-grandmother, I believe. And Mark's old-fashioned tie is simply charming with that shirt!"

"These styles were fads once," commented Dad with a smile, "and everyone wanted them—just like there are clothes today that everyone wants."

Mother nodded. "When it comes to styles, people always seem to want the latest thing," she said. "That's not so bad unless it becomes too important in our lives."

"Yes," agreed Dad thoughtfully, "or unless we apply the principle of copying the latest fads when it comes to some of the sinful activities of the world."

"You mean sinning is a fad?" asked Mark.

"Not exactly," replied Dad, "but sometimes wrong things seem to be very popular. The world changes as far as the things it likes to do, but God's principles never change. As Christians, we need to be careful that we measure the 'in' activities against what He teaches. Right now, the world seems to be teaching, 'If it feels good, it's okay,' but that's not what God says. We must never follow immoral fads."

HOW ABOUT YOU? Do others use bad words, and you find yourself tempted to do the same? Has a friend told a lie, and you find yourself telling the same lie? Don't try to be like others when what they do is sin. Styles of clothing or behavior may change, but God's ways never change. □ G.W.

TO MEMORIZE: *The plans of the Lord stand firm forever, the purposes of his heart through all generations.* Psalm 33:11, NIV

JAN CLASPED HER hands together nervously as the plane taxied down the runway. She had always wanted to fly, and here she was—flying with her brother Don to visit their grandmother. But now she was nervous.

After they were airborne, Jan didn't relax at all. "Do the engines sound funny?" she asked several times. "Should we be flying so high? We're not going to go through clouds again, are we? What if there's another plane in the clouds? Won't we crash?"

"Why don't you go up to the cockpit and take over at the controls?" Don finally asked in disgust. "The pilot knows what he's doing. I'm having fun."

"Me, too," said Jan, but she was very glad when they were finally back on solid ground.

"Did you have a good flight?" asked Grandma.

Don nodded. "I did. But Jan was nervous as a cat. I told her she should take over for the pilot. I'm glad she didn't though, because then I'd have been nervous."

"I guess so!" exclaimed Grandma, putting an arm around Jan's shoulders. "I'm afraid we all lack trust in our Pilot from time to time."

Jan looked at Grandma in surprise. "Are you afraid of flying, too, Grandma?"

Grandma smiled. "Not really," she said. "I was thinking of how we sometimes fail to trust our Pilot through life. Do you know who I mean?"

Jan nodded. "God," she said.

"Yes," said Grandma. "Of course, the airplane pilot wouldn't have let you take over the flight, because it would have meant disaster. I'm glad God keeps control of our lives, too—it's foolish for us to try to take over."

HOW ABOUT YOU? Are you enjoying your "trip through life?" Or do you fret about things that happen over which you have no control? Trust God. Think about how much He loves you and how He knows what is best for you. □ H.M.

TO MEMORIZE: *You will keep in perfect peace him whose mind is steadfast, because he trusts in you.* Isaiah 26:3, NIV

10

Pilot in Control

FROM THE BIBLE:
Shall I look to the mountain gods for help? No! My help is from Jehovah who made the mountains! And the heavens too! He will never let me stumble, slip or fall. For he is always watching, never sleeping. Jehovah himself is caring for you! He is your defender. He protects you day and night. He keeps you from all evil, and preserves your life. He keeps his eye upon you as you come and go, and always guards you. Psalm 121, TLB

Trust God with your life

DECEMBER

11

Underground Railroad

FROM THE BIBLE:

[Jesus said,] "And you will know the truth, and the truth will set you free." "But we are descendants of Abraham," they said, "and have never been slaves to any man on earth! What do you mean, 'set free'?" Jesus replied, "You are slaves of sin, every one of you. And slaves don't have rights, but the Son has every right there is! So if the Son sets you free, you will indeed be free."

John 8:32-36, TLB

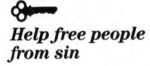

Help free people from sin

KAREN BURST through the front door. "Mom," she called, "guess what we talked about in school today? We learned all about the underground railroad. I wish I could have lived then. I would have helped lots of slaves escape."

"Are you sure?" asked Mother. "Being a part of the underground railroad was very dangerous. Some people were put in jail or even killed for what they did."

Karen thought about that for a minute. "I still would have done it, because no one should have to serve a cruel master. I wish we could go back in time so I could help."

Mother turned to her work. "You don't have to go back in time to help free slaves," she said quietly.

Karen's forehead crinkled. "What do you mean?"

"What is a person before he accepts Christ as Savior?" asked Mother.

"A sinner," Karen replied promptly.

"Exactly," said Mother, "and sin is a cruel master that enslaves people. Only Christ can set them free. I'm thankful that it isn't necessary for us to work undercover to help them, but workers are needed. You can help people escape by telling them about Jesus and what He has done."

"Like how He died on the cross and rose again?" asked Karen. She hesitated. "I guess the kids might make fun of me if I did that."

"Yes, they might," agreed Mother, "and they might try to stop you. But you must keep at it if you want to help the slaves of sin escape to freedom in Christ. You are an important part of God's 'railroad'—His system for moving slaves of sin into the freedom He offers."

HOW ABOUT YOU? Are you trying to help point the slaves of sin to freedom in Christ? Or are you afraid someone will make fun of you? Be a part of God's "railroad"—help "free the slaves." Tell someone about Christ today. □ J.B.

TO MEMORIZE: *Through Christ Jesus the law of the Spirit of life set me free from the law of sin and death.* Romans 8:2, NIV

356

STEVE GLANCED uneasily at the danger signs posted around the old mine shaft. "Come on," urged his older brother John as he climbed over the fence and dropped down inside the enclosure.

"What if someone finds out we came here?" protested Steve. "We're supposed to be gathering wood for the fire."

John shrugged and walked away. Then a horrible, crashing sound filled Steve's ears as John disappeared. "John!" cried Steve. "Where are you?"

"Down here," came the muffled reply. "I can't . . . move."

Steve gulped. "Hang on," he called. "I'll go get Dad." Frantically he ran to the site of the winter church retreat where the men were setting up camp while the boys collected firewood. As soon as Steve saw the tents, he shouted. "Help! John's trapped in an old mine."

The rest of the evening was a blur to Steve. He dimly remembered Pastor Jack calling for help on his ham radio, the wait for the rangers to come in the helicopter, and the wait for his father to return with news from the hospital. How Steve wished he and John had obeyed the instructions to stay within sight of camp! How he wished they had paid attention to the danger signs!

When Dad returned, Steve was relieved to hear that John would be all right. He told his father how sorry he was that he had disobeyed. Dad nodded. "I hope you've learned a lesson from what happened," he said. "What did the signs at the mine say?"

"They said, 'Danger. Keep out!' " replied Steve.

"Exactly," said Dad, "and when you and John didn't obey them, you had to pay the consequences. God's Word also says, 'Danger. Keep out of sin, or you will have to pay the consequences.' Not in those words. But one verse says, 'Be sure your sin will find you out.' Don't ignore God's warning. When you're faced with temptation, run away from it, and ask God to help you."

HOW ABOUT YOU? Do you think you can disobey, cheat, or lie—"just once"—and it won't matter? Do you think nobody will ever find out? God already knows, and very often other people find out, too. Sin is dangerous and has serious consequences. You can't escape forever. □ J.B.

TO MEMORIZE: *Sow for yourselves righteousness, reap the fruit of unfailing love. Hosea 10:12, NIV*

Danger!

FROM THE BIBLE:
Sow for yourselves righteousness, reap the fruit of unfailing love, and break up your unplowed ground; for it is time to seek the Lord, until he comes and showers righteousness on you. But you have planted wickedness, you have reaped evil, you have eaten the fruit of deception. Because you have depended on your own strength and on your many warriors.
Hosea 10:12-13, NIV

Last of all I want to remind you that your strength must come from the Lord's mighty power within you. Put on all of God's armor so that you will be able to stand safe against all strategies and tricks of Satan. For we are not fighting against people made of flesh and blood, but against persons without bodies—the evil rulers of the unseen world, those mighty satanic beings and great evil princes of darkness who rule this world; and against huge numbers of wicked spirits in the spirit world. So use every piece of God's armor to resist the enemy whenever he attacks, and when it is all over, you will still be standing up.
Ephesians 6:10-13, TLB

Sin is dangerous

DECEMBER

13

Wind Wisdom

FROM THE BIBLE:

After dark one night a Jewish religious leader named Nicodemus, a member of the sect of the Pharisees, came for an interview with Jesus. "Sir," he said, "we all know that God has sent you to teach us. Your miracles are proof enough of this." Jesus replied, "With all the earnestness I possess I tell you this: Unless you are born again, you can never get into the Kingdom of God." "Born again!" exclaimed Nicodemus. "What do you mean? How can an old man go back into his mother's womb and be born again?" Jesus replied, "What I am telling you so earnestly is this: Unless one is born of water and the Spirit, he cannot enter the Kingdom of God. Men can only reproduce human life, but the Holy Spirit gives new life from heaven; so don't be surprised at my statement that you must be born again! Just as you can hear the wind but can't tell where it comes from or where it will go next, so it is with the Spirit. We do not know on whom he will next bestow this life from heaven."
John 3:1-8, TLB

Jesus changes you

LOOK AT the wind!" exclaimed Sue as she stood at the window. "The trees are swaying back and forth, and some of the branches are breaking off."

"Wow! It's really blowing!" agreed Todd as he came into the room. "I've never seen such a big wind!"

Dad joined them at the window. "You can't really see wind," he reminded them. "You only see what it does."

"Like making that garbage can roll down the street," remarked Sue.

The three of them watched in silence for a few minutes, then Dad said, "Jesus compared the blowing of the wind to becoming a Christian. We can't see the wind, and we can't see Jesus coming into somebody's life, because it's His Spirit that comes in."

"And spirits are invisible," said Todd. He looked at his sister. "That's why Sue still looks the same. She has a turned-up nose and freckles just like before she invited Jesus into her heart at Bible camp last summer." He loved to tease Sue about her freckles.

Dad smiled. "We see what the wind does, though," he said, "and we also see what Jesus does. When He comes into a person's life, He changes that person. A Christian wants to please the Lord and be obedient. He tries not to do the things that displease God."

Sue nodded. "I still do bad things sometimes, but I try not to," she said. "When I do, I feel awful, and I ask Jesus to forgive me. Before I was saved, I didn't care much."

"And I've noticed that you don't get as mad when I tease you," admitted Todd.

Sue slipped her hand into her father's and looked up at him. "I'm glad the wind doesn't always blow this hard," she said. "But I'm glad Jesus is always in my heart. Even though I can't see Him, I know He's always there to help me live as I should."

HOW ABOUT YOU? Does your life show that you are a Christian? Has there been any change since you invited Jesus to come in? Make sure you're really born again. Then ask God to help you live in such a way that those around you will see what He is doing for you. □ M.N.

TO MEMORIZE: *If anyone is in Christ, he is a new creation; the old has gone, the new has come.* 2 Corinthians 5:17, NIV

358

LORI WAS JEALOUS of her brother Lance. *He gets along with Mom and Dad so much better than I do,* she thought. *Even Todd likes him better than he likes me.*

"Play with me," begged three-year-old Todd, pulling at her arm and interrupting her thoughts.

"No," answered Lori, "play by yourself."

Mother came in from the yard. "Lori," she said, "come help me weed the flower beds."

"Do I have to?" whined Lori, following her mother unwillingly. "Why doesn't Lance ever have to weed?"

"He has other chores," replied Mother. "You start here." Mother guided her to the end of a row.

Lori pouted as she slowly pulled weeds. Suddenly she shrieked, "Oh, that awful mosquito. He bit me!"

"Too bad you couldn't whack him before he got a chance to bite you," said Mother.

Just then Lori noticed a ladybug on one of the plants. "Look, Mom," she said. "A ladybug. Shall I whack it?"

"No," said Mother. "Mosquitoes are pests, but ladybugs are our friends. I read somewhere that ladybugs eat the harmful insects that destroy crops. The article said that they are sometimes caught and shipped to farmers and fruit-growers all over the world, to be released in their fields and orchards. Thank God for ladybugs."

"In other words," said Lori thoughtfully, "ladybugs are popular because they're helpful." A little light was going on in her mind.

Mother nodded. "That's right."

Just then Lance called from the patio. "I finished cleaning the garage, Mom," he said. "Todd wants me to take him to the playground. Is that okay?"

"Wonderful!" said Mother. "Thank you, Lance."

Lori thought hard. "Maybe if I'm more helpful, I'll be appreciated, too—like Lance and the ladybugs. Maybe people would even thank God for me!"

HOW ABOUT YOU? Are you like a mosquito or like a ladybug? Are you "pesky" or helpful? Do others like to have you around? With God's help, become a more useful person. Others will appreciate it, God will be pleased, and you will, too. □ M.N.

TO MEMORIZE: *Whatever you do, work at it with all your heart, as working for the Lord, not for men.* Colossians 3:23, NIV

Ladybug Logic

FROM THE BIBLE:
My son, never forget the things I've taught you. If you want a long and satisfying life, closely follow my instructions. Never tire of loyalty and kindness. Hold these virtues tightly. Write them deep within your heart. If you want favor with both God and man, and a reputation for good judgment and common sense, then trust the Lord completely; don't ever trust yourself.
Proverbs 3:1-4, TLB

Be helpful

15

Grandma's Attic

FROM THE BIBLE:

I remind you to stir up the gift of God which is in you through the laying on of my hands. For God has not given us a spirit of fear, but of power and of love and of a sound mind. Therefore do not be ashamed of the testimony of our Lord, nor of me His prisoner, but share with me in the sufferings for the gospel according to the power of God, who has saved us and called us with a holy calling, not according to our works, but according to His own purpose and grace which was given to us in Christ Jesus before time began, but has now been revealed by the appearing of our Savior Jesus Christ, who has abolished death and brought life and immortality to light through the gospel, to which I was appointed a preacher, an apostle, and a teacher of the Gentiles. For this reason I also suffer these things; nevertheless I am not ashamed, for I know whom I have believed and am persuaded that He is able to keep what I have committed to Him until that Day.

2 Timothy 1:6-12, NKJV

God will reward his children

JILL HAD BEEN having a good time helping her aunt clean out Grandma's attic. It seemed that everything in the attic reminded her aunt of a story. Now Aunt Sarah was reading a letter, holding it up to the light from the small window. "Who's the letter from, Aunt Sarah? Is it from someone you knew?" asked Jill.

"Yes, it is," Aunt Sarah replied. She carefully folded the letter and put it back into the yellowed envelope. "When we were children, we all loved this lady who attended our church. Her husband wasn't so nice. He came to church once in a while, but he was unfriendly."

"But what was the letter about?" asked Jill.

"That lady was Mrs. Alexander, and she went away for quite a long time," said Aunt Sarah. "We thought she was on a trip, but this letter explains what really happened. She had left her husband. This letter is from Mrs. Alexander. She's thanking Mother—your grandma—for praying for her and for encouraging her to continue living the Christian life even though it was so hard for her." Aunt Sarah smiled and shook her head. "We never knew! Mother never said one word about her leaving or giving up. She just went privately to the woman who was suffering and helped her get victory in her life."

"I'm glad that letter wasn't destroyed," Jill said. "Otherwise you wouldn't know how your mother helped that lady."

Aunt Sarah smiled. "It wouldn't matter if I'd never found out," she said. "Jesus knows. He's the keeper of all the good deeds and loving words of His children, and He'll reward them some day."

HOW ABOUT YOU? Are you doing and saying things that will pass the test of time—things that will build rewards for you in heaven? Do you wonder if anyone is noticing when you're kind, helpful, and loving? You can be sure that God is. It doesn't matter if anyone here knows. God does, and He'll reward you for what is done for Him. □ C.R.

TO MEMORIZE: *I know whom I have believed and am persuaded that He is able to keep what I have committed to Him until that Day.* 2 Timothy 1:12, NKJV

As JILL and her aunt cleaned Grandma's attic, Aunt Sarah found a box of her high school souvenirs. As she went through them, she told Jill about each one, remembering the person who had given it to her or the event that it reminded her of. Aunt Sarah held up a long piece of yarn. "This seems like a silly thing to have kept," she said with a laugh. "It's the yarn I wrapped around Tommy's ring so I could wear it. We went steady for a whole month! I haven't thought of him in years."

"I don't think he'd be very flattered to know that a piece of old string reminds you of him." observed Jill with a grin. "Don't you ever forget anything, Aunt Sarah? Everything you see reminds you of something! Your head must be stuffed even fuller than this attic."

"Well, I've heard that people never really forget anything," said Aunt Sarah. "It's all there in the brain, but sometimes it takes something like a souvenir to bring it into the part of our minds where we can use it." She stretched her arms and yawned. "I don't know about you, but I'm getting tired and thirsty. Let's take a break."

Jill agreed, and they went to the kitchen and found some cold lemonade. As they slowly sipped it, Aunt Sarah asked, "Jill, what do you have in your attic?" Jill started thinking about the attic at her home, but Aunt Sarah leaned forward and tapped her on the head. "What I mean is, what do you have stored away up here?" she said. "You know, just as Grandma's attic is full of memories, your mind is storing things too. Are there plenty of Bible verses in your 'storage area'?"

Jill shrugged. "I try to learn as much as I can," she said.

"Once memories are in place, things we see or hear can bring them back," said Aunt Sarah. "It's the same with Scripture. When you've memorized God's Word, He can use people and events to bring it to mind as you need it. That's one way the Holy Spirit helps you each day."

HOW ABOUT YOU? Have you ever seen or heard something that reminded you of a verse you knew? By memorizing God's Word and associating it with everyday things, you make it part of your life. As you become older, it will come back to you in times when you need it. □ C.R.

TO MEMORIZE: *His delight is in the law of the Lord, and on his law he meditates day and night.* Psalm 1:2, NIV

16

Grandma's Attic

(Continued from yesterday)

FROM THE BIBLE:
Blessed is the man who does not walk in the counsel of the wicked or stand in the way of sinners or sit in the seat of mockers. But his delight is in the law of the Lord, and on his law he meditates day and night. He is like a tree planted by streams of water, which yields its fruit in season and whose leaf does not wither. Whatever he does prospers.
Psalm 1:1-3, NIV

Memorize God's Word

17

The TV Recipe

FROM THE BIBLE:

God's truth stands firm like a great rock, and nothing can shake it. It is a foundation stone with these words written on it: "The Lord knows those who are really his," and "A person who calls himself a Christian should not be doing things that are wrong." In a wealthy home there are dishes made of gold and silver as well as some made from wood and clay. The expensive dishes are used for guests, and the cheap ones are used in the kitchen or to put garbage in. If you stay away from sin you will be like one of these dishes made of purest gold—the very best in the house—so that Christ himself can use you for his highest purposes. Run from anything that gives you the evil thoughts that young men often have, but stay close to anything that makes you want to do right. Have faith and love, and enjoy the companionship of those who love the Lord and have pure hearts.

2 Timothy 2:19-22, TLB

Watch good TV programs

M OM, CAN I watch 'Blazing Guns' on TV tonight?" Sammy asked hopefully. "Almost all the kids are planning to watch it. Even my history teacher says it's worth seeing. He says it has a very accurate historical setting."

"How about helping me make a cake, and we'll talk about it," said Mother, taking a box of cake mix from the kitchen cupboard. She poured the chocolate mix into a bowl, and studied the directions on the box. "I know how you love a good chocolate cake, so I want to add the ingredients very carefully. Let's see—eggs, oil, water, what else? Oh, yes. Sammy, please go outside and get a handful of dirt for your cake," she said as she began to stir in the other ingredients.

Sammy laughed. "Very funny, Mom. The box doesn't say 'Add one cup of dirt.' "

"No," said Mother as she plugged in the mixer, "but it would add a little volume to the cake—make it a little bigger. And all the good things will still be there."

"But the dirt would ruin it," Sammy said. "It wouldn't taste good. It might even make me sick!"

"That's true, Sammy," agreed Mother. "So you'd be very unhappy if I intentionally ruined your favorite cake?" Sammy nodded, wondering what Mother was up to. He found out with her next words. "I'm sure God feels that way about your heart," she said as she turned the mixer on low. "The program you want to watch may have some fine things about it, but judging from the ads I've seen, I'm afraid it also has a lot of cursing and violence. Those ingredients don't belong in your heart any more than dirt belongs in cake."

Sammy sighed. "In other words, I need to find a program with a better recipe—one that doesn't call for dirt," he said. Mother nodded and smiled as she poured the cake batter into the pans.

HOW ABOUT YOU? What ingredients go into the programs you watch? Are they good for your heart? Are they pleasing to God? Be choosy. Your mind needs pure ingredients to produce good thoughts. □ D.E.M.

TO MEMORIZE: *Whatever is true, whatever is noble, whatever is right, whatever is pure, whatever is lovely, whatever is admirable—if anything is excellent or praiseworthy—think about such things.* Philippians 4:8, NIV

TIM WRIGGLED INTO the little thicket of shrubs behind the garage. It was his own special hiding place where he always came when he was feeling sad and wanted to be alone. Today he felt very bad because he'd missed a shot in his basketball game, and several kids had mocked him. He sighed deeply as he thought about it.

A little bird rustled in the bushes, and the wind sighed softly overhead in the trees. Tim listened to the pleasant sounds and began to forget his sadness. He always felt better in his hiding place. Then he heard Mother calling, "Tim! Grandpa's here." Tim scrambled out. He didn't want to miss his beloved grandfather's visit.

Tim and Grandpa sat down on the porch to visit—just the two of them. "Where were you just now?" Grandpa asked.

"I was feeling bad about a ball game and went to my special hiding place," Tim said, knowing Grandpa would never tell anyone.

"Say, that's a good idea," said Grandpa sympathetically. "I had a hiding place of my own when I was a boy. It was in the hayloft of the barn." Grandpa's face beamed as he added, "Even at my age, I still have a good hiding place."

Tim looked surprised. "You do?" He wondered what kind of place someone Grandpa's age would use to hide out.

Grandpa nodded. "Run and get your Bible," he said, "and I'll give you a clue as to where I go."

When Tim returned, Grandpa said, "Look up Psalm 143:9, and you'll find the answer."

They read it together: "I flee unto Thee to hide me."

"That's right," said Grandpa. "I go to God with all my hurts and sadness. God's presence is the best hiding place of all."

"Next time I'm sad, I'm going to go to the same hiding place you do, Grandpa," Tim decided. "And I can do that right in my other secret hiding place."

HOW ABOUT YOU? Are you sometimes sad and troubled? Do you take your problems and sadness to God? He's ready and waiting to hear and to help you. He wants to hear about anything that is bothering you—trouble with schoolwork, disappointments with friends, or problems in your family. The next time you need help, go to the best "hiding place" of all—the Lord! □ C.Y.

TO MEMORIZE: *Rescue me from my enemies, O Lord, for I hide myself in you.* Psalm 143:9, NIV

Hiding Place

FROM THE BIBLE:
Answer me quickly, O Lord; my spirit faints with longing. Do not hide your face from me or I will be like those who go down to the pit. Let the morning bring me word of your unfailing love, for I have put my trust in you. Show me the way I should go, for to you I lift up my soul. Rescue me from my enemies, O Lord, for I hide myself in you. Teach me to do your will, for you are my God; may your good Spirit lead me on level ground. For your name's sake, O Lord, preserve my life; in your righteousness, bring me out of trouble. In your unfailing love, silence my enemies; destroy all my foes, for I am your servant. Psalm 143:7-12, NIV

Go to God for help

Cluttered Places

FROM THE BIBLE:

What happiness for those whose guilt has been forgiven! What joys when sins are covered over! What relief for those who have confessed their sins and God has cleared their record. There was a time when I wouldn't admit what a sinner I was. But my dishonesty made me miserable and filled my days with frustration. All day and all night your hand was heavy on me. My strength evaporated like water on a sunny day until I finally admitted all my sins to you and stopped trying to hide them. I said to myself, "I will confess them to the Lord." And you forgave me! All my guilt is gone.
Psalm 32:1-5, TLB

Confess your sins

ROGER EAGERLY SORTED through his things, putting some away in his closet and others in drawers. His family had moved into a new home, and he had a room all to himself at last. He had so looked forward to that.

As Roger worked, his mother came in to see how he was doing. She sat down on his bed. "What a mess!" she said, looking out the window. Roger looked, too. There, at the end of the beautifully landscaped yard, was a huge pile of boxes the family had used to move their belongings. "I'm glad today is trash day," Mother continued. "All those boxes make our beautiful home ugly and cluttered."

"Yeah," agreed Roger. He looked at his own pile of boxes near the door. "I've got to get these out there, too, before the garbage truck comes." He hurried to do so. With the boxes out of his room, it looked so much bigger and more pleasant.

As they finished eating lunch a little later, the garbage truck came. The whole family watched as all the boxes were loaded onto the truck, and they cheered as it drove away. Then Dad reached for the family Bible. "I'm reminded that our lives sometimes get cluttered with trash, too," he said, "and we need to clean it out. We'll read Psalm 32 for our devotions today. Would you like to read it for us, Roger?"

When Roger had finished reading, Dad nodded. "Let's sit quietly and each think over the things that have been going on in our own lives lately. Then we'll have a short time of silent prayer. If there are any sins that have piled up like trash, making our lives ugly, we need to confess those sins to God and allow Him to cleanse us. After a few moments, I'll close in prayer."

HOW ABOUT YOU? Is there sin cluttering your life? Sin that is allowed to accumulate can cover the beauty of your life in Christ. Don't let that happen. Spend some quiet time with the Lord each day. Examine your heart. Is there a bad attitude? A lie you haven't confessed? Anger against a friend? Whatever it is, confess it to the Lord and ask Him to give you victory over it. □ K.R.A.

TO MEMORIZE: *If we confess our sins, he is faithful and just and will forgive us our sins and purify us from all unrighteousness.* 1 John 1:9, NIV

"PRAISE THE LORD," sang Erin as she wrote a note to her friend Bethany, who was sitting beside her in the Sunday morning worship service. "Ask your mom if you may come home with me," the note read. Bethany nodded.

Although Erin continued to sing, bowed her head during prayer, and sat quietly during the sermon, her mind was busily planning what she and Bethany could do together in the afternoon. She did feel a twinge of guilt, because she knew she should be paying more attention to the service. *The Lord will understand. He knows I'm excited about Bethany coming,* she told herself.

Bethany did go home with Erin. After dinner, she noticed a book on Erin's dresser. "Oh!" she exclaimed. "Have you finished this? Could I borrow it?"

"Sure," agreed Erin, thinking that Bethany would take the book home with her. But Bethany sat down and began to leaf through it. Although she continued to murmur replies to what Erin said, she was soon engrossed in the book. She wasn't interested in any of the things Erin wanted to do together. "I really want to read this. You understand, don't you?" said Bethany. Erin felt hurt and disappointed.

That evening, Erin again went to church with her family. Once more, she had Bethany on her mind. *She said she wanted to be my friend, but she didn't really want to be with me,* Erin thought. As she pouted over the events of the day, she again felt some guilt for not paying more attention to the worship service. *Oh, well. I'm upset about Bethany,* she thought. *The Lord understands.* Then she remembered Bethany's words, "You understand, don't you?"

The Lord must feel as disappointed with me as I felt with Bethany, thought Erin.

Erin put Bethany out of her mind. She sang praises with the rest of the congregation, and this time she put her whole heart into it.

HOW ABOUT YOU? Do you worship God in church? Or do you write notes, whisper to friends, or think about what someone is wearing that day? Put such things out of your mind. The Lord wants more than your presence in the church service. He wants your wholehearted worship. □ K.R.A.

TO MEMORIZE: *These people honor me with their lips, but their hearts are far from me.* Matthew 15:8, NIV

20

Whole-hearted Worship

FROM THE BIBLE:
Hallelujah! I want to express publicly before his people my heartfelt thanks to God for his mighty miracles. All who are thankful should ponder them with me. For his miracles demonstrate his honor, majesty, and eternal goodness. Who can forget the wonders he performs— deeds of mercy and of grace? He gives food to those who trust him; he never forgets his promises. He has shown his great power to his people by giving them the land of Israel, though it was the home of many nations living there. All he does is just and good, and all his laws are right, for they are formed from truth and goodness, and stand firm forever. He has paid a full ransom for his people; now they are always free to come to Jehovah (what a holy, awe-inspiring name that is). How can men be wise? The only way to begin is by reverence for God. For growth in wisdom comes from obeying his laws. Praise his name forever. Psalm 111:1-10, TLB

Worship with your whole heart

21

Mary's Part

Be a humble servant

SHELLY WAITED to hear the teacher call her name. She knew she was the perfect one to take the part of Mary, the mother of Jesus. No one could memorize the lines as well as she could. And her mother was the best seamstress in the church. She could have the best costume.

"Julie," said Mrs. Roberts, "I think you would be a good Mary."

Shelly gasped! Who was Julie but a poor, stammering girl who missed church half the time in order to help her sick mother. What kind of Mary would she be? "That's just fine with me," Shelly muttered to herself. "Who wants to be in a dumb old play anyway!" When Mrs. Roberts offered her another part, she made excuses and refused to be in the program at all.

Shelly sat in the front row the night of the program. She had come to laugh at Julie's mistakes. Mrs. Roberts would be embarrassed for making such a foolish choice! Shelly watched as Julie walked up front wearing a drab outfit that looked like it came from a feedsack. *What a peasant!* Shelly thought in disgust.

Hesitantly Julie began reciting from Luke. "For He . . . hath regarded . . . the low estate . . . of his handmaiden. . . ."

"Low estate," grumbled Shelly to herself. "That sure fits Julie." And then suddenly it struck her that Mrs. Roberts was right! Julie was a good Mary! Julie was humble and stood in awe before God like Mary did—a servant willing to obey and carry out His commands. Shelly knew she would have exalted herself, but Julie sought to glorify Jesus.

While the program continued, Shelly bowed her head. Silently she asked God to forgive her proud spirit and make her His humble servant.

HOW ABOUT YOU? Do you think you're better than some people because you feel you are more talented than they are? Do you think you should always be the one chosen to play special music, answer the questions, or lead in prayer because you do it best? Jesus wants obedient servants who are willing to stoop to help others so that He might be lifted up. □ J.H.

TO MEMORIZE: *Whoever wants to be first must be your slave.* Matthew 20:27, NIV

I'M SORRY. Maybe next time." As Jolene hung up the phone, Mother glanced her way. "The junior choir is giving a Christmas program at the nursing home today. Mrs. Wilson wants me to play the piano, but I'm going downtown. I need some notebooks for school," Jolene explained.

Mother raised her eyebrows. "Couldn't you play and still have time to get the notebooks?" she asked. "Playing would be a real service to the Lord."

Jolene shrugged in annoyance. "Oh, Mother! Someone else can do it just as well." She picked up her books and headed for the door.

When Jolene arrived home that afternoon, she not only had two new notebooks, but a small stuffed dog as well. "I've named him Orville," she giggled as she showed Mother. "Isn't he cute? Would you believe he cost only a dollar? I didn't have that much left, but then I remembered that the silver dollar Aunt Jo sent me was still in my purse."

Mother was shocked. "But I thought you knew that coin was actually worth more than a dollar!"

Jolene looked ashamed. "Well, yeah," she admitted, "but Orville was on sale!"

The following Saturday, Jolene went shopping with her mother. They passed a coin shop, and in the window display were several silver dollars, each worth a lot of money. "I don't suppose my dollar was worth nearly that much," sighed Jolene, "but I still wish I had it back."

"It's spent, and you may as well forget it," answered Mother. "I remember the day you spent your dollar. It was the same day you refused to play at the nursing home. You know, Honey, your life is a lot like a coin—you can spend it any way you want to, but you can spend it only once. You need to make sure you spend it wisely."

Soberly, Jolene nodded. "I didn't spend either my dollar or my life wisely that day, did I? I'm going to rename Orville. I'll call him Silver Dollar, and he'll remind me that I need to be careful how I spend my money and my life."

HOW ABOUT YOU? How are you spending your life? Are you "buying" the most you can with it? Are you using opportunities to sing for the Lord? To help someone? The things you do for yourself are soon gone. What you do for the Lord will be rewarded. □ H.M.

TO MEMORIZE: *If what he has built survives, he will receive his reward.* 1 Corinthians 3:14, NIV

22

Silver Dollar

FROM THE BIBLE:
No one can lay any foundation other than the one already laid, which is Jesus Christ. If any man builds on this foundation using gold, silver, costly stones, wood, hay or straw, his work will be shown for what it is, because the Day will bring it to light. It will be revealed with fire, and the fire will test the quality of each man's work. If what he has built survives, he will receive his reward. If it is burned up, he will suffer loss; he himself will be saved, but only as one escaping through the flames.

1 Corinthians 3:11-15, NIV

Spend your life wisely

DECEMBER

23

Hot or Cold?

FROM THE BIBLE:

But godliness with contentment is great gain. For we brought nothing into the world, and we can take nothing out of it. But if we have food and clothing, we will be content with that. People who want to get rich fall into temptation and a trap and into many foolish and harmful desires that plunge men into ruin and destruction. For the love of money is a root of all kinds of evil. Some people, eager for money, have wandered from the faith and pierced themselves with many griefs. But you, man of God, flee from all this, and pursue righteousness, godliness, faith, love, endurance and gentleness. Fight the good fight of the faith. Take hold of the eternal life to which you were called when you made your good confession in the presence of many witnesses.

1 Timothy 6:6-12, NIV

Be content

IT'S SO COLD! I can't stand it a minute longer." Jessie pulled her coat tightly around her.

"Oh, Jessie," said Mom, "you were just as excited about coming downtown to see the Christmas lights as the rest of us! Now you're complaining, and we've only been here ten minutes."

"But I'll freeze to death!" chattered Jessie.

"You will not freeze to death," replied Mother. "I can guarantee that!" She laughed. "Seems to me, I remember a day last July when you complained for an entire morning about the heat. You wished for winter, remember? You put Christmas music on the stereo. Now it's cold for real, and you're wishing for hot weather! Aren't you ever satisfied?"

"But, Mom . . ." Jessie protested

"It's not that cold, honey," said Mother firmly. "I think you should listen to yourself sometimes. You never seem to be happy. If it's hot, you want it cold. If it's cold, you want it hot. The Bible says we're to be content with our circumstances, no matter what they are."

Jessie did remember that day in July when she had complained about the heat! In fact, there had been more than one summer day when she had wished for winter. Suddenly she smiled. "Come on! Let's go see the rest of the Christmas lights. If it were hot, all the beautiful snow would melt."

HOW ABOUT YOU? Do you often wish for something you don't have? Or wish you could be doing something that you can't do? In his letter to Timothy, the apostle Paul wrote that Christians should be content no matter what their circumstances. So, instead of wishing for what you don't have, be thankful for what you do have. Listen to yourself talk. Are you a complainer, or are you content? □ L.W.

TO MEMORIZE: *Godliness with contentment is great gain.* 1 Timothy 6:6, NIV

JEREMY WOKE WITH excitement. "It's an important day, Mom," he announced as he jumped out of bed and ran to the kitchen for breakfast.

Mom looked up from making pancakes. "It is?" she asked innocently. "Why is that?"

"Oh, Mom, you know! It's Christmas Eve," Jeremy replied, "and we open our gifts on Christmas Eve!"

Throughout the day, Jeremy made many excited trips to the Christmas tree to look at the presents. Finally, just when he felt he could stand it no longer, the evening meal was over, the last dish was dried and put away, and the family gathered to open the presents. Jeremy was not disappointed. When it was all over, he looked at the things around him: a sweater, some toys, a book, candy, and what he had wanted most of all—a regular-sized baseball mitt! Already he was dreaming of summer, and he saw himself making spectacular catches and . . .

But Dad was talking. "Let's read about the gifts brought to Jesus on that first Christmas Day," Dad said, turning to Matthew 2. After reading the story aloud, he added, "We've given each other gifts to show our love, and we have a gift for Jesus, too." He picked up a special box. "As you know, this box contains the Christmas offering each of you brought," he continued. Jeremy nodded. He had given some of his own money for Jesus. It made him feel good, and no doubt God was pleased, too. "You each gave money," Dad said. "Now, I'd like to ask you if you've given Jesus what He wants most—your heart? Have you given Him yourself?"

Jeremy thought about that as he went to bed. He knew he had never really given himself to Jesus. Suddenly he jumped up and ran back into the living room. "I want to give myself to Jesus," he cried.

Later, as Mom tucked him back in bed, he looked at her and said, "I told you this was an important day. It's the day I was saved. That's even more important than opening all the presents."

HOW ABOUT YOU? Have you remembered a gift for Jesus this Christmas? If you haven't done so already, won't you make this the most important day in your life? Give Jesus your heart and life. □ H.M.

TO MEMORIZE: *When they had opened their treasures, they presented gifts to Him: gold, frankincense, and myrrh.* Matthew 2:11, NKJV

An Important Day

FROM THE BIBLE:
Wise men from the East came to Jerusalem, saying, "Where is He who has been born King of the Jews? For we have seen His star in the East and have come to worship Him." When Herod the king heard these things, he was troubled. . . . Then Herod, when he had secretly called the wise men, . . . said, "Go and search diligently for the young Child, and when you have found Him, bring back word to me, that I may come and worship Him also." When they heard the king, they departed; and behold, the star which they had seen in the East went before them, till it came and stood over where the young Child was. When they saw the star, they rejoiced with exceedingly great joy. And when they had come into the house, they saw the young Child with Mary His mother, and fell down and worshiped Him. And when they had opened their treasures, they presented gifts to Him: gold, frankincense, and myrrh. Matthew 2:1-3,7-11, NKJV

Give yourself to Jesus

DECEMBER

25

The Empty Box

FROM THE BIBLE:

There were shepherds living out in the fields nearby, keeping watch over their flocks at night. An angel of the Lord appeared to them, and the glory of the Lord shone around them, and they were terrified. But the angel said to them, "Do not be afraid. I bring you good news of great joy that will be for all the people. Today in the town of David a Savior has been born to you; he is Christ the Lord. This will be a sign to you: You will find a baby wrapped in cloths and lying in a manger." Suddenly a great company of the heavenly host appeared with the angel, praising God and saying, "Glory to God in the highest, and on earth peace to men on whom his favor rests."
Luke 2:8-14, NIV

Remember Jesus on his day

OH, MOM! I've never had a birthday party before!" exclaimed Glenda. "You've always said people would be too busy getting ready for Christmas to want to come to another party!" Glenda had been born on Christmas. Now, for the first time, her parents decided to give a special party just for her.

The Saturday before Christmas dawned bright and clear. Soon Glenda's party was in progress, and it was a smashing success. Finally it was time to open gifts, and Glenda was thrilled with each one. Then one of the girls said, "Here! There's just one more gift."

"Who is it from?" Glenda asked. "There's no card."

"Maybe it's on the inside," someone suggested.

Glenda smiled and quickly removed the wrapping. "No, there's nothing inside! It's just an empty box."

Dad had been watching and now he spoke. "Kids, I'm the one who wrapped the empty box," he confessed.

"But why, Dad?" asked Glenda.

"Well, since it's the Christmas season, I wanted to give you an idea of what Christmas must be like for Jesus!" he explained. "You all know it's His birthday, don't you?" The children nodded, and he continued. "It's Jesus' birthday, but we are the ones who receive gifts. It's almost the same as if we had given gifts to each other at this party and given Glenda only empty boxes."

"Oh, I see what you mean," Cathy said thoughtfully. "It's like Jesus is left out of His own birthday party!"

Just then Mother entered the room carrying a beautiful cake which said, "Happy Birthday Glenda and Jesus!" The children at that party never forgot the true meaning of Christmas.

HOW ABOUT YOU? Have you ever treated Jesus as if He were an unwanted guest on His own birthday? Do you get impatient when Mom and Dad take time to read the Christmas story before you're allowed to open your gifts? This year, give Him a place of honor in your thoughts and words and actions. □ R.P.

TO MEMORIZE: *Today in the town of David a Savior has been born to you; he is Christ the Lord.* Luke 2:11, NIV

KATIE TWIRLED in front of the department store mirror, admiring the blue dress she had found on the "clearance" rack. *It's too short, but I bet Mom can fix that,* she thought. *I can always return it if I change my mind.* She had received money for Christmas and decided to use it for a dress.

When Katie brought the dress home, Mother pointed out that the hem was too small to let any out to lengthen it. Besides that, there was a stain on the sleeve. "I'd better take it back to the store," Katie decided. But when she went back the next day, the sales clerk shook her head and pointed to a large sign on the wall. It said: No Refund On Clearance Merchandise.

"That's not fair!" Katie pouted. "I didn't even notice that sign yesterday."

"I'm sorry," said the clerk, "but that's the store's policy, and I can't change it."

Feeling miserable, Katie trudged home and told her mother about it. "I'm sorry, Honey," said Mother. "Maybe we can cut off the sleeves and turn it into a short-sleeved shirt. Then you'd at least get some use out of it."

Katie frowned. "I guess so, but I still wish I could just take it back."

"I do, too," agreed Mother. "But there's a lesson here. Young people are often tempted to do things impulsively, without considering the Lord's will. Perhaps they think they can always change their minds later if it doesn't turn out right. But foolish decisions often carry lasting consequences, and no amount of wishing can turn back the clock. It's so important to ask Jesus to help you make right decisions."

HOW ABOUT YOU? Do you ask God to help you make the right decision whenever you're tempted to lie, cheat, smoke, drink alcohol, or take drugs? You can come to Christ for forgiveness after you've sinned, but you may never be able to undo the awful consequences. Make up your mind to obey God's Word in all things. He will help you do so. □ S.K.

TO MEMORIZE: *Do not be deceived, God is not mocked; for whatever a man sows, that he will also reap.* Galatians 6:7, NKJV

26

No Returns

FROM THE BIBLE:
Do not be deceived, God is not mocked; for whatever a man sows, that he will also reap. For he who sows to his flesh will of the flesh reap corruption, but he who sows to the Spirit will of the Spirit reap everlasting life.
Galatians 6:7-8, NKJV

Pursue peace with all men, and holiness, without which no one will see the Lord: looking diligently lest anyone fall short of the grace of God; lest any root of bitterness springing up cause trouble, and by this many become defiled; lest there be any fornicator or profane person like Esau, who for one morsel of food sold his birthright. For you know that afterward, when he wanted to inherit the blessing, he was rejected, for he found no place for repentance, though he sought it diligently with tears.
Hebrews 12:14-17, NKJV

Sin has lasting consequences

27

Not Garbage

FROM THE BIBLE:

*Let heaven fill your thoughts;
don't spend your time worrying
about things down
here. . . . Your real life is in
heaven with Christ and God.
And when Christ who is our
real life comes back again, you
will shine with him and share
in all his glories. Away then
with sinful, earthly things;
deaden the evil desires lurking
within you; have nothing to do
with sexual sin, impurity, lust
and shameful desires; don't
worship the good things of life,
for that is idolatry. God's terrible
anger is upon those who do such
things. You used to do them
when your life was still part of
this world; but now is the time
to cast off and throw away all
these rotten garments of anger,
hatred, cursing, and dirty
language. Don't tell lies to each
other; it was your old life with
all its wickedness that did that
sort of thing; now it is dead and
gone. You are living a brand
new kind of life that is continually learning more and more of
what is right, and trying
constantly to be more and more
like Christ who created this new
life within you.*
Colossians 3:2-10, TLB

Dress
appropriately

SON, WHAT SHIRT is that you're wearing?"
asked Todd's mother as she cut up broccoli for
freezing.

"This shirt?" Todd asked, looking at the rock
group emblem painted on the front. "It's the one
I got at camp last summer. One of the kids at
school had this special paint, so we all wrote or
put pictures on our clothes."

"Who are you trying to look like?" asked Mother.
"If it's the world, you're succeeding. Todd, you're
a Christian—shouldn't that make a difference in
the way you dress?"

"This isn't so bad," Todd defended himself.

"You know I've never minded the latest styles
as long as they're acceptable," said Mother, "but
what you've been wearing lately isn't acceptable.
Now, go put the garbage out and then go and
change into some presentable clothes."

Todd scowled, but he went out and took the
garbage cans to the curb. When he came back
into the house, his mother was standing at the
front window. "How come we have three cans of
garbage this week?" she asked.

"I don't know," said Todd. "I just took what was
there."

Mother went outside, and Todd followed. "Oh,
no!" she exclaimed when she looked into one of
the cans. "This can is filled with vegetables from
the garden. Dad put them in there to store them
until I have time to freeze them."

"Good thing you noticed the extra can before
the garbage truck came," said Todd with a laugh.
"Dad wouldn't have been happy if they'd been
thrown away."

"That's for sure." Mother laughed, too, but then
she grew serious. "Even though those are good
vegetables, we thought they were garbage because they were stored in a garbage can. In the
same way, even though you're a Christian, you
don't look like one when you dress like the world."

"I suppose you have a point, Mom," admitted
Todd reluctantly. "I'll put the vegetables back into
the garage and then change my clothes."

HOW ABOUT YOU? Do you avoid inappropriate
clothes, such as T-shirts that have bad slogans,
or clothes that imitate the look of an actor or rock
star? Your outward appearance makes an impression. Don't dress like "garbage." Dress like a person who truly loves the Lord. □ L.W.

TO MEMORIZE: *Abstain from every form of evil.*
1 Thessalonians 5:22, NKJV

AT SCHOOL, AMBER kept thinking about the Scripture Dad had read that morning. It was about being a servant of God. She knew Dad was a servant of Jesus Christ. He was a preacher. And Uncle Robert and Aunt Clara were His servants, too. They were missionaries. But how could she, a ten-year-old girl, serve the Lord? Her thoughts were interrupted by the teacher's voice. "Who will stay in during recess and help me with the bulletin board?" Mrs. Powell asked. Amber had planned to play jacks with Sue, but she raised her hand. Later, at lunch time, she helped Mindy study her spelling.

When school was over, Amber hurried home, intending to ask Mother how she could serve God. But as soon as she opened the door, Mother said, "Oh Amber, I'm so glad you're here. Amy is running a high fever. I need you to watch the boys while I take her to the doctor's office." Amber nodded, and willingly entertained her little brothers while Mother was gone. Later, she set the table and put a casserole into the oven. After dinner, Amber washed the dishes. Then she rocked the baby while her Mother put the boys to bed.

It was after the toys were picked up and all was quiet that Amber remembered her question. "Mother, how can I serve God? Daddy's a preacher. Uncle Robert and Aunt Clara are missionaries. You're the church organist. But I'm not anything. What can I do to serve Jesus?"

Mother hugged her daughter. "Oh, Amber honey, you are serving Him!" she exclaimed. "We serve God by serving others. Every day, as you help me around the house and take care of your little brothers and sister, and as you help other people, you're serving God."

Amber was amazed. "That's really serving God?"

Mother nodded. "It certainly is. You're a very special servant of Jesus Christ."

HOW ABOUT YOU? Do you want to "serve the Lord"? Then serve others. When you serve them, you're serving Him. Make up your mind to do something special today for someone else.

TO MEMORIZE: *For you, brethren, have been called to liberty; only do not use liberty as an opportunity for the flesh, but through love serve one another.* Galatians 5:13, NKJV

A Very Special Servant

FROM THE BIBLE:
Don't you realize that you can choose your own master? . . . The one to whom you offer yourself—he will take you and be your master and you will be his slave. Thank God that though you once chose to be slaves of sin, now you have obeyed with all your heart the teaching to which God has committed you. And now you are free from your old master, sin; and you have become slaves to your new master, righteousness. . . . In those days when you were slaves of sin you didn't bother much with goodness. And what was the result? Evidently not good, since you are ashamed now even to think about those things you used to do, for all of them end in eternal doom. But now you are free from the power of sin and are slaves of God, and his benefits to you include holiness and everlasting life. For the wages of sin is death, but the free gift of God is eternal life through Jesus Christ our Lord.
Romans 6:16-23, TLB

Serve God by serving others

Just Different

FROM THE BIBLE:

As we have many members in one body, but all the members do not have the same function, so we, being many, are one body in Christ, and individually members of one another. Having then gifts differing according to the grace that is given to us, let us use them: if prophecy, let us prophesy in proportion to our faith; or ministry, let us use it in our ministering; he who teaches, in teaching; he who exhorts, in exhortation; he who gives, with liberality; he who leads, with diligence; he who shows mercy, with cheerfulness. Let love be without hypocrisy. Abhor what is evil. Cling to what is good. Be kindly affectionate to one another with brotherly love, in honor giving preference to one another; not lagging in diligence, fervent in spirit, serving the Lord.

Romans 12:4-11, NKJV

God made each one special

TWO MORE DAYS," said Jerry, "and we can watch the best ballgame of the year." He picked up the football he had received for Christmas. "The next best thing to playing football," he declared, "is watching the Rose Bowl game."

"Football!" scoffed his sister Beth. "Best thing about football is that the season's almost over." She picked up the sports equipment she had received—a tennis racquet and some bright yellow balls. "Now these are pretty," she declared. "Much better than your dumb old pigskin."

Mother looked up. "Well, I might as well get into this discussion, too," she said. "Now, I think the best ball of all is my new bowling ball. It's big and beautiful. And it's going to help my bowling average—I just know it is."

Dad spoke up. "It's big all right," he agreed, "but if you want to see beauty, you need to take a look at my golf balls." Dad grinned. "Whoever would have thought that buying everybody sports equipment for Christmas would start a family feud?"

Jerry laughed. "As Mother is always saying, we'll just have to agree to disagree, I guess."

"Better yet," said Mother, "let's agree that everybody's sport is great. Not one of these various balls is better than the others—they're just all different. Each has its own special purpose."

"That's true," agreed Dad. "You wouldn't knock many bowling pins over with my golf balls. And that's the way it is with people, too. Some of us are skilled in one area and some in another. Some can sing. Others can speak well. Still others do a good job taking care of little children, or building homes. Some are good in science, sports, or math. Just as it's unfair to compare a tennis ball and a bowling ball, it's unfair to compare people to each other. God made each one different and special."

HOW ABOUT YOU? Do you think someone is better than you because he has skills you'd like? Or do you think you're better than someone else because you can do something he can't? Don't compare people. God wants you to be yourself. Develop the skills He gave you, and don't be envious of those He gave to someone else. □ H.M.

TO MEMORIZE: *Having then gifts differing according to the grace that is given to us, let us use them.* Romans 12:6, NKJV

I SAW THAT new boy, Lon, come out to slide today," announced Beth one evening, "but Jerry and his friends were mean to him, Dad!" Jerry scowled at his sister.

"Is that true?" asked Dad, looking at Jerry.

Jerry shrugged. "We weren't that bad," he said. "But they must be poor or something. Lon was using the cover of a plastic garbage can to slide on!"

"You could have shared your sled," said Beth.

Jerry glared at her. "I didn't see *you* share," he retorted. "Besides, just wait till his sister comes out and wants to play with you—he has a sister, you know."

"He does?" Beth looked startled at the thought. "Does she wear funny clothes, too?"

"I think you're forgetting something," said Dad. "Just yesterday we talked about how tennis balls, footballs, bowling balls, and golf balls are all different, but that doesn't make one better than another, remember? And it's the same with people, right?"

"Well . . . I guess so," said Beth uncertainly.

"The cost of the covering is not the important thing," said Dad. "It's not what makes a ball valuable. And neither does a person's 'covering,' or wealth, determine his value."

"Right," agreed Mother. She looked straight at Jerry. "One person can't afford a sled, and another can't afford a snowmobile. Does that make one better than the other?" Jerry blushed and shook his head. He knew he was the one who couldn't afford a snowmobile. "And," continued Mother, now looking at Beth, "some people buy rings at the discount store, and others own expensive ones. Are people with cheaper rings less valuable than others?"

Beth looked at the cheap ring on her hand. She was glad that didn't make her a less valuable person. "I get the point."

Jerry nodded. "Me, too. I'll be nicer to the new boy."

HOW ABOUT YOU? Do you judge people by the material things they have? God doesn't. In fact, He's very specific about the importance of treating all alike. Be very careful about this. □ H.M.

TO MEMORIZE: *Rich and poor have this in common: The Lord is the Maker of them all.* Proverbs 22:2, NIV

30

Just Different

(Continued from yesterday)

FROM THE BIBLE:
How can you claim that you belong to the Lord Jesus Christ, the Lord of glory, if you show favoritism to rich people and look down on poor people? If a man comes into your church dressed in expensive clothes and with valuable gold rings on his fingers, and at the same moment another man comes in who is poor and dressed in threadbare clothes, and you make a lot of fuss over the rich man and give him the best seat in the house and say to the poor man, "You can stand over there if you like, or else sit on the floor" . . . Don't you realize that it is usually the rich men who pick on you and drag you into court? And all too often they are the ones who laugh at Jesus Christ, whose noble name you bear. Yes indeed, it is good when you truly obey our Lord's command, "You must love and help your neighbors just as much as you love and take care of yourself." But you are breaking this law of our Lord's when you favor the rich and fawn over them; it is sin.
James 2:1-9, TLB

Don't look down on the poor

31

After-Christmas Sale

FROM THE BIBLE:

But now you must rid yourselves of all such things as these: anger, rage, malice, slander, and filthy language from your lips. Do not lie to each other, since you have taken off your old self with its practices and have put on the new self, which is being renewed in knowledge in the image of its Creator. Here there is no Greek or Jew, circumcised or uncircumcised, barbarian, Scythian, slave or free, but Christ is all, and is in all. Therefore, as God's chosen people, holy and dearly loved, clothe yourselves with compassion, kindness, humility, gentleness and patience. Bear with each other and forgive whatever grievances you may have against one another. Forgive as the Lord forgave you. And over all these virtues put on love, which binds them all together in perfect unity. Let the peace of Christ rule in your hearts, since as members of one body you were called to peace. And be thankful.

Colossians 3:8-15, NIV

Develop Christian traits

Y OU SHOULD see all the stuff Mom and I got on sale today," Bonnie told her father one evening. "Cheap, too."

Mother sighed. "Yes," she agreed, "but it was such a hassle getting through the crowds at the mall and pawing through the piles of merchandise. I wondered at times if it was really worth it. But as Bonnie says, it was cheap. It makes you wonder how the stores can afford to sell things at those prices."

"They know what they're doing," Dad assured her. "They're clearing out things that are no longer profitable and making room to restock their shelves with new things from which they *can* make a good profit. We could take a lesson from them."

"Like what?" asked Bonnie curiously.

"There are things on the 'shelves' of our lives that we should clear out from time to time," explained Dad as he reached for his Bible. "Let's read about them for devotions tonight." He read aloud from Colossians 3.

"That makes me feel guilty for getting angry at some pushy women in the store today," confessed Mother. "I need to get rid of anger from the 'shelves' of my life."

"Well, how much do you suppose we can sell our bad qualities for?" asked Bonnie with a mischievous grin.

Dad smiled. "I trust there would be no buyers for them. Forget selling them and just trash them," he advised. "And let's not forget to restock our 'shelves' with this list of traits which are pleasing to God."

HOW ABOUT YOU? What traits are found on the "shelves" of your life? Do you need to get rid of lying, filthy language, or a desire to get even with someone? Do you need to add kindness, a forgiving spirit, or humility? Ask God right now to help you do that. Start the New Year by discarding old, sinful attitudes and adding the things that please God. □ H.M.

TO MEMORIZE: *You have taken off your old self with its practices and have put on the new self, which is being renewed in knowledge in the image of its Creator.* Colossians 3:9-10, NIV

INDEX
of Scripture in
Daily Readings

INDEX
of Scripture
Memory Verses